SHAKESPEARE AND THE CLASSICAL TRADITION

Shakespeare and the Classical Tradition

A CRITICAL GUIDE TO COMMENTARY, 1660–1960

John W. Velz

UNIVERSITY OF MINNESOTA PRESS • MINNEAPOLIS

Printed in the United States of America at
the North Central Publishing Company, St. Paul

 3

Library of Congress Catalog Card Number: 67-14377

PUBLISHED IN GREAT BRITAIN, INDIA, AND PAKISTAN BY THE OXFORD UNIVERSITY PRESS, LONDON, BOMBAY, AND KARACHI, AND IN CANADA BY THE COPP CLARK PUBLISHING CO. LIMITED, TORONTO

To the scholars, past and present, whose labors these pages touch upon

PREFACE

Of problems in the history of Shakespeare scholarship and criticism, few have had broader implications than the question of Shakespeare's knowledge (or ignorance) of the classics. When the Restoration critics interpreted Ben Jonson's ambiguous statement that Shakespeare had "small Latine, and lesse Greeke" as a slur on his friend's "Art,"[1] they forced subsequent commentators to take sides in a controversy which has not died since. Virtually every aspect of Shakespeare study (except commentary on stage history and on Shakespeare's influence on later literature) has concerned itself with the "small Latin" question. Editors have explained cruxes or emended doubtful passages on the authority of putative analogues or sources in ancient literature; interpreters of the characters have repeatedly placed them in juxtaposition with their counterparts in classical culture; students of Shakespeare's thought have traced it to the Greek and/ or Roman philosophers; source-seekers have heard in the plays and poems countless echoes of classical phrases and concepts; recent analysts of Shakespeare's poetic and dramatic techniques have measured his achievement against the classical tradition which in part produced those techniques; chronologists of the canon have used such criteria as incidence or type of mythological allusion to date the plays; disintegrators of the canon have assigned passages to Shakespeare's contemporaries on the basis of their classicism; Baconians and other anti-Stratfordians have argued that Shakespeare the actor did not have the classical learning which the plays and poems imply; psychologists and anthropologists have placed the plays in the context of myth and folklore, usually dwelling on parallels in Greek religion. For three centuries, Shakespeare studies have been touched at all points by the question of Shakespeare's participation in the classical tradition. This bibliographical Guide is an attempt to gather, classify, summarize, and appraise the commentary which has been written since 1660.

This is not, of course, the first time that an attempt has been made to gather secondary materials on Shakespeare's classicism: this compilation is greatly indebted to the bibliographical research of Walther Ebisch and Levin L. Schücking, of Huntington Brown, of Selma Guttman, and of Gordon Ross Smith.[2] The larger purposes of each of the first three of these works necessitated that each be strictly selective, and none of them includes any works published since 1940.[3] The difficulty of finding relevant materials in Smith's bibliography is discussed in my review (English Studies, XLV [1964], 189-191). Moreover, none of the four systematically appraises its entries. That there is need for a more comprehensive compilation of scholarship on Shakespeare's classicism is indicated by T. W. Baldwin's wistful remark in William Shakspere's Small Latine & Lesse Greeke. After discussing in some detail the early history of attempts to trace Jaques's famous "All the world's a stage"

NOTE: Numbers preceded by # refer to entries in this Guide. Keys to abbreviations are found on pages xi-xvii and 381-387.

[1]The term is used here (and, when capitalized, throughout the Guide) in its common seventeenth-century signification: "technical skill derived from study and imitation of one's (classical) predecessors." See G. B. Harrison's brief discussion of the implications of the term in #0312, Appendix 18, p. 1642.

[2]See #0014, #0011, #0019, #0047. The contributions of these standard references to the Guide are designated E-S, HB, SG, GRS.

[3]The present Guide contains almost as many entries from the period 1940-60 as from the preceding 280 years combined.

to a passage in Palingenius' Zodiacus Vitae, Baldwin goes on: "Early in my studies, I came across the passage in Withals [The Little Dictionarie] independently, and located its source in Palingenius. It was thus somewhat irksome to discover later that this prize identification had been made at least thrice before, but had each time failed to enter the tradition. ... Here is another illustration of the fact that it is still utterly impossible to locate without long search what has already been done upon Shakspere." (#0089, I, 653.) The pages of this Guide provide ample evidence that Baldwin's inadvertent duplication of earlier research was not a unique misfortune. The compilation has been undertaken in the hope that it may help scholars to avoid such wasteful duplication.

The Guide includes all the relevant criticism and scholarship in English, French, and German that I could discover except anti-Stratfordian speculations,[4] psychoanalytic studies,[5] most editions of the plays and poems,[6] reviews,[7] and German dissertations and Schulprogramme.[8] Unless they have been published in book form, American doctoral dissertations are listed beginning with the mid-1930's, when the introduction of microfilming made them generally available. I have usually relied on abstracts of these dissertations.[9] At the risk of preserving "ghosts," I have listed several works which diligent search could not locate. For other works listed as "not seen" and for some "seen" materials which are not easily found, I have supplied locations from the National Union Catalogue or the Union List of Serials.

[4]See William F. Friedman and Elizebeth S. Friedman, The Shakespearean Ciphers Examined (CUP, 1957), p. 5, and R. C. Churchill (#0163), p. 17, for impressive evidence of the magnitude of the anti-Stratfordian literature. Of the thousands of books and articles purporting to prove that "Shakespeare" was a mask for another writer or for a group of writers, hundreds have used the argument that the plays display a classical erudition beyond the reach of an illiterate actor from the provinces. But the anti-Stratfordian movement is generally discredited by responsible scholars: see, e.g., Churchill; Friedman and Friedman; Louis J. Budd, "The Baconians: Madness Through Method," SAQ, LIV (1955), 359-368; Louis B. Wright, "The Anti-Shakespeare Industry and the Growth of Cults," VQR, XXXV (1959), 289-303.

[5]See #1979 for objections to the psychoanalytic method; the exclusion has not been adhered to rigidly, however—see index, s.v. "criticism, psychoanalytic."

[6]The multiplicity of editions in the twentieth century and the almost insurmountable technical difficulties to be encountered in cross-referencing the notes on individual plays and passages have made it impossible to include the comments of most modern editors. The introductions to the original and new Arden editions, the New Shakespeare of Quiller-Couch and Wilson, Munro's London Shakespeare, and the one-volume editions by Kittredge, Harrison, Neilson and Hill, Craig, and Sisson stand proxy to numerous others regretfully passed over. A small handful of extended notes by distinguished editors of the New Variorum have been admitted. Because Rowe, Pope, Theobald, Johnson, and Malone made their pronouncements on the "small Latin" question in the introductions to their editions, all of the eighteenth-century editions up to and including Boswell's Malone have been considered relevant.

[7]Reviews of books, of major articles, and of play productions have been excluded on the assumption that an interested reader can readily find them in the standard journals. A few reviews from the London Times Literary Supplement have been admitted because, as leading articles, they constitute essays in themselves. Correspondence in TLS has also been considered relevant, but letters to the editors of other journals have ordinarily been bypassed.

[8]Inaugural dissertations and Programme are not included here in part because they so seldom are available in English and American libraries and in part because they often touch lightly at many points instead of settling firmly on one. For an extreme (but not untypical) case of touching lightly, see Elisabeth Wolffhardt, Shakespeare und das Griechentum, diss (Friedrich-Wilhelms-Universität, Berlin, 1919); Dr. Wolffhardt treats "Die Griechen im Urteil der Römer" in three pages. Richard Mummendey's Language and Literature of the Anglo-Saxon Nations as Presented in German Doctoral Dissertations, 1885-1950 (Bonn, Charlottesville, Va., 1954) lists about thirty dissertations on Shakespeare which would seem to have relevance for this Guide. For Schulprogramme see Fock's Bibliographischer Monatsbericht über neu erschienene Schul- und Universitätsschriften (1889-1943).

[9]In some cases a dissertation is listed without annotation and marked with an asterisk to signify that I have not seen an abstract and that I cannot assure the reader of access to this work. These entries are normally from DDAAU, and their dates may be approximations; DDAAU is ambiguous about the year in which a dissertation was actually accepted.

The forward limit of classical culture is drawn at the death of Boethius (524 A.D.), a date which has some authority in Gibbon, who called Boethius "the last of the Romans whom Cato or Tully could have acknowledged for their countryman."[10] Boethius was a Christian, but it is for his interest in Plato, Aristotle, and the Stoics that he is remembered. In contrast, Augustine and Prudentius, e.g., both of whom died approximately one hundred years before Boethius, are distinguished chiefly as Christian writers and accordingly have not been considered part of classical culture.

The term "tradition," on the other hand, has been taken rather broadly; studies of Shakespeare's direct use of classical sources constitute only a fraction of the entries. The devious paths by which the Renaissance found access to the classics have been explored and mapped in recent years, and studies which follow Shakespeare down those paths are included here. Erasmus, William Lily, Susenbrotus, Palingenius, and Mantuanus, all of them men of the Renaissance, are here considered "classics" because they so obviously draw on their Greek and Roman ancestors and because T. W. Baldwin (#0089), John E. Hankins (#0306), and others have conclusively demonstrated that as grammar school authors they provided Shakespeare with part of his introduction to the classical world. Books and articles on Shakespeare's use of compilations of sententiae, mythological dictionaries, translations, the French Senecan tragedies, and similarly indirect routes to Greece and Rome are also annotated in these pages. Again, comparative studies of Shakespeare and classical literature are here, even when no question of indebtedness is raised, and whether the comparison is based on form, anthropology, philosophy, or characterization. Where Shakespeare is writing on a classical theme, the Guide embraces character and plot studies: Shakespeare's presentation of Volumnia or the siege of Troy is, after all, an index of his response to the ancient world. In short, the aim has been to summarize and appraise as broad a base of criticism and scholarship as feasible without losing sight of classical culture as a focal point.

The Guide is organized around groups of Shakespeare's works. Following the sections of "Bibliographies Consulted" and "General Works" (the latter comprises entries which properly belong in three or more of the other sections of the Guide), there are sections on "The Comedies" (All's W., A.Y.L., Dream, Errors, L.L.L., Meas., Merch., Much, Shrew, T.G.V., Twel., Wives), "The Histories" (1H.IV, 2H.IV, H.V, 1H.VI, 2H.VI, 3H.VI, H.VIII, John, R.II, R.III), "The Plays on Classical Themes" (Antony, Caesar, Cor., Tim., Titus, Troi.),[11] "The Tragedies" (Ham., Lear, Macb., Oth., Romeo), "The Last Plays" (Cym., Per., Temp., W.T.), and "The Poems and Sonnets" (Lov. Com., Lucr., Pass. Pil., Phoenix, Sonn., Venus). Although it inevitably leads to certain distortions,[12] this generic classification has seemed the most convenient means of imposing order on a large and somewhat heterogeneous body of scholarship. Then, too, such a division calls attention to the relative amounts of interest which certain kinds of plays have stimulated.[13] It is, of course, no surprise that the six plays on classical themes have received more than twice as much scholarly attention as the ten histories and the last four plays combined, especially since plot and character studies of the classical plays have been considered relevant. It is surprising, however, to find that the section on the five tragedies is far larger than the section on the twelve comedies—this despite Shakespeare's debt to Roman comedy and classical mythology in several of the twelve. Even more startling is the brevity of the section on the poems and sonnets considering that Venus and Lucr. treat classical myth and legend and Sonn. contain Ovidian, Horatian, and Platonic themes.

Following the section on the poems and sonnets, there are notes on "Shakespeare's Clas-

[10]Edward Gibbon, The History of the Decline and Fall of the Roman Empire, ed. J. B. Bury, 5th ed. (Ln: Methuen, 1923), IV, 197-198.

[11]Troi., Tim., and Titus respectively reflect the Homeric, Periclean, and post-Augustan worlds in a greatly distorting mirror. But Shakespeare and his contemporaries would not necessarily have thought them distortions, and these plays are here accorded the label "classical" without misgiving.

[12]Most notable among them is the fact that the plays on classical themes (with the possible exceptions of Tim. and Troi.) are also tragedies. It should be observed in addition that the Roman plays are histories, and that Venus and Lucr. are poems on classical themes.

[13]For further justification of the organization selected here, see the commentary on Dr. Guttman's bibliography (#0019).

sics," a section devoted to modern editions of the originals and translations which Shakespeare may have used. In this section some flexibility seemed desirable; where one or more responsible authorities suggest that Shakespeare knew a classical author (e.g., Appian [#2469, #1477], Apuleius [#0774, #0565]), modern reprints of the classical or sixteenth-century sources are included, whether or not the prefatory material contains discussion of Shakespeare's debt to the work.[14]

The abbreviations of the titles of the plays and poems are those used in the SQ annual bibliography (#0042).[15] The Oxford Classical Dictionary is normally the authority for the titles of classical works.[16] Where quotations from Shakespeare are given, the Kittredge edition (#0365) has been used. No deliberate alterations have been made in the titles of articles or books, but in paraphrases of their contents wording and lineation have silently been made to agree with Kittredge's. Inconsistency in forms of address for women is deliberate--a response to their wishes when I knew of them and to guesswork when I did not.

I am grateful to Professor Huntington Brown, now emeritus of the University of Minnesota, for first encouraging me to follow the path his own research has marked into the thicket of Shakespeare bibliography. His kindly advice repeatedly was a compass when my ignorance made me uncertain of direction. To Dr. James G. McManaway of the Folger Shakespeare Library I am much indebted for his detailed criticism of the manuscript and for specific information which enabled me to keep the "not seens" to a minimum. A generous grant from Rice University permitted me to make a summer trip to the Widener Library at Harvard University, the Boston Public Library, the Johns Hopkins University Library, the Library of Congress, and the Folger Shakespeare Library. The staffs of these libraries and of the Walter Library at the University of Minnesota, the Fondren Library at Rice University, and the Mirabeau B. Lamar Library at the University of Texas have patiently answered innumerable questions; I am much in their debt.

I wish to thank Dr. F. W. Bateson, Dr. Frederick Sternfeld, Dr. Lester Beaurline, and Dr. Allan H. Stevenson for various suggestions and indispensable bits of information. Acknowledgment is also due to Prof. Dr. Walter F. Schirmer for permission to reprint the final section of the introduction, which first appeared in Anglia. Rice University provided funds for much needed clerical assistance in preparing the manuscript. Mr. Carl P. Daw, Jr., deserves commendation for his painstaking help with the index. To Miss Marcia Strout of the University of Minnesota Press go special thanks for her intelligent care and for her genial good humor--a sine qua non under the burden of an arduous editorial task.

The greatest debt of all is recorded in the dedication.

I, myself, must claim the errors and the omissions, of which there are doubtless many. But if oversights are a bibliographer's spectral nemesis, he can be partially consoled by what he learns as he attempts to avoid them.

J.W.V.

Houston, October, 1967

[14] This section is not systematically cross-referenced to the other sections. Cross-references in general have been held to a minimum--they appear only when a work properly belongs in two sections of the Guide. To be sure that he has found all relevant material, the reader must consult the index.

[15] The set of abbreviations now recommended by MLA, SQ, the New Variorum Committee, and others concerned with Shakespearean scholarship was evolved too late to be adopted here.

[16] I apologize for the absence of Greek capital letters.

TOPICAL KEY TO ABBREVIATIONS

SHAKESPEARE'S WORKS

All's W.--All's Well That Ends Well
Antony--The Tragedy of Antony and Cleopatra
A.Y.L.--As You Like It
Caesar--The Tragedy of Julius Caesar
Cor.--The Tragedy of Coriolanus
Cym.--Cymbeline
Dream--A Midsummer Night's Dream
Errors--The Comedy of Errors
1H.IV--The First Part of King Henry the Fourth
2H.IV--The Second Part of King Henry the Fourth
H.V--The Life of King Henry the Fifth
1H.VI--The First Part of King Henry the Sixth
2H.VI--The Second Part of King Henry the Sixth
3H.VI--The Third Part of King Henry the Sixth
H.VIII--The Famous History of the Life of King Henry the Eighth
Ham.--The Tragedy of Hamlet, Prince of Denmark
John--The Life and Death of King John
Lear--The Tragedy of King Lear
L.L.L.--Love's Labour's Lost
Lov. Com.--A Lover's Complaint
Lucr.--The Rape of Lucrece
Macb.--The Tragedy of Macbeth
Meas.--Measure for Measure
Merch.--The Merchant of Venice
Much--Much Ado About Nothing
Oth.--The Tragedy of Othello, the Moor of Venice
Pass. Pil.--The Passionate Pilgrim
Per.--Pericles, Prince of Tyre
Phoenix--The Phoenix and Turtle
R.II--The Tragedy of King Richard the Second
R.III--The Tragedy of King Richard the Third
Romeo--The Tragedy of Romeo and Juliet
Shrew--The Taming of the Shrew
Sonn.--Shakespeare's Sonnet(s)
Temp.--The Tempest
T.G.V.--The Two Gentlemen of Verona
Tim.--The Life of Timon of Athens
Titus--The Tragedy of Titus Andronicus
T.N.K.--The Two Noble Kinsmen
Troi.--The Tragedy of Troilus and Cressida
Twel.--Twelfth Night; or, What You Will
Venus--Venus and Adonis
Wives--The Merry Wives of Windsor
W.T.--The Winter's Tale

SERIALS AND FESTSCHRIFTEN

AA--Anglistische Arbeiten hrsg. L. L. Schücking
Acad--The Academy (Ln)
Acad (N.Y.)--The Academy (N.Y.)
Accent
The Adventurer
AESG--Annales de l'enseignement supérieur de Grenoble
AFLA--Annales de la faculté de lettres d'Aix
AI--American Imago
AJP--American Journal of Philology
AJPsy--American Journal of Psychology
ALVN--Album des literarischen Vereins in Nürnberg
AM--The Atlantic Monthly
AMB--Antiquarian Magazine and Bibliographer (Ln)
AMS--Joseph Quincy Adams Memorial Studies, ed. James G. McManaway, Giles E. Dawson, and Edwin E. Willoughby. Washington: The Folger Shakespeare Library, 1948.
Anglia
AngliaM--Beiblatt zur Anglia: Mitteilungen über englische Sprache und Literatur und über englischen Unterricht
Anglo-Americana--Anglo-Americana: Festschrift zum 70. Geburtstag von Professor Dr.

Leo Hibler-Lebmannsport, hrsg. Karl Brunner. WBEP, LXII [1955?].
Die Antike--Die Antike: Zeitschrift für Kunst und Kultur des klassischen Altertums
Antike und Abendland
APSR--American Political Science Review
Archiv--Archiv für das Studium der neueren Sprachen und Literaturen
AshSS--Ashland Studies in Shakespeare
Ath--The Athenaeum (Ln)
A-VG--Audio-Visual Guide
AYR--All the Year Round
Baldwin Festschrift--Studies in Honor of T. W. Baldwin, ed. Don Cameron Allen. Illinois UP, 1958.
Bang's Materialien--Materialien zur Kunde des älteren englischen Dramas, hrsg. W. Bang. 44 vols., Louvain, 1902-13.
The Bee--The Bee, or Literary Intelligencer
BEM--Blackwood's Edinburgh Magazine
BFLS--Bulletin de la faculté des lettres de Strasbourg
BHM--Bulletin of the History of Medicine
BJRL--Bulletin of the John Rylands Library
BLM--Bibliothèque des langues modernes
BM--British Magazine
BNYPL--Bulletin of the New York Public Library
The Bookman
BPLB--Boston Public Library Bulletin
BR--Bucknell Review
BRLC--Bibliothèque de la revue de littérature comparée
BUS--Bucknell University Studies
BUSE--Boston University Studies in English
Cahiers du sud
CalcuttaR--Calcutta Review
CamJ--The Cambridge Journal
CAP--Classical Association Proceedings
CarrollQ--Carroll Quarterly
CathW--Catholic World
CE--College English
The Censor
CH--Church History
The Christian Reformer (Ln)
CJ--Classical Journal
CL--Comparative Literature
CM--The Canadian Magazine
ColoradoSLL--Colorado University Studies: Series in Language and Literature
ColSCL--Columbia University Studies in Comparative Literature
ColSECL--Columbia University Studies in English and Comparative Literature
ColSS--Shaksperian Studies by Members of the Department of English and Comparative Literature in Columbia University, ed. Brander Matthews and Ashley H. Thorndike. Col UP, 1916.
CornellR--The Cornell Review
CP--Classical Philology
CQR--Church Quarterly Review
CR--Contemporary Review
Craig Festschrift--Renaissance Studies in Honor of Hardin Craig, ed. Baldwin Maxwell, et al. Stanford UP, 1941. A reprinting of part of PQ, XX (1941).
CRAS--The Centennial Review of Arts and Science
The Criterion
CSE--Carnegie Series in English
CUC--California University Chronicle
CUCE--Columbia University Contributions to Education: Teachers College Series
Culture (Paris)
CUPCP--California University Publications in Classical Philology
CUPE--California University Publications in English
Curry Festschrift--Essays in Honor of Walter Clyde Curry, Vanderbilt Studies in the Humanities, No. 2 (Vanderbilt UP, 1954).
CW--Classical Weekly
DA--Dissertation Abstracts
Darmstädter Tageblatt
DD--Deutsche Dramaturgie: Zeitschrift für die Probleme der darstellenden Künste
DDAAU--Doctoral Dissertations Accepted by American Universities
Discussion (South Africa)
DR--Dublin Review
The Drama
DUJ--Durham University Journal
DVLG--Deutsche Vierteljahrsschrift für Literaturwissenschaft und Geistesgeschichte
EA--Etudes anglaises
EC--Essays in Criticism
Edda--Edda: Nordisk Tidsskrift for Litteraturforskning
EDH--Essays by Divers Hands: Being the Transactions of the Royal Society of Literature
EH--Ewiger Humanismus: Schriften der österreichischen Gesellschaft in Innsbruck
EIE--English Institute Essays
ELH--ELH: A Journal of English Literary History
EM--English Miscellany (Rome)
Encounter
English
ER--Essex Review
Erbe--Das Erbe der Alten
ES--English Studies (Amsterdam)
ESA--English Studies in Africa (Johannesburg)
ESn--Englische Studien

Essays and Studies--Essays and Studies by Members of the English Association
Euphorion
EuropäischeR--Europäische Revue
Europe
Expl--Explicator
FL--Folk-Lore
FM--Fraser's Magazine
FMV--The Flügel Memorial Volume, Stanford University Publications: University Series [XXI], Stanford UP, 1916.
FR--Fortnightly Review
Die Frau--Die Frau: Monatsschrift für das gesamte Frauenleben unserer Zeit (Berlin)
French Festschrift--Essays in Literary History, Presented to J. Milton French, ed. Rudolf Kirk and C. F. Main. Rutgers UP, 1960.
FSUS--Florida State University Studies
GBE--Giessener Beiträge zur Erforschung der Sprache und Kultur Englands und Nordamerikas
Germania (Berlin)
GM--The Gentleman's Magazine
GR--Greece and Rome
GRM--Germanisch-Romanische Monatsschrift
HarLB--Harvard Library Bulletin
Harper's
HCP--Holy Cross Purple
Hermathena--Hermathena: A Series of Papers on Literature, Science, and Philosophy by Members of Trinity College Dublin
HJ--Hibbert Journal
HL--Humanistica Lovaniensia
HLB--The Huntington Library Bulletin
HLM--The Hamilton Literary Monthly
HLQ--The Huntington Library Quarterly
Homage--A Book of Homage to Shakespeare: To Commemorate the Three Hundredth Anniversary of Shakespeare's Death MCMXVI, ed. Israel Gollancz. OUP, 1916.
Home University (Ln)
HowardSHL--Howard College Bulletin: Studies in History and Literature
HR--Hudson Review
HSCL--Harvard Studies in Comparative Literature
HSCP--Harvard Studies in Classical Philology
HSE--Harvard Studies in English
HSNPL--Harvard Studies and Notes in Philology and Literature
HT--History Today
Hunt Festschrift--If By Your Art: Testament to Percival Hunt. Pittsburgh UP, 1948.
HWL--The History of the Works of the Learned
IADD--Index to American Doctoral Dissertations
IBK--Innsbrucker Beiträge zur Kultur-wissenschaft
IJP--International Journal of Psycho-Analysis
Das Inselschiff--Das Inselschiff: Zeitschrift für die Freunde des Insel-Verlags (Leipzig)
IowaHS--University of Iowa Humanistic Studies
Isis
ISLL--Illinois Studies in Language and Literature
Italica
IUS--Indiana University Studies: Contributions to Knowledge Made by Instructors and Advanced Students of the University
JAAK--Jahrbuch für Ästhetik und allgemeine Kunstwissenschaft
JAF--Journal of American Folklore
JEGP--Journal of English and Germanic Philology
JFKA--Jahresbericht über die Fortschritte der klassischen Altertumswissenschaft
JHI--Journal of the History of Ideas
JHUC--Johns Hopkins University Circulars
Jimbungaku--Jimbungaku: Studies in Humanities (Doshisha University, Kyoto)
Jones Festschrift--The Seventeenth Century: Studies in the History of English Thought and Literature from Bacon to Pope, by Richard Foster Jones and Others Writing in his Honor. Stanford UP, 1951.
JP--Journal of Philology
JWCI--Journal of the Warburg and Courtauld Institutes
Klaeber Festschrift--Studies in English Philology: A Miscellany in Honor of Frederick Klaeber, ed. Kemp Malone and Martin B. Ruud. Minnesota UP, 1929.
KN--Kwartalnik Neofilologiczny
KR--Kenyon Review
KSA--Die klassischen Schriftsteller des Altertums in ihrem Einflusse auf die späteren Literaturen
LCUT--Library Chronicle of the University of Texas
LHF--Litterarhistorische Forschungen hrsg. Josef Schick und Frh. v. Waldberg
LHM--American Society Legion of Honor Magazine
Library--The Library: A Bibliographical Quarterly
Liebermann Festschrift--Texte und Forschungen zur Kulturgeschichte: Festgabe für Felix Liebermann. Halle, 1921.
The Listener
The Literary Criterion (Mysore)
Die Literatur--Die Literatur: Monatsschrift für Literaturfreunde
Literature

LL--Life and Letters
LLM--Les Langues modernes
LLT--Life and Letters Today
LM--London Mercury
L&P--Literature and Psychology
LQHR--London Quarterly and Holborn Review
LQR--London Quarterly Review
LV--Lenguas Vivas (Buenos Aires)
MAH--Mélanges d'archéologie et d'histoire
ManQ--Manchester Quarterly
MAR--Manitoba Arts Review
MAS--The Manly Anniversary Studies in Language and Literature. Chicago UP, 1923.
MCMP--The University of Michigan Contributions in Modern Philology
MdeF--Mercure de France
Mélanges--Mélanges de linguistique et de philologie, Fernand Mossé in memoriam. Paris, 1959.
Merkur (Stuttgart)
MF--Midwest Folklore
MiamiSS--Studies in Shakespeare, University of Miami Publications in English and American Literature. Miami UP, 1953.
MichiganPLL--University of Michigan Publications: Language and Literature
MicroA--Microfilm Abstracts
The Mirror
M&L--Music and Letters
MLN--Modern Language Notes
MLQ--Modern Language Quarterly
MLR--Modern Language Review
MM--Macmillan's Magazine
The Month
Monthly Magazine
The Monthly Mirror
Mosher's--Mosher's Magazine
MP--Modern Philology
MQM--Modern Quarterly Miscellany
MR--Massachusetts Review
MSR--Malone Society Reprints
MUM--McGill University Magazine
MUS--University of Missouri Studies: A Quarterly of Research
Museum (Leyden)
Mutschmann Festschrift--Shakespeare-Studien: Festschrift für Heinrich Mutschmann, hrsg. Walther Fischer und Karl Wentersdorf. Marburg, 1951.
NA--New Adelphi
N&A--Nation and Athenaeum
Names
Nation
NBR--North British Review
NC--The Nineteenth Century
Neoph--Neophilologus
NER--New English Review
NewShna--New Shakespeareana
NEYR--New Englander and Yale Review
NIR--New Ireland Review
NJKA--Neue Jahrbücher für das klassische Altertum, Geschichte, und deutsche Literatur, und für Pädagogik
NM--Neuphilologische Monatsschrift
NQ--Notes and Queries
NR--National Review
NS--Die neueren Sprachen
NSST--New Shakspere Society Transactions
NZ--Neuphilologische Zeitschrift
The Observer
OC--The Open Court
Occult Observer
OEP--Old English Plays: Students' Facsimile Edition. . .under the General Editorship of John S. Farmer. 184 vols. n.p., 1907-14.
Our Debt--Our Debt to Greece and Rome
Palaestra--Palaestra: Untersuchungen und Texte aus der deutschen und englischen Philologie
PartR--Partisan Review
PBA--Proceedings of the British Academy
PC--Publishers' Circular
PF--Port Folio
Philologica--Philologica: The Malone Anniversary Studies, ed. Thomas A. Kirby and Henry B. Woolf. Johns Hopkins UP, 1949.
Philologus
The Phoenix--The Phoenix: The Journal of the Classical Association of Canada
PJ--Preussische Jahrbücher
PL--Poet Lore
PM--Penn Monthly
PMA--Papers of the Michigan Academy of Science Arts and Letters
PMLA--Publications of the Modern Language Association of America
PPPLA--Publications of the University of Pennsylvania: Series in Philology, Literature, and Archaeology
PPV--Essays in Dramatic Literature: The Parrott Presentation Volume By Pupils of Professor Thomas Marc Parrott of Princeton University, Published in his Honor, ed. Hardin Craig. PUP, 1935.
PQ--Philological Quarterly
PR--Poetry Review
PRI--Proceedings of the Royal Institution of Great Britain
Propyläen
PS--Philippine Studies: A Quarterly
PSE--Princeton Studies in English
PTPN--Poznanskie Towarzystwo Przyjaciol Nauk: Wydzial Filologiczno-Filozoficzny Prace Komisji Filologicznej
PUB--Princeton University Bulletin
PUM--Publications of the University of Manchester, English Series

QJS--Quarterly Journal of Speech
QR--The Quarterly Review
RAA--Revue anglo-américaine
RB--Revue bleue
RCC--Revue des cours et conférences
The Reflector--The Reflector: A Quarterly Magazine, on Subjects of Philosophy, Politics, and the Liberal Arts
RELV--Revue de l'enseignement des langues vivantes
RenP--Renaissance Papers
RES--Review of English Studies
RG--Revue germanique
RGF--Revue germanique et française
RH--Revue hebdomadaire
RIP--Rice Institute Pamphlet
RLC--Revue de littérature comparée
RPUM--Research Publications of the University of Minnesota
RSH--Revue des sciences humaines
SAB--Shakspere Association Bulletin
SAQ--South Atlantic Quarterly
SatR--The Saturday Review
SBAW--Sitzungsberichte der bayerischen Akademie der Wissenschaften: Philosophisch-historische Klasse
Scrutiny
SEL(T)--Studies in English Literature (Tokyo)
SEP--Studien zur englischen Philologie hrsg. Lorenz Morsbach
SERD--Studies in the English Renaissance Drama, ed. Josephine W. Bennett, Oscar Cargill, and Vernon Hall, Jr., "In memory of Karl Julius Holzknecht." New York UP, 1959.
SewR--The Sewanee Review
SFR--Scholars' Facsimiles and Reprints
ShJ--Jahrbuch der deutschen Shakespeare-Gesellschaft
ShN--The Shakespeare Newsletter
Shna--Shakespeariana
ShR--The Shakespeare Review
ShS--Shakespeare Survey
SKGV--Sprache und Kultur der germanisch-romanischen Völker, germanistische Reihe
SM--Speech Monographs
SouthernR--Southern Review
SP--Studies in Philology
The Spectator
SQ--Shakespeare Quarterly
SR--Studies in the Renaissance
SSP--Shakespeare Society Publications
Standpunte (Kaapstad)
StN--Studia Neophilologica
Studies--Studies: An Irish Quarterly Review of Letters Philosophy and Science
TAM--Theatre Arts Monthly
TAPA--Transactions of the American Philological Association
The Tatler
Taylor Festschrift--A Tribute to George Coffin Taylor: Studies and Essays Chiefly Elizabethan, by His Students and Friends, ed. Arnold Williams. North Carolina UP, 1952.
TBS--Transactions of the Bibliographical Society
Le Temps (Paris)
TennSL--Tennessee Studies in Literature
The Theatre
Theoria--Theoria: A Journal of Studies in the Arts, Humanities and Social Sciences (University of Natal)
Thought
TLS--The [London] Times Literary Supplement
TR--The Texas Review
Traditio--Traditio: Studies in Ancient and Medieval History, Thought and Religion
TRSC--Transactions of the Royal Society of Canada
TRSL--Transactions of the Royal Society of Literature of the United Kingdom
TSE--University of Texas Studies in English
TST--University of Toronto Department of English: Studies and Texts
TT--Time and Tide
The Tudor Translations
TulSE--Tulane Studies in English
UEJ--University of Edinburgh Journal
UKCR--University of Kansas City Review
UMFR--The University Magazine and Free Review (Ln)
UngR--Ungarische Rundschau für historische und soziale Wissenschaften
The Universal Magazine
UR--The University Review
UTQ--The University of Toronto Quarterly
VirginiaES--English Studies in Honor of James Southall Wilson, [ed. Fredson Bowers], University of Virginia Studies, V [incorrectly numbered IV], 1951.
VJ--Vassar Journal of Undergraduate Studies
VM--Vassar Miscellany
VQR--Virginia Quarterly Review
WBEP--Wiener Beiträge zur englischen Philologie
WBFA--Wiener Blätter für die Freunde der Antike
The Western
Westwind (UCLA)
WHR--Western Humanities Review
Wilson Festschrift--Elizabethan and Jacobean Studies Presented to Frank Percy Wilson. . . , ed. Herbert Davis and Helen Gardner. OUP, 1959.
WSLL--University of Wisconsin Studies in Language and Literature

WUS--Washington University Studies: Humanistic Series
WVBPS--West Virginia Bulletin of Philological Studies
WW--Wort und Wahrheit
YR--Yale Review
YSE--Yale Studies in English
YWES--The Year's Work in English Studies
ZDA--Zeitschrift für deutsches Alterthum und deutsche Literatur
ZNU--Zeitschrift für neusprachlichen Unterricht
ZVLG--Zeitschrift für vergleichende Literaturgeschichte
ZVV--Zeitschrift des Vereins für Volkskunde

MISCELLANEOUS ABBREVIATIONS AND SYMBOLS

ArdenSh--The Arden Edition of the Works of William Shakespeare (both the original Arden Edition and the so-called "New Arden")
art(s).--article(s)
Bd.--Band
Boswell's Malone--William Shakespeare, Poems and Plays... with the corrections and illustrations of various commentators... ed. after Mr. Malone's death by James Boswell the Younger. 21 vols., Ln, 1821.
CBEL--Cambridge Bibliography of English Literature
ch(s).--chapter(s)
CLU--University of California at Los Angeles Library
Col UP--Columbia University Press
CSh--The Cambridge Shakespeare, ed. Sir Arthur Quiller-Couch and J. Dover Wilson. CUP, 1921- (in progress).
CSt--Stanford University Library
CT--Chaucer's Canterbury Tales
CtY--Yale University Library
CU--University of California (Berkeley) Library
CUP--Cambridge University Press
CU Riv--University of California (Riverside) Library
DFo--The Folger Shakespeare Library
diss--dissertation
DLC--The Library of Congress
ed.--edition, edited by, editor
E-S--Walther Ebisch and Levin L. Schücking. A Shakespeare Bibliography. See #0014.
F_1--The First Folio, 1623.
FCU--University of Miami (Coral Gables) Library
FQ--The Faerie Queene
GRS--Gordon Ross Smith. A Classified Shakespeare Bibliography, 1936-1958. Pennsylvania State UP, 1963. See #0047.
H.--Heft
HB--Huntington Brown. "The Classical Tradition in English Literature: A Bibliography," HSNPL, XVIII (1935), 7-46. See #0011.
hrsg.--herausgegeben von
HUP--Harvard University Press
IaU--University of Iowa Library
ICarbS--Southern Illinois University Library
IU--University of Illinois Library
LGW--Chaucer's The Legend of Good Women
Ln--London
LSU--Louisiana State University
MA--Converse Memorial Library, Amherst College
MB--Boston Public Library
MdBJ--Johns Hopkins University Library
Meta.--Ovid's Metamorphoses
MH--Harvard University Libraries
MHRA--The Modern Humanities Research Association
MiU--University of Michigan Library
MLA--Modern Language Association
MnU--Walter Library, University of Minnesota
Munro--see #0044.
Munro Sup--John Munro. "More Shakspere Allusions," MP, XIII (1916), 497-544. See #0031.
mythol.--mythological person(s), place(s), etc.
NcD--Duke University Library
n.d.--no date given
NED--The New English Dictionary
New Variorum--A New Variorum Edition of Shakespeare, ed. Horace H. Furness, his son, and MLA. 27 vols. Philadelphia, 1871- (in progress).
n.F.--neue Folge
NjP--Princeton University Library
NN--New York Public Library
NNC--Columbia University Library
NNU--New York University Library (Washington Square)
n.p.--no place of publication given
n.s.--new series
OU--Ohio State University Library
OUP--Oxford University Press
PU(F)--University of Pennsylvania Library (Furness Memorial Library)
PUP--Princeton University Press
Q_1, Q_2, etc.--First Quarto, Second Quarto, etc.
rev.--review
SG--Selma Guttman. The Foreign Sources of Shakespeare's Works: An Annotated Bibliography of the Commentary Written on this Subject Between 1904 and 1940... Col UP: King's Crown, 1947. See #0019.
Sh, Shn, Sh's--Shakespeare, Shakespearean, Shakespeare's
T-D--More Seventeenth Century Allusions to Shakespeare and his Works [collected by George Thorn-Drury]. Ln, 1924. See #0051.
trans.--translation(s), translated

TU--University of Tennessee Library
TxHR--Fondren Library, Rice University
TxU--Mirabeau B. Lamar Library, University of Texas
UP--University Press
vol(s).--volume(s)
WU--University of Wisconsin Library
*--(following a diss entry): the compiler has not seen an abstract of the work; he cannot assure the reader of access to this unpublished material. The entries normally come from DDAAU or IADD.

TABLE OF CONTENTS

SHAKESPEARE AND THE CLASSICAL TRADITION

INTRODUCTION

It is not obvious with what date to begin a compilation of Shakespeare scholarship and criticism. The historians of Shakespeare's reputation in the seventeenth century themselves do not agree on a date after which one can safely say that legitimate criticism had been launched. The Shakspere Allusion-Book (#0044) was begun as a collection of references to Shakespeare and his works made by his own contemporaries; yet it grew until its forward limit was eventually extended from 1693 to 1700 so that it could embrace the nascent Shakespeare criticism of Collier, Congreve, Dennis, Gildon, and others (ibid., pp. xxv-xxvi). Elsewhere in his introduction, its 1909 reviser, John Munro, calls Ben Jonson "the founder of Shaksperean criticism" (ibid., p. xl), and in another place (ibid., pp. xxv-xxvi) he speaks inter alia of Edward Phillips' Theatrum Poetarum (1675), Dryden's Of Dramatick Poesie (1668), Davenant's Gondibert (1650), and Rymer's The Tragedies of the Last Age consider'd... (1678) each as a possible claimant of the honors due an early work of criticism. In 1866 Charles Knight constructed an elaborate argument to demonstrate that Edmund Spenser was the first Shakespearean critic. Knight reasoned that Shakespeare is the "Willy" who is eulogized in the "Thalia" section of "The Teares of the Muses" (1591).[1] Augustus Ralli devotes only eleven of the 1,148 pages in A History of Shakespearian Criticism (#0037) to the sixteenth and seventeenth centuries; he begins with Francis Meres and Gabriel Harvey but spends very little space on any writer before Dryden. T. W. Baldwin naturally begins his three chapters (#0089, Vol. I) on the development of the "small Latin" controversy in the seventeenth and eighteenth centuries with the primary document in the case, Jonson's eulogy prefatory to F_1. Gerald E. Bentley[2] dismisses allusions to Shakespeare before 1601 in order to compare the popularity of Shakespeare with that of Jonson at a time when both had fully begun their careers. He records allusions of all kinds; but of references which can be called criticism, Shakespeare is not accorded more than nine before 1661.[3]

It would appear then that a bibliographer has authority for almost any seventeenth-century terminus post quem he selects. This Guide begins with the year 1660: first because, as the evidence already cited from Bentley shows, relatively little real criticism of Shakespeare appeared before 1660; second because the reopening of the theaters is a convenient (if artificial) boundary line between Renaissance critical standards and the pseudo-classicism which molded the Restoration attitude toward Shakespeare's learning.

I. THE RESTORATION AND THE EIGHTEENTH CENTURY

By 1660 the notion of an untutored Shakespeare was a commonplace beginning to freeze into a tradition.[4] Thomas Fuller's History of

NOTE: Numbers preceded by # refer to entries in this Guide. Keys to abbreviations are found on pages xi-xvii and 381-387.

[1]#0026; see especially Note A, pp. 337-339.

[2]Shakespeare & Jonson: Their Reputations in the Seventeenth Century Compared. 2 vols. Chicago UP, 1945. 149, 307 pp.

[3]Ibid., Vol. I, tables on pp. 99, 103.

[4]Whether Shakespeare's own age thought him as learned as most is a moot question. He was spoken of again and again by his acquaintances as a reincarnation of Terence, Ovid, Catullus, and other classi-

the Worthies of England (#0257), appearing in 1662, crystallized a supposed opposition between Jonson, whom Fuller characterized colorfully as "built far higher in learning" like a "Spanish great Gallion," and Shakespeare, a less ostentatious, but more intellectually agile "English man of War." Fuller's attitude and his language were still sufficiently attractive twenty-five years later to catch the attention of William Winstanley (#0656), who plagiarized Fuller's account of Shakespeare's life and art, and an anonymous plagiarist published Fuller's words again in 1692 (#0333). It may be that Mrs. Aphra Behn was also thinking of Fuller's contrast when she spoke of "Benjamin ... [as] no such Rabbi neither, for I am inform'd his Learning was but Grammar high" (#0099); T. W. Baldwin (#0089, I, 33n) suggests this possibility. The story of Mr. Hales of Eton and his supposed approval of Shakespeare's disregard for the classics was retold in one form or another by Dryden (#0217), Nahum Tate (#1717), Gildon (Miscellaneous Letters and Essays, 1694), Sir Thomas Blount (De Re Poetica, 1694), and Rowe (#0500).

But it is doubtless Dryden, the literary dictator, who sits closest to the center of the general consensus of the age. His is the earliest (1668) version of the story of John Hales mentioned above, and between Dramatick Poesie and 1679 he alludes to Shakespeare's ignorance of antiquity no fewer than five times (#0215, #0216, #0217, #0218, #1274). If Dryden was the author of the Prologue to the refurbished Caesar (#0219), he was prepared in 1672 to deny that Shakespeare knew "what Trope or Figure meant": "He knew the thing but did not know the Name." There is no need arguing that any schoolboy at Stratford knew the terms "trope" and "figure" and a good deal more about classical rhetoric; Dryden's influence, not his accuracy, is at question. There can be no doubt of that influence: Dryden's Laureateship and his lofty reputation as a critic imposed his dogmas about Shakespeare on the age that followed. Rowe (#0500), Samuel Johnson (#0351), and many an Augustan between refer with respect to Dryden's opinions.

Only a few of Dryden's own contemporaries disagreed with him. About 1680 John Aubrey (#0081) recorded the opinion that Shakespeare "understood Latine pretty well: for he had been in his yonger yeares a Schoolmaster in the Countrey." Modern scholars[5] have found good reason to believe that Aubrey was passing along a story founded on truth. About the same time Nahum Tate (#1717) discovered in the Roman plays evidence of Shakespeare's familiarity with "the Manners, the Circumstances, [and] the Ceremonies" of ancient Rome. In a letter published in 1664 (#1204) the Marchioness of Newcastle anticipated Tate's praise of Shakespeare's fidelity to the realities of Roman life. In 1698 an anonymous attack (#0199) on Jeremy Collier saw an illusion of classical unity of time in Macb., Ham., Caesar, and the history plays. Four years later George Farquhar (#0239) laughed at those who demand unity of time--it is Horatian decorum, not Aristotelian unity which Farquhar would judge by, and in the former Shakespeare is rich. Gerard Langbaine recognized Shakespeare's debt to at least one Roman writer; he gives Plautus as a source of Errors (#0833), of Twel. (#0380), and (indirectly, at least) of the mistaken identity in Meas. (#0832). But Langbaine must have thought Plautus available to Shakespeare in English, because he was attacked in The Moderator (#0425) for denying Shakespeare's knowledge of Latin.

Though the critical percipience of these pronouncements has made some of them famous, they are not typical of any large body of opinion at the end of the seventeenth century. Much more representative are references to Shakespeare's ephemeral brilliance (Samuel Butler, #0143), his "wild and native Elegance" (Edward Phillips, #0458), and his "unbounded mind" (Robert Gould, #0281). Thomas Rymer's preposterous attacks on Shakespeare (#2087, #1623) refer repeatedly to his violations of classical decorum, and Edward Ravenscroft advertised his The Rape of Lavinia (1686) by pointing

cal authors--it is not certain whether such flattery implies an assumption of his familiarity with the authors in question. Regardless of what the Restoration critics believed he said, Ben Jonson did say in his famous eulogy in F_1 that Shakespeare had Art as well as Nature: "For a good Poet's made, as well as borne." For the opinions of Shakespeare's contemporaries, see Vol. I of Munro (#0044), passim, and see also T. W. Baldwin's thorough discussion of the implications of Jonson's F_1 poem (#0089, I, Ch. I). Certainly by the time of F_2 (1632) Milton thought more highly of Shakespeare's genius than of his learning (see Munro I, 342), and references to his untutored talent predominate in the decades which followed.

[5]See, e.g., Peter Alexander (#0067, #0068), J. Q. Adams (#0060), Foster Watson (#0628), T. W. Baldwin (#0089, I, 34-38).

out what an "incorrect and indigested piece" Titus, his source, is (#1591). It is not difficult to document the provenance of the prevailing doctrine,[6] but perhaps it is best to leave the final word to John Dryden the Younger, who just before the turn of the century was repeating his father's venerable formula that Shakespeare was deficient in "Learning" (#0220). But if the younger Dryden is looking back toward Leonard Digges,[7] he is also looking forward to eighteenth-century criticism; his pronouncement set a precedent for pre-Romantic critics like Edward Young (#0665) who valued originality: again and again they echo young Dryden's "Had he [Shakespeare] had more Learning, perhaps he might have been less a Poet."

So extreme a position as the Restoration took was almost certain to elicit reaction, at least eventually, but reaction was slow in coming, partly because of the senior Dryden's prestige and perhaps partly because no annotated texts of the Shakespeare canon existed before 1709, and it was not easy to study Shakespeare's classicism in the bulky, misprinted, unannotated Folios. Few men read Shakespeare; the plays they saw produced were Shakespeare "improved,"[8] and there was therefore less interest in reading the originals.[9] When an edition (#0500) of Shakespeare's works did finally appear, the editor was a man of great prestige in the literary world; the fact that Nicholas Rowe repeated and elaborated the myths of the preceding age did much to perpetuate them.

The second editor to turn his attention to Shakespeare was Pope (1725), who enjoyed even greater prestige than Rowe. Pope begins (#0465) with an echo of the younger Dryden on Shakespeare's originality, but he soon is attempting to modify the biases of the seventeenth century. Later in the preface he returns to the concept of Shakespeare as a genius living in a dark, barbarian, preclassical world, but the net effect of Pope's preface is to retract somewhat the excesses of the Restoration critics. It was perhaps Pope's authoritative example which encouraged George Sewell (#0528) to argue three years later in his supplement to Pope's edition that Shakespeare not only knew Latin, but had translated part of Ovid's Heroides.[10]

The editors of Shakespeare's text were not the only contributors to the "small Latin" controversy early in the eighteenth century. George Winchester Stone (#0048), and R. W. Babcock (#0005, #0007, #0008) have defined the provenance of Shakespearean criticism in the periodical literature of the Augustans.[11] Two instances must be made to stand proxy for many others. In The Spectator during 1711, Addison three times refers to Shakespeare's ignorance of or disregard for classical restraints. In these essays Addison appears to be combining Rowe (whom he borrows from for the essay on Ham.

[6]See, e.g., #0526, #1327, #0463, #0171, #0564, and #0430.

[7]Digges was the author of commendatory verses prefixed to John Benson's edition of Shakespeare's poems (1640). They begin with a flat negation of Ben Jonson's thesis (supra, p. 4n):

> Poets are borne not made, when I would prove
> This truth, the glad remembrance I must love
> Of never dying Shakespeare, who alone,
> Is argument enough to make that one.

[8]See the excellent description of some of these "improvements" in Halliday (#0020, Ch. II).

[9]It can be shown that the "small Latin" tradition had an influence on Restoration stage practice. Shakespeare, as an uneducated barbarian (albeit a brilliant one), was in need of "reformation." See #0216, #1274, #1591, and other prefaces and prologues to "Shakespeare re-written." The most striking example is John Dennis' patronizing critique of Shakespeare (#0201) prefixed to his own version of Cor. (1712). There are unclassical absurdities enough in Dennis' Cor., "the dreariest of all adaptations" (Halliday, #0020, p. 61), but that fact does not prevent Dennis from deprecating Shakespeare's classicism.

[10]The translation was Thomas Heywood's. Charles Gildon had anticipated Sewell in his Essay (1710) (see #0269).

[11]Other bibliographers who have culled the Shakespearean criticism in the period are Conklin (#0013), Isaacs (#0024), Knight (#0026), Lounsbury (#0029), Neumann (#0032), Robinson (#0040), Smith (#0046), and Young (#0058).

and Sophocles, #1801) with the younger Dryden (whom he imitates closely in the essay on native genius and labored art, #0063). In 1714 Addison was still expounding the same thesis (#0064). Lewis Theobald published The Censor (#0588) in the second decade of the century; in it, he argued (as Addison had argued) that Shakespeare's genius placed him beyond the classical rules by which literary judgments are normally made. It is interesting to contrast Theobald's attitude toward Shakespeare's classicism in The Censor with the opinions he held two decades later. When Theobald published his edition (#0589) of Shakespeare (1733), he had the announced intention of correcting errors in Pope's work; ironically, however, he appears to have been influenced by Pope's attitude toward the Restoration critics, because Theobald was now prepared to argue in favor of Shakespeare's knowledge of the ancient world.

Theobald's habit of explicating difficult passages by "illustrating" them from the writings of the ancients may have given a cue to John Upton, whose treatise on Shakespeare's learning was first published in 1746. Upton's revision and expansion (#0606) of his argument for Shakespeare's broad knowledge of literature appeared two years later almost simultaneously with a similarly reasoned book by Peter Whalley (#0632). The method of both Upton and Whalley was to place a passage from Shakespeare next to an analogue from another writer (very often classical) and then to conclude that Shakespeare had read his predecessor. Where Theobald had seen only analogues these two entrepreneurs found sources. Each of them had a vast store of obscure classicism at his disposal, but both were ignorant of Elizabethan literature--they repeatedly blundered in according Shakespeare indebtedness to a classical author when the idea, phrase, or situation was a commonplace in sixteenth-century England. Their temporary success encouraged Zachary Grey (#0286) to imitate in 1754 both the methods they employed and the extremes to which they went.

Upton, Whalley, and Grey went as far in one direction as Dryden and his circle had gone in another: now that the pendulum had swung through a wide arc, one might expect it to come to rest in a central position. But the reaction to the new approach to Shakespeare's classicism was no moderate one. In 1767 Richard Farmer exposed (#0238) the ignorance and the bad logic of these three amateurs at the game of parallels, and he included Colman (first ed. of #0175), Theobald (#0589), and Dodd (#0205) as well. Farmer came to the task well prepared with a surprisingly thorough knowledge of Elizabethan culture and with a self-assurance which concealed from himself the fact that his own logic was no better than Upton's, Whalley's, or Grey's. Farmer begins with an unsupported equation between language and learning: i.e., one does not know his classics unless he can read them in the original languages. He then proceeds to show not only that Shakespeare had access to English translations of Plutarch, Ovid, and other ancients, but also that where the translations are incorrect Shakespeare is incorrect too. Ergo Shakespeare used the translations without consulting the originals. Thus far, Farmer had made some contribution to his age's understanding of Shakespeare's reading habits. But he had not established, as he thought he had, that Shakespeare could not read Latin because he sometimes preferred English, or that secondhand knowledge is inferior knowledge, or, indeed, that Shakespeare is somehow responsible for the inanities of the amateur scholars who write about him.

Whatever the limitations of Farmer's Essay, it demolished the partisans of a learned Shakespeare with stunning finality. George Colman's voice of protest (#0175) went almost unheeded, except by Farmer, who criticized Colman's knowledge of Elizabethan literature, and by an anonymous wag who found an embarrassing error in Colman's attack on Farmer. Farmer's Essay was left in undisputed possession of the field of controversy, an advantage it retained for more than half a century. So ended an ill-conceived attempt to study Shakespeare's classicism; had the attempt been made with restraint by competent authorities, it might not have evoked Farmer's Essay, but as it developed no major voice dared counter Farmer until after the beginning of the nineteenth century[12] and even at the beginning of the twentieth H. A. Evans (#0018) was still echoing the opinion of Samuel

[12]Malone's Life (#0406), with its rational approach to Shakespeare's probable education in the classics, was composed before the end of the century; it did not receive wide circulation, however, until it was included in Boswell's Malone in 1821. Dodd's executors bravely brought out a new ed. of the Beauties (#0205) in 1780, but Dodd never had implied Shakespeare's familiarity with the classics used to "illustrate" him. In 1799 Edward Du Bois (#0221) did return to the position of Upton and Whalley, but his voice was not a major one.

Johnson and George Steevens (#0569) that Farmer had settled the matter forever.

While Farmer was castigating anyone who credited Shakespeare with learning, across the Channel M. de Voltaire was castigating Shakespeare for not being learned enough (#1748), and a violent reaction against Voltaire was preparing which would have an important effect on Shakespearean criticism for decades to come. Voltaire's Théâtre de Corneille appeared in 1765. Four years later Elizabeth Montagu (#0426) launched her counterattack, the argument that if Shakespeare did not ape the ancients he does rival them in the excellence of his thought and the validity of his portrayal of what is noble in human nature. She rejects Voltaire's canons of criticism in a scathing attack on French classicism. Mrs. Montagu's approach was anticipated by Hanmer's[13] belief, expressed in the essay on Ham. (#1947), that unity of design is a higher good than unity of place, time, or action. Again, Samuel Johnson argued very much the same point in 1765 (#0351). But it was Voltaire who catalyzed hostility toward neoclassical canons of criticism.[14] He provided sympathetic readers for such works as Edward Young's Conjectures on Original Composition (#0665), which argued the same point made by the younger Dryden at the close of the Restoration and by Addison at the beginning of the age of Pope: i.e., classical discipline (of the kind desired by Voltaire) may stultify genius; perhaps the best poets work outside it.

The eighteenth century ended, then--after two or three violent reactions against preceding movements--much as it began. One new development in the last quarter of the eighteenth century was to have great importance for the nineteenth; Richardson, Davies, and Morgann[15] introduced extended criticism of Shakespeare's plays and characters. But Richardson ignores traditional elements in the character of Timon, many of Davies' references to the classical world are as irrelevant as they are charming, and Morgann finds it possible to deal with Falstaff without discussing the miles gloriosus.[16] Lamb, Hazlitt, and Charles Cowden Clarke, the nineteenth-century inheritors of this innovation in Shakespearean criticism, follow the precedent by discussing Shakespeare's characters, plots, and themes without reference to the classical tradition. Farmer and Young make strange bedfellows, but together they dictated to the second half of the eighteenth century a single message: Shakespeare was no classicist.

II. THE NINETEENTH CENTURY

Samuel Taylor Coleridge is the critic with whom one must begin a consideration of the nineteenth-century response to the "small Latin" question. In the courses of lectures he delivered during the second decade of the century (#0172) he indicated in two ways that he wished to be the harbinger of a new era of Shakespearean criticism. First he depreciated Roman drama--indeed, all Latin literature--to the glorification of Greek culture. This philhellenism appears repeatedly in the Shakespearean criticism of the nineteenth century both in England and in Germany,[17] and its vestiges survive today in the enthusiasm with which psychologists and anthropologists find Greek religion beneath the surface of Shakespearean tragedy.[18] As Coleridge broke with the Augustans' reverence for Rome, he also denied their premise that Shakespeare was a barbarian genius. Coleridge does not argue that Shakespeare's talent was shaped by classical discipline--that argument was to be advanced only later. But he does repeatedly insist on Shakespeare's "judgment," by which he appears to mean his artistic sensibility. He does not indicate that in the Renaissance a man would acquire artistic sensibility in poetic technique from systematic study of Ovid, Virgil, Mantuan, and the Roman rhetoricians. But Coleridge's arguments for a civilized Shakespeare are nevertheless a dividing line between the

[13] If Hanmer did write this distinguished essay. Most authorities do not believe he did.

[14] See #0004 for a full study of this point.

[15] See #1602, #1603, #1004, #1251, #1894, #1895, #0428.

[16] Though he does say that Shakespeare and Milton have done more to immortalize Ovid than Ovid can do to immortalize himself.

[17] See, e.g., Matthew Arnold (#0078), De Quincey (#0202), Swinburne (#0582), Heine (#1386), Ulrici (#0605), Gervinus (#0264), Goethe (#0276).

[18] See, e.g., Ernest Jones (#1979), Maud Bodkin (#1837), Gilbert Murray (#2049), Sarah Davidson (#1893).

views of Young and Farmer and those of some men in the coming decades.[19]

A more dramatic and more specific rejection of the eighteenth-century position came from Charles Armitage Brown (#0126) in 1838, and on its heels came a better known argument from William Maginn (#0403).[20] Brown and Maginn both assailed Farmer's arguments at the vulnerable places indicated on p. 6; they show that the general acceptance of Farmer's conclusion during the half century after 1767 must have been uncritical. Vigorously as Brown and Maginn advance their arguments, the fame of Farmer and the prestige of his supporter, Dr. Johnson, have survived longer; R. W. Babcock (#0005, p. 65n) speaks of Maginn as "vicious" and (ibid., p. 60) of Farmer's Essay as "a splendid specimen of sane scholarship." And, as noted supra, pp. 6-7, H. A. Evans thought, in 1905, that Farmer had had the last word.

While Brown and Maginn failed to persuade most Englishmen that Farmer had been wrong about Shakespeare, some scholars across the Channel after 1850 readily saw the fallacies in Farmer's reasoning. The Germans Elze (#0233) and Gervinus (#0264) and the Frenchman Stapfer (#0563) were not awed by Farmer's arrogant self-assurance; their books proceed from the premise that Shakespeare's intellect could not create art ex nihilo. These books, which prefigure modern assumptions about Shakespeare's use of the resources of his culture, are among the important documents of Shakespearean criticism in the second half of the century. The founding of the Shakespeare Gesellschaft in 1865 and the appearance thereafter of its Jahrbuch (#0043) gave further impetus to serious scholarship in Germany. A surprising number of mid-twentieth-century critical postures are anticipated in early volumes of ShJ. As early as 1867 Albert Lindner (#1469) defined the structure of Caesar as a function of theme as well as of character. Carl Conrad Hense (#2226) saw Temp. in 1880 as recent criticism has seen it--as an eclectic play with a strong affinity for classical themes and conventions. Nicolaus Delius was the first (#1256) to make a close comparison of Cor. with its source in Plutarch; he shows Shakespeare's originality and his indebtedness as Hermann Heuer (#1390) and others have since done. The modern view of Tim. as a Shakespearean rough draft rather than some hack's mutilation of Shakespeare's polished work is as old as Wilhelm Wendlandt's study in ShJ XXIII (#1760).[21]

Yet it would not be just to imply that the Continent had a monopoly on critical study of Shakespeare's cultural heritage.[22] Notes and Queries, founded in 1849, is a rich mine of commentary on Shakespeare's relationship to classical culture,[23] and though the first Shakespeare Society dissolved in scandal, its successor was responsible for the publication of many sound articles. The names F. J. Furnivall, J. O. Halliwell-Phillipps, Brinsley Nicholson, W. Watkiss Lloyd, W. J. Rolfe, Charlotte Porter, and Helen Clarke become familiar as one searches for commentary on Shakespeare's classicism in Shakespeariana, New Shakespeareana, Poet Lore, The Academy, and The Athenaeum.

Again, William Rushton made scholarly studies (#0502, #0503) of Shakespeare's use of the classical rhetoric in Puttenham's Arte of English Poesie, and W. W. Lloyd's brilliant Essays on the Life and Plays of Shakespeare (#0395) is possibly the single work of Shakespearean criticism from the Victorian era most worthy of being brought back to general notice.

[19]It should be noted that August Wilhelm von Schlegel anticipated Coleridge's thought (#0519) and that Coleridge was accused by his own contemporaries of plagiarism. He defended himself by denying that he had read Schlegel before adopting his own critical position. T. M. Raysor, who offers an excellent discussion of the sources of Coleridge's Shn criticism, is inclined to believe that the two men arrived independently at the same conclusion. See the introduction to his ed. of Coleridge's Shakespearean Criticism, 2 vols., Ln, 1930.

[20]Someone identified only as "S" constructed a brief argument (#0507) against Farmer in 1815.

[21]For three other good examples, see #0957 (on the sources of Errors), #2109 (on Plutarch's "Life of Pelopidas" in Ham.), and #1746 (on the structure of Cor.).

[22]It is of interest that in America in this period very little scholarship or criticism relevant to this Guide was produced. See #0055 for a discussion of this phenomenon.

[23]Although it is an unworked mine. On many occasions it has been necessary to indicate in this Guide that a twentieth-century "discovery" was reported in a nineteenth-century vol. of NQ or some other periodical. See supra, pp. vii-viii for a striking instance.

Henry Green's extensive study (#0284) of Shakespeare's use of iconography (some of it classical) has not yet been superseded, and the Collier-Hazlitt collection of Shakespeare's sources (#2421, #2422) is only now being displaced by Geoffrey Bullough's volumes in progress (#2414, #2415, #2416).[24] The nineteenth century also produced some fragmentary comments on Shakespeare's onomastic etymology,[25] a subject studied more fully by Ernst Erler after the turn of the century (#0236); and T. S. Baynes's survey of "What Shakespeare learnt at School" (#0097) was a sketch for the edifice (#0089) which T. W. Baldwin has since constructed.

All these works and more granted Shakespeare some awareness of his classical heritage. But they are not the dominant force in English Shakespearean study before 1900. More typical are the effusions of Swinburne (#0582, #1711) and Charles Cowden Clarke (#1222), the patronizing dismissals of Shakespeare's Latinity by Charles Billson and A. H. Cruickshank (#0103, #0191), Hazlitt's character studies without reference to sources (#1385), and Fleay's ill-conceived attempt to disintegrate the canon on the basis of his conception of Shakespeare the ignoramus (#0242, #0243). The volumes of the New Variorum produced by H. H. Furness in the last three decades of the century summarize very little commentary which would indicate that Shakespeare's plays are in any way traceable to or even comparable with the classics.

In short, though Coleridge inaugurated the nineteenth century by announcing that the new era was to break with the Augustan view of untutored Shakespeare, and though a small corpus of scholarship shows that in a sense he was correct, in 1900 it was not difficult to find critics who spoke of Shakespeare in accents strikingly like Farmer's--it is not impossible to find such critics today.

III. THE TWENTIETH CENTURY

The inheritors of Farmer's interpretation of Shakespeare's "small Latin" encountered energetic antagonists as the twentieth century began. In 1903 Robert K. Root published his doctoral dissertation, an analytic study of Shakespeare's mythological allusions (#0497), which showed that Shakespeare knew his Ovid and, to a lesser extent, his Virgil. Root did not make sweeping claims for Shakespeare; his work is still regarded as reliable.[26] Much less cautious were the articles which J. Churton Collins published in the same year (#0173). Here the game of parallels was played with a verve reminiscent of the essays of Upton and Whalley. Collins had a precedent for arguing that Shakespeare had access to the Greek tragedies through Latin editions; James Russell Lowell had advanced a similar hypothesis in 1870 (#2011). But it is Collins who has usually been attacked as the originator of this explanation of the presence of the Greek tragic spirit in some of Shakespeare's tragedies.[27]

The following year, H. R. D. Anders produced his Shakespeares Belesenheit (#0073), a climax to the German scholarship of the preceding century, and a treatise so authoritative that Selma Guttman regards it as the threshold of the modern attitude toward Shakespeare's sources (#0019, p. xiv), and T. W. Baldwin speaks of Anders as a reference point in the history of the "small Latin" controversy (#0089, I, 74). Anders presents inter alia a list of the Greek and Roman authors Shakespeare probably knew, and he argues convincingly for Shakespeare's "considerable" Latinity. M. W. MacCallum's Shakespeare's Roman Plays and Their Background (#1477), still a standard work on Shakespeare's use of Plutarch,[28] followed Anders six years later; the twentieth century had begun with a flourish.

But the new way with Shakespeare's classi-

[24]Collier-Hazlitt was prefigured in the eighteenth century by Mrs. Charlotte Lennox' Shakespear Illustrated (#2450).

[25]See #0130, #0295, #0505, #2182.

[26]A few among the large number of other students of Shakespeare's mythology in recent years are Douglas Bush (#2327), E. I. Fripp (#0251), Rolf Soellner (#2120), Robert P. Miller (#2367), Paul Elmen (#2337), John Robert Price, S.J. (#0468), Walter F. Schirmer (#0518), DeWitt Starnes, and Ernest Talbert (#0566).

[27]It is common now to trace this tragic spirit to Plutarch's conception of history and of heroic character; see, e.g., #0444, #0594.

[28]James E. Phillips, Jr., has modified MacCallum's criticism slightly by indicating that Shakespeare brought to bear on Plutarch a set of conventional Renaissance doctrines about political life (#1579). These doctrines in turn are traceable to Plato, Aristotle, and Isocrates.

cism did not immediately or entirely displace established traditions. The anthropological approach to Shakespeare's themes so popular in this century[29] bears a curious resemblance to nineteenth-century philhellenism; the Romantic interest in Shakespeare's characters as individuals survives transmuted in psychological studies like those of A. C. Bradley (#1177), John Palmer (#1562), and Ernest Jones (#1979),[30] and Fleay's disintegrationist movement found numerous supporters in the early decades of the twentieth century[31] though it is now generally regarded as heretical to assign to Shakespeare's contemporaries those parts of the canon which suggest familiarity with classical literature.

One of the most remarkable developments of the past fifty years has been the restoration to the canon and to critical favor of the three "classical"[32] plays which had often been thought beneath the talents and the moral sensibilities of Shakespeare. Titus, Tim., and Troi. are currently enjoying an esteem which would have astonished the nineteenth century. Troi. was the first of the three to be reinstated; during the First World War, J. S. P. Tatlock (#1718, #1719), Hyder Rollins (#1613), and W. W. Lawrence (#1461) offered explanations of the peculiarities of tone and structure in the play. All found that the traditional Medieval and Renaissance attitude toward the Trojan legend is reflected in Shakespeare's version. From this point on the effort to purge the canon of the unwanted play diminished, and a contrary effort to recognize merit in Shakespeare's un-Homeric portrait of the Homeric age grew to such proportions that a comprehensive reading list would include at least a hundred books and articles.[33]

The appearance in 1925 of E. K. Chambers' Shakespeare: A Survey (#0158) initiated a movement which eventually placed Titus beside Troi. as a legitimate member of the canon; Chambers' brief (pp. 31-39) but effective criticism of the disintegrators of Titus is a justly famous example of scholarly logic. H. T. Price contributed major articles on Titus in the 'thirties and 'forties (#1585, #1586); the consensus is now that Shakespeare wrote the play[34] and that it has some artistic merits (see, e.g., #1419, #1675, #1750).

Shakespeare's authorship of Tim. has also found apologists in the past twenty years. The play is now more likely to be regarded as an unpolished draft than as the rude treatment by others of Shakespeare's original work (see #1287, #1496, #1554). The pioneer studies on the sources of Tim. by Adams (#1119), Clemons (#1223), and Wright (#1793) have since been followed by Draper's interpretation of the hero's behavior in the light of the humors (#1268) and the reading by Wilson Knight which finds in Tim. the greatest of the tragedies (#1444). It is common now to see irony in the play: some see Ovid's Age of Gold as the standard by which Timon and the Athenians fail (#1272, e.g.); others believe the play reflects the decline of feudal morality under the pressure of Jacobean economics (#1271, #1516). Though few would now agree with Knight, the play does appear to be established as Shakespeare's work--and reasonably good work too.[35]

The disintegrationist movement has been generally rejected in part because scholars are now inclined to believe that Shakespeare knew and used in his plays a substantial portion of that classical heritage which Fleay denied him and which historical scholarship has specified in the past thirty years.[36] There is still debate about how much Latin and Greek Ben Jonson implied

[29]See index s.v. "criticism, anthropological."

[30]It is not to be inferred that Bradley and Palmer share any ground with Jones other than an interest in the private lives of Shakespeare's characters and a tendency to subordinate other dramatic considerations to that interest.

[31]See index s.v. "disintegration."

[32]See supra, Preface, note 11.

[33]See index s.v. "Troi."

[34]See #0030. There are dissenters, of course: see, e.g., #1308, #1397.

[35]Caesar, Antony, and Cor. have by no means been neglected. In ShS, X (1957), an issue devoted to the Roman plays, J. C. Maxwell surveys over 150 twentieth-century books and arts. about the plays from Plutarch (#0030). To this judicious, though selective list one might add a few recent contributions of special importance: e.g., #1166, #1145, #1486, #1253, #1390, #1645. See also index s.v. "Caesar," "Antony," "Cor."

[36]The same logical weapon has been used effectively against the anti-Stratfordian movement.

by "small" and "less" (see #0089, Vol. I, Ch. I; #0654), but most scholars now believe that Shakespeare knew what most Elizabethans knew --most, that is, who were not university men. And if he acquired some of his knowledge of the ancients indirectly, scholars are less likely now to hold this in Shakespeare's disfavor than Farmer was.[37] The last three decades have seen extensive exploration of such indirect routes to the classics as English treatises on rhetoric (#0424), translations (#0381, #1488), mythological dictionaries (#0566, #0923), and Italian comedies (#0695, #0712). William Blisset's comment on the indirect relationship between Shakespeare's Bolingbroke and Lucan's Caesar (#0106) and Gilbert Highet's chapter (#0329) emphasizing that Shakespeare's response to the ancient world was real, though in part secondhand, are typical of much recent commentary on Shakespeare's "classicism."

For many commentators, the limits of "classicism" have been so far expanded that no apology is necessary here for including some works on Shakespeare's use of Renaissance concepts which are only remotely classical. Draper's study, cited above, of the humors in Tim. is one such work. A great many other books and articles have also investigated Shakespeare's use of Elizabethan psychology, with its distant roots in Greek philosophy and medicine.[38] E. M. W. Tillyard (#0598) and Theodore Spencer (#0560), writing in the early 'forties, have shown that Shakespeare's conception of man and the universe he lives in was ultimately based on Greek philosophy. Hiram Haydn's study of Shakespeare's ethical assumptions is a complement (#0318), showing that Shakespeare preferred Christianized classicism to sixteenth-century innovations.

To turn to more direct relationships between Shakespeare and the ancient world: there has been much interest in this century in Shakespeare's English with its aureate diction as an indication of his familiarity with Latin vocabulary.[39] Another group of scholars has studied classical rhetoric as it appears in the plays and poems. Walter F. Schirmer has shown (#0516) that in the early plays Shakespeare used rhetorical formality as Seneca and Marlowe did, to emphasize the isolation of the tragic type against a hostile background; in the mature plays, where conflict is internal, language is not so commonly used as a public veneer. Gladys Willcock also interprets Shakespeare's development as a gradual subordination to dramatic purposes of intrusive, decorative rhetoric (#0643), and Milton B. Kennedy's study of the classical oration in Shakespeare (#0358) leads to a similar conclusion. John E. Hankins has found a connection between Shakespeare's imagery and the rhetoric in Palingenius' neo-Latin Zodiacus Vitae (#0306). The greatest achievement, perhaps, is that of T. W. Baldwin, who shows precisely from which classical and Renaissance treatises Shakespeare derived his knowledge of rhetoric.[40] Baldwin's reconstruction of Shakespeare's probable education at Stratford is regarded by many as one of the most important contributions of this century to knowledge of Shakespeare's mind and art. Of the books which are supplemental offshoots from Baldwin's thorough study of the Stratford curriculum, perhaps the most important is Shakspere's Five-Act Structure, in which Bald-

[37]This may, in part, be because twentieth-century research has proved that the learning of Shakespeare's more learned contemporaries was not always directly acquired. For example, James Earl Applegate, in an unpublished Johns Hopkins diss called "Classical Allusions in the Prose Works of Robert Greene" (1954), shows conclusively that Greene's classicism was often second-rate, often secondhand, sometimes plagiarized, or even occasionally invented. (For an instance of Greene's invented classicism, see NQ, CCX [1965], 195.) Francis Meres relied heavily on florilegia, as Don Cameron Allen shows in "The Classical Scholarship of Francis Meres," PMLA, LXVIII (1933), 418-425; yet Thomas Heywood called Meres "an approved good scholler" in the Apology for Actors (Shakespeare Society ed., 1841, p. 44). Even scholarly Ben Jonson was not above using short cuts to classical erudition. DeWitt Starnes and Ernest Talbert provide evidence in "Ben Jonson and the Dictionaries" (see #0566). See also #0477, where John D. Rea shows that Jonson probably borrowed the lines on the portrait of Shakespeare in F_1 from iconography about Erasmus. Jonson "plunder[ed] from the authors of the Low Countries, through whom he often acquired his classical material at second hand."

[38]See index s.v. "psychology."

[39]See, e.g., #0644, #0120, #0279, #0374. See also index s.v. "aureate diction."

[40]#0089. See especially the first seven chs. of Vol. II.

win studies the dramatic structure of Terence as it appears in Shakespeare's early comedies.[41] This book is at the center of a cluster of recent books and articles on classical foundations of Shakespeare's dramatic technique.[42]

Historical scholarship has apparently persuaded most critics that a responsible estimate of Shakespeare's achievement as a dramatist must consider his direct and indirect relationships to classical culture. The once-prevalent view that Shakespeare and his contemporaries drew their dramatic devices and their conception of tragedy from the Middle Ages without Senecan inspiration[43] is now commonly qualified.[44] John W. Cunliffe's thesis (#0192, #0193) that Shakespearean tragedy owes much to Seneca is (though still regarded as extreme) no longer categorically rejected; and Henry Wells (#2162), Hardin Craig (#1884), Allan Gilbert (#0267), F. R. Johnson (#1978), and T. S. Eliot (#0227)--all of them prepared to grant Shakespeare at least some ties to Seneca--appear now to be in the ascendant.

Lest it be assumed that twentieth-century opinion has moved by general consent toward a more inclusive definition of "classicism" and toward granting Shakespeare a larger awareness of the classical world, some counterpoint to the tendencies discussed above should be indicated. W. W. Greg, whose definition of the classical pastoral denied Shakespeare a place in the tradition (#0285), is often cited as the final authority. F. S. Boas and J. A. K. Thomson speak of Shakespeare very much as Farmer spoke of him,[45] and J. Dover Wilson's article (#0654) defines "classicism" so strictly that none of the scholars cited in the preceding four paragraphs is mentioned in the notes--except Baldwin, whom Wilson cannot find convincing. In 1948 Wilson published an essay on Shakespeare's possible use of Apuleius in Dream in which he postulated a lost source play as intermediary between Shakespeare and the classical themes in the play.[46] In 1949 E. M. W. Tillyard believed that "the notion of an unread Shakespeare, whose first stirrings of mind came from contact with the stage, is still widely prevalent in England" (#1730, p. 44).

There is some evidence that Tillyard's statement about the climate of opinion in England is no longer so appropriate as it once was. In the past fifteen years J. C. Maxwell, Ernest Schanzer, and Kenneth Muir have all published numerous articles on Shakespeare's manipulation of source materials, especially in the Greek and Roman plays.[47] Geoffrey Bullough's comprehensive compilation of Shakespeare's sources is in progress (#2414, #2415, #2416). Of the classical scholars who have turned their attention to Shakespeare, if J. A. K. Thomson circumscribes the term "classicists" so narrowly as to exclude Shakespeare from their number, H. D. F. Kitto (#1987, #1988) defines it broadly enough to permit comparisons between Ham. and the English history plays on the one hand, and Greek tragedy on the other. From England, too, have recently come interesting approaches to Shakespeare's creative process

[41] See #0683; #2320, which treats the classical background of the nondramatic verse, is also a work of scholarly importance.

[42] See, e.g., #0926, #0388, #0466.

[43] This view is sometimes traced to Willard Farnham (The Medieval Heritage of Elizabethan Tragedy [Berkeley: University of California Press, 1936]) and to his successor, Howard Baker (#1137). But Farnham admitted the influence of Seneca on pre-Shn tragedy, and Baker (though rejecting Seneca) argued for the formative influence of Virgil, Lucan, and Ovid. Actually, then, the thesis that the impulse of Elizabethan tragedy is entirely Medieval is a distortion of their positions.

[44] See, e.g., Madeleine Doran in Endeavors of Art (#0206): "Hamlet is certainly not much like any play of Seneca's one can name, but Seneca is undoubtedly one of the effective ingredients in the emotional charge of Hamlet. ...It may be true that Elizabethans did not have to learn from Seneca their taste for the violent and the horrible, true that Virgil had taught them about the classical underworld, true that they had their own ghosts and their own impulses to revenge, true that their preachers had long been warning them against the dangers of worldly ambition and the folly of trust in slippery chance. It is just because of this community of interest that Seneca spoke to them with such authority" (p. 16).

[45] See #0108, #0111; #0591, #0592, #0593, #0594.

[46] #0956. Wilson did not take account of the arguments of DeWitt Starnes (#0565) or of Sister M. Generosa (#0774).

[47] See, e.g., #1490, #1493, #1496; #1631, #1633, #1634, #1636 (and cf. #2469); #1526, #1530.

in Muir's theory of polygenesis (see, e.g., #0860, #1052, #1527) and S. L. Bethell's theory of "multiconsciousness" (#2188). Muir's approach is to accept the multiplicity of sources scholars are proposing for passages like the Mechanicals' playlet in Dream, assuming that a number of discrete but related sources coalesced in Shakespeare's creative imagination when his memory recalled one of them.[48] Bethell believes that similar capabilities were vested in the Jacobean audience, and that Shakespeare directed ambiguities toward those capabilities. Both theories imply that Shakespeare read more widely in both classical and Renaissance literature than has usually been thought until now.

Though there is still disagreement among scholars, the tendency of this century (especially of the years since World War II) has been to reject the assumptions of Farmer and Young. The scholarship of the past three decades has provided a broad foundation of knowledge about Shakespeare's sources and generally about the legacy which came to the Elizabethans from Greece and Rome. Books like Virgil K. Whitaker's Shakespeare's Use of Learning (#0635) and John Vyvyan's Shakespeare and the Rose of Love (#0616) are recent efforts to build criticism on the facts which have been made available. One might predict that similar studies will focus in the future on some of the following areas: the aesthetic and moral significance of mythology in the plays;[49] Shakespeare's continuing interest in pastoral from L.L.L. through Temp.;[50] the relationship between rhetoric and dramatic technique in the mature plays;[51] Shakespeare's participation in the Platonic tradition;[52] the eclectic classicism of the last plays;[53] Plautine and Terentian themes in the mature comedies.[54]

[48]This coalescence was evidently not always subconscious; Muir implies that Sh sometimes deliberately worked with a number of sources as he wrote a given passage.

[49]Thus far, investigations of Sh's mythological allusions have either been source studies (see, e.g., Root, #0497; Starnes and Talbert, #0566) or have been restricted to limited segments of the canon (see supra, note 26). I know of no systematic analysis of the meaning and function of mythology in the plays and poems.

[50]Edwin Greenlaw (#2218), Carol Gesner (#2215), and Northrop Frye (#0766) all have implicitly modified Greg's definition of "pastoralism" (#0285); Richard Cody argues more directly against Greg's position in his diss on the early comedies (Minnesota, 1961).

[51]It has become conventional to define Sh's development as a dramatist as his growth out of rhetoric. But even in the latest plays Sh pauses for rhetorical elaboration (e.g., in Perdita's flower speech, Iachimo's meditation in Imogen's chamber, or Prospero's farewell to his magical powers).

[52]Laurens J. Mills has traced Sh's portrayal of Platonic friendship (#0423); W. C. Curry has discussed occult Neoplatonism in Temp. (#2205); John Vyvyan's book on Shakespeare and Platonic Beauty (N.Y., 1961) and Maria Wickert's art. on "Das Schattenmotiv bei Shakespeare" (#0638) are recent contributions—but no systematic study of Sh's various responses to Platonism has yet been made.

[53]Interpreters of the last plays have traditionally confused the eclectic with the occult. A beginning of serious study of the ancient world in Temp. has been made by Gesner (#2215), Nosworthy (#2269), Knox (#2244), Marx (#2255), and others. Similar brief lists can be made for Cym. and for W.T. as well—but there is no responsible full-length study of the classical world in the last plays as a group.

[54]John Manningham, who saw Twel. in 1601, commented on its relationship to the Menaechmi and to Errors (see #0031, I, 98). Though modern criticism of Shn comedy has been inclined to draw sharp distinctions between the mature romantic comedies and such apprentice work as Errors, it is possible that future commentators may attempt to link Sh's two comic periods through the influence on both of Roman comedy.

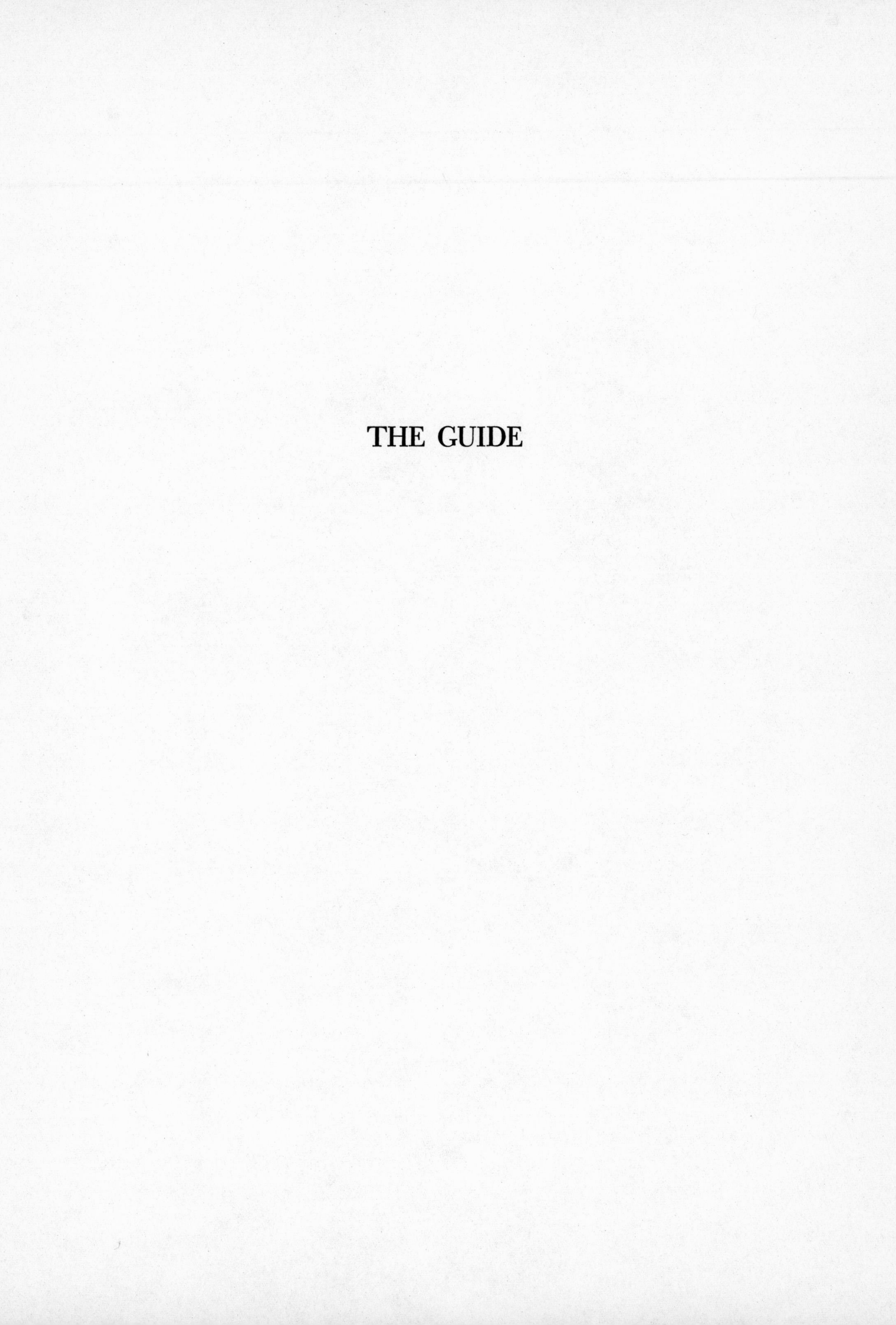

THE GUIDE

BIBLIOGRAPHIES CONSULTED

0001. "American Bibliography for [year preceding current volume]," PMLA, XXXIX- (1924-date).

In the earliest vols., two pages ordinarily suffice to name and even discuss briefly the year's contributions to Shn scholarship. The contrasting size of the Sh section in recent vols. is an index of the acceleration of the Sh Industry since World War II. It should be noted, of course, that the eds. of the "American Bibliography" have in recent years altered the adjective to read "Annual"--PMLA is today one of the best bibliographical sources for Continental materials.

0002. Annual Bibliography of English Language and Literature. Ed. for MHRA, I- (1920-date), CUP.

This annual bibliography is one of the more carefully compiled ones. It contains a section on Sh in the "Sixteenth Century" ch. The MHRA obtains completeness and accuracy at the expense of a hiatus (as long as a decade in some cases) between year(s) surveyed and publication of the vol. The entries are not annotated.

0003. Babcock, R. W. "The Attitude Toward Shakespeare's Learning in the Late 18th Century," PQ, IX (1930), 116-122. E-S (Reprinted with some expansion in The Genesis of Shakespeare Idolatry [1931].)

An enumeration of opinions which concludes that "the late eighteenth century decided against Shakespeare's knowledge of the classics." Babcock's sixty-two footnotes constitute a valuable bibliography of the controversy before and especially after Farmer (1767). Not all of the references he cites are included in this Guide: the allusions he includes have been omitted--only connected discourse on the subject is treated.

0004. Babcock, R. W. "The English Reaction Against Voltaire's Criticism of Shakespeare," SP, XXVII (1930), 609-625.

The art. is so extensively documented as to amount to an excellent critical bibliography of eighteenth-century counterattacks on Voltaire. Only a portion of Babcock's material is relevant here, because Voltaire's objection to Sh's putative lack of classical unity and decorum was only one of the grounds on which such critics as Mrs. Montagu, Tom Davies, Morgann, and Johnson attacked him. Babcock's work appears as always to be thorough. It is to be noted that Babcock regards Voltaire's behavior in the controversy as completely contemptible. F. C. Green, however, sees it from another side ("Shakespeare and Voltaire," Minuet: A Critical Survey of French and English Literary Ideas in the Eighteenth Century. [Ln, 1935], Ch. III, pp. 54-83); to Green, a student of French literature, Voltaire was not only not envious of Sh, but even generous in his judgments of him, at least at the outset.

0005. Babcock, R. W. The Genesis of Shakespeare Idolatry 1766-1799: A Study in English Criticism of the Late Eighteenth Century. North Carolina UP, 1931, 307 pp.

Babcock is an excellent bibliographer; the whole book is filled with valuable bibliographical footnotes (some of which have appeared elsewhere, see #0003, #0004, #0007, #0008). The most important single ch. is V, "Shakespeare's Classical Learning," pp. 57-69. Babcock pays slight heed to the seventeenth-

NOTE: Numbers preceded by # refer to entries in this Guide. Keys to abbreviations are found on pages xi-xvii and 381-387.

century founders of the "small Latin" myth; he even suggests that Rowe may be finally responsible. Babcock also assumes that Farmer's assault on his predecessors was a valid one. He calls the second ed. (1767) "a splendid specimen of sane scholarship," and oddly refers to Maginn's refutation (#0403) as having "too obvious [a] bias and [a] vicious contentiousness." Actually Maginn's ridicule of Farmer is milder than Farmer's castigation of his victims.

0006. Babcock, R. W. "Historical Criticism of Shakespeare," MLQ, XIII (1952), 6-20.

This vigorous defense of scholarship as opposed to impressionistic criticism lists seven legitimate fields of inquiry of which Sh's sources makes one. There are eighty-seven footnotes containing over two hundred citations to books and arts. of historical criticism from Rowe to T. W. Baldwin--the references to source studies constitute a preliminary bibliography in the field.

0007. Babcock, R. W. "A Preliminary Bibliography of 18th Century Criticism of Shakespeare," SP, Extra Ser., No. 1 (1929), 58-76. E-S

Both this list of primary critical works in the Restoration, eighteenth century, and early nineteenth century and Babcock's list of secondary works on Sh criticism in the eighteenth century (#0008) are important bibliographical tools. Neither list is annotated, but both are subdivided, the primary list chronologically, the secondary list topically.

0008. Babcock, R. W. "A Secondary Bibliography of Shakespeare Criticism in the 18th Century," SP, Extra Ser., No. 1 (1929), 77-98. E-S

See #0007.

0009. Bateson, F. W., ed. The Cambridge Bibliography of English Literature. Vol. I [of 4] (1940). With Supplement ed. George Watson (1957).

The Sh ch. in the original CBEL (pp. 539-608) was compiled by the General Editor. David H. Malone is responsible for the compilation (pp. 257-293) in the Supplement. The intelligence with which the entries are classified and arranged makes this one of the most usable of all Sh bibliographies. It is, however, by no means exhaustive.

0010. Boswell's Malone (see Table of Abbreviations).

Vol. I contains over a score of essays, prefaces, "advertisements," etc., on Sh by his eighteenth-century eds. and critics. Some of these are available nowhere else. In Vol. I, pp. 392-401, also appears a "List of [83] Detached Pieces of Criticism on Shakspeare, His Editors, &c" published in the eighteenth century. Vol. II contains Malone's "Life" (#0406). Boswell's Malone is therefore obviously an important bibliographical source.

0011. Brown, Huntington. "The Classical Tradition in English Literature: A Bibliography," HSNPL, XVIII (1935), 7-46.

This pioneer list is selective, but well based on Continental scholarship as well as English and American. The Sh section (pp. 31-34) contains seventy-five entries, and there is a considerable number of other works relevant in part to Sh in other sections. The contributions of Brown's art. to this Guide are marked HB.

0012. Bullough, Geoffrey. Narrative and Dramatic Sources of Shakespeare. 3 vols. [of proposed 7]. Col UP, 1957, 1958, 1960.

Each vol. contains an excellent selective bibliography of primary source materials, eds. of the plays, and commentary on Sh's use of his sources. Very valuable because there is no necessary modern bias: Bullough does not hesitate to include material from the early nineteenth century.

0013. Conklin, Paul S. A History of Hamlet Criticism, 1601-1821. Col UP, 1947, 176 pp.

Though it has no formal bibliography, this book contains a multitude of references in its index and footnotes. Only a very small number are to works which place Ham. in a classical context. This paucity of "classical" criticism of the play is doubtless in part due to the subject and avowed sources of the play, but is nonetheless surprising in an age of neoclassicism. Cf. the paucity of Sh/classics studies in the U.S. at the same time--#0055.

0014. Ebisch, Walther, and Levin L. Schücking. A Shakespeare Bibliography. OUP, 1931, 294 pp. Supplement for the Years 1930-1935 (1937), 104 pp. HB

Though original and supplement together list fewer than a hundred entries in the section headed "Shakespeare and Classical Literature," there are a good many other relevant entries scattered elsewhere in the bibliography, especially in the large section on individual plays and poems. That the format does not readily distinguish books from arts. may be objected; there are also some inconsistencies in naming authors. But this pioneer work is immensely useful. Books and arts. which appear in A Shakespeare Bibliography are marked E-S in this Guide.

0015. Edwards, Philip. "Shakespeare's Romances: 1900-1957," ShS, XI (1958), 1-18.

A somewhat unsympathetic survey of the main critical positions assumed by interpreters of the last plays as a group. The most important section for this Guide is the one entitled "Myth, Symbol, and Allegory," but the entire essay is illuminating; over a score of works are discussed.

0016. Eliot, T. S. "Shakespearian Criticism: 1. From Dryden to Coleridge," A Companion to Shakespeare Studies, ed. H. Granville-Barker and G. B. Harrison (N.Y., 1934), pp. 287-299.

Eliot deals only with major figures in the eighteenth century--this bibliographical ch. is more important for Eliot's advice about how to deal with the critical maze than for its listing of critics or their works. Isaacs (#0023) is more satisfactory as a bibliographer.

0017. Ellis-Fermor, Una. "English and American Shakespeare Studies 1937-1952," Anglia, LXXI (1952), 1-49.

This art. is valuable not so much for its completeness (paragraphs frequently end with tantalizing expressions; e.g., "As usual, [in 1944] there are various notes on sources") as for its perceptions about the trend of Sh scholarship in the period covered. Miss Ellis-Fermor recognizes the contributions of such American historical critics as Baldwin, Stoll, and Craig --a phenomenon rare enough among British commentators. And the judgments about individual works are sound.

0018. Evans, H. A. "A Shakespearian Controversy of the Eighteenth Century," Anglia, XXVIII [n.F. XVI] (1905), 457-476.

Evans regards the Mr.-Hales-of-Eton story as probably authentic and probably a sole survivor of many accounts of the real "wit combates" between Jonson and Sh and between their partisans. He discusses Dryden, Pope, Theobald, Warburton, Upton, Whalley, Capell, Farmer, and Johnson. He oddly regards Farmer's essay as a great piece of scholarship and he seems to think the controversy ended--at least it is "once famous, but now forgotten."

0019. Guttman, Selma. The Foreign Sources of Shakespeare's Works: An Annotated Bibliography of the Commentary Written on this Subject Between 1904 and 1940, Together with Lists of Certain Translations Available to Shakespeare. Col UP (King's Crown), 1947, 168 pp.

Ch. I lists and summarizes works dealing with Latin influence; Ch. II with Greek influence (the remainder of the book deals with Continental sources): Ch. I, 239 entries; Ch. II, 117-- but there are many duplications because the bibliography is arranged alphabetically by Sh's supposed sources. Indeed, the arrangement gives undue emphasis to unreliable critics like Johnstone and Cowl (#0352, #0996), who assert Sh's debt to numerous Greeks and Romans. Though the lists of trans. available to Sh are incomplete (cf. Lathrop's chronological list [#0381] and see Dr. Guttman's comments on her limits, pp. xiv-xv), they are a useful step indicated by T. W. Baldwin's insistence that we read Sh's classics in the eds. Sh probably used. Dr. Guttman regards Anders' Shakespeare's Books (#0073) as a milestone in criticism and accordingly begins her bibliography with 1904. The danger is in the inference an incautious reader may draw that no work written before 1904 has present significance (e.g., she must omit Root #0497 [1903], the standard work on Sh's mythology). The annotations summarize books and arts. without appraisal; only in the Introduction does the author express her opinions, and then of only a fraction of the entries. All entries in the present work which appear in Dr. Guttman's book are marked SG.

0020. Halliday, F. E. The Cult of Shakespeare. Ln, 1957, 218 pp.

With wit, fluency, and a good store of common sense, Halliday traces the rise and fall of fashions in Sh criticism and scholarship from 1616 to the present. The "small Latin" question was often a formative influence on those fashions. At the end of the book Halliday provides a brief but sound ch.-by-ch. bibliography.

0021. Heninger, S. K., Jr. "French Scholarship on Elizabethan Drama: A Survey," EA, XIII (1960), 283-292.

A detailed survey of major French contributions since François-Victor Hugo's Oeuvres complètes de Shakespeare (1859-65). About two thirds of the bibliographical essay deals with works on Sh. If Heninger is a little too gracious about some persistent French heresies (e.g., "Lefrancism"), his essay is most valuable for the thoroughness with which he conveys the content of the books he discusses.

0022. Herford, C. H. A Sketch of Recent Shakesperean Investigation: 1893-1923. Ln, n.d. [1923?], 58 pp. E-S

Herford disclaims the title of bibliographer, but he does discuss several dozen works. The relevant sections are the first, on Sh's life and environment, and the third, on criticism of the plays. There is nothing in either section which is not referred to in other sources, but Herford's book provides a glimpse of the scholarship and criticism of the first two decades of the twentieth century through the eyes of an intelligent contemporary. MnU

0023. Isaacs, J. "Shakespearian Criticism: 2. From Coleridge to the Present Day," A Companion to Shakespeare Studies, ed. H. Granville-Barker and G. B. Harrison (N.Y., 1934), pp. 300-304.

Though very brief, this bibliographical ch. is at least a preliminary guide to the positions of various schools since Coleridge; Isaacs manages to include a number of the most important authors, many of whom appear in this Guide because of their interest in the question of Sh's classicism.

0024. Isaacs, J. "Shakespearian Scholarship," A Companion to Shakespeare Studies, ed. H. Granville-Barker and G. B. Harrison (N.Y., 1934), pp. 305-324.

A historical summary of major trends and documents in Sh scholarship from Dryden to the 1930's. Isaacs' judgment is excellent--he rehabilitates some depreciated talents (e.g., Lewis Theobald, E. Capell) and though he cannot possibly be comprehensive he is able to mention hundreds of important authors and their works, many of which are relevant to the study of Sh's classicism. A valuable introduction.

0025. Jaggard, William. Shakespeare Bibliography: A Dictionary of Every Known Issue of the Writings of Our National Poet and of Recorded Opinion Thereon in the English Language. Stratford-on-Avon, 1911, 729 pp. E-S (Reissued by F. Ungar, 1959.)

The usefulness of this compilation is limited by the fact that all eds., allusions, books of criticism, and arts. are lumped together in a single alphabet. Topical indexes would have made this a better reference work. Only rarely does Jaggard add informational notes.

0026. Knight, Charles. "A History of Opinion on the Writings of Shakspere," in the Supplemental Volume to his Pictorial Edition of the Works of Shakspere. Ln, 1866, pp. 331-400. E-S

Knight gives a colorful account of critics and their positions from Spenser, the first Shn critic, to Samuel Coleridge. The interpretations are sometimes incorrect, but this historical survey shows what a scholarly mind in the mid-nineteenth century thought of the controversies of the preceding age.

0027. Koszul, A. "Troilus and Cressida," BFLS, XV (1937), 167-172. GRS

An excellent preliminary bibliography discussed critically. Koszul thinks it probable that Sh drew the exalted style in which his characters sometimes speak from Chapman's 1598 Iliads, "bien que certains en jugent autrement." The art. contains sections on eds., text, date, authorship, sources, characters, tone, etc. MdBJ

0028. Lockwood, Dean P., and Roland H. Bainton. "Classical and Biblical Scholarship in the Age of the Renaissance and Reformation," CH, X (1941), 125-143. GRS

The classical section occupies pp. 125-138; despite the title, it contains suggestions for research on Renaissance classicism and a general survey of modern endeavors in the field. Two or three relevant books not mentioned elsewhere appear here though Sh himself is not discussed.

0029. Lounsbury, Thomas R. Shakespeare as a Dramatic Artist: With an Account of his Reputation at Various Periods. N.Y., 1901, 449 pp. E-S

Lounsbury's bibliography, pp. 419-434, is a chronological arrangement of primary materials from 1663 to 1838. Many of the entries, and a good part of the book, relate to mutilations of Sh's plays by his eighteenth-century "improvers," but there are some critical works, a few of them not mentioned elsewhere. Lounsbury's studies of Sh and Voltaire and of Sh's English reputation in the eighteenth century have been criticized, but as a bibliographer he is intelligent and accurate.

0030. Maxwell, J. C. "Shakespeare's Roman Plays: 1900-1956," ShS, X (1957), 1-11.

An important listing and appraisal of many studies in this century. Maxwell's good judgment and his command of the trend of scholarship are both indicated by his admission of Titus as a legitimate "Roman play"; to it he accords a special section. For the other three plays there are sections on "Canon, Text, and Chronology" and "Sources and Analogues" followed by a historical survey of critical opinion since Bradley. There are, of course, many omissions, but this ch. is among the best of a good series of bibliographies in ShS.

0031. Munro, John. "More Shakspere Allusions," MP, XIII (1916), 497-544.

A supplement to The Shakspere Allusion-Book... (#0044). Several entries have been drawn from Munro's MP art., which was not incorporated into the latest reissue (1932) of the Allusion-Book. Munro's art. is referred to in this Guide as "Munro Sup."

0032. Neumann, Joshua H. "Shakespearean Criticism in the Tatler and the Spectator," PMLA, XXXIX (1924), 612-623.

An informative summary and analysis of the views of Addison and Steele on Sh's dramatic theory and his abrogation of the unities, among other Shn matters. The notes to the essay constitute a useful bibliographical index to the two periodicals.

0033. A New Variorum Edition of Shakespeare, ed. Horace H. Furness [succeeded by his son and later by MLA]. Philadelphia, 1871- (in progress), 27 vols.

Most vols. contain bibliographies of works consulted. These have been surveyed, together with the appendices to each vol. (the latter have often stood proxy to books and arts. I have not been able to consult). No effort has been made to incorporate all the notes in the New Variorum. Nor in most cases have uninformative titles been run to ground for the classical material they might conceal. The more recent vols. are especially useful (one might single out the Hillebrand-Baldwin Troi. [1953]); some of the earlier vols. are annoyingly vague in their bibliographical citations, but the entire New Variorum is one of the most important single bibliographical sources.

0034. Newald, Richard. "Nachleben der Antike (1920-1929)," JFKA, CCXXXII (1931), 1-122.

A briefly annotated bibliography of contributions during the period (Sh, pp. 82-83). It contains a few items apparently not registered elsewhere. This compilation and Newald's later survey of the years 1930-31 (JFKA, CCL [1935], 1-144 [Sh, pp. 93-94]) are a useful complement to the Warburg Institute's more extensively annotated catalogues for the period 1931-33 (see #0053).

0035. Oppel, Horst. "Stand und Aufgaben der deutschen Shakespeare-Forschung (1952-1957)," DVLG, XXXII (1958), 113-171.

A thorough survey (235 footnotes) of the German contribution for the period. The commentary on books and arts. is detailed and very useful. Oppel mentions a number of English and American publications as well. The bibliographical essay is intelligently subdivided.

0036. Purves, John. "Shakespeare--The English Aeschylus," MLR, XVII (1922), 73-74.

Purves points to the prevalence of allusive comparisons between Sh and Aeschylus from Jonson to Swinburne and cites some French and Italian instances. Sh seems to Purves to have evoked more frequent comparison with Aeschylus than with the other Greek dramatists.

0037. Ralli, Augustus. A History of Shakespearian Criticism. 2 vols. OUP, 1932, 566, 582 pp. E-S

A summary and appraisal of the opinions of over two hundred critics of Sh between Francis Meres and Lascelles Abercrombie. The materials are drawn from England, France, and Germany; though Ralli does not say so, he includes some Americans (e.g., Richard Grant White, E. E. Stoll) among his British critics. The usefulness of so extensive a compendium is obvious.

0038. Raven, Anton A. A Hamlet Bibliography and Reference Guide, 1877-1935. Chicago UP, 1936, 292 pp.

An extremely thorough compilation. A good proportion of Raven's entries are annotated in extenso, and his research has turned up a large number of Continental publications. Especially useful is the long list of commentaries on individual passages in the play; it constitutes a seriatim guide to the text. There are also sections on the character of Hamlet, the other characters, the sources of the legend and of the play, etc.

0039. "Recent Literature of the Renaissance," SP, XIV- (1917-date).

This annual bibliography contains a Sh section; its merits are well known. Not the least of them is that there are informative and critical annotations on many entries, especially for the early years. The great succession of eds., perhaps Hardin Craig most of all, deserves the gratitude of all Renaissance scholars.

0040. Robinson, Herbert S. English Shakesperian Criticism in the Eighteenth Century. N.Y., 1932, 300 pp.

In the body of the book Robinson discusses at some length the critical positions of about thirty Shn critics and briefly summarizes a half dozen more in appendices. But Steevens and Malone do not appear in either place, and the "small Latin" controversy, which other scholars regard as a central theme in Augustan and pre-Romantic criticism is relegated to a minor position: Farmer, Whalley, Upton, and Grey all are treated in appendices.

0041. Sehrt, Ernst Th. "Die Shakespeareforschung 1937-1952 in Deutschland und in der Schweiz," Anglia, LXXI (1952), 50-81.

An intelligently arranged and extensively annotated bibliography of major works by Germans and Swiss for the fifteen-year period. A useful sketch despite its selectivity.

0042. "Shakespeare: An Annotated Bibliography for [year preceding current vol.]," SQ, I- (1950-date).

The SQ annual bibliography is successor to Tannenbaum's SAB compilations, which ceased with the compiler's death. The SQ eds. have sought to preserve Dr. Tannenbaum's inclusiveness--the "committee of correspondents" give the editor access to publications from Europe, the Orient, South America, and even behind the Iron Curtain. This inclusiveness and occasional informative notes, legible format, and scrupulous accuracy make SQ's the best current annual Sh bibliography.

0043. "Shakespeare-Bibliographie für [year(s) preceding current Jahrgang]," ShJ, I- (1865-date).

For a century the Deutsche Shakespeare-Gesellschaft has published exhaustive bibliographical surveys at irregular intervals. The vicissitudes of two world wars have not prevented the Gesellschaft bibliographers from compiling their lists even if they are sometimes several years behind. The importance of the ShJ bibliography is twofold: (1) It is the only comprehensive Sh bibliography for the last half of the nineteenth century (by comparison the bibliographies in the early vols. of the New Variorum are very incomplete). (2) It makes a special point of collecting Continental publications, a valuable feature for the early decades of the present century; but even in more recent years and for British, American, and Canadian materials it is more comprehensive than many English-language surveys. The entries are ordinarily not annotated, and there are many errors in typography which sometimes result in "lost" entries. But the contribution of the ShJ bibliographies has been an insufficiently recognized one; until 1920 they had no serious rival and even today they are a standard current authority.

0044. The Shakspere Allusion-Book: A Collection of Allusions to Shakspere From 1591 to 1700. Originally Compiled by C. M. Ingleby, Miss L. Toulmin Smith, and by Dr. F. J. Furnivall, with the Assistance of the New Shakspere Society: Re-Edited, Revised, and Re-Arranged, with an Introduction, by John Munro (1909), and Now Re-Issued with a Preface by Sir Edmund Chambers. 2 vols. OUP, 1932, 527, 558 pp.

The largest portion of Vol. II embraces the period from 1660 to 1700. The Allusion-Book (referred to in this Guide as "Munro") is the best single source for Sh materials in the seventeenth century, though Bentley (see supra, Introduction, p. 3n) has some strictures on it. Munro is the source of the bulk of the Restoration criticism included in the Guide.

0045. Smith, D[avid] Nichol. Eighteenth Century Essays on Shakespeare. Glasgow, 1903. E-S

Part II of the "Introduction" (pp. xxi-xxvii) contains a useful brief survey of the "small Latin" controversy in the eighteenth century. The positions of Rowe, Gildon, Dennis, Pope, Sewell, Theobald, Warburton, Upton,

Zachary Grey, Whalley, Johnson, and Farmer are clearly stated.

0046. Smith, David Nichol. Shakespeare in the Eighteenth Century. OUP, 1928, 91 pp. E-S

These three lectures constitute an informative and fluent introduction to (1) the staging of Sh, (2) the editorial labors on his texts, (3) the nascent criticism of his characters, all in the Restoration and eighteenth century. In the footnotes which Smith has added for publication are a number of bibliographical hints which have been incorporated into this Guide.

0047. Smith, Gordon Ross. A Classified Shakespeare Bibliography, 1936-1958. Pennsylvania State UP, 1963, 784 pp. (over 20,000 entries).

The section titled "Shakespeare and Classical Literature" contains only 178 entries for the period 1936-58 (some of which are intruders, as they do not deal with Sh—see Nos. A4255, A4292, A4304). But this bulky compilation contains numerous other relevant entries scattered through various sections (especially in the section on the individual plays and poems). Smith does not ordinarily annotate. Entries in this Guide which were first discovered in an examination of Smith are annotated GRS.

0048. Stone, George Winchester, Jr. "Shakespeare in the Periodicals 1700-1740," SQ, II (1951), 221-231; III (1952), 313-328.

Though his interest is in a growing public awareness of Sh which enabled journalists to allude to him with some assurance of being understood, Stone includes connected discourse of a critical nature among the 434 references to Sh which he has uncovered. Some deal specifically with Sh's knowledge of, or difference from the ancients. Stone does not discuss all of his discovered allusions, but the thoroughness of his research suggests that these arts. give us the cream of the bibliography of the subject.

0049. Tannenbaum, Samuel A. Elizabethan Bibliographies. N.Y. (Published by the author in limited eds.)

The relevant vols. in this series are "concise" bibliographies of Oth., Sonn., Troi., Macb., Lear, Merch., and (posthumously published by his wife) Romeo. Dr. Tannenbaum's immense energies and his dedication to Shn studies despite a full psychiatric practice ought to be legendary. These little vols. contain entries (not ordinarily annotated) carefully classified under such headings as "Editions," "Translations," "Book Titles from...," "Burlesques," and the important section for this Guide, "Commentary." Each vol. is indexed. One merit is that Tannenbaum includes chs. from books; another is that he goes back to eighteenth-century commentary. The Guide contains many entries traceable only to their appearance in Tannenbaum.

0050. Tannenbaum, Samuel A. (compiler). "Shakspere and His Contemporaries: A Classified Bibliography," SAB, I-XXIV (1926-49) (succeeded by SQ annual bibliography [#0042]). E-S

Tannenbaum's indefatigable explorations of the nooks and crannies of Sh scholarship make his bibliographies unusually useful; he habitually includes material not found elsewhere either because it is issued by out-of-the-way publishers or because it lies concealed behind misleading titles. But the SAB format leaves much to be desired and, more important, Tannenbaum was not a careful proofreader--many errors limit the usefulness of his compilations. Sh scholars must nevertheless hold themselves very much his debtors.

0051. [Thorn-Drury, George]. More Seventeenth Century Allusions to Shakespeare and his Works Not Hitherto Collected. [Ln], 1924, 52 + iv pp.

About 140 allusions reprinted without commentary, for the most part. Of these, several which postdate 1660 and are relevant to Sh's classicism are annotated in the present Guide; they are designated T-D. MnU

0052. "Twentieth-century Studies in Shakespeare's Songs, Sonnets, and Poems,": 2. "The Sonnets," by A. Nejgebauer; 3. "The Poems," by J. W. Lever. ShS, XV (1962), 10-30.

Excellent bibliographical arts., both of them. Nejgebauer and Lever both are biased in favor of historical criticism. Neither art. is exhaustive, but the most important arts. and books of the past sixty-five years are appraised.

0053. Warburg Institute. A Bibliography on the Survival of the Classics, Vol. I, Ln,

1934 (for 1931); Vol. II, Ln, 1938 (for 1932-33), 333, 382 pp.

Extensively annotated critical bibliographies for the years in question, these vols. are a complement to the two bibliographies which Richard Newald published in JFKA (see #0034). Almost all of the commentary is in German. The few Sh entries appear in each vol. s.v. "Humanism in the Northern Countries: England." Unfortunately the Warburg Institute ceased publication of these very useful compilations after 1938.

0054. Ward, Adolphus W. A History of English Dramatic Literature to the Death of Queen Anne. 2 vols., Ln, 1875 (new and rev. ed., 3 vols., Ln and N.Y., 1899). E-S

The last ch. of Vol. I contains a detailed survey of critical observations on Sh by his contemporaries, many of which are "classical," though Ward does not stress the point. In the large first section of Vol. II there appears a chronological treatment of the canon which summarizes for each play the traditional positions on critical and scholarly problems, some of which are "classical." As a bibliographer Ward deserves praise; this section (pp. 54-209) is packed close with books and arts. which Ward discusses intelligently. Occasionally the modern consensus goes against Ward's view, but this is a reliable standard work.

0055. Westfall, Alfred Van Rensselaer. American Shakespearean Criticism 1607-1865. N.Y., 1939, 305 pp.

In the very short ch. (pp. 274-276) on "American Contributions Concerning the Sources of Shakespeare's Dramatic Material," Westfall lists only seven arts. and books, two of which are relevant (see #2262, #2450). The reason he gives for the paucity of such studies is the unavailability to Americans of primary documents. This does not seem an adequate explanation; neither of the two studies he cites relies on rare primary material and indeed most of the entries in the present Guide are based on study of materials which a modestly equipped library would possess.

0056. "The Year's Contributions to Shakespearian Study," ShS, I- (1948-date).

This is one of the most useful of the current annual Sh bibliographies because it is quite comprehensive and because its informative brief summaries of contents enable the reader to circumvent the ambiguous or unenlightening titles which scholars seem addicted to fastening to their labors. The survey is regularly divided into three parts: "1. Critical Studies," "2. Shakespeare's Life Times and Stage," and "3. Textual Studies," each written by a distinguished authority--not always the same man in successive years. The critical asides on the works included are an honest indication of the compiler's biases, whatever they may be. A very satisfactory map of the jungle.

0057. The Year's Work in English Studies. Published for the English Association by OUP, I- (1919-date).

This annual vol. contains a ch. on Sh which describes in connected prose the criticism and scholarship of the year in question (the vols. are ordinarily two to three years behind). The critiques are brief but often cogent and the descriptions are informative; they disclose relevant material cloaked behind ambiguous or vague titles.

0058. Young, Karl. "Samuel Johnson on Shakespeare: One Aspect," WSLL, XVIII (1923), 146-226.

This erudite study is much more than its title suggests; Young has compiled a closely documented history of the interest in Sh's sources from Dryden and Langbaine to Johnson. Stopping places are Gildon, Pope, Theobald, Hanmer, Charlotte Lennox, and Johnson. Not all of Young's material is "classical," but he is able to show, e.g., that Johnson's remarks about Sh's use of Medieval sources for Troi. are under heavy (unacknowledged) obligation to Charlotte Lennox, for whose book (#2450) he wrote a dedication. Young also recognizes that Johnson was first to discover "Sh's Plutarch" in North. There are very intelligent remarks on Theobald, Warburton, and many other commentators.

GENERAL WORKS

0059. Acheson, Arthur. Shakespeare and the Rival Poet. Ln, 1903, 360 pp.

This special plea seeks to establish Chapman as the rival poet of Sonn. Among Acheson's more fanciful speculations: (1) Troi. was written in 1598 or 1599 as a satire on Chapman's Homer worship and then revised as a further slur on Chapman in 1609. (2) In the "small Latine" passage in F_1, Jonson was defending Sh against Chapman, who had called Sh "ignorant" while Sh was alive. Only less fanciful is the ch. which tries to convict Holofernes' classical pedantries of parodying Chapman's.

0060. Adams, Joseph Q. A Life of William Shakespeare. Boston, 1923, 561 pp. E-S

Adams is master of the documentary evidence for the events of Sh's life and is prepared to interpret that evidence conservatively. The emphasis falls on Sh, not on his art, with the result that the classical tradition does not assume major importance here. Yet there is a ch. on Sh's schooling (with well-informed commentary on the probable curriculum) and another in which Adams argues at some length that Sh did indeed teach Latin literature in Warwickshire. In the discussion of the canon Adams frequently refers to classical sources or themes in the plays and poems. There are some minor misinterpretations: e.g., Adams presents a picture of Sh arriving in London with a draft of Errors in his possession, which Baldwin (#0683) has since shown could not have happened, and he assumes that Sh's father was only semiliterate because he signed his name with a mark. If the Life has a major fault it is that it attempts to impart a specialist's knowledge to a popular audience: erudition and chattiness are awkward companions. But the book is as reliable on the whole as it is readable.

0061. Adams, Joseph Q. "Shakespeare, Heywood, and the Classics," MLN, XXXIV (1919), 336-339.

Documentary evidence appears to support the hypothesis that Sh's company, the King's Men, and Heywood's, the Queen's Company, collaborated in the production of Heywood's four "Ages" plays, his conscientious attempt to "'bring the golden fleece' of Greek culture into the homes of the London middle classes." Sh may have been responsible for the cooperation--he apparently shared Heywood's interest in classical culture.

0062. [Addison, Joseph]. The Spectator, No. 39 (April 14, 1711).

Midway in a discussion of the relative merits of ancient and modern tragedy Addison observes that Sh frequently violates one of Aristotle's canons by elevating and elaborating the expression at moments of crisis. Aristotle recommends the naked style for emotion and more elaborate rhetoric in the quieter interstices.

0063. [Addison, Joseph]. The Spectator, No. 160 (September 3, 1711).

In this essay toward the definition of genius Addison distinguishes between wild, original, untutored talent and the talent that labors within the "restraints of art"; to the first category belong Pindar, Homer, and other "ancients" from the eastern end of the Mediterranean, and Sh, the only northern European worthy of inclusion; to the second class belong Plato, Aristotle, Virgil, Cicero, Bacon, and Milton. Addison appears to prefer Sh's freedom to Milton's discipline.

0064. [Addison, Joseph]. The Spectator, No. 592 (September 10, 1714).

NOTE: Numbers preceded by # refer to entries in this Guide. Keys to abbreviations are found on pages xi-xvii and 381-387.

A witty derogation of the flamboyant stage effects in eighteenth-century productions and a scornful rejection of criticism which ignorantly judges only by the rules lead up to praise of Sh who violates every classic rule and was "born with all the seeds of poetry . . ."

0065. Adler, Jacob H. "Johnson's 'He That Imagines This'," SQ, XI (1960), 225-228.

When Samuel Johnson said (in the Preface to Shakespeare) that if the audience can imagine itself in Alexandria in one scene it "can imagine more" (i.e., can imagine itself in Rome in the next), he was not attacking the doctrine of unity of place. On the contrary, the remark was contemptuous and Johnson remained a neoclassicist in his Sh criticism. This is not a persuasive argument; the tone of Johnson's observations clearly indicates his sympathy for Shn violation of classical dogmas.

0066. Alden, Raymond M. Shakespeare, Master Spirits of Literature. N.Y., 1922, 377 pp.

This biography of Sh and critical study of his plays is conservative and on the whole reliable. Alden tolerates no nonsense about an illiterate provincial bumpkin; he briefly sketches Sh's probable education and attempts to place Sh in a context of classical and Continental influence on English culture in Elizabeth's time. Though the book is intended as an introduction for the general reader, it is full of information of a precise and even specialized kind about Sh's contemporaries, his probable reading, his sources, etc.; and its criticism of the plays is sound.

0067. Alexander, Peter. "The Early Plays of the Schoolmaster from the Country," Shakespeare's Henry VI and Richard III, Shakespeare Problems, III, ed. A. W. Pollard and J. Dover Wilson (CUP, 1929), Ch. III, pp. 117-143. SG

Alexander vigorously defends Heminge and Condell's F_1 canon (especially of the early plays) against the disintegrationist movement that began in the eighteenth century with Farmer and Malone. Accepting Beeston's claim that Sh had been a schoolmaster in the country, Alexander shows that the early works (especially Titus, Errors, Shrew, and Venus) are exactly such as a quondam schoolmaster would have written, based as they are on Seneca, Plautus, and Ovid. Alexander is an able polemicist--his arguments are persuasive.

0068. Alexander, Peter. Shakespeare's Life and Art. Ln, 1939, 247 pp.

Alexander writes to refute the extremists who disintegrate the canon or depreciate Sh's Art. This is a book with no private theories to advance and it is therefore reliable as a reference. While Baldwin (#0089) and others demonstrate Sh's Art by analyzing what he read at school, Alexander argues that Aubrey and Beeston were correct in thinking that Sh taught school himself. The early works are just such as a schoolmaster would write: Titus is a self-conscious imitation of Seneca--its horrors are the products of Art, not of Nature; Errors is Plautine not only in source but also in structure (unity of place and time); Venus is deliberately Ovidian. Alexander is a student of textual problems and he uses the bibliographer's tools to establish Sh's artistic development, but the book contains numerous observations on Sh's classicism: Plato anticipated Sh's practice when in the Symposium he stated that a writer of comedy also has tragic potential. Sh's stage setting for Errors (one exit to the bay and one to the town) is traceable ultimately to Greek drama, which was staged between Athens and the sea. Sh has mythical seacoasts in northern Italy as well as in Bohemia, but he has a distinguished precedent; Plautus gives Thebes a seacoast in Amphitruo. Alexander's is one of the best of Shn literary biographies.

0069. Allen, Don Cameron. "Shakspere and the Doctrine of Cosmic Identities," SAB, XIV (1939), 182-189.

Covering briefly some of the ground later delineated by Tillyard (#0598) and Spencer (#0560), Allen shows the origin of the micro-macrocosm concept in pre-Socratic "elemental" metaphysics and in Plato, Aristotle, and the Alexandrian academies. He cites many references to hierarchy of being in Sh, but many of them can be read as mere pathetic fallacy or as simple metaphor, like Iago's identification of men and beasts. This is not to vitiate Allen's basic contention, however; it is well substantiated.

0070. Allen, Don Cameron. "Some Aspects of the Dispute about Astrology Among Elizabethan and Jacobean Men of Letters," The Star-Crossed Renaissance: The Quarrel about Astrology and Its Influence in England (Duke UP, 1941), pp. 147-189.

"[F]or most men of the Age of Elizabeth and James the influence of the planets was at one with that of fate and fortune." That this faith in astrology was widespread among literary men (including Sh) Allen's impressive array of citations attempts to show. But, as he admits, it is easier to demonstrate that literary allusions indicate popular familiarity with astrology than to demonstrate that the authors themselves believed in planetary influence. The citations to Sh are numerous and embrace almost the entire canon. It can be inferred that Sh's putative belief in astral influence indicates his adherence to the tenets of Renaissance Stoicism: Allen notes (p. 147) the coalescence in the sixteenth century of astrological beliefs and the Fatalism of the classical Stoics. If Shn characters sometimes indicate skepticism about the stars, this is because "Shakespeare, like Cicero, reports all attitudes."

0071. Allen, James Turney. Stage Antiquities of the Greeks and Romans and Their Influence, Our Debt, [No. 28] (N.Y., 1927), 206 pp.

There are about a dozen references to Sh in this book, half of them concentrated in a ch. on "Influences: The Drama." Typical are allusions to Richard's opening soliloquy in R.III as an improvement on the Senecan prologue, to the closing lines of All's W. as an imitation of "the Plautine epilogic tags," and to Temp. as the only play in which Sh did not defy the unities, which he obviously knew.

0072. Anders, Heinrich [R. D.]. "Randglossen zu Shakespeare's Belesenheit," ShJ, LXII (1926), 158-162. SG

Eight entries, of which the following are relevant: (1) Troi. III iii 145-150 ("Time hath, my lord, a wallet at his back ...") is indebted to Aesop [in Latin trans. ?]. (2) The poet's "fine frenzy" passage in Dream V i 4-22 is traceable to Plato, who expresses similar ideas in the Phaedrus, Ion, and Symposium. Anders does not mention the route by which the concept came to Sh, but says in #0073 that Sh did not read the classics in Greek. (6) Points out a parallel between Venus 1111-1118 and the Hellenistic bucolic "On the Death of Adonis." In the light of Jiriczek's art. (#2444) Anders thinks indebtedness likely. (8, misnumbered 9) Points out that in 1582 Gosson mentioned the Golden Ass as having been "ransackt" by English dramatists.

0073. Anders, H[einrich] R. D. "Shakespeare and the Classics," Shakespeare's Books: A Dissertation on Shakespeare's Reading and the Immediate Sources of his Works. (Berlin, 1904), Ch. I, pp. 6-49. E-S HB SG

Brief sections on Latin influence: (William Lily's Latin Grammar, Aesop, Mantuanus, Caesar's Commentaries, Cicero, Ovid, Virgil, Plautus, Seneca, Pliny, Juvenal). Anders cites ch. and verse for echoes of these authors, and though not all of his evidence is convincing, the over-all impression is that "Shakespeare's knowledge of the Latin language was considerable ...he must have read some of the more important Latin authors" (probably not either Horace or Lucan). Greek: "We have no evidence that Shakespeare read any Greek author in the original." Sections on the influence of Plutarch, Homer, Josephus, Heliodorus, Marianus the Byzantine (on the last two Sonn.). An Appendix reprints pp. 1, 2, and part of 3 of Lily's Latin Grammar. This is an important study which has been regarded in recent years as a turning point in the history of the "small Latin" controversy (see, e.g., #0019).

0074. [Anderson, James]. "Critical Remarks on the Othello of Shakespear," The Bee, I (1791), 56-62.

This essay begins with a comparison between Homer and Sh, neither of whom ever borrowed from a predecessor, and both of whom had native genius in abundance. The essay is a forceful indication of the excesses which Farmer's Essay (#0238) encouraged toward the end of the eighteenth century. MnU

0075. Anderson, Ruth L. "'As Heart Can Think'," SAB, XII (1937), 246-251.

In his numerous references to the heart as the controller of the rational faculty, Sh shows that he is an Aristotelian in the sixteenth-century controversy between adherents of Aristotle and of Plato: Plato thought the brain to be the seat of the rational soul; Aristotle favored the heart. Professor Anderson surveys other classical authorities as well: most take the Aristotelian view, e.g., Lucretius, Athenaeus, Alexander of Aphrodisias.

0076. Anderson, Ruth L. Elizabethan Psychology and Shakespeare's Plays, IowaHS, III, No. 4 ([1928]), 182 pp.

The Preface to this excellent introduction to faculty psychology speaks of the subject as "a complex doctrine inherited from Plato and Aristotle, Hippocrates and Galen," but it is Renaissance authorities (Charron, Batman, La Primaudaye, Huarte, Bright, Burton, and many others) who are the chief spokesmen for the doctrine here. In Chs. VII and VIII Plato's Timaeus and Phaedrus are cited as authorities on love and on conflict among the faculties. In numerous places Nemesius (περὶ φυσέως ἀνθρώπου in George Wither's 1636 trans., The Nature of Man) is introduced as a late-classical ancestor of the Renaissance psychologists. Miss Anderson illustrates the theories with scores of quotations drawn from the entire canon; Sh appears orthodox in his thinking about man's faculties.

0077. Anderson, Ruth L. "Kingship in Renaissance Drama," SP, XLI (1944), 136-155.

A discussion of the "principles and imagery associated with kingship" as they appear in Elizabethan drama (especially Sh). There are classical sources for such concepts as the rationale, license, moral responsibility, and disadvantages of sovereignty. Perhaps chief among those sources are Seneca's tragedies, but Plato (by way of Pierre Charron's Of Wisdom), Plutarch's Precepts of Statecraft, and Tacitus are also relevant. Professor Anderson quotes from some ten Shn plays.

0078. Arnold, Matthew. On the Classical Tradition, The Complete Prose Works of Matthew Arnold, Vol. I, ed. R. H. Super (Michigan UP, 1960), 271 pp.

In Arnold's essays "On Translating Homer" and "On the Modern Element in Literature," and in his prefaces to the Poems and to Merope there are over a score of references to Sh. Sh is ordinarily placed in juxtaposition with Hellenic writers with respect to style. Arnold's inclination is to emphasize the differences between Sh and the Greeks.

0079. Arnold, Paul. Ésotérisme de Shakespeare. Paris, 1955, 260 pp.

Arnold finds evidence through much of the canon that Sh was aware of the mystical controversies of his age though he criticized extremists in the occult. Not all of the esoteric lore Arnold finds in Sh is classical, though Orphic love, the music of the spheres, Hermetic Platonism, and the Eleusinian mysteries are liberally mingled with cabalism, Rosicrucianism, the School of Night, alchemy, and Christian mysticism. Typical is Ch. II, in which Arnold argues that L.L.L. and Dream document Sh's belief in a love which transcends the flesh. No one will doubt Sh's reverence for "the marriage of true minds," but it is quite another thing to establish occult sources for such commonplaces of the Middle Ages and the Renaissance, or to win belief for an interpretation of Merch. in which Portia "s'identifie à la Sagesse universelle." Phoenix, Cym., W.T., and Temp. are accorded extended treatment, while Errors, Ham., Macb., Venus, Lucr., and Oth. are discussed more briefly (and more tentatively).

0080. Attwater, A. L. "Shakespeare's Sources," A Companion to Shakespeare Studies, ed. H. Granville-Barker and G. B. Harrison (CUP, 1934), pp. 219-241. E-S

This general, somewhat disorganized ch. deals only briefly with North's Plutarch and not at all with Ovid, Seneca, and Plautus. It does make some very cogent remarks about Sh's manipulation of source material in Troi. (under the heading "The Italian Novel").

0081. Aubrey, John. Aubrey Manuscripts (ca. 1680), Munro, II, 260-261.

The last sentence of this brief bit of gossip about Sh contains the famous attribution to William Beeston of the information that Sh "understood Latine pretty well: for he had been in his yonger yeares a Schoolmaster in the Countrey."

0082. Baker, George Pierce. The Development of Shakespeare as a Dramatist. N.Y., 1907, 329 pp. E-S

There are (passim) a number of passages discussing Sh's manipulation of sources, usually emphasizing his dramatic intention of appealing to his audience. Baker seldom deals with Sh's specific use of specific materials; e.g., Plutarch receives only passing mention in the six pages (286-291) devoted to Cor., and Plautus figures briefly as a foil to Sh's greater art in the eight pages (134-141) on Errors.

0083. Baldwin, T. W. "Nature's Moulds," SQ, III (1952), 237-241.

Baldwin traces Sh's conception of Nature's procreative processes in part to Ovid, in part ultimately to Plato. They were, of course, commonplaces of Elizabethan thought. W. C. Curry argues (SP, XXIX [1932], 15-28) that the Augustinian rationes seminales or the Neoplatonic-Stoic λόγοι σπερματικοί were the ultimate source(s) of Sh's conception. His argument is reprinted as Ch. II of Shakespeare's Philosophical Patterns (#2205).

0084. Baldwin, T. W. "A Note upon William Shakespeare's Use of Pliny," PPV, pp. 157-182. E-S SG

With his characteristically relentless documentation, Baldwin disposes of the traditional assumption that Sh's knowledge of Pliny was confined to Holland's trans. (1601). He presents conclusive evidence that Sh read parts of the Naturalis Historia in Latin, probably in the 1587 Lyons ed. of Jacobus Dalecampius. Sh had at least enough facility to "scour up his old grammar school Latin sufficiently to pull a piece of information out of the original . . ."

0085. Baldwin, T. W. "On Atomizing Shakespeare," ShJ, XCI (1955), 136-144.

As he criticizes those who lose perspective while amassing "infinitesimal facts from infinite modes of approach," Baldwin objects to the use to which his books have been put. "We may [through error] attribute all the learning of his background to [Sh], whereas all that we can demonstrate is that in certain specific instances he reflects a certain degree of acquaintance with that learning." There are brief comments on imago and image, drama as rhetoric, Terence and typed characters.

0086. Baldwin, T. W. On the Literary Genetics of Shakspere's Plays, 1592-1594. Illinois UP, 1959, 562 pp.

Baldwin focuses on Sh's connections with his contemporaries in the theater rather than on his cultural heritage, though at all points, as he says in the Preface, the ultimately classical methods of composition which Sh used are implied as the genetic force in the creation of the early plays. The most important chs. for this Guide are the first, "The Literary Genetics of Robert Greene's Shake-scene Passage," in which Baldwin argues that Greene meant that Sh had supplanted the University Wits, not plagiarized from them,and XXII-XXVI on the tangled relationships of the Titus versions. Baldwin believes that Sh and Peele probably collaborated in a revision of an Ur-Titus in 1593-94. Peele's hand appears more clearly in Act I than elsewhere. The argument is an elaboration of arguments by Parrott, Robertson, and Gray (#1566, #1607, #1354) which have largely been discredited since H. T. Price showed that Titus has unity of construction (#1585). This book is less satisfying, if not less learned, than Baldwin's other studies. The logic of his disintegrationist arguments leaves considerable room for disagreement with his conclusions.

0087. Baldwin, T. W. "Perseus Purloins Pegasus," PQ, XX (1941), 361-370 (also in Craig Festschrift, pp. 169-178).

A discussion of the substitution by Sh and his contemporaries of Perseus for Bellerophon as the rider of Pegasus. Baldwin believes that Sh's confusion stems from the illustrations in the ed. of Ovid he used in grammar school.

0088. Baldwin, T. W. "Shakespeare's Aphthonian Man," MLN, LXV (1950), 111-112.

In two places (Romeo III v 181-184; Twel. I v 277-281) Sh has a character eulogize another in precisely the form laid out by "the grammar school Aphthonius." Moreover, in Troi. I ii 274-278 Sh is obviously thinking of the Aphthonian formula, though he does not follow it exactly.

0089. Baldwin, T. W. William Shakspere's Small Latine & Lesse Greeke. Illinois UP, 1944, 2 vols.: I, 753 pp.; II, 772 pp.

Though Baldwin makes only minimal claims for his achievement, these two vols. represent the most original and at the same time the most painstaking scholarly research into Sh's classicism which has appeared in this century. With enviable erudition and model thoroughness Baldwin shows that whether or not Sh attended Stratford Grammar School, he had at his command the literature and the compositional methods which were probably taught there. Beginning with a survey of the development of English grammar schools and their curricula (a survey which constitutes a preliminary history of this subject, though Baldwin modestly calls it only a beginning), the study attempts to reconstruct by analogy a probable form-by-form curriculum for Stratford and then "examines" Sh on the material and methods presumed to be taught in each form. He passes almost every test—the very great probability is that he completed a normal upper-school education, which made him at least "a learned grammarian," capable of grammaticizing his Latin and his English, of analyzing problems logically, and of applying the rhetorical principles of "imitative variation" which were the essence of prose and verse compositional theory in the sixteenth century. Baldwin finds that among other classics Sh knew Aesop (in Latin), Terence, Plautus, Cicero, Quintilian, Ad Herennium, Ovid, Virgil, Horace, Juvenal, Persius; (possibly) Lucan, Sallust, and Caesar; (doubtfully) Catullus and Seneca. In addition he had studied such Renaissance Latinists as Susenbrotus, Erasmus, Palingenius, and Mantuanus. Sh may have had some Greek in school; the probability is that it did not extend far beyond Scripture. Considering its wealth of documentation Baldwin's book is eminently readable; only the irascible will attribute the jocularity of the style to levity. But if Baldwin's style is pleasing his repeated deference to the disintegrators is not; perhaps the author hopes by deferring to appear not to overstate his case. In point of fact, however, his research provides potent weapons against disintegration: e.g., Ch. XXVII (Vol. I) discusses over twenty probable echoes of Aesop's fables in the canon, and though some are in disputed plays virtually all can be traced with confidence to the school ed. of Camerarius. Disintegration aside, the book is reliable--and useful as well: through the interplay of text and indexes Baldwin offers at least a partial concordance to Sh's classical allusions. This thorough study provides the groundwork of inductive probability on which criticism of Sh's use of his cultural assets can be built. Already such criticism is appearing, vide Whitaker (#0635) who begins with Baldwin's findings and traces the increasingly subtle artistic and intellectual uses to which Sh put what he had learned at Stratford. One cannot say of Baldwin what Dr. Johnson said of Farmer, that he has ended the "small Latin" controversy, but this book takes a long stride toward the truth about Sh's classicism.

0090. Bamborough, J. B. The Little World of Man. Ln, 1952, 187 pp.

Bamborough uses Sh (among many other authors between Chaucer and Pope) to illustrate the complex of Renaissance beliefs about the subtle relationships between the body and the soul. These beliefs are ultimately traceable to Galenic physiology, Platonic psychology, and pre-Socratic, "elemental" metaphysics, but Bamborough emphasizes that the classical doctrines had been greatly modified by the end of the sixteenth century and were being challenged with increasing frequency (in the seventeenth century the discovery of the circulation of the blood caused the quiet and gradual death of the whole system of humoral psychology). A thorough treatment, which like those of Draper, Anderson, Tillyard, Spencer, and Campbell, contributes a background against which we can better interpret Sh's characters.

0091. Baretti, Joseph. Discours sur Shakespeare et sur Monsieur de Voltaire. Ln and Paris, 1777, 186 pp.

The Discours is a witty, agile, and sometimes damaging attack on Voltaire: Sh does not figure centrally in it. The relevant ch. is the fourth, in which Baretti defends Sh against Voltaire's charge that he ignored the three unities. Baretti argues: "Corneille a fait plaisir aux François en suivant les Préceptes d'Aristote. Shakespeare a fait plaisir aux Anglois en ne les suivant point. Pourquoi chicannerons-nous Shakespeare qui a atteint le même but que Corneille, quoiqu'il l'ait atteint par une route différente?" Baretti also anticipates Coleridge's concept of the suspension of disbelief as he points out that an audience must accept an imaginative locus for the play which is not the theater even if there is unity of place in a given play. DFo

0092. Barfield, Owen. History in English Words. Ln, 1926/1954, 239 pp.

Of the ten Sh citations passim, most make some reference to his relationship to the classical world. Sh's coinage, mainly Latin and Greek, has retained its luster because his popularity has kept those words before a large public in their original significations.

0093. Barker, Sir Ernest. "Greek Influences in English Life and Thought," Traditions of Civility: Eight Essays (CUP, 1948), pp. 1-34.

This sensitive essay on Greek humanism as a living force in England twice mentions Sh's reverence for North's Plutarch and in a note (p. 30) speculates about the affinity of Sonn. 53 and Phoenix for the "mysticism" of the Symposium; Barker does not guess at Sh's possible paths to Plato.

0094. Bartlett, Henrietta C. Mr. William Shakespeare: Original and Early Editions of his Quartos and Folios, his Source Books and those Containing Contemporary Notices. Yale UP, 1922. E-S

The fourth section, "Source Books" (83-135), consists of diplomatic transcripts of the titles of ninety printed books which may have served Sh as sources, together with brief notes on the locations of exemplars and on Sh's manipulation of the source material in question. Among the classics are Caxton's Aesop, Golding's Ovid, Underdowne's Aethiopica, Mantuan, North's Plutarch, Hall's Iliad, and W.W.'s Menaechmi. This is an interesting and useful ch.

0095. Baugh, Albert C. History of the English Language. 2nd ed., N.Y., 1957, Ch. VIII.

In Section 172 (pp. 281-282), Baugh illustrates the fecundity of Renaissance coinage from Sh's vocabulary. Most of the examples he cites are from Latin. Sh "would no doubt have been classed among the liberals in his attitude towards foreign borrowing" even though he "could make sport of the inkhorn terms of a pedant like Holofernes." His Latinate words retained their etymological meanings "like recent immigrants who still show traces of their foreign ways."

0096. Baynes, T[homas] S. "An Early Notice of Shakspeare," Ath, No. 2584 (1877), 576-577.

An extended discussion of a passage in Charles Butler's Rhetoricae Libri Duo (1600, 1629, 1635, 1642, etc.) in which Sh is rated in no way inferior to Seneca, Plautus, and Terence. The reference to Sh was probably inserted in 1635 or 1642, supplanting a laudatory reference to Chaucer. That Butler's Rhetoric was a popular grammar school text in the middle decades of the seventeenth century suggests to Baynes that the favorable comparison of Sh with the classic dramatists may have kept his fame alive during the dark days of the theaterless Interregnum.

0097. Baynes, Thomas S. "What Shakespeare learnt at School," FM, n.s. XX (1879), 604-621; XXI (1880), 83-102, 619-641. HB (Reprinted as a single essay in Shakespeare Studies and Other Essays [1894].)

Part I is a fairly reasonable attempt to reconstruct from contemporary documents the curriculum in the sixteenth-century English grammar school. Part II enumerates references in the plays to this curriculum and argues that Sh read Ovid in Latin independently after leaving school and before reading any trans. Part III shows the influence of Ovid on the early works. Most of this work has since been superseded, but it is of considerable interest historically, as it anticipates modern views by finding through scholarship a middle ground between the extremists of the eighteenth century (i.e., Farmer and Upton).

0098. Beattie, James. "On the Similitude Between Shakspeare and Homer in Relation to Their Knowledge of the Human Heart," Memorials of Shakspeare...By Various Writers, collected by Nathan Drake (Ln, 1828), pp. 255-256.

Unlike Godwin (#1339), Beattie considers both poets masters at individualizing characters. Though this abstract from Forbes's Account is very brief, in it Beattie refers to some thirteen Shn characters for illustration. DFo MnU

0099. Behn, Aphra. "An Epistle to the Reader [of The Dutch Lover: A Comedy (1673)]," T-D, p. 10.

In rating Sh's popularity higher than Jonson's, Mrs. Behn takes occasion to say, "by the way 'tis said that Benjamin was no such Rabbi neither, for I am inform'd his Learning was but Grammar high," a tacit disparagement of Sh's classicism as well. T. W. Baldwin (#0089, p. 33n) speculates that Mrs. Behn may be recalling Fuller's contrast (#0257) between Jonson, high in learning like a Spanish galleon and Sh, lower in classicism, but agile like an English fighting ship.

0100. "Ben Jonson's Quarrel with Shakespeare," NBR, LII (1870), 394-427.

A detailed argument to prove that Sh and Jonson attacked one another in plays written before the death of Elizabeth. Sh, who was not studious enough, is Ovid in the Poetaster, while Sh parodied Jonson in the Achilles of Troi. Sh "wanted Art," and Jonson's satire on him was a continuation of lampoons to this effect which began in 1589. The author also weaves in the Essex affair, Sh's coat of arms, and other matters which have nothing to do with the "small Latin" question. Much of the argument substitutes assertion for proof. DLC

0101. Berthelot, René. "La Sagesse shakespearienne," La Sagesse de Shakespeare et de Goethe (Paris, 1930), pp. 9-71.

"Wisdom" here means pastoralism, which Berthelot sees as the dominant ethical theme in Sh from L.L.L. through Temp. He begins with chs. on classical pastoralism and Italian and French modifications (which introduced the Golden Age motif and made Orpheus the ideal man, capable of soothing harsh nature). Then he surveys the canon, pointing out, e.g., that in Merch. Antonio's lack of cupidity places him in the tradition, that Hamlet's quest for wisdom in a corrupt court is again "pastoral," while Friar Laurence meditates on man among his herbs. Berthelot would claim Sh for France and Italy but he offers no real evidence as to the direction of Sh's philosophical obligations. An odd comparison places Act V of Temp. in juxtaposition with Iliad XXIV: both resolve impossible dilemmas of hatred, and each is a quiet close to a story containing much violence. Though stimulating in places, this book does not fill the need for a major study of the pastoral tradition in Sh. DFo

0102. Bieber, Gustav A. Der Melancholikertypus Shakespeares und sein Ursprung, AA, H. 3 (Heidelberg, 1913), 92 pp. E-S

In a brief Ch. II, Bieber traces the evolution of "Temperamentslehre" from its source in Empedoclean natural philosophy through Aristotle and Hippocrates to Galen. The remainder of the book traces the humors through Chaucer and the Renaissance to Sh, laying special stress on melancholy mixed with other humors. Bieber emphasizes Renaissance documents, making no claim for Sh's direct knowledge of the classical psychologists. TxHR

0103. Billson, Charles J. "Shakespeare's Library: An Enquiry into the Sources of Information of the Dramatist Other than Classical," Noctes Shaksperianae: A Series of Papers by Late and Present Members [of the Winchester College Shakspere Society], ed. Charles H. Hawkins (Winchester, 1887), pp. 1-41.

Billson assumes (p. 9) that Ben Jonson meant "thy Latin is so small that only the nullity of thy Greek is less" and that Sh's only practicable access to the classics was trans. (for the most part English). Among the trans. he probably used are North's Plutarch, Chapman's Homer, Golding's Ovid, Phaer's Aeneid, Marlowe's Lucan, and Holland's Pliny. "He may have read some Plautus," but did not know Cicero, Horace, Lucretius, Statius, Seneca, or Persius. This interpretation of Jonson (and of Sh) is obviously untenable. Vide Baldwin (#0089, Vol. I, Section 1). MnU DFo

0104. Black, Matthew. "Enter Citizens," SERD, pp. 16-27.

Sh's use of undifferentiated citizens in bit parts distinguishes him from the classical dramatists. Except for Aristophanes' comedies, where "numeraries" are used for satiric commentary on the action, Greek and Roman tragedy and comedy are devoid of characters who stand somewhere between typed "humors" and mute supernumeraries. The native tradition is Sh's source.

0105. Blake, Harriet Manning. Classic Myth in the Poetic Drama of the Age of Elizabeth. Lancaster, Pa., [1912], 84 pp. HB SG

The emphasis does not fall on Sh in this doctoral diss, but the author finds occasion to express the opinion that Sh knew his Ovid (perhaps in Latin as well as in Golding). For Tim. Sh could have drawn on the conversation of his friends without recourse to Lucian's Greek or the academic play. Dr. Blake is inclined, however, to grant Sh a generous store of Latin and some Greek. She appears favorably impressed with Collins' arguments (#0173). Brief passages on Errors, Romeo, and Venus. DFo

0106. Blissett, William. "Lucan's Caesar and the Elizabethan Villain," SP, LIII (1956), 553-575.

Lucan, who was very popular during the Middle Ages and Renaissance, contributed to Renaissance drama "the figure of the restless, ruthless, impious, and intelligent villain-hero, bent on imposing his will on all the world, at the risk of pulling the whole fabric of things down in ruins." The prototype is, of course, the Caesar of the Pharsalia; though Sh's Caesar is not so malicious as Lucan's, his Bolingbroke does cross precisely a Lucanic Rubicon and his Richard III and Macbeth are clearly in the tradition. Part of the Elizabethan (and Shn) interest is to be accounted for by the sixteenth-century preoccupation with the theme of civil war. A most interesting argument: Sh, it is implied, need not have read Lucan in Latin, since so much of his influence was felt in the pre-Shn drama.

0107. Blythe, Ronald. "Four Villages," ER, LIX (1950), 212-215.

The most famous son of one of them was Arthur Golding, whose life, talents, and influence on Sh occupy most of these pages. "The wonderful Greek hand apparent in the pastoral comedies of A Midsummer Night's Dream and As You Like It; the classical allegory in Venus and Adonis and The Lover's Complaint is Ovid shown to Shakespeare by a masterly guide." Blythe also discusses Temp. Sh, he suggests, probably knew enough Latin to appreciate the excellence of Golding's trans.

0108. Boas, Frederick S. "Aspects of Classical Legend and History in Shakespeare," PBA, XXIX (1943), 107-132. (Annual British Academy Shakespeare Lecture). (Reprinted [very inaccurately] in Queen Elizabeth in Drama and Related Studies [1950].)

Though he begins with the implication that he is familiar with the research of the 'thirties and 'forties in America on Sh's classical education, Boas clings tenaciously to what has come to be identified as the British view of Sh as a semiliterate. Sh's Ovid was probably limited to Golding, his publisher may have inserted the "Vilia miretur vulgus ..." as a heading for Venus, disintegration may exonerate Sh from having quoted Latin authors directly, etc. Boas makes factual slips (e.g., he says that Sh refers only once to the myth of Phaethon), and though he is addressing scholars his tone is more appropriate to the common reader. The address is, however, a useful collection of some of Sh's classical references.

0109. Boas, Frederick S. "Aspects of Shakespeare's Reading" (1948), Queen Elizabeth in Drama and Related Studies (Ln, 1950), pp. 56-71.

The "classical" parts of this essay are subsumed into #0108 which is reprinted in the same vol.

0110. Boas, Frederick S. "How Shakespeare used his Library," An Introduction to the Reading of Shakespeare (OUP, 1927/1930), Ch. IV, pp. 37-45.

Boas describes Plutarch and Holinshed as Sh's two favorite authors; Sh, who believed that character is fate, probed deeply into the characters of the men portrayed in the two historians. Neither Plutarch nor Holinshed was a philosopher: the first cared about character and the second about colorful events; it was Sh who lent significance to the characters and events he borrowed from them. It is noteworthy that to Boas there is no great difference between the Greek historian and the English; he finds no special significance in Sh's classical commitment.

0111. Boas, Frederick S. "Ovid and the Elizabethans" (1947), Queen Elizabeth in Drama and Related Studies (Ln, 1950), pp. 101-121.

Sh does not dominate this essay on the influence of Ovid. Boas briefly compares passages from Temp. and Much with excerpts from Golding--the reader is to infer that Sh was no Latinist. The other miscellaneous remarks on Sh's debt are all in #0108 in much the same form.

0112. Boas, Frederick S. Shakspere and His Predecessors. N.Y., 1896, 550 pp. E-S

Pp. 99-102 are a recapitulation of Baynes's thesis (#0097). Ch. XV (454-503) is a critical analysis of the "Plutarch" plays with many comments on Sh's use of North. A typical aside compares late Republican Rome and Elizabethan England: oriental luxury = Italianate corruption; Stoicism = Puritanism; "by the Thames, as by the Tiber, a centralizing despotism resting upon popular sympathies was in conflict with the inherited rights of an aristocracy and an elective assembly." There are many other references to Sh's classicism passim.

0113. Bolgar, R. R. The Classical Heritage and Its Beneficiaries. CUP, 1954, 592 pp.

Sh receives a two-page comment and a bare handful of scattered references in this major study of the tradition. Bolgar considers the question of how much direct knowledge Sh had of Latin and Greek writers irrelevant, since the indirect paths to the ancient world were so many by the end of the sixteenth century. With Sir Thomas Browne and Montaigne Sh is to the classical learning of the Renaissance what Dante was to the classical learning of the Middle Ages. Bolgar believes Sh may have read Latin with some fluency, but probably not much Greek since his response to Greek culture is so eccentric compared with the realistic portrayal of Rome in the Roman tragedies. Sh doubtless had access to some awareness of Rome other than Plutarch; Plutarch taught him little about Greece. Bolgar says little about Ovid, but stresses Seneca. Kind words for Highet and Baldwin.

0114. Boodle, R. W. "The Theory of the Classical and Shakespearian Dramas," Shna, II (1885), 313-320.

Contrasting Shn practice with Aristotelian theory, Boodle makes a number of provocative, if somewhat oversimplified remarks, among them that the Greeks had no belief in progress and therefore portrayed character as frozen, not developing, as in Sh. Plot and passion are the essence of Greek drama; character rules romantic drama. Greek actors, ensconced behind fixed masks, could not act as Elizabethan actors could; the intimacy of Sh's stage gave him flexibility in introducing detail. The force of these truisms is vitiated in part by Boodle's bland assumption of Sh's almost total ignorance of classical culture.

0115. [Boswell, James the Younger]. "Essay

on the Phraseology and Metre of Shakspeare and His Contemporaries," Boswell's Malone, I, 507-585.

In the first section, "Of Shakspeare's Phraseology," Boswell expresses his conviction that Sh was "remarkably free" from the "pedantry and affectation" of inkhornism. His emphasis falls on the difficulties that arise from Sh's irregularities of grammar, not on his Latinate coinage. About the latter he is hesitant to venture an opinion in the absence of a sure knowledge of the provenance of English Latinisms in Sh's time.

0116. Boyce, Benjamin. "The Stoic 'Consolatio' and Shakespeare," PMLA, LXIV (1949), 771-780.

In this lucid and fluent art. Boyce sketches the rhetorical pattern of the consolatory epistle in the Roman Stoics and briefly traces its impact on the English rhetoricians. He then goes on to analyze four instances of Sh's use of the formulae (in Ham., Oth., Much, and Macb.) and to indicate in passing several other cases of Sh's dramatic use of the consolatio. A reasonable and convincing essay.

0117. Boyce, Benjamin. The Theophrastan Character in England to 1642. HUP, 1947, 324 pp.

Boyce, who believes that Terentian comedy of types in situations is the true bridge between Theophrastus and Renaissance England, finds some response to the tradition in Sh. Maria's depreciatory portrait of Malvolio, Portia's characterization of her various suitors, Jaques's "seven ages" speech, Hamlet's satirical remarks on old men, Berowne's picture of "Monsieur the Nice" are classical "characters" in that they are analytic of society and that they lay little emphasis on individual traits; but Sh in general is too precise in his characterization to be Theophrastan in spirit. Falstaff is much more than a "Thraso-Gnatho" and even Osric and Hotspur are more than fop and hothead respectively. A very interesting study.

0118. Boyer, Clarence V. The Villain as Hero in Elizabethan Tragedy. Ln, 1914, 264 pp. SG

Three chs. of this standard work have relevance: Ch. II (13-20) discusses the villainous protagonists of Seneca's tragedies and the advance the Elizabethans made in adding retributive justice--the paying off of scores in Act V (Sh is not specifically discussed here). Ch. VII (79-98) analyzes R.III to show that the hero is more Machiavellian than Senecan, but that such elements as Margaret (Nemesis) and Richard's "supernatural" defeat preserve their classical origin. Boyer also specifies the audience's reaction of pity and fear according to Aristotelian criteria. Ch. VIII shows that Titus is an Aristotelian hero, while Aaron is Senecan in his joy at the sufferings of others (cf. Atreus' joy at Thyestes' anguish). Iago is Aaron made credible; like Aaron and Atreus he is amused by his victim's contortions, but like Aaron he also has Machiavellian traits. The final ch., on Macb., does not discuss the Senecan elements in the play.

0119. Bradbrook, M. C. Shakespeare and Elizabethan Poetry. Ln, 1951, 279 pp.

In this study of Sh's relationship to the conventions of Elizabethan poetry the emphasis falls on such Medieval survivals as heraldry and Frauendienst, but there are numerous sections devoted to classical themes and treatments. Among them are passages on Venus and Ovid, Titus and the literature of personification, Lucr. and the formal Complaint, Phoenix and Platonic love. A stimulating book, which, unlike some other recent British publications, recognizes and draws on American research in Sh's classics.

0120. Bradley, Henry. "Shakespeare's English," in Shakespeare's England, [ed. C. T. Onions] (Oxford: Clarendon, 1916), II, 539-574.

See especially pp. 560-565 for some illuminating comments on Elizabethan and Shn approaches to coinage from Latin. Most important, perhaps, is the discussion of perfect participles (frequently without -ed endings) formed from Latin verbs (e.g., "The king of Mede had depopulate the country"). Also welcome is Bradley's refutation of "expressions of regretful admiration for the superior 'correctness' of Elizabethan use of Latin derivatives as contrasted with the manner in which the same words are now employed." A very useful ch.

0121. Bradner, Leicester. "The Rise of Secular Drama in the Renaissance," SR, III (1956), 7-22.

This essay ranges across Continental as well as English drama, frequently stressing the additions the Renaissance drama made to the classical: in tragedy, characterization (especially in Sh); in comedy, "an ideal of womanhood."

0122. Brandes, Georg. William Shakespeare: A Critical Study. Ln, 1898/1907, 708 pp. (in the one-vol. ed.).

The scope of this book is much broader than Sh's relationship to the classics, but Brandes does make many passing suggestions, more often comparing than tracing indebtedness. Some insights are provocative (Hotspur is an Achilles who cannot weep or respond to music), some are misleading (R. III is like Greek tragedy because it is the culmination of a tetralogy--Brandes overlooks the fact that the culmination of a Greek tetralogy was a Satyr play). Brandes' criticism must be suspect, since he makes too close an equation between the plays and his conception of Sh's life and character (e.g., Cleopatra is a reincarnation of Sh's cruel mistress, "The Dark Lady"). Yet Brandes intelligently rejects the Romantic conception of Sh the genius without antecedents; he repeatedly refers to Sh as "Romanesque" in spirit and technique.

0123. Brandl, Alois. Shakespeare: Leben--Umwelt--Kunst. Neue Ausgabe, Berlin, 1922, 517 pp. E-S SG

Brandl delineates a Sh who remembered his schooldays (and his schoolbooks) many years later and could put them to artistic use. Numerous brief comments provide evidence: on Senecan tragedy (especially Hercules Furens) in Titus, John, and Lear; on Horace in Sonn., Dream, and Caesar; on De Amicitia in Sonn., on various Adonis traditions in Venus, on the Ciceronian concept "honestum" in Ham., etc. Brandl does not specify the Stratford curriculum except to express doubt that Sh learned Greek. Insofar as it treats Sh's use of his cultural resources this book anticipates a good deal of recent scholarly opinion; it is still a useful guide in the field.

0124. Brewer, Wilmon. Ovid's Metamorphoses in European Culture. 3 vols.: Vols. I, II Boston; Vol. III Francetown, N.H., 1933-57. Vol. I HB SG

Despite its title, this work of twenty-five years is a fuller and more illuminating study of Ovid's sources and of his methods of composition than of his influence on Western culture. Each vol. deals in detail with five books of Meta. At the end of each ch. Brewer lists briefly the European authors indebted to the material in the book of Meta. discussed in that ch., but his field is so broad that he does not often specify ch. and verse. What he says of Sh's mythology in the Introduction (I, 32-34) is a paraphrase of Root (#0497).

0125. Brooke, C. F. Tucker. "Classical Influence in Tragedy," The Tudor Drama: A History of English National Drama to the Retirement of Shakespeare (Boston, 1911), pp. 188-229. E-S

This intelligent analysis of the three currents of the English Senecan stream (academic tragedy; popular, Kydian tragedy; Pembrokism) does not dwell at length on Sh, but it clearly shows his affinity for the subject (Roman history) of the formal Senecans and the thematic and structural elements (revenge, madness, ghosts) of the popular Senecans. Sh follows his Senecan age in several respects: (1) he writes two plays on cruelty and corruption in legendary Britain (cf. Gorboduc, Locrine, Misfortunes of Arthur); (2) he imitates Kyd in Titus and Ham. (what Sh owes to Kyd, Kyd owes to Seneca); and (3) he conveys the vendetta and the cruel luxuriance of Senecanized Renaissance Italy in Romeo. In each case Sh improved on his dramatic predecessors, but he is fully in the traditions they represent. This is an important essay.

0126. Brown, Charles Armitage. Shakespeare's Autobiographical Poems. Being His Sonnets Clearly Developed: With His Character Drawn Chiefly From His Works. Ln, 1838, 306 pp.

The chs. most obviously relevant are "His Learning," "His Knowledge," "His Dramatic Knowledge and Art" (pp. 122-182). The first is an acrimonious attack on Farmer and his admirer, Dr. Johnson. Brown argues from Sh's Latinate vocabulary and from his accurate mythology that he learned as much Latin as he cared to know. Sh did not choose to pursue scholarship in the ancient languages and it is well he did not, since such scholarship might have led to footnoted plays. The second ch. of the three deals more generally with Sh's great store of knowledge (a good bit of it not classical) and the third defends Sh's anachronisms and disregard of the unities, both on the ground that great art makes its own laws and that Sh's contemporaries employ the same practices. Brown's is an important document in the reaction against Farmer in the first half of the nineteenth century. It is vigorous but not so well informed as modern counterattacks have been: e.g., he shows no real knowledge of Sh's probable curriculum at Stratford, assumes that his education would be an expense to his parents, and does not mention Sh's use of classical rhetoric.

0127. Brown, David. "What Shakspere Learned at School," BUS, I (1941), 1-20.

Brown attempts to reconstruct the curriculum at Stratford. He points out that the emphasis was on Latin language rather than on literature: Sh "never penetrated to the deeper influences of the classics"; when Sh quotes, he is remembering a set text from school. His grammar school education "helped him to a vocabulary, to a superficial knowledge of the art of rhetoric, to Ovid [the only "kindred spirit" among the Roman authors he read in school], and to much miscellaneous information."

0128. Brown, Ivor J. C. "'Unwillingly to School'," Shakespeare (N.Y., 1949), pp. 17-34.

Brown assumes that Sh was exposed to dull pedantry at Stratford, chiefly at the hands of Jenkins, but he makes only the briefest effort to specify the curriculum which, he suggests, made Sh restless for rambles in meadow and copse. Brown recognizes the influence of Lily, Caesar's Commentaries, Virgil, Horace, Seneca, and especially Ovid; there is no citation of chapter and verse.

0129. Browne, C. Elliot. "Early Allusions to Shakspeare," 5 NQ, XI (1879), 288.

This note points out that the Earl of Dorset's Commonplace Book contains the remark, "None ever made this saying of Cicero's good so well as Shakespear, that Ingenii bonitas saepe imitatur doctrinam."

0130. Browne, C. Elliot. "Notes on Shakspeare's Names," Ath, No. 2543, 2544 (1876), 112-113, 147-148.

Most of the first installment concerns Sh's fondness for Italian names, but Browne does mention "Shallow," "Dogberry," "Aguecheek," and "Belch" as descriptive character names in the tradition of Roman comedy which Jonson affected more than Sh did. Perhaps Jonson resented Sh's use of the distinguished classical name "Pericles" in his "mouldy tale." In Part II, Browne discusses the names in A.Y.L., W.T., Ham., and All's W. In W.T. many of the names are from Plutarch; "Autolycus" is from Homer and Ovid, not "bodily from one of Lucian's dialogues," as Warburton thought. In Ham. "Horatio" is from the Horatii by way of The Spanish Tragedy, "Marcellus" is from "Mars," "Ophelia" comes ultimately from Horace's "Ofellus(a)" by way of Sannazaro's Arcadia. Browne writes with informed good sense, but much yet remains to be said about onomastics in Sh.

0131. Browne, C. Elliot. "On Shakspeare's Pastoral Name," 4 NQ, XII (1873), 509-510.

Browne advances the hypothesis that Chettle's England's Mourning Garment alludes to Sh under the name "Melicert," and that this name is drawn from the pseudo-classical shepherd Melicertus of Greene's Menaphon. Brinsley Nicholson points out (5 NQ, I [1874], 109-110) that the root meaning of the name ("honeycomb") is appropriate to Sh ("honey-tongued" in Meres and Weever) and that Chettle need have thought only of this epithet without recourse to Greene.

0132. Brunner, Karl. England und die Antike, EH, H. XVII (Innsbruck, 1947), 25 pp.

This monograph is an account of English responses to the ancient world from the fifth century to the twentieth, and it is therefore understandably general. Sh is discussed on pp. 18-19. Brunner mentions Venus and Lucr. as typical of the mythology which was the fashion among Elizabethan sophisticates. Sh's education at Stratford prepared him to make classical allusions beyond the ken of the average graduate of a Latin school today, though Sh may have improved his acquaintance with the classics in after years. Seneca taught Sh and Marlowe "eine rhetorische, packende Sprache," and Plautus provided a gallery of dramatic type characters and the art of complicating and sustaining a plot. But, unlike the French, Sh and his contemporaries went beyond their classical models to create their own dramatic forms (especially Shn romantic comedy and Jonsonian "Charaktertypenkomödie"). CSt NcD NNC

0133. Buchan, John. Augustus. Boston, 1937, 379 pp. GRS

Four quotations from Ham. serve as ch. headings in this study of the historical Octavius, but oddly none of them mentions Rome, though Ham. abounds with Roman allusions. Buchan also makes reference to Twel., Antony, and Caesar. He does not discuss Sh's portrayal of Octavius in Caesar and Antony, but he does make brief remarks about the Shn Cleopatra and Antony.

0134. Buland, Mable. The Presentation of Time in the Elizabethan Drama, YSE, No. 44 (N.Y., 1912), 354 pp.

Dr. Buland shows that the disregard for classical unity and the phenomenon of double time do not originate with Sh, but have wide provenance among his English predecessors. Indeed, double time as a dramatic device has a precedent in Aeschylus' Agamemnon and Sophocles' Antigone (though the author emphasizes that Sophocles' usual practice is to make time concentrated and consistent). The ch. on Sh examines the entire canon in chronological sequence and concludes that Sh's inconsistencies crept into the plays unconsciously, because the sources presented a time scheme longer (usually) than he wished to portray. Sh, like Sophocles, realized that dramatic tension is elicited by the suggestion of action hastening toward climax. In later plays Sh may sometimes have consciously violated consistency, and it seems probable that once a play was written he was fully aware of the double time in it. The conclusions in the book appear justified, but Dr. Buland does not analyze her materials at length--the chs. ordinarily survey quickly the time schemes of plays.

0135. Bundy, Murray W. "Shakespeare and Elizabethan Psychology," JEGP, XXIII (1924), 516-549.

Bundy points out that the language of faculty psychology is nearly absent from the earliest plays in the canon and lacking also in the last plays, while it appears with great frequency and precision of application in the plays of the middle period. The emphasis here falls on Troi., Oth., Lear, and Ham., though several other plays are treated briefly. In these plays disaster follows a dominant conjunction in the protagonist of passion and imagination. This conjunction is to Sh what hamartia was to the Greeks, and it produces a state of dianoia, or inability to reason adequately. Sh's protagonists are often confronted with antagonists in whom the rational process is supreme, though perverted: the result is tragedy. Bundy does not focus on Sh's sources for the concepts here, though he traces faculty psychology to Aristotle, discusses numerous Renaissance theorists, and points out that supposedly unlearned Sh applies the theories to dramatic action more often than Jonson, e.g. One of the best studies of Sh's psychology available.

0136. Bunn, L. H. "The Theatre of Aeschylus and Shakespeare," LQR, CLIII (1930), 266-268.

A somewhat oversimplified comparison of the Zeitgeister of Sh and the Greeks, especially with respect to the religious basis of drama. To Bunn, Sh had shaken off Medieval religion--indeed all influences except the necessity of pleasing an audience craving sensation--while the Greeks preserved a via media inspired by their piety.

0137. Burrill, Edgar W. "Heredity as Fate in Greek and Elizabethan Drama," JEGP, XIX (1920), 486-509. HB

"The Elizabethan dramatists ...were not primarily interested in fate as a controlling factor in their plays, nor were they really concerned with the inheritance of a family curse, whether theological, as with the Greeks, or biological, as with the naturalistic drama since Ibsen." Yet (Burrill contradicts himself), though to Sh (the only Elizabethan discussed) character is fate, Shn tragedy turns on the inherited predispositions of men who are unfitted for the demands fate makes of them (e.g., imagine Hamlet and Othello each in the other's place). We are to note that Edmund, Richard Gloucester, Othello, Cassius, and many another are marked by accidents of birth which dominate their lives. Burrill makes many comparisons between Sh and the Attic drama, but he does not attempt to trace Sh's conception except perhaps to a common awareness of genetic determinism.

0138. Bush, Douglas. Classical Influences in Renaissance Literature, Martin Classical Lectures, No. 13 (HUP, 1952), 60 pp.

Bush's numerous references to Sh are not self-consistent, for he twice speaks of Sh as "unlearned," but later calls Ulysses' "degree" speech the "locus classicus" of classicized Christian humanism. Most of the references to Sh are mere allusions: on his use of Plutarch, Ham. as a Senecan play, the Greek romances as sources for Sh's pastoralism, etc. It should be borne in mind that these are widely ranging lectures; if Bush is not original or thorough on Sh he is certainly stimulating in his general proposition that classicism penetrated the Renaissance in various and turbulent ways.

0139. Bush, Douglas. "Classical Myth in Shakespeare's Plays," Wilson Festschrift, pp. 65-85.

Bush is interested not in sources, but in the use Sh makes of mythological allusions, which "range from Renaissance mythologizing to 'myth'; ...while bookish, rhetorical, and perfunctory items never vanish altogether, they give place increasingly to inspired felicities born of an instinctive and imaginative response to nature and human experience, and ...elaborate patches gratuitously stuck on give place to allusions of integral and dramatic significance for character and the total theme." Though Bush deplores statistics, the essay is in large part a catalogue of references with critical commentary. His conclusion about the development of Sh's approach to mythology is not radically different from Root's (#0497).

0140. Bush, Douglas. "English Humanism," The Renaissance and English Humanism, Alexander Lectures (Toronto UP, 1939/ 1956), Lecture III, pp. 69-100.

See pp. 96-99 for Bush's contrast of Sh's Weltanschauung with ours. Sh's Christian world shared with the classical world the concept that man stands somewhere between heaven and hell with potentialities in him for either. The resulting tension gives tragic stature to Greek and Shn drama which we cannot hope to attain.

0141. Bush, Douglas. "Notes on Shakespeare's Classical Mythology," PQ, VI (1927), 295-302. E-S HB SG

Notes supplementary to R. K. Root's Classical Mythology in Shakespeare (#0497). Bush's emphasis is on Sh's variations on classical legend, and with broad erudition he cites analogues and possible sources in a wide range of Medieval and Renaissance literature, English and Continental, documenting "the currency of certain ideas." Particularly interesting are the note on Narcissus and the indication of parallels between Venus and A. Fraunce's Third Part of the Countess of Pembroke's Ivy-church.

0142. Butler, J. G. "Shakespeare as a Greek Lexicographer," Shna, III (1886), 167-169.

Butler points out some thirty-four citations to Sh in Liddell-Scott's Greek-English Lexicon. They come from seventeen plays and "illustrate" the works of some score of Greek authors. Butler believes that Liddell-Scott's reliance on Sh to explain Greek concepts is attributable to "the kinship of Genius ...not only in thought but in expression." He facetiously suggests that if all the citations illustrated a single Greek author he could, by the Baconian method, be proved to have written Sh's plays.

0143. Butler, Samuel [author of Hudibras]. Characters and Passages from Note-Book (1680). Munro, II, 234.

Jonson, like Virgil, studied long and ergo could attain greater heights than Sh, whose brilliance, like Ovid's, is ephemeral.

0144. C., B. F. "Was Stratford on Avon a 'Bookless Neighborhood' in Shakespeare's Day?" NewShna, VII (1908), 106-110.

A paraphrase of an art. by Charlotte C. Stopes in Ath which gives documentary evidence that in Sh's time Warwickshire was full of books, many of them classics. There is no discussion of Sh's possible acquaintance with any of them, but B.F.C. expresses contempt for Anders (#0073) because he is concerned with internal evidence of Sh's reading.

0145. Camden, Carroll. "Astrology in Shakespeare's Day," Isis, XIX (1933), 26-73.

Parts I and II of this well-documented art. lay out the Renaissance arguments against and for the pseudo-science of judicial astrology. Classical roots are indicated, but not emphasized. In Part III Camden provides in his notes a useful concordance to Sh's numerous allusions to astrology and ventures the plausible opinion that it is impossible to determine Sh's beliefs because his characters argue cogently on both sides of the question.

0146. Camden, Carroll. "The Mind's Construction in the Face," PQ, XX (1941), 400-412. (Also in Craig Festschrift, pp. 208-220).

Camden traces the pseudo-science of physiognomy (or character interpretation from facial features) to Ptolemy, the pseudo-Aristotelian Secreta Secretorum, and Hippocrates. Sh alludes to this system of clues to the moral nature of one's neighbor in Temp., Macb., Lucr., Antony, and Much. He apparently had no interest in the analogous "science" of metoposcopy (character interpretation from the lines on the forehead), which is traceable to Pliny.

0147. Campbell, Lily B. Scenes and Machines on the English Stage During the Renaissance: A Classical Revival. CUP, 1923, 302 pp. E-S

Sh is mentioned only briefly: (1) as the great negator of the classical unities (Troi., H.V); (2) as avoiding the necessity for a personal appearance of Jove ex machina in Lear, yet achieving the same effect through the poetry and off-stage thunder (Miss Campbell oddly does not mention the use of machinery in the epiphany of Jupiter in Cym.); (3) as utilizing some sort of eccyclema in 2H.VI and R.III for bringing lifeless bodies on stage. With respect to the latter device: "It seems ... certain that the suggestion for such a machine is more apt to have come from the Greek dramas, from the definitions in Pollux or from their re-working in Scaliger, and from the earlier scholia of Aristophanes and the other Greek dramatists, all of which sources of information were known to English scholars, than to have arisen independently and spontaneously."

0148. Campbell, Lily B. Shakespeare's Tragic Heroes: Slaves of Passion. CUP, 1930, 248 pp. E-S

Ch. II (pp. 25-38) surveys sixteenth- and seventeenth-century sources to show that "the theory of drama in England during the Renaissance was largely the result of engrafting of the rediscovered classical doctrine of imitation upon [the] tradition ... of teaching by exempla." The "classical doctrine" is a blending of Aristotle, Plato, Horace, and Plutarch.

0149. Campbell, Oscar J. "Shakespeare Himself," Harper's, CLXXXI (1940), 172-185.

In the course of an account for laymen of the inception and fallacy of anti-Stratfordianism, Campbell suggests that Sh's "lesse Greeke" might well have included grammar school study of Demosthenes, Isocrates, Hesiod, Heliodorus, and Dionysius of Halicarnassus, and that Titus and Errors, his first two plays, sprang naturally from his grammar school study [and teaching?] of Seneca and Plautus.

0150. Capell, [Edward]. "Introduction" [to Notes and Various Readings to Shakespeare (1779)], Boswell's Malone, I, 120-171.

Capell's primary interest is textual, and he makes few remarks of criticism, but his enumeration of Sh's sources is surprisingly accurate gauged by modern opinion. Only rarely does he err (as in his belief that Sh used W.W.'s trans., not the original Menaechmi, for Errors). He knows the ballad on Titus and that Sh used both Chaucer and Caxton for Troi., to cite only two examples. Of this Introduction Johnson said that Capell "doth gabble monstrously," but it is full of good sense for all that.

0151. Carrère, Félix. "Shakespeare et la Méditerranée," AFLA, XXXI (1957), 141-161.

Carrère argues that Sh visited the Mediterranean (probably Italy) before writing the large number of "southern" plays in the canon. There he encountered the Mediterranean spirit: an awareness of reality coexistent with an awareness of an ideal which is purely human. Carrère traces the concept to the Odyssey. Another theme in the Odyssey and Aeneid is the sic transit theme, which Sh conveys in Antony. Yet another is the resistance to authority which characterizes the "Latin" temperament. But Carrère's reasoning is fallacious: (1) Sh did not need to travel the Mediterranean to imbibe its spirit through literature; (2) northern peoples are aware of mutability as much as southerners (e.g., in Anglo-Saxon elegiac poetry); (3) Sh could create "northern" rebels like Hotspur without turning to the Mediterranean tradition, while Aeneas, the "Mediterranean" man, is anything but recalcitrant in Virgil's epic. An interesting set of racial hypotheses, but they cannot be sustained. DLC

0152. Carrère, Félix. "Le Théâtre de Shakespeare: Reflet du monde platonicien," LLM, LXV (1951), 368-377.

The treatment of Sh is indefinite. Plato's doctrine that happiness lies in the equilibrium of reason and passion is related to Sh's belief that imbalance produces tragedy. Carrère says very little about Sh's relation to Plato which could not equally be said of any dramatist--indeed the "Platonic" ideas in Sh (e.g., Ulysses' "degree" speech) are all commonplaces of Elizabethan thought. Carrère ignores conventions and sees the Ghost as a projection of Hamlet's desires, Iago as an incarnation of Othello's evil inclinations. The author appears to have little understanding of Elizabethan culture.

0153. [Cartwright, Robert]. Shakspere and Jonson. Dramatic, versus Wit-Combats. Auxiliary Forces:--Beaumont and Fletcher, Marston, Decker, Chapman, and Webster. Ln, 1864, 122 pp.

Cartwright advances the highly implausible thesis that Jonson satirized Sh's lack of a university education in Cynthia's Revels and The Poetaster, launching a quarrel which eventually involved most of the dramatic works of both men. Jonson is Apemantus, Thersites, Don John, Aufidius, etc. This is as extreme a case of reading for topical allegory as can be found anywhere. DFo

0154. Carver, A. J. "A Comparison Between the Female Characters of the Greek Tragedians and Those of Shakespeare," Prolusiones Literariae... [St. Paul's School, 1844] (Ln, 1844), pp. 14-37.

This prize essay argues that because the Greeks kept women in an inferior social position it would have been impossible for an Attic dramatist to create the resourceful, gay, charming, gracious, and accomplished women who appear so often in Sh. There are, however, many points of valid comparison, Carver believes, and he proceeds to a sensitive juxtaposition of Hecuba and Constance, Antigone (Oedipus Coloneus) and Cordelia, Alcestis and Sh's Hermione, Deianira and Desdemona, Aeschylus' Clytemnestra and Gertrude (and Lady Macbeth), Medea and Margaret. Numerous other Greek and Shn women are mentioned in passing. See also #0169, the second-prize essay. DFo

0155. Cassirer, Ernst. The Platonic Renaissance in England. Texas UP, 1953, 207 pp. (The German original, Die platonische Renaissance in England und die Schule von Cambridge, appeared in 1932; this trans. by James P. Pettegrove.)

Cassirer devotes only a dozen pages to Sh, and Platonism barely figures in them (as a conventional element in Sonn.). Shn comedy is seen as related to the Greek Sophists through the element of Lylyan euphuism (Cassirer follows Feuillerat's attribution of Lyly's style to the influence of the First Sophistic--an attribution now generally rejected). The remainder of the insights on Sh in this book are a mistaken interpretation of Portia's "mercy" speech as an endorsement of Divine Grace and an inconclusive attempt to define Shn humor (in 1H.IV, the comedies, and the tragedies). Cassirer appears to have missed Sh's real response to Platonic idealism and ethics.

0156. Castelain, Maurice. "Shakespeare et Ben Jonson," RG, III (1907), 21-65, 133-180.

The first part of this well-informed essay is an examination of primary evidence for any malice that Jonson may have felt toward Sh. Castelain concludes that Jonson felt none, that the critiques he made of Sh were satiric jeux d'esprit aimed at Sh's dramatic theories and practice, not his person. Relevant passages include a discussion of the famous "Caesar doth not wrong," the "nest of antiques" in Bartholomew Fair (a possible reference to the dance of the Satyrs in W.T. IV iv), and Sh's history plays which violate unity of time and place (cf. Prologue to Every Man in His Humor). Castelain's argument sometimes reads like a special plea, as when he maintains that Jonson may not have referred to Sh specifically in the Prologue to Every Man in, but his general conclusion about Jonson's attitude appears well founded. An occasional passing remark has special interest (e.g., Viola's "This fellow is wise enough to play the fool" [Twel. III i 67] belongs to a tradition tracing at least as far back as Lucius Junius Brutus). In the second part, Castelain treats Sh's possible allusions to Jonson in A.Y.L. and Troi. He finds it probable that Ajax is (in part) a parody of Jonson. But Sh was doubtless pushed into the War of the Theaters by his colleagues and never felt bitterness toward Jonson. Castelain suggests that the eulogy of Virgil in The Poetaster may refer to Sh. The art. ends with a commentary on Jonson's F_1 eulogy, "un peu forcée," perhaps, but nonetheless an indication of Jonson's high opinion of Sh's achievement.

0157. [Chamberlain, Mellen]. Notes on Some Writing Which May Be by Shakspeare in the Boston Public Library. [Boston], 1889, 7 pp. + 8 plates.

In this monograph the Librarian weighs the evidence for the authenticity of a signature and the notation "hundred and twenty poundes," which appear on the hinge leaf of a copy of the 1603 North's Plutarch. In his opinion, the evidence points toward authenticity. If the signature is genuine, we have evidence that Sh bought a copy of the 1603 ed. of North although he had already made use of the 1579 ed. (see #0836). Chamberlain does not discuss this matter. DFo

0158. Chambers, E. K. Shakespeare: A Survey. Ln, 1925, 325 pp. E-S

This is a collection of the Introductions to the various plays which Chambers published between 1904 and 1908. They are without exception conservative, intelligent, witty, informative. No more competent guide to the classical part of the canon exists (Chambers' demolition of the logic of the disintegrators of Titus is complete; it set a fashion which has established the present attitude toward the play). Errors, Dream, and other plays are also discussed in their relationship to the classics. Chambers' emphasis falls upon dramatic genres as Sh's plays illustrate or define them.

0159. Chambers, E. K. William Shakespeare: A Study of Facts and Problems. 2 vols., OUP, 1930, 576, 448 pp. E-S

Vol. I begins with an excellent essay on "Shakespeare's Origin" which contains brief but reliable discussion of Sh's probable course of study at Stratford and of his possible experience as an abecedarius in the country before his expedition to London. The bulk of Vol. I consists of prefatory materials for the study of the plays and poems in the canon with some apocrypha as well. As always Chambers is conservative without failing in imagination. His observations about the plays on classical themes and others with classical connections are a place at which a student can begin with confidence. Vol. II deals chiefly with Sh's nonliterary life and has no relevance here.

0160. Chapman, John Jay. "Shakespeare," Greek Genius and Other Essays (N.Y., 1915), pp. 133-217.

See especially Part I, "The Greek Stage and Shakespeare," and Part IV, "Troilus and Cressida" (#1207), but note the large number of incidental references to Sh's classicism passim. In Part I, after pointing to numerous similarities and differences between Greek drama and Sh's, Chapman concludes: "So far as perfection of form goes, the Greek plays are infinitely superior to Shakespeare's. So far as native talent goes, there is no Greek dramatist who stands anywhere near Shakespeare, though Aristophanes suggests him."

0161. Chapman, Raymond. "Fortune and Mutability in Elizabethan Literature," CamJ, V (1952), 374-382. GRS

Chapman defines the peculiar station which Fortune occupied in the Renaissance world picture. She was a special case of Mutability, holding power over men's temporal affairs, yet herself subject to the higher laws of Nature and Providence. This limitation of her power is the reason why the Christian churches accepted this pagan deity and why she appears in Elizabethan drama not as a goddess but as an abstraction, like Time or Virtue. The concept of Mutability is traceable to Aristotle, Lucretius, and especially to Boethius, who first fused Fortuna with Mutability. Other classical authorities cited on the nature of Fortuna are Virgil (Aeneid X), Seneca (Medea), and Terence (Phormio I iv). Chapman illustrates the Elizabethan conception in Sh with quotations from Lear and Sonn. 18 and citations to Tim., John, and A.Y.L.

0162. Chew, Samuel C. "Time and Fortune," ELH, VI (1939), 83-113.

An impressively learned study of the verbal and visual iconography of Fortune and of Time in the sixteenth century. Chew is inclined to emphasize with Farnham the Medieval antecedents of Elizabethan attitudes, but he does point out, e.g., that in Sh's time Fortune became confused with Nemesis and the Parcae as a dispenser of justice. There are a number of references to Sh passim, to Tim., A.Y.L., Much, H.V, Sonn., Temp., etc. It is disappointing that Chew does not relate the pictorial representation of Time to the pre-Socratic conceptions of cyclic time in Book XV of Ovid's Meta.; these concepts were familiar to Sh and his contemporaries and are an analogue to the cyclic motion of Fortune. But this is a very informative art.

0163. Churchill, R. C. Shakespeare and His Betters: A History and a Criticism of the Attempts Which Have Been Made to Prove That Shakespeare's Works Were Written by Others. Ln, 1958, 255 pp.

Of the three major arguments against Sh's authorship which Churchill refutes, the argument that the plays are too full of classical culture to have been his work takes third place behind arguments based on authentic portrayal of court life and accurate knowledge of legal processes. The only ch. to deal in any detail with Sh and the classics is VII, "Some Minor Theories Considered" (pp. 208-218), and it is the most disappointing of the book. Churchill is content to follow Thomson (#0594), ignoring totally the research of Americans on Sh's classicism in the past thirty years (Baldwin's Small Latine, #0089, is barely mentioned in a footnote on Mantuan). It is dismaying that the crusaders must themselves resemble the infidels (cf. Robertson's method of refutation by disintegration, #0489). One must feel that Churchill has not done Sh justice in the ten pages he devotes to the "small Latin" question. (This is not to deny that Churchill's is the best historical survey extant of the various anti-Stratfordian positions.)

0164. Chute, Marchette. Shakespeare of London. N.Y., 1949, 397 pp.

Though she lists Baldwin's Small Latine (#0089) in her bibliography, Miss Chute has apparently not understood the intricate relationship Baldwin traces between the rhetorical excellence of Sh's poetry and the discipline he submitted to in Latin grammar school. She assumes that Sh's educational experience was stultifying and that by and large he succeeded in belles lettres despite it, a position which is hardly tenable in view of twentieth-century explorations of rhetoric in Renaissance compositional theory. This blind spot is a serious defect in a book which shows intelligent command of documentary sources and also has the merit of a readable style. The emphasis falls on Sh's position in the theatrical world of his time; the plays are not analyzed as literature, and their classical background is therefore not a major consideration.

0165. Claflin, Edith F. "The Latinisms in Shakespeare's Diction," CJ, XVI (1921), 346-359. HB

About half (ca. fifty) of the examples offered here are drawn from Ham. and nearly all the rest from four other plays. Even considering the limited space available the author cannot be said to have made a comprehensive survey. She also fails to observe that many of these terms were in common use and that accordingly Sh's use of them cannot constitute proof of his Latinity. Her findings are suggestive, however, and a more comprehensive survey (of other writers as well as Sh) might support the conclusion that Sh "had acquired a considerable acquaintance with Latin in the Stratford Grammar School."

0166. Clark, Cumberland. "Astronomy in Shakespeare," Astronomy in the Poets (Bournemouth and Ln, [1922?]), pp. 1-60.

Like Lowe (#0397), of whose work he is unaware, Clark eclectically combines brief remarks about Sh's astronomical and astrological beliefs with observations about the solar system based on modern scientific discoveries. There are a large number of brief illustrative quotations from Sh, who is shown to have accepted the Ptolemaic system. Clark here states his belief, elaborated elsewhere (#0167, #0168), that Sh used astrology for dramatic purposes while personally remaining incredulous. CU IaU PU(F)

0167. Clark, Cumberland. Shakespeare and Science. Birmingham, 1929, 262 pp.

The running subtitle indicates Clark's scope: "A Study of Shakespeare's interest in, and literary and dramatic use of, natural phenomena; with an account of the astronomy, astrology, and alchemy of his day, and his attitude towards these sciences." The book, intended for the general reader and lacking bibliography and notes, is nevertheless specific about details, informative about Sh's contemporaries, and copious in its documentation from the plays. Clark sees Sh as a conservative adherent of the Ptolemaic school, but at the same time (paradoxically enough) as a skeptic about astrology, which he included in his plays to please a superstitious audience. Clark admits that it is difficult to discern a dramatist's beliefs from what his characters say, but then proceeds to credit Hotspur's attack on Glendower as Sh's opinion. He asserts that Sh's response to scientific systems (e.g., alchemy, Pythagorean cosmology), like his response to scientific phenomena (the firmament, rainbows, snow, motion of planets, changing seasons) is primarily metaphorical: Sh often thought of natural phenomena in the framework of classical mythology.

0168. Clark, Cumberland. Shakespeare and the Supernatural. Ln, 1931, 346 pp.

The discussions of Sh's use of classical mythology and superstitions are scattered and of uneven value. Clark recognizes that Titania comes from the Latin Meta., e.g., but he thinks the "daemon" of Antony (Antony II iii 19) is a Christian guardian angel, apparently unaware of the Plutarchian doctrine of δαίμονες. Clark assumes that Sh put judicial astrology into the canon to please a superstitious audience but surreptitiously inserted negations (by Cassius, Lafew and Helena, Edmund, and Iago) to reveal his own skepticism. DFo

0169. Clay, C. J. "[A Comparison Between the Female Characters of the Greek Tragedians and Those of Shakespeare]," Prolusiones Literariae... [St. Paul's School, 1844] (Ln, 1844), pp. 38-58 (Second Prize).

Sh "is an Aeschylus, in force of language and sublimity of thought; a Sophocles, in the true delineation of nature; and an Euripides in his almost superhuman knowledge of the inmost workings of the human mind." Clay compares Aeschylus' Clytemnestra with Lady Macbeth (and Gertrude), the Helen of the Choral odes in Agamemnon with Cleopatra, Antigone (of both Oedipus Coloneus and Antigone) with Cordelia, Deianira with Desdemona, Hecuba with Constance, Medea with Lady Macbeth, Phaedra with Juliet, Euripides' Helen with Imogen, Alcestis with Sh's Hermione. Clay believes that the difference between the Greek and modern conceptions of woman (originating in the difference between Greek religion and Christianity) should explain why Sh's women are more pleasing, on the whole, to modern sensibilities. See also #0154, the prize essay. DFo

0170. Clemen, Wolfgang [H.]. Die Tragödie vor Shakespeare: Ihre Entwicklung im Spiegel der dramatischen Rede. Heidelberg, 1955, 270 pp. (Trans. as English Tragedy Before Shakespeare: The Development of Dramatic Speech by T. S. Dorsch [1961].)

This extremely valuable book does not treat Sh systematically as it does his predecessors, but it contains many passing references to Sh's relationship to the conventions of the Elizabethan rhetorical tragedy. The conventions (especially set speeches) are traceable in part to Seneca and Euripides. Sh did not abandon these conventions completely (he even preserves stock characters like the consigliere, or Good Counsellor: Kent and Gaunt), but he always modifies them, making rhetoric the servant of the emotion that calls it forth. There are allusions to (or quotations from) about half of Sh's plays. In passing Clemen criticizes the rigidity of Kennedy's categories for Shn set speeches (#0358), though he admits that Sh, like his predecessors, used three basic types: forensic, deliberative, and epideictic. Clemen's most interesting point about Sh is that even in early plays like R. III and John classical rhetoric is made to serve psychological purposes as it is not made to serve them in any earlier Elizabethan dramatist (except possibly Marlowe); Clemen would therefore modify the polarity which some critics have seen between Sh's early and his mature works.

0171. Cobb, Samuel. Poetae Britanici: A Poem, Satyrical and Panegyrical (1700), T-D, pp. 49-50.

Apparently this is a second ed. of #0463, which Munro Sup regarded as an anonymous work and dated 1690.

0172. Coleridge, Samuel Taylor. Lectures and Notes on Shakspere and Other English Poets...Now First Collected by T. Ashe. Ln, 1908, 552 pp. E-S

The vol. consists chiefly of Coleridge's three sets of lectures (1811-12, 1813-14, 1818) which to a considerable extent convey a single corpus of ideas about poetry, drama, and Sh's art. The second lecture of 1811-12 defends Sh from the small men (like frogs croaking in a dark ditch, silenced by light) who would impose Aristotle on Sh. Lecture VII points out that Aeschylus and Sophocles, like Plautus and Molière, created characters so closely attached to the mores of their times that a later time finds them alien; Sh's men and women, by contrast, have universality. The briefer notes on individual plays scattered through the vol. contain many relevant passages: on Dream and classical metrics, on Troi. as a link between Sh's legendary classical plays (Titus and Per.) and his attempts at classical history (Caesar and Cor.), on Antony as Sh's greatest poetic achievement, on Caesar and Cor. as antipopular plays, etc. It is significant that Coleridge holds Roman drama in contempt and compares Sh's work only with Greek literature; yet he finds no close links between Hellenic and Shn art--Sh's plays "are in no respect imitations of the Greeks; they may be called analogies, because by very different means they arrive at the same end." Perhaps Coleridge's real importance in the "small Latin" controversy is not his introduction of Romantic Hellenism but his (largely justified) claim to have first demolished the notion of Sh as a wild, barbaric genius. Coleridge lays heavy stress on Sh's judgment, which is the equal of his imagination. He is interested in that judgment not as a classically trained coordinator of Art, but as a principle visible in the excellence of Sh's poetry; yet the emphasis on Sh's judgment is a first step toward the modern conception of Sh's classicism.

0173. Collins, J. Churton. "Had Shakespeare read the Greek Tragedies?" FR, LXXIX (1903), 618-637, 848-858; LXXX (1903), 115-131. (Reprinted in Studies in Shakespeare [1904] as Ch. I: "Shakespeare as a Classical Scholar.") E-S

Part I reviews the long controversy over Sh's classicism and seeks to establish that Sh obtained a good command of Latin and quite possibly some Greek in grammar school. Collins disregards the hypothesis of many scholars that Sh may have left school before completing the curriculum. He finds echoes of a number of Roman poets in the poems and plays. Part II indicates numerous parallels of language and sentiment between Sh and the Greek tragedians who were available to him, Collins insists, in Latin trans. Part III carries this analogue-hunting further with interesting, if not conclusive, results. Collins attributes Sh's Greek tragic spirit, as in Macb. or Lear, to familiarity with the sixteenth-century Latin trans. of the Greeks, and finds in his plays a true community of tragic outlook with them. The arts. are interesting, but Collins has not established his point, since, as he admits, almost everything he cites could be coincidental, and he does not trace verbal parallels with the Latin trans. The modern consensus is that Sh's

"Greek" tragic outlook comes from Plutarch, not from Greek tragedy.

0174. Collins, J. Churton. "Sophocles and Shakespeare as Theological and Ethical Teachers," Studies in Shakespeare (Westminster, 1904), Ch. III, pp. 127-179. E-S HB

After ten pages of detailed comparison between Sophocles and Sh (there are some very interesting similarities, personal as well as artistic), Collins points out an apparent difference between them: "While Shakespeare, like Aristotle, appears to sever theology from ethics, Sophocles on the contrary appears to subordinate ethics to theology." The remainder of the essay tries to prove that this distinction is invalid. The effort is not entirely successful; Collins' evidence that Sh is not concerned with theological values is better than his evidence that Sh cares for the next world. Collins certainly does not persuade that the two greatest of all dramatists are "teachers." And his analogical faculty becomes easily unbalanced: as when he calls Theseus in Oedipus Coloneus "a companion portrait to Henry V." But Collins offers revealing insights, especially into Shn vice as virtue in excess (in Angelo, Coriolanus, Timon, Hotspur, and Young Siward [and Young Talbot?]).

0175. Colman, George. "Appendix to the Second Edition of the Translation of the Comedies of Terence, Published in the Year 1768," Prose on Several Occasions: Accompanied with Some Pieces in Verse (Ln, 1787), II, 173-178. (Reprinted in Boswell's Malone, I, 367-370.)

In this crisp reply to Farmer (#0238), Colman raises the legitimate objection that Farmer may have proved that Sh read trans. but he has not proved that Sh could not read Latin and Greek. This hits Farmer at his most vulnerable spot, but Colman's almost solitary voice of protest went largely unheeded until the time of Maginn (#0403) and Charles Armitage Brown (#0126). TxHR

0176. Colman, George. "Critical Reflections on the Old English Dramatick Writers," Prose on Several Occasions: Accompanied with Some Pieces in Verse (Ln, 1787), II, 105-148.

This unsigned letter to David Garrick (1761?) is an argument for reviving Massinger's plays on the stage. It begins with the admission that Sh, like Massinger and their contemporaries, violated the unities, but it goes on to compare Sh to Homer in the range of his subject matter and to maintain that Wives (with some of Jonson and Massinger) adheres "more strictly to ancient rules, than most of our later comedies." TxHR

0177. Cooper, Lane. "The Poetics in England," The Poetics of Aristotle: Its Meaning and Influence, Our Debt, [No. 6] (1923/1963), pp. 129-138.

The remarks on Sh (pp. 133-134) call attention to his allusions to the unities in H.V, Ham., and W.T. and his observation of them in Temp. Sh, "though more Roman than Greek in his dramatic origins, is nearer than the formalists to Aristotle and the spirit of Greek tragedy." Jonson's tragedies are more Senecan than Aristotelian. Sh's plays and characters also serve throughout the book to illustrate or to contrast with Aristotelian principles (of comedy as well as tragedy).

0178. Courthope, W. J. A History of English Poetry: Vol. IV, Development and Decline of the Poetic Drama: Influence of the Court and the People. Ln, 1903, 476 pp. E-S

Beginning with a brief comparison and contrast between the development of Greek drama and that of English drama (both are imitations of religious myth, but the Greeks could treat myth as they wished while Sh's predecessors were confined by received attitudes toward Christianity), Courthope goes on to six chs. on the plays and poems. His discussion of each play ordinarily concentrates on its place in Sh's artistic development; he therefore is interested in Sh's sources and the artistic influences on his work. A few examples must suffice: Sonn. show the Platonic reverence for friendship. The classical dream world of Lyly's court comedy is blended with the realism of Greek New Comedy in Sh's best comic efforts. Romeo is based in part ultimately on the Greek romance Anthia and Habrocomes by Xenophon of Ephesus and accordingly carries the burden of "tragic doctrine of moral necessity," while it has acquired from its Medieval peregrinations a sense of the vanity of human wishes. Perhaps the best statement on Sh's classicism is on the background of Errors: "Considering ...that Plautus and Terence were then studied in the English grammar schools, it does not seem unreasonable to suppose that a knowledge of these authors formed part of Shakespeare's stock of Latin, which may well have seemed 'small' to the erudite Ben Jonson without being in itself despicable . . . ." For many other relevant passages passim, see the analytical Table of Contents to the vol.

0179. Courtney, W. L. The Idea of Tragedy in Ancient and Modern Drama: Three Lectures Delivered at the Royal Institution February, 1900. N.Y., 1900, 132 pp.

The first lecture concerns the three Greek tragedians, the second Sh, and the third Ibsen, but Sh is compared and contrasted with his classical predecessors at points in all three lectures. Like the Attic dramatists Sh had the task of molding a corpus of inherited legend which his audience already knew. Like them he could therefore stress anticipatory irony. His central theme like theirs is the struggle between a man's individuality and outside Destiny. These central points are supported by a host of subordinate allusive parallels (e.g., Richard III embodies Aristotle's δεινότης, "intellectual cleverness" gone wrong). There are occasional misstatements (Henry V's bride is not "Margaret"), but the criticism of Sh's plays against a classical backdrop is sensible and illuminating. MnU

0180. Craig, Hardin, ed. The Complete Works of Shakespeare. Scott, Foresman, 1951/1961, 1337 pp.

The General Introduction, the introductions to the four periods of Sh's career, and the prefatory commentary on the individual plays all are more full than one finds in most one-vol. eds. Craig's is plainly intended for undergraduates, and for the beginner makes a reliable guide to the study of Sh's classical heritage, his use of his sources, his education, etc. The criticism is often cogent; see, e.g., the comparison between Lucr. and Venus, p. 439, or the comments on pastoralism in A.Y.L.

0181. Craig, Hardin. The Enchanted Glass: The Elizabethan Mind in Literature. OUP, 1936, 293 pp.

The references to Sh in this standard work of historical criticism are ordinarily allusive, but in the composite they constitute at least a preliminary sketch of Sh's relationship to the learning of his age. Craig investigates such topics as logic, rhetoric, psychology, cosmology, art as imitation, and natural science; in each of them he shows inter alia the ways in which the Renaissance appropriated from the classics what it wished to have. Sh emerges as a typical Elizabethan in every respect except talent.

0182. Craig, Hardin. An Interpretation of Shakespeare. N.Y., 1948, 400 pp.

Craig's opening ch. on "Shakespeare as an Elizabethan" mentions almost every facet of Elizabethan culture except classicism (Craig does, however, show that Sh was a well-educated man). Yet in the succeeding seriatim analysis of the canon there are dozens of passages in which Craig shows acute and imaginative awareness of Sh's classicism. The most brilliant of all is perhaps the observation that Plutarch interpreted history as a function of Nemesis acting on men at the peak of greatness. This Greek tragic view made it simple for Sh to make historical tragedy out of Caesar's life and Brutus'. If Caesar is less desirable than many would wish, this is Sh's mistaken emphasis on Plutarch's hints that men as they fall reveal their weaknesses in little things [cf. "Life of Alexander"]. Craig is also very perceptive on Errors (nine pages of very illuminating contrast with Plautus), and on Titus (Sh's original contribution to his sources is to make the play Senecan by developing Act I from which the horrors proceed logically). But the book is everywhere sound: brief remarks (e.g., on the silences of Hermione and Alcestis contrasted with their husbands' "thin" utterance) scattered throughout are as stimulating a criticism of Sh's use of the classical tradition as any available.

0183. Craig, Hardin. "Motivation in Shakespeare's Choice of Materials," ShS, IV (1951), 26-34.

Though his emphasis does not fall on Sh's classics, Craig includes a number of cogent references to them in this critical essay which defends source study as a path to the understanding of Sh's creative process and his cultural environment.

0184. Craig, Hardin. New Lamps for Old: A Sequel to The Enchanted Glass. Oxford: Blackwell, 1960, 244 pp.

Craig points to lessons which the English Renaissance might offer to the twentieth century; in doing so he makes several passing allusions to Sh's relation to the classical tradition: e.g., on Ham. as a "stoical tragedy" like Seneca's Hercules tragedies and Aeschylus' Prometheus, on Sh as an exponent of Aristotelian psychology, on the un-Aristotelian quality of the pity and fear in R.III. Craig praises Baldwin's Small Latine (#0089) and attacks those who illogically argue that Sh's genius needed no education while maintaining at the same time that the plays bear the stamp of an educated mind.

0185. Craig, Hardin. "Shakespeare and Elizabethan Psychology: Status of the Subject," Mutschmann Festschrift, pp. 48-55.

Sh participates in the Renaissance tradition of psychological theory which goes back to Aristotle, Plato, Theophrastus, and Galen by way of Nemesius. Few changes had been made in that tradition between Nemesius and the last years of the sixteenth century, but beginning with Marston a cult of Stoic philosophy was introduced, proposing that man is the potential victim of abnormal passions. Sh does not allow this new doctrine to dominate his plays as it did the works of numerous Jacobeans; yet Sh is "a great psychologist" because he integrates his characters and their problems into his plots instead of writing plays to illustrate abnormal psychology. Craig's notes to this excellent little essay constitute a valuable critical bibliography of the subject.

0186. Craig, Hardin. "Shakespeare and Formal Logic," Klaeber Festschrift, pp. 380-397. E-S

Craig examines Sh's use of logical formulae (especially the syllogism) and of logical terms and concludes that he was familiar with the system of logic taught in grammar schools in Elizabeth's time and that he uses the terminology in senses closer to their original meanings than we ordinarily do today. He points out that the system of logic Sh learned is basically Aristotelian; despite modern claims that Petrus Ramus made a radical departure from Aristotle, he only simplified Aristotle's system--besides, Ramus was not so likely to appear in a Protestant grammar school curriculum as Melanchthon was.

0187. Craig, Hardin. "Shakespeare and Wilson's Arte of Rhetorique: An Inquiry Into the Criteria for Determining Sources," SP, XXVIII (1931), 618-630.

A thorough and logical examination of the claims which have been made for Sh's direct knowledge of Wilson. Craig concludes that Sh may have known the work, but that claimants have exaggerated the validity of their evidence. Sh obviously understood Wilson's principles as they reflect classical authorities, but there is "no unmistakable evidence" that Wilson provided him this classical knowledge.

0188. Craig, Hardin. "Shakespeare's Depiction of Passions," PQ, IV (1925), 289-301.

All of Craig's quotations come from Renaissance theorists, but he ends by saying that Shn psychology "was, when all is said, the psychology of Aristotle and Bacon and of all the thinkers who lived between them."

0189. Crane, William G. Wit and Rhetoric in the Renaissance: The Formal Basis of Elizabethan Prose Style. ColSECL, No. 129 (Col UP, 1937), 285 pp.

As its subtitle suggests, this pioneer work is not concerned with drama, but in the "Epilogue," on pp. 203-205, Crane alludes to Sh's use of rhetorical terms. "Many . . . passages in Shakespeare's plays, particularly the earlier ones, in which such terms as 'comparisons,' 'circumstances,' 'causes,' 'contraries,' 'distinctions,' 'examples,' 'places,' and 'invention' occur, indicate that his training in rhetoric had been much the same as that of other writers of the time." There are references to Venus, Romeo, Troi., Much, R.II, 1H.IV, H.V, L.L.L., and T.G.V.

0190. Creizenach, Wilhelm. The English Drama in the Age of Shakespeare. Philadelphia, 1916 [Trans. from Vol. IV of Geschichte des neueren Dramas (1909) by Cécile Hugon], 454 pp. E-S SG

This is more than a handbook for German students; it is an impressively erudite work of scope which at the same time gives details and finds space for imaginative and sometimes striking insights. Passages which relate Sh and his contemporaries to their classical forebears are scattered in many places through the book (see the analytical Table of Contents). Creizenach's method of treating Sh as simply one of a group of dramatists writing between 1587 and 1616 is refreshing; the picture of Sh that emerges from this treatment is of a man much like his colleagues in his half-knowledge of Latin literature and much "lesse Greeke"; Creizenach shows that Marlowe, Peele, Beaumont, and Fletcher all are guilty of gross blunders in their Latinizing. One obtains the impression from this study that when Jonson poked at Sh's small classicism he might as well have embraced all the Elizabethans and Jacobeans but himself. There are remarks of interest on Polonius and Terence's Adelphi, on Hotspur and Euripides' Polyneices, on Titus and the burial of Ajax in Sophocles, on Books I, II, and IV of the Aeneid as the favorites of Sh and his colleagues, on the Fool's prophetic anachronism in Lear as an ironic jibe at critics of Sh's "ignorance," and many others. This is a rewarding book.

0191. Cruickshank, A. H. "The Classical Attainments of Shakspere," Noctes Shaksperianae: A Series of Papers by Late and Present Members [of the Winchester College Shakspere Society], ed. Charles H. Hawkins (Winchester, 1887), pp. 43-65. E-S

Though Sh doubtless knew as much Latin as any schoolboy of his time, there is no evidence that he read any Latin author but Ovid after leaving school. "By itself [Sh's] power of classical allusion does not lead us to suppose he obtained it for himself, but rather that he utilized the floating education of the day." The essay examines Sh's use of Latin and Greek words, his mythological allusions, and his English diction. Many of the Latin quotations are found in Lily's Grammar (1549, 1574); Sh's mythology is superficial; but his knowledge of Latin roots does show in his use of aureate diction. The modern scholarly estimate of how "much Latin ...any schoolboy of [Sh's] time" would know is very much higher than Cruickshank's. MnU DFo

0192. Cunliffe, John W., ed., Early English Classical Tragedies. OUP, 1912, c + 352 pp. E-S HB

The plays in this anthology are Gorboduc, Jocasta, Gismond of Salerne, and The Misfortunes of Arthur. The Introduction is a long and detailed essay on the fortunes of classical drama, especially Senecan, from the death of Seneca to Sh. Stopping places are Medieval theorists, the Italian revival, French Italianate tragedy, the development of English tragedy, Kyd, and Sh. Cunliffe believes Shn tragedy to be the child of Seneca, the native tradition, and the demands of the populace. An interesting passage defends the authenticity of Titus, boldly asserting that we dislike not the play, but the genre, and that Sh, not Kyd, deserves the throne of Senecanism. Cunliffe also discusses the Senecan tradition in Sh's history plays.

0193. Cunliffe, John W. "Shakspere," The Influence of Seneca on Elizabethan Tragedy (Ln, 1893), pp. 66-88. E-S HB

Cunliffe points out that for Sh it is especially difficult to distinguish the influence (if any) of Seneca's Latin from the influence of the Senecan tradition in English drama. He believes, however, that cumulative evidence does prove Sh's direct debt and he shows that in several cases Sh is closer to Seneca than to the trans. The parallels, verbal, situational, and philosophical, are between virtually the entire Seneca canon and the early histories, Titus, Ham., Macb., Lear, and the Sh apocrypha. This book has, in the past twenty-five years, been a center of controversy between a group who trace "Senecan" elements in Elizabethan drama to Medieval culture and a group who insist on Seneca's impact on the English Renaissance. The latter group appear to have the better case: it is surely no accident (as Cunliffe points out) that Sh refers to Hercules, Seneca's chief mythological figure, about four dozen times.

0194. Daffner, Hugo. "Der Selbstmord bei Shakespeare," ShJ, LXIV (1928), 90-131.

Daffner devotes nearly thirteen pages to relevant excerpts (in German trans.) from Cicero's treatises and Seneca's letters. These passages, together with Ovid and with Italian and English Renaissance debate on the philosophical issue, formed Sh's attitude, an anti-Christian, anti-Medieval attitude as Daffner sees it. He calls attention to passages from nearly a score of plays and poems, sometimes quoting at length and discussing the revealed attitudes of characters (as in Romeo, Caesar, and Antony), sometimes merely citing a passing allusion (e.g.: Gratiano's cruel taunt, Merch. IV i 364-367; or Parolles' equation of virginity with suicide in All's W. I i).

0195. Dahinten, Gisela. "Zusammenfassung," Die Geisterszene in der Tragödie vor Shakespeare: Zur Seneca-Nachfolge im englischen und lateinischen Drama des Elisabethanismus, Palaestra, Bd. CCXXV (1958), pp. 177-186.

This conclusion contains an "Ausblick auf Shakespeare" to show "wie starke formale und gehaltliche Möglichkeiten eine lange und zum Teil schon starre Tradition in der Hand eines guten Dramatikers noch besitzen kann." Sh is an orthodox Senecan in making his ghosts agents of revenge (R.III, Caesar, Ham., Macb.) and in assigning one of them (Ham.) the function of revealing past events. But Sh lent a credibility to his specters which his predecessors missed by substituting English superstition for Senecan mythology in the circumstances under which the ghosts appear. There were two basic kinds of ghost scenes in sixteenth-century drama: the "isolated," in which the ghost speaks a Senecan monologue as a frame for the human action of the play, and the "dramatized," in which human and supernatural are in contact through action and dialogue. Sh prefers the second type as more in keeping with the interplay of personalities onstage (e.g., he has Hamlet interrupt the Ghost's monologue with questions and exclamations). The author does not discuss Sh's means of access to Seneca, but in the first part of the book she quotes Seneca from the Tenne Tragedies.

0196. Daiches, David. "Guilt and Justice in Shakespeare," Literary Essays (Edinburgh, 1956), pp. 1-25.

This brilliant study of Sh's portrayal of guilt and innocence, evil and regeneration, does not investigate the Elizabethan moral context in which the plays were written, but Daiches finds many opportunities to allude to the classical bases of the plays; and a major section treats Antony as "postlapsarian man" in both Caesar and Antony, and contrasts him with Brutus, Cassius, and Octavius. Antony is not evil, but neither is he naïve. He "manipulates other people's innocence" in Caesar, because he can identify his personal desires with his political aspirations; Antony portrays the divergence of his personal desires and political aspirations with resulting disaster. There are also astute remarks on Meas. (Angelo, like Oedipus, is the judge who discovers his own guilt), and on the last plays (Sh uses myth to suggest that the moral world of the last plays is not "real").

0197. Dawson, Giles E. "Who Wrote Shakespeare?" The Listener, XLIV (1950), 195-196.

In the course of a witty summary and refutation of the basic anti-Stratfordian assumption, Dawson surmises that any Elizabethan child who sat in Stratford schoolhouse for the stipulated time would emerge with definite familiarity with Ovid, Virgil, Cicero, and other Latin writers. Stratford "possessed an uncommonly good school." Dawson also notes that John Davies of Hereford referred to Sh as "our English Terence" in (ca.) 1610.

0198. Deaton, Mary B. "Farewell, and Clap Your Hands," SAB, VIII (1933), 95-96.

Sh borrowed the Roman convention of closing a play with a request for applause, but he transcended the frigid formality of the request, sometimes taking occasion for casual remarks to his audience.

0199. A Defence of Dramatick Poetry: Being A Review of Mr. Collier's View... (1698), Munro, II, 412-413.

This anonymous reply to Jeremy Collier contains praise for the compression of time in Macb. (especially), Ham., Caesar, and the histories, where Sh gives the illusion of adhering to classical unity. Opposed is the flagrant disregard of unity of time in H.VIII and Webster's Duchess of Malfi.

0200. Delius, Nicolaus. "Klassische Reminiscenzen in Shakespeare's Dramen," ShJ, XVIII (1883), 81-103. E-S HB

Delius argues persuasively that the "feathers" which Robert Greene objected to Sh's having borrowed (A Groatsworth of Wit..., 1592) were classical allusions which the Wits thought no mere upstart ought to manipulate as if he were a University man. Delius points out that Sh's allusions to Greek myths and heroic legends are closely imitative of the allusions in Greene, Marlowe, Peele, and Nashe—except that Sh's references are more consistently appropriate than those of his more "learned" predecessors. The body of the art. is an extensive catalogue (unfortunately merely enumerative rather than critical) of Sh's allusions throughout the canon to the chief classical deities and heroes. Delius points out, e.g., that Icarus is alluded to frequently in the Yorkist tetralogy, but he does not explain that the Icarus story (like the Phaethon story) had overtones of political hybris in Elizabeth's time. The catalogue does show, however, that the Trojan War, its antecedents, and its aftermath were Sh's favorite classical story.

0201. Dennis, John. Essay On The Genius and Writings of Shakespear (1712) (Reprinted in Critical Writings of John Dennis, ed. E. N. Hooker [Baltimore, 1939], II, 1-17).

In the form of three letters addressed to his patron, Dennis writes a vigorous attack on the mere idea that Sh had any real acquaintance with Greek and Roman literature. The bias of his conviction is rendered obvious when one notes that the occasion is a justification of his retouched version of Cor. (like Nahum Tate's Lear, Dennis' Cor. observes scrupulous poetic justice). Most of the violations of classical decorum, the anachronisms, the errors in historical fact, and the abrogations of the unities are drawn from Cor., Caesar (which Dennis would have liked to see as a debate in Caesar's great mind whether or not to restore the republic), and Troi. But Dennis finds occasion to deny that Sh could read the Menaechmi with ease (perhaps a friend construed it for him), to point out that Livy, Sallust, and other Roman historians would have been better grist for his Roman tragedies than Plutarch, and to deny that Sh read the Greek dramatists in Latin trans. A good part of the argument is fallacious: e.g., Sh could not have studied the ancients because if he had, English prestige would suffer, since Sh did not profit from them. But Dennis writes with verve and his rhetorical questions are couched in a fluent Ciceronian style.

0202. De Quincey, Thomas. "A Summary Survey," [Conclusion to the art. on Sh in the 7th ed. (1838) of the] Encyclopaedia Britannica (Reprinted in Shakespeare Criticism: A Selection, ed. D. Nichol Smith [OUP, 1916], 379-394).

De Quincey offers the extraordinary hypothesis that Sh's female characters are more attractive than Greek heroines because they are feminine, while the unattractive masculinity of Greek heroines is traceable to the mores of separation of the sexes in Greek culture--only a cataclysm of tragic proportions can break down the wall of the women's quarters and then only a woman of masculine temperament can come out through the breach. De Quincey has, of course, forgotten the selfless love of Alcestis for Admetus, the submission of Iphigenia at Aulis, the timidity of the suppliant maidens, and perhaps other instances of Attic femininity. Carrying on his contrast, he speaks of Greek character portrayal as monochromatic, like Milton's, while Sh's is definitely polychromatic. No Greek could approach the reality of the Ghost in Ham.--Darius' ghost in Persae is only a "state" figure. The Witches of Macb. are worthy of the Furies in the Oresteia. Finally, Sh's verisimilitude in dialogue gives his plays an immediacy lacking in Greek, French, and Italian drama.

0203. Deutschbein, M. "Shakespeare und die Renaissance," NS, XXIII (1915), 9-21. E-S

A general essay. Deutschbein enumerates the characteristics of the Renaissance and then argues that Sh became disillusioned about 1599; after the turn of the century he rejected many Renaissance assumptions: e.g., that the classics are a storehouse of practical wisdom in politics, statecraft, and even military affairs. Deutschbein alludes to R.III as a fusion of Seneca, Marlowe, and Machiavelli, and there are numerous references to other plays and poems, but no detailed analysis.

0204. Dickey, Franklin M. Not Wisely But Too Well: Shakespeare's Love Tragedies. San Marino, Calif., 1957, 205 pp.

Dickey reconstructs the Elizabethan attitude toward sexual love in and out of marriage from a variety of sources, among them the writings of Ficino and other Neoplatonists. The association he finds between lust and other vices (gluttony, wrath, e.g.) he brings to an interpretation of Venus and Lucr., of Romeo, Troi., and Antony. Dickey's basic point is that the Elizabethans' reverence for reason led them to regard doting passion as either comical or dangerous. The pejorative view Dickey takes of Venus is satisfying; his reading of Troi. is also appealing even if it makes too much of love and too little of politics; his interpretation of Antony, though buttressed by a thorough analysis of classical, Medieval, and neo-Senecan portrayals of the moral import of the story, leaves too little room for the nobility we find in the protagonists; about Romeo the objections must be more forceful. Dickey finds the play a "Comical Tragedy" in which the lovers and their environment are comic material for two acts until Sh throws a cloud across the action. Dickey does not consider that Mercutio, Juliet's Nurse, and the quarrelsome servants do not make the love theme of Acts I and II ridiculous any more than Pistol and Nym make Agincourt a joke. Dickey's distrust of neo-Hegelianism in Shn criticism merits praise, but he may have overstated his arguments for the philosophical background of both Romeo and Antony.

0205. Dodd, William, ed. The Beauties of Shakespear... (1752). 3rd ed. revised, Ln, 1780, 3 vols., 264, 263, 312 pp.

Dodd's "Preface" twice mentions Longinus; the editor regards his anthology of chosen passages as an implicit illustration of Longinian sublimity. Indeed for part of Lear he makes no comment except to suggest reading Longinus. There are hundreds of passages drawn from all the plays in F_1. In footnotes Dodd "illustrates" (sometimes in extenso) the quoted passages by comparing them with similar passages from the classics (usually given in trans.) and from English poetry. Scores of classical quotations are provided, some of them sufficiently obscure (e.g., the division, supposed to be by Solon, of man's life into ten stages illustrates Jaques's "seven ages" speech). Each section terminates with "General Observations" on the play in hand, recording the opinions of the notable commentators and proposing Dodd's own interpretations. A most interesting instance of Sh "illustrated";

the comparisons with the classics are suggestive, though Dodd almost never implies Sh's indebtedness. DFo

0206. Doran, Madeleine. Endeavors of Art: A Study of Form in Elizabethan Drama. Wisconsin UP, 1954, 482 pp.

Miss Doran sees form in English Renaissance drama as a vector of opposed forces: (1) the sequential narrative inherited from Medieval drama and romance; (2) the classical desiderata of eloquence and of verisimilitude (imitatio) in character and action, both of them the servants of ethical edification. But the tension between these two forces is not a simple one, nor is the vector a straight line; Miss Doran refuses to oversimplify, and her great erudition carries the reader into widely separated regions of the Renaissance: e.g., she probes the confusing relations between Nature and Art, she discusses the analogy between literature and graphic art in Renaissance Italy and in Medieval England, and she explains the preference for Euripides' more chaotic, more theatrical tragedies (Orestes, Andromache, Iphigenia at Aulis) in the Renaissance as a function of the formal tensions in the Elizabethan drama itself. The greatest importance of the book is in its sensible insights about such modern critical problems as the opposition of classicists and Medievalists. Miss Doran shows that: (1) it is often impossible to distinguish the new injection of Latin eloquentia and copia in the sixteenth century from the Medieval tradition of debased classical rhetoric. (2) The argument over Seneca vs. the Middle Ages is a fruitless one--the combined traditions of De Casibus, slippery Fortune, Medieval Stoicism, homiletic wisdom, and rhetorical elaboration prepared the Elizabethans to listen to Seneca who epitomized them all--indeed, this is the reason for Seneca's popularity in the sixteenth century. Again, Plautus' fondness for verbal trickery as a comic device may explain the various tones and styles of Errors, and Plautus' place in the grammar school curriculum may account in part for Lylyan comedy of verbal wit. Jonsonian comedy is more "eloquent" and more romantic than has often been thought. Latin comedy is not a primary element in any Elizabethan dramatist, but the dramatists can be classified according to the subordinate uses they make of Plautus and Terence. Sh imposed structure on his chronicle plays not by polarizing moral positions (as Bale did in Kynge Johan), but by playing on the pseudo-Senecan De Casibus theme (e.g., in R.II). Sh's later tragedies partake of another ultimately Senecan theme in the machinations of jealousy, revenge, and intrigue (Oth., Ham., Romeo). This is a major landmark of scholarship in Renaissance literature. Sh appears in it as no different from his contemporaries except that he can succeed in working out the vector where they often fail.

0207. Douce, Francis. Illustrations of Shakespeare, and of Ancient Manners: With Dissertations on the Clowns and Fools of Shakespeare... 2 vols. Ln, 1807, 526, 499 pp. 2nd ed., 1839. E-S

To Douce, "ancient" apparently meant "early in the native tradition," and often his intention is to assert the popular culture as a source to be preferred to the classical. Typical is his suggestion that Miranda's offer to be Ferdinand's wife and/or servant (Temp. III i 83-86) is traceable to the ballad of "The Nutbrown Maid" rather than to Catullus. Douce's anticlassical bias in his explications de texte is possibly traceable in part to his familiarity with Farmer, from whom perhaps he also acquired a charming arrogance. This self-assurance does not preclude his being quite wrong at times: e.g., he holds the belief, long outmoded in his time, that Chaucer wrote Henryson's Testament of Cresseid. But many suggestions are valuable, and he does not neglect classical analogues and sources altogether. He must certainly be regarded as among the most important of the early nineteenth-century commentators. MnU

0208. Dowden, Edward. "Elizabethan Psychology," Essays Modern and Elizabethan (Ln, 1910), pp. 308-333.

This pioneer exposition of faculty psychology, the humors, and the micro-macrocosm is deserving of its reputation as a classic. Dowden is accurate, well read in the sixteenth-century authorities, and able to point to at least one fact seldom noted by later commentators ("eucrasy" was the technical term in the Renaissance for the state of perfect balance among the humors). Dowden makes only a brief mention of Aristotle, Plato, Galen, and Hippocrates, the loci classici of Elizabethan psychology. He illustrates the theories from Sh inter alia (about a dozen plays).

0209. Downes, Robert P. Seven Supreme Poets. Ln, 1905. (Sh, pp. 215-268; others are Homer, Aeschylus, Sophocles, Virgil, Dante, and Milton.)

Not seen. Information from Jaggard, #0025.

0210. Drake, Nathan. *Shakspeare and His Times*. 2 vols. Ln, 1817, 735, 677 pp.

This pioneer work of historical criticism touches on Sh's classicism in Vol. I, where (24-33) Drake speculates with informed intelligence about the probable elementary texts in Latin at Stratford in Elizabeth's time, concluding that Sh had some Greek and a sufficient foundation in Latin to have made himself a scholar of note after leaving school; Sh declined the path of scholarship in favor of creative literature, but that does not justify Farmer's contention that Sh was a semiliterate dunce capable of no more Latin than "hig, hag, hog." Drake's criticism of the plays in four substantial chs. of Vol. II is at times excellent, if one can set aside the ill-conceived hypothesis about the chronology of the canon which Drake is at pains to defend. On *Caesar*, *Antony*, and *Cor.* Drake is less copious and illuminating than on *Tim.* and *Troi.*; there are scattered comments on Sh's classics in other plays as well. MnU

0211. Draper, John W. "*Ethiopian* in Shakespeare," *Anglia*, LXXIII (1955), 65-70.

Of Sh's eleven references to Ethiopia and its inhabitants, all but two could be derived entirely from the Greek etymology αἴθειν (to burn) and ὄψ (face) because these nine refer to the dark complexion of the race. There is a possibility also that Sh got his limited knowledge from Leo Africanus, who got his information ultimately from classical geographers. Of the other two Shn references, one (the "rich jewel in an Ethiop's ear" in *Romeo* I v) is probably a variation on a similar image in Lyly and the other (in *Wives* II iii) is probably a reference to a book on Prester John.

0212. Draper, John W. *The Humors & Shakespeare's Characters*. Duke UP, 1945, 126 pp.

In this book Draper epitomizes his many previous arts. approaching Sh's characters through the portal of humoral psychology. Here no character or play receives extended analysis, but dozens of men and women are classified according to their dominant fluids. Draper is more interested in what the Elizabethan medical authorities say than in the classical antecedents of their psychological system, but the Galenic theory is implied at all points and discussed briefly in Ch. I. A useful reference work, but it is possible that Draper's interest in this one aspect of historical criticism has minimized for him the importance of other parts of the Elizabethan background; he tacitly implies that humoral psychology is *the* key to the meaning of every play in the canon.

0213. Draper, John W. "Mistaken Identity in Shakespeare's Comedies," *RAA*, XI (1934), 289-297.

Draper believes that Sh learned the comic worth of mistaken identity from "the Latin comedy that [he] must have known so well." But Sh's use of the convention grows in subtlety: "the fortuitous mistakes of Plautus lead to intentional disguise, which Shakespeare exploits in the high comedies of the second period; and this leads on to the highest types of dramatic irony, misapprehension of the psychology and the mental habits of our fellows," which Sh used as a dramatic device in the tragedies. This is a convincing study of a classical dramatic convention as it develops through Sh's works and is finally transmuted in the later, greater plays.

0214. Driver, Tom Faw. *The Sense of History in Greek and Shakespearean Drama*. Col UP, 1960, 231 pp.

Beginning with a philosophical consideration of the meaning of time to the Hellenes as opposed to the Hebrews, Driver proceeds to a ch. on the relation between time and dramatic form. Then in four perceptive chs. he contrasts Shn use of time with Greek tragic practice, balancing *R. III* against the *Persae*, *Ham.* against the *Oresteia*, *Macb.* against *Oedipus Tyrannus*, and *W. T.* against *Alcestis*. Sh reflects his Judaeo-Christian heritage in which time is a linear continuum: the present is a point on the continuum consisting of memory of the past and anticipation of the future; the past and present to Sh and the Hebrew tradition are a womb that contains the embryo of the future to be delivered by the midwife Providence cooperating with man's free will. To the Greeks, however, time is a circle (the pre-Socratic cyclic view of history); therefore, since the future will merely repeat the present, and the past has been an anticipation of the present, neither future nor past has the importance in Greek tragedy which each has in Sh. In the abstract such a contrast is appealing, but though Driver's analysis of Shn and Greek tragedy is imaginative and thorough, the practical application raises some questions which he perhaps evades rather than answers: e.g., is Oedipus not ensnared by oracular portrayal of the future as much as Macbeth? Is not the pre-history of the House of Atreus even more important than the pre-history of the House of Hamlet? Are the Persians of Aeschylus really divorced from time but not from space to the extent that Driver claims? Is Driver consistent when he describes the Oresteia, Oedipus Tyrannus, and (by implication) the Persae as "poised picture[s] of timeless moral reality" and then says of the Alcestis "[it] becomes another example of that essentially Greek situation in which the past dominates the present"? Driver himself calls attention to the complex tense structure of the Greek language as opposed to the simplicity of Hebrew, and he appears slightly embarrassed by the fact that Greece produced in Herodotus and Thucydides respectively a great recorder and a great analyst of past events. In short, though he is obviously right about the absence from Greek tragedy of a purposive Providence operating through time such as is implied by the form of R.III (e.g.), Driver may be overstating the differences between Greek and Shn conceptions of history and time.

0215. Dryden, John. The Conquest of Granada II: Defence of the Epilogue (1672), Munro, II, 174-176.

Dryden here as in many other places alludes to Sh's lack of learning--he gives as examples of crudity Per., the history plays, W.T., L.L.L., and Meas.

0216. Dryden, John. The Grounds of Criticism in Tragedy [Preface to Troilus and Cressida] (1679), Munro, II, 244-250.

One of Dryden's more extensive explorations of Sh's genius. He ranges far beyond Troi. to Caesar, Ham., R. II, Wives, Romeo, Oth., etc. Sh is to be revered by the Restoration as Aeschylus was by Periclean Greece, yet Troi., one of Sh's earliest (sic) works, is full of barbarisms which Dryden wishes to prune. The scene between Troilus and Hector in Act V bears comparison with the Brutus-Cassius quarrel in Caesar and the Agamemnon-Menelaus quarrel in Iphigenia at Aulis. Sh is a myth-maker in Temp.--Caliban is an original mythological creation. Wives is the most regular of Sh's comedies. The essay ends with an interesting contrast between Sh and Fletcher.

0217. Dryden, John. Of Dramatick Poesie, an Essay (1668), Munro, II, 141-148.

It is in this essay that Dryden makes his most famous pronouncements on Sh's lack of learning: "he was naturally learn'd; he needed not the spectacles of Books to read Nature," etc. At one point he calls Sh the Homer of English drama and Ben Jonson the Virgil. There are other brief references to Sh in his relationship to the classics. This essay had a great influence on opinion of Sh's learning in the first half of the eighteenth century.

0218. Dryden, John. Preface to All for Love; or, the World well Lost (1678), Munro, II, 243.

Includes one of Dryden's many references to Sh's ignorance.

0219. [Dryden, John ?]. "Prologue to Julius Caesar" (1672), Munro, II, 172-173.

In this prologue Dryden (?) makes the obviously erroneous statement that Sh "did not know what Trope or Figure meant" and says that "Those then that tax his Learning are to blame, / He knew the thing but did not know the Name." Despite Sh's ignorance he makes Mark Antony's funeral oration superior to any speech of Cicero's.

0220. Dryden, John, the Younger. "The Dedication [to The Husband His own Cuckold (1696)]," T-D, p. 38.

Dryden's son here says of Sh "had he had more Learning, perhaps he might have been less a Poet." The justificatory approach to Sh's ignorance which some have traced to Edward Young (#0665) in the mid-eighteenth century appears to originate with this earlier statement. T. R[ymer?] attacked this remark: see An Essay, Concerning Critical and Curious Learning... (1698), pp. 30-31, Augustan Reprint Society, Publication No. 113 (1965); the passage also appears in T-D, p. 42.

0221. Du Bois, Edward. "Coincidences and Imitations: Shakespere," The Wreath; Composed of Selections from Sappho, Theocritus, Bion, and Moschus. Accompanied by a Prose Translation, With Notes. To Which are Added Remarks on Shakespere, &c. and a Comparison Between Horace and Lucian (Ln, 1799), pp. 59-84.

Most of the "coincidences and imitations" in these notes involve Greek literature. Plato and Politian on the music of the spheres are juxtaposed with Merch. V i. Sh's reference to mandragora (Antony I v 4) is "an allusion both to Plato and Demosthenes"; Caliban in Temp. II ii is reminiscent of Polyphemus in Odyssey IX; epigrams from the Greek Anthology are compared with lines from Shrew and Wives; Epictetus, Menander, and Marcus Aurelius provide analogues for Sh's observations on consciousness of loss and of injury in Oth.; the Oresteia is a parallel to the situation of Ham., and also gives an analogue to Macbeth's lines on "great Neptune's ocean" (Du Bois ignores Seneca's adaptation of Aeschylus--a closer parallel to Sh); Theocritus' twenty-seventh Idyl provides a parallel to Ophelia's improper song on the loss of virginity, etc. Du Bois does not mention Farmer or the other "small Latin" controversialists of the generation before him, but he remarks that Sh "never appears to have lost his early imbibed (though, perhaps, not far pursued) taste for Latin poetry." He seems unaware of North's Plutarch, arguing for Sh's use of Amyot. A minor, but interesting survival of the approach of Upton and Whalley (#0606, #0632). DFo

0222. Duckworth, George E. "The Influence of Plautus and Terence Upon English Comedy," The Nature of Roman Comedy: A Study in Entertainment. PUP, 1952, pp. 396-433.

The section on Sh (412-418) would grant him enough Latin to read what he wished in Plautus (though Duckworth believes in the mythical Amphitruo trans.). He briefly supplies a sizable number of echoes of Plautus' comedies in Ham., Wives, Shrew, Romeo, and Temp. among others. He stops short of accepting Shylock's debt to Euclio, but he certainly credits Sh with more of Plautus than has been traditional. Duckworth ignores Sh's Terence altogether--an odd omission in the light of his demonstrated knowledge of Baldwin's works on Sh's education.

0223. Eagle, R[oderick] L. "Shakespeare and Catullus," NQ, CCII (1957), 521-522.

Eagle prints eight excerpts from Catullus, gives prose trans., and indicates the supposed indebtedness in Sh. Of the eight, not one is convincing; some have been proposed before without obtaining general consent, and nearly all were Elizabethan commonplaces: e.g., the odi et amo theme, and the poet's capacity for protecting those he celebrates from oblivion.

0224. Eagle, Roderick L. "Shakespeare's Learned Ladies," NQ, CCIII (1958), 197.

Sh's romantic heroines refer frequently to the classics, especially the Meta.; Eagle cites several examples and concludes that Sh is idealizing these women, since education of such caliber was extraordinary for a woman in his day.

0225. Ebrahim, C. "The Drama and Society," Discussion, I (1952), 21-30.

Not seen. According to #0042 (1953), Ebrahim considers Sh's "humanism, his opposition to classical formalism, and his rejection of the unities."

0226. Eliot, T. S. The Classics and the Man of Letters. OUP, 1942, 27 pp.

This presidential address to the Classical Association advances the thesis "that the maintenance of classical education is essential to the maintenance of the continuity of English Literature." The remarks on Sh are very brief, classing him with Bunyan and Lincoln as educationally "ill-furnished," having "fragmentary and secondhand" knowledge of the classics.

0227. Eliot, T. S. "Seneca in Elizabethan Translation" (1927), in Selected Essays, new ed. (N.Y., 1950), pp. 51-88. E-S HB SG

This essay, more modest and more restrained than its contemporary (#0228), is concerned more with Seneca and his influence than with the trans. themselves. Senecan sententiousness and rhetorical devices like stichomythia with echoes appear in R.II and R.III though neither play is Senecan in total conception, and the great language of Lear would have been impossible without the experimental bombast which Kyd's generation thought was a reflection of Seneca's style. But Titus (of which Eliot would purge the canon) is not Senecan at all, being far too crude in conception. The great contribution of Seneca was that his Latin iambics gave impetus to the development of blank verse, the nearest English equivalent to them; Sh learned to write blank verse from Marlowe, who "learned" from Seneca. After Sh the Senecan influence disappears as Sh becomes the model.

0228. Eliot, T. S. "Shakespeare and the Stoicism of Seneca" (1927), in Selected Essays, new ed. (N.Y., 1950), pp. 107-120. E-S HB SG

Sh's debt to Seneca is at least partly indirect. He may have read the plays in school, but he found Senecan Stoicism adrift in the works of Kyd and Peele. In any case, Stoicism is transmuted in the plays of Sh, appearing chiefly in the prideful desire of the tragic heroes to think well of themselves. The essay ranges widely and is full of Eliot's characteristic sweeping generalizations (e.g., "the Roman stoicism was of course a philosophy suited to slaves: hence its absorption into early Christianity").

0229. Ellis, Oliver C. de C. Cleopatra in the Tide of Time. Ln, 1947, 286 pp.

The relevant ch. in this survey of Cleopatra plays is the third, in which Ellis studies both Caesar and Antony. It is preceded by chs. on the historical Cleopatra and on the Senecan tradition, and followed by studies of Fletcher's The False One, Dryden's All for Love, and Shaw's Caesar and Cleopatra. The book is liberally sprinkled with attacks on the Vatican, which are as irrelevant as they are outrageous; when one recognizes also the bias of a special plea (Cleopatra was Isis' saint), he may be pardoned for distrusting Ellis. Caesar is to be regarded as a dramatic failure which Sh wrote to flagellate Elizabeth for her harshness to Essex. Brutus is its tragic hero, though Ellis cannot abide him; Antony speaks Sh's mind in the play. In Antony the crucial moment comes when Cleopatra sees Antony struck by "a Roman thought" (to Ellis "Roman" is a pejorative adjective); from this point on the lovers try to wound one another and only achieve apotheosis in their dying moments. The section on Antony is somewhat diffuse and rambling. Ellis is more provocative in his passing allusions to other plays: e.g., Leontes' reaction to the death of Mamillius may have been inspired by Plutarch's reaction to the death of his daughter; Sh seems to have been thinking of the power which Octavius' spirit had over Antony's when he made Banquo a dominant force in Macbeth's life; the H. VI trilogy is "Greek" in its portrayal of the fall of a great house. But the book is written with a bias and a flippancy which should be a caveat for beginning students.

0230. Ellis-Fermor, Una. "Shakespeare the Dramatist," PBA, XXXIV (1948), 81-96. (Annual British Academy Shakespeare Lecture.)

This analysis of the nature of drama and of dramatic talent is calculated to show that Sh alone of practitioners of the art was inherently a dramatist: i.e., had he lived in an age barren of drama, like the Victorian, he would still have been compelled to express his genius in dramatic form. The argument is continually advanced by thoughtful comparisons between Sh and Aeschylus and Sophocles (and, to a lesser extent, Euripides), as well as Marlowe, Ibsen, and others. A lucid, percipient set of definitions and distinctions.

0231. Elton, Oliver. "Giordano Bruno in England," Modern Studies (Ln, 1907), pp. 1-36.

Elton seeks (pp. 26-28) to deny the contention of numerous German scholars that Sh echoes Bruno's Platonic and pantheistic doctrines in Sonn., Ham., Merch., and Lear. Hamlet, in referring to Alexander's possible progress toward the beggar's guts or the bunghole, is reflecting "atomic materialism," not Bruno's pantheism.

0232. Elton, William. "Timothy Bright and Shakespeare's Seeds of Nature," MLN, LXV (1950), 196-197.

For his several references to the Neoplatonic concept of the rationes seminales, Sh need not have known the "impressive lineage" which W. C. Curry (#0083) traces. Timothy Bright's Treatise of Melancholy would have given him the material ready to hand.

0233. Elze, Karl. William Shakespeare: A Literary Biography, trans. from the German by L. Dora Schmitz (Ln, 1888), 587 pp. E-S

The first ch. contains a passage (35-43) on Sh's education, which is factually correct but fanciful in its speculations. More important is Ch. VI, "Shakespeare's Intellectual Culture" (365-422), which begins with the assertion that Sh was not an ignoramus; it is the scholar's task to explore Sh's whole cultural environment to discover his relationship to it. Elze proceeds to show the weaknesses in Farmer's arguments as Maginn had done earlier, and he maintains that Sh's diction (comic as well as serious), his depiction of Roman culture, and the testimony of his contemporaries assure us of his awareness of the classical world and its languages. Elze goes on to modern languages and other intellectual arenas; the final estimate of Sh's learning places it higher than Jonson's interpreters have usually thought before Baldwin. One of the most interesting features is Elze's effective attempt to place Sh in the same class with Chapman, Marlowe, and others vis à vis Jonson. The whole book is marred by occasional mistaken assumptions resulting usually from Elze's inaccurate chronology of the canon; this reservation aside, Elze's is one of the most significant studies of Sh's classicism in the nineteenth century.

0234. Engel, Jakob. "Die Spuren Senecas in Shaksperes Dramen," PJ, CXII (1903), 60-81.

Engel defends the maligned Seneca in part by arguing that Sh found much to admire and imitate in the Senecan canon. As might be expected, most of the "Spuren" come from Titus, the H.VI plays, R.III, and Macb. But Engel also finds Senecan traces (some of them apparently unnoticed by other commentators) in Ham., Oth., Lear, W.T., and Temp. Engel thinks it probable that Sh studied Seneca in school, but later turned also to the trans., especially those by Jasper Heywood: The Trojan Women, Thyestes, and Hercules Furens. Engel is mainly concerned with verbal echoes and shared ideas in brief passages; he does not compare Sh's conception of the tragic hero with Seneca's, nor does he discuss Stoicism. Some, at least, of his "Spuren" can be as readily traced to other sources (e.g., to Ovid's Meta. in Titus and Temp.).

0235. Enk, P. J. "Shakespeare's 'Small Latin'," Neoph, V (1920), 359-365. HB SG

Enk suggests (following Sonnenschein, #0929, and Fay, #0757) that Sh read Seneca's De Clementia and Plautus' Captivi, Mostellaria, Rudens, and Amphitruo in Latin. He cites parallels between Shrew, Temp., Ham., Much, Errors, and Merch. and Plautus' plays (which, except Menaechmi, were not trans. into English in the sixteenth century); some of these parallels are tenuous, but others are very close. The argument for Sh's having read Seneca is based on striking similarities between Portia's "quality of mercy" speech and De Clementia, which was not available in English before 1614.

0236. Erler, Ernst. Die Namengebung bei Shakespeare, AA (Heidelberg, 1913), 144 pp. E-S

The most extensive study of Sh's onomastics which has yet appeared. Not the least of its merits are its thorough surveys of previous conjectures (see, e.g., the discussions of the source of the name "Sycorax," pp. 47, 122). But Erler's conservative insights are also valuable. His most cogent findings relevant to this Guide are: (1) Sh read more widely in Plutarch than has usually been thought by scholars (this view is now commonly accepted, but less commonly traced to Erler); (2) Sh felt more confident of the etymologies of Latin than of Greek names; (3) Sh frequently used allusive classical names to suggest a character or a situation (e.g., "Hero" in Much). The book is awkwardly arranged and somewhat repetitive, but an accurate index makes it a usable reference. TxHR

0237. Fairchild, Arthur H. R. Shakespeare and the Arts of Design, MUS, XII, No. 1. Missouri UP, 1937, 198 pp.

Fairchild observes (pp. 67-70) that Sh's general references to classical statuary ("Pompey's statua," "old Brutus' statue," "chaste Dian bathing," and the Colossus in 1H.IV, Troi., and Caesar, e.g.) have a literary ring which suggests that he got them from Plutarch, Ovid, and Pliny rather than from direct observation. There is a convincing argument for Ovid's Pygmalion story as the source for the living statue motif in W.T. V (pp. 71-74); Fairchild provides (pp. 134-136) a brief, but detailed account of Sh's possible sources for Fluellen's Fortune "painted plind." A longer section (pp. 139-147) discusses Troy tapestries as a source for the picture of Troy in Lucr.; Fairchild believes that the popular tapestries on the themes of Petrarch's I Trionfi (e.g., the Triumph of Time, the Triumph of Chastity) in which Lucretia appears, may have given Sh the idea of writing Lucr.

0238. Farmer, Richard. An Essay on the Learning of Shakespeare. Cambridge, 1767. E-S HB (Reprinted in Boswell's Malone, I, 300-361.)

This belligerent attempt to deny Sh's knowledge of Latin, Greek, Italian, Spanish, and French is a frontal assault on the evidence for Sh's erudition offered earlier in the eighteenth century by Upton (#0606), Whalley (#0632), Grey (#0286), and others. Farmer's wide reading in Elizabethan literature enables him to point out parallels and sources in English works for many supposed borrowings from the ancients, and he is justified in criticizing the extremes to which his predecessors went. But he draws far too sweeping a conclusion from his source studies: i.e., the fact that Sh used a trans. does not convict him of total ignorance of the original language, as Farmer implies it does. This document had an importance in the "small Latin" controversy far beyond its logical merits; Dr. Johnson seriously believed that Farmer had settled the issue forever, and no major voice offered protest until Coleridge (#0172), Maginn (#0403), and Charles Armitage Brown (#0126). See the discussion supra, pp. 6-8.

0239. Farquhar, George. A Discourse upon Comedy In Reference to the English Stage (1702), ed. Louis A. Strauss (Boston, 1914), pp. 1-35.

This clever invective against slavery to Aristotle has historical significance as an early counterattack against the rules. Sh is contrasted with Aristotle: Shn practice, not Aristotelian theory, is our critical guide. Decorum in the utile and dulce of Horace Sh had and any dramatist must have to be acceptable, but unities of time, place, and action can and should be dispensed with. MnU

0240. Fisher, L. A. "Shakspere and the Capitol," MLN, XXII (1907), 177-182. SG

The misconception of Sh and Heywood that the Roman Senate met in the temple of Jupiter Capitoline (or "the Capitol") is traceable ultimately to a twelfth-century guidebook, Mirabilia Urbis Romae, which gives a fanciful version of what the building looked like. The immediate source is probably some late version of Higden's Polychronicon, which borrows the misconception from the Mirabilia.

0241. Fiske, John. "Forty Years of Bacon-Shakespeare Folly," AM, LXXX (1897), 635-652.

Fiske demolishes the anti-Stratfordians by undermining both premises of their syllogism: the plays are not immensely learned in a Jonsonian/Miltonic sense (though Sh's genius consists in his having noticed vast multitudes of things and recalled them with accuracy and transmitted them with vividness); Sh's plays have a Homeric freshness which more learned poets cannot match. Yet Sh's grammar school days would give him "small Latin and less Greek," about what a Harvard graduate has: "the ability to read Terence at sight, and perhaps Euripides less fluently." A genial, informed, and rational refutation.

0242. Fleay, Frederick G. "Gentle Will, Our Fellow," PL, V (1893), 612-620. (Concluded.)

Fleay, who adopts the persona of John Heminge (writing in 1626), submits on pp. 616-617 that "Jonson truly said of him that he had little Latin and less Greek." Sh is to be conceded no Greek and in Latin only Lily's Grammar, The Accidence, Sententiae Pueriles, and Mantuan. Obviously a more generous concession should be made.

0243. Fleay, Frederick G. Shakespeare Manual. Ln, 1878, 312 pp.

This book is a potpourri of Fleay's previous writings supplemented by original work. The short essays and comments on the canon range from eccentric to wildly speculative. Fleay believes, e.g., that Caesar is an abridgement made by Ben Jonson of a Shn original (this in part because Jonson spells Marcus Antonius' name "Antony" and Sh elsewhere spells it "Anthony"). Again he believes on the most slender evidence that Sh's unfinished Tim. was padded into its present form by Cyril Tourneur to fill the space in F_1 left empty by the shifting of Troi. And so it goes; Fleay's opinions are now largely discredited, as they should be.

0244. Freeburg, Victor O. Disguise Plots in Elizabethan Drama: A Study in Stage Tradition, ColSECL, No. [not given] (Col UP, 1915), 241 pp.

See especially Ch. III (31-60) for a discussion of "The Origin and Extent of Dramatic Disguise." The five types in Elizabethan drama are traceable through French, Spanish, and especially Italian literature to Plautus. It is probable that Menander utilized some of them, but they are of no basic significance in other Greek drama. While Seneca eschews disguise altogether, Terence uses it in one play. Freeburg's study contains passim a large number of brief discussions of Sh's use of this indirectly classical convention.

0245. Friedland, Louis Sigmund. "Dramatic Unities in England," JEGP, X (1911), 56-89, 280-299, 453-467. E-S

The three pages (73-75) on Sh's attitude toward the classical unities occupy only a fraction of the space devoted to Renaissance critical theories and practical applications. But though Friedland briefly points out that there is no clear proof of Sh's knowledge of the formulas, he shows that the Choruses in H.V and W.T. and references in Cym. and Temp. make it probable that Sh knew the rules as a contemporary of Sidney and Jonson ought to. Friedland is uncertain whether Polonius' classifications are a clear reference to dramatic unity.

0246. Fripp, E[dgar] I. "Elizabethan Proverbs," TLS, March 17, 1927, p. 194. SG

The Shn concept of the chameleon as living on air derives ultimately from Ovid's Meta. XV. Sh could have obtained this bit of pseudoscience from Lyly or Erasmus.

0247. Fripp, E[dgar] I. "His Latinity," Shakespeare: Man and Artist (OUP, 1938), I, 114-116.

A long list of Latinate English words Sh uses in the early works; usage indicates Sh's awareness of their roots. Though Sh's only major classical reading was Ovid, he knew his Latin well, yet never paraded it pedantically.

0248. Fripp, E[dgar] I. "His 'Ovid's Metamorphoses'," Shakespeare: Man and Artist (OUP, 1938), I, 102-114.

This brief essay modifies somewhat Fripp's earlier denial (#0251) of Golding's influence on Sh, but still seeks to minimize that influence by a (perhaps unjustified) ridicule of Golding as translator and versifier. A number of Ovidian passages (notably in H.VIII) are added to the evidence he had earlier submitted.

0249. Fripp, E[dgar] I. "School-Plays at Stratford," Shakespeare: Man and Artist (OUP, 1938), I, 116-121.

Repeated references in Sh's plays show that he was familiar with the Latin and English playlets which schoolboys were required to perform. He perhaps acted in Whitsun plays, Acolastus, Menaechmi, and Seneca.

0250. Fripp, Edgar I. "Shakespeare—Boy and Man," ShR, I (1928), 239-248. SG

In this graceful address Fripp finds occasion to point out some of Sh's obligations to Ovid. Meta. I appears in the canon more often than any other of the books just as Genesis appears more often than other Old Testament books (notably both deal with creation). The concept "rudis indigestaque moles" of Meta. I appears in Sonn. 114, 2,3H.VI, and John. In H.VIII the legends of Orpheus and of Ceyx and Halcyone are echoed; the latter may also be reflected in Pisanio's account of the departure of Posthumus to sea (Cym. I iii). Fripp also notes Ovidian sense and sound in Merch. and Oth. A valuable piece of criticism except for its categorical assertion that Sh did not read Golding's "clownish English translation." DFo

0251. Fripp, E[dgar] I. "Shakespeare's Use of Ovid's Metamorphoses," Shakespeare Studies, Biographical and Literary (OUP, 1930), pp. 98-128. E-S HB SG

This close-packed juxtaposition of mythological and pseudo-scientific matter in Ovid's Latin with the same material in Sh is calculated to demonstrate Sh's exclusively direct debt. But Fripp ignores the evidence that Sh did know Golding, and therefore arrives at an obviously untenable conclusion. Nevertheless, the great number of citations does indicate the magnitude of Ovidian influence. See #0248, where Fripp modifies his extreme stand.

0252. Frye, Northrop. Anatomy of Criticism: Four Essays. PUP, 1957, 383 pp.

Frye's ambitious purpose is "to give a rational account of some of the structural principles of Western literature in the context of its Classical and Christian heritage." The first essay classifies literature according to "modes," the kinds of impact characters make on an audience; the second deals with symbols (defined very broadly) as an organizing principle; the third treats archetypes; and the fourth relates genres to rhetorical possibilities. Sh's practice is compared with and contrasted to classical theory (especially Aristotle) and practice at many points in each essay. The scope of Frye's essays precludes any detailed analysis of individual passages, and Sh is only one of hundreds of authors whose works are alluded to. But almost the entire canon appears in one context or another, and some of the brief critical remarks are most interesting: e.g., "Bassanio" may echo βασανίζω (to test character by ordeal); Errors, "though based on a Plautine original, is much closer to the world of Apuleius than to that of Plautus in its imagery"; the resurrection myth of Proserpine is reflected not only in W.T. but in Cym. and Much also, where heroines are "dead" for a time (Sh feels compelled to make the resurrections plausible, whereas the Greek myth simply asks us to accept the miraculous). This is stimulating and original criticism.

0253. Frye, Northrop. "Characterization in Shakespearian Comedy," SQ, IV (1953), 271-277.

Beginning with a definition of classical comedy in a framework of its four main character types (eiron, alazon, agroikos, bomolochos), Frye points to Sh's ingenious manipulation of them from T.G.V. to Temp. "All Shakespeare's characters owe their consistency to the appropriateness of the stock type which belongs to their dramatic function. That stock type is not the character, but is as necessary to the character as a skeleton is to the actor who plays it." This provocative essay contains many interesting remarks: on the continuity of Aristophanic and New Comic conventions, on Katherina in Shrew as a female alazon, on the ultimately Terentian sources of the Gloucester plot in Lear, on Polonius, Duke Senior, and Duke Vincentio as "retreating eirons," and many others. A valuable piece of criticism.

0254. Frye, Northrop. "Comic Myth in Shakespeare," 3 *TRSC*, XLVI, No. 2 (1952), 47-58.

This essay ranges widely: from *The Acharnians* to *The Cocktail Party*, from Euripides to Shaw. Sh is relevant as a master of the romantic comedy of anagnorisis, which Frye contrasts (but not too sharply) with Jonsonian comedy of manners. Sh's *Wives* shares with Plautus' *Casina* the device of subordinating the lovers; *Ham.* is an ironic treatment of the moral paradox at the heart of the *Hippolytus*. There are other original and interesting comments on Sh and Jonson as they participate in comic (and tragic) conventions which Frye explores in a number of Sh's plays: e.g., *All's W.*, *Troi.*, *Temp.*, etc.

0255. Frye, Northrop. "A Conspectus of Dramatic Genres," *KR*, XIII (1951), 543-562.

Emphasizing that Aristotle's "generic criticism" of drama has been neglected as his "formal criticism" has not, Frye sets out to expand the too-limited categories of the *Poetics* to make place for satire, masque, opera, *commedia dell' arte*, etc. Frye establishes his categories according to the impact a play makes on its audience. Sh receives more attention *passim* than any other playwright; the implicit analogies or contrasts with classical drama or with Aristotle's criteria give the art. relevance to the study of Sh's classicism.

0256. Frye, Prosser Hall. "Shakespeare and Sophocles," *Romance and Tragedy* (Boston, 1922), pp. 227-311. E-S

In a singularly obtuse and annoyingly unspecific essay, Frye suggests that Sophocles is somehow more "moral" than Sh, though the reader is not favored with any illustrations from the former. The difference is to be blamed on "the Dark Ages," by which Frye apparently means much of what the Romantic novelists meant by "Gothic." Though Sh was "affected" (in what way is not clear) by the classics, he, like the English commoners, "is a mediaeval overtaken by the immense perturbation of the Renaissance" the result of which "was the erection of incongruity or disorder into a vital principle." This latter misunderstanding of the Elizabethan *Weltanschauung* should be a caveat for readers of Frye's essay.

0257. Fuller, Thomas. "William Shakespeare," *The History of the Worthies of England* (1643?-1662), Munro, I, 483-484.

This is the famous brief eulogy in which Fuller compares Sh to Martial (each has a war-like name), Ovid (who also is "natural" and "witty"), and Plautus (who was a great comedian though "never any Scholar"). In this passage Fuller also opposes Sh to Jonson, the "*English man of War*" against the "*Spanish great Gallion*." Fuller writes with sufficient grace to make one wish he had written about the plays in detail, but he is obviously wrong in assuming that Sh illustrates the adage "*Poeta non fit sed nascitur*."

0258. Furnivall, F. J. "Shakspere," 5 *NQ*, V (1876), 184.

Although some have thought he did, Sh did not read Christopher Ocland's Latin poem, "*εἰρηναρχία sive Elizabetha*" in school because it was not prescribed for grammar schools (nor even composed) until 1582, by which time Sh had doubtless left school.

0259. Furnivall, F. J. "What Did Shakspeare Learn at School?" *Ath*, No. 2554 (1876), 464.

Furnivall prints a communication from a Rev. Lupton of St. Paul's School discussing sixteenth-century statutes specifying texts to be read in various schools. Lupton's informed guesses as to Sh's exposure to grammar school classicism come interestingly near to the findings of the studies carried out by T. W. Baldwin in this century. Lily's Grammar, Erasmus' *Colloquies*, Mantuan, Cicero, Virgil, Ovid, Terence, possibly Sallust, Clenard's Greek Grammar, and pseudo-Cato's *Distichs* are the core of the curriculum. The gist of this letter appears in F. J. Furnivall and John Munro, *Shakespeare: Life and Work* (Ln, 1910), pp. 19-20.

0260. Gallagher, Ligeia Cécile. "Shakespeare and the Aristotelian Ethical Tradition," diss (Stanford, 1956). *DA*, XVI (1956), 1898-99.

This study traces the tenets (prudential, intellectual, communal) of the *Nicomachean Ethics* as they appear in *R.II*, *Merch.*, *Oth.*, and *Lear*. Sh is also drawing on Medieval and Renaissance accretions, not on Aristotle alone. The author considers her thesis a ground for rejecting Stoic and determinist readings of Sh.

0261. Gardner, Helen. "Shakespeare and the Philosophers," *ShN*, V (1955), 3.

A report of a Summer Lecture at Stratford-upon-Avon. Miss Gardner denied that Sh was a Senecan Stoic who revered reason above love and other emotions. Sh had a hope unknown to Seneca. Even "Stoic" characters like Brutus and Horatio are not really Senecan.

0262. Garrett, John. "Shakespeare and Elizabethan Education," ShN, IV (1954), 48.

This report of a Summer Lecture given at Stratford-upon-Avon in 1954 gives the impression that Garrett's treatment was general and that little was said of Sh's use of the Latin he learned at Stratford.

0263. Gayley, Charles M. The Classic Myths in English Literature and Art... Boston, 1893, 597 pp. (in the most recent revision).

Gayley compares (p. 236) the Witches' incantation in Macb. IV i to the chant of Medea as she gathers materials for Aeson's caldron. In the notes and Commentary at the end of the book (pp. 465-540) there are dozens of chapter-and-verse references to Sh as utilizer of various myths. Gayley's makes a convenient if elementary handbook.

0264. Gervinus, G[eorg] G[ottfried]. Shakespeare Commentaries (1849-50), trans. F. W. Bunnètt, 5th ed., Ln, 1892, 955 pp. E-S

This classic of German criticism is still valuable for its insights on the plays (each merits ca. twenty pages), but it should be used with caution as it contains some inaccuracy in fact and a wealth of conjecture (e.g., on the date of Caesar) which has since been shown to be ill-conceived. Gervinus is sufficiently a Romantic to assume that only a German can appreciate Greek culture: that Sh is a typical Englishman in preferring Rome to Athens. He also retails much nonsense about Sh's personal life (especially sexual immorality) based on a credulous reading of Sonn. and the narrative poems, when a more thorough knowledge of Elizabethan literature could have shown him that the poems and Sonn. are conventional, each typical of a genre. But as a critic with insights Gervinus is to be valued. His comparison of Brutus and Horatio as Stoics is masterful, and the ch. on Troi. recognizes what is now a common assumption: that the Greek-Trojan plot is the heart of the play and the Troilus-Cressida plot fills a subordinate role, paralleling the Menelaus-Helen relationship. Gervinus also has enough discrimination to find a middle path between Farmer and the Bardolaters on Sh's knowledge of the ancient world.

0265. Gesner, Carol. "The Greek Romance Materials in the Plays of Shakespeare," diss (LSU, 1956). DA, XVI (1956), 2162.

This diss studies all of the "Sophistic" Greek romances and then traces elements from them in the plots of Errors, Romeo, Much, A.Y.L., Twel., Lear, Per., Cym., W.T., and Temp. "Verbal or incidental elements" from the romances can also be found in T.G.V., Dream, Merch., Oth., and Macb. (the Birnam Wood episode is paralleled in Achilles Tatius). Dr. Gesner admits that much of this material may have come to Sh through his milieu, but suggests that some, at least, may have been directly borrowed.

0266. Gifford, W[illiam]. "Proofs of Ben Jonson's Malignity, from the Commentators on Shakspeare," The Works of Ben Jonson ...in Nine Volumes, ed. W. Gifford (Ln, 1875), I, cxciii-ccxxiv.

A vituperative attack on the eighteenth-century critics, especially Malone, for perpetuating the fiction that Jonson felt malice toward Sh. Inter alia, Gifford casts doubt on the credibility of the Mr.-Hales-of-Eton story, and argues that Jonson understood "Art" in two senses: (1) "information" in the expression Sh "wanted Art"; (2) that which "is opposed to nature" in the F_1 poem. The distinction appears forced. DFo

0267. Gilbert, Allan H. "Seneca and the Criticism of Elizabethan Tragedy," PQ, XIII (1934), 370-381. HB

We miss Sh's intention if we read Romeo, Ham., Lear, Cor., Caesar, Antony, Oth., Macb., and Cym. as purely personal tragedies devoid of public significance. Sh, like his contemporaries, learned from Seneca to value the political implications of the fall of great men. Sh developed character more than his contemporaries did, which is one reason he is preferred to them today--but his intention was always to follow the prevailing critical dicta of neo-Senecanism: to emphasize the social ramifications of personal behavior.

0268. Gilchrist, Octavius. An Examination of the Charges Maintained by Messrs. Malone, Chalmers, and Others, of Ben Jonson's Enmity &c. Towards Shakspeare. Ln, 1808, 62 pp.

Gilchrist attacks those who maintained in the eighteenth century that Jonson felt malice toward Sh. Part of the argument touches on Sh's classicism: e.g., Sh was, as Webster knew, in a class with Dekker and Heywood--capable of "copious industry" [i.e., scholarship?]; Jonson did not attack Sh's history plays in the Prologue to Every Man in His Humor; nor did Jonson refer to W.T. IV iv in the slighting remark about the "nest of antiques" in Bartholomew Fair. The last two arguments are not convincing, but Gilchrist's basic contention about Jonson is doubtless correct. DFo

0269. [Gildon, Charles]. "An Essay on the Art, Rise and Progress of the Stage in Greece, Rome and England," The Works of Mr. William Shakespear. Volume the Seventh [Supplemental to Rowe's ed.] (Ln, 1710), pp. i-lxvii. (Reprinted with minor verbal changes in Pope's ed. [1728].)

Gildon traces the evolution of the rules in antiquity and in England to refute those who maintain that greater knowledge of the ancients would have stultified Sh's genius. "In all that pleases [Sh] is exactly conformable to the Rules, tho 'tis evident by his Defects, that he knew nothing of them." "Yet I can never give up his Acquaintance with the Antients, so intirely as Mr. Rowe has done . . ." Gildon argues for Sh's knowledge of Plautus, Ovid, and the Roman historians, interpreting Ben Jonson's famous aphorism as it is commonly interpreted today: to mean that Sh could (and did) read at least some of the Latin poets, though he was never "a perfect Master of either the Latin or Greek Authors." The bulk of the essay explicates Aristotle's Poetics and applies its criteria for tragedy to Sh and to other writers, ancient and modern; there is a brief discourse on comedy near the end of the essay. Gildon refers to or quotes from a large part of the canon, placing this essay among the first specific critiques of Sh. DFo

0270. Gildon, Charles. The Lives and Characters Of the English Dramatick Poets (1699), T-D, pp. 43-47.

In the Lives of Sir William Alexander, Davenant, Ravenscroft, Rymer, and others, Thorn-Drury has found allusions to Sh, some of them relevant here. Munro's excerpts are only from the Life of Sh (see #0380).

0271. [Gildon, Charles]. "Remarks on the Plays of Shakespear"; "Remarks on the Poems of Shakespear," The Works of Mr. William Shakespear. Volume the Seventh [Supplemental to Rowe's ed.] (Ln, 1710), pp. 257-464.

This is the ancestor of all Sh handbooks. It takes F_1 seriatim, providing plot summaries and pointing out beauties in each play. To Gildon "beautiful" means "classical," i.e., conformable to Aristotelian criteria (Horace also is a reference point); and therefore the "Remarks" are a complement to the "Essay" (#0269), which points out Sh's failures to attain Aristotelian standards. Gildon appends a table of "References to the Classic Authors, &c." (pp. 465-472) citing (though not quoting) Greek and Latin passages comparable in subject and beauty to Sh's passages quoted in the "Remarks." Gildon, then, may be termed the father of "Shakespeare Illustrated" in the eighteenth century. Gildon digresses when he chooses, discussing Sh's learning s.v. Errors (he is inclined to grant Sh more than Rowe would), and discoursing on comedy s.v. Wives. The section on the poems is brief and deals with the question of their authenticity as well as with their artistic merits and relationship to antiquity. Gildon does, however, print the Earl of Winchelsea's trans. of Bion's Adonis Idyl as an "illustration" of Venus, and he states that Sinon in Lucr. is evidence of Sh's knowledge of Virgil. DFo

0272. Gillet, Louis. Shakespeare. Paris, 1931, 348 pp. (Reprinted from RH, XXXIX [1930].)

Gillet announces facetiously at the outset "je déteste les opinions originales." This course of lectures written with wit and grace for the general French public, is traditional in its assumptions about Sh's limited classicism: Sh had Ovid, two or three Senecan tragedies, North's Plutarch, Mantuan, a pre-Chapman Homer, and perhaps a bit of Plautus, but no Virgil or other classics. He shrewdly sees that Caesar is "l'arc romain qui ouvre le passage à tout le tragique de Shakespeare," but he dates the play too late (1603) and oddly assumes that Sh gave unattractive Cassius all the denigration of Caesar because he wished the audience to discredit such denigration. On Antony Gillet is more reliable, tracing Sh's creative use of Plutarch, amusingly defending Sh's anachronisms, and pointing out that the play, like Caesar, is really in two parts not five (the division comes between the eclectic panorama of scenes in the early acts and the focus on the lovers in Egypt at the climax and dénouement). Cor. is a monodrama in which the hero stands above the rest of the cast like a statue "où la figure du roi domine des armées de pygmées." This solitude of the protagonist is Sh's major departure from Plutarch, who makes Coriolanus a Patrician among Patricians. Gillet interprets the love plot of Troi. as a comedy of the sexes in which Troilus is set to school to learn the art of love from Cressida, much as Daphnis is schooled in the art of love in Daphnis and Chloe. Gillet offers a wry but appreciative character sketch of Cressida. The war plot with its atmosphere of "tournoi de chanson de geste" is perhaps "moins loin de l'esprit d'Homère que ne le supposeraient certains archéologues." The remarks about Sh's response to the classics in other parts of the canon are scattered and largely incidental. DFo

0273. "Giordano Bruno in England," QR, CXCVI (1902), 483-508. E-S

See especially pp. 501-503 for a denial that Sh's road to Neoplatonism was through Bruno.

0274. Goddard, Harold C. The Meaning of Shakespeare. Chicago UP, 1951, 691 pp.

Goddard is interested in the dramatist only as he appears in his works and is therefore not at pains to establish his cultural antecedents. But he repeatedly suggests Shn themes which have classical roots: one central theme is the conflict between generations, the great theme of Greek tragedy, which appears in 1H.IV, 2H.IV, Romeo, Lear, Ham., and many other plays; again, the Empedoclean dualism of Lear is a classical concept which runs through "all Shakespeare's tragedies." The most important chs. for this Guide are those on the plays on classical themes. At most points Goddard's criticism is restrained and illuminating, but his tendency is to consider too curiously as when he reads into little Lucius the spirit of Brutus' innocence, seduced by clever Cassius, and then constructs symbolic interpretations of the scenes in which Lucius appears. A more thorough immersion in historical criticism might have shown Goddard the artistic principle behind Titus, e.g., but if he does not appreciate the play, at least he admits it to the canon. There is more to praise than to blame in this book.

0275. Godley, A. D. "Senecan Tragedy," English Literature and the Classics, ed. G. S. Gordon (Oxford, 1912), Ch. IX, pp. 228-247. HB SG

A witty essay on Seneca; the remarks about English drama are very brief. Marston and Jonson are Seneca's chief English debtors. Godley is dubious about Sh's direct indebtedness. "Seneca suffers much from being necessarily compared with the great dramas between which he forms a link: let him at least get credit for being that link."

0276. Goethe, Johann Wolfgang von. "Shakespeare Ad Infinitum" (1813-16), Goethe's Literary Essays, ed. J. E. Spingarn (N.Y., 1921), pp. 174-189.

Part II of this famous essay ("Shakespeare und kein Ende"), states Goethe's doctrine of necessity and freedom. The Greek playwrights dramatized a world ruled by Necessity, the modern drama portrays a world on which the individual will may make a mark. Sh's greatness lies in his fusion of the ancient and modern concepts: the individual will comes into conflict with a moral universal and a struggle results within the character. What Goethe says is true primarily for tragedy, it would seem (his examples are drawn from Ham., Macb., Caesar, and Cor.), and as Lowell pointed out in 1870 (#2011) he oversimplifies both Greek and modern drama.

0277. Golding, Louis Thorn. "Golding and Shakespeare," An Elizabethan Puritan: Arthur Golding the Translator of Ovid's Metamorphoses and also of John Calvin's Sermons (N.Y., 1937), Ch. XV, pp. 212-215.

Golding admits that Sh could and did read Ovid in Latin, but asserts that "there is no reason to doubt that his familiarity with the poet's work was gained from Golding's translation." He supports his assertion with traditional evidence: Prospero's "elves of hills" speech and the description of the boar in Venus. He adds the reference to Meta. in Titus IV i, but of course this bit of evidence does not support his assertion--indeed the allusion would probably be to the Latin text of Ovid.

0278. Goldsmith, Robert H. "The Fool of Tradition," Wise Fools in Shakespeare (Michigan State UP, 1955), Ch. I, pp. 1-14.

This introductory ch. traces the licensed fool of Shn drama to Greek culture by way of Erasmus' Praise of Folly; among the Greek precedents are the phallophoroi, the Cynic philosophers (especially Diogenes), Aristophanic truth-telling, and Socratic irony.

0279. Gordon, George. "Shakespeare's English," Society for Pure English, Tract No. 29 (OUP, 1928), pp. 253-276. (Reprinted in Shakespearian Comedy and Other Studies [1944].)

The sixteenth-century "linguistic freedom [which] had at first been an embarrassment became, as wits grew nimbler, the sport of sports." Sh was the greatest student of the game and coined or first recorded a large number of terms, especially from Latin and Greek. He may well have been indebted in this respect to Puttenham, his great predecessor in neology, who, unlike Sh, felt somewhat uneasy playing a game without a rulebook.

0280. Gould, George. The Greek Plays in Their Relations to the Dramatic Unities. Ln, 1883, 20 pp.

Gould examines the canon of Greek tragedy and comedy to demonstrate (sometimes facetiously) that the idea of the unities, especially of time and of place, is and always has been "nothing better than an idle dream." He shows that the Greeks almost never lived up to the rules which Aristotle extrapolated from their plays. His survey is in part a reply to criticism of Sh by Byron (Preface to Sardanapalus) for not adhering to the unities. DFo

0281. Gould, Robert. "The Play-House, a Satyr" (1685), Munro, II, 295-296.

"Homer was blind yet cou'd all Nature see; / Thou wer't unlearn'd, yet knew as much as He!" This is the poem which praises Sh for the way "his God-like Romans rage" and exalts Tim., Temp., and Lear as "vast Images of [Sh's] unbounded mind."

0282. Gray, Henry D[avid]. "Schoolmaster Shakespeare," TLS, February 5, 1931, p. 99.

Gray finds in II ii of Marston's What You Will a parody of L.L.L. The Pedant of Marston's play is a travesty of Sh, who is portrayed as an inadequate Latinist. If Gray is correct, and it is at least possible that he is, then additional support is given to Beeston's famous remark about Sh's having "been in his yonger yeares a Schoolmaster in the Countrey."

0283. Gray, H[enry] David, and Percy Simpson. "Shakespeare or Heminge? A Rejoinder and a Surrejoinder," MLR, XLV (1950), 148-152.

The inconclusive conclusion to a controversy (which originated in MLR, XLII [1947] and continued in ibid., XLIII [1948]) over whom Jonson wished to imply by the castigated figure of Aesop in The Poetaster. Gray nominates Sh, Simpson, Heminge. Gray's argument is (in part) that Aesop, classically a "poet" (in the sense ποιέω) and actor, would be appropriate to the dual rôle Sh played in the Chamberlain's Company. If Gray is correct, we have an early instance of Sh's being characterized by implied identification with a classical figure.

0284. Green, Henry. Shakespeare and the Emblem Writers: An Exposition of their Similarities of Thought and Expression. Ln, 1870, 571 pp. E-S

Green attempts to demonstrate passim that the vividness with which Sh portrays scenes from the classics is traceable to his familiarity with the emblem literature of the sixteenth century, which Green surveys and exemplifies admirably. Ch. VI, section iii (241-301) deals specifically with mythological allusions. The massed evidence in this book will convince the reader that Sh knew the emblem literature, but Green is on less certain ground when he specifies sources for individual descriptions. The frequent implication is that Sh was merely trans lating into words pictures he had seen, and Green leaves little room for the poet's pictorial imagination.

0285. Greg, Walter W. Pastoral Poetry and Pastoral Drama: A Literary Inquiry, With Special Reference to the Pre-Restoration Stage in England. Ln, 1906, 464 pp. E-S

Of the score of scattered references to Sh's participation in the convention, none suggests his direct interest in its classical background. "It was rarely that in his plays Shakespeare showed any inclination to connect himself even remotely with pastoral tradition."

0286. Grey, Zachary. Critical, Historical and Explanatory Notes on Shakespeare with Emendations of the Text and Metre. Ln, 1754, 2 vols., 400, 346 pp.

Grey "cannot but think from his [Sh's] exact imitation of many of the antient poets and historians, (of which there were no tolerable translations in his time,) that his knowledge in that respect cannot reasonably be call'd in question." Grey's knowledge can repeatedly be "call'd in question"; e.g., he thinks that Sh obtained Ham. directly from Saxo and that Dorastus and Fawnia is based on W.T. rather than vice versa. But if Grey displays judgment and knowledge inferior to those of Farmer (e.g.), he compensates by his genial good will in an age of scholarly malice and by an occasional observation of some interest and plausibility (e.g., his suggestion that Temp. I i 20-21 is an echo of Caesar's famous remark to the sea captain that "Caesar and his fortunes" were aboard). As in the case of Douce (#0207) and many other early commentators, Grey's notes are not nearly all on classical analogues, but a good portion are. MnU

0287. Grierson, H. J. C. "The Drama: Tragedy," Cross Currents in English Literature of the XVIIth Century (Ln, 2nd ed., 1958), pp. 96-129.

Only part of this ch. treats Sh. Sh "refrained from giving to his plays any explicit ethical or religious significance--either that of the Christian feeling of his day, or the crude Senecan religious significance, the doctrine of retribution with which some of his fellow-dramatists essayed ...to justify the horrors of which they invited their audience to sup." The absence of ethical bias is one of the chief differences between Sh and the Greek tragedians; Shn tragedy, unlike Aeschylean and Sophoclean, does not seek to justify the ways of gods to men. This thesis demands qualification: Sh may not be as "theological" as the Attic tragedians, but it is difficult to agree that Ham. (e.g.) is not a Senecan play: Claudius' growing awareness of retribution to come and his vain efforts to forestall it are one key to the terror in the play. The same can be said of Macbeth and Richard III. Grierson appears greatly to oversimplify Sh's ethical position.

0288. Griffin, Ernest G. "The Dramatic Chorus in English Literary Theory and Practice," diss (Columbia, 1959). DA, XX (1960), 3726-27.

Ch. I, "The Elizabethan Chorus," distinguishes between Greek and Senecan Choruses, emphasizing the English humanists' preference for the Senecan mode. The early classical tragedies rely heavily on choral ethos, but in the popular drama (Sh, Jonson, Kyd, e.g.) "only vestiges" remain.

0289. Griffith, Mrs. [E.] The Morality of Shakespeare's Drama. Ln, 1775, 528 pp.

The Preface to this work is in part a pastiche culled from Dryden and Pope, defending Sh against the charge of not imitating the ancients. It is Sh's originality which makes him great. MnU

0290. Groom, Bernard. "Shakespeare," The Diction of Poetry from Spenser to Bridges (Toronto UP, 1955), Ch. II, pp. 26-47.

In Groom's judgment Sh does not use mythological tags (Phoebus, Neptune, Diana, Cynthia, Fortune, etc.) for poetic purposes, though he may use them for such dramatic purposes as characterization (e.g., of the Mechanicals in Dream) or to distinguish a set piece (prologues, Bleeding Sergeant speech, "rugged Pyrrhus" speech) from the rest of the play. Groom also mentions the aureate diction of Troi. as a striking feature of the play.

0291. Guicharnaud, Jacques. "Voltaire and Shakespeare," LHM, XXVII (1956), 159-169.

An introductory, but informed and fluent discussion of Voltaire's reaction to Sh as colored by his own sense of classicism. Of the comments M. Guicharnaud makes, perhaps the most observant is that Voltaire chose Caesar to adapt because "the subject is Roman and thus is akin to the catalogue of traditional subjects of French tragedy." Despite Voltaire's horror at Sh's unclassical irregularity, he must be considered the first in a succession of French critics which finally, in the twentieth century, has arrived at an understanding of the unities subtle enough to allow them to appreciate Sh.

0292. H. "Shakespeare's Favorite Latin Author," PL, I (1889), 323-324.

An appreciation of some similarities and differences between Sh and Ovid, but it is unfortunately full of misinformation: e.g., "of all that he learned at school, his Ovid alone is traceable." H. implies that Brinsley taught Sh at Stratford and that Sh definitely left two years before completion of his studies. The art. is entirely unreliable.

0293. H., J. "Plato and Shakespeare," Ath, No. 2299 (1871), 664.

A suggestion that Sh's knowledge of the Platonic doctrine of music of the spheres may have come through Montaigne's Essais, Book I.

0294. Haight, Elizabeth Hazelton. "Shakspeare's Fatalism," VM, XXIII (1894), 379-386.

A general comment on Sh's portrayal of man as "master of his fate" under the watchful eye of an inscrutable Providence. In this portrayal Sh is more like Sophocles than like Aeschylus, who visualizes Fate as "external power, blind, relentless, and swift." The essay treats Sh developmentally, discussing the histories, dark comedies, tragedies, and last plays. MH

0295. Hales, John W. "Shakespeare's Greek Names," Notes and Essays On Shakespeare (Ln, 1884), Ch. IV, pp. 105-119. (Reprinted from the Cornhill Magazine, February, 1876, pp. 208-216.)

Hales discusses the roots of some of Sh's Greek names to show their significance for the interpretation of the characters who bear them. Ophelia, "ὠφελία," "the helper," is, of course, ironic; Autolycus, "αὐτόλυκος," "wolf's self," preys on the unwary; Desdemona, "δυσδαίμων," or "δυσδαιμονία," "ill-starred," is an innocent victim of circumstances; Sycorax, "σῦς" + "κόραξ," "swine-raven," is an evil and filthy witch; Apemantus, "ἀπήμαντος," the uninjured one," has not been hurt the way Timon has. Hales wisely does not claim that these five names are evidence of Sh's Hellenism; it is to be noted that there are other Greek names in Sh which do not fit the pattern.

0296. Hales, J. W. "Shakspeare's Pastoral Names," Acad, V (1874), 37.

This note suggests that Spenser, who called Sh "Aetion" in Colin Clout's Come Home Again, and Henry Chettle, who called him "Melicert" in England's Mourning Garment (1603), both were ignoring whatever pastoral or other uses the names had been put to before; each was drawing on the Greek etymology of the name to make his compliment. "Aetion" = "The Eaglet"; "Melicert" = "honey-honeycomb" [from μέλι and κηρός]. Correspondents J. A. Symonds and W. Minto respectively advance (ibid., pp. 94-95) (1) the possibility that Chettle was recalling the honorific surname Μελικέρτης given Simonides by the Greeks and (2) that "Aetion" is not Sh, but Drayton.

0297. Hallam, Henry. Introduction to the Literature of Europe in the Fifteenth, Sixteenth, and Seventeenth Centuries, 3 vols. 3rd ed., Ln, 1847. See II, 175-186; III, 80-94.

Hallam must be approached with caution, first because his critical sensibilities leave much to be desired and second because he accepts disintegration and an inaccurate chronology of the canon. But he offers occasional insights: e.g., he praises Farmer for deflating Warburton on "Sh's Sophocles," and he has at the same time the sense to recognize from Sh's Latinisms in Dream that he knew Latin fairly well (though he credits him with a dictionary knowledge, not a literary one). Sh had no Greek, however; apparently Hallam suffers from the misapprehension that Greek was a rarity in Elizabethan England. There are a large number of brief comments on Sh's use of classical materials.

0298. Halliday, F. E. Shakespeare: A Pictorial Biography. N.Y., 1956, 147 pp.

Like Halliday's other books, this is both sensible and readable. The chief merit is in the beautiful photography, but Halliday tells the common reader that "it is high time that the mischievous conception of Shakespeare as an inspired peasant was finally dispelled." He mentions the Stratford curriculum only briefly: "With the aid of Lily's Latin Grammar he would work his way through the easy classics, fall in love with Ovid, read some Virgil, and perhaps some of the comedies of Plautus and tragedies of Seneca."

0299. Halliwell[-Phillipps], J[ames] O., ed., The Remarks of M. Karl Simrock on the Plots of Shakespeare's Plays. Ln, 1850, 144 pp. E-S [for the original German ed.]

In his commentary on Sh's sources Simrock explores analogues in a very large range of oriental, Germanic, and classical literatures, to the annoyance of Halliwell-Phillipps, who repeatedly criticizes Simrock's digressions, not always justly. About half of the canon is represented in this anonymous trans., and for most of this half Simrock has something to say of the classics. Some of his parallels are frequently encountered in other commentators (e.g., Ham. and the story of L. J. Brutus; Romeo and the tales of Hero and Leander and Pyramus and Thisbe). But elsewhere Simrock can teach us something about Sh's re-use of his own early work (Collatine's praise of Lucrece's chastity foreshadows the chastity wager in Cym.; Abbess Emilia is discovered at Ephesus, as is Priestess Thaisa). Simrock also discusses Roman commercial law as a precedent to Shylock's bond; he finds a parallel between the sword of Damocles and Sly's bewilderment; he thinks Sh may have drawn the rivalry between Goneril and Regan for the love of evil Edmund from Livy's story of the rivalry between the daughters of Servius Tullius for the love of evil Tarquin. This is a stimulating book. MnU

0300. Halpin, Nicholas J. The Dramatic Unities of Shakespeare: A Letter Addressed to the Editor of Blackwood's Edinburgh Magazine. Dublin, 1849, 57 pp.

Halpin thinks that after Sh had examined the chaos of native English dramatic form and the unreasonable limitation, especially of time, in classical theory, he devised his own system of unity which he adheres to so strictly that it can be used as an authorship test. Instead of the arbitrary classical maximum of three, six, or twenty-four hours, Sh adopted a time scheme which is always within the limits of the unbroken attention of the audience (ca. fifty hours

[sic]). As to place: space and time are in Sh coordinates on the same graph—no one travels farther than his (ca.) fifty hours will permit (it is not clear how Halpin would explain Antony's grand tour of the Mediterranean Sea). As to action, Sh merely adheres to an ancient principle in "unity of fable." Halpin illustrates his thesis with an extended analysis of Merch. He believes that Sh perhaps had direct access to Greek literature, hinting that he has proof of Sh's attendance at one or both universities (proof which apparently has never appeared in print). But, he adds, even if Sh did not read the Greeks he would have learned their conception of unity from Sidney's Apologie. MnU

0301. Hamilton, Richard Winter. "The Classical Comedy Compared with that of Shakspeare," Nugae Literariae: Prose and Verse (Ln, 1841), pp. 237-287.

"The peculiarity of Shakspeare's Comedy does not easily admit of comparison with the ancient, because it is often introduced into his tragedies." The few points of contact in this essay are contrasts: e.g., Sh's romantic heroines are moral as Aristophanes' Thesmophoriazusae and Ecclesiazusae are not; Parolles is perhaps superior to the miles gloriosus and thraso; the fairies in Dream occupy a middle region between man and God which the Greeks could not dramatize on the stage (they had to bring their gods themselves on the scene). The discussions of Aristophanes, Lucian, and Plautus are superior to the somewhat effusive treatment of Sh. Hamilton treats briefly inter alia Caliban, the Fool in Lear (with other serio-comic characters), and satirists like Casca and Apemantus. Falstaff is given extended appreciation. DFo

0302. Hammerle, Karl. "Das Fortunamotiv von Chaucer bis Bacon," Anglia, LXV (1940), 87-100. GRS

In passing, Hammerle points out that in Aaron's soliloquy (Titus II i) Sh is imitating Marlowe whose Machiavellian characters think themselves above Fortuna's power. In a later passage he adds that Sh always keeps Fortuna in the wings--she never appears personified because Sh's "Charakterprobleme haben das Fortunaproblem verdrängt." At the beginning of the art. Hammerle gives a brief but informative account of Fortuna in Pliny, Boethius, and their Medieval inheritors.

0303. Hanford, James H. "Suicide in the Plays of Shakespeare," PMLA, XXVII (1912), 380-397.

Hanford attacks the position of Churton Collins (#0173) that Sh shared with Sophocles a derogation of suicide. This art. seeks to demonstrate that for dramatic purposes Sh envelops suicide with an aura of dignity, of unbreakable spirit. This is especially true in the Roman plays where Sh has historical warrant and his knowledge of Roman philosophy to justify his presentation of self-destruction; but even in the "Christian" plays (especially Romeo and Oth.) Sh asks us to suspend our Christian morality in Act V in favor of a pagan ethic which motivates the "great of heart" to take their "own way." What Sh thought it is vain to seek; in his art, suicide is noble, if pagan. Hanford's limitation is in assuming that Sh's suicides are all presented in the same light; see #0307 for some cogent distinctions.

0304. Hankins, John E. "Misanthropy in Shakespeare," The Character of Hamlet and Other Essays (North Carolina UP, 1941), pp. 115-130.

The misanthropy of Sh's melancholics often takes the form of loathing for the lust they see in bestial man (Hamlet, Lear, Thersites, Timon). This identification of bestiality and carnal impulse Sh would have found in the Nicomachean Ethics which he could have read in Latin or in Wilkinson's trans., The Ethiques of Aristotle (1547). For a more complete statement on bestiality in Sh, see #2223.

0305. Hankins, John E. "The Pains of the Afterworld: Fire, Wind, and Ice in Milton and Shakespeare," PMLA, LXXI (1956), 482-495.

Sh's conception of punishment after death, unlike Milton's, includes purgatory, referred to certainly in Ham. and Meas. and possibly in W.T. But his vision of purgation is not entirely Christian; it is indebted to Aeneid VI where Virgil distinguishes between the hopeless souls in Tartarus and those being purged, and to Plutarch's "Vision of Thespesius" in De Tarditate Justiciae Divinae (XXII), an even closer approximation to Christian conceptions. Hankins suggests that purgatory was allowed on the stage only if adequately pagan (i.e., classical) and ergo Sh clothed a Christian concept in its classical analogues.

0306. Hankins, John E. Shakespeare's Derived Imagery. Kansas UP, 1953, 289 pp.

Beginning with T. W. Baldwin's evidence that Sh knew Palingenius' Zodiacus Vitae as a grammar text, Hankins proceeds to amass an awesome number of parallels of thought and phrase between Sh's works and both the Latin and Barnaby Googe's English rendering, which Sh probably used as a translation-aid in school. As the author admits, not all the parallels are compelling, but the cumulative effect of the inductive method is convincing, as it is, for example, in Green's Shakespeare and the Emblem Writers (#0284). Hankins concludes that Palingenius was a primary source for some twenty of Sh's favorite image clusters and that Sh, who had an amazingly retentive memory for words and phrases, characteristically reinforced his verbal conception by associative recollection from other sources: frequently the Bible and La Primaudaye's The French Academy. Hankins would have us revise our conception of poetic invention: "Clever inventiveness is not the sole measure of poetic genius. To clarify, sharpen, enrich, and transfer the thoughts of others is an achievement of equal value." The whole book is an interesting and learned study, but of particular interest are Chs. II ("All the World's A Stage"), IV ("Brief Candle"), and VII ("Mental Sickness").

0307. Hankins, John E. "Suicide in Shakespeare," The Character of Hamlet and Other Essays (North Carolina UP, 1941), pp. 222-239.

An interesting classification of Sh's suicides under four headings: (1) "suicide of desperation" (Portia, Ophelia, Goneril, Lady Macbeth, etc.); (2) "suicide to escape earthly ills" (Cassius and Lucrece, successful; Hamlet, Macbeth, and Imogen, contemplated); (3) "suicide of principle," including self-judgment (Othello, Brutus, Enobarbus, Cato); (4) "suicide of friendship" (Antony, Cleopatra, Romeo, Juliet, Titinius, Eros, successful; Horatio, attempted). For Sh's portrayal and attitude there is classical as well as Christian precedent: among classical authorities are Ovid (Meta. is full of suicides for love), Aristotle, Plato, and Cicero (who disapprove), Seneca (who urges (2)), Plutarch (Moralia), and Virgil.

0308. Hapgood, Robert Derry. "A Rebirth of Tragedy: Ritual as Matrix and Element in Shakespeare's Early Tragedies," diss (California, Berkeley, 1956).*

It is presumed that in this diss Shn "rebirth of tragedy" implies the original Greek "birth" and that Sh's "ritual" is made parallel to Greek religion.

0309. Harding, Davis P. "Shakespeare the Elizabethan," Shakespeare: Of an Age and for All Time, The Yale Shakespeare Festival Lectures ([Hamden, Conn.], 1954), pp. 11-32.

This imaginative reconstruction of an apprentice's afternoon at the Globe makes the estimate that at least half the audience would have had a grammar school education, equipping them better than any modern audience to listen to and judge prosody, rhetoric, and meaning.

0310. Harmon, Alice. "How Great was Shakespeare's Debt to Montaigne?" PMLA, LVII (1942), 988-1008.

In a vigorous and well-documented attack on the parallel passage method of "influence grafting," the author shows that Sh had no need to search Florio's Montaigne for the sententious philosophizing in Ham. and Meas. (especially) on such subjects as death, glory, the nature of man, and idleness. Most of the thought is Stoic, ultimately traceable to Seneca, Plutarch, and other classical Stoics, and all of it appears in innumerable anthologies of aphoristic wisdom drawn from the ancients. These florilegia, some of them in English trans., were immensely popular in the sixteenth century. Sh doubtless searched out some of these "places" in classical authors in school, but even had he not done so, he would have found the material without culling Montaigne.

0311. Harrington, Karl Pomeroy. Catullus and His Influence, Our Debt, [No. 11] (Boston, 1923), 245 pp.

See especially pp. 153-156 for the assertion that Sh had enough Latin to read Catullus. Harrington follows McNaghten (#0416) in comparing the Dark Lady of Sonn. to Lesbia. Almost all of the putative echoes of Catullus became commonplaces long before Sh wrote (e.g., marriage as an elm encircled by a vine), but Harrington emphasizes the spiritual affinity of the two love poets.

0312. Harrison, G. B., ed. Shakespeare: The Complete Works. N.Y.: Harcourt Brace, 1948/1952, 1666 pp.

This ed. is intended for college students. Neither the long General Introduction nor the informative Appendices make mention of Sh's probable education or of the rôle of the classics in Elizabethan life. But the full introductions to the individual plays and poems indicate that Sh knew some classics (Plautus, Plutarch, Ovid, etc.), sometimes in Latin (see introduction to Errors), and that he knew how to manipulate classical concepts (see, e.g., the discussion of the rôle of Apollo in W.T.). Harrison's detailed summaries of the content of Sh's sources are very helpful.

0313. Harrison, James A. "Shakespeare as a Foreign Linguist," Shna, I (1884), 148-149.

"Considering the extent of his works and the Latinized taste of the age, the poet was exceedingly sparing of his use of scraps of Latinity." Such scraps as there are are these: some eighty single words, twenty-one quotations from Latin literature, twenty-two proverbs, and eighteen apparently original phrases. Of Greek there are only two words, misanthropos and threnos. Harrison has overlooked Sh's Latinate English diction.

0314. Harrison, Thomas P., Jr. "Aspects of Primitivism in Shakespeare and Spenser," TSE, XX (1940), 39-71.

To Ovid, the primitive life is "delectable"; to Lucretius it is "grim": Harrison compares the responses of Sh and Spenser to this classical paradox, which is related to such Renaissance concepts as the Nature/Art dichotomy, pastoralism, and the idea of the beast in man. Sh's attitudes appear to be more Lucretian than Ovidian, despite his obvious interest in Ovid. At many points Sh's ideas closely parallel those of Spenser, and Harrison is inclined to think that FQ may have been an influence on Shn primitivism, though he does not insist on the point. Act IV of W.T., Temp., the cave scenes in Cym., Act IV of Tim., and, to a lesser extent, Lear and A.Y.L. are Harrison's materials. This is an interesting study, but Harrison only hints at the distinction between the georgic tradition and the pastoral tradition in Temp., a distinction at the heart of Sh's true attitude toward primitivism.

0315. Harrison, Thomas P., Jr. "Shakespeare and Marlowe's Dido, Queen of Carthage," TSE, XXXV (1956), 57-63.

Sh found in Marlowe's play "hints for two lines--in Hamlet and in Macbeth--suggesting the violence of martial exploit; its poetic luxuriance and erotic plot are reflected in A Midsummer Night's Dream; it anticipates Antony and Cleopatra in the famous Cydnus passage and in the management of nonclassical situations involving the protagonists." Marlowe probably also drew on Plutarch in his Dido, but the large number of echoes of Dido in Antony indicate that Sh remembered Marlowe's play.

0316. Hart, Walter Morris. "High Comedy in the Odyssey," CUPCP, XII, No. 14 (1943), 263-278.

Hart finds the center of high comedy in Homer at the same place it appears in Sh: in the relationships between men and women who confront one another as equals. The ironic possibilities of the relationships between Telemachus and Helen, Odysseus and Nausicaa, and Odysseus and Athene are exactly those of the relationships between Benedick and Beatrice, Rosalind and Orlando, Viola and Orsino, Perdita and Florizel, and (Hart might have added) Miranda and Ferdinand. It could also have been noted that the relationship between Imogen and Posthumus is something like that of Penelope and Odysseus. Hart also sees Polonius as much like garrulous Nestor, and the "duel" between Sir Andrew and Viola is reminiscent of the "duel" between Odysseus and Irus. Hart does not imply indebtedness, contenting himself with classing Homer and Sh together as masters of the vis comica.

0317. Hawkes, Terry. "Ficino and Shakespeare," NQ, CCIII (1958), 185-186.

Hawkes believes that the problem of Sh's potential access to Ficino's writings may possibly be solved by his discovery that a very popular book on letter-writing (seven eds. between 1568 and 1621) contains trans. of some of Ficino's Epistles. Hawkes does not take into consideration either Sh's Latinity or the possibility of indirect influence.

0318. Haydn, Hiram. "Shakespeare and the Counter-Renaissance," The Counter-Renaissance (N.Y., 1950), Ch. X, pp. 619-671.

This ch., on Sh's four great tragedies, is preceded by a section on Sh and the various Elizabethan attitudes toward honor (in 1H.IV, Tim., Troi.). Haydn equates "Renaissance" with that humanism which accepted the Platonic-Aristotelian concept of the ethical mean and tempered it with Christian warmth; the "counter-Renaissance" consisted of the extreme ethical positions (Machiavellianism, doctrinaire Stoicism, Epicureanism) which would defeat a moderate approach to life. Sh seems as elusive to Haydn as to any other objective student of the history of ideas, but it is noteworthy that the men of the counter-Renaissance assume the villains' postures in his plays. One can at least say that Sh makes dramatic capital out of conflicts between the ethical values of Christian humanism and those of the counter-Renaissance. The most stimulating analyses are of Ham. (a most satisfying reading of the play as focused on conflicting approaches to honor) and of Troi. (again on the honor theme). On Lear (the conflict between doctrinaire Stoicism and Epicureanism with a mean in Ciceronian Stoicism) Haydn is less original, and the briefer remarks about Oth. and Macb. are distinctly inferior. The total effect of this cultural study is, however, impressive.

0319. Heninger, S. K., Jr. "The Heart's Meteors, A Microcosm:Macrocosm Analogy," SQ, VII (1956), 273-275.

Notes on Renaissance (ultimately Aristotelian) concepts of meteorology, which Sh in a number of plays draws on for analogy with psychological states. As the sky shows certain "exhalations" and vapors drawn up from the earth, the human face makes manifest the emotional states drawn up from the lower parts of the body. For an extension of the concept in L.L.L., see Expl, XVI (1958), item 49.

0320. Hense, C[arl] C[onrad]. "John Lilly und Shakespeare. I. Lilly und Shakespeare in ihrem Verhältniss zum klassischen Alterthum," ShJ, VII (1872), 238-300. E-S HB

"Mit Ausnahme der allegorischen Behandlung finden wir bei ihm [Sh] ähnliche Beziehungen zum klassischen Alterthum, wie wir bei Lilly fanden": (1) a preference for Roman poets (especially Virgil and Ovid) over Greek; (2) anachronistic use of mythology, blending Christian and pagan, ancient and modern. Hense provides numerous illustrations of Sh's use of Ovid, some of them seldom noticed by scholars; there are also several indications of Sh's borrowing from Virgil. Hense goes on to discuss Sh's Senecanism (e.g., Imogen's curse on Pisanio in Cym. IV ii 312-314 is an allusion to Hecuba's curse on the Greeks in Seneca's Troades). Though Sh does not use mythology for topical allegory in Lyly's manner, he does include some topicalities in his plays, and he sees moral significance in classical legend and history. Hense also discusses the use of Latin quotations in Lyly and Sh. In the final analysis, "für ihn [Sh] war alles, was er aus dem klassischen Alterthum kannte, nur Stoff, nur Material, dem er das originale Gepräge seines Geistes, seiner Composition aufdrückt, das er mit souveräner, eigenartiger Behandlung aufnahm und ausbildete." This is a valuable commentary on Sh's classicism, as on Lyly's; it contains a great many intelligent observations on individual passages in both dramatists.

0321. Hense, C[arl] C[onrad]. "Polymythie in dramatischen Dichtungen Shakespeares," ShJ, XI (1876), 245-273. (Reprinted in Shakespeare: Untersuchungen und Studien [1884].)

Hense contrasts Sophoclean unity of action with the multiplicity which enables Sh to use self-parody, mirror-scenes, ironic contrast, and thematic parallels. Sh can broaden the horizon of his drama as much by this "Polymythie" as by the Italian or classical settings he often chooses. Hense comments on much of the canon by way of illustration.

0322. Hense, Carl Conrad. "Shakespeares Naturanschauung," Shakespeare: Untersuchungen und Studien (Halle, 1884), pp. 317-372. (Reprinted from Morgenblatt für gebildete Leser [Stuttgart, 1865, Nos. 49-52].)

Two major passages in this essay explore parallels between Shn use of nature and classical practice: (1) pp. 326-332—unselfconscious comparison between men and animals; (2) pp. 349-355--personification of nature as a method of myth-making. Hense seldom suggests indebtedness (although he points out sources in Ovid for Sh's frequent analogies between men and dogs). The scores of classical examples are more often Greek (Homer, Pindar, Aeschylus, Sophocles, Aristophanes, Euripides, Alcaeus, e.g.) than Roman, though citations to Horace, Ovid, and Virgil are common enough. The number of Shn citations is large, and embraces much of the canon. Hense does not, perhaps, make a sufficiently sharp distinction between Sh's largely rhetorical use of these two devices and the more literal intention of the ancients; but this essay throws considerable light on Sh's dramatic practice--it deserves to be more widely known. DFo

0323. Heraud, John A. Shakspere: His Inner Life as Intimated in his Works. Ln, 1865, 521 pp.

Heraud expresses the opinion (pp. 198 *et passim*) that Sh "must take his place among the most learned poets of the world. His mind was pervaded with examples from Greek and Roman literature, and from the more modern Italian poets, all of them subsisting on classic food and abounding in learned references ..." But

Heraud seldom offers any evidence to support this assertion, and when he does, the "classic food" is likely to be a commonplace (e.g., Falstaff's "Diana's foresters") or generalized (the "Aristophanic" word play of L.L.L.). The book is not a reliable guide to Sh's response to classicism or to other Sh problems. DFo

0324. Herpich, Charles A. "Marlowe and Shakespeare," 10 NQ, I (1904), 1-2.

Herpich adduces almost a score of verbal echoes of Hero and Leander in Sh's early plays and especially poems. Of the most striking, several are classical allusions (e.g., the epithet "rose-cheeked" for Adonis). Some of Sh's classicism appears to have been ready-made.

0325. Herpich, Cha[rle]s A. "'Much Ado,' II.i. 263.--" NewShna, V (1906), 135-137.

In response to a query, Herpich explains Sh's knowledge of the goddess Até (Much, L.L.L., John, Caesar) as acquired from Greene's Friar Bacon and Friar Bungay. Her total absence from Latin literature is one argument (but it is noteworthy that in Appian's Greek she does appear, and Sh probably used Appian in trans. for Caesar and Antony). But the most important evidence is that Greene is also probably Sh's source for the confusion in L.L.L. and Per. between the daughters of Hesperus and the garden they guarded. It is possible also that the "black Hecate" of Macb. is based on Greene's play. Herpich seems to have a valid argument.

0326. Herpich, Cha[rle]s A. "Shakespeare, Ben Jonson, and Pliny," PC, LXXXIII (1905), 120.

A communication which points out the parallel between Heminge and Condell's Epistle Dedicatory to F_1 and the Preface to Pliny's Naturalis Historia; the parallel was recorded in Baconiana [and in NewShna, see #0459]. Since, it is argued, Holland's 1601 trans. of the Latin does not resemble the phrasing in the Epistle, whoever wrote the Epistle must have read Pliny in Latin (Heminge and Condell, presumably, could not qualify). Herpich observes that Jonson might be a candidate.

0327. Hewitt, Joseph W. "Some Aspects of the Treatment of Ingratitude in Greek and English Literature," TAPA, XLVIII (1917), 37-48.

The title is slightly misleading, since Latin literature is also discussed and Sh is almost the only English writer mentioned. The attempt is to contrast Greek and Shn attitudes: Sh makes a great evil of ingratitude by extending its scope to include vices (such as filial impiety or political injustice) which the Greeks kept discrete. Hewitt makes some interesting points: e.g., Seneca classed Pompey and Coriolanus among those ungrateful to a beneficent state while Sh portrayed the state as ungrateful to them, its benefactors. There are many references to the morality of gratitude in Twel., T.G.V., Lear, Tim., etc. The commentary ends with an interesting brief contrast between Lear's demand for gratitude from his children and Oedipus' emphasis on filial duty (at Colonus).

0328. Hickman, Ruby Mildred. "Ghosts in Later World Literature," Ghostly Etiquette on the Classical Stage (Cedar Rapids, Ia., 1938), pp. 161-208. GRS

"Shakespeare in particular [among Renaissance dramatists] shows the effect of this [i.e., Senecan] influence, as do also Dryden, Chapman, and Kyd." The body of the ch. is a presentation in tabular form of the uses made of ghosts by various dramatists. Sh is represented by 2H.VI, R.III, Caesar, Ham., and Macb. The notes contain some odd statements: e.g., Gertrude "was a partner in the crime [of murder]"; "Banquo's ghost is a silent spirit, being only the figment of Macbeth's imagination." The author does not specify Sh's debt to Seneca; this part of the book contains more statistics than criticism.

0329. Highet, Gilbert. "Shakespeare's Classics," The Classical Tradition: Greek and Roman Influences on Western Literature (OUP, 1949), Ch. XI, pp. 194-218.

Though he thinks that Jonson's remark about Sh's Latinity should be taken absolutely, not comparatively, Highet emphasizes that no one in the Renaissance responded more beautifully to the stimulus of classical culture than Sh. Of Sh's interests (Renaissance Europe, English history, the classical world) the third is not the least. Highet discusses Sh's use of Ovid, Seneca, Plutarch, and Plautus, at all times showing familiarity with the opinions of his predecessors. He is particularly wise in accepting and incorporating the findings of Baldwin on Sh's education, though Baldwin leaves the impression of a more literate Sh than Highet does. This ch. and its notes are a useful general introduction to Sh's classicism, but they have limitations: e.g., it is puzzling and annoying to find Plutarch referred to as "a second-rate Greek historian" and North dismissed as an inaccurate translator and bungling stylist.

0330. Hill, A. A. "Ilium, the Palace of Priam," MP, XXX (1932), 94-96.

Sh commits the common Renaissance error of identifying the palace of Priam by the name "Ilium," reserving the word "Troy" for the city. This unclassical distinction is traceable to Benoît de Ste. Maure, who uses this name for the palace in his description, greatly expanded from Dares Phrygius. Benoît's "error" was doubtless deliberate, and it endured until the closing of the theaters, after which more and better trans. of the classics restored the ancient usage.

0331. Hill, R. F. "Shakespeare's Early Tragic Mode," SQ, IX (1958), 455-469.

This astute analysis of Sh's use of rhetoric to convey intense emotion concentrates on 2H.VI, R.II, R.III, Titus, and Romeo. Citing Coleridge's belief that "quibbling is the natural expression of the human mind in deep passion," Hill justifies the elaborated rhetoric of the characters in the Yorkist tetralogy and R.II as a legitimate means of expressing emotion. He traces the "mode" confidently to Seneca (probably in Latin, since in the Tenne Tragedies "the subtler details of wordplay are lost in the rumbling fourteeners"). If the early histories, Titus, and Romeo fail, it is not because rhetorical tragedy is not a valid genre but because Sh consciously or unconsciously blended with it the native tradition of conversational speech, horseplay, and bawdy. The incongruity of the native and Senecan elements perhaps was his reason for abandoning rhetorical tragedy permanently after Romeo. An intelligent study, but Hill has neglected the possible influence of Ovid (on Titus and Romeo) and of grammar school rhetorical exercises (on the histories).

0332. Hirzel, Rudolf. "Engländer: Shakespeare, Bacon, Dryden," Plutarch, Erbe, IV (Leipzig, 1912), pp. 139-150. E-S SG

Hirzel was among the first to argue that Sh read widely in the Lives and drew on them outside the Roman plays; he begins his brief (pp. 140-145) but cogent discussion of Sh's use of Plutarch with evidence that "Shakespeare mag leicht alle Plutarchbiographien gelesen haben." He also defends Sh against charges of having misunderstood and misused Plutarch. The modern reader will not concur when Hirzel argues that Antony's oration owes more to Plutarch than to Appian, but otherwise this is a valuable essay, concerned more with Sh's use of Plutarch's ideas than with his use of North's prose. DLC

0333. An Historicall History of England and Wales in three parts (1692), Munro Sup, No. 77, pp. 537-538.

The passage on Sh in this book is plagiarized from Fuller (#0257), as Munro's note points out.

0334. Holzknecht, Karl J. "Shakespeare's English," The Backgrounds of Shakespeare's Plays (N.Y., 1950), pp. 186-219.

There are references to the influence of Latin diction and usage passim, but see especially the sections labeled "Coinage of Words" and "Native and Foreign Words." Holzknecht's method is to provide a multiplicity of illustrations; his most cogent suggestion is that Sh coined fewer abortions than the most fertile of his contemporaries while coining more surviving heirs than any of them (except the translators of the Authorized Version).

0335. Holzknecht, Karl J. "The Sources of Shakespeare's Plays," The Backgrounds of Shakespeare's Plays (N.Y., 1950), pp. 220-246.

A general, but factual, survey which concludes with a very useful brief statement for each of the thirty-seven plays, naming the source(s) and discussing Sh's manipulation of them. Holzknecht's general attitude is that "it cannot be said that mere respect for his sources very often checked [Sh's] sense of dramatic effect. He read always with the eye of a dramatist interested in character expressing itself in action." There is an excellent brief discussion of Caesar as telescoped Plutarch and many other observations about Sh's use of classical sources. Some of Holzknecht's comments are derivative: the remarks about Sh's reading on pp. 228-229 owe an unacknowledged debt to Attwater (#0080, p. 238).

0336. Honigmann, E. A. J. "Shakespeare's 'Lost Source-Plays'," MLR, XLIX (1954), 293-307.

A tightly constructed argument against the position of Dover Wilson and Malone's other twentieth-century inheritors that Sh was a reviser of earlier plays now lost. Honigmann makes his most vigorous assault on the thesis of Wilson's art. on "Malone and the Upstart Crow" (#1116), but he does not reverse Wilson's evidence completely. There are discussions of putative lost source-plays for nine Shn plays of which only Titus and Shrew have any special relevance to the (possible) classical background.

0337. Hoskins, Frank L. "Shakespeare and the Prodigious Page Tradition," RenP, 1957, pp. 106-110.

Sh's pages in L.L.L., 2H.IV, Wives, H.V, and Tim. are in a tradition of witty, precocious pages which Richard Edwards initiated when he adapted the slave of Roman comedy to the English stage in Damon and Pithias. Lyly fostered the convention, and Sh follows Lyly, but not blindly: Sh always lends his pages individuality. DFo

0338. Hower, Charles C. "The Importance of a Knowledge of Latin for Understanding the Language of Shakespeare," CJ, XLVI (1951), 221-227.

An extension of Edith Claflin's evidence (#0165) that Sh's language is an index of his Latinity. Hower gives etymological explanations of the meanings of some ten obsolete Latinate words in Sh (e.g., "festinate"), discusses another twenty which have changed in meaning radically since 1600, analyzes some of Sh's Latin puns (e.g., "and why indeed Naso, but for smelling out the odoriferous flowers of fancy ..."), and ends with a discussion of typical figures of Latin style which Sh adapted to English: chiasmus, proleptic epithet, hendiadys, correlative repetition ("or ... or"; "aut ... aut").

0339. Hubbell, Lindley Williams. "Shakespeare and Classic Drama," Jimbungaku, No. 48 (July, 1960), 1-87.

Not seen.

0340. Hugo, Victor. "Shakespeare l'ancien," William Shakespeare (Paris, 1864), Livre IV, pp. 161-224. Trans. several times, e.g., in Anderson Baten, The Philosophy of Shakespeare (Kingsport, Tenn., 1937).

Hugo's rambling but vivid essay is chiefly on Aeschylus, who is the ancient Sh. The parallels with Sh are few and scattered. Both were innovators in the drama, the works of both nearly perished through the callousness of their barbarian successors (Hugo is unaware of the publication of F_2, F_3, and F_4 in the seventeenth century), and both were men of genius, though Hugo does not define the concept in terms of Aeschylus' works, nor of Sh's.

0341. Hunter, Joseph. New Illustrations of the Life, Studies, and Writings of Shakespeare. Supplementary to all the Editions. 2 vols., Ln, 1845, 425, 373 pp.

Despite his title, Hunter deprecates "Shakespeare illustrated" unless the passages placed in parallel can actually be shown to have influenced Sh. There are only a handful of brief references to classical authors: Pliny as source for Othello's lines on the Pontic Sea; Ovid and Virgil as source for Prospero's "elves of hills" speech; Proclus and Hippocrates as analogues to Jaques on the division of life into ages. DFo

0342. Ichikawa, Sanki. "A Few Notes on the Rhetoric of Shakespeare," SEL(T), XV (1935), 317-324.

Not seen.

0343. Isaacs, J. "Shakespeare and his World: Sources of Shakespeare's Plays," The Listener, XLII (1949), 183-184, 199.

"We need more sources, for in that way we shall get more Shakespeare." This survey of Sh's chief sources suggests that we can learn most about Sh's mind and art by observing his manipulation of source material; e.g., Sh felt no obligation to Plutarch--he chose ruthlessly what he wished and added to it (the language of love to Enobarbus' description of Cleopatra at Cydnus, for example). Perhaps "To be or not to be" is indebted to Cicero.

0344. J., W. H. "Swan Signifying Poet: 'Swan Song'," NQ, CLXXVII (1939), 311-313.

Jonson's F_1 lines, "Sweet Swan of Avon ..." provoke a detailed survey of loci classici on singing swans: "in Jonson's day people were expected to understand that a swan meant a poet." At ibid., pp. 353-354, Hibernicus supplies an impressive catalogue of supplemental references which include "three [unspecified] places in Shakespeare" (doubtless John V vii 20-24, Oth. V ii 247-248, Merch. III ii 44-45).

0345. Jackson, Henry. "Lecture on Shakespeare: Was Shakspere of Stratford the Author of Shakespeare's Plays and Poems?" (1912), Henry Jackson, O.M. ...A Memoir, ed. R. St. John Parry (CUP, 1926), pp. 272-289.

Jackson's genial refutation of the anti-Stratfordians (especially George Greenwood) argues: (1) that Sh of Stratford would not be so ignorant as Baconians claim; (2) that the plays and poems are not so immensely learned as we (who know the classics less well than the Renaissance did) are likely to assume. The logic is excellent, the tone restrained, and the factual data nearly all correct. Jackson believes that Latin was a living language which Sh, like other men of his time, would not forget once he had learned it in school.

0346. Jacobsen, Eric. "'Amphytrio' [sic] or 'Jack Juggler'," TLS, January 4, 1957, p. 9.

Jacobsen reviews and resolves a controversy which began when R. R. Bolgar (#0113) mistook Jack Juggler for a trans. of Plautus' Amphitruo and claimed to have discovered a Plautine trans. antedating W.W.'s trans. of Menaechmi (1595). J. A. K. Thomson assumed that Sh read this mythical trans. of Amphitruo rather than the original.

0347. Jaggard, W[illia]m. Shakespeare Once a Printer and Bookman: Lecture One of the Twelfth Series of Printing Trade Lectures at Stationers' Hall... (Stratford-on-Avon: Shakespeare Press, 1933), 34 pp. SG

To support his contention that Sh spent the "lost years" working in London as a printer successively for Vautrollier, Field, and the Jaggards, the author gathers a florilegium of some five hundred allusions from the canon. Almost all are scarcely technical (e.g., Juliet's "Was ever book containing such vile matter / So fairly bound?"). Among the five hundred are numerous real or supposed references to classical authors: e.g., Aristotle, Caesar, Cicero, Claudian (De Raptu Proserpinae), Galen, Homer, Horace, Lucan, Lucian, Mantuanus, Ovid, Plautus, Seneca, Socrates, Aelianus (Sh's source for the tale of Philomel), Thucydides (Sh does not refer to him, but "had probably read his folio 'Hystory of the Peloponnesian warre'"), Virgil, and Xenophon (Sh does not refer to the Cyropaedia, but "Xenophon must have been very well known to all bookmen and writers of the sixteenth century"). Jaggard has not, of course, established either Sh's professional background or the source of Sh's "mountain of knowledge." TxHR

0348. Jayne, Sears. "Ficino and the Platonism of the English Renaissance," CL, IV (1952), 214-238. GRS

Jayne includes Sh in a catalogue (p. 225) of English Renaissance poets who responded (indirectly) to Ficino; the pseudo-Platonic cult of love and beauty can be traced to Ficino, whose ideas became known in England chiefly through French Renaissance poetry.

0349. Jenkins, Harold. "William Shakespeare: A Biographical Essay," William Shakespeare: The Complete Works, ed. Charles Jasper Sisson (N.Y., [1953]), pp. ix-xvii.

A conservative and informed account of Sh's career. Jenkins recognizes that Sh's "early schoolbooks left a deep enough impress on his mind to be vividly recollected in some of the compositions of later years ..." Only Lily's Grammar, Mantuan, Terence, and Ovid are named among the school authors Sh knew, but Jenkins plainly regards Jonson's aphorism as a relative, not an absolute statement. There are scattered remarks about Sh's classicism throughout the essay, but Jenkins gives no special attention to Sh's sources.

0350. Jewkes, Wilfred T. Act Division in Elizabethan and Jacobean Plays, 1583-1616. [Hamden, Conn.], 1958, 374 pp.

Rejecting Baldwin's approach (#0089) to Sh's practice through the Renaissance critical theory which he would have learned in school, Jewkes conducts a bibliographic study on 236 extant plays produced during the period. The results for Sh are inconclusive: for some plays (e.g., H.V) it is obvious from internal and external evidence that Sh intended a whole of five parts. For most plays there is no prima facie evidence one way or the other. Such primary bibliographical inspection as Jewkes makes is unquestionably important, but his cavalier dismissal of Baldwin implies that he is not prepared to admit the validity of literary scholarship as a complement to bibliographical analysis.

0351. Johnson, Samuel. "Preface to Shakespeare" (1765), in Johnson on Shakespeare, ed. Walter Raleigh (OUP, 1908), pp. 9-63.

Johnson's famous "Preface" repeats the seventeenth-century legend of Sh's ignorance as it was transmitted by Rowe, but accords Sh enough Latin for construction if not for fluent reading. Sh is granted "no" Greek. Johnson visualizes Sh using mainly, if not only, English trans. (e.g., Sh used the Menaechmi, but no other of Plautus' comedies because only the former was trans. in Sh's day). Perhaps the most important section of this "Preface" is not its consideration of Sh's actual use of ancient culture, but the defense of Sh's neglect of the unities. Johnson comes very close to denying their validity as criteria of dramatic excellence; his substitute criterion is the docere et delectare of the Ars Poetica: if Sh instructs and pleases without cramping his action in one time, or place, or tone, no harm is done. The "Preface" is unspecific about individual plays and passages, but Johnson compares Sh once with Euripides and once with Homer. Johnson was the first to recognize that Sh used North's Plutarch rather than the original. Farmer is sometimes thought to be the discoverer of this fact. Raleigh's ed. contains a selection from Johnson's notes to Sh's text (see #1420).

0352. Johnstone, Julian E. "The Classical Element in Shakespeare," CathW, CVI (1917), 38-52. SG

A totally unreliable art. in which the author returns to the untenable position of Upton (#0606) and Whalley (#0632) that Sh was a great classicist, the rival or even superior of Jonson, Chapman, and the University Wits. The art. is highly speculative (e.g., Sh wrote the Ur-Hamlet ca. 1586) and offers no evidence for many of its sweeping statements (e.g., Sh knew Herodotus in the original). Johnstone misrepresents other scholars (e.g., J. Churton Collins), and repeatedly utilizes bad logic. A good example of what scholarship should not be.

0353. Jorgensen, Paul A. Shakespeare's Military World. California UP, 1956, 345 pp.

There are a large number of references passim to military matters in the Greek and Roman plays, but on the whole Jorgensen emphasizes that Sh's military knowledge is Renaissance knowledge, even in the "classical" armies and wars (e.g., the miles gloriosus is mentioned just twice, both times to stress its irrelevance). Though there are effective analyses, late in the book, of Coriolanus as soldier and citizen and of Tim. as a play about a city corrupted by extended peace, the most important chs. relevant to the classics are 1 and 2. In 1 ("A Fearful Battle") Jorgensen discusses the orchestration of war on the Elizabethan stage, tracing the emphasis on sound in part to the sonorous tones of Virgil's battle scenes and the stentorian rhetoric of the Senecan Nuntius, who describes the scene of battle. In 2 ("Major Discords") he discusses the classical and Renaissance precedents for Sh's interest in military calamities caused by joint command (e.g., Brutus and Cassius at Philippi) and by failure to observe the "specialty of rule" (e.g., the Greek camp in Troi.). This is a learned and readable book.

0354. Kaufmann, Walter. "Shakespeare: Between Socrates and Existentialism," The Owl and the Nightingale: From Shakespeare to Existentialism (Ln, 1959), Ch. I, pp. 1-22.

An emphatic denunciation of the "Anglican" critics, especially of T. S. Eliot, for considering Sh in a Christian context. Sh's ethical affinity is for Socrates (Sonn. are full of echoes of the Symposium) and for Aristotle (Sh's tragic heroes, Hamlet, Coriolanus, Othello, Brutus, and especially Timon are magnanimous men from the Nicomachean Ethics). Again, Sh shares with Sophocles Antigone's view of duty—it must be done without thought of reward: Desdemona and Cordelia are Antigone in miniature. Kaufmann's limitations as a critic are (1) his neglect of Sh's Renaissance cultural context; (2) his failure to consider that what a dramatic character says about life is not necessarily his creator's personal tenet; (3) his silence about the scholarship on Sh's classicism.

0355. Kellogg, A. B. "Place Names and Epithets in Homer and Shakespeare," Names, III (1955), 169-171.

Sh had less reverence for places and their names than did Homer, who graces his proper names with descriptive epithets. Sh was capable of epithetical writing ("still-vex'd Bermoothes," "wat'rish Burgundy," etc.) but ordinarily omitted adjectival tags. Kellogg does not observe that the oral-formulaic epithet is a formal convention of epic poetry, not of drama. A more extensive study might perhaps show that Sh uses epithets as often as his contemporaries in the drama.

0356. Kemp, Harry. "Shakespeare's Response: On Ben Johnson [sic] twitting him that he 'knew little [sic] Latin, less Greek'," ShN, IX (1959), 38. [A sonnet]

Kemp's Sh returns to the long-superseded opinion of the pre-Romantics that it was just as well that he was an untutored man: "Nor need I hark to Horace when I seek / How looks the dawn, for my song's ornament."

0357. Kennedy, H. Arthur. "Small Latin and Less Greek," CR, LVI (1889), 574-585.

Kennedy believes that Sh's knowledge of the classics was secondhand and limited. He makes much of the fact that Sh used what he did have and therefore did not have what he is silent about (an interesting passage substitutes the Orestes story for Hamlet's description of the Murder of Gonzago). It should be noted that Kennedy is writing in the wake of Baconian eulogies of "Sh's" knowledge; he sees himself as a debunker of legends. There are many places where Kennedy has original insights: e.g., he traces the "armipotent Mars" of L.L.L. to the Prologue of Lydgate's Troy Book; he traces Alcides and the Sea Monster of Merch. to Ovid; he shows that Sh, unlike Marlowe and some other Elizabethans, considered Pyrrhus and Neoptolemus as two people and also falsely distinguished between Hippolyta and Antiope. Sh stands outside the succession of classicists: Homer, Virgil, Dante, Chaucer, Milton.

0358. Kennedy, Milton Boone. The Oration in Shakespeare. North Carolina UP, 1942, 270 pp.

Kennedy classifies the eighty-three orations in the Sh canon under the three classical headings: forensic, deliberative, epideictic and finds that (1) over half are epideictic; (2) the largest number appear in early plays and in those (such as Per. and Troi.) which some have tried to expel from the canon; (3) in Sh's best work the orations are fewer, but in better conformity with character and situation--i.e., the later plays conform best to the Aristotelian ideal as stated in the Poetics XIX. Sh differs from his contemporaries in his early departure from the declamatory style which came into English tragedy through Seneca and is traceable ultimately to Gorgias and Protagoras in the "First Sophistic." But Sh is nonetheless classical, as the structure of his orations clearly shows. Ch. VIII (198-216) is a brief excursus on "Elizabethan Education" with the object of showing that Sh had sufficient access to classical models and principles of rhetoric to provide him the foundation for this aspect of his dramatic technique. This book is too early to take advantage of Baldwin's William Shakspere's Small Latine & Lesse Greeke (#0089), but had Kennedy surveyed the scholarship on Sh's learning more fully he would have realized that Churton Collins is not the most authoritative of critics--let alone Delia Bacon and William Theobald. This lack of discrimination in sources is coupled with repetitiveness and an occasional lack of specificity, but the study is nevertheless a valuable contribution to the knowledge of Sh's sources and his dramatic technique.

0359. Kennedy, William S. "Shakespeare's Astronomy: Did He Ever Accept the Fact That the Earth Revolves on Its Axis and Around the Sun?" PL, XIII (1901), 366-379.

Though it is inconceivable that Sh did not have nodding acquaintance with the scientists in London at the turn of the century, there is no clearcut evidence that he ever abandoned classical astronomy in favor of the heliocentric theory introduced in 1543.

0360. Kent, Roland G. Language and Philology, Our Debt, [No. 22] (Boston, 1923), 174 pp.

Contains a passing reference (p. 131) to Sh's knowledge of Lily's Grammar.

0361. Ker, W. P. "Cervantes, Shakespeare, and the Pastoral Idea," Homage, pp. 49-51. (Reprinted in Form and Style in Poetry [1928], Appendix VII, pp. 337-340.)

Ker places Cervantes between Sh (who shows little respect for classical authority) and Sidney (who bows servilely to it). Cervantes shares with Sh a jocular irreverence for the pastoral at the same time that he is using it beautifully (Don Quixote and A.Y.L.). Both men are fond of the Greek romantic convention of "the box of baby-things [which] is produced in the last scene, to bring back the heroine to her own again" (e.g., in W.T.). Ker mentions Polonius' ridiculous fondness for neatly balanced literary genres--the same fondness that caused Sir Philip Sidney's circle to elevate Heliodorus to the status of Homer (the prose epicist "must" balance the verse epicist). Ker also alludes to Sh's use of stichomythia.

0362. Ker, W. P. "A Note on the Form of Shakespeare's Comedies," Edda, VI (1916), 158-163. (Reprinted in Form and Style in Poetry [1928], Appendix VIII, pp. 340-346.)

Sh, who neglected the critical dogma of the unities, but not through ignorance, himself invented a comic form (of which Dream is the supreme exemplar and Temp. a lesser approximation) unexcelled by anything in classical literature. L.L.L. is more orthodoxly unified on classical comic principles, and of course Errors, like Roister Doister, is Plautine. But Sh invented new forms when Latin drama, Gascoigne's "Greek story-play" (Jocasta), and Italian imitations failed to provide sufficient stimulus. E.g., he invented a comédie humaine in the Henriad which anticipates the modern novel--

and it has marvelous symmetry despite its panoramic scope. This is a stimulating comment. MnU

0363. Kerlin, Robert T. Theocritus in English Literature. Lynchburg, Va., 1910, 203 pp.

Though he speaks (p. 32) of Sh and Theocritus as "kindred spirits" and of pastoral scenes in A.Y.L. and W.T. as "the most Theocritean in our literature" (p. 31), Kerlin offers no analysis whatever of the pastoral tradition in Sh except the suggestion (p. 5) that Sh may have read Theocritus in grammar school and the alternative proposal (pp. 31-32) that he found the Idyls in a Latin version or in the Sixe Idillia (1588).

0364. Kitto, H. D. F. Greek Tragedy. N.Y., 1939/1950, 430 pp.

Kitto's astute interpretations of the Attic tragedies are given perspective by his comparisons with Sh's plays. There are a dozen references to Shn practice in this book, some of them especially interesting: e.g., Merch., like Euripides' Ion, is a successful tragicomedy; Caesar's ghost lives on in Acts IV and V the way Ajax' spirit does not; the gadfly in Prometheus is an exit-device analogous to the famous bear in W.T.; Sh and Aeschylus both combine the sublime and the ridiculous to create suspense; Euripides' Cassandra is as terrible in her madness as Ophelia; the concealment of Alcestis at the end of Euripides' play is like the concealment of Hermione except that Euripides obtains an irony lacking in W.T. by having Admetus protest his fidelity to his "dead" wife in her very presence. It is noteworthy that Kitto finds common ground between Sh and each of the Greek tragedians; it has often been implied that Sh bears comparison only or chiefly with some one of the three.

0365. Kittredge, George Lyman, ed. The Complete Works of Shakespeare. Boston, 1936, 1561 pp.

The two-page introductions to the individual plays are packed close with reliable information and sensible judgments. The lack of a general introduction is mitigated by the breadth of Kittredge's commentary: e.g., he argues for Sh's facility in Latin in the introduction to Errors and for his ability to read Homeric Greek in the introduction to Troi. Perhaps the best of the one-vol. eds. of Sh. It is the authority for quotations and line-references in this Guide.

0366. Klein, David. "Shakspere," Literary Criticism from the Elizabethan Dramatists: Repertory and Synthesis (N.Y., 1910), Ch. II, pp. 39-80.

A compilation of Sh's numerous references to his art and to other arts. Klein continually touches on concepts traceable to Greek and Roman thought, but he never comes closer to analyzing them than a few incidental references to Aristotle.

0367. Knight, Charles. Studies of Shakspere: Forming a Companion Volume to Every Edition of the Text. Ln, 1851, 560 pp.

Knight is a professed disciple of Coleridge and he adopts Coleridge's disparagement of eighteenth-century assumptions about Sh's ignorance. Knight's most vigorous attacks come in the essays on Errors and W.T. Of the former he observes that the improbable theories of Malone, Steevens, Ritson, et al. were born "simply because these most learned men are resolved to hold their own heads higher than Shakspere, by maintaining that he could not do what they could—read Plautus in the original." Of the latter he argues that anachronism is an artistic principle in the play; Sh's ability to capture the spirit of Rome in the Roman plays surely indicates that his "lapses" were deliberate, not casual. Knight gives serious consideration to a sizable amount of apocrypha and defends the integrity of Titus, yet he claims to be the originator of the effort to dismember Tim. On the whole Knight shows good judgment as a partisan in the "small Latin" controversy; his criticism ought to be exhumed. MnU

0368. Knight, G. Wilson. Myth & Miracle: An Essay on the Mystic Symbolism of Shakespeare. Ln, 1929, 32 pp. (Reprinted in The Crown of Life [1947].)

This slender treatise is a prospectus for all of Knight's later books, though the emphasis falls on the last plays. Sh, like Plato, is a maker of myth: tempest is the dangerous journey of human life; music and theophany are the sheltering havens in which the tempest-battered ship may be restored. Knight makes too close an equation between Sh and his work, however: he sees Prospero as Sh, served by Ariel (poetry) and Caliban (bestiality) as Plato's charioteer drives one good and one evil horse (Phaedrus, 253). In the storm and the restorative music of Temp. Sh reviews his career in tragedy and romance respectively.

0369. Knights, L. C. "Education and the Drama

in the Age of Shakespeare," The Criterion, XI (1932), 599-625.

A well-informed and well-reasoned attack on the traditional view that Sh wrote for an illiterate audience. Knights quotes extensively from Renaissance authorities on education who have become more familiar since the appearance of Baldwin's study (#0089). The art. shows that grammar school education was widespread and that its emphasis on language (grammar as well as rhetoric) prepared audiences for Sh's poetry. Among the interesting observations: Sh's contemporaries regarded language, not character, as the heart of drama; the license in syntax and the violation of the unities that mark Sh's age were possibly a rebellion on the part of the dramatists against the excessively formal treatment of language in Lily's Grammar which was entrenched as the inescapable nemesis of all schoolboys. The essay ends with brief remarks on Troi. and Ham. More extensive treatments of Knights's subject have since appeared, but his essay remains a valuable introduction to an important problem in historical criticism.

0370. Knobel, E. B. "Astronomy and Astrology," in Shakespeare's England, [ed. C. T. Onions] (Oxford: Clarendon, 1916), I, 444-461.

Knobel explains the astronomical theories of the sixteenth century briefly but clearly. Sh alludes to the Ptolemaic system as laid out in the Almagest in Ham., Dream, Antony, and Troi.; and to the Pythagorean music of the spheres in Per. and Antony. Yet Sh also refers to "perspectives" (in All's W., Twel., and R.II), which may or may not be the English devices which anticipated Galileo's telescope. Knobel assumes that Edmund and Cassius speak for Sh when they reject "starry domination"; this interpretation is now generally rejected (but see #0550). Knobel adduces a number of Shn allusions to astrological matters.

0371. Koch, Max. "Einflüsse des Altertums," Shakespeare (Stuttgart, [1886]), pp. 145-165.

This section of the book is concerned as much with Elizabethan culture in general as with Sh. Koch sketches a world steeped in the classics, some of them imported indirectly, through Renaissance Italy. Sh was very much a part of that world, responding to the ancients much as did his German near-contemporary, Hans Sachs, whose reading was "ungeheure." Among the Greeks and Romans Sh probably read (many of them in trans.) are Cicero, Suetonius, Ovid (Amores as well as Meta.), Livy, Sallust, Horace, Caesar (Commentaries), Quintus Curtius, Seneca, Plautus, Homer (Chapman's trans., but not for Troi.), Virgil (Sh, like his age, preferred Virgil to Homer), and Ammianus Marcellinus (for unspecified elements in Temp.). Koch supplies also a substantial catalogue of trans. of other classics which Sh would have access to. There is little attempt to supply chapter and verse here, but nevertheless Koch demonstrates a detailed knowledge of Elizabethan culture. Suetonius, Quintus Curtius, and Ammianus Marcellinus are not generally listed among Sh's classical sources even by those modern commentators who grant Sh a respectable education and a considerable literary curiosity. DFo TxHR

0372. Koenigsberger, Hannelore. "The Untuned String--Shakespeare's Concept of Chaos," diss (Columbia, 1951). DA, XII (1952), 66.

This diss studies the tragedies, histories, Sonn., and last plays as responses to disorder. Ingratitude is the great sin of disorder in the tragedies; rebellion and tyranny produce chaos in the histories; Sonn. complain against the disruptive influence of Time; but in the last plays Sh portrays "fairyland" where Time does not destroy and where order can triumph. Most of these concepts are "classical," though the abstract does not indicate whether the roots of Sh's thought are a concern of the diss.

0373. Koeppel, E. "Randglossen zu dem Anders-schen Werk über Shakespeares Belesenheit," Archiv, CXIII (1904), 49-55. E-S SG

Koeppel would add these notes to Anders' ch. (#0073): (1) Sh knew Claudius Aelianus (probably in Abraham Fleming's 1576 trans.). (2) A considerable part of Meta. was trans. in A. Fraunce's Third Part of the Countesse of Pembrokes Yvychurch, which would have been available to Sh. (3) Lady Macbeth's satanic invocation (I v 41-55) is more likely to be indebted to The Misfortunes of Arthur than to Seneca.

0374. Kökeritz, Helge. "Shakespeare's Language," Shakespeare: Of an Age and for All Time, The Yale Shakespeare Festival Lectures ([Hamden, Conn.], 1954), pp. 33-51.

This survey of what has been done in the field and the huge amount yet remaining takes the view that Sh reflected the spoken and written language of his time—that he was not a neologist (Latin or native) to the extent that scholars have thought him. Kökeritz believes that the NED is not an adequate guide to provenance or date of a term since it neglects private documents and the spoken language. There is an extended passage on Sh's illogical interchange of Latinate adjectives in -ive and -ible, but this does not prove Sh's lack of Latin since, as Kökeritz indicates, Latinists like Jonson and Milton made similar "errors."

0375. Kraemer, Casper J., Jr. "Some Latinisms in English," CW, XXI (1927), 57-61.

A close-packed listing of brief passages from Kraemer's casual reading in English literature in each of which the sense turns on the meaning of the Latin original of an English word. There are over thirty instances from Sh. See also Claflin (#0165) and Hower (#0338).

0376. Kranz, Walther. "Shakespeare und die Antike: Drei Beiträge," ESn, LXXIII (1938), 32-38. SG

Kranz's first note quotes phrasing in Greek from Porphyrius' Life of Pythagoras which is strikingly like Merch. V i 63-65, and observes that a passage from Iamblichus' Life of Pythagoras is only less so. He does not suggest the route Sh took to the Neoplatonic doctrine, but notes that the context in V i is steeped in classical allusions. The second note points to Plato's Alcibiades I (132-133) as the ultimate source of Caesar I ii 51-58 as well as of Troi. III iii 95-111. In each passage two men discuss the fact that a man can see his own soul only by reflection and in each case the analogy is that a man must use a mirror to see his own eye. "Wieder wird es nicht möglich sein zu sagen, wie Shakespeare Kenntniss von dem antiken Motiv erhalten hat." But Kranz points out that Sh himself referred to the concept as "familiar" in Troi. The third note is a most interesting discussion of the ancient world as a pervasive element in Lear. Kranz finds traces of Seneca, Horace, and Lucretius, and interprets "learned Theban" as a reference to Oedipus; he also notes allusions to raving Ajax, Ixion, and the Centaurs. The religion of the play is almost consistent in its polytheism, but where it seems to be monotheistic Sh has a precedent in Seneca.

0377. Laffan, R. S. de Courcy. "Aeschylus and Shakespeare," NC, LV (1904), 585-594.

A proposal to produce at Stratford-on-Avon the Oresteia in juxtaposition with Ham., Lear, R.II, and Temp. prompts Laffan to consider Aeschylus and Sh together. Both lived in times of nationalism induced by the repulsion of enemy naval forces; both watched emerging democracy and decaying religious traditions. Both convey in their plays a sense of the unknown Infinite which lesser men like Corneille, Molière, and Milton do not convey, but Aeschylus conveys his sense through bas-relief simplicity; Sh conveys his through panoramic complexity of detail. Both men believed in the principle πάθει μάθος; both show in their plays that "Men at some time are masters of their fates." And for both there is the possibility of reconciliation at the end of tragic action; they end on a calm note "which links the eddying of the play to the vast flow of the river of continuous life." A rewarding piece of criticism which contains excellent illustrations from both playwrights.

0378. Laffan, R. S. de C[ourcy]. "Shakspere's School," The Rambler, I (1892), 41.

Not seen. NcD

0379. Landor, Walter Savage. "The Abbé Delille and Landor," Imaginary Conversations (1846). (Reprinted with some deletion in Shakespeare Criticism: A Selection, ed. D. Nichol Smith [OUP, 1916], pp. 396-399.)

The Abbé, as might be expected, defends the unities, while Landor points out that a forest is not a garden and should not be called one. There is an interesting interchange on Euripides' Cyclops as a possible ancestor of Caliban; Landor believes that whereas no Roman dramatist could have created Cyclops, he still falls short of Caliban in uniqueness and self-consistency.

0380. Langbaine, Gerard. Some Account of the English Dramatic Poets (1691). Munro, II, 346-373.

In these pages are reprinted the passages relevant to Sh; many of them are concerned with Sh's learning. Langbaine appoints himself antagonist to critics like Ravenscroft and Dryden, but he does not attack them frontally on the question of Sh's classicism. Not the least interesting passage lists the canon (Langbaine extends hospitality to a considerable body of apocrypha) and discusses sources in some detail. Langbaine's source study is a mixed bag of insight (he recognizes Plautus as the ultimate source of the Sebastian-Viola plot in Twel.) and carelessness (he has read Cor. and Plutarch so casually that he does not see the latter as the sole source of the former). For Charles Gildon's condensation of Langbaine and his own slender additions, see Munro, II, 417-422.

0381. Lathrop, Henry B. Translations from the Classics into English from Caxton to Chapman, 1477-1620, WSLL, No. 35 (Madison, 1933), 350 pp. E-S HB SG

Lathrop refers to Sh some ten times, but in each case accords him only a phrase or sentence. There are references to Sh's use of the Tudor trans. of Appian, the Tenne Tragedies, Golding's Ovid, possibly Drant's Horace, W.W.'s Menaechmi, Adlington's Apuleius, etc. An appendix contains an excellent chronological list of trans.

0382. Law, Robert A. "On Certain Proper Names in Shakespeare," TSE, XXX (1951), 61-65.

Law indicates loci in Plutarch's Lives for nearly three dozen names in Sh's plays. (Others are traced to the Chanson de Roland and to literal scrambling.) It is noteworthy that Sh's selections were often "fortuitous"--i.e., the connotations of the name do not suit the character--but if the names do trace to Plutarch (and in most of Law's cases there can be little doubt), then the influence of Plutarch on Sh was pervasive from the time of 2H.VI and Titus to that of W.T. The most striking case is in Tim., where all but one of the dramatis personae are drawn from North--and that one, "Phrynia," may well be a combination of two Plutarchian names.

0383. Law, Robert A. "Porcia's Curiosity: A Tale Thrice Told by Shakespeare," TSE, XXVII (1948), 207-214.

Sh dramatized three times Plutarch's story of Porcia's desire to know the cause of Brutus' unrest: (1) in the lighthearted exchange between Hotspur and Lady Percy in 1H.IV II iii; (2) in Caesar II i where Sh follows North more closely; (3) in Macb. III ii where Lady Macbeth questions her husband about the plan he has laid to murder Banquo and Fleance. In Caesar Sh minimizes Plutarch's central point--that Porcia stabbed herself to prove her constancy--and he omits this element altogether from 1H.IV and from Macb. "possibly on aesthetic grounds." Law's analysis shows Sh's facility in re-using a story, altering details in accordance with his dramatic purpose.

0384. Lee, Sidney. "Aspects of Shakespeare's Philosophy," Shakespeare and the Modern Stage (N.Y., 1906), pp. 142-169. E-S

The first section (142-148) contrasts Sh with Bacon with respect to their attitudes toward and knowledge of formal philosophy, specifically of its origins in Aristotle and Plato. Lee's conclusion is not only that the two differ but that Sh was almost totally ignorant of Greek philosophy and felt an antipathy toward syllogistic reasoning and scientific studies. Lee goes on in the later sections to discuss Sh's ethics and politics (but not often in the light of their sources). It is strange that Platonic doctrines, the pre-Socratics (as transmitted by Ovid's Meta. XV), and the Stoics receive no attention. The mid-twentieth-century consensus grants to Sh a more generous store of ancient wisdom than Lee would assent to.

0385. Lee, Sidney. Life of Shakespeare. Ln, 1898/1929, 776 pp. E-S

This standard work has not been superseded in the past thirty-five years because Lee's caution prevented him from rash conjectures. There are passim a very large number of passages on Sh and the classics. Most are as succinct and full of information as the summary (pp. 15-21) of Sh's probable education and his use of it. The book contains as much critical insight as fact: typical is the passage on Antony, where Lee points out that Sh's compression of Plutarch's time scheme gives a distorted picture of Antony, who historically interspersed his hegiras to Egypt with vigorous political and military activity.

0386. Leech, Clifford. "Shakespeare's Prologues and Epilogues," Baldwin Festschrift, pp. 150-164.

Leech iterates Lüders' point (#0400), that the Shn prologue and/or epilogue owes something to the practice of Latin comedy, something to Seneca's "monologuizing chorus," and something to the moralizing "expositors" of the native tradition. He adds that between 1599 and 1608, Sh eschewed such direct statement to the audience as old-fashioned and unsophisticated, but returned to the practice with Per., perhaps because romance is a "more relaxed dramatic kind."

0387. Leech, Clifford. Shakespeare's Tragedies and Other Studies in Seventeenth Century Drama. OUP, 1950, 232 pp.

Of the relevant essays in this book, the first four as a group explore the nature, subjects, style, and impact of tragedies at the end of the sixteenth century (especially Sh's) to determine the reasons for the brief floruit of Elizabethan tragedy as a form. The thoughtful criticism begins with the Poetics and suggests that Sh succeeds to the extent that he is Stoic, not Christian, because Christianity and tragedy are incompatible. There are interesting observations on stylistic differences between mature Shn tragedy and earlier, Senecan works. A later essay proposes Tim. as the link between the politically conservative Roman plays and the emphasis on individual power in the later plays. The simplistic psychology of the last plays is prefigured in Timon's one-sidedness, and puritan themes in Tim. appear in the romances as well.

0388. Leech, Clifford. "Shakespeare's Use of a Five-Act Structure," NS, n.F. I (1957), 249-263.

Leech believes that Sh followed, but varied, an Elizabethan tradition when he organized the actions of his plays so as to indicate five distinct stages (acts) yet did not interrupt the action for scene breaks. For the act-division Sh had authority in the commentators on Terence (as Baldwin has pointed out, #0683), in the works of Plautus and Seneca, and in the dictum of Horace. In Leech's judgment Baldwin errs in not considering tragedy as well as comedy and in stopping short of Sh's great plays where the theatrical effectiveness of interrupted action is greatest. The argument is advanced by analyses of Twel., Merch., Dream, John, Titus, Caesar, Macb., Lear, Oth., and Ham., with references also to some non-Shn plays. An interesting approach.

0389. Legouis, Emile. "The Bacchic Element in Shakespeare's Plays," PBA, XII (1926), 115-132. E-S (Annual British Academy Shakespeare Lecture.)

This serio-comic lecture interprets Sh's dramatic career as a function of his changing attitude toward toping. "He was not only the interpreter of the Bacchic or anacreontic traditions. He also voiced the instincts and beliefs of the common people, of his London surroundings, or of his countryside. The two streams flow together, mixed or separate, through his plays." Unfortunately, Legouis is more specific about the anacreontic tradition in Spenser, Jonson, and in Milton than in Sh.

0390. Leo, F. A. "Shakespeare's Ovid in der Bodleian Library zu Oxford," ShJ, XVI (1881), 367-375. E-S HB

A detailed commentary on the flyleaf and title page notations and the marginalia in the Bodleian Meta. Three facsimiles assist the reader. Leo argues for the authenticity both of the Shn signature and of T.N.'s notation (1682) that Sh once owned the book. But he doubts that Sh used this vol. as the source for the plays; only one of the passages annotated marginally possibly found its way into a Shn play: Meta. II 846-847 on politics and love may be the source for Laertes' caveat for Ophelia (Ham. I iii 14-28). And even this is not a striking parallel.

0391. Levitsky, Ruth Mickelson. "Shakespeare's Treatment of the Virtue of Patience," diss (Missouri, 1957), DA, XIX (1959), 2940.

This diss interprets the ethics of almost the whole Sh canon as a progressive movement from a code of honor calling for impassioned vengeance through Stoic negation of passions and the world toward Christian patience in the later tragedies and the last plays.

0392. Lichtenstein, S. Shakespeare und Sophocles: Ein Beitrag zur Philosophie der Geschichte. München, 1850 (no pagination available).

Not seen.

0393. Lloyd, Michael. "Plutarch's Daemons in Shakespeare," NQ, CCV (1960), 324-327.

Sh accurately reflects Plutarch's theology of daemons (spirits, angels, geniuses) which, as ministers of the gods, move men to action good or evil. There are many indications (e.g., in Lear, Macb., Antony, Caesar) that Sh was familiar with the Moralia, probably in Holland's version (1603), which he may have seen before its publication.

0394. Lloyd, Robert. "Shakespeare: An Epistle to Mr. Garrick," [a poem] A Complete Edition of the Poets of Great Britain [no editor given] (Ln, 1794), X, 632-633.

A witty attack on Greek tragedy, especially for its formalities (e.g., Chorus) which interpose between the action and the spectator's reaction to it. Sh indulges in no such artificialities and is to be preferred. He "travers'd all the human heart / Without recourse to Grecian art." This is the poem (1760) for which Churchill praised Lloyd in The Rosciad. MnU

0395. Lloyd, William Watkiss. Essays on the Life and Plays of Shakespeare... Contributed to the Edition of the Poet by S. W. Singer, 1856. Ln, 1858, [no pagination].

This collection of Lloyd's insights is a

monument of nineteenth-century criticism and bears reading on its own merits today. The entire canon is studied critically (in random order), each play receiving ten to fifteen pages of close print. The whole is prefaced by a thorough and critical study of the documents and traditions related to Sh's life; Lloyd gives minimal attention to the "small Latin" controversy, but what he says is sensible: he believes that Sh knew Latin well in his youth and had some Greek but allowed both to rust in later years. Aubrey may well have been correct in his belief that Sh taught Latin to country boys. The criticism of the plays is invariably thoughtful: e.g., Lloyd juxtaposes Caesar and Antony, the former a play in which Rome is shown touched by Greek philosophy, the latter a play in which Rome is shown touched by oriental luxury. But it is not only on the Greek and Roman plays that Lloyd shows insight into Sh's classicism. Sh's "translation" of Bottom is compared with Aristophanes' translation of "litigious citizens and hazy philosophers" into wasps and clouds. Again Lloyd compares Hermione with Alcestis and shows that Hermione (at Leontes' urging) violates "Homer's better rule to speed the parting guest." A rewarding book which deserves reprinting. MnU

0396. Lloyd, W[illiam] Watkiss. "Shakspeare Notes," Ath, No. 2597 (1877), 143.

Lloyd discusses Sh's probable debt to Palingenius' Zodiacus Vitae (in Googe's trans.) in Meas. and 2H.IV and (possibly coincidental) in Cor. The parallel with Meas. is the only striking one. Lloyd is unaware that Palingenius was a grammar school text.

0397. Lowe, Thomas. Shakespeare Under the Stars; Or His Genius and Works in the Light of Astronomy. Stratford-on-Avon, 1887, ix + 118 pp.

This strangely disjointed book combines a consideration of Sh's astronomical and astrological allusions with an account of the author's experiences as an amateur astronomer, an attack on anti-Stratfordianism, warm enthusiasm for Sh's original genius (Lowe thinks of Sh as Fancy's child), and miscellaneous notes on nineteenth-century astronomical discoveries. Lowe makes no effort to establish the assumptions about the stars which Sh inherited from the ancient world. But he does compare Sh with Homer (both refer magnificently to astronomical phenomena and both have been disintegrated by unworthy critics) and with Euripides (Sh portrays Nemesis in operation from the moment of moral decision; Euripides portrays Nemesis only after the crime itself has been committed). MA

0398. Lucas, F. L. Euripides and His Influence, Our Debt, [No. 3] (N.Y., 1923), 188 pp. HB SG

"Euripides' individual influence on the Elizabethans, except vicariously through Seneca, remains slight." Lucas offers severe strictures on the parallel passage method of Collins, but he does see some resemblance between Eteocles' protestation (Phoenissae, 504-506) and Hotspur's "By heaven methinks it were an easy leap ..." (1H.IV I iii 201-208). Gascoigne's Jocasta and Plutarch's On Brotherly Love both stand between the Shn passage and the original. "Far the most truly Euripidean thing in Shakespeare is the biting realism of Troilus and Cressida," which is only "the coincidence of great minds in disillusion."

0399. Lucas, F. L. "Seneca in the Elizabethans," Seneca and Elizabethan Tragedy (CUP, 1922), Ch. V, pp. 110-133. E-S HB SG

Lucas, who is less concerned with "English Seneca" than with "Roman Seneca," devotes only six pages to Sh (117-123) in which he alludes to Titus, R.III, H.VI, Macb., and Ham. The scene of Bassianus' murder, the stichomythia in R.III and Richard as tyrant, two or three verbal echoes in Macb., and the Ghost in Ham. are almost the only Shn vestiges of the Roman tragedy: "In short though Shakespeare almost certainly had read Seneca, though he may even have read him in the original, and though he seems here and there to echo him, the number and importance of such echoes seem to have been very much exaggerated."

0400. Lüders, Ferdinand. "Prolog und Epilog bei Shakespeare," ShJ, V (1870), 274-291.

Lüders discusses the prologues, epilogues, inductions, choruses, dumb shows, and "presenters" of Elizabethan drama. The conventions are traceable to Medieval drama, but were reinforced by classical example (Terence, Euripides, Seneca). Sh is fully aware of the tradition: Lüders finds evidence in about half the canon, including W.T. (in which "der Zeitgott" is a "deus ex machina"), 2H.IV (Rumour is based on the Fama of Aeneid IV and Meta. XII), R.III (Richard's opening monologue is "fast nach Art des Euripides"), and Romeo (Benvolio's facetious remarks on "Cupid hoodwink'd with a scarf" and the "without-book prologue, faintly spoke / After the prompter" [I iv 4-8]).

0401. Lumley, Eleanor P. The Influence of Plautus on the Comedies of Ben Jonson. N.Y., 1901, 121 pp.

In a ch. designed to emphasize the popularity of Plautus in sixteenth-century Europe, there are eight pages (40-47) on Sh. The author traces Plautine elements in Twel., Shrew, Temp., Per., Merch. (Shylock), A.Y.L. (possibly the "thrasonical brag"), Wives, 1H.IV, Ham. ("assume a virtue if you have it not"), and less palpably in L.L.L. (Armado) and All's W. (Parolles). It appears quite probable that the author mistakes Renaissance commonplaces (such as the Ham. quotation), which may or may not be ultimately Plautine, for immediate echoes. She would grant Sh enough Latin to read what he wished (possibly with Ben Jonson's help) in Plautus, but she adds the highly improbable alternative that W.W. had trans. all of Plautus by 1595 and allowed Sh to read it in manuscript. One oversight may illustrate the remainder: the author hears an echo of the steward of Asinaria in Malvolio but she does not mention the more obvious debt to the conjuring scene of Menaechmi which is the basis of Twel. IV ii as it had been the basis of Errors IV iv.

0402. Madan, Falconer. "Two Lost Causes, and What May be Said in Defence of Them: (a) The Oxford 'Jerome' of '1468'. (b) A Supposed Shakespeare Autograph," 3 Library, IX (1918), 89-105. E-S

The second of these "lost causes" is the case of the Sh signature in the Bodleian Ovid. This part of the art. is a reply to E. Maunde Thompson's assertion (ibid., VIII [1917], 193-217) that the signature and accompanying note are clumsy forgeries. It is difficult for a reader untrained in paleography to judge, but Madan appears to have marshaled better documentary evidence and to have considered the probabilities more plausibly. It is noteworthy that Madan does not argue positively for the genuineness of the signature; he rather pleads that Thompson's assurance is not warranted.

0403. Maginn, William. "Dr. Farmer's Essay on the Learning of Shakespeare Considered," FM, XX (1839), 253-273, 476-490, 647-666.

A bristling critique of Farmer's famous Essay (#0238), which in the first third of the nineteenth century was still considered to constitute the final word on Sh's classicism. Maginn justifiably objects to Farmer's arrogance, and with even more reason ridicules the fallacies in his syllogistic deduction. That a trans. existed does not mean ipso facto that Sh consulted it, nor if he did does it ergo follow that he could not read Greek or Latin. Again, the ignorant blunders and enthusiastic excesses of the early eighteenth-century critics cannot logically be a detraction from Sh; yet Farmer implies that the follies of Whalley, Upton, and others are proof of Sh's ignorance. Maginn's effort to strike a compromise between Upton and Farmer is of great historical importance; but he unfortunately overstates the case for Sh's learning with resulting loss of credibility: e.g., (1) Sh wrote Troi. to rival Homer whom he probably knew in Greek; (2) Sh may have consulted Plutarch's original (or at least Amyot's French) as well as North. Yet there are numerous well-made points; typical is the alert recognition that Sh drew on both Golding and Ovid's original in Temp. The first part of the essay deals with Greek, the second with Latin, and the third with modern languages, but Part Three also contains several remarks on the classics.

0404. Magnus, Laurie. "Shakespeare," English Literature in its Foreign Relations, 1300-1800 (Ln, 1927), Ch. III, pp. 47-86. E-S

This ch. is concerned primarily with Continental literature, but it contains numerous passing references to the classics, especially Seneca and Plutarch. Magnus is an enthusiast, inclined to treat speculation as fact (e.g., Sh studied law, arrived in London in 1586, could not read Virgil in Latin, etc.); and he is an adherent of the school of thought according to which Sh acquired his culture in conversation at the Mermaid. One ought to accept his conclusions with hesitancy.

0405. Mair, A. W. "Praise of Shakespeare," Homage, pp. 292-305.

A dialogue (in Greek with facing English) which emphasizes that Sh's practice followed the principle of Aristotle: his poetry is universal, recording not what is, but what might be.

0406. Malone, Edmond. The Life of William Shakspeare, Boswell's Malone, II, 1-287.

To this day Malone's antiquarian researches demand the respect of Sh scholars. His was the first systematic attempt to sort truth from legend in the traditions concerning Sh's life, and the documentary evidence he amassed is a tribute to his patience and energy. Malone died with the Life unfinished--it is to be assumed that he intended to add a major critical study of the plays to his biography and his attempt to arrange the canon chronologically. The most important section for the Guide is VII, in which

Malone confronts the mare's-nest of Sh's ignorance. He does not make any detailed analysis of Sh's possible studies in the classics, but he tries to lay to rest the myth that Sh could have attended school without learning any Latin to speak of. He recognizes as curricular Lily's Grammar, Sententiae Pueriles, Cato's Distichs, Cicero's Offices, Mantuan, Virgil's Eclogues and Aeneid, some of Ovid, and ("probably") Cornelius Nepos. Despite Sh's "moderate knowledge of Latin" (which Malone realizes that Farmer has not disproved), he turned to trans. from "indolence" and "desuetude in the progress of life." Malone's modification of an extreme eighteenth-century position is important historically, but it is interesting to note that he devotes a great deal less space to the "small Latin" question than to (e.g.) the deer-stealing myth or Sh's father's supposed professions.

0407. Manly, J. M. "The Influence of the Tragedies of Seneca upon Early English Drama," The Tragedies of Seneca, trans. F. J. Miller (Chicago, 1907), pp. 3-10. E-S HB

This is a brief essay, but a challenging one: e.g., (1) we ought not to underestimate the importance of private theaters in transmitting to the public drama the Senecan modes; (2) the influence of Latin comedy on English tragic form has been neglected; (3) Senecan eloquentia, not the bare stage, encouraged rhetorical description in English drama; (4) only Sh was able to escape from Seneca's chief legacy--melodrama--which results from tragic action stripped of its theocratic halo. Sh substituted for the Greek theocracy which Seneca had abandoned a "web of circumstance" from which his tragic protagonists futilely attempt to extricate themselves. Manly has praise for Cunliffe (#0193). There are several references to Sh passim.

0408. Marder, Louis. "Aspects of Shakespeare's Education," diss (Columbia, 1950). MicroA, X, No. 4 (1950), 219-220.

Marder's study of Sh's knowledge of music as revealed in his vocabulary is prefaced by a review of the long controversy over Sh's learning, with some attention to the "small Latin" question. Marder sees Sh as a "learned grammarian" who may well have served as a schoolmaster; he assumes that this view is now generally accepted.

0409. Maxwell, J. C. "The Ghost From the Grave: A Note on Shakespeare's Apparitions," DUJ, XLVIII (1956), 55-59.

Sh defied traditional Senecanism when he made his ghosts (both those that appear and those referred to) tenants of "the grave" rather than of Tartarus or any other underworld. References in Temp., W.T., Ham., Macb., Dream, and elsewhere support Maxwell's contention that Sh's characters believe they are seeing the body of a once-living human when they see a ghost, but there are many instances in which infernal regions are obviously intended. By fusing the literary and the popular traditions, Sh gave an effectiveness to his pneumatological scenes that no contemporary could rival.

0410. Maxwell, J. C. "Virgilian Half-Lines in Shakespeare's 'Heroic Narrative'," NQ, CXCVIII (1953), 100.

Maxwell attempts to show that Sh deliberately imitated the Aeneid by writing truncated lines in Errors, the Prologue to Troi., Ham., and Macb. The argument is interesting, but in the case of Errors, metrical peculiarities may result instead from Sh's attempt to imitate Plautus' metrical legerdemain.

0411. McAvoy, William Charles. "Shakespeare's Use of the Laus of Aphthonius," diss (Illinois, 1952). DA, XIII (1953), 97.

When Sh's characters praise one another they do so in a formal rhetorical scheme which can be traced in large measure to two grammar school texts: the "Laus" from Aphthonius' Progymnasmata and the "Amatoria Epistola" from Erasmus' De Conscribendis Epistolis. Sh sometimes varies the prescribed formulae, but evidence of his early rhetorical training is discernible throughout his career.

0412. McCullen, Joseph T., Jr. "Brother Hate and Fratricide in Shakespeare," SQ, III (1952), 335-340.

Though McCullen justly stresses the Cain/Abel story as the most influential source of Elizabethan horrified fascination with the theme of fratricide, he also includes Plutarch's discussion in the Moralia, where the suggestion is made that the theme is full of dramatic significance. McCullen does not attempt to pinpoint Sh's access to the theme, but he shows that it was important to him from R.III to Temp., included in A.Y.L., Ham., Much, Lear, etc. An original treatment of a subject of importance.

0413. McDonnell, Robert Francis. "The 'Aspiring Minds': A Study of Shakespearean Characters Who Aspire to Political Sovereignty, Against the Background of Literary and Dramatic Tradition," diss (Minnesota, 1958). DA, XIX (1958), 1365-66.

Three traditions form the conventional Elizabethan political villain: De Casibus literature, Senecan drama (which proved that politics and theater could mix), and the Mystery plays with their ranting Herods. Sh also had precedent in Sackville and Norton, Peele, Marlowe, and other earlier dramatists. Sh's "aspiring minds" are Richard Gloucester, Bolingbroke, Julius Caesar, Edmund, and Macbeth. Macbeth is the last and greatest of Sh's usurpers, a climax to a tradition that had faded by the time of Sh's death.

0414. McKnight, George H. "Shakespeare and Rhetoric," Modern English in the Making (N.Y., 1928), Ch. IX, pp. 151-165.

A ch. full of intelligent observations. Typical is the suggestion that Sh was able to unlearn his Warwickshire accent and acquire London Standard rapidly perhaps because he had had experience with linguistic analysis in teaching school in the country. Again, Sh admired rhetorical art, but only when it suited the circumstance; Art must be consonant with Nature. Sh probably knew Cicero's Orator in Latin: from it he may have learned to suit language to speaker. A rewarding ch.

0415. McKnight, George H. "Shakespeare and the Language of His Time," Modern English in the Making (N.Y., 1928), Ch. X, pp. 166-211.

Though a large part of the ch. deals with such topics as accidence, syntax, orthography, and pronunciation, McKnight does make some extended comments on Sh's use of Latinate diction. In this ch., Sh is made out to be more a pawn of his times than in Ch. IX on his rhetoric (#0414). Indeed much of Ch. X is a study of Elizabethan practice, not of Sh.

0416. McNaghten, Hugh. The Story of Catullus. Ln, 1899, 83 pp.

This appreciation of Catullus' life and work, interspersed with verse renderings of many of his poems, contains passim numerous comparisons with Sh, the only English poet to merit such parallel treatment. An extended passage enthusiastically compares the Dark Lady with Lesbia and insists on identifying the former with Mary Fitton. Again the "odi et amo" theme is shown in Oth. and Cym., and Romeo is called Catullus' only rival in love poetry: "Shakespeare, who, far more than Sophocles, 'saw life steadily and saw it whole,' and Catullus, who saw but a single side, alone attain perfection here, because they alone are absolutely true." If McNaghten ignores Catullus' more obvious inheritors in England, perhaps one should in justice indicate his intended audience: "a scholar here and there, ...a barrister, a businessman, ... an Eton boy ...or the sister of an Eton boy."

0417. McPeek, James A. S. Catullus in Strange and Distant Britain, HSCL, No. 15 (HUP, 1939), 411 pp. SG

The numerous allusions to Sh passim and the extraordinarily full notes make this certainly the most exhaustive work in which Sh's relationship to Catullus is treated. McPeek suspects a connection, but no direct or conscious imitation; e.g., perhaps Sonn. 30 ("When to the sessions of sweet silent thought") was written after Sh had heard Jonson read aloud Carmen XCVI on the death of Quintilia. There are also specific references to Venus, Cym., Temp., and L.L.L. as well as many more general allusions. But McPeek finds Sh's works free of those expressions from Catullus which the Elizabethan sonneteers had made stock.

0418. Meissner, Paul. "Das Goldene Zeitalter in der Englischen Renaissance," Anglia, LIX (1935), 351-367.

In A.Y.L. Sh applies the classical concept of the Golden Age to the Middle Ages, substituting Robin Hood for the fortunate men of the classical myth. But in Lucr. (1. 60) he equates the Golden Age with virtue, placing himself in a Platonic tradition. In 1H. VI (I vi 4) the Dauphin associates Joan with Astraea, who left the earth when order was abrogated (Meta. I); if "Astraea's daughter" has returned, then order has returned too. By the time of Temp. Sh regards the Golden Age as a dream, and removes it to "eine elegische Ferne." An interesting essay which treats numerous other Elizabethans also.

0419. Mendell, Clarence W. "Conclusion," Our Seneca (Yale UP, 1941), Ch. XI, pp. 189-200.

The body of Mendell's book deals with Seneca's works, their background and dramatic merit. But in this Conclusion, he analyzes briefly and effectively the Senecan modes in

Elizabethan drama. There are cogent remarks on Sh passim: e.g., Sh abandoned stichomythia early in his career because "rhetorical fireworks" do not advance plot or characterization, both of which Sh considered important; the Shn soliloquy owes something to Seneca's monologues. Perhaps the most illuminating comment is on the fusion of Senecan and native elements in Macb.

0420. "[The Merits of Elizabethan Drama]," The Athenian Mercury, V (December 1, 1691), Munro Sup, No. 75, pp. 536-537.

The third of a series of questions and answers compares Elizabethan with Restoration drama and in doing so names Sh first of "those who first brought our Stage any thing near the Ancients"; the Elizabethans had the advantage of Greek and Latin tragedy and "all the Fable of the World to work upon."

0421. Messiaen, Pierre. "L'Érudition de Shakespeare," RB, LXXVII (1939), 181-184.

Aimed at the general French reader, this art. is general, if not superficial. Messiaen is an enthusiast, but he makes an occasional cogent observation (e.g., Portia's "mercy" speech is probably indebted to Elyot's Governour rather than directly to Seneca's De Clementia).

0422. Mézières, A. Shakspeare: Ses oeuvres et ses critiques (1860). 2nd ed., Paris, 1865, 511 pp.

This book is of uneven value. Mézières claims in Ch. I to establish a middle ground between the partisans of the omniscient Sh and the believers in the ignoramus from Stratford, but at the same time he speaks of Sh's "peu de latin et point [sic] de grec, comme le disait Ben Jonson," and he denies that Sh could read the Menaechmi in Latin. In Ch. VI Mézières sagely observes of Coriolanus that Sh "lui donne de la grandeur, ce qui ne signifie pas qu'il le propose pour modèle"; but he assumes that Sh used the Greek text of Plutarch for Caesar (p. 350—how Sh did this with his "point de grec" is not explained). In short, the book is unreliable factually but often sound and sometimes original in its critical insights: e.g., Lear and Cym. are Homeric in spirit because they "degage[nt] des moeurs encore barbares les plus grands et les plus nobles sentiments de l'âme humaine." DFo

0423. Mills, Laurens J. One Soul in Bodies Twain: Friendship in Tudor Literature and Stuart Drama. Bloomington, Ind., 1937, 470 pp. (See in Ch. V especially pp. 239-284 passim.)

This thorough study surveys in Ch. I the classical basis of Renaissance concepts of friendship, distinguishing the several contributions of Plato, Aristotle, the Stoics, the Epicureans, and especially of Cicero's De Amicitia as a repository of earlier thought. Then after discussing Medieval accretions (especially romantic love), Mills shows by ample illustration the immense popularity of revivified classical ideals before 1590 and their importance as dramatic material after 1590. Sh, unlike his predecessors and successors, made minimal use of the theme. Sonn., of course, set up a dichotomy between friend and mistress--it is the mistress who is castigated, not the friend. Here Sh is following a classical convention, probably not revealing his private life. Then in two early plays, T.G.V. and Merch., Sh used received attitudes toward friendship as the skeletal structure--in T.G.V. it is the conflict between love and friendship that moves the plot; in Merch., the classical triumph of friendship over love (Bassanio's loyalty to Antonio in Acts III and IV) assures a happy marriage for Bassanio, because it proves his virtue. Shylock poses as Antonio's friend when he offers the bond, and this hypocrisy makes him a classical villain, who is ironically punished in Act IV when justice requires him to share his property with his "friend" Antonio according to classical precepts of communal ownership. After Merch. Sh used friendship only as incidental material, preferring less trite themes, but it appears in several plays, including Romeo, Oth., Ham., W.T., Twel., and Cor.; though Tim. is largely a product of the malcontent tradition, it is possible to read the play as a tragedy of "failure to perceive the truth of the classical doctrine regarding the number and quality of friends," i.e., quantity defeats quality. A well-informed and perceptive study.

0424. Miriam Joseph, Sister, C.S.C. Shakespeare's Use of the Arts of Language, ColSECL, No. 165 (Col UP, 1947), 423 pp.

This book approaches Sh's grammar, logic, and rhetoric not from the foundation of the grammar school curriculum as Baldwin (#0089) does, but from the treatises, especially those in English, which were so widely studied by adults in the Renaissance. There is strong evidence that Sh read at least some of them (Puttenham's Arte of English Poesie, Peacham's

Garden of Eloquence, Silvayn's Orator, Wilson's Arte of Rhetorique, etc.). Sister Miriam Joseph classifies the logicians and rhetoricians under three headings: (1) the Traditionalists (Melanchthon, Cox, Wilson, Rainolde, Lever, Blundeville) who are directly indebted to Aristotle, Cicero, Quintilian, and Ad Herennium; (2) the Ramists (Ramus, Talaeus, Fenner, Fraunce, Butler, and Hoskyns) who modified Aristotle's method and terminology; and (3) the Figurists (Susenbrotus, Sherry, Peacham, Puttenham, Day), who appear to emphasize eloquence at the expense of logic and grammar. Despite their differences all three groups in effect expound the same concepts, and Sh shows that he was thoroughly familiar with those concepts. After preliminary explanations Sister proceeds to a long second section of the book in which she illustrates Sh's use of an immense number of logical, grammatical, and rhetorical devices. This second part is valuable not only for its conclusive proof of Sh's linguistic knowledge but especially for its classification, definition, and illustration of scores of those awesome Greek terms which have fallen out of common use as our educational system has deteriorated. The third part of the book gives further definitions, this time with illustrations from the treatises. An unusually satisfying book which admirably complements the studies of Craig, Baldwin, Whitaker, and Madeleine Doran.

0425. The Moderator, No. 3 (June 23, 1692). T-D, pp. 33-34.

This anonymous leaflet in part attacks Langbaine for crediting Sh with Italian and French in one place and in another denying him French, Latin, and Aristotle. An early recognition of an inconsistency which still persists among those who will credit Sh with Italian or French which was not taught at Stratford, but not with Latin which was.

0426. [Montagu, Elizabeth]. An Essay on the Writings and Genius of Shakespear, Compared with the Greek and French Dramatic Poets. Ln, 1769, 288 pp. E-S

Mrs. Montagu's famous treatise is in part praise of Sh, in part comparison of Sh and classical drama, in part derogation of Racine and (especially) Corneille, in part ridicule of Voltaire for his incompetent trans. of Sh and for his critical inadequacies. Theseus in love during a plague, speaking rhymed French, dressed as a French fop in a play with no action is far more ridiculous and unclassical than anything Sh ever created on the model of the ancient world. The most interesting chs. are the comparisons between Sh and the ancients: Sh is like Tacitus in his analysis of human motives in history in 1,2H.IV; the Ghost in Ham., unlike his counterpart in the Persae, is an agent in the plot of the tragedy; Lear cursing his daughters is more persuasive than Oedipus lecturing his son (at Colonus); Aristotle would have enjoyed discussing Sh's history plays because they illustrate the Greek belief that history exemplifies moral philosophy. The most interesting passage of all applies to Macb. the precept of Bishop Hurd that "Gothic" mythology is superior to classical mythology as poetic material. The last ch. defends Caesar from Voltaire's charge that it is "a monstrous spectacle." Antony's oration, e.g., "popular [in its] address and manner," is entirely appropriate to its audience of Plebeians. Mrs. Montagu still talks about Sh and "Nature," but she has profited from the canons of Pope and Johnson. MnU

0427. Moorman, F. W. "Shakespeare's Ghosts," MLR, I (1906), 192-201.

After tracing the dramatic ghost from Aeschylus' Darius and Clytemnestra and Euripides' Polydorus through Seneca and the Italian and French Senecans to Sh's immediate predecessors (in a previous art., ibid., [1905], 85-95), Moorman shows that Sh gave the Senecan ghost a personality and a direct influence on the action of the play, while he was stripping away the Senecan rhetoric about Tartarus and Ixion's wheel which Kyd and his imitators had adopted as a trademark. For classical eschatology Sh substituted popular Elizabethan beliefs (e.g., the lights burn blue at a ghost's approach). The plays discussed are R.III, 2H.IV, R.II, Caesar, Macb., and Ham. The ghost to Sh is an instrument of Nemesis, divine justice. Other scholars maintain that Hamlet Senior is a pagan ghost, and many disagree with Moorman's belief (and Bradley's) that Banquo's specter is only in Macbeth's mind, and that the ghost of Caesar is likewise a figment of Brutus' imagination.

0428. Morgann, Maurice. An Essay on the Dramatic Character of Sir John Falstaff. Ln, 1777, 185 pp.

Morgann speaks (pp. 65-66) of Sh's learning as too small for his age, but "too much for the reach of his genius." He also defends Sh against the charge that he violated the unities by insisting that Aristotle would have applauded Sh's larger scope had he known of it (p. 70).

Morgann alludes to the miles gloriosus to deny its relevance to Falstaff, but he neither defines the miles nor discusses Sh's rejection of it. MnU

0429. Moulton, Richard G. Shakespeare as a Dramatic Artist: A Popular Illustration of the Principles of Scientific Criticism. 3rd ed., OUP, 1906, 443 pp.

In this reaction against impressionism Moulton pleads for analytical criticism of drama and illustrates his proposed method in several Shn plays. Chs. relevant to this Guide are V on Nemesis in R.III, a ch. which should be read in conjunction with VI on Nemesis and Destiny (in their classical senses) in Macb. Two further chs., VIII and IX, deal with the characterization and the rising/falling action of Caesar. Moulton's pioneer criticism is not sufficiently appreciated today; these four chs. (especially the brilliant essay on R.III) deserve and reward attention.

0430. Mr. Turbulent: Or, The Melanchollicks. A Comedy... (1682), T-D, p. 18.

In this anonymous play a character refers to Sh and Jonson as "mere Oafs" by contrast with Aristophanes, Menander, and Terence.

0431. Muir, Kenneth. "Shakespeare and Rhetoric," ShJ, XC (1954), 49-68.

The classical rhetoric taught in sixteenth-century schools was not for Sh a mere exercise which his mature plays outgrew. He valued it as a means of subtly conveying thought, and we make a serious omission when we neglect (or merely tolerate) all rhetorical devices in Sh except metaphor and simile. Sh cared enough about rhetoric to read at least three treatises on the subject (including Pyott's trans. of Silvayn's Orator) after leaving school. Muir's thoughts should be compared with those of T. W. Baldwin in the early chs. of Vol. II of #0089.

0432. Muir, Kenneth. Shakespeare's Sources: I, Comedies and Tragedies. Ln, 1957, 267 pp.

A useful compendium of what is known or surmised about Sh's sources and his manipulation of them. A second vol. is projected. Muir appears intelligently conservative, and his awareness of scholarship in the field will convince the reader of the validity of his conclusions. Naturally only parts of the book deal with classical sources, but Muir makes scattered observations and suggestions about Sh's use of classical material.

0433. Munro, H. A. J. "Seneca's Tragedies," JP, VI (1876), 70-79.

In prologue to a critique of an ed. of Seneca, Munro briefly cites parallels between Macb. and Hercules Furens, Ham. and Hercules Furens and Hercules Oetaeus, Caesar and Troades, 1H.IV and Thyestes; he adds an interesting verbal resemblance between Ham. II ii 26-32 and Marcus Manilius, "once read more than he is now."

0434. Munro, John, ed. The London Shakespeare. 6 vols., Ln and N.Y., 1957, 1690 pp. [total].

Munro's ed. begins inauspiciously with an introduction to Errors which will posit a lost source-play or a Shn debt to Italian comedy (cf. the introduction to Temp. in Vol. II) rather than acknowledge that Sh could read easily the Latin of Plautus (Munro admits that Sh may have consulted the Menaechmi but would deny him knowledge of the Amphitruo). Yet Munro's other introductions are relentlessly documented from the tradition of scholarship and criticism and frequently credit Sh with indirect knowledge of classical authors (see, e.g., IV, 1020 for Pliny in H.V) and sometimes of direct knowledge (see, e.g., IV, 1282, 1324 on Ovid in Venus and Lucr.). There are some provocative comparisons with classical literature as well: Shylock broods over the action of Merch. as inexorable Fate did over Greek tragedy; "Silvius and Phebe, the passionate swain and reluctant nymph [in A.Y.L.], are as old and immortal as Pan and Syrinx whose story was danced by Daphnis and Chloe ..." This is, taken as a whole, a valuable ed. See also #0639.

0435. Musgrove, S. Shakespeare and Jonson, The Macmillan Brown Lectures 1957: Auckland University College Bulletin, No. 51, 55 pp.

The first lecture (pp. 3-20), for which the series is named, explores intelligently and conservatively the probable relationship between the two playwrights. To Musgrove it is obvious that Sh was no illiterate, and his analysis of Jonson's poem dedicatory to F_1 is, like Baldwin's (in #0089), admirable for its consideration of the context and its awareness of the contemporary implications of terms like "Nature," "Art," and "Latin and Greek." This is an interesting study which sees the two men not as polar rivals, but as mutual complements —Musgrove does justice to both of them. MnU

0436. Neilson, W[illiam] A[llan], and A[shley] H. Thorndike. "Shakespeare's Reading," The Facts About Shakespeare (N.Y., 1913), Ch. III, pp. 50-66. E-S

"Shakespeare, if not a scholar, was a man of wide and varied reading." The authors trace Sh's probable education in the classics and his use of that education in the plays; they also point out indirect routes to classical culture in the translators and in Continental adaptations of the classics. This ch. is on the whole an intelligent and reliable guide, though recent research would modify the conclusion on Sh's Senecanism (Neilson and Thorndike consider it --direct and indirect--the greatest single influence on him) and would grant Juvenal and Persius a place in his experience (Neilson and Thorndike deny Sh any knowledge of the two satirists).

0437. Neilson, William Allan, and Charles Jarvis Hill, eds. The Complete Plays and Poems of William Shakespeare. Cambridge, Mass.: Houghton Mifflin, 1942, 1420 pp.

The claims for Sh's education in the general introduction are rather understated: he had "begun an acquaintance while a boy" with "the works of some half-dozen Latin writers" but knew no Greek. Nevertheless the introductions to the individual plays portray an intelligent Sh aware of his cultural heritage and eminently capable of making good art out of classical materials. See, e.g., the introductions to Errors, Troi., and Caesar for typically reliable commentary. A satisfying companion to Sh, though as might be expected it summarizes received opinion more than it introduces new insights.

0438. Nicoll, Allardyce. Shakespeare, Home Study Books (Ln, 1952), 181 pp.

The most important relevant ch. is III, "The Young Dramatist At Work" (64-99), in which Nicoll makes some interesting points about Sh's learning. In the early plays Sh crowds his dialogue with Latin tags, "is delighted to be able to out-Plautus Plautus," and takes on Roman "history" in Titus. He later becomes less aggressive about showing the world his knowledge. It is of interest also that he lacks classical restraint in 1, 2, 3H. VI, Titus, and Errors. He writes three H. VI plays where one would do, piles up atrocities in Titus and doubles Plautus' already complex plot. The learning which Sh parades in his early works is respectable by modern standards. There are other remarks of interest scattered through this readable introduction to Shn study.

0439. Nicoll, Allardyce. "'Tragical-Comical-Historical-Pastoral': Elizabethan Dramatic Nomenclature," BJRL, XLIII (1960), 70-87.

The Elizabethan concern with generic classification of drama, parodied in Polonius' catalogue of dramatic types, derives from the nature of drama itself: the dramatist holds a colored glass between his audience and the action; the color of the glass determines the audience's reaction and the genus of the drama. "Shakespeare, who may never have known more of Sophocles than his mere name, has viewed his characters in Hamlet in the same light as that which illumined for his Athenian predecessor the characters in Oedipus." Sh, himself, or perhaps his publishers, first introduced some of the terms later used to classify plays, but the two key terms, "comedy" and "tragedy," were adopted with Plautus and Seneca, though the Elizabethans changed their meanings.

0440. Niva, Weldon N. "Significant Character Names in English Drama to 1603," diss (Pennsylvania, 1959). DA, XX (1959), 2296.

Though the use of tag names was common in Medieval drama, the sixteenth-century humanists vitalized the convention by means of an infusion from Latin comedy. Lyly, Peele, Chapman, Jonson, Marston, Dekker, Heywood, and Middleton inherited a device which heightened dramatic interest and multiplied the possibilities for wit; but the "master" of wit and wordplay with names is Sh.

0441. Nixon, Paul. Martial and the Modern Epigram, Our Debt, [No. 18] (N.Y., 1927), 208 pp.

Fuller's observation (#0257) that Martial, with Ovid and Plautus, was "compounded" in Sh causes Nixon to include Sh among Martial's seventeenth-century inheritors (p. 65); Fuller was, of course, joking about Sh's martial name, as Nixon points out.

0442. Norwood, Gilbert. "The Nature and Methods of Drama," Euripides and Shaw: With Other Essays (Boston, 1921), pp. 109-209.

None of the numerous comments on the methods of Shn drama is analytical or extended; Norwood's aim is to illuminate his general principles by allusion, not by analysis. However, Sh frequently comes into juxtaposition with the Greek dramatists, and the implied analogies are sometimes suggestive.

0443. Norwood, Gilbert. Plautus and Terence, Our Debt, [No. 29] (1932/1963), 212 pp.

Norwood repeatedly illustrates problems in Plautus/Terence scholarship and criticism by making comparisons with the Sh industry. He also points to echoes in Ham. of the Eunuchus and Mercator and in Romeo of the Eunuchus. An appendix gives the Menaechmi and Amphitruo as sources for Errors; Miles Gloriosus as source for L.L.L. (Armado), All's W. (Parolles), 1H.IV (Falstaff), 2H.IV (Falstaff and Pistol), H.V (Pistol), and Wives (Pistol).

0444. Oakeshott, Walter. "Shakespeare and Plutarch," Talking of Shakespeare, ed. John Garrett (Ln, 1954), pp. 111-125.

Oakeshott elaborates the argument of J. A. K. Thomson (#0594) for the importance of Plutarch in Sh's development, indicating Caesar as the turning point in Sh's career. "This is what Shakespeare derived from Plutarch: a sense of history as being the record not of God's intervention continuously taking place in order to prevent man being too big for his boots, but of history as a record of events that develop out of character." This view of history and character is not in Seneca or the Greek tragedians; in an important sense, therefore, Plutarch is a more pervasive influence than Seneca.

0445. O'Brien, Gordon Worth. Renaissance Poetics and the Problem of Power, Institute of Elizabethan Studies: Publication No. 2 (Chicago, 1956), 127 pp.

The Renaissance quest for beatitude through power (energy and potentiality) and its servant, knowledge, sometimes approached belief in the possibility of apotheosis: i.e., man's capacity to ascend to godlike stature through the degrees of a hierarchy of being. This view is to some extent indebted to the metaphysics of Plotinian Platonism, although there is a Christian ancestry as well. Some Renaissance poets (Chapman, Milton, e.g.) felt an obligation to lend tangibility to this beatitude by treating it in sensuous imagery ("avatar"). Sh shows acquaintance with "the problem of power" in several plays: Meas., Oth., Lear, Macb., Antony, e.g., but his most interesting treatment is in Temp., where Prospero is a "materialization of man become the Word," i.e., man become god in a Platonic sense for benevolent purposes. Prospero may also bear some relationship to Simon Magus, who according to an ancient Greek text forswore his magic arts and threw his instruments and books into the sea.

0446. O'Connor, Evelyn. "A Possible Source of Shakespeare's Culture," PL, XXIII (1912), 114-124.

This art., a combination of good sense and baseless speculation, suggests that Sh's "small Latin and less Greek" (the quantity of which the author estimates approximately as received authorities do today), together with his French and Italian, may have been acquired in part under the clandestine guidance of some popish priest hiding near Stratford between the date of Sh's withdrawal from school and his arrival in London. The author gives some interesting accounts of secret chambers and "priest holes" in the mansions of recusant families in the Midland counties, but there is not the slightest evidence that this suggestion is anything more than an improbable guess.

0447. Ogle, M. B. "The Classical Origin and Tradition of Literary Conceits," AJP, XXXIV (1913), 125-152.

With impressive primary documentation (which he modestly says is not exhaustive), Ogle analyzes the tradition of the Elizabethan formula for praise of a lady: golden hair, starry eyes, rosy cheeks, ruby lips, tapered fingers, etc. etc., tracing the elements ultimately to the Alexandrian poets. The main line of descent is through Latin erotic poets to late rhetoricians, to Medieval literature, to Italian and French Renaissance to English Renaissance. Sh ridicules the clichés (e.g., in L.L.L. IV iii 183-186), but he is fully in the tradition: e.g., of all his heroines, only Rosaline (L.L.L.) is dark. There are numerous citations to the poems and plays passim.

0448. Ogle, M. B. "The 'White Hand' as a Literary Conceit," SewR, XX (1912), 459-469.

Largely subsumed into #0447. Ogle here deals chiefly with white hands as a feminine asset from Homer to Sh, whose sources are the French and Italian imitators of the Roman erotic poets.

0449. Ord, Hubert. "The Child and Education in Shakespeare," CR, CIV (1913), 737-741.

Ord suggests that Sh advocates the trivium and quadrivium as the foundation of education but that all the Latin a boy learns will do him no good unless he acquires "that thorough knowledge and creation of faculty which is the aim of true education." Ord gets Sir Hugh Evans into the wrong play and he appears to ignore totally the context and speaker of lines about education in the plays, but this is a pleasant, brief collection of Shn references—from Ipswich and Oxford to Rheims and the Inns of Court.

0450. Owen, S. G. "Ovid and Romance," English Literature and the Classics, ed. G. S. Gordon (OUP, 1912), Ch. VII, pp. 167-195. HB

Owen includes Sh (pp. 185-191) with Chaucer, Gower, and Spenser as one of Ovid's four chief English inheritors. He follows the lead of R. K. Root (#0497) in stating "that the influence of Ovid on Shakespeare was at least five times as great as that of Virgil." Owen expresses confidence that Sh read Ovid in school, but also points out many echoes of Golding's trans.

0451. Parrott, Thomas Marc. Shakespearean Comedy. OUP, 1949, 417 pp.

Parrott's subject is much broader than his title would suggest: the book is a studied analysis of the entire canon prefaced by chs. on the native, classical, and romantic elements which fused to form Elizabethan comedy, on Sh's predecessors in this fusion, and on Sh's probable life before he achieved success in the theater (including an intelligent discussion of his education and his possible service as a schoolmaster). The analyses of the plays are exceptionally good; they include study of sources, the development of dramatic (comic) technique, and character studies. Though the emphasis falls naturally on comic elements in the plays, this book nevertheless is an excellent general guide to the canon; only on Tim. does Parrott appear to be misguided.

0452. Parrott, Thomas Marc. William Shakespeare: A Handbook. N.Y., 1934, 266 pp. E-S

Intended as it is for undergraduates, this handbook ordinarily summarizes briefly passim the received attitudes on given aspects of Sh and the classics, but occasionally Parrott makes an original observation: e.g., if Sh adapted Plautus in Errors while he was a country schoolmaster he must have completely revised the manuscript after going to London because the poetry is Marlovian blank verse which Sh could only have heard and seen in London; perhaps Sh, who had irritated Jonson and the other neoclassicists by the romantic license of W.T., wrote Temp. to poke fun at them by proving he could write according to the classical unities. Altogether a readable and reliable introduction.

0453. Parrott, Thomas M[arc], and Robert H. Ball. "The Drama in Transition: Native, Classical, and Romantic," A Short View of Elizabethan Drama... (N.Y., 1943), Ch. II, pp. 27-44.

The central section of this ch. describes the features of Roman comedy and tragedy as Sh's Elizabethan predecessors adapted them to English tastes. The authors repeatedly call attention to Sh's later use of these classical innovations: the Senecan confidant (Horatio, Juliet's Nurse), the interior conflict in the tragic hero (Shn "soul tragedy"), the Nuntius (the Bleeding Sergeant in Macb.), Terentian wit as a substitute for obscenity (Sh's comic wordplay), Gascoigne's adaptation of Plautine and Terentian comedy (as well as Italian, of course) in Supposes as a source for Shrew, etc. A fluent ch. which, unlike many handbooks, imparts its information gracefully.

0454. Partridge, A. C. "A Comparative Study of the Accidence of Shakespeare and Ben Jonson...," The Accidence of Ben Jonson's Plays, Masques and Entertainments... (Cambridge, 1953), Appendix II, pp. 273-322.

See Section 5, "Gender" (pp. 281-283), the only section to stress a relationship to Latin accidence. "Natural gender, although clearly in operation for general purposes, was still shackled by obscure ties to the grammatical gender of Latin (and sometimes of other languages), but ...the difficulty was generally overcome by the device of personification, more or less consistently used by Jonson, and with the utmost freedom by Shakespeare."

0455. Percy, Thomas, and Richard Farmer. The Correspondence of Thomas Percy and Richard Farmer, The Percy Letters, Vol. II, ed. Cleanth Brooks (Louisiana State UP, 1946), 218 pp.

The exchange of letters about Farmer's

famous *Essay* (#0238) can be found pp. 120-141 *passim*. The letters afford interesting insights into the private opinions of two *litterateurs* on Sh's learning.

0456. Perry, T. S. "A Possible Autograph of Shakspere," *Acad*, No. 477 (1881), 474-475.

A communication describing the supposed Sh signature on the binding of a 1603 North's Plutarch. Perry believes that it is genuine, but the Editor of *Acad* is dubious. Modern opinion remains divided, as it still is on the signature in the Bodleian Ovid.

0457. Pettet, E. C. "Shakespeare's Conception of Poetry," *Essays and Studies*, n. s. III (1950), 29-46.

Pettet sees Sh as a conservative about the nature of poetry, accepting the classical concepts of inspiration (traceable to Plato's *Ion* by way of Sidney) and *mimesis* (traceable to Aristotle) as well as Petrarchan associations of love and the poetic impulse. By "feigning," Sh ordinarily means "imagination," but there are contexts in which he means "dissimulation"; (Pettet does not observe that this latter concept is also ultimately Platonic, deriving from the ostracism of poets, ὅι ψευδαί, from the Republic).

0458. Phillips, Edward. *Theatrum Poetarum* (1675). Munro, II, 221-223.

Phillips refers some half-dozen times to Sh, usually with the "small Latin" concept implied; the most overt statement: "His Learning was not extraordinary, he pleaseth with a certain wild and native Elegance."

0459. Platt, Isaac Hull. "Had Heminges and Condell Studied Law or Read Pliny's Natural History?" *NewShna*, III (1904), 103-106.

The absurd suggestion that Bacon wrote the "Epistle Dedicatorie" to F_1 is based in part on interesting parallels between the Preface to Pliny (in a modern trans., not in Holland) and the Epistle. Most are quite close enough to warrant the suggestion that the Epistle is based on the Preface. But it does not follow that Bacon or Jonson or anyone other than Heminge and Condell wrote it.

0460. "Plautus and His Imitators," *QR*, CLXXIII (1891), 37-69.

Ostensibly a review of Karl von Reinhardstoettner's *Spätere Bearbeitungen plautinischer Lustspiele* (#0479), this is really a full-length essay on the Plautine tradition. It contains some challenging remarks about Sh (e.g., Jonson was correct in saying that Sh had dimmed the fame of Plautus and Terence; his comedies have made the modern world forget the Roman comedians altogether, though Aristophanes remains popular). The author claims for Sh much too extensive an indebtedness to Plautus, but in doing so makes the interesting observation that "'Rudens' ... is Plautus's 'Tempest'." He makes the curious remark that Sh owed nothing direct or indirect to Seneca, yet he seems prepared to guess that Sh obtained assistance in plumbing the Greek tragedies. This is stimulating criticism, but it is not very reliable.

0461. Plimpton, George A. *The Education of Shakespeare: Illustrated from the School-books in Use in his Time*. OUP, 1933, 140 pp. E-S SG

This brief description of a number of books from Plimpton's private library is attractively printed and contains numerous plates showing title pages, hornbooks, etc., but Plimpton is no authority either on Sh's education or on what would be taught in a sixteenth-century grammar school. When he goes beyond Watson (#0627) and Anders (#0073) he is at a loss. Perhaps the most misleading feature of the book is that it treats "Arithmetic and Geometry" in twelve pages and "Rhetoric" in two (and those two imply that Sh's rhetoric would be in English, e.g., Wilson's *Arte of Rhetorique*). T. W. Baldwin shows (in a *JEGP* rev., XXXIV [1935], 444-445) that Plimpton is mistaken about his bibliographical facts in some particulars as well. But Plimpton does recognize "that Shakespeare's brief schooling must have resulted in considerably more learning than the layman has credited him with."

0462. Ploch, Georg. "Über den Dialog in den Dramen Shakespeares und seiner Vorläufer," *GBE*, II (1925), 129-192. SG

After a sketch of evolving technique in nineteen pre-Shn plays, Ploch focuses on Sh in the last thirty pages. Sh follows his predecessors in adopting numerous ultimately Senecan devices: bad news brought by a messenger (*L.L.L.* V ii; *R.III* II iv, III ii), question-and-answer dialogue, stichomythia (*R.III* especially), manipulation of more than two characters in dialogue, monologue placement in scene structure, etc. Ploch's enumeration of the leading features of the dialogue in a dozen plays shows that Sh moved away from markedly Senecan mechanical devices in the mature plays. "Alles in allem aber ist Shakespeare nicht so sehr Neuerer als vielmehr meisterhafter Beherrscher der überkommenen Technik." MdBJ

0463. "Poetae Britannici, A Poem" (1690), Munro Sup, No. 71, pp. 534-535.

A passage of some twenty-eight lines in this poem makes Sh the equal of Plautus, Aeschylus, Ovid, and Cicero, each in his forte, "Tho' Art ne'er taught him how to write by Rules, / Or borrow learning from Athenian Schools." See also #0171.

0464. Pogson, Beryl. In the East My Pleasure Lies: An Esoteric Interpretation of some Plays of Shakespeare. Ln, 1950, 120 pp.

This critical study is ingenious if unconvincing. Unlike some other occult readings, this one does not explore the ancient mysteries in any detail; most of the assertions are only allusive. The duality of sex in Sh's disguised heroines symbolizes the ancient belief that both sexes must be fulfilled in the individual. The anachronisms in Cym. are Sh's deliberate acknowledgment of his cultural debt to ancient Rome and Renaissance Italy. Sh's heroes, like those of Greek tragedy, are of noble birth, symbolizing their "innate Divinity as [children] of God." Angelo in Meas. is a man who, like the Greek heroes, can transcend humanity (as his name suggests) and the arbitrary justice of Act V is like the arbitrary justice of the Areopagus in the trial of Orestes. The Labyrinth of Minos is implied in the forest outside Athens in Dream: Theseus has escaped it; the lovers are still in it. Underlying several plays (e.g., Meas., Dream, Tim.) is a scale of being which recalls the mysteries and Plato. Cleopatra symbolizes the mystical glories of the mystery religion while Rome symbolizes the mundane interests which keep a man earth-bound. The same difficulty intrudes in this book as in others of its kind: if occult meanings lie in the stories Sh used, they must lie also in the sources Sh drew those stories from. Since Sh cast a wide net for his materials, the whole culture of Elizabethan England must ergo have been occult. The author does not face this difficulty; there is very little source study here.

0465. Pope, Alexander. "Preface to the Works of Shakespear" (1725), The Works of Alexander Pope, Esq. With Notes and Illustrations by Himself and Others..., ed. William Roscoe, 10 vols. (Ln, 1824), VII, 403-426.

Despite the claims for Sh's originality advanced in the first two paragraphs, this famous essay would modify considerably the view of Milton, Dryden, and the other late seventeenth-century eulogists that Sh was Fancy's child, unschooled in his predecessors' achievements. Pope finds abundant evidence of Sh's accurate awareness of antiquity and he makes a distinction between learning and language which Richard Farmer and many another detractor could have profited from heeding; he also makes the wise observation that his seventeenth-century forebears took unnecessarily extreme postures in the Art/Jonson—Nature/Sh debate: Jonson and Sh share both Art and Nature. However, Pope's only defense of Sh's violation of the unities is to plead that he wrote in ignorance of them in a pre-Jonsonian age. Much else of what Pope considers crudity he blames on (1) Sh's association with low actors, (2) the demands of a boorish audience, (3) the helter-skelter method of publication which produced F_1 and the quartos without benefit of Sh's supervision. This ed. is elaborated by the commentary of Warton (Thomas?).

0466. Price, Hereward T. Construction in Shakespeare, MCMP, No. 17 (Michigan UP, 1951), 42 pp.

This brilliant lecture attacks that Shn criticism which mistakes the part (poetry, imagery, characterization, e.g.) for the whole (dramatic structure). The fallacy began, Price thinks, with the misunderstanding of Aristotle and Horace by seventeenth-century critics: if the unities are construction and Sh disregards the unities, then Sh does not construct. But Price shows that Shn unity is repetition with a difference and concentration on thematic material. The address ranges widely; among the best passages are analyses of Sonn. 116, of 1H.VI and of Titus. Price makes two interesting comparisons between 1H.VI and the classics: IV vii is a Homeric way of degrading the dead; the whole play is like Aeschylus' Persae —a dramatization of a theme, not of a story.

0467. Price, Hereward T. "Shakespeare's Classical Scholarship," RES, IX (1958), 54-55.

A letter to the Editor insisting that Sh "had wide intellectual interests ranging far beyond what the theatre demanded of him and that his 'Latine' was not 'small'." Price's evidence is the signature "W. Shakspere" in the Folger Library's copy of W. Lambarde's Latin/Old English ed. of the Anglo-Saxon Laws, 'αρχαιονομια. This signature has been given at least tentative credence by J. Q. Adams, Giles E. Dawson, and T. W. Baldwin, all of whom Price cites.

0468. Price, John Robert, S.J. "Shakespeare's Mythological Invention," diss (Wisconsin, 1959). DA, XX (1959), 1355.

Price believes that those who confidently locate Sh's source for a given image in a single classical or Renaissance author are neglecting the commonplace character of mythological imagery in the sixteenth century. "Invention" consisted of finding and manipulating commonplaces for artistic effect, not of original formulation or imitation of a single author. The background of Sh's invention lies in the rhetorical curriculum of the Renaissance grammar schools. Price gives five conclusions: (1) we cannot be certain that either Golding or the Latin Meta. was Sh's primary source of information about Greek mythology; (2) mythology had, for the Renaissance, "humanistic" and rhetorical values which were delineated in schoolbooks; (3) and (4) Sh's mythology makes use of these values (especially rhetorical)--Sh never regarded myth as mere decoration; (5) Sh's originality lies in "creative adaptation of commonplace imagery to the theatre," not in the revelation of new concepts or images.

0469. Prölss, Robert. "Shakespeare," Das neuere Drama der Engländer, Geschichte des neueren Dramas, Bd. II, H. 2 (Leipzig, 1882), Ch. V, pp. 86-154. E-S

Prölss considers it "wahrscheinlich" that Sh learned a certain amount of Latin at Stratford School and that he improved his acquaintance in after years. But there is no attempt to specify the discipline Sh underwent; nor is there any real attempt to explore his varying responses to classical culture, even though Prölss gives inter alia an adequate brief survey of nineteenth-century received opinion on Sh's sources. Antony, Caesar, and Cor. are classed with the histories, Titus and Tim. with the tragedies, and Troi. by itself, as in F_1. DLC

0470. Quiller-Couch, Sir Arthur. Notes on Shakespeare's Workmanship. N.Y., 1917, 338 pp. (Republished with minor changes under title: Shakespeare's Workmanship [1918].)

References to Sh's classicism are scattered passim: e.g., the analogy of Macb. to Greek tragedy, pp. 55-59; the interesting reminder that the convention of mistaken identity was more credible on Plautus' stage than on Sh's because Roman actors wore masks, pp. 65-66; the observation that Sh's Yorkist histories are doomed as tragic art by the Aristotelian dictum that history is not so philosophical as poetry: while Macbeth, Cymbeline, and Lear were mythical figures like those of the Greeks, Richard III was too real to be tragic, p. 116; the definition of Per., Cym., and W.T. as successful fusions of epic theme and dramatic form, pp. 218-219.

0471. Raleigh, Walter. Shakespeare, English Men of Letters Series (N.Y., 1907), 233 pp.

The most important relevant ch. is III, "Books and Poetry," which discusses inter alia Sh's use of Plutarch, his response to mythology (an early cult of beauty which Sh later abandoned in favor of a more ethical religion), his use of Ovidian and neo-Ovidian materials, etc. Raleigh also scatters remarks of lesser interest all through the book: on Sh's grammar school Latin in Ch. II, on Cleopatra and Octavia in Ch. VI, on Sh's attitude toward the Graeco-Roman world in Ch. V. But Raleigh is interested in Sh as a person, as a thinker, and as an artist; only incidentally does Sh emerge as a classicist.

0472. Ralli, Augustus. "The Uses of the Classics," Later Critiques (N.Y., 1933), pp. 41-50.

This defense of classical study against its pragmatic critics from Cato the Censor to Oswald Spengler defines classicism in spiritual terms and treats Sh as a classic to be compared with the Greeks and Romans. Passages from several plays are cited and specific comparison is made to Horace, Virgil, and Catullus.

0473. Rand, Edward K. Ovid and His Influence, Our Debt, [No. 13] (Boston, 1925), 184 pp.

English Renaissance literature does not receive the attention one might expect in a survey of this scope; Sh merits a single paragraph. Rand observes that "there is hardly an aspect of Ovid's genius and art that one will not see reproduced somewhere in Shakespeare," but he does not specify, being content to suggest that Sh and Ovid shared freedom of the spirit, "'the elegancy and golden cadence of poesy'," and perhaps "a lack of religion."

0474. Ransom, John C[rowe]. "On Shakespeare's Language," SewR, LV (1947), 181-198.

Sh's habit (in his mature verse) of making a brilliant contrast between native monosyllables and Latinate polysyllables ("incarnadine," "superflux," "multitudinous," etc.) demonstrates his profound Latinity and may well have saved the Latinate element in English diction from becoming naturalized the way the Norman element became naturalized by 1400. Thanks to Sh, then, we have a specialized diction which retains its foreign flavor and can serve specialized functions in English poetry. Ransom's observations about Sh's technique are unquestionably valid, but he is less convincing when he extends them into the field of linguistic and literary history.

0475. Rây, P. C. "Learning of Shakespeare," 3 CalcuttaR, LXXVI (1940), 235-246; LXXVII (1940), 1-10, 131-140. (The three arts. are parts X, XI, and XII of Rây's longer series titled "Shakespearean Puzzle —Endeavours After Its Solution.")

Rây is in essence correct in his belief that Sh could read some Latin classics in the originals. But these essays should be credited only with great caution, as they contain numerous errors of fact (Apollo is a "goddess"; "The Rape of Lucrece has been [i.e., 'was'] definitely based upon Ovid's Metamorphosis [sic]," etc.). There are also several misquotations of secondary sources. The essays are somewhat disjointed and written in a style which (though pleasant and informal) shows only an imperfect command of English syntax. DLC

0476. Rea, John D. "The Dyer's Hand," SAB, VII (1932), 82-87.

This selection from Sh's many references to his trade as actor emphasizes several by "classical" characters (in, e.g., Cor., Troi., Cym., W.T.) which are distinctly anachronistic. In passing: the reference to Aristotelian imitation in drama in Ulysses' attack on Patroclus and Achilles (Troi. I iii 150) "is evidently an attempt to give some Greek flavor to the comments on actors and acting."

0477. Rea, John D. "'This Figure That Thou Here Seest Put'," MP, XXII (1925), 417-419.

Rea traces to the iconography of Erasmus the sentiment in Jonson's lines on the Sh portrait in F_1. Jonson suggests that the writings of Sh show him better than his portrait can. Exactly the same concept appears in the Greek and Latin inscription on a medallion portrait of Erasmus (1519), in Erasmus' own writings, and especially in a laudatory Latin poem which Gilbertus Cognatus wrote opposite a Holbein portrait of Erasmus in a 1533 ed. of the Adagia. Rea calls Jonson's verses a paraphrase of Cognatus'. It is ironic that Jonson, who "accused" Sh of minimal classicism, should, as Rea puts it, "plunder from the authors of the Low Countries, through whom he often acquired his classical material at second hand."

0478. Reese, M. M. Shakespeare: His World and His Work. Ln, 1953, 589 pp.

Though references to Sh and the classics are scattered through the book, the most important relevant ch. is III, "Classical Influences in the Sixteenth Century," which constitutes a responsible introduction to English use of classical dramatic models during Elizabeth's reign. The conclusion about Sh: "Traces of the Morality, the romantic and the classical exist side by side." In another part of the book Reese makes the point that if Beeston was right in saying that Sh had been a schoolmaster in the country he would have been an abecedarius, lacking the university degree and divine orders necessary for mastership.

0479. Reinhardstoettner, Karl von. Plautus: Spätere Bearbeitungen plautinischer Lustspiele, KSA, Bd. I (Leipzig, 1886), 793 pp. E-S HB

This immensely learned and relentlessly documented tome makes reference to fourteen of Sh's plays. Though he has been much criticized for granting Sh too broad an acquaintance with Plautus, actually von Reinhardstoettner argues against the received opinions of his day only on the character of Falstaff, whom he thinks closer to Parolles and to the miles than Morgann's successors would grant (and in this, of course, he anticipates the position of Stoll in this century). For the rest, Sh appears most often as one whose characters bear interesting resemblances to Plautine characters—it is seldom claimed that Sh borrowed themes, characters, scenes from Plautus directly, though the author sometimes quotes from scholars who do make such claims.

0480. Ribner, Irving. Patterns in Shakespearian Tragedy. Ln, 1960, 205 pp.

Ribner takes a developmental approach to Shn tragedy--from Senecan Nemesis Sh progressed to an ethical system founded on freedom of choice and moral responsibility in the great tragedies which owe much to the Morality tradition. But even in the early, Senecan plays personal responsibility and the alternatives of salvation and damnation are crucial. The first ch. analyzes Titus, R. III, and Romeo, each as a tentative departure toward Christianity from Kydian Senecanism. Other relevant sections analyze the theme of public and private morality in Caesar and the rejection of man and God in Tim. (Troi. is not considered relevant). The last ch., on Antony and Cor., discusses the paradox of heroes damned by their vices, yet glorious in their damnation. Ribner's book is more rewarding in its criticism of individual plays than in its over-all thesis, which may be an oversimplification of philosophical values (e.g., he does not give sufficient consideration to Sh's portraits of Stoicism and the Aristotelian virtues, or to hamartia as the prelude to Nemesis). It would seem that Ribner is imposing Christian standards where they are not applicable, especially on the Roman and Greek plays in which Sh makes some special effort to surround the action with classical ethics (e.g., Cassius' Epicureanism, Brutus' Stoicism, Antony's magnanimity).

0481. Richards, I. A. "The Places and the Figures," KR, XI (1949), 17-30.

Richards is dubious of the validity of the equation made by Baldwin (#0089) and Sister Miriam Joseph (#0424) between Sh's putative education in Renaissance rhetoric and the "places and the figures" in his plays. He is inclined toward the view that Sh could easily have picked rhetoric out of the air around him as he doubtless picked law and medicine. (It is interesting that Richards is very much less dubious about Donald L. Clark's similar equation for Milton in John Milton at Saint Paul's School). Richards appears to share in the common modern suspicion of rhetoric as one of the dishonest arts (it does not deal with facts stripped naked); historical critics with some exposure to Renaissance theory and practice will probably not take his side of the question.

0482. Richardson, L. J. "Repetition and Rhythm in Vergil and Shakespeare," CUC, XXXII (1930), 177-182. HB

An interesting study of the metrical effect of verbal repetition in Sh and Virgil. Of the four possible methods, Sh, like Virgil, prefers the three "musical" ones, not because Sh imitated Virgil, but because both had ears sensitive to music. Richardson draws most of the "unmusical" examples in Sh from Venus. It would be of interest to pursue the study, determining the ratio of musical to unmusical echoes in Sh's later works as a possible criterion of the development of his poetic technique.

0483. Rick, Leo. "Shakespeare und Ovid," ShJ, LV (1919), 35-53. E-S HB SG

An erudite and well-documented study. Verbal, thematic, and stylistic parallels show conclusively that Sh knew both Golding and the Latin Meta. In addition, Rick finds traces of the Heroides, Ars Amatoria, Remedia Amoris, Amores, and Fasti, especially in the early works. As Sh matured he was less inclined to echo Ovid directly, but Rick shows that the Ovidian style remained part of Sh's literary equipment throughout his career. Some of the direct echoes of Ovid have not been widely noted (e.g., Luciana's homily [Errors III ii 1-28] is a recollection of Amores III 14; Kate's "Happy the parents of so fair a child! ..." [Shrew IV v 39-41] reflects the praise of Hermaphroditus by Salmacis in Meta. IV). Rick is fully aware of the broad provenance of Ovidian themes and rhetoric in Elizabethan England and therefore does not claim too much for Sh; this important art. is an informative complement to Root's groundwork on Sh's Ovid (#0497).

0484. Riddle, J[oseph] Esmond. Illustrations of Aristotle on Men and Manners from the Dramatic Works of Shakspeare. Oxford, 1832, 134 pp.

A florilegium from the Rhetoric and the Nicomachean Ethics juxtaposing passages from over a score of Shn plays. Aristotle is represented in Greek without comment. The brief "Advertisement" announces at the outset that Aristotle and Sh were "accurate and independent observers of human nature" and Riddle expresses the intention of seeing "how far Aristotle was a poet, and how far Shakspeare was a philosopher." The large number of abstract nouns and infinitives in the Greek and the concrete directness of much of the Shn material suggest that philosophy and poetry are some distance apart in this book. Topics illustrated include "Anger," "Jealousy," "Shame," "The Aged," "Human Society," "Force of Habit." DFo

0485. [Ritson, Joseph]. Remarks, Critical and Illustrative on the Text and Notes of the

Last Edition of Shakspeare. Ln, 1783, 240 pp.

The "last edition" was that of Johnson and Steevens (1778), but Ritson comments sarcastically on Warburton, Malone, Farmer, and Upton as well. His tone is belligerent and pontifical. About two score of the hundreds of brief notes here are relevant: several treat etymology from the classical languages, some discuss Sh's use of North's Plutarch, some interpret difficult passages of ultimately classical origin. DFo

0486. Robbins, Edwin W. Dramatic Characterization in Printed Commentaries on Terence 1473-1600, ISLL, XXXV, No. 4 (1951), 122 pp.

Robbins attempts to do for the Tudor drama at large what Baldwin (#0683) did for Sh, except that Robbins is concerned with techniques of characterization, the relative importance of plot and character, the ethical import of character, types and individuals, and other matters connected with the characters in Renaissance drama. He is able to show a definite debt to Terence and especially to his eds. and annotators, though he stresses that the influence comes into English drama as early as Medwall and thereafter the question of direct or indirect indebtedness is difficult to answer. Sh is mentioned only infrequently, but each time the allusion implies that he is fully in the tradition: Shylock has some elements of Sannio, the Terentian usurer; Falstaff has both thraso and gnatho in him (and of course more besides); Romeo is on the theme of almost all the Terentian comedies, the desire of youth to marry against the wishes of the older generation, but the tone is definitely different--no Terentian character is ever in any danger of death.

0487. Roberts, Donald R. "Shakespeare and the Rhetoric of Stylistic Ornamentation," diss (Cornell, 1936).*

0488. Roberts, W. Rhys. Greek Rhetoric and Literary Criticism, Our Debt, [No. 7] (N.Y., 1928), 164 pp.

Roberts makes two passing allusions to Sh: the first (pp. 16-17) contrasts Sh's relatively infrequent parodies (Dream, Ham., L.L.L., A.Y.L., and Falstaff's parody of King Cambyses' vein in 1H.IV) with the "amazing opulence of fancy and ingenuity shown in the parodies of Aristophanes"; the second (p. 39) mentions Falstaff's parody (1H.IV II iv 439-461) of euphuism, which Roberts traces to Gorgias in the First Sophistic—he points out that Diodorus applied the term εὐφυής to Gorgias' disciples.

0489. Robertson, J[ohn] M. The Baconian Heresy: A Confutation. Ln, 1913, 612 pp. SG

Ch. VII (pp. 178-252) is a detailed and contemptuous "confutation" of those Baconians who base their claims for Baconian authorship on "the alleged classical scholarship of the plays": Lord Penzance, Ignatius Donnelly, George Greenwood (The Shakespeare Problem Restated), R. M. Theobald, and W. Theobald are the authors most harshly treated. Ch. VIII (pp. 253-375) is a laborious analysis of R. M. Theobald's list of 230 "Latinisms" in Sh which, Theobald claimed, proved the erudition of Sh. Robertson shows, chiefly through the use of the NED, that most were common English terms in Sh's day. Robertson has done a thorough and useful job, but he has two chief faults: (1) insufficient bibliographical information—he occasionally even leaves one guessing as to a man's full name or the title of his book; (2) occasional refutation by disintegration of the Sh canon, a procedure which, unfortunately, may cast suspicion on the part of the job which he does well.

0490. Robertson, John M. "The Learning of Shakespeare," UMFR, X (1898), 166-180.

Robertson attacks Baynes (#0097) and Fiske (#0241) as much because their arguments for Sh's Latinity give aid and comfort to the Baconians as because their evidence is inadequate. Robertson resurrects Farmer to praise him and excuse his faults as jocularity. This essay is convincing enough in its demonstration that Sh used Golding in Venus and Temp., and that "Adonis' gardens" (1H.VI I vi 6-7) were a Renaissance commonplace. But the reader may be dubious when Robertson postulates unrecorded manuscript trans. as intermediaries between Sh and his ultimate sources in Latin literature. DLC TxHR

0491. Robertson, J[ohn] M. Montaigne and Shakespeare and Other Essays on Cognate Questions. Ln, 1897/1909, 358 pp. SG

In his eagerness to establish the formative influence of Montaigne on Sh's mind, Robertson minimizes all other influences, especially classical. In Ch. IV ("Shakespeare and the Classics") and elsewhere passim he suggests that Sh absorbed Senecan and Ciceronian influences chiefly through Montaigne's Essais. Robertson accounts for classical influence before 1603 (Florio's trans.) by suggesting that Sh saw the manuscript before publication and by disintegrating the Sh canon, and he vigorously attacks J. C. Collins (#0173) though he uses Collins' methods to some extent.

0492. Robertson, John M. "The Originality of Shakspere," UMFR, X (1898), 577-608.

Robertson here answers the reviewers of Montaigne and Shakespeare (#0491), who objected that Robertson's source studies and disintegration conspire to deprive Sh of his genius (i.e., originality). Robertson repeats some of his arguments for Montaigne as intermediary between Sh and the classics. He also endorses Fleay's view of Caesar as an abridgment of a two-part play by an earlier dramatist; the popularity of Roman plays in the 1590's caused Sh to adapt his predecessors' works in Caesar. Robertson's arguments are vigorous but not persuasive. DLC TxHR

0493. Robertson, John M. Shakespeare and Chapman. Ln, 1917, 303 pp.

The heart of Robertson's book is an effort to assign Chapman a hand in Tim., Per., Troi., the masque in Temp., the theophany in Cym., and the "rugged Pyrrhus" speech in Ham. Robertson calls attention to the fact that these plays and passages "are all founded on 'classical' themes," but he does not probe Sh's (or Chapman's) classicism, contenting himself with verbal and prosodical tests which have since fallen into disuse and disrepute. Robertson has proved very little—see, e.g., the caustic criticism of his rationale on Troi. in the New Variorum, p. 372.

0494. Robinson, Edwin Arlington. "Ben Jonson Entertains a Man from Stratford," Collected Poems (N.Y., 1922), pp. 20-32.

In this dramatic monologue Robinson gives a vivid, imaginative, false picture of Sh as he thinks Ben Jonson saw him. Sh is ignorant of the classics, but doesn't care, careless of his artistry, and ambitious chiefly for money and "that House in Stratford." His Dark Lady tortures him into producing Cleopatra and other dramatic explosions. An amusing, but greatly misleading poem.

0495. Rolfe, W. J. "At School," Shakespeare the Boy (N.Y., 1896), pp. 93-118.

An elementary account of Sh's probable schooldays with references from the plays. Rolfe suggests Lily, Sententiae Pueriles, The Accidence, and Mantuan as sources of Sh's "small Latin," but he concedes him a bare minimum of Greek (if any) and attributes the ignorance to Sh's having left school at thirteen; then (illogically enough) Rolfe uses this newly established ignorance to justify the legend that Sh did leave school young.

0496. Rolfe, W. J. "Shakespeare at School," Shna, IV (1887), 208-212.

Superseded by #0495.

0497. Root, R. K. Classical Mythology in Shakespeare, YSE, No. 19 (N.Y., 1903), 134 pp. E-S HB

This compilation is doubly useful as an index to Sh's mythological allusions because Part I is an alphabetical list of persons, places, and things in classical myth with loci cited in Sh's plays and poems while Part II is a presentation (chronological according to Root's judgment) of the Sh canon with brief discussion of the use and source of myth in each play or poem. The twenty-four-page introduction contains Root's deductions from the evidence of I and II: (1) Ovid and (much less) Virgil are Sh's almost exclusive sources for myth. (2) Sh's attitude toward myth changed during his career. (3) (1) and (2) can serve as partial guides in debate about the Sh canon and about the chronology of plays. (4) Sh responded most deeply to "that original aspect of the system which gives a divine personality to the great forces of nature," and though he did not find the profound meanings in Ovid that he would have found in the Greeks, he himself supplied "the deeper spiritual significance which [mythology] implies." (1) and (4) are convincing arguments; (2) and especially (3) perhaps go beyond the evidence. This is an important work which has not been superseded by later scholarship. But note the supplement (#0141) published by Douglas Bush in 1927.

0498. Root, R. K. "Some Notes on Shakespeare," JEGP, IV (1902), 452-459.

Explanations based on mythology of cruxes in Lear (II ii 131-132), A.Y.L. (III ii 155), Ham. (I v 31-34), Lucr. (265-266), Dream (III ii 378-393). In each case the opinions are restated in Classical Mythology in Shakespeare (#0497).

0499. Rowe, Nicholas. "Prologue to The Ambitious Stepmother" (1701), Munro, II, 252n.

Rowe boldly asserts that Sh "durst not"

portray "famous Greek and Latian Beauties." How he would classify Troi., Caesar, Antony, and Cor. is not clear.

0500. Rowe, Nicholas. Some Account of the Life &c. of Mr. William Shakespear (1709). Ed. Samuel H. Monk, Augustan Reprint Society Extra Ser., No. 1 (1948), xl pp.

This is Rowe's famous preface to the first ed. of Sh in the eighteenth century. Though it perpetuates the Restoration's extreme polarity between Jonson's labored Art and Sh's unlearned Nature, and though it contains as much myth as fact about Sh's life, Some Account contains some surprising information considering its date. Rowe knows that Errors is based on the Menaechmi (but not that W.W. had trans. the latter in 1595); he also recognizes Plutarch as the source of the characters of Brutus and Antony and of much else in the Roman plays. Most interesting of all, however, is Rowe's recognition of the similarities between Ham. and Sophocles' Electra. His is apparently the first analysis of the two plays in juxtaposition (Addison [#1801] apparently is Rowe's debtor, at least in part). Too much attention has been given to Rowe's retailing of stories about Sh's deer-stealing, leaving school young, and knowing no classical literature; more in justice should be given to his pioneer and responsible criticism of the plays.

0501. Rüdiger, H. "Shakespeare und die Antike," Darmstädter Tageblatt, November 27, 1938. GRS

Not seen.

0502. Rushton, William Lowes. Shakespeare and "The Arte of English Poesie". Liverpool, 1909, 167 pp. E-S

An extensive catalogue of passages in Sh which exemplify or comment upon Greek and Roman rhetorical devices defined and discussed in Puttenham. Some of them have evidently not been noticed by other scholars. Rushton relies rather heavily on verbal parallels, and does not persuade that Sh is recalling The Arte of English Poesie in every instance. But he presents a good case for Sh's knowledge of the treatise and an excellent case for Sh's familiarity with the rhetorical devices at issue. It is obvious, for example, that Sh is deliberately using the device of κλῖμαξ (or gradatio) in passages quoted from John, Much, Errors, and A.Y.L., whether or not he has Puttenham's definition in mind; in Ulysses' "degree" speech in Troi. the device is particularly effective since Ulysses' subject is itself "gradation" (pp. 67-70). Again, Hamlet, in his "Look here upon this picture, and on this" (III iv 53-65) may not be referring to portraits actually in Gertrude's closet, but following instead the formulas for hypotyposis and prosographia, both of which describe persons or things absent or dead (pp. 38-43). It seems probable moreover that Holofernes is referring directly to Puttenham's discussion of barbarismus and solecismus in his complaints to Nathaniel about mispronunciation of Latinate English words and about mutilated Latin (L.L.L. V i 18-32); in both Sh and Puttenham Priscian appears as the standard for grammatical correctness (pp. 46-50). Rushton also occasionally argues with cogency for emendations in F_1 on the basis of verbal analogues in Puttenham. DFo

0503. Rushton, William L[owes]. Shakespeare Illustrated by Old Authors, [in two parts]. Ln, 1867, 84, 64 pp.

This is a collection of parallel passages which Rushton earlier had published in Archiv. Rushton's main interest is the law, but his intensive reading in Greek literature enables him to "illustrate" many passages in Sh by excerpts from Homer, Aristophanes, Euripides, Demosthenes, Aristotle, and others. There is considerably less illustration from Latin literature. Occasionally Rushton will infer indebtedness, as when he suggests that Sh and Aristotle share an allusion to a distich of Anacreon on love, but more often he is content to permit the Greek and the English to complement one another. Of major interest is the number of close parallels between Sh and the explanations of classical rhetoric in Puttenham's Arte of English Poesie. Rushton induces a good case for Sh's knowledge of Puttenham. MnU

0504. Rushton, W[illiam] L[owes]. "Shakespeare's Books," 9 NQ, VIII (1901), 78-79, 180-181, 321; 10 NQ, I (1904), 465; II (1904), 464.

A number of examples of Sh's use of such rhetorical formulae as anaphora and antistrophe which Puttenham discusses in The Arte of English Poesie. The parallel passages here are a supplement to those offered in #0503. Rushton's case seems stronger in the original than in this supplement.

0505. Ruskin, John. "Government" (1863), Munera Pulveris: Six Essays on the Elements of Political Economy, in The Works of John Ruskin, ed. E. T. Cook and Alexander Wedderburn (Ln, 1905), XVII, 231-261.

On pp. 257-258, in a well-known passage, Ruskin etymologizes the names of some dozen of Sh's characters, most from Latin and Greek roots. Some of the etymologies are ingenious and have since been largely accepted, but in several cases Ruskin overlooks the obvious: e.g., deriving "Titania" from "τιτήνη" ("the queen"), Ruskin forgets that Sh found the Latin form in Meta.; so also with "Valentine" from "valens," when St. Valentine is the patron of lovers.

0506. Rylands, George H. W. Words and Poetry. Ln, 1928, 244 pp.

Sh is the central subject in this approach to the diction and prosody of English poetry. The most important single observation about Sh's use of classical materials is in Part II, "Notes and Quotations Preparatory to a Study of Shakespeare's Diction and Style." At the end of the third ch., Rylands points out that Sh's sublime effects in his verse before 1600 are achieved by sculptured railing about set topics (Time, Learning, Women, Death, Opportunity) on the model of Ovid. [Wolfgang Clemen has since shown that Sh's predecessors in tragedy also relied heavily on set speeches—see #0170.] In his mature style Sh makes the soliloquies of his characters reflect not rhetorical structure but conflict between passion and reason. But Sh still retains rhetorical utterance for special occasions (e.g., in Caesar, Meas., Troi.).

0507. S. "On Shakspeare's Learning," Censura Literaria, ed. Egerton Brydges, 2nd ed. (Ln, 1815), IX, 334-339.

An intelligent dissent from the views of Richard Farmer (#0238); the first half shows that Farmer proved only that Sh did not use Latin and Greek originals, not that he could not. The argument by analogy is conducted with some flair. MnU

0508. Saintsbury, George. "Shakespeare: Life and Plays," "Shakespeare: Poems," The Cambridge History of English Literature, ed. A. W. Ward and A. R. Waller (CUP, 1910), V, Ch. VIII, Ch. IX, 186-263. E-S

Saintsbury gives little attention to the "small Latin" controversy. He considers that investigating Sh's probable education is of importance only as a weapon against anti-Stratfordianism; as he neglects the importance to criticism of a knowledge of Sh's cultural heritage he also minimizes source study generally—he merely mentions Plutarch and Plautus and regrets briefly that Sh did not borrow extensively from Chaucer for Troi. Yet his criticism is sane (he rejects disintegration as an idiosyncrasy) and sometimes very stimulating (on the stanzaic patterns of Venus and Lucr.; on the "classical" contrast between Ariel and Caliban, etc.).

0509. Salter, Charles Henry. "Poetry and Politics," PR, XXX (1939), 345-361. GRS

Salter points out inter alia that Sh thought of politics in the same way that Aeschylus and Euripides did: as "synonymous with human life as a whole." The Greeks thought of politics in its root sense "what [goes] on in the city," and therefore generalized; Sh thought of the effect of politics on the individual. When Sh and the Greek tragedians do enunciate "political" dogmas, the effect is banality because, not wishing to offend any segment of their audiences, they speak truisms which all can accept.

0510. Sandys, J[ohn] E[dwin]. "Education," Shakespeare's England, [ed. C. T. Onions] (Oxford: Clarendon, 1916), I, 224-250. E-S SG

Though Part I, "Schools and School-Books," 224-238, has been superseded by the massed evidence of T. W. Baldwin's two-vol. William Shakspere's Small Latine and Lesse Greeke (#0089), Sandys' essay is desirable for the general reader because of its brevity. It is among the first serious attempts to assess Sh's learning through informed conjecture about the curriculum he would have to pursue at Stratford Grammar School. Cf. Baynes (#0097) and Plimpton (#0461) and (of course) Baldwin. Part II, "Universities and Learned Societies," shows passim that Sh was familiar at least with the jargon of higher education.

0511. Sandys, John Edwin. A History of Classical Scholarship. [3 vols.] Vol. II: From the Revival of Learning to the End of the Eighteenth Century (In Italy, France, England, and the Netherlands). CUP, 1908. 498 pp. (Reprinted, 1958.)

The three brief references to Sh record his familiarity with North's trans. (which Sandys at one point attributes to Florio) of Amyot's Plutarch and with Golding's Meta.

0512. Sandys, J[ohn] E[dwin]. "Scholarship," Shakespeare's England, [ed. C. T. Onions] (Oxford: Clarendon, 1916), I, 251-283. E-S SG

Section (2), "Classical Scholars," makes a passing contrast between Sh's interpretation of mythology and Bacon's. (3), "Translators" (259-283), is one of the best short essays on Elizabethan trans. It needs supplement from Lathrop's more complete survey (#0381), but Sandys' compilation has the merit of being readable—it is more than a list. He closes with an admirable brief review of the history of the "small Latin" controversy.

0513. Schelling, Felix E. "History and Tragedy on Classical Myth and Story," Elizabethan Drama, 1558-1642 (Boston, 1908), II, Ch. XIII, 1-50. E-S

This strangely uneven ch. is more edifying on Sh's contemporaries than on Sh himself. Troi. and Antony, through misguided organization, have been excluded altogether from this survey while none of the other plays on classical themes receives anything like a just treatment. Not even Schelling's obvious intention of emphasizing Sh's contemporaries can defend the sketchy and misleading remarks about the Greek and Roman plays. Yet, curiously enough, Schelling is informative and critically sound on Fulke Greville, Ben Jonson, and many of Sh's other contemporaries.

0514. Schirmer, Walter. "Chaucer, Shakespeare und die Antike," Kleine Schriften (Tübingen, 1950), pp. 57-82. (Originally published in England und die Antike [1930-1931]. E-S HB)

Though Sh lived after the high point of the English classical revival, he deserves inclusion with Sidney, Spenser, and the rest because he had a genuine reverence for the ancient world. To Chaucer, the first English classicist, the classical myths were everyday data of which he spoke casually; in Sh's works "wir essen nicht mehr mit den Göttern und Heroen am selben Tisch." Sh appreciated the solemnity of the double strain of Senecanism (the Tenne Tragedies and the French imitations) and he read Plutarch as Dryden later did: "All history is only the precepts of moral philosophy reduced into examples." Unlike Ben Jonson and Sir William Alexander, who tried to recreate the letter of antiquity, Sh idealized what he thought was its spirit, and, if he sometimes misunderstood that spirit (as in the idealization of Antony's irresponsibility in Antony), he rivaled it, especially in the last plays where he successfully synthesized Chaucerian naturalism and heroic classicism. A stimulating essay.

0515. Schirmer, Walter. "Der englische Humanismus," Kleine Schriften (Tübingen, 1950), pp. 7-23.

See Section 11, pp. 22-23, for the opinion that Sh, the last man of the Renaissance, is an example of the "Sich-Selbst-Finden des nationalen Genius unter dem durchlebten Einfluss der Antike." Brief mention of Macb., Lear, Oth., R. III, Ham. Much of what is said here is to be found verbatim in "Chaucer, Shakespeare und die Antike" (#0514).

0516. Schirmer, Walter. "Shakespeare und die Rhetorik," ShJ, LXXI (1935), 11-31. E-S (Reprinted in Kleine Schriften [Tübingen, 1950].)

Defining the rhetorical drama which Sh inherited from Marlowe (ultimately from Seneca) in terms (1) of its verbal decoration and (2) of its action and character, Schirmer shows by what steps Sh submerged the Marlovian elements as he grew in dramatic and linguistic power. Metaphor as a cloak for meaning and formal oratorical tricks which do not advance the action are far more common in the early plays than after Caesar, though Sh never completely dropped Wilson, Cicero, and Quintilian from his Art. More important, however, than language are character and plot. In Sh's early Marlovian plays (especially Titus) the conflict is an external one as in Seneca, and rhetorical formality emphasizes the loneliness of the tragic type as he stands against a hostile background. In the mature plays the action springs from internal conflict (character is fate) and thus the need for rhetoric is less as Sh wishes to reveal psychological states, not public veneers. The major emphasis falls on Titus, the two tetralogies, Caesar, Ham., and Cor. One of the most interesting passages juxtaposes Brutus and Coriolanus and Antony and Menenius, all four as orators dealing with the Roman mob. Such public images as are projected by characters in the later plays suggest that "er sah dankbar auf seine Lehrmeisterin Rhetorik zurück, aber er brauchte sie nicht mehr, er hatte selbst die Kunst, das Menschenherz zu rühren."

0517. Schirmer, Walter. "Shakespeares klassizistische Gegenspieler," Anglia, LXXVI (1958), 90-116.

In the course of an informative account of

the activities and aspirations of the Countess of Pembroke's circle and of other English Renaissance classicists in drama, Schirmer indicates that this academic group regarded itself as the opponent of Sh and the Art-less drama he wrote: "nie galt er als fehlerlos; erst die Romantik machte ihn zum Gott."

0518. Schirmer, Walter. "Die Verwendung der klassischen Mythologie," Antike, Renaissance und Puritanismus: Eine Studie zur englischen Literaturgeschichte des 16. und 17. Jahrhunderts (München, 1924), pp. 24-71. E-S

In the first part of this ch., Lyly and Sh are placed together as opponents of a main stream of Renaissance mythologizing which culminates in Milton and which seeks moral (preferably Christian) significance in ancient myth. Whereas Lyly (especially in Euphues) ignores or distorts the moral import of a classical myth regarding it simply as a good story, Sh thinks of classical mythology as a storehouse of decoration to grace his work regardless of moral or temporal appropriateness. Both are therefore anti-puritan. MnU

0519. Schlegel, August Wilhelm von. A Course of Lectures on Dramatic Art and Literature, trans. John Black, revised ed. (Ln, 1846), 535 pp. E-S

The five lectures on Sh, XXII-XXVI (pp. 338-446) are an avowed effort to defend him against two charges of barbarism. Schlegel skillfully refutes the accusation of semiliteracy and with even greater dexterity shows that Sh's works are not formless and barbaric, but have organic, if not classical, unity. He is often wrong on matters of fact, but his critical instincts are excellent on most points (e.g., he has little leisure to bestow on disintegrators). Schlegel's interest in the drama of antiquity causes him to make repeated analogies and contrasts between classical culture and Sh. This is a major study of Sh which doubtless deserved its accrued fame in the nineteenth century.

0520. Schmidt, Alexander. Shakespeare-Lexicon: A Complete Dictionary of All the English Words, Phrases and Constructions in the Works of the Poet. Berlin, 1875, 2 vols.

Appendix III (II, 1425-29) gives "Words and sentences taken from foreign languages." Section I lists the three Greek words Schmidt has found in Sh; Section II (1425-27) lists alphabetically: (a) single Latin words appearing in the plays and poems, (b) phrases and sentences quoted from Latin authors, (c) popular and proverbial Latin phrases, (d) Latin phrasing which appears to be Sh's own. Schmidt cites chapter and verse for each entry and provides English trans. This is a useful concordance.

0521. Schoell, Franck L. Études sur l'humanisme continental en Angleterre à la fin de la renaissance, BRLC, XXIX (1926), 270 pp. E-S

Schoell's erudite treatise focuses primarily on Chapman: the allusions to Sh are few and brief. There are two passing references to Venus as a mythological poem; Schoell ranks Sh with Castiglione, Montaigne, Chapman, and Hans Sachs as a debtor to Plutarch; in a ch. on Epictetus in England, Schoell notes that the Stoicism of Horatio and Brutus is strictly Roman in its origins; Clenardus' Greek grammar was not a literary source for Sh and his contemporaries as Lily's Latin grammar was.

0522. Schöne, Annemarie. "Shakespeares weise Narren und ihre Vorfahren," JAAK, V (1960), 202-245.

This art. contains two paragraphs on possible analogues in the classics to Sh's fools. One mentions the mimes (especially as dignified by Theocritus), and the other mentions the Aesop of Plutarch's τῶν ἑπτὰ σοφῶν συμπόσιον. But the author notes that wise folly is lacking in both of these ancient analogues: the fools of the mime are crafty, not wise, and Plutarch's Aesop is merely stupid.

0523. Scott, John A. Homer and His Influence, Our Debt, [No. 1] ([1925]/1963), 164 pp.

Scott grants Sh knowledge of Chapman's Homer (p. 133) because (1) Thersites is lacking from Chaucer and Medieval romance, (2) in Medieval versions Achilles returns to battle because of Troilus' exploits while in Homer and Sh it is the death of Patroclus which stirs him to action. In 3H.VI IV ii 18-21 Warwick summarizes the action of the tenth book of the Iliad (Scott does not note that 3H.VI antedates Chapman's trans.). See also pp. 85-86 for Sh's allusions to Proteus in 3H.VI III ii 188-192 and T.G.V. and for Puck's Protean boast in Dream III i 111-114: "Sometime a horse I'll be, sometime a hound, / A hog, a headless bear, sometime a fire ..." These allusions like "most literary references depend on" Homer's account of Menelaus and Proteus in Odyssey IV.

0524. Seccombe, Thomas, and J. W. Allen. The Age of Shakespeare (1579-1631), Vol. II, The Drama (Ln, 1903). E-S

Ch. II, "William Shakespeare," pp. 54-142, is not entirely reliable, usually because it is incomplete or sketchy (as in the one-sentence account of Sh's probable education), or because its critical observations are obtuse ("Politically [Coriolanus] is simply a revolutionist"; "[Troi.] ends with the apotheosis of the brute, Achilles.") There are better handbooks available.

0525. Sedgwick, W. B. "The Influence of Ovid," NC, CXXII (1937), 483-494. SG

See especially pp. 489-492, in which brief space Sedgwick makes several challenging observations. He hears echoes of Dido's epistle to Aeneas in Cleopatra's "farewell to Antony"; he suggests that the tomb scene of Romeo is indebted to the legend of Pyramus and Thisbe; and most challenging of all, he proposes that Sh's "Senecan" tragedies (and those of his contemporaries) are indirectly indebted to Ovid, because what is "Senecan" about Seneca was to be found in Ovid's lost tragedy, Medea. Sedgwick writes with enviable precision and fluency.

0526. Sedley, Charles. "Prologue" to the Wary Widow (1693), Munro, II, 392.

Contains a conventional Restoration allusion to Sh as "the shame of Schools, / Born to Create, and not to Learn from Rules."

0527. Selby, H. M. The Shakespeare Classical Dictionary: or, Mythological Allusions in the Plays of Shakespeare Explained. For the Use of Schools and Shakespeare Reading Societies. Ln, [1887], 56 pp.

Nearly two hundred mythological personages, events, and things defined clearly, accurately, and in detail ("Hercules," the longest entry, occupies seven columns in this pocket pamphlet). Selby gives chapter and verse in Sh and in the standard classical authors as well. Appended are (1) trans. of and comment on eight Latin quotations in the canon (Selby omits Titus, Troi., and Per. from his book as of no interest to his readers); (2) a one-page discussion of the classical view of the afterlife. DLC

0528. Sewell, G[eorge]. "Preface," to The Works of Mr. William Shakespear: The Tenth Volume [Pope's Ed.] (Ln, 1728), pp. v-xii.

Sewell speaks of Sh's "Wildnesses," "And yet I cannot place his Learning so low as others have done, there being evident Marks thro' all his Writings of his Knowledge in the Latin Language, and the Roman History." Sewell (following Gildon, #0269) attributes Heywood's trans. of two of the Heroides to Sh and rates it above Golding's [?] Meta. But he sees the folly of assigning knowledge of Greek to Sh merely on the ground that Sh and the Greeks both use compound epithets. Sewell offers criticism of Sh for not portraying Julius Caesar as nobly as even Cicero, his enemy, did. DFo

0529. Seznec, Jean. "The Influence of the Manuals," The Survival of the Pagan Gods: The Mythological Tradition and Its Place in Renaissance Humanism and Art, trans. Barbara F. Sessions, Bollingen Series, No. 38 (Pantheon, 1953), pp. 279-323.

In this widely ranging study in comparative literature Sh merits only a single paragraph (pp. 114-115) which cites some standard authorities on Shn mythology (Root, Anders, Fripp, e.g.) and suggests that though they believe he obtained his knowledge directly from Ovid and Virgil there is other evidence (Henry Green, e.g.) that emblem literature provided his mythology ready-made. Seznec is not aware of the research of Baldwin (#0089) on Sh's education and use of Renaissance compendia; since Seznec's book appeared Starnes and Talbert (#0566) have illustrated Sh's debt to the dictionaries.

0530. Seznec, Jean. "Les manuels mythologiques italiens et leur diffusion en Angleterre à la fin de la renaissance," MAH, L (1933), 276-292.

Seznec argues that Sh's access to classical myth was partly (perhaps largely) indirect. He would look first for Sh's mythology in Ravisius Textor and the emblem books of Alciatus, Sambuc, Whitney, Symeoni, and Cartari. Though he objects that Anders (#0073) and Root (#0497) offer little evidence for Sh's direct obligation to Ovid and Virgil, Seznec himself offers very little evidence for Sh's debt to the mythographers of the Renaissance, being content largely to refer for support to Green (#0284) and Schoell (#0521).

0531. Shackford, Martha H. Plutarch in Renaissance England with Special Reference to Shakespeare. [Wellesley, Mass.], 1929. E-S HB SG

Ch. V (35-45) consists of (1) "Plutarch as

a Source and as an Influence" and (2) "A Parallel Between Plutarch and Shakespeare." (1) suggests that though Plutarch was second only to Holinshed as Sh's creditor, the latter was a greater formative influence because Sh learned characterization from the Chronicle in the 1590's. Though North's prose is of great importance for Sh, it should be remembered that Plutarch also came to Sh filtered through the whole humanistic movement of the sixteenth century. "Shakespeare was, then, acquainted with Plutarch's Lives: Julius Caesar, Brutus, Antonius, Coriolanus, and he probably had read parts at least of Theseus, Alcibiades, Cicero, Cato Major and Minor, and Pelopidas." (2) draws a comparison and contrast between the two writers in the manner of Plutarch himself. The conclusion is that despite differences of philosophy they had a spiritual kinship. Both of these brief essays are full of insights (e.g., it is a mistake to neglect Plutarch's comparisons as a source for Sh; "the appearance of the 1603 edition [possibly] re-awakened [Sh's] interest in Plutarch and led to the writing of the later Roman plays"). This is a valuable little book.

0532. Shackford, Martha H. "Stichomythia, Chorus, Soliloquy, as Dramatic Forces," Shakespeare, Sophocles: Dramatic Themes and Modes (N.Y., 1960), pp. 25-44.

A lucid analysis of the characteristics and dramatic effect of each of the three elements. Though soliloquy first developed in the declamatory style of Seneca, in Sh it is "always dexterous, magnetically powerful in arousing sympathy for a speaker haunted by problems." Sh probably learned this technique of character-revelation first from Daniel's Cleopatra, Tamburlaine Part I, The Jew of Malta, and especially The Spanish Tragedy.

0533. "Shakespeare's Education," Home University (Ln), September, 1898, [no pagination available].

Not seen. Information from #0043, XXXVI (1900).

0534. "Shakespeare's Learning," TLS, May 15, 1943, p. 235.

A general comment. "To Shakespeare, in the long view, the ancient world stood for wisdom, power and integrity, as well as for passion and beauty; his little learning in it opened a little window over a wide and noble view." Praise for F. S. Boas' British Academy Lecture (#0108).

0535. "[Shakespeare's Moon, Jewish Folklore and the Classics]," NewShna, III (1904), 71-73.

The author dismisses the notion that the vaporous drop which Hecate will catch as it falls from the moon (in Macb. III v) is the venomous drop which in Jewish folklore could make food inedible. He appears to prefer the description of the preparations Erictho made for Sextus in Pharsalia VI. He also discusses the meaning of Antony's reference to Lichas on the horns of the moon (Antony IV xii) in relation to Seneca, and finally "Moon's" reference to the bush and the dog in Dream V i.

0536. "Shakespeare's School," 3 AYR, VI (1891), 17-19.

The author is as interested in the appearance of the school to a visitor to Stratford as in what Sh may have learned in it, but he does find occasion to side with T. S. Baynes (#0097) in defending Sh's knowledge of Latin; "the poet could read Latin fluently and fairly, and any author he cared for he would be able to read for his pleasure and information." The instruction was rigorous as the Quiney Latin letter proves.

0537. "Shakespear's Merits as a Comic Writer considered," BM, VIII (1767), 561-563.

Sh is here ranked above Homer (Batrachomyomachia), Virgil (satire on woman in Aeneid —"Varium et mutabile semper femina" is surpassed by "Frailty, thy name is woman"), Plautus (Falstaff lying "to cloak his cowardice" in 1H.IV II iv is "not to be equalled by any thing in the Miles Gloriosus"), and Terence (Thraso is "but a faint sketch in comparison" to Falstaff). Only Lucian could rival Sh in comedy, but Lucian, unlike Sh, never approached the sublime. The essayist, like many other eighteenth-century critics, regards Wives as one of Sh's greatest achievements. DLC

0538. Sheppard, J. T. Aeschylus and Sophocles: Their Work and Influence, Our Debt, [No. 23] (N.Y., 1927), 204 pp. SG

See "Elizabethans" (120-140, especially 126-128, 134-140). Though "there is nothing to prove conscious borrowing or direct acquaintance with the Greek originals" Sh possibly knew Sophocles (especially Ajax) in a Latin or French version; he did not know Aeschylus at all. Nevertheless, Macb. is a very Aeschylean play with its Apaté leading Macbeth to abandon virtue, its Erinyes (Witches), and its juxtaposition of foul and fair. Through Plutarch more than Seneca Sh derived the spirit of Greek tragedy to which he is indebted. Sheppard speaks of Antony III xiii 111-115 as being "in the tone and almost in the phrases of Aeschylus." Brief comparisons: Ophelia to Io, the Nurse in Romeo to the Nurse in Eumenides, the ghosts in Macb. and Ham. to Darius' ghost in the Persae, Sh's Cassandra to Aeschylus'. An informed ch., more restrained than Collins' (#0173), which Sheppard criticizes.

0539. Sheppard, J. T. "Shakespeare's Small Latin," RIP, XLIV, No. 3 (1957), 70-86.

This fluent and gracious address gives T. W. Baldwin due credit for his achievement in delineating the Stratford curriculum. Sheppard briefly sketches that curriculum and the method of instruction which combined with it to lend Sh a style that "reflects a high poetic ancestry." Sheppard gives Sh more Greek than many have done, and there seems no reason to contradict him. But the best of the lecture is the account of the response Sh made to Ovid (in Temp., Dream, and W.T. more than in the "Ovidian" poems), to Virgil (the Eclogues and II, IV, and VI Aeneid, especially in Ham.), and to Cicero (the Somnium Scipionis in Act V of Merch.). There is an original insight on the motivation of the "rugged Pyrrhus" speech and another on Hamlet's (not Sh's) "error" in introducing the "Hyrcanian beast" from Book IV of Virgil into Book II. This is an unusually satisfying paper.

0540. Shorey, Paul. "Platonism and English Literature," Platonism Ancient and Modern (California UP, 1938), pp. 175-236.

In the passage on Sh (pp. 179-182), Shorey points to numerous parallels between Sh and Plato, some of them not noted by other scholars. He admits that some of these may be coincidental, and suggests Cicero (Tusculans), Plutarch, Montaigne, Erasmus, Mulcaster, Ascham, Elyot (Governour), "the conversation of Ben Jonson," Spenser (FQ), Chapman (Iliad), and Du Bellay as possible intermediaries for others. Shorey hesitantly grants that Sh may also have seen Ficino or "some French version." The theme of immortality through art (Sonn.) comes ultimately from Symposium; Sh's "ethical nihilists" (e.g., Richard III at V iii 310-311) summarize the doctrines of Callicles in the Gorgias and Thrasymachus in the Republic. The contempt for life which the Duke urges on Claudio in Meas. (III i) is ultimately traceable to the apocryphal Axiochus. Shorey also comments on passages in Oth., Cor., Caesar, Troi., H.V, Temp., and Merch.; see also scattered allusions to Sh elsewhere in this reasoned, well-informed book.

0541. Sigismund, Reinhold. "Uebereinstimmendes zwischen Shakespeare und Plutarch: Aus den Lebensbeschreibungen sowohl wie aus den moralischen Schriften des Letzteren," ShJ, XVIII (1883), 156-182. HB

Sigismund offers a large number of parallels between Plutarch's Moralia and Sh's sentiments on death, suicide, the life of the after-world, melancholy, the rôle of imagination, love, wine and its effects, and some miscellaneous matters of natural history. The parallels are of considerable interest but do not establish an unquestionable indebtedness. Sigismund himself leaves the matter partly open: "Ob Shakespeare wirklich die Moralia des Plutarch gelesen habe, wage ich nicht zu entscheiden, doch scheint mir sicher, dass er wenigstens Auszüge daraus zu Gesicht bekommen haben muss." He does not mention those trans. (e.g., by Elyot, Holland) which might have been accessible to Sh and he quotes Plutarch in German and/or Greek. Sigismund also notes a possible echo of Plutarch's "Life of Phocion" in 2H.IV.

0542. Sills, Kenneth C. M. "Virgil in the Age of Elizabeth," CJ, VI (1910), 123-131. HB

See especially pp. 126-127 for five Virgil allusions in Sh and for the assertion that Sh's knowledge of Virgil is revealed by them (e.g., "In such a night / Stood Dido with a willow in her hand ..."). Those who deny Sh's familiarity with "the one poet who was then regarded not only as the laureate of Rome but as the supreme poet of all literature" are ignorant of poetry and of Elizabethan classicism. But Sills does not insist that Sh read Virgil in Latin.

0543. Simpson, Percy. "Shakespeare's Use of Latin Authors," Studies in Elizabethan Drama (OUP, 1955), pp. 1-63.

A close-packed listing of parallel passages in Sh and Plautus, Ovid, Horace, Virgil, Catullus, Terence, Seneca, Juvenal, Statius, Silius Italicus, Tibullus, Publilius Syrus, Apuleius, Cicero, Caesar, Quintilian, Justinus, and Erasmus. Though Simpson asserts that he has eliminated commonplaces, many of the concepts were deeply embedded in Elizabethan culture, e.g., Horace's "Semper ad eventum festinat et in medias res / non secus ac notas auditorem rapit" is given as the (presumably direct) source of Troi. Prologue (26-28) "our play / Leaps o'er the vaunt and firstlings of those broils, / Beginning in the middle." A good many of the other parallels cited have been scholarly property for many decades, but Simpson does useful service in several instances: e.g., he revives Plautus' Rudens as a source for Per. III-V, and apparently clears up the difficulty over Aristotle and moral philosophy (cf. Campbell [#1197] and Ford [#1315]).

0544. Sisson, Charles Jasper, ed. William Shakespeare: The Complete Works. N.Y., [1953], 1376 pp.

Despite their brevity and their intended general audience, Sisson's introductory essays on the plays are a mine of percipient criticism and informed scholarship. On virtually every controversial issue concerning Sh's classicism Sisson stands on the side of intelligent conservatism, refusing, e.g., to disintegrate the canon, to regard Troi. as either a farce or a mark of soulsickness, or to see Sh as a political polemicist in Cor. Some of the passing remarks are of special interest: e.g., Sh's classical training shows in the rhetoric of 2H.VI V ii 31-65; beginning with "classical" works like Titus, Errors, and the poems was de rigueur for an ambitious young writer in the 'eighties or 'nineties. One of the best of the one-vol. eds.

0545. Small, Samuel A. "The Iuventus Stage of Life," Philologica, pp. 235-238.

An illustration in a Dutch ed. of Bartholomaeus Anglicus serves as an analogue to Sh's technique of characterization because like Sh's tragedies it stresses the centrality of the age Juventus among the other six. In A.Y.L. Sh gives the seven ages mechanically equal importance, perhaps a result of his rhetorical training in school; but in Oth., Ham., Antony, Romeo, and Lear Sh maintains a realistic flexibility in the boundaries among the ages, allowing Lear, Othello, Romeo, and Hamlet all to "grow" in years as their respective plays move on.

0546. Smart, John S. "Scholarship," Shakespeare: Truth and Tradition (Ln, 1928), pp. 149-190. SG

A convincing defense of Elizabethan culture from the charges of barbarism implicit in much criticism of Sh. Such charges are the children of nineteenth-century faith in creative progress, and are entirely fallacious; in fact, Smart suggests, the gallery for which Sh wrote (he despised the groundlings) was far better educated than modern audiences, alert to French, Latin, Italian, mythological, and historical allusions. Despite the usual assumption, it is possible that Sh did attend a university where he would have acquired not Ovid, Virgil, and Greek, but decayed Scholasticism, which was still rampant in the 1580's. Sh's most learned contemporaries were self-taught, like Keats, Burns, Meredith, Stevenson, Hardy, and Dickens--against none of whom are charges of barbarism brought. "Baconism" would die if we abandoned the paradox of a "Janus-headed monstrosity," too stupid to appreciate the value of wide reading, but bright enough to write the greatest plays in the language. This is a lucid, reasoned, fluent essay, which expresses several incidental insights into Ovid and Roman comedy as they appear in Sh's plays. MnU

0547. Smith, Hal Hampson. "Elizabethan Symbolism and the Unity of Troilus and Cressida," diss (Princeton, 1958). DA, XX (1960), 2810-11.

The first two chs. deal with Elizabethan emblems and mythography as they affected presentational imagery in the theater. Scenes from Lear, Cor., and A.Y.L. illustrate the thesis. The last five chs. deal with Troi. as a presented myth: among the matters considered are classical costume, emblematic grouping of characters on the stage, plot, theme (the identification of love with war), and metaphorical language. Smith argues that the mythographical background reveals the unity of the play.

0548. Smith, Hallett. Elizabethan Poetry: A Study in Conventions, Meaning, and Expression. HUP, 1952, 355 pp.

The most important relevant ch. is II, "Ovidian Poetry," which contains critical discussions of Venus and Lucr. among many other poems. Both poems are treated as variations on conventions, but Smith fails to recognize the irony of Venus or the dramatic characterization of Lucr., and he regards both poems as inferior to Sh's contemporary work in the drama. He says little of the classical sources or of Sh's approach to myth, but he recognizes that through Marlowe, Lodge, and others Sh's work can be traced to Ovid. In other chs. (especially "Satire" and "Pastoral Poetry") there are passing references to classical elements in almost a dozen plays (e.g., the Golden Age in A.Y.L. and Horatian satire in Ham. and A.Y.L.). The ch.

on "The Sonnets" makes no reference to Sh's interest in pre-Socratic conceptions of time or Platonic attitudes toward beauty and friendship.

0549. Smith, N. A. The Latin Element in Shakespeare and the Bible, George Peabody College for Teachers, Contributions to Education, No. 32, 2 vols. (Nashville, Tenn., 1929), [no pagination]. HB

This awesome work of tabulation lists the entire vocabularies of the King James Version and of Sh, giving etymology, number of occurrences, locus of first occurrence, etc. The author concludes that Sh has a substantial proportion of Latinate words: 7739/19217 (Sh); 3609/8707 (Bible). No naturalization dates are given for the words, and the derivations are all ultimate (e.g., "air" from "ἀήρ"; "joy" from "gaudium"). Therefore this reference work does not really contribute to the resolution of the "small Latin" controversy, but it does demonstrate that Sh was in command of the resources Latin had lent to English by his time. MnU

0550. Smith, Warren D. "The Elizabethan Rejection of Judicial Astrology and Shakespeare's Practice," SQ, IX (1958), 159-176. GRS

This art. amasses impressive evidence to show that the official position of Elizabethan church and state was rejection of judicial astrology as a "pagan superstition." He does not observe, however, that the very vehemence and frequency of such condemnations argues for the diffusion of the pagan superstition in Renaissance England. Smith is also less than persuasive in his assertion that we can read Sh's rejection of celestial augury through the rejections made by Cassius, Edmund, Hotspur, and several others. Smith does not discuss the mythological antecedents of the doctrine, though he does speak of Sh's acceptance of Ptolemaic astronomy.

0551. Smith, William Henry. "Shakspere and Shake-speare: Shake-speare and Pallas Athene," 7 NQ, IV (1887), 66.

Smith points out that "Pallas" can be derived from "πάλλειν" ("to brandish"); Athena's attribute is therefore "Shake-spear" which may perhaps bear on the epithet "Hasta-vibrans" which Thomas Fuller gave to Sh.

0552. Soellner, Rolf H. "Anima and Affectus: Theories of the Emotions in Sixteenth Century Grammar Schools and Their Reflections in the Works of Shakspere," diss (Illinois, 1953). DA, XIV (1954), 351.

After presenting evidence that Renaissance theorizing on psychology has been inadequately studied, Soellner traces the probable education in psychology Sh would obtain from the Stratford curriculum (he uses Baldwin, #0089, as a model). There was no systematic study of the soul in grammar schools, he concludes, but Sh would learn a great deal incidentally about faculty psychology from rhetorical treatises, the comedies of Terence, and elementary Latin schoolbooks (e.g., Lily's Grammar, Latin dictionaries, etc.). Not all of the background is classical, however.

0553. Soellner, Rolf [H.]. "The Four Primary Passions: A Renaissance Theory Reflected in the Works of Shakespeare," SP, LV (1958), 549-567.

The "tetrachord of passions" (joy, grief, hope, fear) under which the Renaissance classified all emotions had classical authority as old as Plato. The Stoics introduced the emphasis on opposed extreme passions which Sh so often reflects. The three most likely sources for Sh's attitudes toward the tetrachord were Cicero's Tusculan Disputations, Virgil's Aeneid VI (Anchises lectures to Aeneas on the subject), and a scene in Terence's Andria. Sh's Stratford schoolmaster could have imparted this psychological theory in any or all of these loci classici. Soellner discusses many references to the theory of the tetrachord in Sh and refers to many more in footnotes. The most interesting analysis is of R.II. Soellner is on firm scholarly ground--he makes a definite contribution to knowledge of the background of Sh's characters.

0554. Sondheim, Moriz. "Shakespeare and the Astrology of His Time," JWCI, II (1938-39), 243-259.

Sh accepted astrologia naturalis (the influence of the stars on the four elements), but seems to have rejected both horoscopy and astrologia iudicialis (the influence of the stars on the spiritual affairs of men). In making this distinction Sh follows the Ptolemaic doctrines: "inclinant astra non necessitant" and "sapiens dominabitur astris." The arguments both for and against judicial astrology in the sixteenth century were classical: e.g., the "Renaissance" argument that twins have a single horoscope but differing destinies was raised by Nigidius Figulus (1st cent. B.C.). Sondheim surveys a large number of Shn allusions to illustrate the theses.

0555. Sonnenschein, E. A. "Shakespeare's Knowledge of Latin," TLS, March 17, 1921, pp. 179-180. HB SG

Notes on Latinity in Titus, 2H.VI, and H.V to suggest that Sh knew classical prosody and vocabulary better than many have said. Sonnenschein's preface on the debt of Portia's "mercy" speech to Seneca is criticized by C. C. Stopes (ibid., March 24, 1921, p. 196 SG), and the central thesis is attacked by John Sargeaunt (April 7, 1921, p. 228). G. G. Greenwood in turn attacks Sargeaunt (April 28, 1921, p. 276), and in the same columns Sonnenschein adds fuel, insisting that the Golden Age of Temp. II i 147-168 is indebted to Seneca as well as to Florio's Montaigne.

0556. Sonnenschein, E. A. "Shakspere and Stoicism," UR, I (1905), 23-41. SG

Sonnenschein argues that Milton's notion of the Artless Sh is completely false. Sh learned enough Latin at Stratford to read Seneca's De Clementia, from which he borrowed Portia's sentiments on mercy. But, more important, Sh imbibed from the classics their essential, ethical spirit. Sh makes no errors in dramatizing classical philosophy (except in the case of Brutus' attitude toward Cato's suicide, where North's mistranslation of Amyot's French makes Brutus change his mind about suicide in the middle of a speech). Sonnenschein includes an excellent excursus on the mutual affinity of Stoicism and Christianity (Pauline and Augustinian), and brief remarks on the historical Brutus as a Platonist, on Stoicism in Ham., on condemnation of suicide in Lear and Cym., etc. A plausible approach to Sh's classicism. MH

0557. Spencer, Hazelton. The Art and Life of William Shakespeare. N.Y., 1940, 495 pp.

Certainly among the best systematic introductions to the plays. Spencer is orthodox and entirely reliable in his judgments, including many comments on Sh's classical antecedents, and at the same time he writes with imagination, fluency, and wit. To each play is reserved ca. 6-10 pages.

0558. Spencer, Terence. Fair Greece Sad Relic: Literary Philhellenism from Shakespeare to Byron. Ln, 1954, 312 pp.

This interesting compendium of English attitudes toward contemporary Greece from the fifteenth to the nineteenth centuries contains in its first seventy pages some fifteen references to Sh, some of which indicate that Sh's attitude toward classical Greece was colored by Elizabethan sentimentality and prejudices about Greece under the Turks (e.g., the sadly ironic lines about Troy in ruins, Troi. III ii 192-196, or the many Shn references to Greeks as carefree scapegraces).

0559. Spencer, Theodore. Death and Elizabethan Tragedy: A Study of Convention and Opinion in the Elizabethan Drama. HUP, 1936, 288 pp.

Spencer joins with those who minimize the impact of Seneca on Sh and his contemporaries; he places great emphasis on fifteenth-century traditions like the danse macabre. Yet Sh is shown in relation to other classical traditions from the bride-of-death metaphor (in Romeo, Meas., and the Greek Anthology), to the negation of death through poetry (in Sonn., Ovid, and Horace), to the Platonic concept that the body is a prison from which the soul is released by death (John III iv 17-19). There is surprisingly little emphasis on Stoic attitudes toward death, considering their importance in Sh's Roman plays and Chapman's tragedies.

0560. Spencer, Theodore. Shakespeare and the Nature of Man, The Lowell Lectures. N.Y., 1942, 233 pp.

Spencer begins with a ch. on the hierarchy of being and man's nexal position in it; he shows that the concepts are Christian but were repeatedly buttressed in the Renaissance by analogues from classical philosophers (Plato, Aristotle, Cicero, the Neoplatonists, Plutarch). This optimistic homocentricity came under assault from pessimistic philosophies (Skepticism of Montaigne, pragmatism of Machiavelli, and especially the doctrine of Original Sin). It is interesting to observe that the materials of the first ch. are what Haydn (#0318) calls "the Renaissance" while those of the second are what he calls "the Counter-renaissance"; Spencer's book also bears comparison with Tillyard's (#0598), which advances essentially the same propositions about Sh's classical-Christian philosophical heritage. Spencer traces the use of these concepts in drama from Medieval literature through Sh's early plays; then follows detailed analysis of Ham. and Troi. which portray the difference between man as he ought to be and man as he is, Oth. and Lear in which the bestial is contrasted with the angelic, Macb.

and Antony in which catastrophe follows a clear moral choice, and the last plays (including Cor., Tim., and T.N.K.) in which Sh progresses toward an optimistic view of man opposed to the dark pessimism of much in the tragedies. This is a major work of historical criticism.

0561. Spitzer, Leo. "Classical and Christian Ideas of World Harmony: Prolegomena to an Interpretation of the Word 'Stimmung,' I, II," Traditio, II (1944), 409-464; III (1945), 307-364.

The brief passage (III, 333-335) on Sh in this exhaustive study places him in the Christianized classical tradition in his emphasis on music as a structural principle reflecting the order of the cosmos, of man, and of the state. Among other interesting points in the close-packed discussion, Spitzer observes that in Merch. Sh equates musical harmony with Grace, thus participating in a Christianized tradition of classical Pythagoreanism. Spitzer also interprets allusions to music as order and morality in Caesar, Troi., and R.II.

0562. Stanford, W. B[edell]. "Ghosts and Apparitions in Homer, Aeschylus, and Shakespeare," Hermathena, LVI (1940), 84-92. GRS

Despite its brevity, this is one of the best commentaries on the impact of ghost scenes in Homer (one in the Iliad, three in the Odyssey), Aeschylus (Persae, Agamemnon [Cassandra's vision], Eumenides, Prometheus [Io's vision of the ghost of Argus]), and Sh (2H.VI, R.III, Caesar, Ham., Macb., Cym.). Stanford also glances briefly at Virgil's use of Homeric ghosts and Seneca's use of Greek tragic ghosts. The emphasis falls on the Greeks—Sh is repeatedly brought in for comparison: "No foolhardy attempt [is] made to argue that Shakespeare had any direct knowledge of Homer's work, or, less likely still, of Aeschylus'." Among numerous interesting points is a comparison between Homer's onomatopoetic use of the verb "τρίζω" ("to squeak") and the noun "τετριγυῖα" ("shrill cry") and Sh's use of "shriek" and "squeal" in Caesar II ii 24 (Stanford might have added "squeak" and "gibber" from Ham. I i 116). Stanford ends his graceful and witty essay with the observation that Sh did not have the advantage Homer and Aeschylus had of living in a pre-Aristophanic age; Greek comedy made ghosts laughable and spoiled most of the dignity and terror that once was their hallmark. MdBJ

0563. Stapfer, Paul. Shakespeare et l'antiquité: Première partie, l'antiquité grecque et latine dans les oeuvres de Shakespeare. Paris, 1879, 490 pp. [New ed. in two vols., 1884]. Trans. Emily J. Carey, Ln, 1880, 483 pp. E-S HB SG

A reasoned attempt to dispel the enduring fiction that Sh's classical plays and poems were the progeny of brilliant ignorance. The emphasis falls on the Roman trilogy, Troi., and Tim. (Titus is passed quickly by), but there are also chs. on the mythological poems and Errors. Stapfer is well informed, not only about Sh and the criticism of his works but also about Elizabethan culture generally. He is aware, e.g., that Antony's oration in Caesar is strikingly similar to passages in Appian, an insight often credited first to MacCallum (#1477), and he knows of the academic Timon, considering it a crude adumbration of Sh's Tim. Stapfer's critical judgment is as sound as his knowledge of the Elizabethan period; he refutes extremists of all kinds with genial wit and he is possibly the first Frenchman to read Sh without either condescending to the barbarian on the question of the rules or rejoicing that the barbarian escaped being fettered by them: as he shrewdly observes of the English attacks on Voltaire's Sh criticism, Sh's eighteenth-century defenders and detractors sound very much alike. Like Gervinus (#0264), for whom he expresses admiration, Stapfer is a harbinger of the mid-twentieth-century view of Sh's as a disciplined mind alert to its classical heritage.

0564. Stapleton, Sir Robert. "Prologue to The Slighted Maid" (1663), T-D, p. 6.

A conventional depreciation of Restoration talent by contrast with the greater worth of Beaumont, Fletcher, Jonson, and Sh. The latter two are, respectively, representations of Art and Nature.

0565. Starnes, DeWitt T. "Shakespeare and Apuleius," PMLA, LX (1945), 1021-50.

Starnes presents evidence for Sh's knowledge of Apuleius, probably in the Adlington trans. (1566). He cites echoes of The Golden Ass in Errors, T.G.V., Venus, Dream, Macb., Antony, Cym., W.T., and Temp. Some of his parallels are convincing (W.T., Cym., T.G.V., Venus) but others (especially Antony where he finds traces of Apuleius in Enobarbus' description of Cleopatra) are strained. Starnes's discovery is important, but he perhaps claims too much for it.

0566. Starnes, DeWitt T., and Ernest W. Talbert. "Shakespeare and the Dictionaries," Classical Myth and Legend in Renaissance Dictionaries: A Study of Renaissance Dictionaries in their Relation to the Classical Learning of Contemporary English Writers (North Carolina UP, 1955), Ch. V, pp. 111-134.

Following the organization of Root (#0497), the authors divide the essay into two parts: Part I discusses a generous dozen classical names from "Absyrtus" to "Xanthippe" as they appear in Cooper's Thesaurus and briefly compares Shn allusions in an attempt to show his indebtedness to Cooper. In some cases the evidence is striking, and the cumulative impression is that Sh obtained ready-made classicism from the mythological dictionaries. Part II analyzes at greater length Sh's alleged debt to Cooper in Lucr. (especially the Argument) and Antony. The remarks on Antony are perhaps least satisfactory--the chief limitation of the whole ch. is the lack of extended analysis: so important a possible source for Sh as Cooper deserves more, perhaps, than a twenty-four-page treatment.

0567. Staunton, H. "A Mistaken Allusion to Shakspeare," Ath, No. 2415 (1874), 193-194; No. 2418 (1874), 292; No. 2421 (1874), 391.

Staunton's effort to identify Nashe (in place of Lodge) with the "young Juvenal" of A Groatsworth of Wit comes under fire from C. M. Ingleby. They agree that perhaps Chettle did not refer to Sh, but to "young Juvenal" in his famous apology prefatory to the Kind Heart's Dream. The suggestion has not been generally accepted--at least Dover Wilson's recent essay (#1116) on Greene and Sh assumes that Chettle was apologizing to Sh for Greene's pejorative classical allusion.

0568. S[teevens], G[eorge]. "Advertisement to the Reader," [Prefixed to his ed. of twenty Shn quartos (1766)], Boswell's Malone, I, 109-119.

Steevens refers in passing to the desire of the Elizabethans to Latinize their English grammar, especially to write a suspended, Ciceronian style. Sh, in Steevens' judgment, never participated in the craze, contenting himself with a direct and lucid discourse.

0569. [Steevens, George]. "Ancient Translations from Classic Authors," Boswell's Malone, I, 371-391.

This list, with some supplements from Malone, is a surprisingly extensive one. It has, of course, been superseded by Lathrop (#0381) and others, but it has great historical significance as demonstrating that the late eighteenth century had a broader and more accurate familiarity with Elizabethan literature than is often thought. Steevens appended this list to his ed. of 1773 as an indication that he considered the "small Latin" controversy settled in favor of Farmer's position: i.e., Sh could read no Latin or Greek and ergo had to rely on the trans. in Steevens' list.

0570. Stevenson, W. H. "Shakespeare's Schoolmaster and Handwriting," TLS, January 9, 1920, p. 21.

Stevenson provides information about Thomas Jenkins, who may have taught Sh his Latin at Stratford in the late 'seventies. Jenkins used the "Italian hand" in writing both English and Latin, while Sh appears to have used the "secretary hand." The custom was ordinarily to write English in the secretary hand and Latin in the Italian hand. Stevenson does not observe that the discrepancy between Jenkins' practice and Sh's is no clue to the riddle whether Sh studied under Jenkins, since Sh would have been deeply entrenched in his "secretary" habits long before Jenkins arrived (1577) in Stratford.

0571. Stoll, E[lmer] E[dgar]. "Art and Artifice in the Iliad: The Poetical Treatment of Character in Homer and Shakespeare," ELH, II (1935), 294-321. Johns Hopkins Alumni Magazine, XXIV, pp. 13-43. (Revised as Ch. XI, pp. 362-393 in Shakespeare and Other Masters [1940].)

With the major emphasis falling on Homer's Achilles and Hector, the essay repeatedly shows points of comparison with Hamlet, Brutus, Macbeth, Lear, Romeo, Coriolanus, and others of Sh's characters to illuminate the thesis: "The great dramatists absolutely must be poets, have small need to be psychologists." Stoll assumes a close congruence between drama and epic--an assumption which is perhaps debatable.

0572. Stoll, E[lmer] E[dgar]. "The Dramatic Texture in Shakespeare," The Criterion, XIV (1935), 586-607. (Revised and expanded as Ch. I, pp. 11-58 in Shakespeare and Other Masters [1940].)

Stoll points passim to a number of parallels between Shn drama and Hellenic, the chief of which are: (1) suspense of anticipation, not of curiosity; the audience is not curious about the outcome, but about the manner of its arrival, ergo the opportunity for irony. (2) Drama of passion, not of psychologically devious or complex character. With both (1) and (2) Stoll sharply contrasts the modern drama. Stoll does not suggest, however, that Sh was aware that he was working with a conception of the drama formulated and practiced by the Greeks before him.

0573. Stoll, Elmer Edgar. "Shakespeare Forbears," MLN, LIV (1939), 332-339.

Stoll vigorously objects to attempts to find sexual significance in Lady Macbeth's "to bed, to bed, to bed," or to seek "evidence" that Othello had seduced Emilia before meeting Desdemona, or to interpret Ophelia's improper songs as proof that Hamlet had compromised her. Like Aeschylus and Sophocles Sh kept his heroines in the background and gave physical love a minor role; the later Jacobean dramatists, like Euripides, brought it forward. There is no question of Sh's indebtedness to the Attic tragedy.

0574. Stoll, Elmer E[dgar]. Shakespeare's Young Lovers, The Alexander Lectures at the University of Toronto, 1935. OUP, 1937, 118 pp.

There are three chief observations on the classical tradition in these three lectures: (1) Sh's men and women love one another primarily for their beauty, a convention that can be traced to the reverence for physical beauty in the Greek and Roman epics; and, like the heroes of the epics, they have epithetical virtues ("wily" Odysseus, "pius" Aeneas, "holy" Silvia, "good" Imogen). (2) Sh expresses no real interest in the Ovidian ars amandi tradition of dramatizing the sex-chase. Except for the coquetry of Cleopatra and Cressida there is no amorous intrigue in Sh (Stoll has forgotten Sh's Venus). (3) Sh's lovers are like Achilles, Odysseus, Antigone, and Oedipus, "without a psychology," and like all great literary creations they mean only themselves, not something else as well.

0575. Stopes, Charlotte C. "Shakespeare's 'Industry'," Shakespeare's Industry (Ln, 1916), pp. 1-11.

Mrs. Stopes calls attention to Webster's attribution to Sh of "right happy and copious industry" in the preface to The White Devil, and suggests that he meant that Sh labored diligently to acquire enough knowledge to rival the University Wits. She suspends judgment about the vexed problem of how much Sh may have learned in school; instead she suggests that Sh read in London "industriously" the many books which Vautrollier and later Richard Field had ad imprimendum solum. Among them were North's Plutarch, Puttenham's Arte of English Poesie, "the new Ovid" (by which she appears to mean both the Meta. and the Amores), and many nonclassical works including Florio's Firste and Seconde Fruites. Some credit is given to her contention by the fact that Field and Sh were fellow townsmen, but there is no justification for Mrs. Stopes's implication that the antecedent probability is higher for Sh's being self-taught after coming to London than for his having learned what he knew at Stratford School. MnU

0576. Stopes, Charlotte C. "Shakespeare's Treatment of his Originals," Shakespeare's Industry (Ln, 1916), pp. 12-42.

Mrs. Stopes discusses Sh's manipulation of his sources (1) to obtain approval of censor and audience; (2) to accommodate the talents of his Company; (3) to please his own taste; (4) to maintain fidelity to the original. The fourth was ordinarily least important to Sh as Mrs. Stopes shows in her analysis of the enveloping action of Errors; yet she says that Sh felt an obligation to adhere closely to North in the Roman plays (to Caesar he did add the funeral oration from Appian and the story of Caesar's leaping into the sea [Tiber] from Suetonius). The essay contains many interesting remarks: e.g., on Nemesis in 1, 2, 3H. VI as the sequel to Henry V's marriage to an idiot's daughter; on the rôle of Apollo and the Platonic relationship between Leontes and Paulina, both in W.T., etc. An illuminating study. MnU

0577. Stopes, Charlotte [C.]. "Text-books on Rhetoric in Shakespeare's Time...," Shna, VIII (1891), 42-43.

Mrs. Stopes briefly describes Brinsley's Ludus Literarius, Hoole's New Discovery, Wilson's Arte of Rhetorique, Cox's Arte or Crafte of Rhethoryke, The Artes of Logike and Rethorike (1584), and Fenner's The Artes of Logike and Rhetorike (1588). She makes no suggestions about Sh's use of any but Wilson, who, as a Warwickshire man, might have been especially interesting to Sh. She emphasizes that all the treatises were in English—a hint as to her opinion of Sh's Latinity.

0578. Stowe, A. Monroe. English Grammar

Schools in the Reign of Queen Elizabeth, CUCE, No. 22 (N.Y., 1908), 200 pp. E-S

This is a thorough study which contains a wealth of information about the schools and their masters and curricula, but it does not trace the impact of education on the artistic works of the Elizabethans. There is little about Stratford and nothing of importance about Sh. The early chs. of Baldwin (#0089) have largely superseded Stowe, at least on curriculum.

0579. Strachan, L. R. M. "The Spelling 'Anthony'," NQ, CLXVII (1934), 85-86.

In response to a query about the insertion of the false "h" in "Antony," Strachan points out that in Caesar Sh always uses the Roman form but elsewhere in his plays the Anglicized name often appears. Strachan does not indicate that the typographers, not Sh, could be responsible; V.R. adds some other relevant Shn references.

0580. Stronach, George. "Shakespeare's Scholarship," 10 NQ, I (1904), 33-34. SG

With verve Stronach defends Collins (#0173) against his detractors. The dog-Latin of L.L.L. is intended to disparage Holofernes. Stronach comments on spelling and pronunciation in Troi., Temp., and Merch.

0581. Strowski, Fortunat. "La Dramaturgie Moderne: III De Sophocle à Shakespeare, de Racine à Musset," RCC, XXXI (1930), 242-248.

A general essay: "Dans la pièce classique, c'est la spiritualité qui domine. Dans la pièce shakespearienne, c'est la pittoresque et la poésie." Both approaches are valid, but an age which accepts one fully has difficulty finding attention for the other.

0582. Swinburne, Algernon C. Shakespeare. OUP, 1909, 83 pp.

This impressionistic appreciation touches lightly at all points, never lingering for elaboration or proof; it alludes sometimes to the classics, always comparing Sh favorably: H.V is worthy of the Persae, A.Y.L. is more idyllic than Theocritus, Errors is better than its original in Plautus, Per. recalls Homer in the storm and Virgil in the reunion, the Witches in Macb. are like the Eumenides of Aeschylus, etc. The eulogy of the Roman plays, especially of Antony, occupies several pages.

0583. Symmes, H. S. Les Débuts de la critique dramatique en Angleterre jusqu'à la mort de Shakespeare. (Thèse, Université de Paris, 1903.) Paris: Leroux, 1903. HB

See pp. 171-177 for Symmes's analysis of Sh's implicit dramatic criticism. Symmes does not relate Sh directly to the classical theorists whom he treats elsewhere in the book, but he does discuss Sh's attitudes toward "classical" questions such as art as imitation (in pronouncements of Hamlet and Holofernes) and the unities (in H.V, W.T., and Troi.). MnU

0584. Taine, H[ippolyte]. "Le Théâtre anglais de la Renaissance I, II," RGF, XXV (1863), 209-254, 425-465. E-S

Taine considers Sh on pp. 452-465. The value of his credulous observations can best be estimated from this misstatement: "Shakespeare n'avait eu qu'une demi-éducation, savait 'peu de latin, point de grec,' à peu près le français et l'italien, rien d'autre."

0585. Taylor, Alfred Edward. Platonism and its Influence, Our Debt, [No. 19] (N.Y., 1932), 151 pp.

A passing reference (p. 26) places Sh with Marlowe as having "close familiarity with the whole Pythagorean-Platonic mythology of the soul." Sh carries his knowledge gracefully—he did not obtain it "by burning the midnight oil."

0586. Thaler, Alwin. "Shakespeare and Our World," TennSL, II (1957), 105-120. GRS

As he shows Sh's continuing relevance to problems and aspirations in the twentieth century, Thaler expresses the belief that Sh's learning "was anything but beneath contempt." He may well have been a schoolmaster in the country, but "he was no bookworm." Thaler illustrates Sh's moderate attitude toward the scholarly life with a commentary on the "academe" of L.L.L.: "a super-graduate Institute of Advanced Studies" which Sh satirizes through Berowne's sensible reactions to the extremists around him.

0587. Thaler, Alwin. Shakespeare and Sir Philip Sidney: The Influence of The Defense of Poesy. HUP, 1947, 100 pp.

Thaler cites scores of Shn passages which illustrate passages in the Apologie, and he has no difficulty in establishing that Sh is very often the example to Sidney's precept. He admits that there are differences between the two (e.g., on the validity of the imagination), but his belief is that Sh consciously recalled the Apologie which he knew well and put it into practice in his plays. The antecedent probability that Sh knew so famous a treatise by so reverently regarded a critic is enormous (as Thaler points out), but the actualities of establishing indebtedness are considerably less convincing. In the first place, as Thaler recognizes, Sidney's theories are Platonized Horace; Sh could have had access to them in other ways which Thaler does not discuss (notably his study of the classical rhetoricians in grammar school; cf. Baldwin, #0089). Secondly Thaler has a tendency to slide across difficulties (it is absurd to imply that Sh and Sidney agreed about the fusion of dramatic genres, e.g., tragicomedy). But at the least Thaler's book provides a series of practical illustrations of Sidneyan precepts; it is an interesting study.

0588. [Theobald, Lewis]. The Censor, 3 vols. Ln, 1717, 211, 230, 247 pp. (The essays were composed for The Censor during the period 1715-17.)

In some of the essays (e.g., Nos. 7, 10, 70), Theobald conveys the Augustan preoccupation with "the Rules of Aristotle, and the Tragedies of the Ancients," with both of which Sh was, unfortunately, "unacquainted." But Theobald sees Sh's merits and is not content merely to state his barbarism. In the essay (No. 36) on Oedipus Tyrannus, e.g., he ranks Oth. with Sophocles' best because in both plays the flaws of curiosity and impetuosity precipitate catastrophe for the hero, though he may appear to be manipulated by an oracle or an Iago. Again, Theobald places Sh and Aeschylus together as majestic despite a tendency toward bombast (No. 60); he would defend them both with reference to Longinus. In No. 73 he describes Sh as Horace described Pindar "as an inimitable Original whose Flights are not to be reach'd by the weak Wings of his Followers." No. 70 values the quarrel scene in Caesar higher than its counterparts in The Maid's Tragedy and Iphigenia in Aulis. The Censor is an interesting source of early Sh criticism which should be reprinted. DFo

0589. Theobald, Lewis. [Preface to Shakespeare] (1733). (Reprinted in #0045, pp. 63-91.)

One of Theobald's purposes is to restore the text of Sh; another is to get back at Pope in the Dunciad quarrel. But a third is to show in his notes that Sh was not so ignorant of the ancient world as he was thought by Dryden's age to be. Theobald does not give any specific evidence of Sh's classicism in the Preface—indeed he passes along the old legend that Sh left school very young--but he promises to provide evidence in his notes on individual passages. Theobald's general position has been shown by succeeding centuries to be closer to the truth than that of his more highly rated contemporaries; his reputation is only now (and slowly) recovering from the raking Pope gave it.

0590. Thompson, Marvin Orville. "Uses of Music and Reflections of Current Theories of the Psychology of Music in the Plays of Shakespeare, Jonson, and Beaumont and Fletcher," diss (Minnesota, 1956). DA, XVI (1956), 2448-49.

In Ch. III, Thompson includes the Pythagoreans among authorities for the Renaissance belief that music is a "reflection of the divine" and a salubrious moral influence on the listener. In Chs. IV, V, and VI Thompson evidently examines much of the canon, although W.T. and Temp. are the only Shn plays named in this abstract.

0591. Thomson, J. A. K. The Classical Background of English Literature. Ln, 1948, 272 pp.

The passage on Sh (pp. 183-189) expresses the same unfounded assumption of his ignorance of Latin that appears in Thomson's other books. But Thomson is willing to concede to Sh the credit for having given vividness to the classical world in his plays on classical themes. Sh's access to classical culture was chiefly through imitations of classical literature by his predecessors, but it was North's Plutarch that gave Sh his conception of history as the influence of men on their surroundings. Thomson dismisses Troi. and speaks somewhat contemptuously of Venus and Lucr.; this is not the most thorough or thoughtful of the commentaries on Sh and the classics.

0592. Thomson, J. A. K. Classical Influences on English Poetry. Ln, 1951, 271 pp.

In the chs. on tragedy and comedy (pp. 97-137), the emphasis falls more on the classical dramatists than on their English inheritors, but there are a number of passing allusions to Sh, some of them of special interest: on the Ghost in Ham., on Senecan elements in Titus, on Plautus in Errors and Shrew, and on Terence in A.Y.L. and Twel.

0593. Thomson, J. A. K. Classical Influences on English Prose. Ln, 1956, 303 pp.

The nine scattered references to Sh's relationship to ancient prose works allude to such matters as the Attic style in Brutus' oration over Caesar, Holland's Pliny and Sh's pseudo-scientific misinformation, Sh's contempt for pseudo-classical pastoralism, and Plutarch and Sh's tragic view of life. Unfortunately, none of the comments is expanded into a discussion.

0594. Thomson, J. A. K. Shakespeare and the Classics. Ln, 1952, 254 pp.

Thomson, who equates classicism with direct and extensive knowledge of the ancients in the original languages, finds Sh sadly lacking in this asset; he sees Sh's Latin as minimal and his Greek as nonexistent (for a list of trans. Sh probably used, see pp. 36-37). Thomson puts his emphasis on mythology (at the expense of rhetoric and the five-act structure, e.g.). He casts light in passing on some disputed passages in L.L.L. (pp. 71-73). There is a long aside (162-191) on Chapman and Jonson with some interesting observations on Chapman's character, scholarship, and relation to Sh. Among the more perceptive analyses are sections on Troi., Caesar, and Antony (192-221). There follows a passage on style and then the concluding argument "that it was from [North's] Plutarch that Shakespeare learned how to make a tragedy of the kind exemplified in Hamlet and Othello, Macbeth and Lear." (Oakeshott [#0444] elaborates this interesting thesis.) The book is somewhat uneven: Thomson's logic is not consistent, and his analyses often ignore context and speaker (e.g., pp. 100-101 on Hotspur's "Senecan" speech). The book also suffers from lack of any index, bibliography, or chapter division.

0595. Thomson, J. A. K. "Studies in Elizabethan Drama by Percy Simpson," RES, VII (1956), 424-427.

Ostensibly a rev. of Simpson's book, these four pages are actually an attack on Sh's Latinity. Thomson places the burden of proof on those who deny that Jonson had a foundation for his pejorative reference to Sh's "small Latine." He finds flaws without difficulty in Simpson's method of parallel-hunting, but he ignores in his argument for Sh as Nature's child the conclusions of T. W. Baldwin, e.g., on Sh's obvious competence in Latin.

0596. Thorndike, Ashley H. "Shakspere as a Debtor," ColSS, pp. 163-184. E-S

This rather general essay argues that recognition of Sh's literary indebtedness should not diminish his stature as a creative artist. A considerable part of the evidence is a recapitulation of Thorndike's earlier attempts to show Sh's indebtedness to contemporary dramatic conventions (see, e.g., #2302). The remarks on Sh and the classical tradition are brief and general: Plutarch, Ovid, the miles gloriosus, and pastoralism are mentioned, but Sh "did not crowd his mind with the great literature of antiquity ..."

0597. Thümmel, Julius. "Über die Sentenz im Drama, namentlich bei Shakespeare, Goethe und Schiller," ShJ, XIV (1879), 97-114. E-S

A general commentary: the function of the Chorus in ancient drama—to comment on the action—is taken over in Sh and other modern dramatists by sententious utterance from various characters. Thümmel does not go into Sh's use of classical materials for his sententiae. He does, however, compare the Athenians' exultation at their recent victory over Persian tyranny to the Elizabethans' glorying in newfound freedom from the tyranny of the Middle Ages and Catholic Spain.

0598. Tillyard, E. M. W. The Elizabethan World Picture. Ln, 1943, 108 pp.

This classic of historical criticism refers to Sh some two score times, to illustrate from his works the Elizabethan acceptance of such concepts as Platonic hierarchy, classical pseudo-science, and pre-Socratic doctrines of the mutability of nature, all tempered with Christian ethics and Old Testament theology. Tillyard finds this material in over a dozen plays. The book makes an excellent guide to Sh's assumptions, though its intent is to expound the assumptions of his fellow Elizabethans as well.

0599. Tillyard, E. M. W. Shakespeare's History Plays. N.Y., 1946, 336 pp.

Tillyard's main thesis is that the philosophical basis of Sh's English history plays is the concept of degree expressed in Plato, in Genesis, and in Ulysses' "degree" speech in Troi. The book traces these conceptions through the histories and Macb. Sh's source may have been the Christian homiletic tradition, not the classics. This is as excellent a book for its passing remarks as for its central thesis, witness the brilliant comparison (pp. 135-141) among Errors (Sh's ambitious classical comedy), Titus (his ambitious Senecan-Ovidian tragedy), and 1H.VI (his ambitious chronicle play).

0600. Tison, John L., Jr. "The Dramatic Consolatio in Shakespeare," diss (North Carolina, 1953).*

0601. Tison, John L., Jr. "Shakespeare's Consolatio for Exile," MLQ, XXI (1960), 142-157.

Aware not only of the rhetorical and philosophical tradition of consolation for exile but also of its dramatic possibilities, Sh employed banishment "by decree" in "almost one-third" of his plays. The tradition stems from Seneca, Plutarch, and Cicero, modified by such Christian philosophers as Boethius; consolation books were immensely popular in the sixteenth century. Tison takes Seneca's Ad Helviam as typical of the formal structure and Stoic philosophy of the consolatio for exile, and then analyzes banishment scenes in 1H.VI, R.II, T.G.V., 2H.VI, A.Y.L., Titus, Cor., and Romeo. Sh "follows, or breaks, the conventions in order to console, to create dramatic irony, or to intensify the suffering." An excellent piece of scholarly criticism.

0602. Tolman, Albert H. "The Early History of Shakespeare's Reputation," Falstaff and Other Shakespearean Topics (N.Y., 1925), pp. 169-210. E-S

This survey was originally an address and bears some vestigial marks of the speaker's approach, especially generalization. Rymer and Dryden are the only Restoration critics discussed, and the very early references to Sh are somewhat slighted, though Tolman is following Munro (#0044). Much of what Tolman says of the relative reputations of Jonson, Beaumont, Fletcher, and Sh and of their relationships to the classical tradition would call for more extensive treatment. But his address is fluent and informative within its limits.

0603. Tschernjajew, Paul. "Shakespeare und Terenz," Anglia, LV (1931), 282-295. E-S HB SG

Tschernajajew finds parallels to Terence in more than a score of Sh's plays and poems. He recognizes what is plainly the case: that many of the coincidences of thought are commonplaces (e.g., love as fire, fever, madness, or slavery; gods taking on shapes of beasts for love). But he insists "dass dem englischen Dramatiker der Inhalt der Schauspiele des römischen Komikers zweifellos sehr gut bekannt gewesen sein muss." Eunuchus is cited nearly three times as often here as Andria or Adelphi, and there are only eight citations to Hecyra, Phormio, and Heautontimorumenos combined. The conclusion that Eunuchus was Sh's favorite among Terence's comedies is verified by Baldwin's thorough study (#0683). Tschernjajew does not discuss dramatic structure or Sh's probable reading in Terence at Stratford School --indeed, he ends with indications that Terence was available to Sh in English trans.

0604. Tupper, Frederick, Jr. "The Shakespearean Mob," PMLA, XXVII (1912), 486-523.

A scholarly approach to Shn crowd scenes, finding their impact on audiences not a product of Sh's prejudices but of contemporary history and classical convention. Virgil and Horace are jointly responsible for the concepts mobile vulgus and bellua multorum capitum. Most important, however, is Plutarch, whose anti-popular bias was intensified by the trans. of Amyot and North. Tupper sketches the influence of Shn mobs on later drama. This is a valuable art.

0605. Ulrici, Hermann. Shakspeare's Dramatic Art: And His Relation to Calderon and Goethe, trans. from the German by A. J. W. M. Ln, 1846, 554 pp.

Ulrici writes "on the high principles of aesthetical criticism," which he somehow confuses with moral sensitivity and the Christian Weltanschauung. The result is some very odd contradictions: e.g., after implying repeatedly that Sh was a convinced and profound Christian, Ulrici observes, p. 354, that it is impossible for a Christian to recapture the spirit of the ancient world; yet, he concludes, Sh "has succeeded better than any modern poet in treating ancient subjects." Ulrici believes Errors a "satire on man's boasted wisdom and discernment"; he refuses to believe that Sh imitated Plautus (he must have remade an older play). There is very little in Ulrici of any permanent value, though he is to be commended for his attempt to study the plays generically (the Roman plays are "histories") and for his attempt to revive aesthetic criticism in what he thought was imitation of Hazlitt and Coleridge.

0606. Upton, John. Critical Observations on

Shakespeare (1746). 2nd ed. Ln, 1748, 415 pp.

Upton proposes passim a number of emendations of Sh's texts and criticizes the emendations of others, both in many cases on the basis of classical authority. The book is perhaps more a parade of the author's obscure classicism, some of which he thinks he shares with Sh, than a reasoned estimate of Sh's probable debt to antiquity. MnU

0607. Ure, Peter. "On Some Differences Between Senecan and Elizabethan Tragedy," DUJ, X (1948), 17-23.

Ure counts himself among those who are convinced by Howard Baker and Willard Farnham that it is time to discount the Senecan influences on Elizabethan drama spelled out by Cunliffe (#0193) and T. S. Eliot (#0227). But he does not look only to the Middle Ages as the Elizabethan progenitor; the influence of "romanitas," as he terms Roman political, philosophical, mythological, and literary culture, is also to be considered a major one; and Seneca is only a small part of "romanitas." Ure makes a striking comparison between divinized emperors and English kings who rule by divine right and he shows that the controlling principle in English drama in the creative period of Sh's life was the stability of the social order (hierarchy). Those who, like Puritans and dissolute noblemen, sought to undermine the social compromise evoked merciless satire from the dramatists; similar conditions evoked similar satire from Horace, Persius, and Juvenal. This brilliant brief essay relies mainly on Jonson and Chapman for illustrations; Sh is a participant only by inclusive implication.

0608. Vandiver, E. P., Jr. "The Elizabethan Dramatic Parasite," SP, XXXII (1935), 411-427.

Bushy and Green, Falstaff, Parolles, Iago, Sir Toby Belch, Timon's coterie, Nathaniel, and possibly Armado represent Sh's varied use of the classical parasite. Bushy, Green, and Iago are corrupters; Parolles, Sir Toby, and Iago are procurers; Falstaff and Sir Toby are gluttons; Nathaniel, Armado, and Timon's train are flatterers; Armado, Falstaff, and Parolles are braggarts. Sh's parasites betray their classical lineage but they also are close in spirit and conception to their English forebears (who in turn owe much to the classics). The observations on Iago and his relationship to Jonson's Mosca are especially astute. This is an interesting study which makes its point that the Elizabethans surrounded the gnatho with a variety of dramatic tones and put him to a variety of dramatic uses.

0609. Van Doren, Carl. "Shakspere on His Art," ColSS, pp. 403-427. E-S

"Being a poet could not make [Sh] a partisan of poets." Sh portrays only three professional poets, and all three are in his sources (Cinna and the Cynic in Caesar and the nameless Poet in Tim.); in each case he portrays the poet as worse than he appears in the source. Sh apparently did not accept Plato's theory of poetic inspiration: "there is no reason to think that, to [Theseus in Dream], the poet's frenzy is authoritative." Yet Sh was capable of "the poet's show of pride"--the opening lines of Sonn. 55 have "a Roman ring of confidence." Much of the essay treats Sh's allusions to actors and the stage and is therefore not relevant to this Guide.

0610. Van Doren, Mark. Shakespeare. N.Y., 1939, 344 pp.

Van Doren states at once that Sh was greater than (and, implicitly, independent of) his age, with the result that this criticism stands at polarity with those of Craig, Baldwin, Tillyard, Whitaker, and the other historical critics who have examined Sh's use of the donnés of his culture, including classicism. Yet Van Doren has the classical world at hand occasionally as in his list of the classical allusions of 1,2,3H.VI, his briefest (and unappreciative) discussion of Venus as an "Ovidian" poem, his references to Plutarch, etc. The metaphorical imagination of his criticism is brilliantly illuminating (as when he sees Antony as a play of men at home in bright sunlight and gigantic spaces), but he gives Sh credit for more than is just by implying that he is his (classical) sources and for less than is just by disregarding his Art: a creative imagination working on traditional materials through the medium of classical rhetoric.

0611. Vatke, Th[eodor]. "Bildung und Schule in Shakespeare's England," ShJ, XX (1885), 172-189.

Vatke's art. is more valuable for its reprinting of numerous relevant extracts from treatises, plays, poems, etc., than for its presentation of the Renaissance system of education in the classics. It is rather disjointed, ranging freely from fourteenth to seventeenth centuries.

The references to Sh's education and his reaction to it are brief and incidental.

0612. Vatke, Theodor. "Shakespeare und Euripides: Eine Parallele," ShJ, IV (1869), 62-93. E-S HB

The first half of the essay is a general commentary on Seneca's response to Euripides and on Medieval and Renaissance classicism. Some of the parallels which Vatke later sketches between Sh and Euripides are accidental (both men lived in times of military and religious stress; both men went into provincial seclusion late in life). But some are more significant: both were reformers of language and critics of linguistic excess; both were lovers of music; "es giebt nicht zwei Dichter, bei denen das Für und Wider mit ähnlicher Heftigkeit besprochen, bei denen die Schaale der Anerkennung in gleicher Weise geschwankt hätte"; both use parallel structure to highlight the main action (though Sh is more artful here); both are masters of dramatic irony. The most extended analysis is of the Bacchae: here the comparisons with Sh (Antony, Lear, Oth., R.III, Romeo, e.g.) are often parenthetical. Vatke also discusses, inter alia, Medea (comparison with Macb. and Oth.), Hippolytus, Alcestis (comparison between Hercules and the Fool in Lear), Iphigenia in Aulis (comparison with the quarrel scene in Caesar), and Phoenissae (comparison with Troi.).

0613. Vedel, Vald. "Shakespeare und die Renaissance," GRM, III (1911), 633-648. E-S

Sh shared the Renaissance taste for romance, including the romantic conventions of Greek and Roman antiquity (see pp. 636-637). The heroine wandering in search of her lover (Imogen and Helena), the heroine returning unexpectedly to life (Hermione--and, one might add, Hero and Thaisa), the girl who drinks a sleeping potion and awakens in the grave (Juliet), and the lover who kills himself in the mistaken belief that his beloved is dead ("Pyramus" and Romeo) are only a few. Love and adventure by land and sea are the two chief ingredients of this classical romanticism.

0614. Venezky, Alice S. Pageantry on the Shakespearean Stage. N.Y., 1951, 242 pp. GRS

Ch. I of this informative, but somewhat repetitive book explains the Elizabethan convention that a pretentious triumphal procession anticipates a casus; the concept has a classical basis which Sh capitalizes on in Titus I i, Caesar I ii, and Cor. II i. By contrast Sh's English kings (especially the two Richards) enter in "muted" fashion. Ancient dread of being led in triumph appears in Act V of Antony, though the author points out that Cleopatra's dread of proximity to the spectators is greater than her fear of disgrace. Ch. III contains a discussion of mythological entertainments in Elizabeth's progresses. Sh imitated this Ovidian, moralizing pageantry in L.L.L. and especially Dream (in the woodland scenes as well as in Act V). Numerous passages on the classical basis of Shn pageantry appear elsewhere in the book (see, e.g., pp. 151-152 for a discussion of Pistol's Latin motto, 2H.IV V v 30-31). The final ch., on "Shakespeare's Pageant Imagery," is a rewarding treatment of passages in the plays which take on significance when seen as allusions to Elizabethan classical pageantry. Two sections of interest deal with Sh's probable allusions to Brut's struggle with the giants Albion and Gogmagog, traditionally dressed as Romans, and with Sh's use of Petrarchan pseudo-classical "triumphs" in the Yorkist histories where he portrays the Stoic relationship between Fortune and Death.

0615. Vines, Sherard. The Course of English Classicism From the Tudor to the Victorian Age, Hogarth Lectures on Literature, XII (Ln, 1930), 160 pp.

Of the more than two dozen references to Sh, most portray him as "modified" by the classical revival, but at the same time modifying it to harmonize with his romantic predispositions. Vines's bias may be seen in his contempt for everything Medieval and his distrust of everything romantic. Nonetheless there are illuminating comments on such things as Sh's indirect debt to the Greek romances, the Nurse in Romeo as a Plautine lena, and transmuted Senecanism in the tragedies after R.III.

0616. Vyvyan, John. Shakespeare and the Rose of Love: A Study of the Early Plays in Relation to the Medieval Philosophy of Love. N.Y., 1960, 194 pp.

Vyvyan believes that in L.L.L., T.G.V., Romeo, Meas., and W.T. Sh used the Terentian five-act structure with its protasis, epitasis, and catastrophe as a framework for the dramatization of a psychomachia. The forces of evil (within the character or within the plot) make their trump play in the third act; the forces of good counter at the end of the epitasis (during the fourth act). The catastrophe of the fifth act is precipitated by the success or failure of "Good's" countermove. Vyvyan's thesis appears valid, at least in these five plays. The forces of good are often Love in one of three forms: the Medieval Rose of Love, Platonic beauty, Christian Love. In this book Vyvyan is concerned primarily with the first, but references to Sh's use of Platonic concepts sometimes occur (Vyvyan's later book, Shakespeare and Platonic Beauty, falls ahead of the terminus ante quem of this Guide), and of course Christian values are repeatedly introduced as well. Vyvyan's book is a largely successful effort to construct a critical system on the scholarly pilings of Baldwin's book on Sh's Terence (#0683).

0617. Wade, James Edgar. "Mediaeval Rhetoric in Shakespeare," diss (Saint Louis U., 1942). MicroA, V, No. 2 (1944), 72.

Wade's thesis is that Sh reflects in the narrative poems and at least a dozen plays the alterations which the Medieval rhetoricians made in the tenets of the classical authorities (Quintilian, Cicero, Ad Herennium). The chief of these is the fusion of rhetoric and poetic under the head of elocutio (i.e., "the study of style, almost entirely from the point of view of the figures of speech"). Wade's work comes just too early to profit from the work of T. W. Baldwin (#0089), who shows conclusively that Sh was schooled in the Roman masters themselves.

0618. Wagner, W. "Seneca und Shakespeare," ShJ, XI (1876), 319-321.

For the benefit of German readers, Wagner summarizes the parallels brought together by H. A. J. Munro in #0433. He suggests a detailed examination of Sh's plays in juxtaposition with Seneca's Latin and the Tenne Tragedies to determine whether Sh used the original, the trans., or both.

0619. Waldo, Tommy Ruth Blackmon. "Musical Terms and the Complexity of Shakespeare's Style: An Illustration of the Style and Its Relationship to Rhetorical Precept," diss (Florida, 1960).*

0620. Walker, Roy. "The Celestial Plane in Shakespeare," ShS, VIII (1955), 109-117. GRS

Walker makes a critical survey of the commentaries of the past century on Sh's astrology, which he himself ties to imagery of light, sight, storms, and love. There are several passing remarks on classical connections (e.g., "Thunder and lightning, as interpreted by Oedipus [at Colonus] and the chorus, is as portentous as it is in King Lear"). Walker illustrates his thesis with short discussions of passages in Lucr., Romeo, Ham., Oth., Lear, Macb., and Temp.

0621. Walker, Roy. "The Northern Star: An Essay on the Roman Plays," SQ, II (1951), 287-293.

This imaginative essay proposes that Sh's conception of Rome was a living, growing conception; the Roman plays and those like Cym. and 1, 2, 3H. VI in which Caesar is referred to must be seen as parts of a total view of Rome which culminates in Cym. Sh may have believed that Britain and its kings are the legitimate and purer inheritors of Rome and its Caesars. That is why Henry V is stellified (1H. VI I i) as Caesar stellifies himself in Caesar III i. Walker adduces a large number of references to the guiding influence of the stars and planets in association with Rome; Sh may have come to associate the reincarnation of Roman greatness in English greatness with Providence as hinted at by astral influence. This is a stimulating essay which rewards attentive consideration. But it is difficult to reconcile Walker's concept of Sh's developing attitude toward Rome with the consistency which he finds in the plays.

0622. "[Warburton's Edition of Shakespeare]," HWL (1740), I, 1-34.

The author approves of Warburton and his methods which are allowed to speak for themselves through extracts from his notes on sixteen plays. Sometimes the interpretation of Sh is plausible (Charmian's reference to figs and long life in I ii of Antony is an ironic anticipation of figs as the death-bringer of Act V). But more often Warburton is ingenious rather than plausible (e.g., Henry IV's "I stole all courtesy from heaven"—1H. IV III ii 50—is "an Allusion to the Story of Prometheus's Theft, who stole Fire from thence; and as with this he made a Man, so with that Bolinbroke [sic] made a King ..."). DLC

0623. [Warner, Richard]. A Letter to David Garrick, Esq. Concerning a Glossary to The Plays of Shakespeare... Ln, 1768, 110 pp.

In this prospectus Warner finds occasion (pp. 7-19) to discuss the "small Latin" question and to attempt to steer a middle course between the extravagant claims which Upton (#0606) made for Sh's learning and the contemptuous denial by Farmer (#0238) that Sh had any learning at all. He avers that Sh had enough Latin to read Terence, Plautus, Horace, and Seneca, and that "he understood at least as much of the language as a school-boy, never suppos'd to be an idle one, might be allow'd to have done." Much of Warner's evidence is linguistic (e.g., "ear" [to till] from Latin aro); some of the evidence is Sh's familiarity with ancient customs and concepts (e.g., "Corinthian" [1H.IV II iv 13] means "brazen-fac'd" because "Corinthian brass was famous among the antients"). Warner's moderate stand on the "small Latin" question appears not to have greatly affected the prejudices of his contemporaries. DFo

0624. Waters, Robert. "Shakespeare's Education," Shna, V (1888), 245-250.

Waters counters the Baconian gambit that Sh the actor was not formally educated by attacking classical education as a stultifier of genius. He supplies a list of self-educated men (Lincoln, Bunyan, Charles J. Fox, et al.) to support his thesis. If Sh had no Latin or Greek (Waters seems to think he had none), tant mieux, as Emerson, Hazlitt, Voltaire, and Bagehot would agree.

0625. Watkins, W. B. C. "Shakespeare's Banquet of Sense," Shakespeare & Spenser (PUP, 1950), Ch. I, pp. 3-35.

A perceptive study of Sh's changing presentation of carnal relationships from Venus to Antony. Watkins makes critical observations on Sh's use of sensual language and situations and on his portrayal of sensualists. Sh is more like the Ovid of the Amores and the Heroides than are Marlowe and the other "Ovidians" because he admits the trivial and the sordid into sexual relationships, but as he matures (Watkins endorses a developmental approach to Sh's art) two major differences from Ovid emerge: (1) Sh's carnal characters (Antony, Troilus, Othello, e.g.) are driven by genuine emotions; passion is not auto-induced as in Ovid; (2) the frank physical desire of some of Sh's characters (Juliet anticipating her bridal night, e.g.) is suffused by a spirituality totally lacking from Ovid.

0626. Watson, Curtis B. Shakespeare and the Renaissance Concept of Honor. PUP, 1960, 471 pp.

Watson's concern is with Sh's reflection of honor both as a private guide to ethical behavior and as a public principle organizing the social order. Between Christianity and the "pagan humanist" values Sh almost always chooses to portray the pagan ethical system as it descends from Plato, Aristotle, Cicero, and (to a much lesser extent) the Stoics, through countless Renaissance moral treatises, to the Elizabethans. In this system, reputation is a key to immortality and therefore a more important goal than any other on earth. Reputation is the reward both of rank, which itself is sacrosanct, and of virtue; the classical virtues Sh portrays are chiefly magnificence, wisdom, justice, bounty, gratitude, temperance, gentility, beauty with other outer graces, valor, virility, patriotism, plainspokenness, fidelity to friends, fortitude, and constancy. In some of these virtues (e.g., wisdom, justice, temperance) it is more difficult to distinguish the classical from the Christian than Watson implies, but there is no doubt that his basic position is tenable: especially in the tragedies, where crucial ethical questions are at stake, Sh is writing for an audience which accepted the complex of values handed down by the classical moralists (though paradoxically enough the Elizabethans simultaneously espoused the Christian ethical system). Watson's historical approach is a corrective to that criticism which reads modern notions into the plays (he exposes the fallacies in Eliot's attack on Sh's dying heroes and in Granville-Barker's defense of Goneril and Regan). This is an important contribution to knowledge of the donnés of Elizabethan culture, and it is well written, if one discounts an annoying repetitiveness.

0627. Watson, Foster. The English Grammar Schools to 1660: Their Curriculum and Practice. CUP, 1908, 548 pp. E-S

This classic in the history of education is a source of information about the classical discipline Sh probably was submitted to, though Watson makes no effort to relate the educational theories and practices of the sixteenth century to Renaissance literature. (Baldwin's Small Latine [#0089], Vol. I, complements Watson in that it focuses on the literary results of grammar school training.)

0628. Watson, Foster. "Was Shakespeare Ever a Schoolmaster?" NC, LXXXVIII (1920), 643-654.

An argument for the validity of Aubrey's casual remark about Sh's "lost years." Watson supports the hypothesis by indicating the teacher-shortage occasioned by the closing of the monasteries, by showing that most Elizabethans wanted their children educated, and by proving that Beeston, Aubrey's authority, had direct access to Sh's circle in and around the theater. Watson is exceptionally well informed about the state of English education in the sixteenth century, though this is an essay, not a treatise. This essay evokes an attack on Watson and Aubrey by the Baconian George Greenwood in NR, LXXIX (1922), 230-239.

0629. Watt, Lauchlan M. Attic & Elizabethan Tragedy. Ln, 1908, 356 pp. E-S HB

Watt begins with a brief comparison between the elation that followed the repulse of the Persians and the elation that followed the repulse of the Spaniards; both triumphant emotions led to the writing of great tragedy. Then, after nearly two hundred pages of criticism of the Greek tragic canon, Watt turns to Elizabethan drama and Sh. The criticism is effusive and emotional, full of hyperbole, personification, simile. And it contains surprisingly few direct and cogent comparisons between Sh and his Greek predecessors. An occasional remark has special interest: Othello's "prurient curiosity" is, like Oedipus', the cause of his downfall. But for the most part the comparisons are either hackneyed or fanciful: e.g., "The pride of Aeschylus in Athens finds an echo and parallel in Gaunt's immortal eulogy of England"; Sh need not have known the story of Clytemnestra as he could model Ham. on the Darnley murder. There are passages on the tragedies, the Greek and Roman plays, and the tragic English histories. Watt's poetic enthusiasm should put the reader on guard against distortions like these: "His college was the fields and woods of Stratford: his professors, hunger, and the love of all things, and, very often, misunderstanding ... Shakespeare was one of Nature's aptest scholars."

0630. Way, Arthur S. "Relics of Ancient Aryan Folk-Lore in Shakespeare," LQR, CV (1906), 258-275.

Way sees analogous relationships between ancient Sanskrit writings and Celtic, Teutonic, and Greek folklore. Therefore he suggests that some of Sh's Greek mythology (the phoenix bird of H.VIII V v, e.g.) is related indirectly to the Vedic myths. The emphasis falls on astronomical and meteorological mythology. An interesting study; there are over a score of Shn quotations, but not all, of course, illustrate his Greek mythology.

0631. Weisinger, Herbert. "The Myth and Ritual Approach to Shakespearean Tragedy," CRAS, I (1957), 142-166.

Weisinger distinguishes between the participant in the realities of ritual and the spectator of the symbols of tragedy. His definitions of myth and ritual lead him closer to Hebraic religion than to Greek, but his comments on the four great tragedies, on the Roman plays, and (briefly) on the dark comedies and the last plays can be illuminated by the reader's awareness of Greek myths lying at the tragic root. The most challenging statement is insufficiently developed: the fertility and resurrection myths of the last plays are not an outgrowth of Sh's tragic conception but a negation of it, a superposition on the final plays which Sh never took seriously.

0632. Whalley, Peter. An Inquiry into the Learning of Shakespeare with Remarks on Several Passages of his Plays... Ln, 1748, 84 pp. E-S

The last third of the essay is a collection of parallels between Sh and various Greek and Roman authors, each of which Whalley feels is too close to be coincidental. But most are commonplaces and Whalley's ignorance of Elizabethan literature (e.g., he assumes that Sidney is attacking Per. in the Apologie for Poesie) is such as to cast doubt on all his findings and to explain the vehemence with which Farmer (#0238) took a diametrically extreme stand in 1767. It is of interest that Whalley has little to say of Plautus and Ovid and nothing of Plutarch. MnU

0633. Wheatley, Henry B. "Shakespeare As A Man of Letters," TBS, XIV (1919), 109-132.

Part I is a long list of Shn allusions to the technical terminology and processes of publishing. Wheatley can show that Sh was "a man of letters" (i.e., a man who has scholarship but not pedantry, who loves books, who is catholic in his literary tastes, and who is "a man of the world"). Part II is a group of disorganized remarks about Sh's artistic development. Wheatley does not specify the classics as the letters Sh was a man of, but he does mention them and he suggests that Sh was master of a respectable amount of Latin.

0634. Whitaker, Virgil K. "Shakespeare's Use of His Sources," PQ, XX (1941), 377-389. (Also in Craig Festschrift, pp. 185-197.)

"The study of Shakespeare's sources is no infallible guide to an understanding of his plays; but it does afford an insight into his mind and habits. Often what it shows merely confirms what we may infer from other studies of Shakespeare, but occasionally it clears up an obscurity. It is therefore useful as one of many avenues to a better appreciation and enjoyment of the plays—the proper end of all Shakespeare studies." References passim to Sh's use of Plutarch and Plautus.

0635. Whitaker, Virgil K. Shakespeare's Use of Learning: An Inquiry into the Growth of his Mind and Art. San Marino: The Huntington Library, 1953, 366 pp.

Beginning with a précis of and commentary on Baldwin's study of Sh's education (#0089), Whitaker shows that Sh's knowledge of the world and of classical and Christian moral philosophy developed gradually during his career, at least up until the period of the last plays. We can trace the growth of his mind as we can trace the growth of his art. The method is to show the significance of deviations from established sources, especially sources, like Plutarch, which Sh ordinarily followed closely. "Learning" means much more than "classicism"; Whitaker also discusses theology, Scripture, contemporary literature, English history, courtly handbooks, political theory, astrology, humoral psychology, and scientific lore. But mythology, rhetoric, and classical allusion appear frequently in the discussion of the phases in Sh's intellectual development. The basic finding is analogous to those of Bush (#0139) and Kennedy (#0358), i.e.: in the early works Sh used classical allusions as fillers to give texture to the action; as his general knowledge increased he found it less necessary to impose allusions, and myth and rhetoric become naturally integrated into the structure of the plays. The book contains any number of intelligent suggestions: (1) Elizabeth's Act of Uniformity was responsible for the classical wedding masques in Sh because it forbade the portrayal of Christian services; (2) "The fact that Shakespeare's characters [in the history plays] always find analogies or illustrations in Latin writers and never in English history surely justifies an assumption that he was himself almost completely ignorant of it at the time he wrote these plays"; (3) John II i 437-438 ("He is the half part of a blessed man, / Left to be finished by such as she;") "indicate Shakespeare's familiarity with Platonic theories about love." Whitaker's general conclusion is that Sh was "a busy playwright with a curious mind and an interest in contemporary affairs, not a student or an omnivorous reader." This book is of great value, even though it does not always compel agreement (see discussion of Whitaker's ch. on Caesar [#1765] and note also the ch. on Troi. [#1766]).

0636. White, Harold O. Plagiarism and Imitation During the English Renaissance, HSE, No. 12 (HUP, 1935), 209 pp.

This is a successful effort to establish a correlation between the practice of Elizabethan authors and their theory of literary borrowing. The theory, of course, is traceable to the classical rhetoricians by way of France and Italy, and White begins with a ch. surveying the classical and Continental precursors of English critics. Sh receives rather less attention than one might expect: in five pages White disposes of the idea that Greene's Groatsworth of Wit refers to Sh as a plagiarist (the primary reference is to his acting); in another three pages White discusses briefly passages in L.L.L., T.G.V., Romeo, and Sonn. in which Sh ridicules or otherwise derogates improper imitation (i.e., pedantry, affectation, insincerity, lack of variation of the material borrowed). White could have found dozens of references to art as imitation in later plays--Ham. and Temp. alone contain perhaps half a dozen--but White makes it plain that in both theory and practice Sh is an orthodox classicist on the subject of imitation as a literary principle.

0637. Whitmore, Charles E. "The Elizabethan Age in England," The Supernatural in Tragedy (HUP, 1915), pp. 203-288.

Whitmore calls the revenge-ghost virtually an Elizabethan invention, formed by fusing Medieval traditions and Senecan decorative ghosts. Seneca's major contribution was to make the ghost an accepted member of the dramatis personae; the Elizabethans themselves gave him a real part to play in the action. In R.III Sh's ghosts have no classical parentage--indeed in none of Sh's plays does a ghost prattle of Tartarus. Sh used the ghost of Caesar to unify Caesar and he wisely brought him on stage only briefly and used allusions to him by other characters as a substitute for a Greek Chorus. In Ham. the Ghost is an active participant in the action—not at all classical. In Macb. Sh returned to a classical concept—the Goddesses of Destiny, whom he introduces at first as witches to make the alien seem familiar as Aeschylus did in the Eumenides. The cold impartiality of the Goddesses in Macb. makes this the most terrifying play since the Oresteia.

0638. Wickert, Maria. "Das Schattenmotiv bei Shakespeare," Anglia, LXXI (1953), 274-309.

A commentary on Sh's use of the Platonic concepts of appearance and reality, shadow and substance, as they relate to being, to beauty, to love, and to art. Among Sh's works discussed are Venus, Sonn. (27, 43, 53, 98, 99), R.III, R.II, Ham., Temp., 1H.VI, John, Caesar, T.G.V., Merch., and 2H.IV. An interesting passage compares Ficino on Narcissus with Venus 162-163. Another suggests that Cassius' lines about Brutus' inability to see his own "worthiness" (Caesar I ii 55-58) may be traceable to a misinterpretation by Ficino of the concept ἀρετή in Plato's Alcibiades I. Still another interprets Talbot's "practical joke" on the Countess of Auvergne as an important part of 1H. VI, symbolizing the main plot in its play with the contrast between shadow and substance. On the whole one of the best arts. which has yet appeared on Sh's use of Platonic concepts.

0639. W[ickham], G[lynne]. "General Introduction," The London Shakespeare, ed. John Munro, 6 vols. (Ln, 1958), I, xi-xl.

Wickham takes an eminently reasonable approach to the "small Latin" question. Whether Sh attended Stratford School or whether he was made a page in an aristocratic household, he probably received a standard Renaissance education in the classics—"a firm grounding in Latin and an acquaintance with Greek . . . a reading, in the original, of Ovid, a little of Plautus and Terence, 'sentences' from Seneca, Cicero and Horace and maybe some Virgil." Therefore, Jonson's remarks about Sh's Art are not depreciation of his knowledge, but regretful acknowledgment that Sh did not choose to order his plays according to "a classical sense of form."

0640. Wickham, Glynne. "Shakespeare's 'Small Latine and Less Greeke'," Talking of Shakespeare, ed. John Garrett (Ln, 1954), pp. 209-230.

The implication here is that Sh is exclusively immersed in the Medieval dramatic tradition and virtually uninfluenced by the classics. Wickham sets up an artificial dichotomy between Jonson's realistic formalism and Sh's native license. The essay is full of fallacious assumptions (e.g., Sh's tragedies are melodramas because the audience always has hope for the hero until the catastrophe; "Jonson embraced the new words of Greek and Latin stock. Shakespeare clung to the traditional vocabulary"). The whole case appears vastly oversimplified, and a marked contrast to Wickham's later thoughts on the "small Latin" question (#0639).

0641. Wiles, Roy McKeen. "'In My Mind's Eye, Horatio'," UTQ, XVIII (1948), 57-67.

Sh often abrogates the dictum of Aristotle and Horace that portrayed action is preferable to narration except where it is impossible or offensive to show an event. That Sh uses narration to good purpose Wiles demonstrates by an examination of a large number of passages from the plays. Among Sh's motives chief is to impart a tone to the action: if it is described by biased lips (e.g., Casca's as he watches Caesar reject the crown), action takes on an emotional color that could not otherwise be produced. An interesting approach to Sh's deviation from a classical precept.

0642. Wilkinson, L. P. "The Renaissance: Sweet Witty Soul," Ovid Recalled (CUP, 1955), Ch. XII, pp. 399-438.

An informed and sensitive discussion of the Renaissance Ovidian tradition especially in England. See particularly pp. 406-427 passim for commentary on Sh. Wilkinson acknowledges his debt to Root, Bush, Baldwin, and Thomson; he gives emphasis to several of their suggestions: e.g., Sh may well have encountered Ovid first in school in Mirandula's Flores Poetarum and Veltkirchius' annotated Copia of Erasmus; the balance and antithesis of Venus is the most Ovidian part of the poem; it was from Ovid that Marlowe learned the art of the closed couplet; Dream and Temp. are more truly Ovidian in spirit than Sh's epyllia. Altogether a most satisfying ch.

0643. Willcock, Gladys D. "Language and Poetry in Shakespeare's Early Plays," PBA, XL (1954), 103-117. (Annual British Academy Shakespeare Lecture.)

Concerned with the "Elizabethan" Sh of before Ham., the address concentrates largely on rhetoric—not just oratorical formulae from the classical mentors, but also the verbal decoration and elaboration which Miss Willcock calls elocutio. This latter material is, of course, also classical in origin. She makes some cogent distinctions between the rhetorical conceits of the 1590's and those of the metaphysical poets. The remarks on prosody and diction are more brief and general.

0644. Willcock, Gladys D. "Shakespeare and Elizabethan English," A Companion to Shakespeare Studies, ed. H. Granville-Barker and G. B. Harrison (CUP, 1934), pp. 117-136. E-S

Though Chapman may have coined more terms (cf. Holzknecht [#0334]), Sh has had a greater influence on the language because he is at the heart of real speech--a happy blending of native resources ("Pray you, undo this button") and Latinate neologism ("the multitudinous seas incarnadine"). He was fortunate to live at a time when education was beginning to expand beyond the restrictions the dissolution of the monasteries had placed on it and when both puritan and pedant were being held at bay so that the language was a plastic, flexible medium.

0645. Willcock, Gladys D. "Shakespeare and Elizabethan English," ShS, VII (1954), 12-24.

In this attempt to refute the hallowed concept that the Elizabethan age was a time of unbridled license in neology, grammatical usage, and other linguistic practices, Miss Willcock stresses in Sh, as in his contemporaries, those aspects of Art which organized and controlled a writer's Nature. The evolution of a received literary dialect and the attempt to apply Latin grammar to English were two, but perhaps most important was the use of classical rhetoric, in which Sh participated fully, especially early in his career. The numerous citations of rhetorical passages from the plays show that the Restoration was very wrong to assume that "'he did not know what trope or figure meant'."

0646. Willcock, Gladys D. "Shakespeare and Rhetoric," Essays and Studies, XXIX (1943), 50-61.

Modern readers of Elizabethan literature make the error of equating "rhetoric" with "inflated decoration." Actually, this conception is only half right; the 1590's saw a transition from decorative rhetoric to persuasive (classical) rhetoric, and Sh participates in the change. The early plays exemplify the inflated style, but by the time of Meas. and Troi. (both of which are examined toward the end of the essay), Sh had mastered forensic, deliberative, and epideictic oratory.

0647. Willcock, Gladys D. Shakespeare as Critic of Language, Shakespeare Association Pamphlets, 1934, 30 pp. E-S

Sh's response to the linguistic ferment of his age was to criticize language as well as to utilize it. In L.L.L. appears the first English use of the term "critic" and the play represents a brilliant criticism of linguistic excess in the court (Armado) and the schoolroom (Holofernes); Armado the innovator goes to one extreme in Latinate neology while Holofernes the conservative tries to impose classical orthography, pronunciation, and syntax on a flexible language. But Sh does not confine his jibes at language-jugglers to L.L.L., as a glance at 1H.IV (Falstaff and Hotspur), A.Y.L., Ham., and R.II will show. This is a sensible essay.

0648. Williams, Charles. "William Shakespeare," Stories of Great Names (OUP, 1937), pp. 112-140. GRS

This sketch of the known facts is conservative and reliable. It does not give details of Sh's probable schooling, but does posit that "he had a good grounding in Latin, learning to speak in it and to read certain Latin writers, especially Ovid." Williams also explains that Jonson's famous aphorism does not imply Sh's ignorance of the classics.

0649. Williamson, George. "Elizabethan Drama and Its Classical Rival," CUC, XXXI (1929), 251-256.

The emphasis is on "the comparative sterility of Elizabethan classicism," which is partly a result of the failure of Elizabethan theorists like Sidney and Jonson to add anything to the Italian critics from whom they obtained their classical doctrines. At the same time the English populace refused pure Senecanism with the result that the University men added only bits of Seneca to the native stream (Marlowe contributed rhetoric, Kyd blood). Sh is a spokesman for the Elizabethan preference for introspection (Hamlet is compared with Orestes, Lady Macbeth with Medea). And Sh also represents his age in the abandonment of the unities, perhaps a result of the neglect of the classical Chorus and perhaps a habit learned from life story plays in the Medieval Morality tradition.

0650. Willis, William. The Baconian Mint: Its Claims Examined. Ln, 1903, 110 pp.

This is a word-by-word refutation of the claim made by R. M. Theobald in Shakespeare Studies in Baconian Light that coinage from Greek and Latin, characteristic both of the plays and of Bacon's writings proves that Bacon wrote the Shn plays. Willis' method is to show that supposed neologisms in Bacon and/or Sh are very often found in many previous writers. After examining hundreds of words, Willis concludes "that Lord Bacon did not enrich the English language by the addition of a single new word, nor by the use of a word, in a new or unusual sense. The Author of the folio may have done both these things, in some few instances." Modern opinion grants Sh more originality in his Latinate diction.

0651. Wilson, F. P. "Marlowe and Shakespeare," Marlowe and the Early Shakespeare, The Clark Lectures, Trinity College, Cambridge, 1951 (Oxford: Clarendon, 1953), pp. 104-131.

Wilson's emphasis falls on the history plays, H.VI, R.III, and John, especially. He speaks of the tradition that Sh was a country schoolmaster as "the most attractive ... and the most respectable." Such a professional background would explain Sh's knowledge of Plautus, Seneca, and Ovid which he shows in Errors, Titus, and Venus. Wilson compares and contrasts Marlowe and Sh at many points; especially interesting is the view that Sh was more inclined than Marlowe to use "figures of speech" as Quintilian defines the term. There are also thoughtful remarks on the concept of order (degree) in Errors. Altogether a satisfying essay.

0652. Wilson, F. P. "Shakespeare's Reading," ShS, III (1950), 14-20.

A general discussion: only pp. 14-15 deal with classical reading. Wilson admits the definitiveness of Baldwin's William Shakspere's Small Latine & Lesse Greeke (#0089), but nevertheless minimizes the importance of direct borrowing.

0653. Wilson, J. Dover. "The Schoolmaster in Shakespeare's Plays," EDH, n.s. IX (1930), 9-34. E-S

It is possible that Sh did not attend Stratford Grammar School after all, but studied as a page in some noble house. However that may be, "Shakespeare found something in those who lived by the instruction of youth which he disliked, and worse still, something which he could not bring himself to forgive." Perhaps the "something" was pedantry expressed best in Holofernes' "husks" of Latinity which he mistakes for the grain of learning. Wilson does not consider Sh's attitude toward the literature he studied under the pedants he hates.

0654. Wilson, J. Dover. "Shakespeare's 'Small Latin'—How Much?" ShS, X (1957), 12-26.

This strangely obtuse brief survey confines itself to Sh's use of Ovid, concentrating on mythology and direct allusions at the expense of rhetoric, and depreciating Sh's Latinity without sufficient warrant. Wilson shares with J. A. K. Thomson (#0594) a patronizing attitude toward Sh's use of trans., suggesting that only inability to read Latin fluently would have driven him to Golding. Wilson's cavalier dismissal of Baldwin's conclusive evidence (#0089) of Sh's familiarity with the Meta. and the Roman rhetoricians, with Horace, Virgil, and many other Latin authors is surprising, coming as it does from a normally responsible scholar. Wilson omits Hardin Craig, H. T. Price, John E. Hankins, Milton Kennedy, Sister Miriam Joseph, and other important names from his very brief list of contributors to the knowledge of Sh's classicism.

0655. Wilson, J. Dover. "Shakespeare's Universe," UEJ, XI (1942), 216-233.

An admirably lucid discussion of the general propositions about the universe which Sh's plays show that he accepted. Sh's world view was basically Neoplatonic not Aristotelian; he accepted the Platonic concepts of hierarchy and harmony (music of the spheres). His astronomy was Ptolemaic—the naked sky "described and systematised by successive Greek philosophers." His metaphysics was Pythagorean (the concept of the elements and related concept of the humors). Wilson relates these basic tenets to offshoots like alchemy and astrology. He illustrates with quotations from almost a dozen plays. MdBJ MH

0656. Winstanley, William. The Lives Of the most Famous English Poets... (1687), T-D, pp. 22-26.

A pastiche plagiarized from Fuller (#0257), William Basse ("On Mr. William Shakespeare," 1622—see Munro, I, 286), and others. The relevant part of this biography is entirely Fuller's.

0657. Withington, Robert. "'Vice' and 'Parasite': A Note on the Evolution of the Elizabethan Villain," PMLA, XLIX (1934), 743-751. E-S

The Morality Vice prepared English theatergoers for the adoption of the gnatho of Roman comedy. Of Shn characters who may owe something direct or indirect to the gnatho, Withington discusses Iago ("thus do I ever make my fool my purse"), Falstaff (who also owes much to the miles gloriosus), Richard II's wicked councilors Bushy and Bagot ("caterpillars of the commonwealth"), Proteus (he is false and self-seeking in his betrayal of Valentine), and Borachio and Don John (whose punishment, like that of the traditional gnatho, is deferred until after the play).

0658. Wolff, Emil. "Shakespeare und die Antike," Die Antike, XX (1944), 133-174. (Apparently expanded in Antike und Abendland, I [1945].)

Most of Wolff's observations on Sh's use of classical materials have often been made by other critics (e.g., Plautus and Terence in Shrew, Plautus and the Greek romance in Errors, Ovid in Venus, A.Y.L., L.L.L., Lucr., etc.). But in a few cases Wolff sees relationships which are not generally noticed elsewhere: (1) Ovid not only is a more important influence on Titus than Seneca, but may well be a major influence on Sh's whole conception of tragedy; Ovid was himself much under the influence of the Greek tragedians. (2) Lear's plea that he not weep and his unspecified threat against his daughters (II iv 279-289) echo Procne's similar plea and similar threat in Meta. VI, 610--probably in Golding's trans. (3) Sh is not alone in fusing classical with native elements (e.g., chivalry and Christianity with Roman legend in Lucr., English folklore at Athens in Dream); Milton (Comus) and Pope (Rape of the Lock) work in the same tradition, and both are respectable classicists. (4) The rôle of Theseus as benevolent protector of the oppressed in Dream derives from Plutarch, who calls benevolence the greatest of his virtues.

0659. Wolff, Max J. "Zu Arden von Feversham," NS, XXXV (1927), 424-427. E-S

Sh could not have written Arden because "der Verfasser steht vollständig unter dem Einfluss Senekas und der klassizistischen Schablone, sogar die antike Schicksalsidee suchte er nachzubilden." Sh's tendency was in an entirely opposed direction. Wolff argues that the unknown author consciously fused recent history with the Agamemnon story from Seneca's tragedy.

0660. Wright, Celeste Turner. "The Amazons in Elizabethan Literature," SP, XXXVII (1940), 433-456. GRS

An impressively learned study which shows that the Elizabethans "regarded the Amazons as picturesque ornaments to a pageant or a romance but their social system as a dangerous example of unwomanly conduct, a violation of ... traditional order." Two hundred seventy-three footnotes document the lore of militant women in a wide range of classical and Renaissance literature. Sh is represented by references to Twel., Dream, 1,3H.VI, John, Macb., Antony, Tim., Titus, and Lear. He emerges as sharing the views of his contemporaries and as having a respectable store of general information, though he shows no knowledge of such esoteric matters as the Amazons in the New World or Amazons as "unimamians" (i.e., mutilated by removal of one breast).

0661. Wright, Louis B. Shakespeare's Theatre and the Dramatic Tradition, Folger Booklets on Tudor and Stuart Civilization. (Washington, D.C.: Folger Shakespeare Library, 1958), 36 pp.

Wright remarks briefly (pp. 7-8) that Sh may have studied Plautus in grammar school.

0662. Wyndham, George. "The Poems of Shakespeare," Essays in Romantic Literature, ed. Charles Whibley (Ln, 1919), pp. 237-388.

Section ii (251-259) recapitulates Baynes' account (#0097) of Sh's education.

0663. Yardley, E. "Bacon on Hercules," 9 NQ, XI (1903), 65.

Yardley begins an enduring controversy with his observation that Bacon was in error about the means of transportation Hercules took in journeying to the Caucasus to free Prometheus. See ibid., pp. 154, 199, 352, by which point a "Baconian" debate over Sh's errors in classicism is in full voice. The controversy brings forth more heat than light; the chief Baconian is George Stronach. See ibid., XII (1903), 54-55, 156-157, 275-276, 427; 10 NQ, I (1904), 33-34.

0664. Yoder, Audrey. Animal Analogy in Shakespeare's Character Portrayal. Col UP: King's Crown, 1947, 150 pp.

Observing that Sh's four thousand references to animals include allusions to supernaturalized beasts, "unnatural natural history," and analogies between men and beasts, Dr. Yoder elects to concentrate on the third type which she traces to the Aesopic fables Sh learned at school. Like Baldwin (#0089), she believes that Sh used the Camerarius ed., and she is able to supplement Baldwin's list of Sh's echoes of Aesop. The second section of the book is an interesting enumeration of Sh's references to animals for the purpose of characterization. Villains, characters Sh wishes to satirize, and weak but decent people are most often given the attributes of various kinds of animals, but Dr. Yoder also shows that Sh characteristically brands warring factions, abstractions, and mankind generally with the moral features of animals. In his use of animal analogy Sh is following the classical tradition of physiognomy which traces to Aristotle. Among the more interesting points is the observation that Falstaff is compared more often (sixty-seven times) to animals than any other Shn character; in 2H.IV these comparisons become progressively more pejorative, a prefiguration of his rejection by Hal and Sh. The book has a statistical orientation; the appendices give, inter alia, graphs and lists showing frequency of occurrence, etc., and the body of the text is largely an enumeration and classification of allusions, but the author is very well informed, as her endnotes show. Within its limits this is an informative study.

0665. Young, Edward. Conjectures on Original Composition In a Letter to the Author of Sir Charles Grandison. Ln, 1759. (Reprinted in Edward Young's "Conjectures on Original Composition" in England and Germany, by Martin W. Steinke [1917], pp. 41-73.)

Insofar as it concerns Sh, this famous essay forms a link between the Augustan critics and the Romantics, since Young enthusiastically praises Sh for his ignorance of the classics. He compares him to untutored Pindar and contrasts him with pedantic Jonson and tasteless Dryden. "Who knows if Shakespeare might not have thought less, if he had read more?"

0666. Zandvoort, R. W. "Dramatic Motivation in Macbeth," LLM, XL (1951), 110-120. (Reprinted in Collected Papers [1954].)

In passing: "To the Greeks, Fate and the Gods were evil; man, despite the crimes he was made to commit, was fundamentally innocent. In Shakespeare ... it is the other way round: man himself, not the gods is evil ..."

0667. Zbierski, Henryk. Shakespeare and the "War of the Theatres": A Reinterpretation, PTPN, Tom XVI, Zeszyt 5 (Poznan, 1957), 150 pp.

Zbierski argues (persuasively, on the whole) that the "War" was fought on ideological, more than personal, grounds. The conflict was between the private theaters, which Jonson wished to make "classical" on lines traceable to the Apologie for Poesie, and the public theaters, personified in Sh, who neglected the classical formulae. The author is inclined to discount Jonson's F_1 praise of Sh's Art and to maintain that for four decades he persisted in his critical view of Sh's unclassical artistic standards; yet he insists that Jonson felt no malice toward Sh and that the safe scholarly position is the middle ground between those who believe in a vindictive Sh flagellating Jonson through the central segment of the canon and those who try to remove Sh altogether from the ancient-modern controversy. Zbierski believes that Sh's "purge" was administered not so much to Jonson as to the private theater, his chosen ground, and that Ham. II ii is Sh's sardonic answer to Jonsonian criticism of the public theaters. DFo

0668. Zupitza, Julius. "Shakespeare über Bildung, Schulen, Schüler, und Schulmeister," ShJ, XVIII (1883), 1-31. E-S

Zupitza's "einleitender Vortrag" marshals scores of quotations from the canon to show that Sh was fully conscious of education from the "absey book" to the university. Surprisingly little of Zupitza's commentary focuses on instruction in Latin language and literature, which was the core of education in the English Renaissance. These quotations and the analyses of Hugh Evans, Holofernes, Pinch, and other schoolmasters in Sh Zupitza would regard as support for John Aubrey's contention that Sh was himself once "a Schoolmaster in the Countrey." In any case, he remembered his own schooldays well. Excerpts in trans., Shna, I (1884), 277-279.

THE COMEDIES

0669. A., E. S. "'Measure for Measure,' II.i. ('O thou wicked Hannibal')," 8 NQ, V (1894), 363.

A. questions whether Elbow is thinking of a reference to the fiend Anaballe in one of the Towneley Mysteries or whether Sh knew Lucian's portrait of the quarrelsome, boastful Hannibal in the twelfth Dialogue. Two correspondents (ibid., VI, p. 44; ibid., VII [1895], 203) emphasize that Elbow is a malapropist; one suggests "cannibal," the other "Ananias."

0670. A., G. E. P. "The Death Songs of Pyramus and Thisbe," 10 NQ, V (1906), 341-343, 401-403.

A. prints two songs which he believes were intended for plays put on for the Queen by children. The first is based on a story in Xenophon. A. conjectures that Sh parodies these two songs (or similar ones) in the death songs of Pyramus and Thisbe (without any clear evidence he assumes that the final lines of Sh's hero and heroine are sung, not recited). The argument is interesting if not entirely persuasive. Recent scholarship has discovered so many analogues to the Mechanicals' playlet that it is risky to specify any one as the target for Sh's parody.

0671. Addington, Marion H. "'Juno's Swans'," NQ, CLXIV (1933), 7.

A number of scholars have speculated on the source of Celia's confusion of Venus and Juno in A.Y.L. I iii 77. Juno had no swans, but Kyd gave her some in Soliman and Perseda and this is probably Sh's source, as Professor Addington indicates.

0672. Addis, John. "'Fortune': Chaucer and Shakespeare," 4 NQ, IX (1872), 339.

The domesticity of Chaucer's setting for the Goddess Fortuna in the Book of the Duchess ("Now by the fire, now at the table") anticipates Sh's allusions in A.Y.L. (I ii 34) and Antony (IV xv 44) to the goddess as a "housewife." Sh has been thought to have originated the association of Fortuna with the distaff.

0673. Arnold, Paul. "Occultisme elisabethain," Cahiers du sud, No. 308 (1951), 88-101. GRS

In this essay Arnold announces his book on Sh (#0079) and devotes more than half of his space to an analysis of Merch. which exemplifies his critical method in the book. "Portia ... a renouvelé vis-à-vis de tous les personnages le miracle d'Orphée, domptant, élevant, réaccordant toutes les âmes par tous les procédés usités à Eleusis et chez Pythagore: la réflexion juste, la musique, le symbole, enfin et surtout la terreur qui déchire le voile de la logique et dénude le coeur." Antonio is (because of his malice toward Jews) most in need of this mystic purification of spirit, and he is accorded it through the horror of the courtroom scene, but Bassanio, too, must undergo the rites of initiation as he successfully chooses a symbolic casket. Arnold maintains that Sh echoes Quintilian's De Musica (i.e., Institutio Oratoria, X) in Act V; there the combination of music and moonlight is from the Eleusinian liturgy. An ingenious, but unpersuasive interpretation of the play. One can see philosophical significance in Acts IV and V without reading the play allegorically.

0674. Arterus. "Shakspeare Correspondence: 'As You Like It'," NQ, VIII (1853), 383-384.

This note prints more than forty lines from Palingenius' Zodiacus Vitae in Latin, itali-

NOTE: Numbers preceded by # refer to entries in this Guide. Keys to abbreviations are found on pages xi-xvii and 381-387.

cizing those phrases that are reminiscent of Jaques's phrasing in "All the world's a stage." Arterus does not know which passage is creditor and which debtor. Curiously, he does not identify the author or work, and even the editor's plea does not elicit any identification.

0675. Ashe, Geoffrey. "'Several Worthies'," NQ, CXCV (1950), 492-493.

The opinion is expressed here that in the "several worthies [that] make one dignity" in L.L.L. IV iii 236 Sh is anagramming the name "Wriothesley" in its Latin form: "H. Wriotesleus Earl." The suggestion that Southampton or anyone else could read through to this meaning is patently absurd even when Ashe hypothesizes a similar anagram antedating the play. The noun "worthies" appears in a similar sense (i.e., not referring to the Nine Worthies) in T.G.V. at II iv 166.

0676. Auden, W. H. "Music in Shakespeare: Its Dramatic Use in His Plays," Encounter, IX (1957), 31-44.

Auden makes the passing remark (p. 40) that only Jaques of all the sojourners in Arden is in true harmony with the Neoplatonic cosmos, because in Act V he chooses to remain in the forest to hear the music of the spheres.

0677. B., C. W. "Ducdame, Ducdame," TLS, February 15, 1934, p. 108.

B. suggests a Greek origin for the puzzling word "ducdame" in Jaques's song (A.Y.L. II v 56): δεῦρο δὴ, "come hither." This guess is no more improbable than dozens of others that have been made; δεῦρο δὴ is far from "ducdame" phonologically, however.

0678. B., C. W. "'Merchant of Venice,' II.ii. 80," 10 NQ, VI (1906), 325.

B. cites a witty epigram from Menander on the different relationships between mother and child and father and child to illustrate Sh's use of the proverb "It's a wise father that knows his own child."

0679. Bacon, J. R. "Plautus and Posterity," CAP, XXXIII (1936), 37-38. (A summary of an address.)

Miss Bacon is certain that Sh read Plautus, and she hears echoes in the plots and diction of Dream, Merch., and Caesar. The summary does not give details. Sh had precedent for his interest—thirteen different Plautine comedies were produced at Cambridge between 1547 and 1590. MnU

0680. Baldwin, C. S. "Pastoral and Rustic Comedy," Renaissance Literary Theory and Practice: Classicism in the Rhetoric and Poetic of Italy, France, and England 1400-1600 (Col UP, 1939), pp. 146-154.

After some fumbling attempts by Lyly and Peele, Sh finally "found the dramatic solution of myth and pastoral, folklore and rustics, for court show in the Midsummer Night's Dream." The result is "a one-act play, Greek dramaturgy beyond Garnier's or Tasso's. But instead of saying that Shakspere conformed to the dramatic unities, we should rather say that he learned the dramatic importance of holding fairyland together."

0681. Baldwin, T. W. "Commentary on Dr. Pope's 'Shakespeare on Hell'," SQ, I (1950), 296.

Sh is not reflecting Christian concepts of hell in Meas. III i 126-128 as Miss Pope claims (#0886). Claudio's "doubts" and vivid portraiture are derived from Cicero's Tusculan Disputations "which Shakespeare knew well." Lines 126-128 constitute a reference to pagan philosophers who are outside the Hebraic law and therefore only imagine hell. A very effective argument.

0682. Baldwin, T. W. "'Respice Finem: Respice Funem'," AMS, pp. 141-155.

Baldwin analyzes Dromio's coarse Latin-English pun (Errors IV iv 44-46), tracing the adage respice finem directly to the Greek Anthology. He discovers no one source for respice funem, but his exhaustive research enables him to point out a multitude of analogues (classical, pseudo-classical, scriptural, and Elizabethan) for the two phrases.

0683. Baldwin, T. W. Shakspere's Five-Act Structure: Shakspere's Early Plays on the Background of Renaissance Theories of Five-Act Structure from 1470. Illinois UP, 1947, 848 pp.

This detailed study is a special application of the thesis of William Shakspere's Small Latine & Lesse Greeke (#0089) that Sh was at least "a learned grammarian" and knew what classics any graduate of a grammar school ought to know. The focus in this book is on Terence, the preferred author for lower forms in Sh's day. Baldwin's minute inspection of a host of eds. of Terence has enabled him to trace with enviable precision Renaissance indebtedness to the classical commentators (especially Donatus and Servius). These commentators and their descendants evolved from the six comedies of Terence a three-part organic structure (protasis, epitasis, catastrophe) which is worked out precisely in five stages or acts. This structural formula Sh knew very well as Baldwin's analysis of L.L.L., Errors, Twel., T.G.V., All's W., and Romeo clearly shows. Eunuchus appears to have been Sh's favorite Terentian comedy, followed by Andria and Heáutontimorumenos (all three were well represented in Udall's Floures, which Sh doubtless used as a pony in school for difficult passages). Sh's school text of Terence was probably the Willichius ed. (1550); the structure he uses is spelled out there. Baldwin uses the evidence of Sh's knowledge of Terentian structure to propose a chronology of the canon which he would oppose to Chambers' traditionally accepted one: L.L.L. (between August, 1588, and August, 1589) followed by All's W., Errors, T.G.V., and Romeo, all before 1592. (L.L.L. and Romeo were revised later in the 1590's). One may be hesitant about accepting the chronology, but the scholarly criticism of the individual plays is extraordinarily good. The most rewarding, perhaps, is on the classical (Lylyan) elements in L.L.L. and the multiplicity of sources for Errors. This is, next to #0089, Baldwin's most satisfying book.

0684. Barber, C. L. "The Saturnalian Pattern in Shakespeare's Comedy," SewR, LIX (1951), 593-611.

Barber, a mythicist, argues that Sh, like Aristophanes, made comedy out of the folk rituals of his culture, especially the inhibition-releasing holidays. This essay is largely subsumed into #0685.

0685. Barber, C. L. Shakespeare's Festive Comedy: A Study of Dramatic Form and its Relation to Social Custom. PUP, 1959, 266 pp.

Barber, like Janet Spens (#2126) and Frye (#0766), is concerned with native English folkways and their relationship to the form Sh's comedy took, but like them he also sees certain connections with the classical tradition. In the first place, he repeatedly makes a loose equation between the festival comedy of Sh and the Greek Old Comedy, sometimes comparing passages, but never suggesting indebtedness. Secondly, he distinguishes between Dream and Sh's earlier comedies: the latter were imitations of imitations of the classics (Plautus and Terence especially), but with Dream Sh launched a native form based on the dances, games, and rituals of folk holidays, a form which was to preoccupy him until the period of the great tragedies. After Twel., festive comedy relinquishes its dominant position and assumes a subordinate rôle as counterpoint to more sober themes in the tragedies and romances. Barber's explanation of Shn comic form is interesting, but does not take adequate account of other traditional elements: pseudo-classical pastoral, Greek romance, Medieval romance, humoral satire, etc.

0686. Baskervill, C. R. "Bassanio as an Ideal Lover," MAS, pp. 90-103. E-S

The casket choices made by Morocco, Arragon, and Bassanio (Merch. II vii; II ix; III ii) symbolize respectively sensual, rational, and ideal love in the Platonic distinction made by Castiglione's Courtier. That the whole play is permeated by Platonic doctrine reinforces this interpretation of the casket scenes, according to Baskervill. The art. contains extensive documentation from sixteenth-century sources; an analysis of the scenes themselves could support the argument, which appears well founded.

0687. Benham, A. R. "A Note on the Comedy of Errors," MLN, XXXVI (1921), 377-378. SG

Sh derived his conception of the pathetic Aegeon of I i from Plautus' prologue to the Menaechmi (lines 34-36) where the bereaved father is said to have died of grief.

0688. Bennett, Josephine W. "Jaques' Seven Ages," SAB, XVIII (1943), 168-174.

Mrs. Bennett reviews the controversy over the source of Jaques's speech and suggests that Palingenius' Zodiacus Vitae is as close to Jaques's words as anything yet brought forward. She then goes on to show very close parallels to the Onomasticon of Julius Pollux (second century A.D.) which was trans. into Latin in 1541. As it was a thesaurus, Sh may have dipped into the Onomasticon for the erudition he needed to compete with the University Wits. The portrait of Jaques is satirical--he speaks "rhetorical commonplaces" rather than sincere wisdom. John Hankins (#0306) presents a very similar view of Palingenius' relationship to "All the world's a stage."

0689. Bernad, Miguel A. "The Paradox of Shakespeare's Golden World," PS, IV (1956), 441-458.

The golden world of A.Y.L. is not classical ("it is doubtful whether Shakespeare had ever read the Metamorphoses or the Georgics . . .") but Christian—a paradise in which man has no right to remain because he merits the "penalty of Adam." Yet, while he sojourns in the golden world he "fleet[s] the time carelessly" (i.e., sine cura--Sh's Latinate word still retained its original meaning). DLC

0690. Blistein, E. M. "The Object of Scorn: An Aspect of the Comic Antagonist," WHR, XIV (1960), 209-222.

Blistein distinguishes between comic characters we laugh with and those we laugh at; the latter share with the Aristotelian tragic hero the sin of hybris or overreaching. Two of his four examples are Parolles and Malvolio who provide us an Aristotelian catharsis of scorn and mockery rather than of pity and fear. Parolles is more complex than the Plautine braggart because he sees his own status and may possibly reform. All of these insights are not so original as Blistein appears to assume.

0691. Boas, F[rederick] S. "The Soldier in Elizabethan and Later English Drama," TRSL, n.s. XIX (1942), 121-156.

For Parolles as a miles gloriosus see #0977.

0692. Boll, Franz. "Die Lebensalter..." NJKA, XXXI (1913), 89-145.

A relentlessly documented study of the evolution of the concept of man's life as divided into stages. The first part discusses numerous classical texts in which three, four, five, six, eight, ten, twelve, or fifteen "Lebensalter" appear. In the second part Boll turns his attention to the seven ages, beginning with Ptolemy, and following the developing concept through the late classical and Medieval periods to the Renaissance. Here Sh is introduced, and Jaques's lines in A.Y.L. are seen to reflect the classical identification of each of the seven ages with a planet (Mercury for the schoolboy, Venus for the lover, Mars for the soldier, etc.). Boll insists that Sh has not combined two discrete images in Jaques's speech: the Stoic view that man is only a player on the stage of life had been associated with the ages of man in classical times. The tone of Sh's lines is Stoic (i.e., pessimistic and sardonic). Boll gives minimal attention to Sh's means of access to the classical concept. The treatise ends with remarks on Schopenhauer's place in the tradition and an appendix on Greek hebdomadal literature. A learned study which should serve as a standard reference, especially for the concept in antiquity. DLC

0693. Bond, R. Warwick. "The Framework of 'The Comedy of Errors'," Studia Otiosa (Ln, 1938), pp. 43-50. SG

The essay is an attempt to trace the enveloping action of Errors to an Italian source, but the first half of the ch. (43-46) contains interesting remarks on Sh's debt to the classics, especially Roman comedy.

0694. Borinski, Karl. "Dante und Shakespeare," Anglia, XVIII (1896), 450-454.

In refutation of a Baconian who had pointed to the word "honorificabilitudino" in Bacon (cf. L.L.L. V i 44), Borinski points out that Dante uses the term in his De Vulgari Eloquentia and suggests that Sh could have found the Latin term in Dante or its Italian equivalent in Trissino's Italian trans. See Herrmann (#0805) and Hutton (#0814).

0695. Boughner, Daniel C. The Braggart in Renaissance Comedy: A Study in Comparative Drama from Aristophanes to Shakespeare. Minnesota UP, 1954, 328 pp.

Beginning with a discussion of Aristophanes, who invented the cowardly braggart in Dionysos of The Frogs, Boughner goes on to Menander and then to a detailed characterization of the eight exemplars in Latin comedy. After showing the revival and modernization of the type on the Italian stage in the sixteenth century, he focuses on England, where, he believes, hospitality was prepared for classical and Continental imports by the Herodian tyrant of the Mystery plays and the Vice of the Moralities. Boughner makes no systematic effort to fit Sh into the pattern, but he finds opportunity to discuss briefly Falstaff, Parolles, Bully Bottom, Ancient Pistol, and Sir Andrew. The last two chs. are on Spanish and French participation in the tradition. This is an important study, valuable for its information and its responsible judgments.

0696. Boughner, D[aniel] C. "Sir Toby's Cockatrice," Italica, XX (1943), 171-172.

The death-dealing glance referred to by Sir Toby (Twel. III iv 214-215) is a reference to Italian comedy in which the cowardly braggart often compared himself to a basilisk. The mediate source is Plautus.

0697. Bowers, R. H. "A Medieval Analogue to 'As You Like It', II, vii, 137-166," SQ, III (1952), 109-112.

Bowers prints a sixty-line Middle English poem depicting the seven ages of man, but the parallel to Sh is not particularly close. As T. W. Baldwin points out in his extensive survey of the problem (#0089, I, 652-673), Sh's source for the passage is likely to have been classical or pseudo-classical.

0698. Bracy, William. "'Humour' Comedy in the Merry Wives," The Merry Wives of Windsor: The History and Transmission of Shakespeare's Text, MUS, XXV, No. 1 (Missouri UP, 1952), Ch. X, pp. 113-120.

Bracy argues that the play should be dated 1597, i.e., before Jonson made humor comedy his special province. Sh was, then, not in Jonson's debt but something of an innovator: "The tendency to exaggerate Ben Jonson's great learning and Shakespeare's lack of learning has ...been a decided barrier in giving the latter his due credit as an original and creative artist." There is no comment on how much "learning" about the classical humors is implicit in Wives.

0699. Bradbrook, M. C. "Shakespeare and the Use of Disguise in Elizabethan Drama," EC, II (1952), 159-168.

In passing: of the five types of disguise in Shn plays, all derive from the classical comedy, but Sh made capital only of the girl-as-boy device.

0700. Brandl, A. "Zur Quelle der 'Komödie der Irrungen'," ShJ, XXXIX (1903), 233.

Brandl refers to C. Bardt, who in the preface to his Roman Comedies suggests that Sh came to knowledge of Plautus' Menaechmi by way of Warner's trans. (published in 1595), which, like Sh's play, usually has "Epidamnum" (the accusative) where Plautus shows a nominative. The opinion of G. B. Harrison (#0312, p. 270b) is that "Warner" (Harrison does not consider "W.W." identified as yet) possibly saw Sh's play; or perhaps Sh saw the trans. in manuscript; it was entered in the Stationers' Register in 1594.

0701. Bray, F. W. "Shakespeare As a Critic," PL, IX (1897), 238-256.

This survey of Sh's judgments of literature and litterateurs contains a section "Of Foreign Affectations—Italian, Spanish, Latin." Here are brief remarks on Holofernes' Latinate pedantry—a travesty of theoretical knowledge which has no practical reference. Bray believes that Sh hated this kind of abstract intellectualism.

0702. Brooke, C. F. Tucker. "Classical Influence in Comedy," The Tudor Drama: A History of English National Drama to the Retirement of Shakespeare (Boston, 1911), pp. 147-187. E-S

A fluent and penetrating study of the nature of Latin influence and its means of infiltration into the native stream. Sh is not the primary concern of this ch., but Brooke refers several times to his comedies as culminations of adaptations begun as early as the 1530's and 'forties. Brooke regards Errors as the closest imitation of Plautus in the English Renaissance. The romantic emphasis on mistaken identity (A.Y.L., Twel., Much, etc.) is more Plautine and Terentian than the Jonsonian comedy of types is. Another classical influence on Sh's comedies is Ovidian mythology. Dream is an effort to combine myth and pastoral as Lyly had done; Lyly's experiments with mythology also taught Sh to combine stark realism with "the impalpably imaginary" (Bottom and Titania, Armado-Moth-Jaquenetta).

0703. Brooks, Robert Giles. "An Edition of W.W.'s 1595 Translation of Plautus' Menaecmi," diss (Illinois, 1951). DA, XII (1952), 59.

Brooks's diss contains considerable material on Sh's use of Plautus in Errors, and on the probability that W.W. was influenced by Sh, not vice versa. W.W. and Sh may well have known one another as they worked on the same materials at the same time under the same patronage.

0704. Brown, John Russell. "Introduction," The Merchant of Venice (1955/1959), ArdenSh, pp. xi-lviii.

See pp. xxvii-xxviii for a brief explanation of the Roman Law of the Twelve Tables as an analogue to the bond plot in Merch.

0705. Burnet, J. "Shakespeare and Greek Philosophy," Essays and Addresses (Ln, 1929), pp. 163-168. HB SG (First printed in Homage.)

In Lorenzo's speech (Merch. V i 54-88), Sh has expressed the true Pythagorean doctrine of music as ἁρμονία (or order) and κάθαρσις (or spiritual purgation). Sh's version is uncluttered by "the Aristotelian and Scholastic accretions which disfigured the doctrine." This even though Sh's only access to Plato's Timaeus in which they are expressed was through the Medieval tradition with its "Aristotelian and Scholastic accretions." Provocative, but unconvincing. Burnet makes some interesting asides on the importance of the Timaeus in the Middle Ages.

0706. Bush, Douglas. "The Tedious Brief Scene of Pyramus and Thisbe," MLN, XLVI (1931), 144-147.

An effective attack on Miss Farrand's evidence (#0756) that Sh was parodying Mouffet. The most telling argument is that no parody is worthwhile unless the audience knows the model; Mouffet had not appeared in print in 1595. Bush cites numerous verbal echoes of other Elizabethan versions of Ovid's story to show that Sh was burlesquing butchered mythology, "a popular bygone fashion in drama," not any single source.

0707. C. "Shakspeare, Sidney, and Essex," 3 NQ, III (1863), 82-84, 103-106, 124-126.

As part of this unconvincing effort to posit a devoted relationship between Sh and Sidney, C. in the third letter (p. 124) suggests that L.L.L. is modeled exactly on Sidney's proposals for comedy in the Apologie. Sidney rejects native elements in favor of the thraso, the lover, the pedant, and the traveler of Latin comedy. As Furness points out in the New Variorum, L.L.L. probably antedates 1595, the date of publication of the Apologie.

0708. C., H. C. "Plautus and Shakespeare," 4 NQ, V (1870), 594.

Falstaff, Tranio and Grumio, and Duke Theseus' speech on the Poet's eye "in a fine frenzy rolling," indicate that Sh had read in the originals Miles Gloriosus, Mostellaria, and Pseudolus respectively. Only the second suggestion is ordinarily accepted today.

0709. C., R. "'Than Music From the Spheres' (Twelfth Night Act iii. sc. i)," 5 NQ, VII (1877), 186.

Without explanation, C. prints in juxtaposition to Olivia's passing allusion a passage (in Greek) from Fabricius' Bibliotheca Graeca which explains the motion of the spheres and their music. Sh's means of access to this ubiquitous doctrine are impossible to specify, but reprinting a commentary from 1712 does not appear to illuminate Olivia's commonplace remark.

0710. Cambillard, [C.]. "Le Songe D'Une Nuit D'Été: Thème Astrologique," EA, III (1939), 118-126. GRS

This interpretation of the fairy plot is more restrained than some "solar" readings. Cambillard sees Titania as the moon (Lucina as well as Diana-Hecate-Cynthia—there are several images of childbirth associated with her) and Oberon as the sun. The analysis follows the two astrological entities through the zodiacal patterns for Mayday and Midsummer-day, showing the conjunction of Mercury (reversal of rôles) and Venus (love). The astrological lore employed dates from the Renaissance, but Cambillard appears aware of its roots in classical mythology.

0711. Campbell, Oscar J. "Love's Labor's Lost," Shakespeare's Satire (OUP, 1943), pp. 24-43.

Campbell reads the play as Sh's "barbed shafts of ridicule" against pedantic reverence for ancient authorities, Latin and Greek inkhornism, the stargazing Raleigh group who rejected feminine companionship to speculate idly on impracticalities, anti-Petrarchism—in short all intellectual pretentiousness divorcing itself from humane relationships. Much of what Campbell says about Holofernes, Armado, et al. is a readable digest of earlier work, including his own. But he emphasizes the responsible opinion that specific topical reference is only secondary to the more general satiric meaning of the play.

0712. Campbell, O[scar] J. "Love's Labour's Lost Re-Studied," MichiganPLL, I (1925), 1-45.

A substantial part of this study is an attempt to trace Don Armado, Moth, Holofernes, and Nathaniel to the commedia dell' arte. Ultimately they are related to the miles gloriosus, servus, pedant, and gnatho respectively of Latin comedy, but numerous details appear to indicate a proximate Italian source. An informed and effective argument.

0713. Carleton, Hugh. "'Measure for Measure'," 7 NQ, V (1888), 181-182.

Carleton rejects some interpolated plurals in Claudio's description of the pains of the after-life. The analysis of the speech is calculated to show "that Shakespeare draws throughout upon the stores of his own learning, which was multifarious and extensive." There are Latinisms in the passage, with probable references to the Aeneid, Cicero, Euripides, and Hermetic writings. Some objections and additions are elicited ibid., pp. 382-383.

0714. Carruthers, C. H. "The Shakespearian 'Ducdame'," PQ, XII (1933), 37-43. SG

Carruthers proposes a twelfth derivation for Jaques's puzzling word (A.Y.L. II v 56) which he adds to the eleven earlier ones he summarizes (See #0677 for a thirteenth). Because Jaques is parodying the pastoral and refers to magic, the source should be sought in a combination of the two. This source is Virgil's Eclogues VIII, where a maiden uses the magic incantation "ducite Daphnim" to call her lover. The phrase was probably taken early into English folklore (under the influence of the Medieval notion of Virgil the necromancer) and by normal English sound changes evolved into "ducdame" (trisyllabic) by the end of the sixteenth century. The theory is as plausible as any yet proposed, but Carruthers is much less convincing when he attempts to use his hypothesis to explain a supposed crux in Errors IV iii.

0715. Charlton, H. B. "Shakespeare's Recoil from Romanticism," BJRL, XV (1931), 35-59. E-S SG (Reprinted in Shakespearian Comedy [1938].)

Sh "recoiled" from romance twice early in his career: after L.L.L. he turned to classical comedy in Errors; then again after T.G.V. he recoiled to Shrew. In each case the recoil was precipitated by the almost insurmountable difficulties which Sh encountered in trying to harmonize incompatibles—drama and romance. But in the case of Errors, at least, he was unable to strip himself of the sentiments (chivalry, Frauendienst, sympathy for the unfortunate) which are the legacy of Medieval romance. Renaissance England and ancient Rome were different milieux, as Charlton shows in a brilliant exposition of the basis of Latin comedy in Roman social ethics. Because Sh was an Elizabethan, his recoils were incomplete, and after each of them he returned to romance as philosophically more congenial. What Charlton does not account for is the dramatic (and theatrical) success of Jonsonian comedy which (perhaps he would concede) does have a consistent basis in the social ethics of Rome.

0716. Charlton, H. B. "The Taming of the Shrew," BJRL, XVI (1932), 353-375. E-S (Reprinted in Shakespearian Comedy [1938].)

This lecture is a continuation of the thesis stated in "Shakespeare's Recoil from Romanticism" (#0715). Shrew is a satire on romantic wooing; Sh has thrown the clichés of courtship into a rollicking context of mercenary "wiving" and conniving duplicity out of Roman comedy. "For the moment [Sh's] mood was to exhibit the love of woman more in the spirit of the Roman market-place than in that of his own modern Europe ..." Sh's road to the Roman market-place was marked by directional signs in Italian.

0717. Cheney, David Raymond. "Animals in A Midsummer Night's Dream," diss (Iowa State, 1955). DA, XV (1955), 2188.

The abstract indicates that literary sources for Sh's connotative use of animals in the play are a major concern of this diss. Aesop is not mentioned in the abstract, but is presumably treated among those sources.

0718. Chew, Samuel C. "'This Strange Eventful History'," AMS, pp. 157-182.

Expressing contempt for Quellenforschungen of Jaques's "seven ages" speech (A.Y.L. II vii 139-166), Chew himself launches into a sweeping and detailed survey of the literature and iconography of the theme and its association with other concepts like Fortune and Father Time, all as a background to Sh's passage. Among the classical authorities mentioned are Aristotle, Pythagoras, Horace, Ovid, Varro, Solon, Hippocrates, Galen, and Proclus.

0719. Churchill, George B., and Wolfgang Keller. "Die lateinischen Universitäts-Dramen in der Zeit der Königin Elisabeth," ShJ, XXXIV (1898), 221-323.

Churchill and Keller consider that Holofernes is modeled on the pedant of Pedantius, which Sh's small Latin was entirely adequate to read. They believe that the university play definitely antedates 1591 and that it is inconceivable that Sh did not know of it. Nathaniel corresponds to Dromodotus, the learned friend of Pedantius. The Latin play is traceable to Plautus, directly or by way of Italian or German models. Churchill and Keller note that pedants are rare in English literature before L.L.L.

0720. Clark, Donald L. "Ancient Rhetoric and

English Renaissance Literature," SQ, II (1951), 195-204.

For rhetoric in Merch. see #2329.

0721. Claus, W. Über die Menächmen des Plautus und ihre Nachbildung besonders durch Shakspere. [Stettin, 1864, 61 pp.]

Not seen. NcD

0722. Coghill, Nevill. "The Basis of Shakespearian Comedy," Essays and Studies, n.s. III (1950), 1-28.

This fascinating critical essay distinguishes between the satirical comedy of Jonson and the romantic comedy of Sh by tracing both to their ultimate sources in the dicta of the Latin grammarians of the fourth century A.D.: Euanthius, Diomedes, and Donatus. Jonsonian satire is directly traceable to late Latin theory, while Shn romance is transmuted by the Medieval emphasis on narrative and the happy ending. Plot serves character in Jonson; character serves plot in Sh. From the Middle Ages Sh also learned the double vision of allegory. This he exemplifies in his comedies (analysis of Merch. and Temp.) in defiance of orthodox Renaissance theory of comedy, which calls almost exclusively for satire as a moral corrective. But the basis of Shn comedy does lie in classical theory, as Coghill's discussion of the grammarians clearly shows.

0723. Cohen, Herman. "The Seven Ages of Man," TLS, January 30, 1930, p. 78. E-S

Cohen finds an "'all English' source" for Jaques's catalogue in the Promptorium Parvulorum (ca. 1440) of Geoffrey of Lynn which Sh might have studied at school. His small Latin could easily unravel the passage in question. Baldwin and others have shown that Palingenius' Zodiacus Vitae is a more likely source.

0724. Connely, Willard. "When Plautus is Greater than Shakspere (Imprints of Menaechmi on Comedy of Errors)," CJ, XIX (1924), 303-305. HB SG

In rebuttal of the many critics who have praised Sh's additions to Plautus in Errors, Connely interprets the accretions as marks of immaturity, which by the time of Twel. (with its single pair of twins) Sh had outgrown. Plautus has ten characters, eight of them well defined; Sh has sixteen, most of them ill defined. "Let us remember that since Shakspere could not read Menander his genius had to feel its way." Connely fails to appreciate the structural excellence of Errors with its romantic picture frame setting off a classical farce.

0725. Conrad, Hermann. "Zu den Quellen von Shaksperes Twelfth Night," ESn, XLVI (1912), 73-85. E-S

Conrad is inclined to reject any suggestion that Sh knew and used for Twel. the Latin university play, Laelia, on the Gl'Ingannati theme. His arguments are reasonable.

0726. Cook, Albert S. "Notes on Shakespeare," MLN, XXI (1906), 147-149.

The first note discusses the pejorative attitude in a wide range of classical literature toward the baying of hunting dogs and contrasts this disapproval to the obvious pleasure Theseus takes in the music of his hounds (Dream IV i 109-130). Other "classical" attributes of hounds are cited. Ovid, Virgil, and Seneca are probable sources for Sh's major canine references.

0727. Cook, Albert S. "Shakespeare's 'Pattens of Bright Gold'," J[E]GP, IV (1902), 481-482.

If Sh erred in speaking (in Merch. V i) of the stars as plates of gold he was in good company, since his term "patens" is an accurate trans. of πέταλα, the word in Plutarch's Moralia used to describe the stars as Anaximenes saw them. Sh might have read Amyot's French or he might have encountered the concept in Eusebius, Stobaeus, Galen, or Achilles Tatius, all imitators of Plutarch.

0728. Coulter, C. C. "The Plautine Tradition in Shakespeare," JEGP, XIX (1920), 66-83. E-S HB SG

A survey of Plautine (and Terentian) influence, especially on the early plays (Errors, Shrew, Wives, T.G.V., Romeo, All's W.). The author does not insist on exclusively direct borrowing; she points to the Italian comic and romance traditions and to German intermediaries between the English drama and the Roman. A learned art.

0729. Crane, Milton. "Twelfth Night and Shakespearian Comedy," SQ, VI (1955), 1-8.

An analysis of the structure of the play to show that "Shakespeare [was] working effectively within the tradition of classical comedy and enlarging it to encompass a rich and harmonious development of fundamentally comic matter."

That tradition traces to the "fourth-century Latin grammarians, such as Donatus." Cf. Coghill (#0722), to whom Crane refers.

0730. Creizenach, W[ilhelm]. "Shakespeare und Ovid," ShJ, XLI (1905), 211. E-S HB SG

Creizenach proposes that T.G.V. II vii 24-32 was inspired by Ovid's remark about the violence of dammed streams (Meta. III 568 ff.). Sh knew his Meta., but perhaps did not need Ovid to tell him this truth about nature, physical and human.

0731. Cuningham, Henry. "Introduction," The Comedy of Errors (1907/1933), ArdenSh, pp. xi-xlv.

Cuningham argues at length that Sh used either the lost Historie of Error or W.W.'s trans. of the Menaechmi, not having sufficient Latin or inclination to read Plautus in the original. The considerable list of verbal parallels between the trans. and Errors is not at all convincing. More appealing is the suggestion that Sh intended to name his twin heroes "Antiphilus" [i.e., ἀντιφιλία "mutual affection"]; he could have found the name in Sidney's Arcadia. Cuningham also provides a detailed comparison between Errors and the Menaechmi and indicates that Sh's adherence to the unities is an incidental carry-over from the source. Among the more interesting suggestions is that the aura of mystification which hovers over the play may be derived from Lyly, who himself learned how to mystify from Plautus.

0732. Cuningham, Henry. "Introduction," A Midsummer-Night's Dream (1905/1930), ArdenSh, pp. ix-lxiii.

Cuningham traces the Athenian setting of Dream and the events concerning the lovers to Plutarch's "Life of Theseus" and to Chaucer's "Knight's Tale." The Mechanicals' burlesque is chiefly Ovidian (in Golding's trans.), though Cuningham believes that "no doubt" Sh knew the ballad on Pyramus and Thisbe by I. Thomson. The name of Titania is regarded as evidence that Sh knew Ovid in the original as well, though Cuningham claims without evidence that Sh "more probably only referred to" than read the Latin.

0733. D., C. "An Essay upon Shakespear's Learning," BM, II (1761), 404-405.

For "learned" plot construction in Wives, see #1891. DLC

0734. Danks, K. B. "The Case of Antonio's Melancholy," NQ, CXCIX (1954), 111. GRS

Antonio's melancholy foreshadows danger, as melancholy was thought to do in the Renaissance. The result is "Sophoclean irony" because the audience sees the danger while Antonio does not.

0735. Dannenfeldt, Karl H. "Egypt and Egyptian Antiquities in the Renaissance," SR, VI (1959), 7-27.

Sh's two references to "mummy" (Wives III v, where Falstaff imagines himself drowned, bloated, "a mountain of mummy" and Oth. III iv where the potent handkerchief was "dy'd in mummy") constitute his participation in an interest in Egyptology which was characteristic of Elizabethans. The primary authorities were classical.

0736. Davenport, A. "Weever, Ovid, and Shakespeare," NQ, CXCIV (1949), 524-525.

For the influence of Ovid on Dream see #2334.

0737. David, Richard. "Introduction," Love's Labour's Lost (1951/1956), ArdenSh, pp. xiii-lii.

The academy of L.L.L. is probably based on La Primaudaye's account of French academies imitative of Plato. Similarly indirect classicism provides Sh with a miles (Armado), pedant (Holofernes), rustic boor (Costard), and gnatho (Nathaniel), all by way of the commedia dell' arte.

0738. Davies, Thomas. "All's well that ends well," Dramatic Miscellanies... (Ln, 2nd ed., 1785), pp. 5-51.

A discussion of Lavatch in I iii leads Davies to trace him to the Roman sannio by way of the Italian Harlequin and Scapin. His authority is Riccoboni's history of the Italian theater; Riccoboni cites Cicero on the sannio. MnU

0739. Desai, Chintamani N. Shakespearean Comedy. Agra UP, 1952, 204 pp.

This book is an attempt to trace the elements of Greek comedy as found in Aristophanes and Menander through Roman comedy and the Italians to Sh. The work suffers from oversimplification, disorganization, and diffuseness. It is not a very useful study.

0740. Dickins, Bruce. "'Pythagoras concerning Wilde-Fowle': (Twelfth Night, IV, ii, 52-58)," MLR, XX (1925), 186.

Sh borrowed Feste's interrogation of Malvolio from Golding's "Epistle" dedicatory to his trans. of the Meta. The doctrine of psychic transmigration appears also in Book XV of the Meta. (which is, of course, why Golding discusses it in the "Epistle"), but the verbal similarities between the "Epistle" and the colloquy of Feste and Malvolio make it apparent where Sh got his comic lines.

0741. Dickins, Bruce. "Two Queries on Twelfth Night," MLR, XXIX (1934), 67. SG

(1) Asserts that "tongues" (I iii 97) refers specifically to Greek and Hebrew and therefore adds to the comedy. (2) Suggests sources in Ovid's Meta. and astrology for II iii 23-25.

0742. Dillingham, William B. "Antonio and Black Bile," NQ, CCII (1957), 419.

Antonio's sadness in Merch. I i is the key to his character as faithful friend later in the play. According to Ficino's commentary on Plato's Symposium, the melancholy type is firm in his love for either man or woman. This appears a convincing explanation of a long-standing problem of interpretation.

0743. Doran, Madeleine. "A Midsummer Night's Dream: A Metamorphosis," RIP, XLVI, No. 4 (1960), 113-135.

To establish her thesis that anachronism and verisimilitude complement each other in Renaissance art, Miss Doran analyzes Sh's fusion of classical, Medieval, and Elizabethan materials in Dream, especially in the characters of Theseus and of Titania. With respect to historical accuracy, Sh stands somewhere between Chaucer's nonchalance and DeMille's agonizing efforts, and as a result, he can achieve (e.g., in Theseus) characters who give us "a comfortable sense of being in country we have been in before," and yet who are more than the sum of their sources, classical or otherwise. An intelligent argument clearly expressed.

0744. Dowlin, Cornell M. "Two Shakspere Parallels in Studley's Translation of Seneca's Agamemnon," SAB, XIV (1939), 256. SG

For A.Y.L. see #1901.

0745. Draper, John W. "Court vs. Country in Shakespeare's Plays," JEGP, XXXIII (1934), 222-232.

One of the first comic themes Sh evolved was the contrast between urban and rural life. He did not derive it from Latin comedy, which is purely urban as Errors shows (only the Mostellaria has a hint of the theme); The Acharnians is a treatment of the theme in Greek comedy, but Aristophanes was virtually unknown to Sh and his contemporaries. Horace and Virgil praise the bucolic life under pastoral as well as Epicurean influence, but the most potent influence on Shn practice was his own observation of the severe tension between London and the provinces. Draper appears to share in the common, but fallacious assumption that the pastoral meant little to Sh.

0746. Draper, John W. "Jaques' 'Seven Ages' and Bartholomaeus Anglicus," MLN, LIV (1939), 273-276.

Draper finds previously suggested (see New Variorum A.Y.L., pp. 122-124) sources for Jaques's famous speech "too remote" or "too different" to be plausible. He suggests the 1582 trans. by Stephen Batman of De Proprietatibus Rerum of Bartholomaeus Anglicus de Glanvilla (thirteenth century). In the 1940's and since, it has been shown that Palingenius' Zodiacus Vitae is a more likely source.

0747. Draper, John W. "Shakespeare's Orlando Innamorato," MLQ, II (1941), 179-184.

Draper interprets Orlando as Fortune's minion in A.Y.L. As hero he does little to merit the success that comes to him, but this is to be expected because his is a simple case of the sanguine humor under the influence of Jupiter. Draper's argument would be more convincing if his Renaissance authorities on psychology did not repeatedly contradict one another (as Draper himself points out). It is better to think of Orlando as a literary type in a conventional setting than as a Renaissance version of a pseudo-classical psychological "case." Draper's insistence on humoral psychology as the key to the plays (see, e.g., #1903, #1270, #1267, #1268) is perhaps too limiting an approach to their dramatic impact.

0748. Draper, R. P. "Shakespeare's Pastoral Comedy," EA, XI (1958), 1-17.

"What we have [in A.Y.L.] is proof that at least in England at the end of the Sixteenth Century the pastoral was a vital and sufficiently varied tradition to become in the hands of genius a means of exploring instead of escaping from life." Of the "varied" pastoral elements in the play, Draper traces Silvius and Phebe to Virgil's tenth Eclogue and to Theocritus' eleventh Idyl; the Forest of Arden in part to the classical concept of the Age of Gold; Corin, the "real" shepherd, to the first and ninth Eclogues, where Virgil speaks for the farmers dispossessed by Octavius' grasping veterans, and to the realistic passages of Mantuanus' Eclogues. Cf. W. W. Greg (#0285), who finds no vestigial classicism in the play.

0749. Dunbabin, R. L. "A Rhetorical Figure in Shakespeare," MLN, XLI (1926), 469-470.

Rosalind's explanation of the stages by which Celia and Oliver fell in love (A.Y.L. V ii 35-40) is an example of κλῖμαξ, or gradatio. A famous instance is in one of Demosthenes' orations which Quintilian translated as an epitome of the figure, but Sh need not have read Quintilian, as he might have learned the art of gradatio in school. It does not occur to Dunbabin that Quintilian may well have been Sh's textbook.

0750. E[bsworth], J. W. "'Earthlier Happy': 'Midsummer Night's Dream,' Act I. sc. i. l. 76," 5 NQ, X (1878), 383.

To defend the F_1 reading of Theseus' observations to Hermia on single and married life, Ebsworth cites a parallel in Erasmus' Colloquia (which he does not recognize as a grammar school text) in which a young suitor tries to persuade a maiden that the rose is happier which dies in a man's hand than one that withers on a bush. Since T. W. Baldwin has shown (#0089, I, Ch. XXX) that Sh probably used the Colloquia in school, there can be no doubt that Sh is recalling a "Latin speaking" assignment in this passage, which Baldwin does not mention in his discussion of this very Colloquy.

0751. Eichoff, Theodor. "Interpolationen in The Comedy of Errors," Unser Shakespeare: Beiträge zu einer wissenschaftlichen Shakespeare-Kritik (Halle, 1903), I, 30-88.

Eichoff begins by rejecting the theory that Sh used Plautus directly for Errors, proposing a lost source-play as alternative. The elevated tone of Errors is entirely different from that of the Menaechmi. If "Anklänge" are to evidence Sh's knowledge of Latin, French, Spanish, and Italian, we might as well grant him Sanskrit, too. Then on the ground that they are not consistent with the action (or that they do not advance it), Eichoff excises "Interpolationen": the Courtesan's scenes and several passages in which the Dromios play the fool. The essay also proposes a number of emendations of the text. This is not a convincing approach to the play; the external evidence points to Sh's authorship as Eichoff admits, and the internal difficulties are better accounted for by recognizing Sh's immaturity as a dramatist than by dismembering the play. DFo

0752. Elliott, G. R. "Weirdness in The Comedy of Errors," UTQ, IX (1939), 95-106.

Elliott believes that the comedy in Errors is comedy of relief; the real loss of identity is a frightening prospect which Sh toys with all through the play. The serio-comic tone is produced by the aura of witchcraft, cozenage, conjuring, and mysterious behavior which causes Antipholus of Syracuse and his Dromio to fear Ephesus. Elliott also admires the structure of the play in which serious and happy elements in the picture-frame plot set off the serious, yet comic possibilities of mistaken identity in the central plot. He believes that Sh consciously preserved the unities in Errors, but does not consider the amount of Plautus' contribution important. This is an interesting critical study, but Elliott neglects St. Paul as the source of the weird elements in the play, Terence as a contributor to the admirable structure, and Plautus (as mentioned) for the serio-comic possibilities in the violation of identity.

0753. F. "Horaz und Shakespeare," ShJ, IX (1874), 336.

Though no trans. of Horace's Odes had appeared by the time of Sh's death, Sh had enough Latin to read them in the original and the coincidence of phrase between "The poet's eye, in a fine frenzy rolling" (Dream V i 12) and "amabilis insania" of Odes II, iv shows that he did. Whether he remembered unconsciously or deliberately imitated is a moot question. The author reinforces his argument by indicating that Francis' 1742 trans. of the Odes renders the phrase: "pleasing frenzy," but the question would appear to be still open, especially since the idea is Platonic and had much currency in the sixteenth century.

0754. F., J. C. H. "'The Comedy of Errors':

Antipholus or Antiphilus," 3 *NQ*, V (1864), 230.

Though Sh was not a great linguist he might have had enough Greek to derive "Antipholus" from ἀντίπολις referring to the opposed cities of the two brothers. He definitely did not intend "Antiphilus," which would make friends of the two brothers who were no friends, but strangers.

0755. Fairchild, A. H. R. "'Mummy' in Shakespeare," *PQ*, I (1922), 143-146.

For Sh's reference to Egyptian mummy in *Wives*, see #1916.

0756. Farrand, M. L. "An Additional Source for *A Midsummer-Night's Dream*," *SP*, XXVII (1930), 233-243. E-S SG

The Pyramus-Thisbe burlesque in *Dream* is more likely indebted to Thomas Mouffet's verse treatise on *The Silkwormes and Their Flies* (which recounts the legend) than to Golding's Ovid. The argument rests on verbal parallels. For a more thorough and more convincing analysis of the relationship see A. S. T. Fisher (#0761), and for an effective attack on the thesis see Douglas Bush (#0706).

0757. Fay, Edwin W. "Further Notes on the Mostellaria of Plautus," *AJP*, XXIV (1903), 245-277. HB

In Section A, "The Mostellaria and the Taming of the Shrew," Fay argues that Sh may have borrowed more from Plautus than the names of his comic servants: "the rôles of Tranio and Grumio correspond rather minutely in point of dramatic business in both plays, and so do the rôles of Tranio's young and old masters." In Section B, "Tell-tale Names in the Mostellaria" (248-260), Fay briefly points out similarities (1) between the abusive invective hurled at Grumio by Tranio in the *Mostellaria* and the derogatory epithets Prospero attaches to Caliban in *Temp.* I ii; (2) between this same Plautine invective and Petruchio's violent language to the tailor in *Shrew* IV iii; and (3) between Plautus' use of tag names for comic purposes and Sh's punning foolery with names like "Simple" in *Wives*. The remainder of the art. is textual notes on Plautus.

0758. Feipel, Louis N. "A Perennial Witticism *versus* a Shakespearean Crux," *PL*, XXIII (1912), 341-347.

Dromio of Ephesus' puzzling remark identifying riches and ropes for hanging (*Errors* IV i 21) partakes of a tradition traceable as far back as Lucian's *Dialogues of the Dead* and Ausonius. Feipel cites numerous modern instances as well.

0759. Fergusson, Francis. "*The Comedy of Errors* and *Much Ado About Nothing*," *SewR*, LXII (1954), 24-37.

In contrasting the prearranged clockwork of the comedy in *Errors* with the poetic comedy of *Much*, Fergusson makes brief remarks about Sh's use of Plautus: in *Much* part of the comedy arises from the festive and ceremonial aspects of the play; of these elements there is nothing in Plautus or *Errors*.

0760. Finney, Gretchen L. "Ecstasy and Music in Seventeenth-Century England," *JHI*, VIII (1947), 153-186.

This well-documented study treats the classical bases of the Renaissance belief in the power of music to draw the soul temporarily apart from the body. Among those bases are the magical powers of music in the myths of Orpheus and Arion, the mystical significance of musical numeration in the Pythagorean doctrines, Plato's distrust of the inspirational potency of aulic music, and the Greek emphasis on the ethical value of music. All these Hellenic sources were reinforced by the story of Saul and David and similar biblical accounts. Sh refers to the ecstatic potentiality of music at least four times: in *Dream*, *Twel.*, *Merch.*, and *Cym*.

0761. Fisher, A. S. T. "The Source of Shakespeare's Interlude of Pyramus and Thisbe: A Neglected Poem," *NQ*, CXCIV (1949), 376-379, 400-402.

A scholarly analysis of the relationship between Mouffet's *The Silkwormes and Their Flies* and Sh's burlesque. The verbal parallels Fisher adduces are impressive, if not compelling, and he tries to account for Sh's apparent "interest" in entomology by showing that both Dr. Mouffet and Sh were beneficiaries of William Herbert's patronage. Sh would have had to see the poem in manuscript. An interesting case, which (Fisher admits) cannot be proved or disproved, but it has won credence from some, including Kenneth Muir (#0862). Fisher was anticipated by M. L. Farrand's 1930 art. (#0756), but he makes a better case of it. See Douglas Bush (#0706) for an attack on the thesis that Mouffet is a source.

0762. Fisher, Peter F. "The Argument of

A Midsummer Night's Dream," SQ, VIII (1957), 307-310.

The tetrapartite structure of Dream focuses attention on its argument: the polar opposition of passion (the lovers) and reason (the Athenian court), of instinct (the Mechanicals) and fantasy (the fairies). The dénouement leaves reason supreme, with passion in subordination, entertained by instinct, with fantasy as a commentator. The setting is Saturnalian, but not specifically "Greek" in its folk-religion. All this is less original than Fisher assumes, but he does make two interesting points: (1) the four worlds are represented by four "languages" --prose for instinct, blank verse for reason, couplets for passion, song for fantasy; (2) the theme represented by Puck, that harmony is inherent in strife, is reminiscent of the metaphysics of Heraclitus, who found "the unlike ...joined together" and disparity the mother of concord.

0763. Forsythe, R. S. "A Plautine Source of the Merry Wives of Windsor," MP, XVIII (1920), 401-421. E-S HB SG

Plautus' Casina contains sufficient situational parallels to Wives to convince Forsythe that Sh knew the play, though no English version appeared until long after Sh's time. A detailed argument in which some of the evidence is less than persuasive, though there is no reason why Sh could not have read Casina since "it seems probable that Shakespeare read Latin with fair proficiency."

0764. Fripp, Edgar I. "A Shakespeare Problem," TLS, August 16, 1928, p. 593.

Fripp points out some half-dozen incidental echoes of Marlowe's Dido (printed in 1596) in Dream and suggests that Sh inserted them in his play when he revised it in 1598. Some of them are quite close.

0765. Fritz, A. Menaechmi des Plautus und die Comedie of Errors. Triest, 1874, [no pagination available].

Not seen. NjP

0766. Frye, Northrop. "The Argument of Comedy," EIE, 1948 (Col UP, 1949), pp. 58-73.

"Shakespeare's comedy is not Aristotelian and realistic like Menander's, nor Platonic and dialectic like Aristophanes', nor Thomist and sacramental like Dante's, but a fourth kind" which, like Spenser's, sets up a tension between the "green world of comedy" (the forests of nearly every Shn comedy) and the "red and white world of history" (the normal social structure to which events and characters return at the resolution). Nonetheless, there are elements both of Aristophanes' mythography and of Menander's social formulae in Shn comedy. By some obscure means Sh sensed in Plautus and Terence the underlying "argument" of Greek comedy--the theme of death and resurrection which always fringes on tragedy. (Frye does not mention the Symposium where Plato suggests the close affinity of tragedy and comedy.) This is a stimulating essay.

0767. [Furness, H. H.] "Duration of the Action --Aeschylus," New Variorum Merch., pp. 341-345.

Following suggestions made in private communications from W. W. Goodwin, Furness analyzes the Agamemnon to show that in it Aeschylus deliberately utilizes a double time scheme as Sh does in Merch. [and Oth.]. The three months of Antonio's bond correspond to the voyage of at least a week from Troy to Argos and the casket plot corresponds to the continuous presence of the Chorus on stage enforcing the "fact" that "Troy has fallen this very day." The dusty Herald, preceding Agamemnon, is a link between Aeschylus' two time schemes; Furness does not offer any corresponding link in Merch., though Bassanio's importance in both plots might be one.

0768. [Furness, H. H.] "[Shylock and the Law of the XII Tables]," New Variorum Merch., pp. 416n-417n.

This long footnote to a section on the law behind the trial scene cites a work by James Muirhead in which the ancient Roman Law of the Twelve Tables is interpreted as meaning that an insolvent debtor could be sold into slavery, his creditors dividing up the price. The ambiguous passage has often been interpreted as meaning that an insolvent debtor could be cut into pieces, each of his creditors taking flesh in proportion to the extent of his bond. Thus, if Muirhead is correct, Roman law is not a precedent for Shylock's bond.

0769. Furnivall, F. J. "Scraps," 1 NSST, VII (1877-79), 470-471.

A transcription of two passages from Googe's trans. of Palingenius in juxtaposition with Jaques's "All the world's a stage."

0770. Gabele, Anton. "Das Schicksal in Shakespeares 'Sommernachtstraum'," Die Literatur, XXXVII (1934), 28-30.

As part of his argument that Dream is a play in which Puritan Christianity is set off by Stoic Fatalism, Gabele points out the irony that Helena, an ectype of Helen of Troy, is, despite her beauty, unloved early in the play.

0771. Galloway, David. "'Alcides and His Rage': A Note on The Merchant of Venice," NQ, CCI (1956), 330-331.

This note proposes that "rage" be emended to "rag" (in preference to "wag," "page," "rogue," etc., which have been proposed) in Morocco's remark about Hercules and Fortune (Merch. II i 32-35). That Lichas, Hercules' companion, should be referred to as a "rag," a base servant, is in keeping with Morocco's arrogant character.

0772. Gardner, Helen. "'As You Like It'," More Talking of Shakespeare, ed. John Garrett (N.Y., 1959), pp. 17-32.

"For the learned and literary this is one of Shakespeare's most allusive plays, uniting old traditions and playing with them lightly." Pastoral romance and pastoral love eclogue are combined with moral eclogue in the Theocritean tradition of moral debate between urban and rural life (the former closes the play with its own deity, Hymen). Miss Gardner goes no closer to specifying classical sources, but this is a stimulating essay on the play.

0773. Gaw, Allison. "The Evolution of The Comedy of Errors," PMLA, XLI (1926), 620-666. E-S SG

The author begins with an intelligent comparison between Errors and its two Plautine sources, a comparison which shows that the five additions to the original materials are all contributors to a tight and effective dramatic structure. At this point, however, the author feels it necessary to excuse Sh from having written so well and disintegrates Errors into a whole progression of stages of development; of the five well-chosen additions to the Plautine original Sh can be credited only with the character of Luciana. The fallacy in this reasoning is the assumption that Sh could not have written a well-constructed comedy at the same time that he was writing not-so-well-constructed histories and tragedies. It has since been shown (#0683) that Terence was the model for Sh's early comedies; it can further be demonstrated that chronicles provided him no such convenient pattern, nor in tragedy did Seneca and the Senecans bequeath him a coherent tragic pattern. These disintegrationist speculations are altogether unnecessary and have been generally rejected in recent years.

0774. Generosa, Sister M. "Apuleius and A Midsummer-Night's Dream: Analogue or Source, Which?" SP, XLII (1945), 198-204.

Sister cites situational, not verbal parallels to support her contention that Sh read either Adlington's trans. (1566) or the original Golden Ass. The chief relationship is, naturally, between the problems of Lucius-turned-ass and the ordeal of Bottom, but there is also a possible hint from the Cupid and Psyche legend in The Golden Ass: Puck behaves very much like Cupid, who also is ordered to make a woman fall in love with a vile creature. This similarity, coupled with the striking resemblance between Titania and the woman who loved Lucius the ass, makes it probable that Sh used Apuleius--freely, as Sister points out; Sh modified sharply the promiscuity of The Golden Ass.

0775. Genouy, Hector. L'Élément pastoral dans la poésie narrative et le drame en Angleterre, de 1579 à 1640. Paris, 1928. E-S HB

See pp. 356-359 (on A.Y.L.) and pp. 369-372 (on Act IV of W.T.). Genouy objects to the view of Smith (#0924) and Greg (#0285) that A.Y.L. and W.T. owe nothing (or little) to classical pastoral. He shows that both create the illusion of arcadianism (though both draw on proximate rather than Greek and Roman sources). Two suggestions are of special interest: (1) the sexual "metamorphosis" of Rosalind is very much like that of Eurymene in The Maid's Metamorphosis which in turn comes from Ovid. (2) The genuine rustics of W.T. are worthy of (though probably not indebted to) the realism of Theocritus. Genouy's basic position on the two plays is in harmony with a growing tendency to re-examine the position of Greg (see supra, p. 13n). MnU

0776. George, J. "'Laelia' and 'Twelfth Night'," NQ, CXCIV (1949), 29-30.

A note which proposes the highly improbable hypothesis that in 1600 Sh learned the story of the Latin comedy Laelia from Dr. John Hall, who later married his daughter, and then put it to use in Twel. The only semblance of evidence offered is that Dr. Hall was (presumably) on the campus of Queen's College, Cambridge, when the play was produced there ca. 1594.

0777. Gilbert, Allan H. "Jacques' [sic] 'Seven Ages' and Censorinus," MLN, LV (1940), 103-105.

Gilbert recognizes Draper's argument (#0746) for Bartholomaeus Anglicus as the source of this disputed passage, but points to Censorinus' De Die Natali as another possible source (which Sh probably would have had to read in Latin). His ground is dubious.

0778. Gill, Erma. "A Comparison of the Characters in 'The Comedy of Errors' with Those in the 'Menaechmi'," TSE, V (1925), 79-95. E-S SG

"In The Comedy of Errors the plot overshadows the characters in interest, and yet the play is a better play than its source largely because the characters are more fully developed than those in the older play." The additions and omissions which Sh made were chiefly designed to further this development of character: e.g., Sh exaggerates Plautus' sketchy contrast between the twin masters to make one a foil to the other and thereby heighten interest in each; and again, he adds Luciana, not just as a fifth-act mate for Antipholus of Syracuse, but as a sharp contrast to Adriana. Sh also, of course, alters the morality to suit English taste.

0779. Gill, Erma. "The Plot-Structure of 'The Comedy of Errors' in Relation to its Sources," TSE, X (1930), 13-65. E-S HB SG

An exhaustive seriatim analysis of Sh's play which concludes: (1) Sh had assimilated thoroughly both the Menaechmi and the Amphitruo so that he blended them effectively and perhaps unconsciously; (2) the enveloping action (the Aemilia-Aegeon plot) is traceable to the legend of Apollonius of Tyre, probably from Gower; (3) the Amphitruo (the most serious of Latin comedies) may have taught Sh how to blend the somber tone of his enveloping action with the buffoonery of the central plot; (4) Errors shows signs of indebtedness to an early Renaissance interpolation which filled a lacuna in the Amphitruo. This is a thorough study, which makes a number of interesting incidental suggestions (e.g., Twel. is deeply indebted to Latin comedy).

0780. Gray, Arthur. "The Comedy of Errors," TLS, February 17, 1927, p. 108. SG

Gray speculates on Sh's sources for two elements in the play: names (some perhaps from Golding), and an error in geography (perhaps from Cooper's Thesaurus).

0781. Greenlaw, Edwin. "Shakespeare's Pastorals," SP, XIII (1916), 122-154. E-S

For the influence of the classical pastoral tradition in A.Y.L. see #2218.

0782. Griston, Harris Jay. Shaking the Dust From Shakespeare: An Authentic Renovation of the Merchant of Venice. N.Y., 1924, 342 pp.

Griston, an attorney, argues unpersuasively that the setting of Merch. is not Renaissance Italy, but early fourth-century Aquileia (ancestor of Venice), where the pre-Justinian Law of the Twelve Tables was in force. The Third Table provided that a bonded debtor's body became the property of his creditor upon forfeiture, and that a plurality of creditors could divide up his body among them. This is a special plea which digresses, repeats itself, and twists the evidence in order to label Renaissance allusions (e.g., "Rialto") anachronisms. Sh was, Griston maintains, aware that he was writing a "Roman play"; his knowledge of Roman law may have come from allusions in Lazarus Pyott's Orator. It is quite possible that Sh knew Pyott, but Griston fails totally to persuade that Sh intended the plot, characters, and legal forms to appear in a late-classical setting. Indeed, the large number of analogues to the pound-of-flesh motif which Griston adduces in Ch. XII suffice to refute his argument, since almost all are Medieval or Renaissance in provenance. DFo

0783. Groene, Joh. "Zwei neu entdeckte Quellen zu Shakespeare's Komödie der Irrungen," ShJ, XXIX/XXX (1894), 281-287. E-S

Groene's two new sources are Chaucer's "Knight's Tale" for I i (the alien runs the risk of death to seek a loved one in a hostile land) and the close of the Arcadia where mistaken identity is clarified, saving a condemned person from death. Groene suggests that opposing classical and native sources was Sh's usual habit of composition, but his argument for Chaucer and Sidney is now almost universally rejected; certainly both motifs are fairy tale commonplaces.

0784. Gummere, Richard M. Seneca the Philosopher and His Modern Message. Our Debt, [No. 16] (Boston, 1922), 150 pp.

This brief survey, which emphasizes the prose works at the expense of philosophical values in the tragedies, finds Sh's debt (pp. 111-113) only in Meas. (III i 5-41, 118-132) on death, and in Merch. (IV i 184-205) on mercy (for which latter point Gummere credits Sonnenschein, #0929).

0785. Haight, Elizabeth H. Apuleius and His Influence, Our Debt, [No. 17] (N.Y., 1927), 190 pp. SG

Two sentences (p. 140) suffice Professor Haight to dismiss Sh's debt to The Golden Ass in Dream. She sees no connection except the indirect relationship of Oberon to Cupid through "Huon de Bordeaux" and the fact that Bottom "dimly recalls" Lucius.

0786. Halio, Jay Leon. "Rhetorical Ambiguity as a Stylistic Device in Shakespeare's Problem Comedies," diss (Yale, 1956).*

It is presumed that Halio studies classical rhetoric as it appears in All's W. and Meas.

0787. Halliday, William Reginald. "The Classical and the Medieval Traditions," Greek and Roman Folklore, Our Debt, [No. 44] (N.Y., 1927), pp. 115-144.

For Greek antecedents to Jaques on the world as a stage and on the seven ages of man, see #1941.

0788. Halliwell[-Phillipps], James O. An Introduction to Shakespeare's "Midsummer Night's Dream". Ln, 1841, 104 pp. E-S

There are a number of references to the classical background of the play, especially in Sections 1, 3, and 4. Halliwell-Phillipps believes Sh drew chiefly on the "Knight's Tale," on the "Legend of Thisbe" from LGW, and on Golding, but he offers a number of interesting analogues and possible sources in Elizabethan literature, venturing the implication that Sh's classicism was imaginative but pretty much indirect. An interesting passage discusses Greek concepts of fairies, though the author does not consider that Sh ever gave such concepts a thought, and another discusses the Indian locus of fairyland in Elizabethan folklore. MnU

0789. Halliwell-Phillipps, J[ames] O. Memoranda on the Midsummer Night's Dream, A.D. 1879 and A.D. 1855. Brighton, 1879, 47 pp. E-S

This booklet consists of an Introduction to the play, modified from his earliest thoughts (#0788) and this, in turn, qualified by the opinions he held in 1879. Halliwell-Phillipps believes that Sh read both Chaucer's "Knight's Tale" and Plutarch's "Life of Theseus," though he took little but names from either. There is a full list of versions of the Pyramus-Thisbe story in the sixteenth century. Halliwell-Phillipps briefly suggests that Sh may deliberately have fostered the anachronistic juxtaposition of English fairies and Athenian court life; the remote setting might make the fairies acceptable to an intellectual audience. MnU

0790. Hammerle, Karl. "The Poet's Eye (MND 5. 1. 12): Zur Auffassung Shakespeares vom Wesen des Dichters," IBK, I (1953), 101-107. (Ammann Festgabe, 1. Teil).

Hammerle argues that Sh drew part of Theseus' observations on the poet in Dream V i from a passage in North's trans. of Plutarch's "Life of Brutus." On the morning of the battle at Philippi, Cassius explains Brutus' vision of the evil spirit as a fabrication of imagination. Part of Hammerle's evidence is verbal coincidence, which is notable, though not striking. Less obvious coincidences of diction suggest to Hammerle that the passage in Plutarch may also be the source of two passages in L.L.L.: V ii 769-774 (Berowne's observation on the rôle of imagination in love) and IV ii 67-74 (Holofernes on his creative gifts). But Plutarch offers no hint for the rolling eye which appears both in Berowne's speech and in Theseus'. Hammerle would trace this element to Plato's "Ideenwelt" and would trace to the Phaedrus Sh's concept of "fine frenzy." Sh might have gained his knowledge of Plato (possibly the Theaetetus as well as the Phaedrus) "durch verschiedene Kanäle." WU

0791. Hammerle, Karl. "Shakespeares platonische Wende," Anglo-Americana, pp. 62-71.

In Dream Sh turned toward Platonism as a means of justifying his untrained genius against the University Wits and Spenser. Theseus' lines on the lunatic, lover, and poet are an echo of Socrates' praise of inspired madness in the Phaedrus. Sh's point is that inspired genius is to be preferred to plodding scholarship, represented by the Mechanicals with their insistence on explanatory prologues and explication de texte (in the manner of E.K.'s glosses on the Shepherds' Calendar and Spenser's own Letter to Raleigh). An ingenious interpretation which

Hammerle supports with the facts that Sh makes several glancing allusions to Spenser in other places in the play, and that Dream is concerned with both of the two favored Neoplatonic subjects: love and poetry.

0792. Hammerle, Karl. "Das Titanialager des Sommernachtstraumes als Nachhall des Topos vom Locus Amoenus," ShJ, XC (1954), 279-284.

Sh's description of Titania's bower is "unmistakably" a participant in the rhetorical tradition of the locus amoenus which (though Hammerle does not mention this) apparently goes back as far as Cicero. Sh's immediate sources were Spenser's Garden of Adonis, Bower of Bliss, and Isle of Phaedria, all of which Sh combined. At the same time he was treating it half seriously in Titania's bower, Sh parodied the locus amoenus theme in Bottom's concern that the Mechanicals smell fragrant to set the right mood for the Pyramus-Thisbe interlude. Hammerle covers much of the same ground at greater length in "Das Laubemotiv bei Shakespeare und Spenser," Anglia, LXXI (1953), 310-330.

0793. Harrison, Charles T. "The Ancient Atomists and English Literature of the Seventeenth Century," HSCP, XLV (1934), 1-79. HB

Concerned not with drama but with "more reflective literary forms," Harrison points out nonetheless in passing (pp. 2-3) the Lucretian basis of Duke Vincentio's speech on death (Meas. III i 5-41) with its "many a thousand grains / That issue out of dust." Harrison admits that scholars do not ordinarily credit Sh with a knowledge of Lucretius, but finds it "difficult not to suspect an indebtedness."

0794. Harrison, G. B. Shakespeare at Work, 1592-1603. Ln, 1933, 325 pp.

Harrison's interest in the day-to-day life of the Elizabethans causes him to stress the relationship between the plays and topicalities. But at several points he makes stimulating suggestions about Sh's literary sources; the two most interesting are: (1) Sh found Plutarch's portrait of Caesar somewhat "cold," and he therefore fell back on the Herodian tyrant of the Mystery plays to characterize his title figure; (2) Sh names Jaques for Ajax, the prototype of melancholy to the Elizabethans; perhaps Harington's Metamorphosis of Ajax, which caused a scandal three years before A.Y.L., suggested the connection to Sh.

0795. Harrison, Thomas P., Jr. "Flower Lore in Spenser and Shakespeare: Two Notes," MLQ, VII (1946), 175-178.

The second note, "Shakespeare's 'Cupid's Flower' and 'Dian's Bud'," (Dream IV i 78) suggests that Henry Lyte's Newe Herball may have taught Sh that Cupid's flower is the rose, which received its red color from Venus' blood, shed by its thorns as she hastened to her Adonis; or again, Lyte adds, perhaps Cupid spilled the gods' nectar on some roses, turning them red. Dian's bud is less easy to trace, but Lyte calls mugwort "Parthenis, that is to say Virginal," associating it with Diana.

0796. Hart, H. C. "Introduction," Love's Labour's Lost (1906/1930), ArdenSh, pp. vii-lv.

Hart looks at the bits of Latin sprinkled through L.L.L. as evidence that the play is early work. He notes that Lyly's pages and (especially) Sir Philip Sidney's Rombus (The May Lady, 1578) indulge in this pedantic inkhornism. Hart also offers evidence of Sh's use of Golding's Ovid in the play.

0797. Hazlitt, William. Characters of Shakespear's Plays (1817), Liber Amoris and Dramatic Criticisms, ed. Charles Morgan (Ln, 1947), pp. 159-426.

For Hazlitt's opinion of Sh's classicism in Errors, see #1385.

0798. Heath-Stubbs, John. "The Mythology of Falstaff," Occult Observer, I (1949), 21-30.

For Falstaff as Actaeon in Wives, see #1024. DLC

0799. Henneberger, Olive Pauline. Proximate Sources for the Italianate Elements in Shakespeare. Urbana, Illinois, 1937, 14 pp. SG (an abstract of a University of Illinois diss.)

The thesis rejects the contention of O. J. Campbell and K. M. Lea that Shn comedy owes much to Italian drama. The plays treated are L.L.L., Errors, T.G.V., Wives, Shrew, Dream, and Temp., of which only T.G.V. and Errors are discussed in any detail here. The assertion is that T.G.V. is modeled in part on Errors (and therefore ultimately on the Menaechmi and the Amphitruo). Speed, e.g., is a clever servus, not an Italian buffoon. A good part of the argument rests on Baldwin's evidence for Sh's knowledge of Terentian structure and of other aspects of classical literature in #0089 and #0683 (both at that time unpublished). The inspiration of Shn comedy (including Temp., though here Dr. Henneberger is less positive) is not Italian (though the Italian tradition indirectly affected Sh); it lies closer to home in the grammar school curriculum and native literature. DLC

0800. Hense, Carl Conrad. "Shakespeare und die Philosophie (Pythagoras)," Shakespeare: Untersuchungen und Studien (Halle, 1884), pp. 619-641.

Hense begins with evidence that Sh was not a systematic philosopher in the classical sense: the rejection of philosophy by unhappy sufferers like Brabantio, Romeo, Bertram, and Leonato; the deprecatory remarks of Hamlet, Lafew, and Tranio; and the parody of philosophical jargon and methods by Sh's fools (e.g., Feste on metempsychosis). But Sh was attracted by classical Stoicism, and even more by some of the doctrines of Pythagoreanism; Pythagorean ethics (spiritual harmony) has much in common with Stoicism. Sh accepted both Pythagorean cosmology (music of the spheres) and Pythagorean ethics. The last half of the essay documents these assertions from Merch. Hense's analysis of the play finds more Pythagorean doctrine than other critics have found--the analysis is convincing on the whole. Portia and Shylock stand at opposite ends of a harmony/disharmony spectrum. Shylock is a wolf (like appetite, the "universal wolf," the opposite of order in Troi.). Even Gratiano's clowning, the characters of Morocco and Arragon, and Antonio's friendship for Bassanio can be interpreted in Pythagorean terms. Hense implies that Sh's access to Pythagoras may have been in part through Quintilian and Cicero's Tusculans, but he oddly does not mention Boethius or Ovid's Meta. XV, both of which Sh knew. As illuminating criticism of Merch. this little-known essay merits reprinting. DFo

0801. Herpich, Chas. A. "'The Penalty of Adam,' 'As You Like It,' II. i. :—" 10 NQ, II (1904), 524.

The note proposes that Golding's Golden Age "moralisé" in the "Epistle" dedicatory to Meta. may have suggested the concept and the phrase to Sh.

0802. Herpich, Chas. A. "The Source of the 'Seven Ages'," 9 NQ, IX (1902), 46-47.

Herpich would add Lodge's A Margarite of America (1596) to the New Variorum sources and analogues of Jaques's speech. Herpich quotes seven stanzas from Lodge who gives his source as Plutarch. E. Yardley points out (ibid., p. 197) that Lodge may have been echoing Sidney's Arcadia in his description of the wailing child of the first Age. Yardley also suggests that Jaques's whole speech is reminiscent of a passage in Horace's Ars Poetica. Later (p. 298) Yardley suggests that Sh was echoing Holland's Pliny in the wailing child of Lear who regrets his entry onto "this great stage of fools," and finally at the same place John McCarthy offers Tertullian's De Anima as yet another analogue to Jaques's speech.

0803. Herrick, Marvin T. Comic Theory in the Sixteenth Century. ISLL, No. 34 (1950), 248 pp.

Herrick's interest is in theory, not in practice, and he establishes the positions of French and Italian as well as English critics; Sh, therefore, like other dramatists, assumes a minor place in this study of the rhetorical theory of Terence's commentators as it affected the Renaissance conception of comedy. When Sh is referred to, however, it is always to suggest that his practice is a reflection of theory. Such features as tag names, double love plots (as in Much), rhetorical questions (Falstaff's "catechism"), exchanges of insults (Hal and Falstaff), etc., are all derived ultimately from Terence or from his annotators. One striking oddity: Herrick does not mention the research in the Renaissance Terence by his colleagues Baldwin (#0683) and Robbins (#0486).

0804. Herrick, Marvin T. Tragicomedy: Its Origin and Development in Italy, France, and England, ISLL, No. 39 (1955), 331 pp.

For a study of All's W. and Meas. and (to a lesser extent) Merch. as tragicomedies on an ultimately classical plan, see #2227.

0805. Herrmann, Max. "Honorificabilitudinitatibus," Euphorion, I (1894), 283-293.

A close-packed study which traces Sh's comic term (L.L.L. V i 44) as far back as the thirteenth century. It is impossible to designate Sh's source precisely among so many possibilities, but a very interesting analogue to parts of L.L.L. (especially the character of

Costard) exists in the sixteenth-century Narrenschulen, vernacular German plays ridiculing grammar school instructional methods. Herrmann discusses two of them, one of which uses the term "honorificabilitudinitatibus" in an amusing parody of school exercises in Latin syllabification. MnU

0806. Hibernicus. "Actaeon: Myth and Moralizing," NQ, CLXXV (1938), 74-76.

Among numerous English instances of Actaeon moralisé stands Twel. I i 21-23, where Orsino's desires are the hounds that harry him and Olivia is the goddess Diana.

0807. Hoepfner, Theodore C. "M. O. A. I.— 'Twelfth Night'," NQ, CCIII (1958), 193.

The note suggests the Latin sentence, "Malevolus omnino amore [sui] infelix facitur," as the meaning behind the mask of the initials in the letter that tricks Malvolio in II v. It is difficult to agree that "even most of the pit" would find this construction "obvious in context," even if they knew their Latin.

0808. Hollander, John. "Musica Mundana and Twelfth Night," Sound and Poetry, ed. Northrop Frye (Col UP, 1957), pp. 55-82.

This interesting essay sketches the Renaissance concepts of music, which derive proximately from Boethius' De Musica and ultimately from Cicero and Plato. Boethius spoke of "musica mundana" (music of the spheres), "musica humana" (self-consistent harmony of the human soul), and "musica instrumentalis" (audible, practical music). It is to the third division that Sh most often refers, but Hollander indicates reference to the first in R.II V v and Merch. V i, and to the second in Caesar IV iii. "The general concern of Twelfth Night ... is musica humana, the Boethian application of abstract order and proportion to human behavior." Sh skillfully plays with the relationship between musica instrumentalis and musica humana in Twel.'s atmosphere of revelry, for the time being unconcerned with the higher value of musica mundana, to which he returned in his last plays.

0809. Howell, Wilbur Samuel. Logic and Rhetoric in England, 1500-1700. PUP, 1956, 411 pp.

In passing (p. 337): the rhetoric of the trial scene in Merch. may have been based in part on speeches in Lazarus Pyott's The Orator (1596). Pyott presents both sides of a case in which a Jew claims the pound of flesh which a Christian has posted as security for a debt. The rhetoric here is classical; Pyott announces his debt to Livy and "other ancient Writers" on the title page. The place of Merch. in the chronology of the canon would, of course, be affected if Pyott were to be accepted as a source.

0810. Hudson, Hoyt H. The Epigram in the English Renaissance. PUP, 1947, 178 pp.

This book, left unfinished at Hudson's death, contains three brief references to Sh's possible use of the classical epigram; in each case there is a Renaissance intermediary, twice Sir Thomas More, once Buchanan. Sh's possible debts are in Jaques's "seven ages" speech, Falstaff's "catechism" of honor, and the song "Tell me where is fancy bred" (Merch. III ii).

0811. Hulme, Hilda M. "On the Meaning of Copy (Comedy of Errors, V.i.62)," Neoph, XLII (1958), 73-74.

When she says "[scolding] was the copy of our conference," Adriana means "it was the plenty ..." from the original Latin signification of "copia."

0812. Hulme, Hilda. "Wit, Rage, Mean: Three Notes on The Merchant of Venice," Neoph, XLI (1957), 46-50.

The second of the three notes defends the F_1 reading "So is Alcides beaten by his rage" (II i 35). Theobald's emendation to "page" was motivated by his assumption that x = Lichas, an eighteenth-century assumption, since Sh was less interested in antithesis and parallel structure than the Augustans were. The word "rage" here means "foolish, rash, indiscreet behavior," and the passage means that even Hercules can be overcome if he gives himself up to chance as Morocco is proposing to do in this scene. A convincing argument.

0813. Hunter, G. K. "Introduction," All's Well That Ends Well (1959), ArdenSh, pp. xi-lix.

Hunter observes in a note (p. xxviii) that All's W. is reminiscent of Terence's Hecyra, where a woman is identified as a man's wife by a ring he had taken from her earlier after sleeping with her. But he points out that the motif had a broad Renaissance provenance and doubts the direct influence of Terence. He regards Parolles as more a foppish gnatho than a miles (pp. xlvii-xlviii).

0814. Hutton, James. "Honorificabilitudinitatibus," MLN, XLIV (1931), 392-395.

Hutton points out this Shn hapax legomenon (L.L.L. V i 44) in Erasmus' Adagia in an epigram which ridicules a certain Hermes for his pretentious diction. Erasmus' source is unknown; Hutton indicates a later analogue in a Scotch work and another in its source, a 1529 French trans. of Cebes' Tabula and Lucian's Dialogues. There are, of course, many other instances of this term, which G. B. Harrison has called "a scholars' joke."

0815. Hutton, James. "Some English Poems in Praise of Music," EM, II (1951), 1-63.

A study of a number of sixteenth- and seventeenth-century poets, including Sh (see especially pp. 1-38), Davies, Milton, Dryden. To establish that Sh did not himself synthesize the various elements of Lorenzo's disquisition on music (Merch. V i 54-88), Hutton makes an exhaustive and most learned survey of the encomium musicae as an epideictic convention traceable to the Hellenistic age. Some of the elements in the encomium are, as scholars have pointed out, Pythagorean and Platonic, but the important point is that the association of concepts in Sh's thirty-five-line passage is entirely conventional, the result of an evolutionary process that long antedates Quintilian and ends with Ficino, who added the concept that the spheres and angels sing in concert (Sh, lines 60-62). Thus it is useless to attempt tracing individual elements to specified classical sources. The immense number of classical, Medieval, and Renaissance names in the rhetorical current should discourage any such attempt. Hutton is a classics scholar who knows and appreciates Renaissance literature. This essay is a valuable contribution to knowledge which deserves wider circulation than it has had.

0816. Isaac, H. "Shakespeares Comedy of Errors und die Menächmen des Plautus," Archiv, LXX (1883), 1-28. E-S HB

The Menaechmi is represented by W.W.'s trans. in this comparative study, because Isaac believes Sh's possible knowledge of the original to be irrelevant in the presence of an English version which had been circulating among W.W.'s friends for some time in 1595. The first half of the essay employs the parallel passage method extensively—but inconclusively, since (1) no comparisons or contrasts with Plautus' Latin are made; (2) many of the verbal coincidences are scarcely evidential (e.g., "Let go ye varlet" / "Masters let him go"); (3) several of the parallels are situational and therefore apply to Plautus as much as to W.W. The second half of the treatise is more pleasing as it places the major characters of the two plays in juxtaposition and concludes that Sh's additions to the Plautine cast give his play an advantage in revelation of plot and of character.

0817. Jackson, James L. "The Use of the Five-Act Formula in Richard II and Twelfth Night," ShN, II (1952), 26.

For Terentian structure in Twel., see #1030.

0818. Jhering, Rudolf von. Der Kampf um's Recht (1872), 4th ed. (Wien, 1874), 96 pp.

On p. 59 in a long footnote Jhering observes of the injustice which Shylock suffers from in the trial scene: "Man möchte fast glauben, dass die Geschichte von Shylok [sic] schon im ältesten Rom gespielt habe"; this because the authors of the Law of the Twelve Tables felt it necessary to specify that the creditor who operated on the body of his debtor should do so with a free hand, regardless of the size of the pieces of flesh he removed. Several more recent critics have used Jhering's statement as authority in their arguments for a Roman legal basis for Merch. DLC

0819. Kalepky, Theodor. "'Die Freude am Tragischen'--Shakespeare--Aristoteles," GRM, XVI (1928), 168-171.

For Sh's "Aristotelian" concept of imitatio in Dream, see #1983.

0820. Keller, Wolfgang. "Die Entstehung des Sommernachtstraums," Anglia, LIX (1935), 376-384. E-S

The world of Dream is a Lylyan-Chaucerian world; "die klassische Antike wird von Shakespeare durch die heimische Welt mittelalterlichen Volksglaubens ersetzt." Keller denies the influence of Apuleius on Bottom's "translation," preferring Lyly's Midas as source. He traces Titania's name to the Latin Meta.

0821. King, Virginia Wetmore. "Shakespeare's

Use of His Sources in The Comedy of Errors," ShN, II (1952), 20.

According to this précis of a paper given at the Ninth Annual Renaissance Meeting at Duke University (1951), the author argued that Sh recalled the Menaechmi, Amphitruo, and Apollonius from "some time considerably removed from the composition of [Errors]," i.e., Sh did not read the three works while he was composing.

0822. Kishimoto, G. S. "On the End of 'Love's Labour's Lost'," SEL(T), XVIII (1938), 506-512.

An ingenious explanation of the meaning of the extraordinary lines that end L.L.L. "The songs of Apollo" are, of course, the ditties on spring and winter just previously sung; "the words of Mercury" are the eloquence of an epilogue, which, Kishimoto suggests, was regarded by the Elizabethans as rhetorical exornation superadded to a play. Since Mercury was the god of eloquentia, the connection with epilogue is complete. The lines mean that after such music as the audience has just heard, an epilogue would be superfluous, even harsh, so the audience are to depart through one door, while the actors leave by another.

0823. Koeppel, E. "Bottoms 'Ercles' und Studleys Übersetzung von Senecas Hercules Oetaeus," ShJ, XLVII (1911), 190-191. SG

Bottom's "Ercles Vein" (Dream I ii 27-43) is not a generalized ridicule of bombast, but a specific mockery of Studley, whose (1581) trans. of the Hercules Oetaeus sometimes reads "Hercles" for "Hercules." Sh exaggerates the error by dropping Bottom's "H". The link with the Senecan trans. is made more clear by the parody of excessive alliteration in Quince's "Prologue" (V i 147-148) and (Koeppel might have added) elsewhere in the play. Excessive alliteration is a common feature of the Seneca-translators' "art"--as many as six initial rhymes in a single line.

0824. Korner, Sinclair. "Solar Myths in 'A Midsummer-Night's Dream'," PL, III (1891), 17-20.

Dream is "a beautiful mosaic of old-world myth and modern folklore. The solar element is as pronounced as in the poems of Homer." Hippolyta, Theseus, Oberon, and Titania were all associated, directly or not, with sun worship in primitive religion, Greek and Teutonic. Korner's statements are bare of qualification or documentary support, and his conclusions should therefore be more tentative than they are. See, e.g., the skeletal discussion of Oberon's mythological ancestry.

0825. Krapp, George P. "Parolles," ColSS, pp. 289-300. E-S

Though Parolles is a braggart, a soldier, and a coward, "to the Elizabethan audience witnessing a performance of 'All's Well,' it seems probable that the comparison which the character of Parolles suggested was not with any Miles Gloriosus or with Falstaff, but with those villainist and modernist time servers who walked the streets of London in gaudy splendor." Krapp is perhaps overstating a distinction between classical conventions and topical realities; as Boughner (#0695) has pointed out, the modern ectype is what makes the classical prototype delightful to an audience.

0826. Krieger, Murray. "'Measure for Measure' and Elizabethan Comedy," PMLA, LXVI (1951), 775-784.

Krieger explains the apparent inconsistencies of morality in the play as stemming from Sh's attempt to merge two comic forms: (1) the classical (satiric) and (2) the romantic (pastoral). The argument is ingenious, but if in 1604, as Krieger says, Sh was moving away from his purely romantic comedies toward a classic form under Jonsonian influence, how are we to account for Errors and Shrew, early and predominantly classical plays?

0827. Kuhl, E. P. "Hercules in Spenser and Shakespeare," TLS, December 31, 1954, p. 860.

Kuhl explores the connotations of Hercules to the late Elizabethans and seeks to prove that to Spenser and Sh alike he was a symbol for Essex. Kuhl suggests that we miss some of Sh's meanings if we ignore topical ambiguity such as the Hercules references in Merch. (II i 35, III ii 60, III ii 85), and Ham. (II ii 378). Kuhl's argument for the identification of Hercules with Essex is more convincing for Spenser than for Sh.

0828. L., G. G. "Chapman and Holofernes," NQ, CLXXII (1937), 7.

L. argues that Holofernes' insistence (L.L.L. V i) that silent consonants in Latinate English words be pronounced (e.g., "debt") is a caricature of Chapman, whose rhymes in his trans. from the classics show that he did pronounce the gh in "thought" and the b in "debt."

0829. Landau, L. "Some Parallels to Shakespeare's 'Seven Ages'," JEGP, XIX (1920), 382-396. E-S

Landau cites a number of divisions of man's life into stages; Hesiod, Pythagoras, Plato, and Staseas are the only classical authors. There is no question of any direct connection to Sh who surpassed all his predecessors in "poetic conception."

0830. Landmann, F. "Shakspere and Euphuism: Euphues an Adaptation from Guevara" (1882), NSST, [IX] (1880-85), Part II ([1884]), 241-276. E-S

Landmann believes that in L.L.L. Sh does not parody euphuism but four other styles: Spanish estilo culto, Petrarchism, Latinate pedantry ("soraismus") which was very popular at court, and excessive alliteration (which the author distinguishes from the artificial consonance of Euphues). It is only in 1H.IV II iv that Sh travesties the true features of euphuism--interlocking alliteration, balance, antithesis, and pseudo-scientific allusions from the classics. Landmann points out that Nashe believed euphuism to be derived in part from "Plutarch, Ovid, and the choicest Latin authors," and he also shows that the raids on classical pseudo-science are appropriate enough in Guevara, who was writing on Marcus Aurelius, but are sadly out of place in the English prose which imitated Guevara's style without taking over his subject matter. Landmann's inclination is to blame euphuism and the stylistic exaggerations Sh ridicules in L.L.L. on English feminism, on misplaced enthusiasm for classical literature, and on the desire to elevate the vernacular.

0831. Lang, Andrew. "The Comedies of Shakespeare. X—Love's Labor's Lost," Harper's, LXXXVI (1893), 900-913.

Lang makes two remarks about the classics, both of them misinformed: (1) he thinks Moth's remark about the scraps from the feast of languages is "curiously" close to Aeschylus' disclaimer, "scraps from the great feast of Homer"; the orts of a banquet have been used metaphorically often between Aeschylus and Sh. (2) Lang confuses Mantuanus with Tennyson's "Mantovano," assuming that Holofernes' "Fauste precor" is a quotation from Virgil.

0832. Langbaine, Gerard. An Account Of The English Dramatick Poets (1691). T-D, pp. 30-31.

One passage, not noticed in Munro, gives Meas. as an example of a play turning on mistaken identity; Langbaine traces Meas. and all similar plays to Plautus.

0833. Langbaine, Gerard. "Preface to Momus Triumphans" (1688), Munro, II, 332.

Sh and Jonson are placed together as intelligent, selective borrowers from the ancients (Sh in Errors); like Virgil, Ovid, and Terence they "manage what they borrow."

0834. Lascelles, Mary. "Shakespeare's Pastoral Comedy," More Talking of Shakespeare, ed. John Garrett (N.Y., 1959), pp. 70-86.

This essay explores various kinds of pastoral influence on Sh; with the Daphnis and Chloe strain of pastoral (it is the only real pastoral among the Greek romances) Sh blended Montemayor's Diana, the Robin Hood legends, oracular prophecy from Greek gods, tales of chivalry, etc. Sh had an eclectic imagination. An interesting approach to each of the various "sources": for example, Miss Lascelles points out that while in Greek myth oracular prophecy symbolized the inescapability of man's destiny, in Sh it becomes associated with "the second chance."

0835. Law, R[obert] A. "Some Books that Shakespeare Read," LCUT, I (1944), 14-18.

In describing the University of Texas' collection of thirteen exemplars of sixteenth-century books which Sh probably read, Law makes the suggestion that Sh was indebted to North's Plutarch (1579) in Dream and Titus, but offers no evidence.

0836. Law, R[obert] A. "The Text of 'Shakespeare's Plutarch'," HLQ, VI (1943), 197-203.

Law suggests that there are few textual variants between the 1579 and 1595 eds. of North, fewer than Brooke implies in his ed. #2413. Sh probably used the 1579 ed. for Dream [late 1594? early 1595?] and then did not bother to obtain a new copy after 1595 because it differed so little from his own. The conclusion may be plausible, but Law's premise that there is little difference between the eds. makes it a conclusion of more interest to bibliophiles than to students of Sh's creative process.

0837. Lawton, Robert O., Jr. "Stock Comic Characters in Shakespeare: A Study of Their Relation to the Plot," diss (Duke, 1953).*

It is presumed that some of the "stock comic characters" discussed in this diss are traceable to Roman comedy.

0838. Le Comte, Edward S. Endymion in England: The Literary History of a Greek Myth. Col UP: King's Crown, 1944, 189 pp.

Le Comte convincingly analyzes the "moonlight" speeches in Merch. V i as unified by the Endymion myth (pp. 63-64); he points to some striking similarities between Titania's promises to Bottom in Dream and Phoebe's promises to Endymion in Drayton's poem of about the same date (p. 93). This latter point could be reinforced by emphasizing that Ovid identifies Diana with "Titania." Sh appears elsewhere in this learned book, but the allusions are chiefly incidental.

0839. Lee, Sidney. "Shakespeare and the Italian Renaissance" (1915), PBA, [VII] (1915-16), 121-143. (Annual British Academy Shakespeare Lecture.)

For Italian culture as an influence on the classicism of Merch. V, see #2356.

0840. Lees, F. N. "'Loue Labours Wonne'," TLS, April 10, 1959, p. 209.

To establish that A.Y.L. was the Love's Labor's Won to which Meres referred in 1598, Lees interprets this title and L.L.L. as referring to Hercules' labors and then indicates the plurality of Hercules allusions in the two plays. Not the least of them is the character of Orlando, whose name, through Greene's Orlando and Harington's Ariosto, came to connote the madness of Hercules. A very interesting argument.

0841. Lees, F. N. "'Shakespeare's Love's Labor's Won'," TLS, March 28, 1958, p. 169.

This letter to the editor contains the germ of Lees's more convincing argument of 1959. In this early version Lees sees the Hercules allusions of L.L.L. and A.Y.L. as one of five reasons for suggesting that the latter is the play Meres referred to as Love's Labor's Won. In L.L.L. the pageant of the Worthies is to have Hercules strangling a snake while in A.Y.L. Orlando performs some of Hercules' feats--wrestling, defeating a lion and a serpent.

0842. Legouis, Émile. "La Psychologie Dans Le Songe D'Une Nuit D'Été," EA, III (1939), 113-117.

This brief posthumous essay argues cogently that the psychological inconsistencies of Dream, especially in the four lovers, are Sh's deliberate device to suggest that "les sentiments sont inexplicables par la logique humaine." In making his characters puppets, Sh reminds us of classical myths in which man is at the mercy of divine whims. As in the Iliad, the gods are themselves subject to passion with the result that the puppet strings are sometimes rudely jerked.

0843. Levy, Milton. "Did Shakespeare Join the Casket and Bond Plots in The Merchant of Venice?" SQ, XI (1960), 388-391.

Three classical allusions in the play, all associated with the casket plot, suggest to Levy that Sh used Il Pecorone as his source for this plot, himself making the fusion with the bond plot. Two of the three are to Hercules and the concept of quest through labor and effort; the third compares Bassanio to Jason and Portia to the fleece. Levy's point is that while these allusions do not appear in Fiorentino's novella the theme is the same (e.g., the power of sleep appears in Fiorentino's plot and in the Jason story). The evidence is not persuasive; nor is the logic: why could not a hypothetical combiner of the two plots have added mythological allusions to Fiorentino, and Sh in turn have borrowed the result from him?

0844. Lievsay, J. Leon. "Shakspere's 'Golden World'," SAB, XIII (1938), 77-81.

A discussion of Renaissance precedent for Sh's use of this phrase (A.Y.L. I i 125) instead of the more common "Golden Age," which had Ovidian authority (Meta. I). There were variants of the phrase in classical times (Hesiod, Virgil, Boethius), but the word "world" is modern. Lievsay mentions two possible derivations of the identification of "age" with "world": (1) wer-eld (OE), "man-age"; (2) saeculum, saecularis (Latin). He prefers the second explanation.

0845. Lloyd, W[illiam] Watkiss. "Shakespeare

Platonizes," Ath, No. 2585 (1877), pp. 605-607.

Merch. V i 58-65 is Pythagorean and Platonic cosmology transmuted by Medieval theology. See Burnet (#0705) for a contrary view.

0846. Lord, John Bigelow. "Certain Dramatic Devices Studied in the Comedies of Shakespeare and in Some of the Works of His Contemporaries and Predecessors," diss (Illinois, 1951). DA, XII (1952), 66-67.

Lord studies eleven dramatic devices (reform, vow, law, reward, bribe, love token, misdelivery, betrayal, substitute, hidden character, disguise) as they descend from Aristophanes through Roman comedy to the English Renaissance. He traces Sh's use of the devices as structural members of comic plots and as functional fillers in comedy from L.L.L. through Temp.

0847. Lord, Louis E. "Aristophanes' Influence on English Writers," Aristophanes: His Plays and His Influence, Our Debt, [No. 4] ([1925]/1963), pp. 155-173.

Sh is accorded one paragraph (p. 164) in which Lord suggests indirect influence of Lysistrata and Ecclesiazusae on Shrew through Beaumont and Fletcher's The Woman's Prize (sic). Aristophanes' (sic; Antiphanes'?) lost Timon "may have furnished through Plutarch and Lucian some of the material for [Tim.]." But it is "fanciful" to infer "any relation between the world's two greatest masters of comedy."

0848. Luce, Morton. "Ovid and Shakespeare," 10 NQ, VII (1907), 301. SG

Luce suggests Ovid's Pontic Epistles, II ix as the source of Portia's "mercy" speech in preference to De Clementia of Seneca as proposed by Sonnenschein (#0556, #0929). N. W. Hill suggests (10 NQ, VIII [1907], 505) the possibility that Seneca derived the sentiments from Ovid and in turn transmitted them to Sh.

0849. Mackenzie, Agnes M. The Women in Shakespeare's Plays. Ln, 1924, 474 pp. E-S

For Portia as a classical "scholar" and for Julia and her maid as "classical" characters, see #1478.

0850. Mackie, W. S. "Shakespeare's English: And How Far It Can Be Investigated With the Help of the 'New English Dictionary'," MLR, XXXI (1936), 1-10.

Drawing on the research of one of his graduate students, Mackie points out that the vocabulary of L.L.L. is inaccurately and incompletely recorded in the NED partly because the date of the play is there given as 1588, but chiefly because the reading for the dictionary was so highly selective. A large part of the word list given in exemplification is of Latin derivation.

0851. Martin, L. C. "Shakespeare, Lucretius and the Commonplaces," RES, XXI (1945), 174-182.

Martin points to "Lucretian" passages in Lear, Meas., and Ham. and suggests that though De Rerum Natura had not been trans. by 1600 and though there were "few signs before 1600 of any real interest in the original Latin," Sh might have encountered the work in manuscript trans. The argument is wisely stated in very tentative terms (see #0886 and #0681). Martin prefaces his suggestions with some cogent remarks on the values and dangers that inhere in approaching Sh through "the commonplaces."

0852. Mauntz, Alfred von. "Honorificabilitudinitatibus," ShJ, XXXIII (1897), 271-274.

Mauntz analyzes the word semantically and syllabically. He points out that it is Medieval Latin (earliest known use eighth century); he suggests that it reached England and Sh through the popular Catholicon of Joannes de Balbi (thirteenth century).

0853. Maxwell, J. C. "Creon and Angelo: A Parallel Study," GR, XVIII (1949), 32-36.

Maxwell observes that though Sh is not indebted to Sophocles, Antigone and Meas. have much in common, and a comparative study can throw light on each. Creon and Angelo are both more tragic figures than they have been thought to be, and the dramatist's conception of each is a key to the meaning of the whole play. A brief, but interesting comment.

0854. Maxwell, J. C. "'Hero and Leander' and 'Love's Labour's Lost'," NQ, CXCVII (1952), 334-335.

Baldwin is in error when he argues

(#0683, p. 644) that Sh (L.L.L. IV iii 340-341) and Marlowe (Hero and Leander II 297-298) were the only Elizabethans confused about Hercules' relationship to the daughters of Hesperus and their garden; the garbled version of the myth was common in the sixteenth century. Maxwell's point is well taken.

0855. McCartney, E. S. "A Possible Indebtedness of Shakespeare to Athenaeus," CJ, XXIV (1928), 213-214. SG

McCartney suggests that Moth's facetious remark about Nathaniel and Holofernes (L.L.L. V i 39-40) is reminiscent of Athenaeus (VII 347E), where Aeschylus is made to speak of his works as "scraps" of Homer. A similar metaphor in Much (II iii 21-23--inaccurately cited by McCartney) need not convict Sh of having dipped into the Greek or even into a commonplace book. It is surely no rare achievement to compare thoughts and/or words to nourishment. Andrew Lang (#0831) made a similar identification in 1893.

0856. McNeal, Thomas H. "The Names Hero and Don John in 'Much Ado'," NQ, CXCVIII (1953), 382.

The note suggests Hero and Leander, which Sh obviously knew, as the source of Sh's heroine's name. If McNeal is right, Sh must have applied the erotic connotations of Marlowe's classical protagonist ironically to his chaste Hero; indeed she is falsely accused of exactly what Marlowe's Hero does.

0857. Merrill, Elizabeth. The Dialogue in English Literature, YSE, No. 42 (1911), 131 pp.

The author gives to Sh only a page (34-35) on which she exemplifies the debt of English drama to the dialogue from L.L.L. V ii, with its brilliant conversation and from Falstaff's "catechism" in 1H.IV V i, in which Sir John takes both sides of the débat. Though the author stresses Medieval antecedents throughout, she consistently looks to Plato as the father of the perfect dialogue in which truth is pursued as character is being revealed. Sh's dialogues are "Platonic" in this sense. There is no mention of the débats in Venus and Lucr.

0858. Miller, Donald C. "Titania and the Changeling," ES, XXII (1940), 66-70.

An argument that Sh's Titania, unlike Ovid's Diana who bears the same name, is not chaste, but wanton and has made a sexual partner of the changeling boy she refuses to part with. Sh achieved comic irony in Dream by inverting the usual conception of Diana and of fairies as patrons of chastity. The thesis hinges on the sixteenth-century meanings of several key adjectives: "brown," "proud," "jealous," "rash," etc. The argument is not entirely persuasive, but if the interpretation is accepted, it will successfully account for the entire action of the Oberon-Titania plot.

0859. Moore, John R. "The Transformation of Bottom," IUS, XIII, No. 72 (1926), pp. 45-50.

Moore believes that episodes in Medieval and early Tudor drama are a closer analogue to Puck's "translation" of Bottom in Dream than Apuleius or any other often-suggested source. The objection to Apuleius is that Lucius transforms himself (Bottom is transformed) and he becomes entirely an ass (Bottom has only the ass's head). Moore objects to several other suggested sources on the ground that they do not contain a love element (Titania and Bottom); he does not mention the fact that Lucius the ass is beloved by a woman in Apuleius' account.

0860. Muir, Kenneth. "Pyramus and Thisbe: A Study in Shakespeare's Method," SQ, V (1954), 141-153.

An argument, on the whole convincing, that Sh parodied a number of discrete sources of the Bottom episodes and especially of the Mechanicals' playlet. Muir convincingly shows the use of Golding, Thomas Mouffet, I. Thomson (in A Handful of Pleasant Delites), and less convincingly Painter, A Gorgeous Gallery, Chaucer (LGW), Dunstan Gale, and others. Muir implies that Sh consciously read around in the subject before writing; is it not equally probable that having read a number of versions over a period of time he subconsciously recalled them and coalesced them in his creative imagination? (See Introduction, p. 13.)

0861. Muir, Kenneth. "Shakespeare and Erasmus," NQ, CCI (1956), 424-425.

Before writing Meas., Sh may have read Erasmus' Funus (for its information on friars). It probably provided him with the names "Barnardine," "Francisca," "Vincentio" (oblique case of "Vincentius"), and with the Order of St. Clare.

0862. Muir, Kenneth. "Shakespeare as a Parodist," NQ, CXCIX (1954), 467-468.

The multiplicity of Sh's sources for his Pyramus-Thisbe burlesque in Dream served at least five artistic purposes for him. The sources: Mouffet's The Silkewormes and Their Flies, Chaucer, Golding, A Gorgeous Gallery of Gallant Inventions, A Handful of Pleasant Delites. Muir advances very much the same thesis in #0860; he was anticipated by Douglas Bush (#0706) in 1931.

0863. Muir, Kenneth. "The Sources of 'Twelfth Night'," NQ, CC (1955), 94.

Among Muir's arguments for Barnabe Rich's Apolonius and Silla as a source for Twel. is the fact that in Rich "a man tries to reform his shrewish wife by treating her as a lunatic, shutting her in a dark house." He does not observe, however, that Sh had used the idea before he applied it to Malvolio in IV ii. Errors, which, like Twel., has a heavy debt to Roman comedy, employs this Plautine device.

0864. Nash, Ralph. "Shylock's Wolvish Spirit," SQ, X (1959), 125-128.

Nash argues that Gratiano's lines (Merch. IV i) about Pythagorean transmigration and the hanged wolf whose spirit Shylock inherited are a reference to the venerable custom of hanging animals as malefactors. He also urges that Antonio's despairing characterization of Shylock as a merciless and rapacious wolf in the same scene is an echo of lines from Aeneid IX as they were quoted in Natalis Comes' Mythologiae. While it is true that pitilessness is a lupine quality (cf. Lucr.), the identification of Shylock with the lupus is much more probably a punning topical reference to Lopez, the Portuguese Jew who was hanged for (alleged) murderous designs on Elizabeth in 1594, as Furness long ago pointed out (in Shna, V [1888], 355-356). Furness and A. H. Smyth (ibid., 513-516) also anticipated Nash's point about punishing animals by hanging.

0865. Nearing, Homer, Jr. "Caesar's Sword (Faerie Queene II.x.49; Love's Labour's Lost V.ii.615)," MLN, LXIII (1948), 403-405.

If Sh meant by the "pommel of Caesar's falchion" the death-dealing sword Julius Caesar was said to have left behind in England, the insult to Holofernes would be the greater, as great antiquity would be implied in the simile. The possibility is reinforced by Spenser's reference to Caesar's sword said "yet to be seene this day"; perhaps both Spenser and Sh are referring to some sword in the Tower of London reputed in their day to be Caesar's.

0866. Nemerov, Howard. "The Marriage of Theseus and Hippolyta," KR, XVIII (1956), 633-641.

In the conversation between Theseus and Hippolyta (Dream V i 1-27) about the lovers' experiences in the wood, Sh states the two possible views of poetry: Theseus, art is entertainment; Hippolyta, art is mystery. "It is perhaps ironic that Theseus' views should seem allied with those of the mysterious and fable-minded Plato, while in Hippolyta's 'great constancy' we hear some echo of the plain-spoken [Aristotle]." It does not seem apparent that Sh has any Plato/Aristotle antinomy in mind here.

0867. Nicholson, Br[insley]. "'Atalanta,' 'As You Like It,' III.ii.137," 6 NQ, IV (1881), 244.

"Atalanta's better part" in Orlando's catalogue of female assets was her physical beauty which Ovid hints was striking. The answer does not seem clearly given by this interpretation--as Nicholson admits, another explanation is her virginity; perhaps Orlando simply means her fleetness of foot.

0868. Nitze, William A. "'A Midsummer Night's Dream,' V,i,4-17," MLR, L (1955), 495-497.

Nitze traces these lines to Plato's Phaedrus I, where Socrates says that love, madness, and poetry have something in common. Nitze does not insist that Sh read Plato, but points out that Ficino's Latin trans. would have been available to him.

0869. Noble, Richmond. Shakespeare's Use of Song with the Text of the Principal Songs. OUP, 1923, 160 pp. E-S SG

See pp. 88-90. The song, "Take, oh take those lips away," which opens Act IV of Meas. has only one stanza in Sh's play, but in John Benson's 1640 ed. of Sh's poems it appears as part of Pass. Pil. with a second stanza (presumably by Fletcher). Both stanzas appear to be based on the lyric "Ad Lydiam" attributed (perhaps erroneously) to Cornelius Gallus, the contemporary of Virgil.

0870. Oeftering, Michael. "Heliodor auf der Bühne: c) England," Heliodor und seine

Bedeutung für die Litteratur, LHF, H. XVIII (1901), pp. 149-155.

Oeftering mentions briefly Sh's direct allusion to the Aethiopica in Twel. (V i 120-122) and his use in T.G.V. of Heliodorus' plot device in which the hero becomes a noble leader of a band of robbers. Hamlet's "he might not beteem the winds of heaven / Visit her face too roughly" recalls a passage in the Aethiopica also. DLC

0871. Olson, Paul A. "A Midsummer Night's Dream and the Meaning of Court Marriage," ELH, XXIV (1957), 95-119.

In a well-documented and plausible study, Olson interprets Dream as an integrated allegory (of order in marriage) on the model of masques, Lyly's comedies, and FQ. The English Renaissance attitudes toward reason and passion, male and female sovereignty, earthly and spiritual love, order and chaos are all mirrored in the characters and action of the three plots: e.g., Theseus, reason, has conquered Hippolyta, passion, before the play opens, setting the ideal standard against which the audience is expected to measure the unreasonable, passionate behavior of the lovers, Titania, and "Pyramus" and "Thisbe." The Renaissance attitudes on which the play is based were a blend of Christianity and classical culture. Olson indicates elements from Plutarch, Macrobius, Plato, Boethius, Ovid, and Apuleius.

0872. Oswald, Eugene. The Legend of Fair Helen as told by Homer, Goethe and Others. Ln, 1905, 211 pp.

For Sh's attitude toward Helen of Troy in A.Y.L., see #1557.

0873. P., S. T. "George Buchanan," 4 NQ, XII (1873), 406.

P. points very briefly to the possible connection between Buchanan's "Quis puer ales? Amor." and "Tell me where is fancy bred" (Merch. III ii 63-72). Hudson (#0810) picks up the suggestion, giving S. T. P. credit for originating it, and pointing out Buchanan's importance as transmitter of classical materials and forms.

0874. Palmer, J. Foster. "'Twelfth Night,' II. iv. 116: 'Green and Yellow Melancholy'," 10 NQ, VI (1906), 325.

The etymology of "melancholy" with its emphasis on "black" does not coincide with the "green and yellow" which Sh attributes to the disorder. Palmer suggests that Sh is describing chlorosis, of which a greenish pallor and melancholia are characteristic.

0875. Parks, George B. "Shakespeare's Map for The Comedy of Errors," JEGP, XXXIX (1940), 93-97.

Parks presents evidence that Sh's knowledge of classical geography in Errors is reasonably accurate and fits closely a probable source in an atlas by Ortelius of Antwerp (1570). Parks believes that only Ortelius could have supplied Sh's knowledge, but T. W. Baldwin (#0683, Ch. XXVIII) constructs a complicated argument to show that Sh could have arrived at his information and misinformation from a complex of more accessible scriptural, classical, and Renaissance materials.

0876. Perott, Joseph de. "Eine portugiesische Parallele zum Heiligen Dreikönigsabend," Anglia, XXXVIII (1914), 255-260. E-S SG

Perott provides a summary of a seventeenth-century Portuguese romance which illustrates the "kontamination" (sic l.c.) between the disguise motif in Twel. and elements in Achilles Tatius' Leucippe and Clitophon. In passing he also notes that the ready pardon in T.G.V. (V iv 77-83) is prefigured by a passage in Achilles Tatius which he prints in Italian trans.

0877. Perott, Joseph de. "Noch eine eventuelle Quelle zum Heiligen Dreikönigsabend," ShJ, XLVI (1910), 118-120. E-S SG

Perott cites some parallels between Twel. and Achilles Tatius' romance Leucippe and Clitophon, suggesting that Sh may have seen it in an Italian trans. But all of the similarities are either superficial or conventions of the romances: e.g., Olivia and Melitte have in common that they are powerful and influential women; Clitophon, like Malvolio, is mystified by false news while he is incarcerated. The attempt to identify Feste with a fool in an Italian comedy is no more convincing.

0878. Perott, Joseph de. "Shakespeare and Diodorus Siculus," CJ, XVIII (1923), 571. SG

Perott suggests the possibility that Dogberry's confused antinomy of Fortune and Nature (Much III iii 14-16) may have been suggested by Diodorus Siculus' aphorism on corrupt

Nature and education (XII 13). The connection seems very unlikely, as the contrast between Nature and Fortune was a commonplace in Sh's day (cf. A.Y.L. I ii 34-57).

0879. Perott, Joseph de. "Die Vorgänge im Heiligtum der Artemis zu Ephesus bei Achilles Tatios und in der Abtei daselbst bei Shakespeare," GRM, III (1911), 247-248. SG

This note points to striking similarities between the conclusion of Errors and the last two books of Leucippe and Clitophon. In both finales: (1) the scene is Ephesus, (2) an impending execution is prevented through discovery of identity, (3) a man who is pursued by a woman, (4) takes refuge in sanctuary where (5) he discovers a long lost relative and (6) all ends happily with a banquet. Perott does not discuss the question of Sh's access to these motifs in Achilles Tatius.

0880. Perry, Henry Ten Eyck. Masters of Dramatic Comedy and Their Social Themes. HUP, 1939, 428 pp. GRS

Sh is "the master of what may be called humane as distinguished from social comedy," and therefore he is not discussed in detail in this treatment of the satiric tradition from Aristophanes to Shaw. An occasional passing reference, however, places Sh near the edge of the main stream (e.g., Prospero's island is briefly compared to Cloud-Cuckoo-Land as an "airy region"). The most challenging suggestion is that Sh may have derived his twin servants in Errors not from the Amphitruo, but from the confusion over the identity of the slave in the last act of the Menaechmi.

0881. Perry, Thomas A. "Proteus, Wry-Transformed Traveller," SQ, V (1954), 33-40.

Perry points out, inter alia, that "Proteus" was a name with ready-made connotations in the 1590's. The classical legend had been adapted to Renaissance customs, and the Italianate traveler, young, fickle, clothes-conscious, was sometimes called "protean." In T.G.V. Sh is not himself inventing the Renaissance application of the classical myth.

0882. Pettet, E. C. "Shakespeare's 'Romantic' Comedies," Shakespeare and the Romance Tradition (Ln, 1949), pp. 67-100.

The prologue to this ch. is an excellent study of the Latin comic elements in Errors, Shrew, and (to a lesser extent) Wives. Bourgeois society, urban life, loveless marriage, knockabout fun, intrigue-for-intrigue's sake, and middle-aged or old characters—these are the chief elements Sh borrowed from the comedies of Plautus and Terence. Among other things Pettet points out that the so-called romantic subplot of Shrew is a good deal less romantic (i.e., more classical) than it is often said to be. Lucentio and Bianca are not lovers so much as schemers, intriguing to outwit the older generation. This is among the best studies of Roman survivals in Shn comedy. Unfortunately it is brief, and Pettet does not go on to a full-fledged study of Plautine and Terentian conventions in the later comedies. There is need for a comprehensive study of the subject.

0883. Pierpoint, Robert. "'All the World's a Stage,' 'As You Like It' II. vii.," 10 NQ, III (1905), 184.

Pierpoint reprints the entire aphorism of Democritus (Ὁ κόσμος σκηνὴ ...) with some of the commentary on it from a seventeenth-century ed.

0884. Poggioli, Renato. "The Oaten Flute," HarLB, XI (1957), 147-184.

Section XIV (180-182) briefly considers the pastoralism of A.Y.L. Three sets of characters represent three "levels" of pastoralism and each is a commentary on the conventions: the noble cast come into the "golden world" as refugees, not as seekers after la vie douce, and they find bad weather, cold, and hunger, but redeem themselves by making a virtue of necessity (a very unclassical pastoralism). Of the conventional shepherds, Corin, Silvius, and Phebe, Corin refuses shelter to Rosalind and Celia and thus violates the conventional virtue of pastoral hospitality. Phebe's conventional inconstancy excites Rosalind's (and Sh's) distaste. Audrey and William are "real" rustics, an earthy contrast to the traditional ideals represented by the other two sets of characters. The art. is "a concise resumé of a work in progress by the same title."

0885. Pooler, Charles Knox. "Introduction," The Merchant of Venice (1905/1935), ArdenSh, pp. vii-lvi.

Pooler calls attention briefly to Sonnenschein's thesis about the debt of Portia's mercy speech to Seneca (see #0556, e.g.). He also recalls Douce's comment (1839 ed., p. 486) on the mediate relationship between the casket plot and Prometheus' ruse which caused Zeus to choose bones in preference to meat. He quotes the Law of the Twelve Tables in Aulus Gellius' version but points out differences between this Roman law and the bond plot.

0886. Pope, Elizabeth Marie. "Shakespeare on Hell," SQ, I (1950), 162-164.

Professor Pope objects to the suggestion of L. C. Martin (#0851) that Sh derived the skepticism of Meas. III i 126-128 from Lucretius. She gives evidence that some Renaissance theologians thought the physical pains of hell as described in Scripture are a metaphor for the real pain, which is not to be understood sub specie temporis. Her evidence and conclusion are of interest, but she obviously has not disposed of the problem of Sh's affinity for Lucretian doctrines, as she implies she has (see #0681).

0887. Post, L. A. "The Genius of Menander," QR, CCL (1928), 353-367.

In passing: Sh's comedies are not Menandrian, but farcical or romantically historical. Sh wrote greater poetry; Menander had greater "intensity of purpose in the characters."

0888. Price, Hereward T. "Shakespeare as a Critic," PQ, XX (1941), 390-399. (Also in Craig Festschrift, pp. 198-207.)

For use of classics as weapons of parody in Shrew, see #1071.

0889. Price, Thomas R. "Love's Labour's Lost," Shna, VII (1890), 67-91.

Price observes inter alia that Holofernes does not move the plot, yet occupies much time in the play; Sh considers his pedantic affectations the antithesis to the courtly affectations of Don Armado. "All that he [Holofernes] says is said in the worst form of that hideous classical pedantry which the scholars of the sixteenth century England had got by inheritance from the scholars of the fourteenth and fifteenth."

0890. Q., D. "Shakespeare's Little Latin," NQ, CXCIII (1948), 150.

The note ridicules E. D. Johnson for arguing in Baconiana (January, 1948) that two Latin phrases, coincidental to Bacon's Promos and to Titus and Twel., make Bacon the author of Sh's two plays.

0891. Q[uiller-Couch, Sir Arthur]. "All's Well That Ends Well: Introduction," All's Well That Ends Well (1929), CSh, [XII], vii-xxxv.

The editor alludes to Helena's pursuit of Bertram as a variation on the Psyche tale. He suggests that Sh's skill with blank verse in parts of All's W. (but only in parts) illustrates Aristotle's dictum that iambics are the "'most conversational'" meter. He notes that Lavatch is inadequate for the rôle which Sh usually assigns to his clowns: a Greek Chorus puncturing hybris. Finally, he notes that All's W. is homocentric, which makes Sh as unclassical as he is unecclesiastical.

0892. Q[uiller-Couch, Sir Arthur]. "As You Like It: Introduction," As You Like It (1926), CSh, [X], vii-xviii.

The remarks on classical antecedents are brief but of considerable interest. Rosalind appeals to Jupiter "as a Ganymede should" (II iv 1). Though there are artificialities in A.Y.L., "the heart of it is as sound as the heart of an Idyll of Theocritus or an Eclogue of Virgil." "The classical nuptials . . . wildly incongruous with . . . English Arden" are not finally jarring: "if the deus Terminus of our woodland be the altar of Hymen, who shall gainsay? Surely no one who has known Catullus."

0893. Q[uiller-Couch, Sir Arthur]. "The Comedy of Errors: Introduction," The Comedy of Errors (1922), CSh, [V], vii-xxiii.

Sh may have read Menaechmi in Latin (perhaps at school), he may have seen W.W.'s trans. in manuscript, or (the editor's preference) he may have revised a lost source-play. Quiller-Couch oddly assumes that research on the sixteenth-century grammar school curriculum is fruitless: "In the result we get little for certain, and that little certainly, for critical purposes, of no great matter." He traces the theme of mistaken identity to Poseidippus among practitioners of New Comedy and provides a detailed summary of the Menaechmi. His conclusion is that Sh's play is inferior to the original: (1) in probability (Sh achieves neither Aristotle's "impossible probability" nor his "possible improbability," but "an impossible improbability"); (2) in unity of tone (Sh mixes farce and romance).

0894. Q[uiller-Couch, Sir Arthur]. "The Merchant of Venice: Introduction," The Merchant of Venice (1926), CSh, [IX], vii-xxxii.

The bond plot meets all the Aristotelian criteria for tragedy: Antonio errs through hamartia, not through a malicious nature, and until Portia asks "Why doth the Jew pause?", the course of this plot is "up towards pure tragedy." Bassanio's quest for Portia is traceable, finally, to the Circe episode in the Odyssey, where a man also arrives from the sea to be tested by a woman with love as a reward for success and severe penalties for failure. Portia is not, of course, a witch, and countless variations on the theme lie between the Odyssey and Merch., but Sh is, nevertheless, working here in the Homeric tradition.

0895. Q[uiller-Couch, Sir Arthur]. "A Midsummer-Night's Dream: Introduction," A Midsummer-Night's Dream (1924), CSh, [VIII], vii-xxi.

Quiller-Couch points out the absence of a source for Dream, or rather the multiplicity of sources, of which the Pyramus/Thisbe story in Meta. IV is one: "we know that Shakespeare knew his Ovid--if not, as many contend, in the original, at any rate in Arthur Golding's translation." Ovid also provided a hint for Bottom's ass's head in the story of Midas (Meta. XI). The editor provides an informal and imaginary account of the process by which Sh evolved the play; he suggests that the mistaken identity of the lovers may have suggested itself because Sh had already used Plautus' mistaken identity of husband and wife in Errors.

0896. Q[uiller-Couch, Sir Arthur]. "Twelfth Night: Introduction," Twelfth Night (1930), CSh, [XIII], vii-xxviii.

As part of his thesis that Twel. is a brilliant pastiche of themes and devices Sh had used before, the editor points out that mistaken identity and eventual reunion are central in Plautus' Menaechmi whence Sh "had dipped a pailful" for Errors. The conclusion of Twel. is an anagnorisis thrilling and "truly Aristotelian." Malvolio's self-deception reminds us of the great tradition of comic characters turned inward, e.g., in Menander's Self-Tormenter and Self-Pitier.

0897. Q[uiller-Couch, Sir Arthur], and D[over] W[ilson]. "Love's Labour's Lost: Introduction," Love's Labour's Lost (1923), CSh, [VII], vii-xxxix.

The editors repeat (p. xxviii) the suggestion of J. S. Reid (#0903) that the phrase "living art" (I i 14) echoes the Greek Stoic τέχνη τοῦ βίου and the Roman ars vivendi. But they doubt that Sh was "scholar enough to know all about this."

0898. Quirk, E. P. "Shakespeare's 'Less Greeke'," PL, II (1890), 526-528.

Quirk explains the puzzling F_1 reading "An-heires" in Wives II i 228 as the Host's Anglicization of Greek "ἀνήρ" or "ἀνέρες." This reading would suit the context and the Host's proclivity toward foreign terms of address. The suggestion has not been accepted, but it seems as reasonable as the proposed alternatives.

0899. R., R. "'Cherubim' in the 'Celestial Hierarchy', Milton and Shakspeare," 7 NQ, II (1886), 517-518.

In response to a suggestion that Dionysius the Areopagite [i.e., pseudo-Dionysius] may have been Sh's source for Merch. V i 62, R. points out that this Platonic concept was available to Sh in Batman upon Bartholomew and Reginald Scot's Discovery of Witchcraft among other places.

0900. Rea, John D. "Jaques in Praise of Folly," MP, XVII (1919), 465-469. E-S

Much of what Jaques says about folly and wisdom is to be found in Erasmus' Praise of Folly, and other characters in A.Y.L. apparently draw on Erasmus also. E.g., Touchstone in V i distinguishes between the fool and the wise man in the same terms that Erasmus says Socrates used on the same subject.

0901. Rea, J[ohn] D. "Jaques on the Microcosm," PQ, IV (1925), 345-347. SG

Rea discusses the concept of the micro-macrocosm (since made familiar by E. M. W. Tillyard's The Elizabethan World Picture) and shows that Jaques's speech on the seven ages of man (A.Y.L. II vii 139-166) can be interpreted as a statement of micro-macrocosm if one recognizes the source as Ficino's trans. of Proclus, where the ages of man are equated analogically with planets (cf. MP, XXVI [1928], 208, where Rea reaffirms his thesis). Jaques leaves out the astrology because he is a skeptic.

0902. Reich, Hermann. "Der Mann mit dem Eselskopf: Ein Mimodrama vom klassischen Altertum verfolgt bis auf Shakespeare," ShJ, XL (1904), 108-128. E-S SG

Reich believes that he can trace an unbroken chain which links Sh's low comedy (and to some extent his romantic comedy) to the ancient Greek and Roman mimes which had a broad provenance in the early centuries of the Roman Empire. The fusion of the risible and the romantic, the theme of adultery, the large rôles of artisans and fools (i.e., stupidi), the frank earthiness, and the blending of verse with song and prose all were handed on to the jongleurs of the Dark Ages who passed the conventions into French Medieval farce whence they came to the Renaissance. One of the most popular miming devices in classical times was putting animal heads on people. Of these heads far the most common was the ass's head which Sh could have heard about in such Medieval works as Higden's Polychronicon, or perhaps even seen in some folk play. Reich points out, however, that Apuleius' Golden Ass is the most probable source of Bottom's "translation" because it includes a woman's passionate love for the donkey and contains roses as an important plot device (Titania mentions roses in Dream and flowers are, of course, a major plot device in the play). But, like Petronius' Satyricon, The Golden Ass is heavily indebted to mimes—so Sh's ultimate source remains the mime.

0903. Reid, J. S. "Shakespeare's 'Living Art'," PQ, I (1922), 226-227.

This phrase (L.L.L. I i 14) Reid would interpret as a reference to the Greek Stoic τέχνη τοῦ βίου which by the time of Cicero and Seneca became identified with philosophy itself. The King is thus saying that the men will live in continual contemplation of ethical philosophy. This interpretation (which has been largely accepted) is reinforced by the reference to "Academe" in the preceding line; Reid does not notice that the term would infallibly recall Plato and ergo connote Greek moral philosophy generally.

0904. Reresby, Tamworth. A Miscellany of Ingenious Thoughts and Reflections, in Verse and Prose; With some Useful Remarks. To which are added, for the Sake of Variety and Entertainment, Characters, Pleasant Narratives, Moral Observations, and Essays. Ln, 1721, 422 pp.

On pp. 340-341 Reresby classes Sh with the writers of "great Characters" (presumably Theophrastan—see Chester N. Greenough, A Bibliography of the Theophrastan Character in English with Several Portrait Characters [HUP, 1947], p. 185, col. b). As evidence he reprints Jaques's "seven ages" speech. DFo

0905. Roberts, John H. "The Nine Worthies," MP, XIX (1922), 297-305. E-S

This is an attack on part of Abel Lefranc's "evidence" that Stanley wrote L.L.L. Roberts shows that the pageant of the Worthies is not a burlesque of Richard Lloyd's Briefe discourse of...the Nine Worthies (1584) (Lloyd was Stanley's tutor), but rather a good-humored travesty of traditional pageantry and of the wealth of Elizabethan Worthies literature. Among other points Roberts discusses Sh's introduction of Pompey and Hercules into the canon of the Worthies, his burlesque of the physical features of Hector, and his use of the traditional conception of Alexander the Great.

0906. Root, R. K. "Shakespeare Misreads Chaucer," MLN, XXXVIII (1923), 346-348.

When Sh implies (Merch. V i) that Troilus "sigh'd his soul" toward Cressida in bright moonlight he mistakes Chaucer, his source. In the corresponding passage Chaucer makes it plain that there is no moon—Creseyde promised to return to her lover when the moon again shone. Sh may have misread the passage or [very likely] he may have remembered it inaccurately.

0907. Rowse, A. L. "Haud Credo: A Shakespearian Pun," TLS, July 18, 1952, p. 469.

Rowse makes the pleasing suggestion that "haud credo" (L.L.L. IV ii) in Elizabethan pronunciation would come out "awd grey doe," which irritates Dull, who keeps insisting the deer was not an old grey doe, but a pricket (i.e., a young buck).

0908. Sackton, Alexander H. "The Paradoxical Encomium in Elizabethan Drama," TSE, XXVIII (1949), 83-104.

Adoxiography, the oratorical art of praising that which is unworthy or dispraising the worthy, is a common device in Renaissance literature from the Encomium Moriae to Sh. It traces as far back as Gorgias in the First Sophistic and had a distinguishable development in classical and Medieval rhetoric. The device was appropriated by the Elizabethan dramatists;

examples from five of them are given and analyzed. At first the adoxiograph was intruded as a set speech without dramatic necessity, but Sh assimilated it into the dramatic texture of the play, sometimes even making it virtual dialogue (e.g., Parolles' argument to Helena in dispraise of virginity in All's W. I i or Feste's preference of enemies to friends, Twel. V i). There are also Shn examples in Tim. and A.Y.L.

0909. Salingar, L. G. "Messaline in 'Twelfth Night'," TLS, June 3, 1955, p. 301.

Salingar explains this puzzling geographical name as deriving from the Menaechmi, which Sh probably used as one source of the play.

0910. Sargent, Ralph M. "Sir Thomas Elyot and the Integrity of The Two Gentlemen of Verona," PMLA, LXV (1950), 1166-80.

Sargent believes that Sh blended with Montemayor's Diana the story of Titus and Gisippus as told by Elyot in The Governour. In Boccaccio's pseudo-classical tale, which was most popular in the sixteenth century in England, the moral appears: happiness in love comes to those who are noble in friendship. This moral (with variations) appears in The Arcadia, Endimion, The Old Wives' Tale, Euphues, and of course, in T.G.V. Elyot gives as his authorities Aristotle and Cicero, but he goes beyond them in placing friendship on the highest pedestal of all. Seen as modeled on Elyot's classical ethics, the final scenes of T.G.V. are not a moral blot on the play but a fitting conclusion to the action. This is a satisfying thesis.

0911. Schanzer, Ernest. "The Moon and the Fairies in A Midsummer Night's Dream," UTQ, XXIV (1955), 234-246.

A discussion of the classical background of the lunar symbolism in the play, including Sh's precedents for identifying Diana with the Fairy Queen. Schanzer makes his points well, but in some cases they have been part of the tradition for many years.

0912. Schlauch, Margaret. "Roman 'Controversiae' and the Court Scene in Shakespeare's 'Merchant of Venice'," KN, VII (1960), 45-56.

An interesting study which shows that the trial scene contains the two basic elements of the rhetorical exercises of Seneca the Elder: controversia (a legal dilemma) and colores (emotional pleas—in this case for mercy). In addition the scene contains many stylistic devices (e.g., anaphora, epizeuxis, apostrophe) which were recommended to orators in Seneca's Controversiae. Even if Sh did not read the elder Seneca at Stratford School, the Controversiae may lie behind Merch.: Lazarus Pyott's The Orator is in the tradition—and it contains a controversia in which a Jew demands a pound of flesh as a penalty for forfeit of a bond. Interestingly enough, Sh refers to Antonio's trial as a "controversy" (IV i 155). Professor Schlauch also points out that Meas. may be based on the same ultimate sources (a hypothetical legal dilemma combined with eloquent colores), and Per. "goes back to the well-known romance of Apollonius of Tyre which owes a fundamental element in its plot to the controversia entitled Sacerdos prostitua (Seneca, I, 2)." DLC

0913. Schrickx, W. Shakespeare's Early Contemporaries: The Background of the Harvey-Nashe Polemic and Love's Labour's Lost. Antwerp, 1956, 291 pp.

Schrickx believes that mythological names became pseudonyms for political and literary personages and concepts in the 1580's and 1590's; he argues at length that Ganymede = intellectual aspiration = Earl of Derby, that Cerberus = Nashe, that Bellerophon = Harvey, that Mercury, prosaic eloquence and learning, is opposed to Apollo, poetic inspiration. On these equations he constructs a hypothesis which ties the Marprelate controversy to the Harvey-Nashe flyting and both to the School of Night, at least in L.L.L. and A.Y.L., where contemporary cults and affairs are ridiculed in mythological garb. He then uses the supposed interconnections to date L.L.L. in 1592 and a first draft of A.Y.L. in 1593. Schrickx' research has been thorough, but he does not convince, because in his mind a slender analogy too often becomes a certain connection. Reading this book one obtains a growing impression that the evidence is prearranged. Part of the problem is that the last major ch., the analysis of L.L.L., is not intimately tied to the evidence which precedes—it is not the most coherent ch. in the book.

0914. "Select Passages from Shakspeare, IV," The Universal Magazine, LXXXVIII (1791), 283-286.

According to this art., the mocking remarks of Rosalind on what men die of (A.Y.L. IV i) show that Sh knew his classics either in the originals or in trans. (Troilus and Leander are referred to in the passage.) MnU

0915. Sen Gupta, S. C. Shakespearian Comedy, OUP, 1950, 287 pp.

Sen Gupta ranges across almost the whole of the canon in his quest of the Shn vis comica but he seldom looks back in any detailed way to classical antecedents in form, stock characters, myths, etc. Aside from brief remarks (e.g., on Parolles as a miles gloriosus, Moth as a witty servus), the only passages of relevance for this Guide are seven pages on Errors and ten on Troi.

0916. Seronsy, Cecil C. "The Seven Ages of Man Again," SQ, IV (1953), 364-365.

The note suggests Lodge's Margarite of America (1596) as the source of this disputed passage. Not a convincing argument, despite Seronsy's insistence on the community of tone in the two passages. Lodge refers to Plutarch. Seronsy is unaware that he has been anticipated (see #0802).

0917. Shaw, John. "Fortune and Nature in As You Like It," SQ, VI (1955), 45-50.

Both plot and characterization in A.Y.L. are a function of the traditional polarity between the goddesses Fortuna and Natura. The tricks of Fortune bring undeserved adversity early in the play to those characters in it whom Nature has blessed most (Orlando, Duke Senior, Rosalind, Celia, et al.). But the gifts of Nature (intellectual and moral) enable them to "flout at Fortune" until she improves their lot as she does in Act V. Meanwhile, the opposed group of characters, less blessed by Nature (Duke Frederick, Oliver, and their friends) ally themselves with Fortuna and attempt by "policy" to obtain Fortuna's gifts. This they do until fickle Fortune deserts them (Acts IV and V) whereupon they quickly shift allegiance to Nature, who gives them her greatest gift, self-knowledge. An interesting approach to the play; Shaw wisely emphasizes that it provides only a structure: the play is hardly a didactic philosophical treatise.

0918. Sheldon, W. L. "The Antigone of Sophocles and Shakespeare's Isabel," PL, IV (1892), 609-612. HB

Though their external circumstances are different, Antigone and Isabella are both loyal to principle, which makes them seem cold. A general, and somewhat impressionistic comment.

0919. Sheppard, J. T. "Music at Belmont," Music at Belmont and Other Essays and Addresses (Ln, 1951), pp. 129-151.

This sensitive analysis of Act V of Merch. traces its delicate balance of philosophy and idyl to Pythagoras and Theocritus. For the music of the spheres, Sh had intermediaries like Plato's tale of Er, the Somnium Scipionis, and Aeneid VI, the latter two of which he knew well. The beautiful recollection of the first Idyl of Theocritus ("how sweet the moonlight sleeps") he would have had to get from the Greek (it was not in the Sixe Idillia of 1588); perhaps he did, but "pastoral was in the air and Shakespeare's magic is his own." In an interesting passage, Sheppard shows that for the "in such a night" dialogue, Sh carefully chose the classical names (Troilus, Cressida, Thisbe, Dido, Medea) in order to characterize Lorenzo and Jessica who use them.

0920. Sidgwick, Arthur H. The Influence of Greek Philosophy on English Poetry: The Chancellor's Essay, 1906. Oxford: Blackwell, 1906, 30 pp.

For Sh's allusions to ancient philosophy in Merch. as "dead" classicism, see #2385. MH

0921. Simonini, R. C., Jr. "Language Lesson Dialogues in Shakespeare," SQ, II (1951), 319-329.

Simonini advances the hypothesis that the language lessons in Sh and much else besides (including the love-making courtesies of his gallants) were drawn from instructional books in French and Italian, perhaps specifically the Firste Fruites and Seconde Fruites of John Florio. This despite the fact that of the three lessons he cites, two are in Latin (Wives and Shrew) and despite the fact that Baldwin (#0089) has plainly shown that those two lessons embody the standard classical method of classroom instruction in the sixteenth century. Simonini appears to indulge in the common desire to make Sh know what we know and at least by implication to deny him that classical education which it is much more plausible to grant him.

0922. Sims, Ruth E. "The Green Old Age of Falstaff," BHM, XIII (1943), 144-157. GRS

For Falstaff's age and humoral complexion in Wives, see #1085.

0923. Sledd, James. "A Note on the Use of Renaissance Dictionaries," MP, XLIX (1951), 10-15.

With impressive erudition Sledd discusses the dictionaries of the Renaissance, pointing out their complex interrelationships (he is able to enumerate twelve distinct sources of Baret's Alvearie), and cautioning scholars not to confuse parallels with sources. Sledd indicates dictionary parallels inter alia to: (1) the Nurse's recognition (in Romeo) of "R" as the dog's letter (traceable ultimately to Persius); (2) Jaques's "seven ages" speech (traceable ultimately to Cicero's De Senectute); (3) Hecate as "triple" in Dream.

0924. Smith, Homer. "Pastoral Influence in the English Drama," PMLA, XII (1897), 355-460. E-S

The section on A.Y.L. (pp. 378-382) does not trace the pastoralism of the play beyond Lodge's Rosalynde. Sh subordinated the pastoral element of Lodge's romance "as much as possible" seeing, perhaps, "how little dramatic power existed in the pastoral theme." He allowed pastoralism to dominate Dream I i and II ii but did not use the elements in any other play (Smith rejects Perdita as shepherdess). Sh's debt to the pseudo-classical Italian conventions would appear to be larger than Smith will admit; T.G.V., Temp., W.T., and Cym. all contain pastoral scenes of some importance.

0925. Snuggs, Henry L. "Observations on the Theory of 'Correlated' Plot-structure and Act-division," ShN, IX (1959), 30.

This paper, delivered at the Southeastern Renaissance Conference in 1959, is largely subsumed into #0926, which appeared in the following year. Snuggs attacks Baldwin (#0683) and his "Andrian formula."

0926. Snuggs, Henry L. Shakespeare and Five Acts: Studies in a Dramatic Convention. N.Y., 1960, 144 pp.

Snuggs assails the contention of Baldwin (#0683) that the practice of Terence as expounded by Donatus and his successors was Sh's mentor for the construction of comedies. He begins by analyzing Greek tragedy, Old Comedy, New Comedy, Plautus, Terence, and Seneca; and he concludes that only Seneca can properly be said to have constructed his plays in five parts--Seneca was probably influenced by Horace's insistence in the Ars Poetica that plays should have five acts. The other dramatists may or may not have intended their plays to fall into structural units, but the number of such units was certainly not regularly five. Then, after showing that there is little textual evidence that Sh wrote with act-structure in mind, Snuggs analyzes the plots of Errors, Much, Twel., and Romeo, arguing that Sh did not design the plays under the influence of Willichius or any other commentator on the ancient dramatists. It is of interest that of Snuggs's examples Much and Twel. are not among Sh's 'prentice plays, and would be less likely than the earliest comedies to show the influence of his grammar school lessons in dramatic structure; at the same time, Snuggs doesn't discuss L.L.L. and T.G.V. (and All's W., possibly also an early play) which are early, and which in Baldwin's analysis clearly reflect the "Terentian" pattern. Snuggs is probably right in his claim that there is little warrant for the traditional assumption that the ancients wrote in five acts. What he ignores is that it matters not at all--what Sh and the Renaissance commentators thought about Terence (and Plautus) is here of the essence. Baldwin's thesis need not be greatly modified by Snuggs's arguments.

0927. Sochatoff, A. Fred. "Much Ado About Nothing," Shakespeare: Lectures on Five Plays, CSE, No. 4 (1958), pp. 3-17.

The ultimate source of Much is Chaereas and Callirhoe, the "tear-soaked" romance by Chariton. (The proximate source is, of course, Bandello.) The Hero-Claudio plot is essentially that of the Greek romance, but Sh redeems it by skillful motivation, by the low comedy of Dogberry, et al., and especially by the realistic wit of Beatrice and Benedick.

0928. Soellner, Rolf [H.] "The Troubled Fountain: Erasmus Formulates a Shakespearian Simile," JEGP, LV (1956), 70-74.

Sh twice compares a troubled mind to a muddied fountain (Shrew V ii 142-145; Troi. III iii 310-315). The ultimate source of the comparison is classical Stoicism, whence Plutarch derived it; Erasmus elaborated the analogy in De Parabolis Sive Similibus, which is probably Sh's proximate source.

0929. Sonnenschein, E. A. "Latin as an Intellectual Force in Civilisation," NR, XLVII (1906), 670-683. SG

In the course of a brilliant analysis of Stoicism as a binding force in Roman culture and as one of the creditors of the modern world, Sonnenschein reiterates his argument (#0555) for Seneca's De Clementia as the immediate source of Portia's "mercy" speech (Merch. IV i 184-205).

0930. Spencer, Terence. "Three Shakespearian Notes," MLR, XLIX (1954), 46-51.

The first note, "The Vile Name of Demetrius," explains Lysander's exclamation (Dream II ii 106-107) as a reference to Demetrius Poliorcetes, who was noted for his lechery and his inconstancy to women. Lysander is referring to Demetrius' perfidy to Helena. Sh's source is the Comparison between Marcus Antonius and Demetrius Poliorcetes in North's Plutarch. A convincing argument. The second note, "Old John Naps of Greece," defends the F_1 text listing Sly's cronies in Shrew. The ground is that Greek mercenary soldiers ("estradiots") were found in England in the sixteenth century—Sh may be referring to a retired veteran who settled near Stratford (the area that produced Sly's other friends). If he had a long name with a "-nopoulos" suffix, the truncation to "Naps" would be natural.

0931. Starnes, D[eWitt] T. "Actaeon's Dogs," Names, III (1955), 19-25.

Starnes traces the nomenclature of Actaeon's mythological hounds through sixteenth-century dictionaries and trans. of Meta. Sh refers to the hound named last in Golding's Ovid ("Ringwood") in Wives. Starnes also suggests that Sh may be referring obscurely to the Actaeon legend in Macb. where Macbeth addresses a catalogue of hounds to the murderers (III i 92-101).

0932. Starnes, DeWitt T. Renaissance Dictionaries: English-Latin and Latin-English. Texas UP, 1954, 427 pp.

In passing (p. 71), Starnes corrects an error in Anders' Shakespeare's Books (#0073). The Latin tag "Redime te captum ..." in Shrew I i derives from Terence by way of Lily's Grammar, as Anders observes, but Anders is wrong to suggest that along another bypath Udall borrowed it from the Bibliotheca Eliotae; the indebtedness is the other way round. Starnes does not choose Sh's immediate source from among Lily, Udall, and Elyot.

0933. Stetner, Samuel Cabot V. "Old Men, Young Men, and Slaves (A Study of Some Stock Types in Shakespeare's Comedies)," diss (Columbia, 1959). DA, XX (1959), 663.

Stetner traces Sh's use of the three stock male comic characters defined in the Onomasticon of Julius Pollux. Epicharmus, Aristophanes, Herodas, Plautus, Terence, Theophrastus, the Tractatus Coislinianus, and the commedia dell' arte are the background for an analysis of Sh's comic men. When Sh departs from the conventional type (as he often does) it is in the interest of good theater.

0934. Stevenson, David L. The Love-Game Comedy. Col UP, 1946, 259 pp.

Ch. II, "Ovid and Sixteenth-Century Amorous Controversy," contrasts Marlowe, Chapman, Marston, and Sh with Ovid. None of them imitated the tone of Ovidian verse closely because their Medieval and Renaissance heritage prevented them from regarding love primarily as a sensual passion. Indeed, Ch. XIII, in conclusion, suggests that Catullus is more suited to the Renaissance temperament than Ovid, since the former originated the tension between conflicting views of love which Sh utilized and resolved in his sex-duel comedies. (Catullus, of course, is not directly responsible for Sh's approach to comedy.)

0935. Stone, W. G. "Shakspeare, Cicero, and Dante," 5 NQ, XI (1879), 286-287.

Stone suggests that Claudio's description of the pains of the after world (Meas. III i 124-126) may be in part a recollection of Dante ("the viewless winds") and of Cicero's Somnium Scipionis in Macrobius' Comentarii (being "blown with restless violence round about / The pendent world.") Stone does not observe how appropriate this Ciceronian punishment for the lustful is to Claudio and to the entire theme of the play.

0936. Stopes, C[harlotte] C. "[Correspondence]," New Shna, VI (1907), 73. SG

Mrs. Stopes proposes a thesis (which she restates in TLS, March 25, 1921) that Portia's "mercy" speech is indebted not to Seneca direct, but to the Senecan sentiments on the subject in English "Meditations and Prayers" by John Conway of Warwickshire. This thesis has not won many adherents.

0937. Stopes, Charlotte C. "'Honorificabilitudinitatibus' in Warwickshire," Ath, No. 4221 (1908), 334-335.

Mrs. Stopes reports that she has discovered in the parish register of a Warwickshire village the words "Honorificabilitudinitatibus, Constantinopolis," obviously written by a scribe to test his handwriting before beginning to copy the register. The hand appears to be that of a William Palmer—it probably antedates L.L.L. Mrs. Stopes regards her discovery as evidence that Sh did not coin the term; it has since been shown that Erasmus and other Renaissance writers used it long before Sh's time.

0938. Stratton, Lowell D. "The Nine Worthies," AshSS (1956), 67-97 + ix-xiii.

This informed study focuses on the Medieval origin and development of the concept of the Worthies, and devotes little attention to L.L.L. But in passing (p. 73) Stratton explains that Boyet's facetious remark about Nathaniel's nose (V ii 568) reflects the common Renaissance belief that Alexander had a crooked nose. CU Riv

0939. Stull, Joseph S. "Shakespeare and Plutarch's 'Life of Pelopidas'," NQ, CXCVIII (1953), 512-513.

For a link with Wives, see #2137.

0940. Sullivan, Edward. "Two Notes on 'Hamlet' I,1. and 'Merchant' V,2. [sic]," ShJ, XLIV (1908), 145-146.

The second note suggests that Lorenzo's lines to Jessica on the music of the spheres may have been inspired by Nashe's Unfortunate Traveller in a passage which describes a "summer banketting house." Sullivan's assurance is unwarranted; the commonplace character of the Pythagorean doctrine in the sixteenth century makes attribution of sources extremely difficult.

0941. Symonds, John A. "The Rise of Tragedy," Shakspere's Predecessors in the English Drama (Ln, 1884), Ch. VI, pp. 211-245. E-S HB

For Symonds' view of the classical influence on Elizabethan comedy, see #2138.

0942. Sypher, Wylie. "Nietzsche and Socrates in Messina," PartR, XVI (1949), 702-713.

Sypher contrasts the rôle of Socratic eiron, rational and gentle, with the rôle of the Nietzschean or Dionysiac eiron, emotional and violent. Benedick and Beatrice have something in common with the Socrates of the Phaedrus and Crito; like Socrates they are constrained to submit to the social order (in their case, marriage), but like him they are still capable of the gentle irony of "a cock for Asclepius." The connection between Much and the Socratic personality may seem more tenuous to the reader than to Sypher.

0943. [Tannenbaum, Samuel A.]. "The Names in As You Like It," SAB, XV (1940), 255-256.

Etymological analysis of the entire dramatis personae to show that the root-meanings and/or connotations are appropriate to the characters. The conclusion is that Sh was more learned and more careful about significant detail than is often thought. Five or six names are traced to Greek or Latin; some are standard ("Celia," e.g.), but it is not probable that Sh or his audience would recognize in "Dennis" the derivation from "Dionysius."

0944. Tannenbaum, Samuel A. "Notes on 'The Comedy of Errors'," ShJ, LXVIII (1932), 103-124. SG

Tannenbaum sides with T. W. Baldwin against Dover Wilson on Sh's single authorship, the date, sources, geography, and topical significances of Errors. Two notes are directly concerned with Sh's classicism: (1) Tannenbaum adds three possible echoes of W.W.'s trans. to the list of fifteen got up by Henry Cuningham in the Arden Errors (#0731); none is obviously more than coincidence of phrase; (2) Tannenbaum defends Sh's Latinity: he believes that "Erotes" (also "Errotis") given as a stage direction is a compositor's error for "Erratus," an appropriate epithet for the wandering Antipholus. The compositor may also have misread Sh's "Surreptus" (from "Subreptus"--"kidnapped"), writing "Sereptus."

0945. Taylor, George Coffin. "Is Shakespeare's Antonio the 'Weeping Philosopher' Heraclitus?" MP, XXVI (1928), 161-167.

The extraordinary contrast in Merch. I i between Antonio's melancholy and the gaiety of his companions recalls the conventional débat between weeping Heraclitus and laughing Democritus which reached its high point in Milton's L'Allegro and Il Penseroso. The closest analogue to Sh's scene is Sylvester's Du Bartas—Taylor adduces verbal parallels between the Divine Weeks and Merch. However, as Taylor admits, Sylvester's English did not appear in print until long after Merch. and even Du Bartas' French was not complete when Sh wrote.

0946. Thorndike, Ashley H. "Shakespeare: The Earlier Comedies," English Comedy (N.Y., 1929), pp. 95-119.

Despite Thorndike's awareness (manifested in an earlier ch.) of the classical antecedents of Renaissance comedy, there are only two allusions to Sh's use of Plautus here and no substantive references to the classics in the following ch., "Shakespeare: The Later Comedies." The first allusion is to Errors as a brilliant adaptation of Plautus to the English stage--for Plautus' prologue Sh substitutes a romantic picture frame in which Aegeon provides the audience with indispensable information about the identical twins and their history. The second allusion is to the fact that Twel. reuses an element (identical twins and the purse) which Sh had borrowed from Plautus for Errors.

0947. Thümmel, Julius. "Der Miles Gloriosus bei Shakespeare," ShJ, XIII (1878), 1-12. E-S HB

For Sh's use of the miles in All's W., L.L.L., and Wives, see #1097.

0948. Tierney, Michael. "The New Menander and the Origins of High Comedy," Studies, XIX (1930), 295-308.

This interesting critical study ends with the suggestion that Greek drama had an "oblique influence" on the Elizabethans. Menander coarsened by Plautus is the source of Errors; "Pinch the conjuror is an Elizabethan version of a Greek comic physician."

0949. Tilley, M. P. "Notes on Twelfth Night," Archiv, CXXXIV (1916), 133-138.

The first of three notes points out that Malvolio's reference to Feste's "infirmity" in I v ought to be taken as a reference to lust or inordinate love. The echo is of a proverb about the incompatibility of love and reason which goes back to classical times (Publilius Syrus, Plutarch). Sh need not have learned from the classics as the proverb was a moral commonplace in his day.

0950. Tillyard, E. M. W. The Nature of Comedy and Shakespeare, English Association Presidential Address (OUP, 1958), 15 pp.

Tillyard places his emphasis on the concern of comedy with the relationship between the individual and his society. Though this concern has a classical basis, Tillyard does not trace the Greek and Roman roots of the genre. Only when touching on tone does he remember Latin comedy: Plautus' Rudens is proof that the Romans were as capable of stage reconciliations and of gentle humor as Sh, and Coghill (#0722) is wrong to establish too straight a boundary line between Roman and Medieval backgrounds of Shn practice.

0951. Watt, H. A. "Plautus and Shakespeare--Further Comments on Menaechmi and The Comedy of Errors," CJ, XX (1925), 401-407. HB SG

Watt criticizes Connely (#0724) for assuming that Errors is an inaccurate imitation of the Menaechmi. He points out that Sh's deviations from Plautus are all in response to romantic convention and he insists on Sh's right to be eclectic, though he does not defend what he regards as the inadequacies of Errors.

0952. Wedgwood, Julia. "The 'Midsummer Night's Dream'," CR, LVII (1890), 580-587.

Among Miss Wedgwood's suggestions about the play: (1) there are fewer classical and mythological allusions than might be expected in a play set in ancient Athens; (2) what allusions there are are more tolerable in Sh than they would be in any modern play because we recognize that the Renaissance paralleled the mythology of ancient Greece with Teutonic folklore and made both meaningful; (3) Theseus, elaborated and brought to life from his grave in Plutarch's "withered legend," is distinctly reminiscent of Sophocles' Theseus, who shelters Oedipus as Sh's Theseus protects the disobedient lovers. But "Shakespeare can hardly have read Sophocles, and Sophocles certainly never read Plutarch."

0953. Weichberger, Konrad. "Die Urquelle von Shakespeare's 'Much Ado about Nothing'," ShJ, XXXIV (1898), 339-345. E-S

Two central events in Much are traceable ultimately to Chariton's Chaereas and Callirhoe: the heroine is falsely accused of infidelity because her maid's love-making is mistaken in the dark for her own; the living heroine is later taken for dead. Weichberger provides a detailed summary of the relevant parts of the Greek romance and discusses the provenance of these plot devices among Chariton's Italian and Spanish Renaissance inheritors. There is no suggestion that Sh had direct access to Chariton.

0954. Weitzmann, Francis W. "Notes on the Elizabethan Elegie," PMLA, L (1935), 435-443.

Of the at least eight discrete meanings the Elizabethans attached to their Anglicization of the Greek and Latin terms, Sh uses only one. In both A.Y.L. and T.G.V. the term obviously refers to the plaints of a disappointed lover. In this sense "elegie" owes its connotations directly to the Petrarchan sonneteers, but those connotations are based mediately on the erotic elegiacs of Ovid, Tibullus, and Propertius.

0955. Welsford, Enid. "The Court-Fool in Elizabethan Drama," The Fool: His Social and Literary History (Ln, 1935), Ch. XI, pp. 243-270. E-S

See especially pp. 249-270 for three suggestions about Sh's fools: (1) Touchstone as a point of realistic reference in an idyllic environment offers A.Y.L. the same service that the Chorus offered a Greek play; (2) Feste as licensed instigator of "misrule" in Twel. is in an ancient Saturnalian tradition; unlike Touchstone he is participant not critic; (3) Lear violates Sidney's classical precepts about keeping fools and royalty apart, yet a neoclassical author, Erasmus, is the best running commentator on Sh's use of the Fool in the play. The Encomium Moriae makes the same points about sane lunatics in a mad world that Lear's Fool makes.

0956. Wilson, J. Dover. "Variations on the theme of 'A Midsummer-Night's Dream'," Tribute to Walter De La Mare on his Seventy-fifth Birthday (Ln, 1948), pp. 25-42.

Part of this essay (pp. 35-42) is an attempt to suggest that Dream is Sh's rewriting of a now lost play which was mythological in the manner of Lyly. The hypothetical source was in turn based on Apuleius' Golden Ass: Titania = Psyche, Puck = Cupid, Oberon = Venus, Bottom = Lucius, etc. In rewriting, Sh substituted for some of the Apuleian material his own childhood recollections of English folk mythology, but the original material shows through in places. It is easier to accept Sh's direct use of Apuleius than Wilson's "lost-play" theory. He appears unaware of Sister Generosa's study (#0774) and admits that he has not read Starnes (#0565). MnU

0957. Wislicenus, Paul. "Zwei neuentdeckte Shakespearequellen," ShJ, XIV (1879), 87-96. E-S (Reprinted with revision from Die Literatur, Nos. 1, 3 [1874].)

Wislicenus is the first scholar to notice that Sh blended Plautus' Amphitruo with the Menaechmi to form the main plot of Errors and that he molded the enveloping story of Aegeon and Aemilia out of the romance Apollonius of Tyre, the source of Per. The use of the Amphitruo can be seen not only in the doubled servants and the device of shutting a man out of his own house, but in the comic concern of Errors with the nature of human identity as well. The argument for Apollonius rests on the setting at Ephesus, the shipwreck which separates the family, and the discovery of the lost wife in a religious institution. Wislicenus' evidence is compelling and has been generally accepted in this century.

0958. Wolff, Max J. "Aristophanes im Urteil von heute," GRM, XVI (1928), 257-274.

The brief allusions to Sh in this critical essay compare his comic art with that of Aristophanes. Wolff gives no attention to the sources of Sh's comic spirit; but he observes that Sh stated Aristophanes' philosophy adequately in Twel. (I iii 2): "care's an enemy to life." Like Aristophanes, Sh relied chiefly on language to convey setting, and like Aristophanes and Ariosto, Sh was the master of a form in which reality and fantasy are successfully blended.

0959. Wood, Henry. "Custom and Myth in the Midsummer Night's Dream," JHUC, XVI (1897), 50-51. (An abstract of a paper read before the University Philological Association.)

The main contention of the paper is that the play turns on the Germanic custom of a trinoctium of waiting before the consummation of marriage. In the second part of the paper, "It is shown that [Dream] marks the close of a long development of folk-lore conceptions, which include Proserpina, Queen Mab and Titania ... particular attention is paid to the Pervigilium Veneris, the Roman Lamuria, the May Marriage, and the lyrics of Thomas Campion."

0960. Woodhouse, Tho[ma]s. "'All the World's a Stage'," 6 NQ, IV (1881), 311.

In response to a query from Br[insley] Nicholson asking for patristic references to the world as a stage, Woodhouse points out the remark attributed to Democritus: ὁ κόσμος σκηνή, ὁ βίος πάροδος. Another correspondent cites a similar metaphor in Erasmus' Praise of Folly.

0961. "The World's A Stage. As You Like It, II.7., " 1 NSST, VIII-X (1880-86): Appendix (December 9, 1881), 9-11.

An account of a meeting in which Brinsley Nicholson noted a parallel between Jaques's speech and a passage in Withals' Dictionary (1586). In reply F. J. Furnivall called attention to his transcription (#0769) of relevant passages from Googe's trans. of Palingenius. T. W. Baldwin (#0089) has since shown Withals' debt to Palingenius (see supra, p. viii).

0962. Yates, Frances A. "Italian Teachers in Elizabethan England," JWCI, I (1937), 103-116.

In passing Miss Yates suggests that a passage on love's mythological associations from the Twelfth Dialogue of Florio's Seconde Fruites may lie behind "For valour, is not Love a Hercules, / Still climbing trees in the Hesperides" (L.L.L. IV iii 340-341) and "Never durst poet touch a pen to write / Until his ink were temp'red with Love's sighs" (L.L.L. IV iii 346-347). Neither suggestion is persuasive.

0963. Yates, Frances A. "Shakespeare and the Platonic Tradition," UEJ, XII (1942), 2-12.

For the Platonism of Bruno and of Pseudo-Dionysius in L.L.L., see #2179. MdBJ MH

0964. Yates, Frances [A.] A Study of Love's Labour's Lost, Shakespeare Problems, ed. A. W. Pollard and J. Dover Wilson (CUP, 1936), 224 pp.

Miss Yates is primarily interested in the topical significances of L.L.L., and though she admits the relationship of the characters in the subplot to Italian and ultimately to Latin comedy, she is inclined to trace Holofernes' pedantries to French and Italian teachers in Sh's London more than to the classical pedant or to contemporary classicists.

0965. Young, G. M. "Master Holofernes," TLS, July 3, 1937, p. 496.

For an adumbration of Holofernes' pedantic foolery with language, see #2406.

0966. Zandvoort, R. W. "Fair Portia's Counterfeit," Collected Papers (Groningen, 1954), pp. 50-57. (Reprinted from Rivista di letteratura moderne [1951].) GRS

Bassanio's description of Portia's portrait which he finds in the leaden casket (Merch. III ii 114-129) is orthodox Renaissance art criticism: the great virtue Bassanio finds in the painting is its ability to deceive the beholder into thinking that the object lives. This trompe l'oeil school of criticism is classical in its antecedents; Zandvoort cites Zeuxis of Heraclea and the legend of his lifelike grapes (from Pliny) and also the lifelike statue of a cow by Myron of Eleutherae which became a conversation piece at Athens. Sh's rhetoric in this passage includes chiasmus, a device favored by Sidney in an analogous description in the Arcadia.

THE HISTORIES

0967. Alderson, E. S. "Shakespeare and Cicero," 9 NQ, V (1900), 288-289.

The line "Lord Say hath gelded the commonwealth and made it an eunuch" (2H.VI IV ii 174-175) is a close echo of a phrase in De Oratore (III 41) which was quoted by Quintilian: "Nolo dici morte Africani castratam esse rem publicam."

0968. Allen, D[on] C[ameron]. "Hotspur's Earthquake," MLN, L (1935), 171-172. SG

Hotspur's explanation (1H.IV iii i 27-33) of earthquakes as caused by wind within the earth may derive ultimately from Virgil's cave of the winds (Aeneid I), but it is essentially a Medieval interpretation of classical science (found in Bede, Caxton, Isidore of Seville, e.g.) and out of date in Sh's time.

0969. Alspach, Russell K. "A Note on 2 Henry IV," SAB, XV (1940), 191-192.

Alspach recalls the comment of Samuel Whyte (#1105), an eighteenth-century Irish litterateur that Ulpius Trajan (thirteenth Roman emperor) was the source for the scene (V ii) in which Hal, now Henry V, bestows the sword of office on the Lord Chief Justice with the admonition to use it as he had used it against Prince Hal himself. Pliny the Younger, Aurelius Victor, Dio Cassius, Zonaras, Xiphilinus the Younger, and Suidas all relate that Trajan told the leader of the Praetorian Guard to use his sword of office in Trajan's defense if he ruled well, against him if he did not. Of Sh's possible sources all were available in Latin: if Sh "had Trajan's symbolism in mind, then we have not only a source for the lines discussed, but also a hint that Shakspere had a wider knowledge of Latin literature than has been supposed."

0970. Armstrong, W. A. "The Elizabethan Conception of the Tyrant," RES, XXII (1946), 161-181.

Seneca thought of tyranny as a crime against reason; the Medieval world thought of it as a crime against God; the Renaissance kept both of the earlier views and added the concept of crime against the commonweal. The Renaissance view was also indebted to Aristotle, Plato, and Plutarch. This essay is a prelude to Armstrong's later consideration of Seneca and Machiavelli (#0971). Sh's R.III and Macb. are analyzed as typifying the conventional views.

0971. Armstrong, W. A. "The Influence of Seneca and Machiavelli on the Elizabethan Tyrant," RES, XXIV (1948), 19-35.

See especially II (pp. 20-25) for a discussion of Seneca's contribution to the Elizabethan conception. The Senecan influence preceded the Machiavellian, and gave the Tudor dramatists such concepts as the Stoic faith in reason and nature rather than passion, Fortuna as an avenger (although the English dramatists are more specific about this than Seneca is), titanic stature of protagonists, tragedy as a moral debate, dynastic guilt. Armstrong draws some useful contrasts between Senecan and Machiavellian villains and distinguishes between revenge tragedy and tyrant tragedy. The villain (Claudius in Ham.) is a private machiavel; the tyrant (Richard III, Macbeth) makes his country bleed because of public evil. The discussion centers on Hughes, Greville, and Sh (Macb. and R.III). Cf. Armstrong's earlier RES art. (#0970) and Ruth L. Anderson (#0077).

NOTE: Numbers preceded by # refer to entries in this Guide. Keys to abbreviations are found on pages xi-xvii and 381-387.

0972. Baker, H. K. "Hamlet: Three Notes," NQ, CLXXV (1938), 158.

Baker attacks C.T.C. (#1856) for his doubt that Sh could read De Oratore, and then claims that the Hostess' description of Falstaff's symptoms (H.V II iii 14-28) accurately reflects Hippocratic medicine which Sh might have learned from reading Bacon.

0973. Benjamin, Edwin B. "Fame, Poetry and the Order of History in the Literature of the English Renaissance," SR, VI (1959), 64-84.

Sh's use of Rumour in the Induction to 2H.IV is traceable to the Fama of Aeneid IV and Meta. XII. Edward V's reference to Caesar's fame (R.III III i 84-89) is Sh's hit at Richard, whose infamy is implicitly contrasted with Caesar's fame.

0974. Bennett, Josephine Waters. "Britain Among the Fortunate Isles," SP, LIII (1956), 114-140. GRS

An erudite study which traces the ancient beliefs that Britain was "another world," the locale of the Blessed Isles (garden of the Hesperides), and (sometimes) the domicile of departed spirits. Sh seems to be thinking of the first of these concepts in Cloten's observation that "Britain is / A world by itself" (Cym. III i 12-13) and of the second in Gaunt's eulogy of England (R.II II i 40-66). The ancients cited include Virgil, Horace, Claudian, Homer (Ogygia, Calypso's isle, was sometimes believed to be off the coast of Scotland), Julius Caesar, Diodorus Siculus, Dionysius Periegetes, Pomponius Mela, Plutarch, Hesiod, Tibullus, Lucian, and Procopius of Caesarea. Natalis Comes brought many of the classical allusions to Britain together and transmitted them to the Renaissance. An interesting corollary is the Elizabethan fondness for deriving "Albion" from "ὄλβιος," "fortunate." Mrs. Bennett goes on to argue that this classical tradition offers evidence that Spenser equated fairyland with fortunate Britain.

0975. Berdan, J. M. "Shakespeare's Learning," Nation, XCII (1911), 241. SG

For an echo of the Aeneid in 3H.VI see #1830.

0976. Birch, W. J. "Shakespeare and Lucretius," 7 NQ, II (1886), 202. HB

Birch notes the parallel between 2H.VI III i 210-216 and De Rerum Natura II on the subject of cows bereft of their calves by the butcher. There is no apparent indebtedness; "the Latin and the Englishman were alike only in their study of nature."

0977. Boas, F[rederick] S. "The Soldier in Elizabethan and Later English Drama," TRSL, n.s. XIX (1942), 121-156.

See pp. 131-132 for Boas' brief dismissal of the miles gloriosus as a major influence on the Elizabethan stage. It is interesting that in Pistol, Parolles, and possibly in Falstaff's "honor" speech (though not in Falstaff himself) Boas credits Sh with as much participation in the tradition as anyone else he mentions, including Jonson.

0978. Bond, R. Warwick. "Falstaff as 'Vox Populi'," Studia Otiosa (Ln, 1938), pp. 51-68.

"The braggart Miles of Latin Comedy was probably known to Shakespeare, but those witless personages could be of very little service here [in 1H.IV]," a play expanded into two by the sheer charm and wit of Falstaff.

0979. Boughner, Daniel C. The Braggart in Renaissance Comedy: A Study in Comparative Drama from Aristophanes to Shakespeare. Minnesota UP, 1954, 328 pp.

For Falstaff and Pistol as partakers of the tradition, see #0695.

0980. Boughner, Daniel C. "Traditional Elements in Falstaff," JEGP, XLIII (1944), 417-428.

Boughner traces Falstaff's mythological allusions, his claims that in battle he was heavily outnumbered, and his pretentious erudition, among other elements, to the braggart soldier of Italian Renaissance comedy who was the miles gloriosus of Latin comedy given an arrogant and ill-fitting veneer of humanistic learning. Sh individualizes Falstaff, but he bases him on Latin comedy Italianized. This is a very erudite art.

0981. Boughner, Daniel C. "Vice, Braggart, and Falstaff," Anglia, LXXII (1954), 35-61.

A broad survey of the cowardly bullies and buffoons in English Renaissance drama before Sh. Falstaff partakes of some of their characteristics, but he is also the child of Roman and Continental comedy. Like Boughner's other studies, this one is well informed and convincing.

0982. Bryant, J. A., Jr. "The Linked Analogies of Richard II," SewR, LXV (1957), 420-433.

A typological reading of R.II which tries to show that in writing the play Sh "had given to secular fable a significance that it had achieved only rarely in drama since the days of Aeschylus and Sophocles." Richard is a microchristus and the ritual through which he is deposed and killed bears the same relationship to the drama of the Mass and Calvary that the plays of the Attic dramatists bear to the fertility rites of ancient Greek religion. The result in both cases is a universality of application in the story; it transcends its own framework and assumes cosmic significance. Bryant's reading is not a persuasive one; the audience may not agree with Richard that he is a Christ betrayed by twelve thousand Judases (IV i 170-171).

0983. Butler, James D. "Platonic Allusions in Shakespeare," Shna, III (1886), 230-232.

Butler traces to Plato's Phaedrus the lines in 1H.VI about the rapidity with which plants grow in Adonis' gardens. Butler criticizes other commentators for tracing the reference to the Odyssey or for maintaining that classical literature does not contain any reference to Adonis' gardens. He feels sure that Sh derived the concept directly from Plato. Henry G. Langford makes exactly the same identification in NewShna, I (1901), 29-30.

0984. C., H. C. "Plautus and Shakespeare," 4 NQ, V (1870), 594.

For Falstaff and the miles gloriosus, see #0708.

0985. Caine, T. H. Hall. Richard III and Macbeth: The Spirit of Romantic Play in Relationship to the Principles of Greek and of Gothic Art, and to the Picturesque Interpretations of Mr. Henry Irving: A Dramatic Study. Ln and Liverpool, 1877, 46 pp.

"The critic or actor who brings principles of Greek or Roman art to bear upon ... [Sh] must necessarily very widely miss his mark," because Sh is essentially "Gothic" (i.e., pictorial) rather than classical (i.e., statuesque). Yet Sh is capable of Hellenic "metrical chastity" in the "strophe and antistrophe" in which Elizabeth and Richard speak (R.III IV iv). The body of the essay is a critical analysis of Richard and Macbeth without explicit or specific contrast with Attic tragedy. DFo

0986. Cairncross, Andrew S. "Introduction," The Second Part of King Henry VI (1957), ArdenSh, pp. xi-liv.

At the end of this introduction, Cairncross points out that the animal imagery which establishes the notion of anarchy in the play comes in part from Aesop. He also points out, inter alia, Sh's debts to Ovid (Tristia, Meta.), Virgil, and Lucan. Earlier (pp. xlii-xlv), Cairncross reviews the controversy over the meaning of the "upstart Crow" insult and proposes that Greene meant Sh was fond of dropping allusions in his early works--he was tricked out in "plumes" from Ovid, Plutarch, and the other authors named above. A convincing argument.

0987. Camden, Carroll. "Three Notes on Shakespeare," MLN, LXXII (1957), 251-253.

Note III explains that "Charles' wain" (1H.IV II i 2) refers to the North Star, as it does in Holland's Pliny.

0988. Campbell, Lily B. "Theories of Revenge in Renaissance England," MP, XXVIII (1931), 281-296.

We oversimplify when we lump revenge tragedies of Sh's age under the label "Senecan." It is only necessary to survey the ethical tracts of the sixteenth century to see that the tradition was complex. St. Paul (especially), Socrates, Alexander [the Great?], Epictetus, Seneca, Theophrastus, and Plutarch all condemned private revenge for wrongs done. Miss Campbell discusses briefly the extent of Sh's participation in this Christian-classical ethical system in R.II, R.III, and Ham.

0989. Chapman, Raymond. "The Wheel of Fortune in Shakespeare's Historical Plays," RES, n.s. I (1950), 1-7.

In the Lancastrian tetralogy, "Shakespeare had in mind a literary convention much older than the chronicle-histories of his dramatic predecessors." He repeatedly used the concept of the turning wheel of Fortune--a concept which traces to Imperial Rome, and the goddess of childbirth. Sh did not, of course, go to the fountainhead, but drew on the Medieval tradition. Chapman implies that Sh was almost unique among his fellow dramatists in making capital out of Fortune's turning wheel. This is, of course, a misleading implication: Fortuna dominates Marlowe's Edward II, e.g.: see Mortimer's lines at V ii 53, V iv 69, and (especially) V vi 59-63.

0990. Chubb, E. W. "Shakspere's Cicero," Acad (N.Y.), V (1890), 108-112.

For Sh's reference to Cicero in 2H. VI see #1220.

0991. Clemen, Wolfgang [H.] Clarences Traum und Ermordung (Shakespeare: Richard III 1,4) SBAW, V (München, 1955), 46 pp. GRS

In passing Clemen cites Aeneid VI as one possible source for Clarence's descent into an underworld which is partly classical and partly Christian. He also lists Greek tragedy, Seneca (Troades), Homer, and Virgil among Sh's predecessors in the use of dreams for foreshadowing, presentiment, and warning. But both for the underworld and for the dream Clemen stresses the greater importance of the Mirror for Magistrates as source.

0992. Clemen, Wolfgang H. "Tradition and Originality in Shakespeare's Richard III," SQ, V (1954), 247-257.

R. III is an important milestone in dramatic history because it marks an effort to manipulate conventional elements of drama in original ways. Specifically, Sh blended the chronicle play with Senecan tragedy; the manipulation of the elements indicates the play's success. E.g., in Queen Margaret, Sh embodied both the Senecan Até or Nemesis and the Chorus; again, Sh used stichomythia in Richard's wooing of Anne, but unlike Seneca, he made it a characteristic of the speaker, not just a literary convention. Clemen's analysis is lucid and penetrating; a rewarding essay, but it seems to overstate the importance of R. III as a "milestone": e.g., the authors of the Tudor interludes were also manipulating conventional elements of drama in original ways when they secularized the Morality drama of the fifteenth century. Cf. Ribner, #2080, who argues on the same grounds that Romeo is a milestone.

0993. Coghill, Nevill. "Shakespeare's Reading in Chaucer," Wilson Festschrift, pp. 86-99.

A survey of the scholarship which has adduced parallels between the two poets. To those parallels, Coghill would add several of which one is relevant to Sh's classicism: Bolingbroke's exclamation (R. II I iii 294-295), "Oh, who can hold a fire in his hand / By thinking on the frosty Caucasus?", which has usually been traced to Meta. VIII, is closer (in Coghill's opinion) to the lines in the "Wife of Bath's Tale": "Taak fyr, and ber it to the derkeste hous / Bitwix this and the mount of Kaukasous ..."

0994. Conklin, Willet T. "Two Further Notes on Shakespeare's Use of Elyot's 'Governour'," TSE, X (1930), 66-69.

The first note would add to D. T. Starnes's compilation (#1088) of Shn echoes of Elyot Fluellen's reference to the death of Clitus at the hands of Alexander the Great (H. V IV vii 35-41).

0995. Cowl, R. P. "Some Literary Allusions in 'Henry the Fourth'," TLS, March 26, 1925, p. 222.

In this art. Cowl cites many parodies of contemporary drama (especially Marlowe) in the comic subplots of both parts of H. IV. Pistol's references to Pluto's lake and Cerberus, to Hector and Caesar, are among them. When Pistol confuses "Hannibal" with "cannibal" Sh may be satirizing Samuel Brandon's Virtuous Octavia (1598) in which "cannibal" is placed as a pejorative appositive to "Hannibal."

0996. [Cowl, R. P.] Sources of the Text of Henry the Fourth Parts I and II. Bruges: The Saint Catherine Press, 1928, 54 pp. With eighteen supplements (some Ln: Murray; some Glasgow: W. McDougall; some n.p. or publisher--1929-42). E-S SG

Sources are indicated in a vast range of classical, Medieval, and Renaissance literature for a multitude of phrases in both plays. In some cases, the (ultimate, at least) source is obviously correct, but Cowl's extensive reading has led him into two fallacies: (1) Sh "must" have read everything that Cowl has read, even when antecedent probability is against that conclusion; (2) Sh was incapable of conceiving a phrase without prodding from some source at his elbow. One example can illustrate both fallacies: the fact that Sh characterizes Mercury with the epithet "feathered" (1H. IV IV i 106) rather than with the conventional "winged" indicates that he was drawing on Arnobius (a fourth-century Christian polemicist against the pagans) even though not another passage in the play shows any Arnobian influence. Cowl, like Johnstone (#0352) displays more erudition than critical judgment (though Cowl's erudition is far superior to Johnstone's). Consult SG, who itemizes the "sources" in this somewhat rare book. She takes no cognizance, however, of the eighteen supplements, which range far beyond H.IV in the Sh canon, and which (passim) deal with classical "sources" often through the medium of Italian poetry. MnU

0997. Craig, Hardin. "Shakespeare and the History Play," AMS, pp. 55-64.

Craig discusses the rhetorical features of Titus and the Yorkist tetralogy and contends "that Shakespeare made his way into the history play through the door of Senecan tragedy" rather than exclusively through imitation of Marlowe. In the mature histories, rhetoric is a subordinate dramatic device associated "with special situations and characters."

0998. Creighton, C. "Falstaff's Deathbed," BEM, CXLV (1889), 324-336.

Creighton attacks Theobald's famous emendation (in H.V II iii 18) on the evidence of Hippocrates' Prognostica, which he believes Sh knew, possibly in the Latin ed. of Copus (1511) or that of Laurentianus (1508). There is a possibility that Pliny or a Renaissance Dr. Caius (perhaps the model for the Caius of Wives) also contributed to his knowledge. Creighton's is a very early and thorough study of the classical background of Falstaff's death; it has, however, been largely ignored by later students of the passage.

0999. Crundell, H. W. "Shakespeare, Lyly and 'Aesop'," NQ, CLXVIII (1935), 312. SG

The note suggests that Suffolk's contemptuous correction of the Captain who has captured him (2H.VI IV i 109) is a mocking reflection of a curious distortion in Lyly of the fable of the eagle and the scarab. That Sh knew the true Aesopic version is evident from a reference in Cym. III iii.

1000. Cumberland, Richard. "[Falstaff]," The Observer, II (1808), No. 73, pp. 144-150. (The essay may antedate 1808.)

In passing: Falstaff is a Silenos in size, a satyr in sensuality, and a "bacchalian" in intemperance; Pistol speaks a "tissue of old tags of bombast" reminiscent of the parody in Greek Middle Comedy. DFo

1001. Cumberland, Richard. "[Macbeth and Richard III]," The Observer, II (1808), Nos. 69-72, pp. 117-144.

For R.III "illustrated" by the classics, see #1887. DFo

1002. Cunningham, F. "Euripides and Shakspeare," Ath, No. 2316 (1872), 346.

Stimulated by the remarks on Ham. and Euripides made by Latham (#1997) the previous year, Cunningham recalls the observations of earlier commentators on the parallel between the Alcestis and Queen Katherine's farewell to her servants (H.VIII IV ii).

1003. Davenport, A. "Notes on Lyly's Campaspe and Shakespeare," NQ, CXCIX (1954), 19-20.

The third of four notes points out that Falstaff's comic rebuke to Prince Hal (1H.IV II iv 439-461) is an exact parody of Hephestion's rebuke to Alexander in Campaspe for falling in love with a slave girl. The sun, truancy, blackberries, and rhetorical questions are all in both places. Davenport is less convincing when he tries to trace part of Falstaff's "honor" speech to another passage in Campaspe. Davenport does not observe that the identification of Alexander with Hal also occurs elsewhere: in H.V where Fluellen compares the two military leaders and (perhaps) in Henry IV's advice to his son (1H.IV III ii 39-84) about dealing with the people (see #1021).

1004. Davies, Thomas. Dramatic Miscellanies: Consisting of Critical Observations on Several Plays of Shakspeare. . . Vol. I (of three), Ln, 2nd ed., 1785, 451 pp.

This first vol. discusses only the history plays: John, R.II, 1,2H.IV, H.VIII. Charming with their anecdotal style, Davies' scholia ramble on, chiefly commenting on eighteenth-century actors, productions, and attitudes toward the plays; but Davies inserts numerous allusions to classical literature and history as they can enlighten us on individual passages. He shows a marked preference for Greek literature; again and again he cites Homer, Aeschylus, Euripides, Plutarch, et al. Constance is more moving than Clytemnestra, Hecuba, and the other great suffering women of antiquity; Richard eulogizing England on his return from Ireland is like Ulysses glad to be in Ithaca again; Falstaff's remark about fish-eaters who "get wenches" calls for an excursus from Pliny, Diodorus Siculus, and a supporting array of authority on fish and sexuality. Davies deserves to be exhumed and dusted off. MnU

1005. Dean, H. P. "Falstaff's Death," TLS, April 23, 1925, p. 284.

Dean suggests that Sh went to classical sources for his description of Sir John's last moment. The "facies Hippocratica" in Cardan's version of the Prognostica would explain "chloros": "Who does not know that in Greece the face of a dying man is of a green color?" The pen is Falstaff's nose, his face a table, the green induced by acute disease. In Dean's opinion there is no need to tamper with the text of F_1 as Theobald did.

1006. Dollarhide, Louis E. "Shakespeare's Richard III and Renaissance Rhetoric," diss (North Carolina, 1954).*

1007. Draper, John W. "Falstaff and the Plautine Parasite," CJ, XXXIII (1938), 390-401.

While Falstaff is vividly Elizabethan, Sh probably obtained some part of his conception from the miles gloriosus and even more from the parasites of Roman comedy. Lechery, gluttony, wit, willingness to be the butt of humor are all "parasitical" traits. This is a plausible argument.

1008. Eagle, Roderick L. "The Death of Falstaff," NQ, CCII (1957), 240.

Lewis Theobald's emendation of H.V II iii 18 to "'a babbled of green fields" was unnecessary. Hippocrates' Prognostica gives Falstaff's six symptoms of approaching death in the same order; Eagle translates the fifth: "The whole face of a pale green colour." Sh, indeed, understood the meaning of χλωρός ("pale green") better than many Renaissance commentators who rendered the word "pallidus." Note that Baker (#0972) made a similar suggestion in 1938. See Fogel (#1014) for a survey of (nonclassical) explanations of the passage.

1009. Eagle, R[oderick] L. "'The Phoenix and the Turtle': Translation of Pliny," NQ, CLXXX (1941), 51.

On Pliny and R.II see #2371.

1010. Evans, Maurice. "Metaphor and Symbol in the Sixteenth Century," EC, III (1953), 267-284.

The source of the theory of correspondences on which the Elizabethans founded their respect for metaphor, symbol, allegory, and fable was the Platonized Christianity of pseudo-Dionysius' Celestial Hierarchies (fifth century) which maintained that man's lack of perfection necessitated that he contemplate truth through its shadows (e.g., man "understands" the Trinity only through its reflection--faith, hope, and charity). This Platonic concept led naturally to analogical interpretation of Scripture and later of the classics. In the sixteenth century, classic myth was seriously regarded as a shadow of divine truth. Therefore, when Sh compares Richard II to Phaethon "wanting the manage of unruly jades" the analogy is not mere pretty decoration, but a serious ethical commentary. Evans gives numerous similar examples from sixteenth- and seventeenth-century literature.

1011. Fansler, Harriott Ely. The Evolution of Technic in Elizabethan Tragedy. Chicago, 1914, 283 pp. SG

For Senecanism in R.III, see #1919.

1012. Finney, Gretchen L. "Music: A Book of Knowledge in Renaissance England," SR, VI (1959), 36-63 (see especially p. 58).

When Richard II refers to time and his own life in musical analogies, he is following an English Renaissance pattern traceable finally to Pythagoras: Music is tempus (structured intervals), but it is also the process temperare, "to adjust harmoniously." When Richard expropriated Gaunt's lands he violated harmony, sinning against the Pythagorean cosmos.

1013. Foakes, R. A. "Introduction," King Henry VIII (1957), ArdenSh, pp. xv-lxv.

See especially pp. xxxvii-xlv, lxi-lxii. Foakes sees in H.VIII most of the themes which criticism has found in the other last plays; but where birth, death, and rebirth (e.g.) are conveyed by Ceres and Proserpina in Temp. and W.T., in H.VIII Sh locates his theme in human events (e.g., the deaths of Buckingham, Wolsey, and Katharine and the birth of Elizabeth). Myth gives place to history in this last of Sh's plays.

1014. Fogel, Ephim G. "'A Table of Green Fields': A Defense of the Folio Reading," SQ, IX (1958), 485-492.

After an admirably clear survey of opinion on one of the most complex of Shn cruxes (H.V II iii 14-18), Fogel propounds the thesis that the Hostess is reciting the "facies Hippocratica" in which a marked paleness or greenness of complexion is a fatal sign. Her words mean: "his nose was as sharp as a goose-quill and the very picture of green fields (i.e., as green as grass)." Cf. Eagle and Baker (#1008, #0972), who anticipated Fogel but who do not give his survey of the question. He does not mention either of them.

1015. Forsythe, R. S. "Tacitus, 'Henry VI, Part III,' and 'Nero'," MLN, XLII (1927), 25-27. HB

The passage in 3H.VI II v in which the slaughter of father by son and son by father is lamented stems mediately from Tacitus' Historiae III 25. The immediate source may be Hall's Chronicle. The author of the tragedy Nero probably borrowed the idea from 3H.VI.

1016. Gilbert, A[llan] H. "Falstaff's Impresa," NQ, CLXIV (1933), 389. SG

Gilbert traces Falstaff's boast (2H.IV IV iii 55-59) to Horace's Odes I xii by way of an Italian emblem writer. But the verbal similarity is not striking and the thought is a commonplace.

1017. Graf, Herman. Der Miles Gloriosus im englishen Drama (1892) (no complete pagination available).

As abstracted and trans. in the New Variorum 1H.IV, Graf says that Sh "split" the classical miles gloriosus, embodying the attractive characteristics in Falstaff and the despicable ones in Pistol. Graf apparently believes that the English dramatists approached the Latin stock character through the Capitano Spavento of the commedia dell' arte.

1018. Graham, Thomas H. B. "Venus and Adonis," GM, CCLXXXII (1897), 500-508.

Graham traces the Adonis legend as far back as Ishtar and Dumuzi, the Mesopotamian fertility symbols; by the time of Ovid the fertility symbolism had very much dropped away, and the story was regarded only as a charming love tale. In Greece women annually lamented dead Adonis, carrying about pots of lettuce which they called "Adonis' gardens" because, like Adonis, lettuce comes early to fruit but fades soon. Sh is thus more nearly correct about the Adonis' gardens in 1H.VI (I vi 6-7) than Milton and Spenser are; they follow Pliny, who erroneously assumed that the gardens were fertile, delectable places, not mourning symbols.

1019. Gudeman, Alfred. "A Classical Reminiscence in Shakespeare," MLN, VI (1891), 106-107.

Gudeman shows that Sh's echo of Horace's Satires II in H.V (III v 50-52) cannot be coincidental. Sh refers to "The Alps [which] doth spit and void his rheum upon" the valleys. Horace has "Furius hibernas cana nive conspuet Alpis." Sh misunderstood "Furius" as an adjective ("furiosus") instead of the proper name it is and therefore took "Alpis" for a singular nominative. This is why Sh here uses the word "Alps" as a singular noun.

1020. Hanford, J. H. "A Platonic Passage in Shakespeare's Troilus and Cressida," SP, XIII (1916), 100-109. E-S SG

For the Platonic basis of H.V I ii, see #1374.

1021. Harrison, Thomas P., Jr. "The Folger Secret of Secrets, 1572," AMS, 601-620.

The discovery of an apparently unique exemplar of the 1572 English ed. occasions a discussion of the influence of this pseudo-Aristotelian work. The "Aristotelian" advice given to Alexander the Great about how to comport himself with respect to his subjects is almost identical to that given by King Henry to Prince Hal (1H.IV III ii 39-84). The argument is reinforced by the possibility that Lear's foolish question-and-answer session with the Fool (I v and [erroneously cited] III iv) is a parody of the Sydrac question-and-answer book which appears with the Secret of Secrets in this 1572 ed.

1022. Hart, H. C. "Introduction," The First Part of King Henry the Sixth (1909/1930), ArdenSh, pp. vii-l.

Hart observes inter alia debts in 1H.VI to Puttenham's Arte of English Poesie (the reference at I vi 25 to "the rich-jewell'd coffer of Darius" seems to be an echo of Puttenham, not of Plutarch or Pliny) and to Golding's Ovid (mainly echoes of diction, not of thought).

1023. Hart, H. C. "Introduction," The Second Part of King Henry the Sixth (1909/1931), ArdenSh, pp. vii-lii.

On p. xl there is a brief citation of sixteen passages in 2H.VI which parallel Golding's Ovid, "a favourite volume with Shakespeare in his early days." The parallels are chiefly verbal, not thematic, and few of them are striking.

1024. Heath-Stubbs, John. "The Mythology of Falstaff," Occult Observer, I (1949), 21-30.

The mythology in this essay is mainly native folklore, but Heath-Stubbs makes three suggestions which relate Falstaff to the classics: (1) Sir John as a gigantic glutton is in a tradition also discernible in the Hercules of Euripides' Alcestis; (2) the rejection of Falstaff by Hal is a parallel to the desertion of Dido by Aeneas, also a king who must choose between sensuality and political responsibility; (3) in Wives the identification of Falstaff with Actaeon in a question of cuckoldry may suggest that there is some validity in the theory which traces the cuckold's horns to Actaeon. Heath-Stubbs also proposes that Falstaff's feeble lechery may reflect ancient myths about the decline of fertility gods. DLC

1025. Herrick, Marvin T. Comic Theory in the Sixteenth Century, ISLL, No. 34 (1950), 248 pp.

For Terentian influence on the comic subplots of Sh's history plays, see #0803.

1026. Hollander, John. "Musica Mundana and Twelfth Night," Sound and Poetry, ed. Northrop Frye (Col UP, 1957), pp. 55-82.

For "classical" music in R.II, see #0808.

1027. Honigmann, E. A. J. "Introduction," King John (1954), ArdenSh, pp. xi-lxxv.

In passing (p. lxv) in the excellent section on the interpretation of the play, Honigmann points out the dominant rôle of Fortune and her wheel in John.

1028. Hudson, Hoyt H. The Epigram in the English Renaissance. PUP, 1947, 178 pp.

For a possible echo of classical epigram in 1H.IV see #0810.

1029. Humphreys, A. R. "Introduction," The First Part of King Henry IV (1960), Arden Sh, pp. xi-lxxxii.

The observations on Falstaff as miles and gnatho are brief (pp. xlii, xliii) and emphasize that Sir John is more than the sum of the sources and conventions which lie behind him; Humphreys devotes more commentary to the Morality Vice than to Plautine types.

1030. Jackson, James L. "The Use of the Five-Act Formula in Richard II and Twelfth Night," ShN, II (1952), 26.

A précis of a paper given at the South Central MLA meeting at LSU (1951). Major Jackson applied the criteria of Baldwin (#0683) to R.II and Twel. and concluded that both plays fit the Terentian pattern.

1031. Jorgensen, Paul A. "Alien Military Doctrine in Renaissance England," MLQ, XVII (1956), 43-49.

For Sh's "unclassical" attitude toward military policy in H.V, see #2238.

1032. Keirce, William F. "Henry V," Lectures on Four of Shakespeare's History Plays by Members of the Department of English, Carnegie Institute of Technology, CSE, No. 1 (1953), pp. 53-69.

The lecture, intended for undergraduate engineering students, analyzes the plot and characterization of H.V according to the criteria of the Poetics. Sh falls short of Aristotelian standards because he has a preconceived intention of idealizing Henry and he sacrifices plot and character to that end. For example, the ironic possibilities of the discovery of treason against Henry, son of a traitor, are bypassed in II ii, lest it be thought that Henry sits unjustly on his throne; again Henry allows the legalistic bishops to make his decision to invade France for him--Sh bypasses the ethical implications of a choice which Henry might have made for himself. Keirce also draws some interesting analogies to Sophocles' Electra (evidently produced in 1953 at Carnegie).

1033. Kitto, H. D. F. "A Classical Scholar Looks at Shakespeare," More Talking of Shakespeare, ed. John Garrett (N.Y., 1959), pp. 33-54.

For an Aeschylean theme in Sh's history plays, see #1987.

1034. Koeppel, E. "Shakespeares 'Richard III', und Senecas 'Troades'," ShJ, XLVII (1911), 188-190. E-S SG

Koeppel believes that Royster (#1079) is wrong in seeing a close similarity between R.III IV iv and the grieving Marys of the Middle English drama. Sh is closer in spirit to the next-to-last scene of Seneca's Troades, in which Andromache, Hecuba, and Helen lament the news that Pyrrhus has taken Polyxena for his concubine. Though Sh's scene is a lyric interlude, unlike Seneca's which advances the plot, there are sufficient similarities to suggest to Koeppel the possibility that Sh borrowed, either from the Latin or from Jasper Heywood's trans. One might raise the same objection to Koeppel's hypothesis as to Royster's (see commentary on #1079).

1035. Koller, Katherine. "Falstaff and the Art of Dying," MLN, LX (1945), 383-386.

In an attack on the theory that the Hostess' account of Falstaff's death is a parody of Plato's account of Socrates' death (see #1051), Miss Koller traces the passage to the ars moriendi tradition which dates from the fifteenth century; Sir John's last moments parody the method of holy dying. Alfred Adler argues (MLN, LXI [1946], 72) that the background is pagan as well as Christian; he points out that the carefree relationship between Hal and Falstaff is a folk motif, and he gives (inter alia) "the association between youthful Dionysos and Silenos" as an analogue.

1036. Krappe, Alexander H. "Shakespeare Notes," Anglia, LII (1928), 174-182. SG

The first note deals with "The Source of 'King Richard III', Act I, sc. ii [sic] ll. 1-4," which Krappe finds in Claudian's De Bello Gallico. The contexts are similar, and the phrasing is close, but in the absence of full knowledge of the Claudian tradition in the sixteenth century, Krappe wisely claims this as "only ultimately the source" of Richard's "winter of our discontent" lines.

1037. Landmann, F. "Shakspere and Euphuism: Euphues an Adaptation from Guevara" (1882), NSST, [IX] (1880-85), Part II ([1884]), 241-276. E-S

For Sh's parody of euphuistic classical allusions in 1H.IV, see #0830.

1038. Langenfelt, Gösta. "'The Noble Savage' until Shakespeare," ES, XXXVI (1955), 222-227.

Montaigne and the voyagers were not Sh's only sources for his references to primeval man. He was also indebted to the millennium and Golden Age traditions, traceable at least as far back as Hesiod. This theme, so popular with the Roman authors (Virgil, Tibullus, Tacitus, Ovid), was transmitted to the humanists by Boccaccio, who is a pillar in the bridge between the ancient and Renaissance worlds. Sh could also have found some of what he found in Montaigne in Golding's Meta. Sh was too much a realist to be sentimental about the theme; in both Jack Cade (2H.VI) and Gonzalo (Temp.) he satirizes the utopian idealist. A responsible brief study.

1039. Law, R[obert] A. "An Echo of Homer in Henry the Fifth?" TSE, XXII (1942), 105-109.

Law attempts to trace the King's attitude and behavior before the battle at Agincourt (H.V IV i) to Chapman's trans. (1598) of Iliad X, where Agamemnon is also restless at night. It would seem more reasonable to call the two passages analogues with a common source in human nature.

1040. Leon, H. J. "Classical Sources for the Garden Scene in 'Richard II'," PQ, XXIX (1950), 65-70.

Leon shows that in III iv Sh is utilizing an old story originating in Herodotus and echoed in Aristotle, Livy, Ovid, Dionysius of Halicarnassus, and Notker Balbulus' Gesta Karoli Magni (ninth century). Leon wisely does not insist on any one of these as source, contenting himself with pointing out the tradition of Sh's device: the parallelism between gardening and political policy.

1041. Lloyd, Roger. "Socrates and Falstaff," TT, XXXIX, No. 1 (1958), 219-220.

Sh's source for Hostess Pistol's putting her hands higher and higher on Falstaff's legs and finding them cold (H.V II iii 24-28) was the death scene in the Phaedo where the jailer did the same thing to Socrates. Lloyd tries to justify the ludicrous connection of the two men in Sh's mind by suggesting that both were conscious of vocation (1H.IV I ii 116). Sh would have had to read the Phaedo in trans. "since all the authorities seem to be agreed that Stratford Grammar School did not teach Greek." See #0089 passim for an authority who disagrees.

1042. Lynn, W. T. "'1Henry VI.,' I.i.," 9 NQ, I (1898), 284.

When the Duke of Bedford's invocation to the ghost of Henry V is interrupted at I i 56, he is comparing Henry's soul to Caesar's and (presumably) to some similarly stellified spirit. Lynn suggests that he is about to speak of the stellification of Callisto, Lycaon's daughter, in recollection of Virgil's Georgics I.

1043. McAvoy, William C. "Falstaff, Erasmus, and Ficino," CarrollQ, XI (1957), 10-14.

Not seen.

1044. McAvoy, William C. "Form in 'Richard II', II.i.40-66," JEGP, LIV (1958), 355-361.

McAvoy shows that John of Gaunt's famous lines clearly follow the formula for praise given in Aphthonius' Progymnasmata with Lorichius' scholia as used in the sixteenth-century grammar school.

1045. McDiarmid, Matthew P. "A Reconsidered Parallel Between Shakespeare's 'King John' and Kyd's 'Cornelia'," NQ, CCI (1956), 507-508.

This note adduces possible echoes in John of Kyd's trans. of Garnier (especially of a dialogue between Cassius and Brutus) to support the parallel long noticed between Falconbridge's impassionedly patriotic "Shall we, upon the footing of our land" and Cassius' equally patriotic "Shall we then, that are men and Romains borne." None of McDiarmid's evidence is so convincing as what it seeks to support, but he appears to be correct when he makes Sh the debtor to this neoclassical play.

1046. Mendilow, A. A. "Falstaff's Death of a Sweat," SQ, IX (1958), 479-483.

The "sweat" of which Falstaff dies in H.V is the plague, induced by the wild life he has led and by his grief at being rejected by Hal. Mendilow marshals an array of Renaissance medical authorities who based their treatises on the descriptions of plague symptoms in Thucydides, Lucretius, Pliny, Hippocrates, and Galen. Closest parallels to Falstaff's symptoms are from Peter Lowe's trans. of Hippocrates' Prognostica (1597, a date well before the 1599 composition of H.V). See Fogel (#1014) for a survey of the scholarship on Sir John's death.

1047. Merrill, Elizabeth. The Dialogue in English Literature, YSE, No. 42 (1911), 131 pp.

For Falstaff's "catechism" as an example of the classical dialogue, see #0857.

1048. Modersohn, Anna B. "Cicero im englischen Geistesleben des 16. Jahrhunderts," Archiv, CXLIX (1925), 33-51, 219-245. E-S HB

For "Tully" in 2H.VI, see #1513.

1049. Monaghan, J. "Falstaff and his Forbears," SP, XVIII (1921), 353-361. E-S

Monaghan sees Falstaff's inception in Derrick, the clown in the Famous Victories of Henry the Fifth—a tacit negation of classical influence. Most authorities now agree with Boughner (#0695) that Sir John owes at least something to the Italianized Roman comedy.

1050. Moore, Ella Adams. "Moral Proportion and Fatalism in Shakespeare: 'King John' and Conclusion," PL, VIII (1896), 139-145.

The culmination of a series of arts. (only two of which have been considered relevant—#1516, #1517), this essay on John contains a comparison between Greek and Shn concepts of Fate. To the Greeks Fate was an inexorable exterior force against which man had no recourse; to Sh, man is free until by succumbing to passion he becomes the slave of exterior force. In Greek tragedy we feel "pity and resignation"; "but in Shakespeare, behind the real, the terrible 'now' stand forever the spectral figures of the 'once', the 'might have been'." "If Greek tragedy was a Colossus, Shakespeare's is a human soul." Mrs. Moore oversimplifies; Greek tragedy is full of regret for lost opportunities, and R.III is a play whose opening lines indicate that there can be no alternative to an evil course for the hero.

1051. Moore, John Robert. "Shakespeare's Henry V," Expl, I (1943), item 61.

"The fat knight who drank sack died like the fat philosopher who drank the hemlock." The symptoms of Falstaff's approaching death are similar to the symptoms of Socrates' approaching death as Plato describes them "however Shakespeare had come to know [them]." For some strictures, see ibid., II (1943), item 19. See also #1035.

1052. Muir, Kenneth. "Shakespeare Among the Commonplaces," RES, X (1959), 282-289.

The first of two notes on sources of R.II attempts to trace the elements of Gaunt's consolatio dialogue with Bolingbroke (I iii 275-304) to a variety of sources including Plato (in Euphues), Valerius Maximus, Cicero, and Ovid. Muir justifies his conclusion (that a plurality of sources coalesced in Sh's mind) by referring to J. L. Lowes on Coleridge; he neglects the fact that there were at least seventy-one consolation books current in England in the sixteenth century (see Tison, #0601). Under such circumstances specific attribution of sources is next to impossible.

1053. Muir, Kenneth. "Shakespeare and the

Tragic Pattern," PBA, XLIV (1958), 145-162. (Annual British Academy Shakespeare Lecture.)

For R.II and R.III in relation to tragic theory, see #2045.

1054. Muirson, Patrick. "Passage in 'King John' and 'Romeo and Juliet'," NQ, VIII (1853), 384.

The first of two notes suggests that John II i 143-144 ("[the lion's skin] lies as sightly on the back of him [Austria] / As great Alcides' shows upon an ass") is a reference to the mysteries ("shows") of Hercules which were transported by donkey: "Asinus portat mysteriae." Muirson's interpretation is not persuasive; Sh more obviously is referring to the skin of the Nemean Lion and to the ass in Aesop whose pose as a lion was betrayed by his long ears.

1055. Mustanoja, Tauno F. "I King Henry the Sixth, I.iii.30: Piel'd Priest," Mélanges, pp. 342-347.

The insulting epithet which Gloucester hurls at Winchester does not refer only to the tonsure. It has sexual overtones (fornication, syphilis, virility, etc.), some of which go back to early oriental and western folklore. Among classical antecedents are a story in Macrobius about Augustus' daughter Julia, Suetonius' account of Caesar's sexuality and baldness, references in Phaedrus and Diodorus Siculus. The proximate source is, of course, Medieval; doubtless the fabliau is the meeting ground of bald priest and sexual irregularity. This is a learned philological study.

1056. Mustard, Wilfred P. "Virgil's Georgics and the British Poets," AJP, XXIX (1908), 1-32.

The passage on the commonwealth of the bees in H.V I ii is an illustration of Georgics IV 153ff. Mustard notes the "interesting parallel" between Virgil's "praetoria" and Sh's "tent-royal of their emperor."

1057. Nearing, Homer, Jr. "Julius Caesar and the Tower of London," MLN, LXIII (1948), 228-233.

Sh's two anachronistic references to Julius Caesar as the builder of the Tower of London (R.III III i 68-74; R.II V i 2) probably derive from Lydgate's Serpent of Division (1422), a life of Caesar. Reputable sixteenth-century historians disbelieved this fanciful story.

1058. Nearing, Homer, Jr. "The Legend of Julius Caesar's British Conquest," PMLA, LXIV (1949), 889-929. GRS

This is an erudite study of the evolution of various myths about Caesar's adventures in Britain: e.g., that he had a poisoned sword which he was forced to leave behind, that he had a stone "pavilion" which his men demolished and carried about in pieces when he traveled, that he succeeded in gaining a foothold in Britain only because of treason in the British ranks, that his motive in invading Britain was greed for the pearls of the Britons. Sh alludes to Caesar's invasion in the closing lines of John, in R.II (V i 2), R.III (III i 68-74), and in Cym. (see especially III i and also I i 28-30, II iv 20-23). Sh alludes to very few of the oddities of the legend; he, like his contemporaries, was more interested in Caesar's Roman affairs. Nearing does not discuss the question of consistency in Sh's attitude toward Caesar: e.g., in Cym. Sh voices the anti-Caesarian bias of the Britons; in R.III he has praise for Caesar, again by Britons.

1059. Nearing, Homer, Jr. "A Note on 'King John,' V,vii,112-114," NQ, CXCII (1947), 256-257.

The Bastard is referring in the last speech of the play to the "only" time England was conquered by an outsider, when Julius Caesar (after two fruitless attempts) finally conquered the island through the treasonable help of Androgeus, the Briton who defected to the Roman cause--indeed invited the Romans to invade. Sh's source would be The Mirror for Magistrates or one or more of the Elizabethan chroniclers. The original source is an anecdote told by Caesar himself [in De Bello Gallico V], but Geoffrey of Monmouth deserves the credit for preserving the story. Sh would regard William the Conqueror as a legitimate heir seeking his throne, and other invaders (Claudius, Hengest, et al.) have similar exonerations from the charge of being "conquerors." Nearing has found no comment on these lines: Post's note in MLN (1926) offers a more generalized interpretation of the lines and traces the thought to Sallust and Plato (#1069).

1060. Nel Mezzo. "'2 Henry IV.,' II.iv.21: Ulysses and Utis," 11 NQ, IV (1911), 83-84.

This note recalls the ingenious explanation given by Bishop Samuel Butler of the First Tapster's "By the mass, here will be old utis."

Butler thought the reference was to Ulysses' cleverness in disguising himself and his companions to escape from Polyphemus, and his concomitant adoption of the name "οὖτις." The reference is appropriate since the Prince and Poins are about to disguise themselves as tapsters to deceive Falstaff. Sh probably "had heard" the story of the Cyclops' cave. Nel Mezzo also points out the similarity between Ajax' pejorative reference to Ulysses as a fox in Sophocles' play and Thersites' appellation for him, "dog-fox," in *Troi.*, but he concludes that the conjunction could well be coincidental. A correspondent (ibid., p. 243) gives some later iterations of Butler's suggestion.

1061. Nel Mezzo. "'Richard II.,' III.ii.155-6: Sitting on the Ground," 11 *NQ*, I (1910), 165.

Parallels in Sophocles' *Trachiniae* and *Oedipus Coloneus*, the Book of Job, and a modern novelist to Richard's desire to "sit upon the ground." But none is a close parallel; in none of them does anyone "tell sad stories of the death of kings."

1062. Nosworthy, J. M. "The Integrity of Shakespeare: Illustrated From *Cymbeline*," *ShS*, VIII (1955), 52-56.

For the influence of Plutarch on the Chorus to *H.V* III, see #2267.

1063. Palmer, John. *Comedy* (The Art and Craft of Letters) (N.Y., [1914]), 64 pp.

The first half of this analysis of the English *vis comica* frequently refers to Falstaff as an Aristophanic character whose gross wit is our defense against the calamity of being imprisoned in flesh and blood. There are also brief remarks on *Troi.* as Sh's almost successful attempt "to write the pure comedy of reason."

1064. Parr, Johnstone. "Shakespeare's Artistic Use of Astrology," *Tamburlaine's Malady and Other Essays on Astrology in Elizabethan Drama* (Alabama UP, 1953), pp. 57-69.

Parr believes that Sh's knowledge of celestial augury was entirely superficial and that it is impossible to determine his own attitudes toward divination. Only one of the scores of Shn astrological references cited here appears to have been informed by a classical author: the vision of Edward and Richard (*3H.VI* II i) of the three suns in one heaven is "almost certainly" from Pliny's *Naturalis Historia.*

1065. Pearce, Josephine A. "Constituent Elements in Shakespeare's History Plays," *MiamiSS*, pp. 145-152.

Sh wrote his history plays at a time when the purpose of historiography was in flux between Cicero's doctrine of "history as the teacher of life" (i.e., as the interpreter of "providential causation") and the Raleigh-Bacon-Machiavelli doctrine that history has the "pragmatic value of the interpretation of human behavior." Sh therefore had no single set of fixed rules to follow; he found room for English chronicles, the mirror tradition, and classical rhetoric. Seneca influenced Sh not in materials, but in construction and decoration; the ghost in *R.III* V iii 132-139 is not Seneca's—it is Clarence's—but the rhetorical irony and rhetorical patterns are derived from Seneca. The conclusions here are well founded, if not startlingly original.

1066. Pearce, T. M. "The Braggart-Soldier in Jacobean Drama," *ShN*, II (1952), 36.

Sh appears briefly in this *précis* of a paper read at the Rocky Mountain MLA sixth annual meeting. Pistol and Bardolph are more Plautine than Falstaff, who, like the roaring boys of Sh's later contemporaries, is more an Englishman than a Roman.

1067. Platt, Isaac Hull. "'First Henry VI.' I. vi.6-7—" *NewShna*, III (1904), 65-68.

A somewhat sardonic critical review of the controversy over Sh's source for the gardens-of-Adonis passage in *1H.VI*. "Still so far as I can discover the passage in Plato is the only other one in which exactly the same characteristic [rapidity of fructification] is mentioned as is in Henry VI." With this statement Platt rejects Bacon's *Promus*, Erasmus' *Adagia*, and *FQ* III.

1068. Poel, William. "The Five Act Divisions in Henry V," *TLS*, October 6, 1927, p. 694. E-S

This letter suggests that Sh did not write the play with a five-act structure in mind, because in F_1 there is no choral prologue for Act IV and a Chorus in Act I is inserted disproportionately close to the Prologue to the play. The act divisions were made by Heminge and

Condell "as being in accordance with classical drama."

1069. Post, L. A. "Note on Shakespeare's King John," MLN, XLI (1926), 535.

The patriotic sentiment expressed in the last three lines of the play is traceable to Sallust's Ad Caesarem Senem de Republica Oratio. Post feels "practically certain" that Sallust borrowed the concept that a people can be defeated only by subversion, not by assault, from Plato's Menexenus which in Jowett's trans. is very similar to the Bastard's words. There is no suggestion that Sh owes either Sallust or Plato a direct debt.

1070. Price, Hereward T. "'Like Himself'," RES, XVI (1940), 178-181.

In reply to J. M. Robertson, who thought the phrase (H.V Prologue) unworthy of Sh, Price compiles a list of Elizabethan and later uses of the expression and its cognates. He begins with Whytynton (1532) and Erasmus (1534), where the phrase is a literal trans. of "sui similis." It gradually acquired the connotation of incomparability which the term carries in H.V.

1071. Price, Hereward T. "Shakespeare as a Critic," PQ, XX (1941), 390-399. (Also in Craig Festschrift, pp. 198-207.)

Price conceives Sh's criticism chiefly in the form of parody and Sh as the greatest parodist in English literature. At two points Price indicates Sh's use of the classics for parody: (1) in 2H.VI Suffolk, the self-important poser, is made to look a fool when he equates his capture by "pirates" (IV i) with famous analogues in classical history; (2) the integrity of Shrew is manifested by parallel passages in different styles like the use of classical analogy by sentimental Lucentio (I i 153-181) and by hard-boiled Petruchio (I ii 66-74).

1072. Pruvost, René. "Robert Greene a-t-il accusé Shakespeare de plagiat?" EA, XII (1959), 198-204.

Pruvost disagrees with Wilson's interpretation of the famous passage in A Groatsworth of Wit (#1116). He marshals evidence to support his contention that the feathers which the Aesopic/Horatian crow has "borrowed" here are the lines which an actor recites on stage (as in the H.VI plays), not the words or plots which a thieving playwright steals from another.

1073. R., V. "'Henry V.,' Act IV. Chorus:—," 11 NQ, IV (1911), 84.

This note cites Lydgate's Troy Book as evidence that by "umber'd face" Sh means "vizarded face." He suggests that the word may imply "shaded," from the Latin root.

1074. Radcliffe, W. "'And There Is Salmons in Both'," TLS, March 18, 1926, pp. 217-218.

Fluellen's remark about Macedonia (H.V IV vii 33) is patently false; salmon have never been known there. Indeed there is no reference to salmo in all of Greek literature, and in Latin only Pliny, Ausonius, and Sidonius refer to the species. Sh may just possibly have been confused by a reference to a speckled fish in Macedonian rivers in Aelian (the locus classicus of fly fishing). About Aelian Radcliffe accepts the counsel of W. Theobald (The Classical Element in the Shakespeare Plays), who is not deemed relevant to this Guide because of his Baconian affiliation (see supra, p. viii); Theobald is hardly a reliable authority on Sh's classicism. A more plausible hypothesis is that Sh has Fluellen refer to Macedonian salmon because it does not occur to a Welshman that rivers exist independent of salmon.

1075. Reeves, W. P. "The Gardens of Adonis," MLN, XVII (1902), 31.

Reeves points out references to the Garden in Colin Clout's Come Home Again and FQ II as well as iterating the usual identification of FQ III. Reeves also points to the earlier research of Frazer's Golden Bough and Gollancz's eds. of 1H.VI and Venus.

1076. Ribner, Irving. "The Tudor History Play: An Essay in Definition," PMLA, LXIX (1954), 591-609.

Ribner distinguishes two main streams of historiography, the Medieval and the humanist. The latter bears some considerable mark of its classical ancestry (e.g., history, in the judgment of Polybius, teaches men how to bear misfortune with calm of mind). Sh blends both streams in his history plays and also in his Roman plays which are histories as well as tragedies. Ribner's erudition is extensive; he ranges across a large body of primary and secondary material from Aeschylus and Herodotus to Tillyard. Among the most interesting passages is the discussion of the influences of tragedy and history on one another in antiquity and in the Renaissance. Sh's Cor. is, like his R.II, a successful attempt to write tragical history.

1077. Ross, Lawrence J. "The Meaning of Strawberries in Shakespeare," SR, VII (1960), 225-240.

Sh's three allusions to strawberries (H.V I i with reference to Hal; R.III III iv in the Hastings affair; Oth., on Desdemona's handkerchief) are not gratuitous. Each is meaningful if one recognizes that to the Elizabethans the fruit symbolized evil in a fair disguise; this emblematic meaning is traceable to Virgil's warning that snakes lurk beneath strawberry plants (Eclogues III). In Oth., the irony of the emblem is accentuated by the rival use of strawberries as symbolic of the Blessed Virgin—fruitful but chaste: in the minds of Iago and Othello the Virgilian symbol applies; in reality it is the Christian symbol which is valid for Desdemona. This is a valuable study.

1078. Round, P. Z. "A Classical Quotation in Henry VI," TLS, June 14, 1928, p. 450. SG

Round traces the Latin quotation "Gelidus timor occupat artus" (2H.VI IV i 117) to Lucan (Pharsalia I). But a week later (p. 468) Edgar I. Fripp (SG) shows that Sh could have more easily obtained the quotation from Ovid (Meta. III). Over a score of years earlier Fripp's point was made by Yardley (#1117).

1079. Royster, J. F. "Richard III, IV,4 and the Three Marys of the Medieval Drama," MLN, XXV (1910), 173-174. SG

Royster thinks this scene with its three lamenting women is an analogue closer to the three Marys of the Resurrection plays than to the Greek Chorus. Royster does not observe that the set speech of complaint is a stock device in pre-Shn tragedy (cf. Clemen, #0170); moreover, the tragedies of the 'eighties often grouped characters in threes (cf. David Bevington, From "Mankind" to Marlowe, HUP, 1962, Ch. XIV et passim).

1080. Savage, J. J. "'The Winter of Our Discontent'," CW, XXI (1928), 115.

The association of unhappiness and winter in Gloucester's mind (R.III I i 1) is in a literary tradition as old as the Phaenomena of Aratus, trans. by Cicero. Other Latin participants are Virgil and Marcus Manilius.

1081. Schanzer, Ernest. "Hercules Oetaeus and King John," NQ, CCI (1956), 509-510.

Schanzer points to the previously unnoticed connection between John's description of the effects of the "hot" poison within him (V vii 28-48) and Hercules' extravagant exclamation in a similarly agonizing situation. Studley's loose rendering of the Latin is in some specifics nearer to Sh than the original is. Schanzer's argument carries conviction.

1082. Schmidt, Karl. Margareta von Anjou vor und bei Shakespeare, Palaestra, LIV (1906), 286 pp. E-S SG

Schmidt discusses (p. 246) Asmath's ambiguous prophecy (2H.VI I iv). Sh "strengte seine Schulerinnerungen an . . . uns noch das Muster mitzugeben, nach dem er den Ausdruck bildete," the passage in Cicero's De Divinatione on the ambiguous prophecy made to Pyrrhus when he set out to war against the Romans. Schmidt also points (pp. 252-253) to interesting parallels between Margaret (more a man than her husband) and Seneca's Medea, whose vilification of her enemies may have influenced Sh's portrait of Margaret. Schmidt cautions against pushing the comparison too far.

1083. Sigismund, R[einhold]. "Ueber die Bedeutung des Mandrake bei Shakespeare, sowie über die historische Entwickelung dieses Begriffes," ShJ, XX (1885), 310-319.

This interesting study traces Sh's mandrakes (Romeo IV iii 48, 2H.VI III ii 310, 2H.IV I ii 17, III ii 339) as far back as "moly," the magical root which Hermes gave to Odysseus to protect him against Circe's witchcraft (Odyssey X). A survey of mystic plant lore in the ancient world includes references from Theophrastus, Pliny, and Aelian and from Egyptian, Persian, and Judaic writings. Sigismund remains uncertain where shrieking mandrakes and the madness or death they produce came into the tradition.

1084. Simpson, Percy. "The Theme of Revenge in Elizabethan Tragedy," PBA, XXI (1935), 101-136. (Annual British Academy Shakespeare Lecture.)

For R.III and the Senecan revenge play, see #2111.

1085. Sims, Ruth E. "The Green Old Age of Falstaff," BHM, XIII (1943), 144-157. GRS

This extensively documented study shows that Falstaff is portrayed as on the borderline between "green old age" (50 to 65 years) and "dotage" (65 years to death) in the divisions of man's life which go back to Galen, Hippocrates, Pythagoras, and Cicero's *De Senectute* (among other writers). The symptoms are largely humoral: i.e., the humor of "green old age" is choler, which is Falstaff's natural disposition, but he shows signs of melancholy, the humor of "dotage." At the same time, Falstaff feigns the sanguine humor which is associated with youth; he tries in vain to induce this youthful complexion by application of sweet wine (sugar and sack), which was believed to stall off the approaching "cold of age and melancholy." A convincing interpretation, which applies to *Wives* as well as to the last three Lancastrian plays.

1086. Spargo, John W. "An Interpretation of Falstaff," *WUS*, IX, No. 2 (1922), 119-133. (Heller Memorial Volume.)

Spargo objects to the identification of Falstaff with the *miles gloriosus* because, unlike the *miles*, Falstaff is not unquestionably a coward, not "antipathetic" to the author, not stupid, not unsuccessful in love, and not a braggart for personal glorification. Spargo interprets *1,2H.IV* as the struggle between Falstaff as Vice (Gluttony and Lechery) and the Lord Chief Justice as Virtue generally; Hal, Everyman, chooses correctly in the end as Everyman is expected to do in the Morality tradition. Spargo's view has been endorsed by many, but it ignores Falstaff's rôle as soldier and his polar opposition to Hotspur in *1H.IV*.

1087. Stampfer, Judah Leon. "Ideas of Order in Shakespeare's Histories and Tragedies," diss (Harvard, 1959).*

This diss is presumed to consider classical ideas of order.

1088. Starnes, D[eWitt] T. "Shakespeare and Elyot's *Governour*," *TSE*, VII (1927), 112-132.

Starnes suggests (116-132) Elyot as the source for the Platonic concepts of order expressed in *H.V* I ii, Ulysses' "degree" speech (*Troi.* I iii), and Coriolanus' arguments against majority rule in *Cor.* III i. For the first two passages Baldwin (#0089, II, 472-479) prefers Willichius' commentary on Virgil's *Georgics* as source at least for the figure of the bees. Others have found Plato (#1374), or Hooker's *Laws of Ecclesiastical Polity*, or even Rabelais attractive. For comprehensive surveys of the question, see Gayley (#1331) and especially Baldwin (#1141). For an objection to Starnes's view on *Cor.*, see #1229.

1089. Steadman, John M. "Falstaff's 'Facies Hippocratica': A Note on Shakespeare and Renaissance Medical Theory," *StN*, XXIX (1957), 130-135.

Steadman gives a learned survey of Renaissance medical opinion on the ῥίς ὀξεῖα or "sharpnesse of the nosethrils" which Hippocrates placed first in his list of symptoms of approaching death. Oddly, however, he regards the relationship between the *Prognostica* and the Hostess' description as a subject given "superficial" treatment by Sh scholars (see index, s.v. "Hippocrates"); he further incorporates Theobald's emendation (quoting from Dover Wilson's ed.) without comment and he believes that the sharp nose was the only detail from Hippocrates which Sh borrowed.

1090. Steadman, John M. "'Perseus upon Pegasus' and *Ovid Moralized*," *RES*, IX (1958), 407-410. GRS

This note points to fourteenth- and fifteenth-century moralizing commentaries on Ovid as precedents for the common Renaissance belief that Perseus rode Bellerophon's horse Pegasus. Steadman notes that Bellerophon had a disastrous fall from his horse and therefore "comparison with Bellerophon could confer no credit on a horseman." Sh, like Jonson and Peele, wished to praise a horseman by using the Pegasus allusion (*Troi.* IV v 185-187; *H.V* III vii 13-17, 21-22), so he placed Perseus on the horse.

1091. [Steele, Richard]. *The Tatler*, No. 47 (July 28, 1709).

Part of this number concerns the great merit Sh has of expressing sorrow rather than describing it (cf. Addison, #0062). The example given is Northumberland's simile (*2H.IV* I i 68-75) comparing his (probable) loss of his son to Priam's discovery of Troy in flames. When Hotspur's death is confirmed Northumberland abandons both the classics and rhetoric to vent his anguish in simpler terms.

1092. Stemplinger, Eduard. *Horaz im Urteil*

der Jahrhunderte, Erbe, Zweite Reihe, H. V (Leipzig, 1921), 212 pp.

Stemplinger hears echoes of the Odes in 3H.VI (Warwick's dying realization: "My parks, my walks, my manors that I had, / Even now forsake me" V ii 24) and in Antony (Antony's threat that in Caesar's triumph Cleopatra will "Most monster-like be shown / For poor'st diminutives . . ."), and of Satire II in "The Alps [which] doth spit and void his rheum upon [the valleys]" (H.V III v 52). The other comments on Sh are brief and general. DLC

1093. Stoll, E[lmer] E[dgar]. "Falstaff," Shakespeare Studies: Historical and Comparative in Method (N.Y., 1927), pp. 403-490. E-S

See Section 8 (427-431) for a terse, but effective analysis of the features of the miles gloriosus and Falstaff's participation in them. The section is based on Stoll's 1914 art. in MP. Brief as Stoll's treatment of the miles is, it has earned him the reputation of being chief of the partisans of Latin comedy as a source for Falstaff.

1094. Stronach, G[eorge]. "Shakespeare's Knowledge," Acad, LX (1901), 111.

Stronach cites Adonis' garden of 1H.VI as evidence that Sh could read Greek; to his knowledge only the Phaedrus in pre-Shn literature alludes to this mythical fertile spot. A. Lang supplies a reference to Frazer's Golden Bough (ibid., p. 130) which cites Theophrastus, Gregorius Cyprian, "and others." Stronach points out (ibid., p. 193) that Frazer's authorities were all in Latin or Greek in the sixteenth century, but at the same place notes Spenser's description in FQ III vi. At ibid., p. 236, an American correspondent observes that the N.Y. Sh Society debated the question with Baconian coloring in 1894.

1095. Thompson, A. Hamilton. "Introduction," The Tragedy of King Richard the Third (1907/1932), ArdenSh, pp. vii-xxxi.

The tendency of this introduction is to minimize the relationship of R.III to the classical tradition; Thompson notes the paucity of classical allusions, denies that a meaningful Nemesis (in the Greek sense) is operative, and considers irrelevant any comparison between Margaret and "the models of antique tragedy." He does admit the influence of Senecanism, but suggests that the woodenness of the play is a product of the influence.

1096. Thompson, Dorothy B. "The Colossus at Rhodes," SQ, II (1951), 270.

For Sh's reference to the Colossus in 1H.IV, see #1727.

1097. Thümmel, Julius. "Der Miles Gloriosus bei Shakespeare," ShJ, XIII (1878), 1-12. E-S HB

This Vortrag makes two provocative suggestions: (1) Sh combined the Roman miles with the gnatho and colored the result with touches from the licensed fool of English tradition: the result is that Sh's boastful soldiers (Falstaff, Don Armado, Parolles, Pistol) are also parasites who play the fool for their bread. Falstaff is wise enough to play the fool in 1,2H.IV, while the other three are fools natural. (2) Sh may have had Plautus' Miles Gloriosus specifically in his recollection when he wrote Wives. Thümmel also offers a brief but thoughtful survey of the braggart soldier from Aristophanes' Acharnians through Menander and Philemon to Plautus and Terence and on into Western European literature.

1098. Tolman, Albert H. "Shakespeare Studies III: The Epic Character of Henry V," MLN, XXXIV (1919), 7-16.

A defense of the play as deliberately nondramatic. Sh sought to convey epic scope and the heroic ideal of kingship; his play is in the manner of the Iliad, the Aeneid, and Paradise Lost. Tolman makes no detailed comparisons with the classical epics.

1099. Trapp, J. B. "['The Garden of the World']," TLS, December 5, 1952, p. 797. GRS

Trapp responds to a query (ibid., p. 732) by giving (inter alia) Plutarch's De Facie in Orbe Lunae (XXVI) as an analogue to Sh's reference to England as a "demi-paradise" (R.II II i 42). Plutarch alludes to Ireland as a mild and fragrant island where Cronus sleeps.

1100. Tyler, Parker. "Phaethon: The Metaphysical Tension between the Ego and the Universe in English Poetry," Accent, XVI (1956), 29-44.

Under this inclusive title, Tyler deals chiefly with R.II, which he interprets as (in part) a reflection of classical mythology: the Prometheus/Phaethon/Icarus theme, in which he who aspires to the prerogatives of the gods must fall through Nemesis. Tyler, who bases his argument on Richard's comparison of himself to Phaethon in III iii 178-179, does not observe that Richard's simile is more appropriate to Bolingbroke than to himself, especially if one conceives of the Lancastrian tetralogy as a unit, for Bolingbroke, like Phaethon, tried to take the place of the Sun/king, and though he was more successful than Phaethon, 1H.IV and 2H.IV are the Nemesis of his hybris.

1101. Ure, Peter. "Introduction," King Richard II (1956), ArdenSh, pp. xiii-lxxxiii.

In passing, p. liii, Ure mentions Leon's art. (#1040) on the classical background of III iv and iterates the suggestion that the simile, "like an executioner, / Cut off the heads of too fast growing sprays / That look too lofty in our commonwealth," is of classical origin. "It seems likely that the classical echo did not originate the analogy [in R.II] but only helped to consolidate it." At p. liv: Sh's use of vegetation for analogical purposes here owes something ultimately to Plato, despite Socrates' insistence that urbanized man is more worthy than nature of study.

1102. Walter, J. H. "Introduction," King Henry V (1954/1960), ArdenSh, pp. xi-xlvii.

Walter argues convincingly that Sh's Henry partakes of the qualities of ideal kingship which were first treated by Isocrates and which were much discussed in the Renaissance. The scope, theme, and hero of the play all are epic: the qualities which Henry shares with Virgil's Aeneas, "rectitude and uprightness, ...stoicism, ...[and] unswerving obedience to the Divine Will" have "laid them both open to charges of priggishness and inhumanity." And "Dido and Falstaff are sacrifices to a larger morality they both ignore." The Introduction contains several other interesting comments on the relevance of the classics to H.V.

1103. Webb, Henry J. "English Translations of Caesar's Commentaries in the Sixteenth Century," PQ, XXVIII (1949), 490-495. GRS

In passing Webb points out that Clement Edmondes' Observations Upon the Five First Bookes of Caesars Commentaries (1600) "was a military book such as Shakespeare's Fluellen might have read." It sided with the theorists in the Elizabethan "controversy over experience versus precept and example in education." The book appeared, of course, a year too late for Fluellen to have studied it.

1104. White, Richard G[rant]. "Glossaries and Lexicons," Studies in Shakespeare (Boston, 1886), pp. 280-363.

White, in his characteristic dogmatic fashion, asserts Sh's knowledge of Plato's Phaedrus (pp. 296-297) and Alcibiades I (298-299). The first assertion is based on 1H.VI I vi 6-7; the second on Troi. III iii 102-111 and Caesar I ii 52-53. The implication is that Sh knew Plato better than did either Spenser or Milton.

1105. [Whyte, Samuel]. "Progress of Plagiarism, III," The Monthly Mirror, II (1796), 336-340.

Whyte ends his comment on Sh's indebtedness to other writers with a very close parallel between Ulpius Trajan and the words of Hal to the Chief Justice as he mounts the throne (see #0969). MnU

1106. Wilder, M. L. "Shakespeare's 'Small Latin'," MLN, XL (1925), 380-381. SG

Wilder points to Seneca the Elder as a source for two passages in 1H.IV. G. L. Kittredge (ibid., p. 440. SG) tersely points to alternative and more accessible sources.

1107. Wilhelm, Friedrich. "Zu Seneca und Shakespeare ('Richard III.')," Archiv, CXXIX (1912), 69-73. E-S SG

Because the research of Cunliffe and Fischer has made plain the extent of Senecan influence on Elizabethan drama before Sh, we must always consider the possibility that Sh borrowed indirectly. The scene (I ii) where Richard woos Anne is based ultimately on Hercules Furens 329-523 where Lycus, the murderous enemy of Megara, woos her after the (supposed) death of Hercules. However, the key elements are also in Legge's Ricardus Tertius (1573), and if we assume that Sh supplemented Legge with Seneca's Phaedra we can accept Legge as the direct source. That Sh saw in performance (and remembered) a neo-Latin play seems at least as unlikely as that he read Hercules Furens in school or afterwards.

1108. Williams, Philip. "The Birth and Death of Falstaff Reconsidered," SQ, VIII (1957), 359-365.

In the course of a defense of J. I. M. Stewart against E. E. Stoll's vigorous attack,

Williams emphasizes the psycho-anthropological substratum of the Lancastrian plays. Falstaff is a substitute for Hal's father, and as Jove displaced Saturn, Hal must displace his father figure, Falstaff, by rejecting him so that the land may be ritually purified and the hero-king can bring new life to it. This is surely a strained interpretation of the Henriad.

1109. Wilson, J. Dover. "Falstaff High on Fortune's Wheel," The Fortunes of Falstaff (CUP, 1943), Ch. V, pp. 82-113.

In the section (82-88) entitled "The Classical Braggart and the Old Soldier," Wilson denies Stoll's thesis that Falstaff is essentially a miles gloriosus. Emphasizing that in Latin comedy the braggart was not only a coward, but ignorant of war besides, Wilson emphasizes that in the ways of Elizabethan war Falstaff is very wise. Falstaff "is ready to play the part [of miles gloriosus], after Gad's Hill and again at Shrewsbury, for the Prince's amusement" but he would be recognized by Sh's audience as an Old Soldier, "one they often met in the field and at the tavern." Wilson appears to be hedging in trying to make Falstaff simultaneously a miles and not a miles.

1110. W[ilson], J. D[over]. "Introduction," The First Part of "King Henry VI" (1952), CSh, [XX], pp. xi-l.

"That trick of bookish window-dressing, so common with the 'university wits', so alien to the mind of Shakespeare," is common enough in 1H.VI to convince Wilson that Nashe and Greene had a hand in the play, Greene a major one. Sh's rôle was that of reviser, but the original, classical "window-dressing" shows through.

1111. W[ilson], J. D[over]. "Introduction," King Henry V (1947), CSh, [XIX], pp. vii-xlvii.

In passing (pp. xii-xiii): Sh treated his national hero in an epic form in which, despite digressions, Henry "dominates the play as Aeneas dominates the Aeneid." Later (p. xxxi) Wilson compares Agincourt to (inter alia) Thermopylae.

1112. W[ilson], J. D[over]. "Introduction," Richard III (1954), CSh, [XXIII], pp. vii-xlv.

Wilson speaks of R.III as a successful Senecan melodrama and he summarizes and praises Moulton's analysis of Nemesis in the play (#0429).

1113. W[ilson], J. D[over]. "Introduction to Henry VI, Parts II and III," The Second Part of "King Henry VI" (1952), CSh, [XXI], pp. vii-liii.

Wilson reiterates the argument of "Malone and the Upstart Crow" (#1116). In another passage he would assign Jack Cade's assertion that "Lord Say hath gelded the commonwealth and made it an eunuch" (2H.VI IV ii 174-175) to Nashe; Nashe refers elsewhere to Talaeus' Rhetorica which quotes Cicero's De Oratore on the subject of castrated commonwealths. The many other specialized or obscure classical allusions in the three parts of H.VI Wilson would assign to Greene, who was "in artibus magister," while the superficial or erroneous allusions in the plays may still be attributed to Sh--Wilson asserts that Sh's classical learning "at this early date" was mainly drawn from Chaucer's LGW and Golding's Meta. See pp. l-liii for Wilson's analysis of several of the allusions. Wilson is unaware of the superficiality of Greene's own classicism: see the unpublished diss by James Earl Applegate, "Classical Allusions in the Prose Works of Robert Greene" (Johns Hopkins, 1954), a thorough study which shows that much of Greene's learning was secondhand, plagiarized, or even invented.

1114. W[ilson], J. D[over]. "Introduction to Henry VI Parts II and III," The Third Part of "King Henry VI" (1952), CSh, [XXII], pp. vii-xxxviii.

In passing Wilson observes that the Yorkist tetralogy portrays the downward turning of Fortune's wheel for the house of Lancaster as the Lancastrian tetralogy portrays the upward turning. The wheels of Fortune and of Time come "full circle" in the eight plays.

1115. W[ilson], J. D[over]. "King Richard II: Introduction," King Richard II (1939), CSh, [XVI], pp. vii-lxxvi.

Wilson regards the wheel of Fortune (which is nowhere overtly mentioned in R.II) as a key to the plot structure (Richard falls as Bolingbroke rises) and to the moral structure (Bolingbroke is not to be seen as flagrantly guilty; "he takes what Fortune and Richard throw in his path" and "is an opportunist, not a schemer").

1116. Wilson, J. Dover. "Malone and the Upstart Crow," ShS, IV (1951), 56-68.

In his Dissertation on the Three Parts of Henry VI (1790), Edmond Malone expressed the belief that Greene's reference to Sh as an "upstart Crow, beautified with our feathers" can be taken as evidence that Greene thought Sh plagiarized in the H.VI plays. That view, held for over a century, has been challenged by Greg, Alexander, and others in recent decades. Wilson maintains that Malone was correct, because the "crow" is not Aesop's only, but also Horace's cornicula of the third Epistle in which he attacks literary plagiarism. "Horace's crow and Aesop's were so closely associated in readers' minds in Shakespeare's day" that Greene's meaning would be unmistakable. Wilson's thesis comes under fire from Janet Spens (TLS, June 15, 1951, p. 373), who points out that both Horace's crow and Aesop's were beautified with the feathers of a variety of other birds: ergo Greene did not accuse Sh of wholesale theft, but of derivative writing. Dr. Spens also emphasizes the point made in Wilson's footnote that Chettle's supposed apology to Sh contains a deliberate comparison of Sh to Virgil (the observation is originally due to an unpublished comment of J. A. K. Thomson). Wilson replies with vigor ibid., p. 405. See also ibid., p. 501, 517. Sidney Thomas (MLN, LXVI [1951], 483-484) does not discuss the classical basis, but supports Wilson's position on Greene's meaning. See #1072, #0986 for dissent.

1117. Yardley, E. "'Henry VI.,' Part II, IV. i.:—" 10 NQ, VI (1906), 324. SG

Yardley proposes Meta. III as the source of Suffolk's "Gelidus timor occupat artus"; many commentators have thought Sh was misquoting a line from Aeneid VII.

1118. Yates, Frances A. "Queen Elizabeth as Astraea," JWCI, X (1947), 27-82.

For the appropriateness of Charles's identification of Joan of Arc with Astraea in 1H.VI, see #1796.

THE PLAYS ON CLASSICAL THEMES

1119. Adams, Joseph Quincy. "The Timon Plays," JEGP, IX (1910), 506-524. HB SG

Adams discusses the sources of the three English Renaissance dramatizations of the Timon legend: Beaumont and Fletcher's Triumph of Time, the academic Timon (which Adams thinks was written for schoolboys, not for university production), and Sh's Tim. In Section III it is pointed out that Sh used everything in the Plutarch version, several nonclassical details which must have come from the academic Timon or from its sources, and a single detail (the incident of the dowry) which appears in Lucian's Misanthropos but nowhere else. Thus, it appears probable that Sh knew (1) Plutarch's brief version, (2) the academic play, (3) Lucian (but only indirectly, since Sh omits a wealth of Lucian's incident which could effectively be dramatized), (4) Painter, possibly—there is little evidence on this last point, for Painter was drawing on Plutarch as Sh was. An excellent brief essay.

1120. Addis, John. "'Fortune': Chaucer and Shakespeare," 4 NQ, IX (1872), 339.

For the Goddess Fortuna as a "housewife" in Antony, see #0672.

1121. Addis, John. "'Troilus and Cressida', Act IV., Sc. 5, l. 59," 3 NQ, XII (1867), 122-123.

Addis discusses briefly the merits of the F_1 reading "a coasting welcome" and Theobald's emendation "accosting welcome." The Latin root costa will serve for both terms. Addis is inclined toward the F_1 reading.

1122. [Addison?; Steele?]. The Tatler, No. 53 (August 11, 1709).

This number praises Sh for portraying Caesar in his dressing gown at home where he appears "a great soul." With only his wife for audience, Caesar need not pose; he appears as a man, not as a public figure. This view is counter to the usual modern view of the thrasonical Caesar.

1123. Adler, Fritz. "Das Verhältniss von Shakespeare's 'Antony and Cleopatra' zu Plutarch's Biographie des Antonius," ShJ, XXXI (1895), 263-317. E-S

A detailed seriatim comparison of play and source in the manner of Delius (#1256, #1257). Adler explores the extent of Sh's reliance on Plutarch for incidents, characterization, and language, and concludes for Antony as Delius does for Cor. and Caesar "'dass Shakespeare der Plutarchischen Biographie quantitativ wie qualitativ weit weniger zu verdanken hat als man gewöhnlich anzunehmen geneigt ist'." The most interesting section is the third, in which Adler scrutinizes some of the minute alterations which Sh made in North's language—sometimes compressing, sometimes vivifying, always improving. The second section is also of interest, as it shows that Sh clearly departs from Plutarch in his conception of the principals; there are also briefer comments on Octavia (whom Sh pushes into the background), Octavius (very much Plutarch's cold politician), and Enobarbus (only a name in Plutarch), as well as other minor characters. An interesting study, but Adler's eagerness to underline Sh's creative genius tempts him to minimize the significant indebtedness of Antony to North's trans.

1124. Aldus, Paul J. "Analogical Probability

NOTE: Numbers preceded by # refer to entries in this Guide. Keys to abbreviations are found on pages xi-xvii and 381-387.

in Shakespeare's Plays," SQ, VI (1955), 397-414.

Following the lead of H. T. Price (#0466) and others who have stressed structural analysis of the plays, Aldus analyzes scenes to show their mirror-like reflection of the total action of the plays they appear in. The most interesting and convincing argument is that Flavius and Marullus in Caesar I i are adumbrations of the conspirators in their desire to strip Caesar of honors; at the same time they persuade like Antony and (though Aldus does not mention it) they are, like the conspirators, "put to silence" by Caesar's power. A less convincing attempt to find Actium mirrored in the revels on Pompey's galley meets with an acid rejection by L. J. Mills (SQ, VII [1956], 133), who offers an equally unsatisfactory reading of the last part of the scene. See also Aldus' lively reply (loc. cit.).

1125. Allen, Joseph C. "The Julius Caesar of Shakespeare and of History," PL, XIII (1901), 560-575.

A scornful précis of Sh's character, who is a distorted exaggeration of depreciatory hints in Plutarch. Taking his standard from Mommsen's encomium of the historical Caesar, Allen asserts that Sh's Caesar "differs from the real personage as much as a pug differs from a mastiff." Sh's ignorance of classical history is much to blame in this, but so are the Elizabethan Zeitgeist and Sh's desire for dramatic contrast between Brutus and Caesar.

1126. Allinson, Francis G. "Lucian's Creditors and Debtors," Lucian: Satirist and Artist, Our Debt, [No. 8] (N.Y., 1927), Ch. VIII, pp. 121-187.

For Lucian in Tim. see #1806.

1127. Andersen, Donald K., Jr. "Shakespeare's Use of Plutarch in Julius Caesar," ShN, II (1952), 20.

This précis of a paper given at the Ninth Annual Renaissance Meeting at Duke University (1951) suggests that Sh's primary source for Caesar was the "Life of Brutus" and that the "Life of Caesar" only provided details which Sh subordinated.

1128. Arnold, Aerol. "The Hector-Andromache Scene in Shakespeare's Troilus and Cressida," MLQ, XIV (1953), 335-340.

Arnold believes that (1) Tatlock was incorrect in saying that Sh added V iii to the legend--both Caxton and Lydgate provide Sh his materials, including Andromache's dream, Hector's inflexibility, and the vain intercession of other members of the family; (2) Sh deliberately avoided Homer's poignancy in the parting scene because he did not want Hector to seem anything but honor-bound; when Hector is killed Troilus recognizes the inadequacy of honor as a battle motif and himself adopts revenge as his raison de se battre. About this second point there is some room for disagreement; it hinges on the possibly fallacious assumption that Troilus is the protagonist of the play.

1129. Ayres, H. M. "Shakespeare's 'Julius Caesar' in the light of some other Versions," PMLA, XXV (1910), 183-227. E-S SG

Where Sh differs from Plutarch in his conception of Caesar, the difference is traceable to the conventional sixteenth-century interpretation (e.g., Muret's Caesar, "carefully modelled on the braggart Hercules of Seneca"), but Plutarchian Stoicism remains to dignify the character. This is an erudite and convincing art.

1130. Azzalino, Walther. "Stilkundliche Betrachtung der Reden des Brutus und des Antonius in Shakespeares 'Julius Caesar' (III, 2)," NM, XI (1940), 249-271. GRS

A close reading of the two Forum speeches to show that Sh characterizes Brutus and Antony and distinguishes them from each other by the grammar and rhetoric they use. As one might expect, Azzalino treats chiasmus, rhetorical questions, and verbal repetition, but he also considers epithetical adjectives and even the use of particles ("the"). A convincing analysis which shows precisely how Antony's speech achieves its emotional impact while Brutus' remains abstract, neutral utterance. The only discussion of the classical background contrasts Brutus' oratory with Cicero's, in which irony plays a larger rôle. TxU

1131. B., A. "An Echo of the 'Paragone' in Shakespeare," JWCI, II (1938-39), 260-262.

In passing: the Poet in Tim. indicates that his allegorical poem portrays Fortune enthroned on a hill (I i 63-89). Sh here participates in a tradition which goes as far back as the Greek painter Apelles of Colophon (fourth century B.C.), whose Fortuna sedens is mentioned by Stobaeus.

1132. Bacon, J. R. "Plautus and Posterity," CAP, XXXIII (1936), 37-38. (A summary of an address.)

For an unspecified echo of Plautus in Caesar, see #0679. MnU

1133. Baildon, H. Bellyse. "Introduction," The Lamentable Tragedy of Titus Andronicus (1904), ArdenSh, pp. ix-lxxxiv.

A generally effective (if repetitive) argument for Sh's authorship of Titus, and a defense of the play on aesthetic and ethical grounds. Oddly, Baildon pays almost no heed to the classical element in the play: he considers classical allusions gratuitous—a sign of Sh's immaturity—but he places Titus with Euripides' Medea and Aeschylus' Agamemnon, plays which raise the gruesome to tragic heights. The most interesting feature of this introduction is its perceptive comparisons of Titus with Lear, Cor., Ham., and (especially) Dream.

1134. Baker, Arthur E. A Shakespeare Commentary (N.Y., 1938/1957), 2 vols., 965 pp. [continuous pagination].

This students' reference book gives for fifteen of the plays (among other things) a discussion of sources (with selections from them), character explication, and explanation of allusions (many of them classical). The usefulness of Baker's work for students of Sh's classicism is sharply limited by the fact that of plays with unquestioned classical bases, only Caesar is treated, but the discussion of the historical figures portrayed in the play is of value.

1135. Baker, Donald C. "The Purging of Cleopatra," ShN, X (1960), 9.

Baker believes that the Clown's sexual puns in Antony V ii are an epitome and a purge of Cleopatra's sexual language earlier in the play. Once the Clown has summed up Cleopatra's sexuality, the Queen is free to leave her base elements to base life and to indulge in immortal longings. This is an interesting explanation of V ii, but it seems equally possible that the Clown's language reminds us that we are witnessing the death of a woman whose sexuality is her chief characteristic.

1136. Baker, George P. "'Tittus and Vespacia' and 'Titus and Ondronicus' in Henslowe's Diary," PMLA, XVI (1901), 66-76.

Baker elaborates the theory of Fuller (#1326) that these two plays were combined artfully by Sh into Titus. They are (according to both Fuller and Baker) respectively the sources of the German play and the Dutch play which now survive. Baker's major emphasis falls on the probable theatrical history of the two plays before Sh united them.

1137. Baker, Howard. "The Spanish Tragedy, Titus Andronicus and Senecanism," Induction to Tragedy: A Study in a Development of Form in Gorboduc, The Spanish Tragedy and Titus Andronicus (LSU Press, 1939), Ch. III, pp. 106-153.

Part ii of this ch. is a vigorous assault on J. W. Cunliffe's ascription (#0193) to Seneca of major influence on Titus. The primary source of the plot is Ovid's tale of Philomel (Meta. VI) available and popular in Gower, Chaucer, Pettie, Gascoigne, and Golding. There may have been some hints from Virgil, but of Seneca no trace (except two inconsequential tags from the Phaedra). Nor can Seneca be assigned such elements as act-division, ghosts, rant, revenge, and sensational horrors; they are all Medieval, not Senecan. The remainder of Baker's book extends this argument to militate against Senecan influence in Elizabethan drama generally. This extreme view is not now widely accepted—nor should it be: Sidney's Apologie for Poesie and Nashe's Preface to Greene's Menaphon both indicate that the Elizabethans thought they were imitating Seneca. A compromise between Baker and the unrestrained "Senecans" may approximate the truth. See H. W. Wells (#2162) for such a view.

1138. Bald, R. C. "Shakespeare and Daniel," TLS, November 20, 1924, p. 776.

Bald traces the "strong Egyptian fetters" which imprison Antony in Antony I ii 120-121 to Daniel's Argument to the "Letter from Octavia." The attribution has since been generally accepted.

1139. B[aldwin, T. W.] "Faculty Psychology in Troilus and Cressida," New Variorum Troi., pp. 416-418.

A close-packed treatment of some of the passages in the play where Sh gives his audience a clue to his attitude by "diagnosis" of characters through the system of psychology in which the senses and the imagination (common sense) must be in balance to permit "discourse of reason." Sir John Davies' Nosce Teipsum is Baldwin's Elizabethan key for interpreting Troi.

1140. Baldwin, T. W. "Structural Analysis

of Troilus and Cressida," Mutschmann Festschrift, pp. 5-18. (Condensed by the author in the New Variorum Troi., pp. 450-454.)

An analysis of the play with sixteenth-century dramatic theory as a guide shows that the main thread is the death of Hector and that the Troilus/Cressida plot is an appurtenance which doesn't even appear in Act II. Key events in the Greek and Trojan camps end each act and are balanced against each other to focus attention on the approaching catastrophe of Hector's death. Baldwin thinks that Pandarus' promise of more in two months is to be taken seriously, i.e., that "the author" (Baldwin refrains from blessing the play with Sh's name) intended to write a second play on the death of Troilus and the leprous fate of Cressida and possibly a third on the death of Achilles. Such a scheme would have fulfilled the conventional course of the Troy story (as found in Cooper's Thesaurus and Heywood's Iron Age, e.g.). Baldwin believes that Troi. is indebted to Chaucer for the Troilus/Cressida plot and to Book II of the Iliad colored by Medieval points of view for the main plot. The ingenious theory that the play is only the first of two or even of three parts accounts for such seeming irrelevancies as Polyxena, but it is difficult to accept the lovers as superficial padding, especially in the light of their importance in traditional literature.

1141. B[aldwin, T. W.] "[Ulysses on 'Degree': I.iii.84-141]," New Variorum Troi., pp. 399-410.

An admirably compact and detailed exploration of the "literary genetics" of the famous speech. Baldwin treats it as a structured argument and shows that a germ in Iliad II may have been expanded in "our author's" mind by accretions from Cicero's Tusculans, Virgil's Georgics, Ovid's Meta. I (the account of chaos), Chaucer, and probably Lydgate. The Hesiod-Plato tradition, with its "mystic" belief in love as the organizing principle in the universe, is notably absent—Ulysses instead stresses degree as the cohesive force—this emphasis he shares with Chapman's Iliad. Baldwin self-consciously refrains from attributing the passage to Sh and emphasizes that if Sh did write it, he was somewhat out of character in doing so, since his usual inclination is to Hesiod-Plato's love, not to Chapman-Lydgate's "degree."

1142. Barker, Ernest. "A Shakespeare Discovery," The Spectator, CLVIII (1937), 615-616. SG

The immediate source of Sh's classical concept in Ulysses' "degree" speech (Troi. I iii 75-137) is Elyot's Governour I and II. Barker's finding is a rediscovery; J. M. Robertson called Elyot the ultimate source twenty-four years before in The Baconian Heresy (#0489), pp. 204-206, and Starnes (#1088) also anticipated Barker.

1143. Barnet, Sylvan. "Recognition and Reversal in Antony and Cleopatra," SQ, VIII (1957), 331-334.

Two of Aristotle's ingredients for tragedy, anagnorisis and peripeteia, can be found in Antony. Antony kills himself (peripeteia) when the false news of Cleopatra's death causes him to recognize (anagnorisis) the love he had not entirely comprehended in himself before. Similarly, Antony's death gives Cleopatra insight (anagnorisis) into "the high Roman fashion" and she too cheats Caesar (peripeteia) of his victory. The Aristotelian criteria appear to fit Cleopatra better than Antony.

1144. Barroll, J. Leeds. "Antony and Pleasure," JEGP, LVII (1958), 708-720.

Antony's tragic flaw is "Pleasure," the Elizabethan term for the common conjunction of vices: sloth, gluttony, and lechery. To emphasize this flaw, Sh repeatedly departs from his source in Plutarch. Barroll does his usual thorough job of documenting the Elizabethan background, and his interpretation of the play accounts for such elements as the juxtaposition of food and sexuality in the imagery. But Barroll's thesis leads to the inevitable identification of Antony with a Morality abstraction; in his last sentence Barroll attempts to extricate Antony from this predicament, and in so doing virtually negates his preceding argument.

1145. Barroll, J. Leeds. "Enobarbus' Description of Cleopatra," TSE, XXXVII (1958), 61-78.

With massive documentation, Barroll places Enobarbus' portrait (II ii 196-245) in the Renaissance tradition of voluptas-descriptions. Sh expected his audience to see Cleopatra at this point in the play as a sort of Aphrodite-Omphale symbol, representing the kind of life which Antony is drawn to, but is capable of transcending. Antony's tragedy is that, like Hercules, he succumbs to voluptas despite his obvious capability of self-denial. Sh, of course, characterizes Cleopatra, and the last act is entirely hers, but the symbolic interpretation of the play lends added depth to Antony's catastrophe. A very interesting argument; Barroll is most convincing when he discusses the rationale of Enobarbus' speech in the light of his character and of dramatic consistency in the whole play.

1146. Barroll, J. Leeds. "Scarrus and the Scarred Soldier," HLQ, XXII (1958), 31-39.

Barroll adduces evidence for the identity (in Antony) of Scarus and the Soldier, both of whom are scarred and neither of whom appears in Plutarch. If they are one, and only misleading stage directions make them seem two, then the rôle gains in importance as an emphatic commentary on Antony's fortunes, for which reason Sh added it to his source materials. (Scarus is from Appian.)

1147. Barroll, J. L[eeds]. "Shakespeare and Roman History," diss (Princeton, 1956). DA, XVII (1957), 626-627.

A study of Antony and Caesar as Sh's response to classical, Medieval, and Renaissance interpretations of the Roman civil wars.

1148. Barroll, J. Leeds. "Shakespeare and Roman History," MLR, LIII (1958), 327-343.

A comprehensive, but detailed survey of the backgrounds (classical, Medieval, and Renaissance) of Elizabethan concepts of Roman history at the time of Augustus, with brief remarks about Sh's reflection of those concepts in Caesar and Antony. As always, Barroll is in thorough command of his materials, both primary and secondary; this is a valuable piece of scholarship.

1149. Batchelder, Merrit C. "The Elizabethan Elements in Shakespeare's Troilus and Cressida," diss (Iowa, 1935).*

1150. Bates, E. F. "Aristotle and Moral Philosophy," 10 NQ, I (1904), 405.

Bates cites lines from Beaumont and Fletcher's Valentinian which say a young man "should not dare to read / His moral books, till after five-and-twenty." At p. 472 John Wainewright denies that Aristotle has been misinterpreted in Troi. or by Bacon. (Sh's reference to Aristotle, young men, and moral philosophy is at Troi. II ii 165-167.)

1151. [Bathurst, Charles]. "Coriolanus"; "Antony and Cleopatra," Remarks on the Differences in Shakespeare's Versification in Different Periods of His Life and on the Like Points of Difference in Poetry Generally. (Ln, 1857), pp. 126-130 [reprinted in the New Variorum Cor.]; 130-134.

The poetry of Cor. comes under the domination of North's prose, a "stiffening" influence. Another strain on the poetry is the great store of "dry thought" which Jonson's example encouraged Sh to acquire. The intellectual tenor of the play defeats characterization as it does in Tim. and Troi., which are like Cor. also in the difficulty of their verse. Antony has less "crampness" except "in the political parts." Plutarch's anecdotal style accounts for the lack of dignity in the play as well as for its "looser and softer character." Plutarch did not, however, inspire Sh's Cleopatra, whose "passions are those of a mere ordinary woman, who has no respect for herself." Sh elevates Antony to a level of which the historical Antony was not worthy. DFo

1152. Baumgarten, Eduard. "Gemeinschaft und Gewissen in Shakespeares 'Coriolan'," NS, XLIII (1935), 363-384, 413-425.

Baumgarten analyzes Coriolanus' relationships to the people, Aufidius, his mother, the aristocratic party, and his wife to establish that the play is an ironic portrayal of "Für-sich-selbst-sein-Wollen." Having arrived at this conclusion before reading North's Plutarch, the author finds evidence to support it in the Comparison between Coriolanus and Alcibiades, where Plutarch records Plato's opinion that "solitariness" is a quality "which a governor of a commonwealth ... should shun." Sh embodied this critique of the hero in the dialogue of the two Officers at the Capitol (beginning of II ii), which Baumgarten regards as the key to the meaning of the whole play. Individual conscience must fuse with the common good or disaster follows.

1153. Beckingham, C. F. "Seneca's Fatalism and Elizabethan Tragedy," MLR, XXXII (1937), 434-438.

For Seneca's "ethical" fatalism in Caesar, see #1828.

1154. Behrens, Ralph. "Cleopatra Exonerated," ShN, IX (1959), 37.

Behrens tries to acquit Cleopatra of the main charge of infidelity to Antony. It is not difficult to do so, but it does not appear that Behrens exculpates Cleopatra when he speaks of her flight from Actium as "a case of feminine fear" and of the treason of her fleet as a case "probably of neglect." The pejorative comments of Scarus and Philo are labeled "common gossip in Rome and court circles," without any observation that such gossip has a firm foundation in fact. For further objections, see Betty Bandel, ibid., IX, X (1959/1960), 10.

1155. Bekk, Adolf. "Speersänger, Speerschüttler und Speerfreund," Shakespeare und Homer: Ein Beitrag zur Literatur und Bühne des englischen Dichters (Pest, Vienna, and Leipzig, 1865), pp. 1-25. E-S HB

The "Speersänger" is Homer, the "Speerschüttler" is (of course) Sh, and the "Speerfreund" is Gervinus (Old Germanic Gêr and wine), whose approach to Troi. does not please Bekk (see #0264). Bekk thinks of Sh as "aristofanisch," a satiric critic of his own times, but not a mocker of Homer. Sh individualized the dramatis personae of the Iliad and therefore may seem to parody Homer, but if Ulysses is a Machiavellian, the criticism is of Il Principe, not of the Iliad. Bekk discusses Sh's use of Chaucer, Caxton, and Chapman, and he offers brief interpretative passages on the characters and action. The essay rambles (the Vandals in Spain somehow find a place in it, e.g.). It is noteworthy that Bekk gives more attention to the war plot than to the lovers, though he sees Troilus as the prototype of youth and Cressida as "nicht besser und nicht schlimmer als Hundert und Hunderte ihres Geschlechts." The essay is an introduction to Bekk's trans. and free adaptation of Troi., which occupies the remainder of the book. DFo

1156. Berger, [Alfred] Freiherrn von. Studien und Kritiken. Wien, 1886 (no complete pagination available—as trans. and abstracted in the New Variorum Caesar).

An unsatisfactory reading of Caesar as symbolic--Caesar = "power"; Brutus = "men who cannot endure such power." To Berger Brutus is an alter Judas; he cites Nietzsche on Brutus as a manifestation of Sh's spiritual torment.

1157. Berkeley, David S. "On Oversimplifying Antony," CE, XVII (1955), 96-99.

As a corrective to critical adulation, Berkeley proposes an extraordinary interpretation of Antony as a "double-crosser" who, to avenge the wrong he thinks Cleopatra has done him, cleverly attempts to betray her into Caesar's power by implying (IV xv 48) that Proculeius is reliable when he knows him to be Caesar's trusted friend. To the shocked protest of F. S. Hook (ibid., XVII [1956], 365-366), Berkeley replies vigorously (ibid., XVIII [1957], 286-287). Berkeley had suggested the possibility of such a reading of Antony's character in 1950 (NQ, CXCV, 534-535) without, however, endorsing it. A delayed rejection of the possibility of a treasonable Antony comes from Cynthia Grill (NQ, CCV [1960], 191).

1158. Bertram, Franz. Die Timonlegende: Eine Entwicklungsgeschichte des Misanthropentypus in der antiken Literatur. [Greifswald], 1906, 99 pp. SG

Not seen. According to SG, Bertram argues (pp. 83-88 et passim) for Sh's use in Tim. of both Plutarch and Lucian (the latter in French or Italian trans.). Sh's characterization is superior to that in his sources. NjP

1159. Bethell, S. L. Shakespeare and the Popular Dramatic Tradition. Ln, 1944, 164 pp.

Bethell supports his "multi-consciousness" theory (see #2188) by analyses of Troi. (pp. 98-105) and Antony (116-131) among other plays. Bethell sees Troi. as a product of the tension between outer beauty and inner ugliness (Cressida, Helen, the knight in "sumptuous armor" who has a "most putrified core," etc.). Sh debunked the romanticized Marlovian Helen, and even Hector is greedy, but nevertheless Sh does not treat the characters realistically—they are symbolic, and what they say is more important than the dramatic situations in which they speak. On Antony, Bethell is percipient: the key to the play is its language which in the mouths of all the characters is "Brobdingnagian," especially when the reference is to the protagonists. The effect is grandeur which removes any possibility of our regarding Cleopatra as a strumpet and Antony as an old ruffian. The defense of the play's formlessness and the exploration of Sh's conception of Imperial Rome are both sensitive, but Bethell forces the evidence when he suggests that Sh implies an underlying Christian ethic in the antinomy between Octavius' calculating malice and Cleopatra's spiritualized carnality.

1160. Binder, Rudolf. Der dramatische Rythmus

in Shakespeares "Antonius und Cleopatra". Würzburg-Aumühle, 1939, 173 pp. GRS

Not seen. According to Robert Fricker's rev. (ES, XXV [1943], 113-115), Binder focuses on the character of Cleopatra as he delineates the internal coherence of Antony. His method is said to be not unlike that of Wilson Knight. CU MiU

1161. Birrell, T. A. "The Shakespearian Mixture: Recent Approaches to Shakespeare's Handling of the Comic and Tragic Kinds," Museum, LXIII (1958), 97-111.

See pp. 106-108, 109 for brief remarks on Sh's manipulation of Plutarch in Antony and Cor. "Shakespeare transmutes not only the sense of grandeur of the imperial theme that he got from North's Plutarch, but also the strong moralistic implications of the source material. The climax of Antony and Cleopatra is suicide, and suicide is the height of human folly." Cor. is Sh's "most classical, most Jonsonian piece."

1162. Boas, Guy. "'Troilus and Cressida' and the Time Scheme," NER, XIII (1946), 529-535.

A fanciful and witty juxtaposition of Troi. with plays of O'Casey and Shaw; the conclusion is that Sh's "Helen is no more Homer's than she is Marlowe's ..." Like Cressida, she is "a 'heroine' of twentieth century comedy." Sh was not "guying ... the grand manner of Homer and of himself" but anticipating modern literature by almost four hundred years.

1163. Boecker, Alexander. A Probable Italian Source of Shakespeare's "Julius Caesar". N.Y., 1913, 130 pp. E-S

Boecker's thesis is that Pescetti's Il Cesare, Tragedia (1594) was a funnel transmitting to Sh elements of the Caesar story from Lucan, Suetonius, Appian, and perhaps other historians. The argument is based on parallels between the action of Sh's first three acts and Pescetti and on similarities in characterization of Caesar, Brutus, and some minor figures. But Boecker adduces no evidence which cannot otherwise be accounted for; and, more important, he himself shows (1) that there is no action at all in Pescetti's hyper-Senecan play, whereas Sh's play is full of movement; (2) that Pescetti's four thousand lines of verbiage are ninety-nine per cent feeble, whereas Sh's spare language forms eminently quotable lines of distinguished poetry. It is not without reason that Boecker's thesis has failed to gain general acceptance in fifty years.

1164. Bolton, Joseph S. G. "Titus Andronicus: Shakespeare at Thirty," SP, XXX (1933), 208-224.

Bolton believes that Sh made a thorough and sympathetic revision of the work of someone else in Acts II, III, and IV, shifting the emphasis from Tamora to Aaron. The argument is conducted with vigor, but it can be shown that there are Shn elements in every scene of the play; there is no longer any need to dismember it.

1165. Bond, R. Warwick. "Lucian and Boiardo in 'Timon of Athens'," MLR, XXVI (1931), 52-68. E-S HB SG (Reprinted in Studia Otiosa [1938].)

Bond argues that Sh's access to Lucian's Misanthropos was through Boiardo's Timone, which includes in its first four acts virtually everything in Lucian. The last two acts of Tim. are based on this material and (significantly) also on several hints from Boiardo's Act V, which is his original addition to Lucian. Bond appears to have a strong case, but he does not observe that Sh could have acquired at least some of the Lucianic material from the English academic Timon.

1166. Bonjour, Adrien. The Structure of Julius Caesar. Liverpool UP, 1958, 81 pp.

Bonjour emphasizes three chief elements which hold the play together: (1) the dual tragedies of Caesar and Brutus; (2) thematic repetition (suicide, superstition, sleep); (3) verbal repetition (the imagery of rising and falling especially). The most interesting ch. is certainly the first, in which Bonjour argues for Caesar as a "drama of divided sympathies" with both Caesar and Brutus our objects. The analysis of Brutus is more effective than the defense of Caesar, though Bonjour is certainly right that the latter is not a tyrant like the butchers Richard III and Macbeth. Bonjour takes a dimmer view of Cassius than is usual in recent criticism. The second ch. shows what dramatic ironies lie in the subthemes which illuminate the central subject of the play. The least satisfactory section is the third; like many image-hunters Bonjour "may seem to consider passages a little too curiously," to use the words of Kenneth Muir's Preface. There are many brilliant insights: e.g., Brutus' pose before Messala about Portia's death is like Caesar's earlier "Northern Star" speech—both men wish others to think them constant under duress because both wish to think so of themselves. But one is left with the impression of a fragmented approach to the play. A fuller treatment might have shown the "flow" of characters from the first two acts through the third and on into the fourth and fifth. Limitations considered, this is an important study which should become a standard work.

1167. Bonnard, Georges. "Note sur les Sources de Timon of Athens," EA, VII (1954), 59-69.

Assuming that Sh invented very little, if any, of the legend, Bonnard urges a search in Byzantium (where Lucian was revered) for extensions and redactions of the Misanthropos. He also believes that Italian literature may produce a predecessor other than Boiardo's Timone, to which Sh owes nothing. The anonymous English farce Timon apparently is based on Sh, not vice versa. So Sh's debt would appear to be to some combination (probably Italian) of Lucian, Plutarch's "Life of Antony," and further details of the legend. Cf. Bond (#1165), who argues for Sh's debt to Boiardo.

1168. Bowden, William R. "The Human Shakespeare and Troilus and Cressida," SQ, VIII (1957), 167-177.

Operating under the possibly fallacious assumption that a dramatist wishes his audience to know where he stands on moral issues, Bowden attempts to construct a view of Troi. "a little nearer to the center than [Wilson] Knight's": i.e., Sh sides with the Trojans (who allow emotion to dominate them) and he expects us to do so, too. Bowden, in unconsciously applying to Troi. the vestiges of a Romantic movement which Sh never dreamed of, makes the error of thinking he has found the Sh "for all time" when he has only proposed the Sh "of an age"--the critic's age, not Sh's. This is not to say that Bowden is incompetent as a polemicist--he observes that sympathetic characters like Leonato (Much), Brabantio, Hamlet, and Romeo reject in their grief the rational consolations of philosophy. Such an observation is telling until we remember that the consolations of philosophy are offered to these characters in clichés by unintelligent or morally unattractive people. As for Troi., Bowden is not wrong to suggest that Troilus is attractive; he is wrong to suggest that Sh approved of his conduct, or expected a Jacobean audience to do so.

1169. Bowling, Lawrence E. "Duality in the Minor Characters in Antony and Cleopatra," CE, XVIII (1957), 251-255.

A stimulating and persuasive analysis of the characters of Pompey, Lepidus, Octavia, and Enobarbus, who share the trait of indecision. Each is unable to decide between alternatives and each suffers for his inertia. Though Bowling does not specifically say so, these minor characters can be seen as miniature reflections of Antony, who hovers until Actium (and perhaps even after) between the poles of Rome and Egypt. A difference is that while Antony makes his full commitment to Cleopatra before his death, each of the other four remains self-divided. Bowling shows that in the case of Octavia Sh definitely departed from Plutarch, who describes her as wholly Antony's. An illuminating comment, which Bowling might have expanded into a study of Sh's creative process in Antony.

1170. Bowman, Thomas D. "Antony and the 'lass unparallel'd'," ShN, VII (1957), 47.

Bowman sees Antony IV iv as the scene in which Cleopatra first shows that nobility which characterizes her in Act V. He analyzes the scene, supplying probable stage business, to show that Cleopatra's concern is to conceal from Antony her premonition of defeat and death. This "stoical" restraint, a prologue to the dignity of her death in "the high Roman fashion," is especially evident in the fumbling with Antony's armor; Cleopatra pretends clumsiness to make Antony laugh. Bowman is not entirely convincing, especially about the opening line of the scene.

1171. Boyle, Robert. "Troilus and Cressida," ESn, XXX (1902), 21-59. E-S

Boyle disintegrates Troi., assigning what he does not like (i.e., the Hector plot, especially the last seven scenes) to Marston and splitting the rest of the play between the period of Romeo, with which the love plot is compatible (sic) and the period of the mature tragedies (the Ulysses plot). Boyle is a member of the Sturm und Drang school of Sh interpreters: those who believe that the soul of the poet shows in everything he wrote.

1172. Bradbrook, Frank W. "Thomas Nashe and Shakespeare," NQ, CXCIX (1954), 470.

An unconvincing attempt to persuade that Sh is echoing a passage in Christ's Tears over Jerusalem in Cleopatra's glorious "dream" of her dead lover. The verbal resemblances are so tenuous that the irony Bradbrook detects in Sh's supposed echo of Nashe could not conceivably be noticed by the audience for whom he wrote Cleopatra's lines.

1173. Bradbrook, M. C. "What Shakespeare Did to Chaucer's Troilus and Criseyde," SQ, IX (1958), 311-319.

"Compression and inversion direct Shakespeare's use of Chaucer." What to Chaucer had been an interior development of mental states is to Sh only external action: the result is a brutalization of Chaucer's story. Miss Bradbrook mentions Caxton, Henryson, and other participants in the tradition, but does not fully distinguish Sh's own distortions of the pseudo-classical love story from the distortions he inherited from the fifteenth and sixteenth centuries.

1174. Bradford, Gamaliel, Jr. "The Serpent of Old Nile: A Study of the Cleopatra of Tragedy," PL, X (1898), 514-532. (Reprinted in Elizabethan Women [1936].)

A detailed comparison of Antony with Dryden's All for Love and Fletcher and Massinger's The False One (about Cleopatra's early career). In part the discussion deals with the fidelity with which each writer adheres to Plutarch. Sh includes too much of Plutarch's incident and thus lacks dramatic coherence by comparison with Dryden and Fletcher-Massinger. "It may be said that Shakespeare does not follow Plutarch in everything; but I really do not see why we should be grateful to him for what he has left out."

1175. Bradley, A. C. "Coriolanus," PBA, V (1912), 457-473. (Annual British Academy Shakespeare Lecture.) E-S

This famous defense of Coriolanus as a tragic protagonist is one of the best essays on the play. At one or two points it is difficult to agree (e.g., that Cor. is a play of reconciliation, not a tragedy), but the criticism is generally sound and sharply observant, especially of what Sh added to and omitted from Plutarch's story. Bradley's main point about the hero is that he is an aristocrat, not a potential tyrant; Sh softened Coriolanus' most unpleasant characteristics and intensified the friction in his relationship to the Plebeians to make him more noble than Plutarch does. There are thoughtful comments on Volumnia and Virgilia as well; but Bradley appears blind to the effectiveness of Aufidius' pragmatism as a foil to the unyielding absolutism of the hero.

1176. Bradley, A. C. Shakespearean Tragedy: Lectures on Hamlet, Othello, King Lear, Macbeth. Ln, 1904, 498 pp. E-S SG

For Bradley's passing remarks on the substance and structure of the plays on classical themes, see #1842.

1177. Bradley, A. C. "Shakespeare's Antony and Cleopatra" (1905), Oxford Lectures on Poetry (Ln, 1909), pp. 277-308. E-S

This distinguished critical interpretation makes the major point that Antony is not an inadequate imitation of the four great tragedies but a successful play of a different kind. First, it lacks passion and action in the first three acts; second, the characters are not wholly attractive; third, Sh seems to diminish the world of the play as he diminishes the world of Troi. (cf. Lear, where a small island takes on cosmic significance in the moral order). Bradley makes intelligent observations on Sh's use of Plutarch here as he does in his essay on Cor., but the most valuable feature of the lecture is the striking character analysis. Octavius, Antony, and Cleopatra all emerge in sketches which are lifelike even if they run the risk of exceeding the play. It is not always possible to agree with Bradley (e.g., that Cleopatra's suicide is entirely a product of her fear of Octavius' plans for her), but it is never possible to read him without obtaining new insights.

1178. Brandl, A. "Horaz und Shakespeare," ShJ, XXXIX (1903), 233-234. HB

Marullus' description of the echoing shouts of the Roman mob (Caesar I i 49-52) may itself be an echo of Horace's description of the echoing shouts of the Roman mob in Odes I 20. Brandl offers evidence from Dream, L.L.L., and Titus that to Sh Horace was a "beliebten Schulautor" and recommends a systematic study of Shn Horatianisms.

1179. Brewer, D. S. "Brutus' Crime: A Footnote to Julius Caesar," RES, n.s. III (1952), 51-54.

Dover Wilson (#1782) notwithstanding, Sh did not apotheosize Brutus as the Renaissance humanists did; Sh partakes to a considerable extent of the Medieval tradition (Dante, Chaucer, Lydgate, et al.) which saw Brutus as guilty, betraying the noble Caesar. Sh's references to Caesar and Brutus before Caesar obviously show that he regarded Caesar as a great man--even Caesar can be read as a story of "murder most foul."

1180. Breyer, Bernard R. "A New Look at Julius Caesar," Curry Festschrift, pp. 161-180.

The two most controversial cruxes of Caesar can both be cleared away if we regard Caesar as a portrait of the classical/Renaissance tyrant and Brutus as a justified tyrannicide. With this approach, Caesar's boasting, capriciousness, subjection to flattery, etc., are explained and Brutus' soliloquy (II i 10-34) is no expression of confused republicanism but justified fear of Caesar's predisposition to a form of tyranny condemned from Plato to Erasmus. Breyer's explanation does not solve all the problems of the play, but it does clear the ground a bit.

1181. Brittin, Norman A. "Coriolanus, Alceste, and Dramatic Genres," PMLA, LXXI (1956), 799-807.

Brittin argues that Cor. slides across the boundary toward comedy as Le Misanthrope slides across the boundary toward tragedy. Coriolanus offends against manners early in the play, and offenses against manners are the materials of one kind of comedy. Sh's hero dies--a severe punishment for a comic fault--but he dies without anagnorisis and cannot therefore be tragic. Sh has fused dramatic genres in Cor. Brittin only briefly considers Plutarch (who, after all, shaped Sh's plot and character for him) and then it is only to emphasize Plutarch's social didacticism. But the art. makes several interesting points: e.g., (1) Coriolanus shares the fault of egotism with Cordelia, Brutus, and Molière's Alceste, though Cordelia and Brutus are not nearly so reprehensible as he; (2) Coriolanus is a Hotspur without a Worcester or Glendower to rebuke him. An interesting paper at all points, but it is by no means certain that Sh regarded his hero as a comic type to be castigated for his bad manners in social situations.

1182. Brooke, Stopford A. "Coriolanus," On Ten Plays of Shakespeare (Ln, 1905), pp. 221-252.

Like John Palmer (#1560), Brooke detracts from the greatness of the hero in order to give a modicum of dignity to the people and their Tribunes. Though he tries to maintain the ignobility of the Patricians and the essential righteousness of the people, when he abandons the political question for a close examination of the protagonist, he gradually attributes greater stature to Coriolanus until in the culminating discussion of the persuasion scene Brooke echoes the effusiveness of Swinburne. But inconsistent as his analysis is, Brooke makes interesting suggestions: e.g., (1) Sh encountered Coriolanus in Painter as well as in North, but chose to follow the latter version exclusively; (2) Coriolanus is in an ironic position vis à vis the Second Citizen: he is the rash advocate of misguided Patricianism as Second Citizen is the "great toe" of misguided Plebeianism; (3) at Coriolanus' exile we are given a great sense of his solitude, and all through the play he is a rock surrounded by a stormy sea. At other points Brooke is less convincing: e.g., Menenius should not be regarded as a "Roman Polonius."

1183. Brooke, [C. F.] Tucker, "Shakespeare's Study in Culture and Anarchy," YR, XVII (1928), 571-577. SG

The crudity of Sh's characters and action in Troi. is traceable to Chapman's Homer, not to Caxton or Chaucer. Brooke is here more speculative than dogmatic and offers little evidence.

1184. Brown, David. "'My Gracious Silence'," SAB, XV (1940), 55-56.

Sh did not find many hints in Plutarch for a dramatic characterization of Virgilia, so he cleverly made a dominant trait of her silence. He may have taken Coriolanus' famous greeting to her from Jonson's Volpone which refers (perhaps) to Sophocles' Ajax on the attractiveness of silence in woman.

1185. Brown, Huntington. "Enter the Shakespearean Tragic Hero," EC, III (1953), 285-302.

The technique by which Sh engages our sympathy with his tragic protagonists is to introduce them early in the plays as (1) passive, or responsive, rather than active; (2) divided between an individual, public, outer self and a universal, private, inner self with which the audience can identify. Of the classical heroes, Brutus and Antony are introduced as private men (Brutus with a friend and Antony with his lover) whereas Titus makes a public address, Timon appears at the center of his sycophants, and Coriolanus harangues a mob. It is significant that these last three protagonists are men with whom we feel no kindred humanity, whereas Brutus and Antony are, like the heroes of the great tragedies, men we can feel with.

1186. Brown, J. M. Julius Caesar: A Study. Ln, n.d. (no complete pagination available--as abstracted in the New Variorum Caesar).

Brown regards Caesar as Greek in its austerity, its lack of comic relief, and its theme of Nemesis. Sh followed Plutarch closely but ennobled the conspiracy, at least in Brutus, who is haunted by the "Et tu Brute" and by Caesar's last look--indeed the ghost of Caesar is Brutus' recollection of that "upbraiding look." Brown denies that Sh used any source other than Plutarch (with the possible exception of Suetonius for Caesar's dying words). He regards Brutus' oration as "obituary eloquence compared with the manly broken-hearted eloquence of Antony." On this last point and on the objectivity of the ghost, Brown's criticism is not a good guide to the play.

1187. Brown, Macmillan. "Shakespeare and Classical Learning," Julius Caesar ([Auckland University College?], 1894), no pagination available. (Part of a series of lectures.)

Not seen. Discussed briefly and praised in #0435.

1188. Browning, I. R. "Coriolanus: Boy of Tears," EC, V (1955), 18-31.

A potent argument against Enright (#1296). Browning maintains that in Cor. "we are given the unhappy irony of a man who performed bloody and pitiless deeds in order to feel loved." Though he refrains from any deeper depth psychology than this, Browning does emphasize the personal relationship at the expense of the public one. He has, however, shown that Plutarch's Coriolanus and Sh's are both much more than mere fighting machines.

1189. Brubaker, Edward S. "A Note on Titus Andronicus IV.ii.32-6," SQ, III (1952), 140.

This passage, in which Aaron claims to have "braved" Marcus earlier in the play, suggests that originally such a scene had a place in one of the first three acts, but that Sh deleted it when revising an old play in order to make Aaron a behind-the-scenes villain. An interesting speculation.

1190. Büchler, Hermann. Shakspeare's Dramen in ihrem Verhältnisse zur griechischen Tragödie. Nürnberg, 1856, 86 pp. HB

The running subtitle gives some idea of Büchler's scope: "in besonderer Hinsicht auf Shakspeare's 'Julius Cäsar' und Hindeutungen auf 'Hamlet'; die 'Orestias', 'Agamemnon', 'Choëphoren', 'Eumeniden' des Aeschilos; die 'Trachinierinnen' und 'Oedipus auf dem Kolonos' des Sophokles." Büchler's method is to compare, not to attribute, but his appreciations are frequently vague ("in seinem Innern fand [Sh] den wahren Grund allen Handelns und Dichtens, dort fand er die Urbilder, die auch die Alten in ihren Schöpfungen leiteten"), and the relevance of his extended quotations is not always apparent. Yet he makes some stimulating suggestions (e.g., about Sh's use of the crowd in Caesar for choral purposes). MnU

1191. Buck, Eva. "Cleopatra, eine Charakterdeutung: Zur Interpretation von Shakespeares 'Antony and Cleopatra'," ShJ, LXXIV (1938), 101-122. GRS

This interesting interpretation concentrates on the gradual integration of Cleopatra's love for Antony with the masculine virtues she loves in him. Early in the play she loves his masculinity but does not comprehend the Roman world which symbolizes that maleness--she is unsure of herself. But gradually she takes on political as well as personal stature (references to Cleopatra as "Egypt" are more common in the last half of the play). She deals with Thyreus and Octavius on a political level and finally dies like the Roman man she loves. Meanwhile Antony, who has been torn apart by conflicting worlds of value, brings the two together in his death (he seeks to join Cleopatra and to defeat Octavius in one gesture). This reading of Antony makes Cleopatra both more consistent and less commanding than she has often been thought to be. The author points to the irony implicit in Cleopatra's tragedy: her love for Antony inevitably destroys those masculine virtues she loves in him. The polarities of the play and the protagonists' response to them the author would trace to Plutarch's account of "Cleopatra's lamentation over Antonius' tomb"; here the grieving queen underlines the irony that her Roman lover is buried in Egypt while she, the Egyptian, will be buried at Rome.

1192. Burke, Kenneth. "Antony in Behalf of the Play," SouthernR, I (1935), 308-319.

An imaginary address to the audience by Antony after Caesar's death, analyzing Caesar as a product of dramatic devices and especially delineating his own character as Caesar's alter ego in the last half of the play. The treatment is flippant and does not remove the difficulties of dramatic structure in the play.

1193. Burns, Winifred. "The Character of Marcius Coriolanus," PL, LII (1946), 31-48.

This study, though at times elementary, makes some significant points: (1) Cor. "approaches the Aristotelian theory of classical tragedy as nearly as any of the other great Elizabethan plays"; (2) Coriolanus' hamartia, pride, and resultant wrath (the flaw of many Greek heroes) fit him for war, not politics, but it is to be noted that even in battle he leads best when he restrains his passion; (3) the name "Marcius" by which Aufidius calls him at Corioli in Act V is as much a taunt as "boy" or "traitor" because it reminds Coriolanus of the honors that the Romans once accorded him and have now stripped from him.

1194. Bush, Douglas. "Julius Caesar and Elyot's Governour," MLN, LII (1937), 407-408.

Sh's source for Caesar's pride in not examining the warning which Artemidorus gives him in III i was Elyot, who speaks of Caesar as "beinge radicate in pride." North's Plutarch mentions the incident, but not Caesar's pride. But as Elyot provides no source for Caesar's self-characterizing statement, "What touches us ourself shall be last serv'd" (perhaps the key to the pride in this scene), Bush has not established any necessary connection between Elyot's conception of Caesar and Sh's.

1195. Büttner, Richard. "Zu 'Coriolan' und seiner Quelle," ShJ, XLI (1905), 45-53. E-S SG

Sh carefully founded his hero on the character in Plutarch, but he left out irrelevancies and petty matters in order to make Coriolanus appear the grander. Büttner observes that Delius (#1256) did not examine the Comparison of Coriolanus with Alcibiades, from which Sh took a detail or two, as he also did from North's marginal summaries. Büttner's points are interesting, but none will significantly affect the interpretation of the play.

1196. Byrne, M. St. Clare. "Classical Coriolanus," NR, XCVI (1931), 426-431.

A lucid and percipient exposition of the reason why Cor. is, though one of his best plays, Sh's most unpopular tragedy. In its lack of pathetic fallacy (no icy winds blowing over Elsinore) and its simplicity of characterization (we care more about the salvation of Rome than about its great hero), the play is distinctly unromantic. Coriolanus, who, like Antigone, is single-minded, succumbs in classical fashion to what is closest to his nature--in his case his mother, who also represents Rome. Thus we experience the same shock in coming to Cor. from the other Shn tragedies that we would in coming to Greek drama from them.

1197. Campbell, L[ily] B. "A Note for Baconians," MLN, LIII (1938), 21-23. SG

The fact that Bacon's Advancement of Learning and Troi. II ii 165-167 both refer incorrectly to Aristotle's Nicomachean Ethics does not make Bacon the author of Troi. since the error also occurs in Nicholas Grimald's Cicero and probably originated in some sixteenth-century Latin ed. of the Ethics. See #1315, #1542 for earlier discussions of the matter.

1198. Campbell, Olwen W. "Troilus and Cressida: A Justification," LM, IV (1921), 48-59.

This critical analysis partially anticipates Meyer (#1509); Sh "has shown us ... how not only cities, but judgment and character and love itself, may be laid waste in war: and how in the turmoil of so unnatural a struggle vanity, folly, and cynicism may be left standing when what is brave and virtuous and gentle has perished." Unlike Meyer, however, Mrs. Campbell does not stress the injustice of the war or the depravity of all the characters, and she gives more centrality to the love plot than Meyer does. She suggests that the passions of hatred (the Greeks) and improper love (the Trojans) are a thread which ties the play together.

1199. Campbell, Oscar J. Comicall Satyre and Shakespeare's Troilus and Cressida. San Marino, Cal.: Huntington Library, 1938, 246 pp. SG

Campbell proposes that Troi. is Sh's attempt at writing what Jonson called "comicall satyre," the satiric play which quickly assumed popularity after verse satire was banned in 1599. Beginning with an interesting ch. on Renaissance views of classical satire, Campbell shows how the confusion of satire and comedy evolved and why Jonson could regard satire as a middle ground between comedy and tragedy. Then, after four chs. on Jonson and Marston as dramatic satirists, we are given a substantial (fifty-page) analysis of Troi. Campbell argues with verve and is unquestionably persuasive as he discusses such points as the inconclusive dénouement of the play (appropriate to satire as to no other dramatic form) or the vestigial chivalry and sexual libertinism of Elizabeth's factious courtiers as they may be reflected in the play. But there are two aspects of the play which his interpretation does not adequately account for: (1) Troilus is too likable to be the Italianate roué Campbell thinks him and (2) the burden of philosophy stated in magnificent verse is incompatible with the derisive tone the whole play is said to have. Perhaps the truth is that Sh was influenced by Jonson and Marston but did not abandon his idealism, his poetry, and his habit of eliciting sympathy for his characters.

1200. Campbell, Oscar J. Shakespeare's Satire. OUP, 1943, 227 pp.

Of the three chs. on the Greek and Roman plays, the first (98-120) is a fluent condensation of Campbell's longer ch. on Troi. in #1199. The second (168-197) interprets Tim. not as a tragedy, but as a tragical satire on the general plan of Volpone and Sejanus. Sh did his best work on Acts IV and V which are most satiric of the malcontent Timon but lost interest in I-III and never polished the play, going on to Cor. as a second, and final, effort at tragical satire. The ch. on Cor. (198-217) is at once the most interesting and the least convincing: Cor. is not a tragedy, but an exemplum of political impropriety on the part of its hero and of the Plebeians. Campbell's thesis is appealing when he exemplifies the foul language Coriolanus uses in his tirades and when he emphasizes that people in the play talk chiefly of Coriolanus and from pejorative viewpoints; but the argument loses force when Campbell reads Menenius' genial banter as the laughable railing of a Thersites, Apemantus, or Carlo Buffone, and he is certainly wrong to call Coriolanus' concessions to his mother puerile cringing. In short Campbell's theory of Shn satire obviously has some foundation, but he has greatly overstated it; Sh was influenced by Jonson and Marston, perhaps, but he certainly was not their ape.

1201. Carson, R. A. G. "The Ides of March," HT, VII (1957), 141-146.

An interesting account of the circumstances surrounding Caesar's death with several references to Sh's (authentic) portrayal of his sources. The most significant observation is that Sh wrote a funeral oration which the historical Marcus Antonius would have liked to give: to reassure the Senators, inflame the mob, and establish himself as "the heir to Caesar's designs."

1202. Case, R. H. "Introduction," The Tragedy of Antony and Cleopatra (1906/1930), ArdenSh, pp. vii-xxvi.

In relating Antony to its source in the "Life of Marcus Antonius," Case defers to Wyndham's detailed study (#2487). In considering the place of the play among Sh's tragedies he offers a view not unlike that of Bradley (#1177). Sh's portrait of Antony is not really milder than Plutarch's, he argues, since Plutarch's Antony offends most in his early life which Sh omitted. At the same time, Sh's Cleopatra fears the shame of Caesar's triumph, while Plutarch's dies entirely for love of Antony.

1203. [Case, R. H.] "Introduction," The Tragedy of Coriolanus (1922), ArdenSh, pp. ix-xxvi.

The comparison here between the Plutarchian and Shn versions has largely been assimilated by more recent students of the play. Case in turn acknowledges his debt to Bradley (#1175) and MacCallum (#1477).

1204. Cavendish, Margaret. CCXI Sociable Letters Written by the Lady Marchioness of Newcastle (1664): Letter CXXIII (as it is quoted in Munro, II, 131-133).

Among Sh's triumphs is his projection of himself into his Roman characters; "I believe that Antonius and Brutus did not speak better to the people than he hath feigned them." Brief mention also of Caesar, Octavius, and Cleopatra. This letter is important historically as one of the very first attempts to write Shn criticism that is more than mere allusion.

1205. Cecil, Lord David. "'Antony and Cleopatra'," Poets and Story-Tellers (Ln, 1949), pp. 1-24. (Originally composed as a lecture, 1943.)

The theme of Antony is not love, but success. Sh presents four aspirants to political power and shows why three of them (Lepidus, Pompey, Antony) fail. If the play is amorphous, it is because Sh is counterpointing this theme with the vivid portrait of the lovers' fascination for each other. Sh selected from Plutarch what he wanted and transmuted much of what he selected. The structure of the play contributes to a sense of inevitability; Antony begins at a peak and slides more and more rapidly down into the abyss of defeat through Acts II, III, and IV. Then, too, the Soothsayer is an important element--his admonitions about Antony's genius and Octavius' suggest that mysterious powers control the fates of men, and Enobarbus reinforces this hint with his emphatic denial that Antony has the power to leave Cleopatra. Wholly an interesting interpretation of the theme and structure of the play, but as Cecil expounds it, Act V must largely be an appendix.

1206. Chambers, R. W. "The Expression of Ideas--Particularly Political Ideas--In the Three Pages, and in Shakespeare," Shakespeare's Hand in the Play of Sir Thomas More [a symposium] (CUP, 1923), pp. 142-187.

A convincing argument that the 147 lines thought to be in Sh's hand express the respect for authority, attitudes toward the commoners en masse, and emphasis on the evil effects of successful insurrection which are to be found in the Shn history plays and especially in Caesar, Cor., and Troi. The analysis of the mob scenes in Caesar and Cor. is especially good; Chambers points out Sh's deviations from Plutarch in Cor. to make the mob humanly likable, if absurd. The same ambivalent attitude can be inferred from this mob scene in Sir Thomas More.

1207. Chapman, John Jay. "Troilus and Cressida," Part IV of "Shakespeare," [see #0160] in Greek Genius and Other Essays (N.Y., 1915), pp. 173-190.

Chapman finds in the play no "character-interest," no plot, no unity, "and yet it is full of the greatest talent for writing that a man ever possessed. This talent seems to roll about like a hulk in the trough of the sea." There is no consideration here of the tradition behind Sh's play. More recent critics have found much more to praise in the play than Chapman can discover.

1208. Charlton, H. B. "The Dark Comedies," BJRL, XXI (1937), 78-128.

Charlton offers the hypothesis that Sh wrote the dark comedies, of which Troi. was the first, as a withdrawal from Falstaff's intellectualized materialism. The implication that Sh trained himself to write romantic comedy by experimenting with "dark" comedy is not warranted, but Charlton makes interesting observations about Troi., Meas., and All's W.: about Troi., e.g., the catastrophe of the love plot has the salutary effect of rendering Troilus more useful to the Trojans and Cressida less harmful to her future lovers. Again, in the sources of his two plots Sh found epitomes of classical idealized heroism and Medieval romanticism--he plays them against each other and shows the deficiencies of each; but then he had already debunked romantic love in Dream and he had ample precedent for portraying mythological heroes as "filibusters."

1209. [Charlton, H. B.] "The Senecan Tradition in England," [part of the Introduction to] The Poetical Works of Sir William Alexander Earl of Stirling, ed. L. E. Kastner and H. B. Charlton, PUM, No. X (Manchester UP, 1921), pp. cxxxviii-cc. (Reprinted as Charlton's in The Senecan Tradition in Renaissance Tragedy, PUM, No. XXIV [1946].) E-S HB

Charlton makes only two passing allusions to Sh: (1) "The period from 1590 to 1603 is that of the highest achievement in English tragedy; and in that achievement Seneca, through Shakespeare and lesser men like Marston, has his share, often fragmentarily but palpably, often extensively but obscurely" (cxliv). Only Titus is offered as support for this assertion; the play, like Locrine and The Spanish Tragedy, is in the current of "naturalised" Seneca. (2) Sh inserted the Choruses into Romeo "to throw over succeeding action a Senecan force of fatal compulsion."

1210. Charlton, H. B. Shakespeare, Politics, and Politicians, English Association Pamphlet No. 72 (1929), 24 pp.

The last part of this address (19-24) advances the thesis that Sh wrote Caesar down to write Caesarism up. Caesar is a history play which is concerned with the view that social forces not personalities made Roman history (as opposed to English history, which was made by strong and weak men). Charlton gives a contemptuous analysis of Caesar as he appears at the Lupercalia and with Calphurnia at home. He regards Brutus as no more important in Caesar than Hotspur is in 1H.IV, an unpersuasive view.

1211. Charlton, H. B. Shakespearian Tragedy. CUP, 1948, 246 pp.

Charlton begins with Bradley as a donné and treats Shn tragedy developmentally. The passages relevant to Sh's classical background are pp. 18-24 on Titus and 69-82 on Caesar. The former measures Titus against Aristotelian canons on probability and spectacle and finds the play lacking. The latter considers the character of Brutus against a background of Plutarch's sense of history as conveyed in the Moralia and in the Lives: part of the reason for the depreciation of Caesar in the play is that Plutarch, Sh's source, concerned himself with the rôle of Fortune in the affairs of men while to Sh history (in the earlier history plays) is the record of the deeds of great men--Caesar falls between the stools of Sh's earlier practice and Plutarchian theory.

1212. Charney, Maurice. "An Anachronism in 'Julius Caesar'," NQ, CXCVIII (1953), 267.

Charney asks who first pointed out the anachronism of striking clocks in Caesar. He does not find any reference in Ben Jonson, often said to be the first to point out Sh's "error." There apparently has been no published answer to Charney's query.

1213. Charney, Maurice. "The Dramatic Use of Imagery in Shakespeare's Coriolanus," ELH, XXIII (1956), 183-193.

The verbal imagery of Cor. is sparse; Sh uses "presentational" (i.e., visual) imagery to reflect the character and the Rome he lives in. Coriolanus is Sh's least introspective protagonist (only one brief soliloquy) and also the least eloquent (Sh characterizes him by his long silences at moments of emotional tension). The effect on the play of these theatrical elements (body contact, silence, costume, etc.) is to concentrate its spare action into a single thread--Sh's success is indicated by the fact that though Cor. is contained within a structure similar to that of Caesar, it succeeds in its series of climaxes where Caesar "seems to fall apart."

1214. Charney, Maurice. "The Imagery of Food and Eating in Coriolanus," French Festschrift, pp. 37-55.

Food and its consumption, almost always in a pejorative sense, serve to characterize Coriolanus, the mob, and the tense action that involves them both. For this unifying image Plutarch gives a bare hint in the popular agitation over grain and its price.

1215. Charney, Maurice. "Shakespeare's Antony: A Study of Image Themes," SP, LIV (1957), 149-161.

Charney finds three kinds of images associated with Antony which hint at the course of his fortunes as the action progresses. First (and most interesting) is the large number of references, literal and figurative, to swords and armor which become equated with manhood. Second are visual effects of altitude (Antony sits after Actium, while others stand, e.g.), and third are the many references to dissolution, especially in Acts IV and V, suggesting the fading of Antony's "Roman" life. Charney is stimulating if not always convincing.

1216. Charney, Maurice. "Shakespeare's Roman Plays: A Study of the Function of Imagery in the Drama," diss (Princeton, 1952). DA, XIV (1954), 118-119.

A prefatory ch. in this diss attempts to isolate Sh's response to Roman history, Roman character, and Roman mores. The body of the thesis treats imagery, especially "presentational" imagery (i.e., imagery conveyed visually, not verbally), as it contributes to the correct interpretation of each of the Roman plays.

1217. Charney, Maurice. "Shakespeare's Style in Julius Caesar and Antony and Cleopatra," ELH, XXVI (1959), 355-367.

In Caesar, Sh attempted to reflect the soberness of Rome by means of a simplified style (limited vocabulary, few images, direct equational similes); in Antony, he attempted to reflect the rich exotic culture of Egypt by means of a florid style (large vocabulary, hyperbole, suspended statement). The second experiment was more successful than the first, and Sh never again attempted the naked style. Charney does not consider that the plays are almost a decade apart; he juxtaposes them as if they were successive experiments.

1218. [Chesterton, A. K.] "An Aspect of 'Timon of Athens'," ShR, I (1928), 19-23.

Chesterton observes that Tim. has no ethics but then extracts some moral wisdom from the play; the chief point: Timon was born and died but never lived because he equated all mankind with the flatterers who had betrayed him. There is no discussion of the tradition behind the play. DFo

1219. Chislett, William, Jr. "On Shakespeare's 'Julius Caesar'," FMV, pp. 76-78.

Chislett believes that Sh presents Caesar satirically. Julius is a pseudo-Senecan hero, pompous, thrasonical, and inclined toward King Cambyses' vein. Sh's reason for this portrayal can be found in Cym., where British patriotism in the face of Roman imperial ambitions is a key theme. Chislett suggests that under the influence of Holinshed Sh colored his view of Roman history with an anti-Julian bias, remembering that Caesar had gained a foothold on sacred British soil. Chislett forgets: (1) that Sh speaks in some half-dozen plays of Caesar as a very great man (hardly a candidate for satire); (2) that Sh and his contemporaries regarded themselves as "Brutans," descendants of the ancestors of the very Romans Chislett believes Sh derogated. In fairness, however, Chislett does regard the satire as veiled, at least by comparison with the parody of pseudo-Senecanism in Dream.

1220. Chubb, E. W. "Shakspere's Cicero," Acad (N.Y.), V (1890), 108-112.

Chubb examines Sh's two references to Cicero outside of Caesar (in Titus IV i and 2H.VI IV i) and the four passages in Caesar in which Cicero is present or referred to. Sh shows some sophistication by having Cicero speak the cosmopolitan language, Greek, and he recognizes the courage Cicero demonstrated in delivering the Philippics when he rejects Plutarch's version of the conspirators' refusal to include him. Plutarch says that the assassins feared Cicero's cowardice, but Sh makes Brutus distrust his self-centered arrogance. On Chubb's evidence Sh obviously regarded Cicero as a great Roman.

1221. Clark, Eleanor Grace. "Titus and Vespasian," MLN, XLI (1926), 523-527.

An effective attack on the frequent assumption that the lost Titus and Vespasian referred to by Henslowe was a source for Titus. Aside from the name "Titus" and a glorying in carnage there is no connection between Sh's pseudo-classical play and the Medieval Christian story of the revenge taken by Vespasian and his son Titus on the murderers of Christ.

1222. Clarke, Charles Cowden. "Shakespeare's Philosophers and Jesters," GM, n.s. X (1873), 306-325, 392-423, 514-539, 634-660.

Part I, "Philosophers," contains, inter alia, discussion of Apemantus as a "professed" philosopher; Ulysses and Nestor as classical figures whose names connote wisdom; Brutus, the gentle Stoic; and Timon (as contrast to Apemantus). In Part IV, "Shakespeare's Philosophy," Clarke touches on a range of concepts from "natural philosophy" to Sh's attitude toward oratory; many of the examples are from the Greek and Roman plays, but Clarke never relates any of them to their classical sources, nor does he ever explore the roots of Sh's ideas in classical philosophy.

1223. Clemons, W. H. "The Sources of 'Timon of Athens'," PUB, XV (1904), 208-223. SG

An erudite survey of the Timon legend from Aristophanes and his successors in Greek comedy through Lucian and into the Renaissance serves as a prologue to consideration of Sh's sources. Clemons provides a Timon allusion-list not only for ancient literature but also for the Elizabethan period. He points out that Sh shares with Lucian a motive for Timon's misanthropy and a somber tone which is unlike the usual comic treatment of the theme; he believes that Sh may have read Lucian in a French or Italian trans. But an appended table of coincidence in plot elements shows that Sh used other sources as well: Painter's account in The Palace of Pleasure, the academic Timon, and, of course, Plutarch's "Life of Marcus Antonius" which doubtless got Sh interested in Timon at the outset. An interesting corollary is Clemons' observation that twenty basic elements from these four sources appear in the undisputably Shn parts of the play: i.e., Sh, not some other writer, actually did the reading and manipulated the sources. This remains the best study of Sh's sources for the play, and could serve as a model for source studies in general. It is significant that Clemons anticipates modern attitudes toward polygenesis at a time when most critics believed in single sources, even when they had to postulate "lost plays" to do so. DLC MH

1224. Coad, O. S. "Shakespeare and Aeschylus," JEGP, XX (1921), 556-557. HB

For a parallel between Caesar and the Choephori, see #1876.

1225. Cobden-Sanderson, T. J. "A Passage in 'Julius Caesar'," TLS, July 17, 1913, p. 306.

By omitting a speech-attribution, F_1 makes it appear that Young Cato calls himself

"Cato" at V iv 6 and then "Brutus" at V iv 7. Rowe set a precedent for editors by assigning the speech beginning "And I am Brutus, Marcus Brutus I—" to Brutus. Cobden-Sanderson does not think this flamboyance consistent with Brutus' characteristic self-restraint and would assign the speech to Lucilius, the next speaker. He presumes that Brutus has exited and that Lucilius seeks to rally the Brutan forces by crying out that he _is_ Brutus; Lucilius then works his deception on Antony's soldiers to give the real Brutus time to escape or to kill himself. An interesting argument, but it is supported by no real evidence. Cf. Crawford, #1243.

1226. Coles, Blanche. _Shakespeare Studies: Julius Caesar_. N.Y., 1940, 281 pp.

A detailed _seriatim_ paraphrase of the play, expounding phrases and concepts which would be difficult for those uninitiated into Elizabethan and/or Roman culture. The author writes from a vigorously pro-Caesarian bias which greatly vitiates the objectivity of her passages of criticism; certainly the book should be given to beginners (for whom it is apparently intended) only with caution.

1227. Collins, A. S. "_Timon of Athens_: A Reconsideration," _RES_, XXII (1946), 96-108.

Collins sees _Tim._ as peculiarly Shn because it is experimental: i.e., a Morality play in a classical setting; Timon represents Liberality (or Friendship and Bounty), and he is opposed and destroyed by Vices who, taken _en bloc_, represent Commercialism. This interpretation certainly accounts for the pasteboard characterization in the play, but Collins may be too sanguine in his implication that such a reading makes the play an artistic success.

1228. Conklin, Willet T. "Shakespeare, 'Coriolanus,' and Essex," _TSE_, XI (1931), 42-47.

Conklin believes that after the accession of James Sh felt compelled clearly to dissociate himself from the old Essex rebellion with which his name had been connected. He therefore added (to the account of Coriolanus in North's Plutarch) the characteristics of Hotspur with which he had already alluded to Essex' hotheadedness in _1H.IV_. From hotheadedness to treason is an easy move both for Percy and for Coriolanus as it was for Essex. Sh shows by this addition that he sides with the state against any individual, however great. The parallels with Hotspur are interesting, but it is not obvious that in _Cor._ Sh is consciously recalling his earlier work.

1229. Conklin, Willet T. "Two Further Notes on Shakespeare's Use of Elyot's 'Governour'," _TSE_, X (1930), 66-69.

The second note suggests that Plutarch is a more likely source for _Cor._ III i 107-118 than Elyot, despite Starnes's proposal (#1088).

1230. Conley, C. H. "An Instance of the Fifteen Signs of Judgment in Shakespeare," _MLN_, XXX (1915), 41-44. SG

For a Medieval alternative to Lucan as source for the portents in _Caesar_, see #1877.

1231. Conrad, Hermann. "Shakespeares Timon: Urheberschaft, Abfassungszeit und Entstehung," _ZVLG_, n.F. XVII (1909), 337-384. E-S

Without offering conclusive evidence, Conrad asserts that Sh read Lucian's _Timon_ in the French trans. of Bretin (1582); he hears verbal echoes of Lucian's Thrasycles in Apemantus' speeches. He argues in addition that Sh read Lucian's _Peregrinus_ and _Cynicus_, where he learned to hold Cynicism in contempt. The body of the essay is an effort to dismember the play on stylistic grounds (some metrical, most verbal), and to date the remainder (shortly before 1603). Conrad refrains from naming the "other hand" in the play. DLC

1232. Conrad, Hermann. "Shaksperes 'Troilus und Cressida': Eine Rettung," _PJ_, CLXIX (1917), 22-44, 199-218. E-S

Troi. is not to be interpreted as a travesty of Homer, but (in part) as a parody of Sh's own surroundings. E.g., the Greeks' "schulmeisterlich" speeches in council (I iii) may be a parody of the complicated periods and reciprocal flatteries which characterize the Ciceronian speeches Sh's contemporaries were so fond of. Sh had ample precedent for this kind of parody. The _Batrachomyomachia_ is an early example; Sh may also have taken hints from Ovid (_Meta._ XIII, the character of Ajax) and Virgil (_Aeneid_ II, the character of Helen). In any case Sh was more interested in recreating people as he saw them than in reproducing antiquity accurately or in parodying it. Most of the first part of the art. is concerned with the love plot (date, relationship to Sh's biography, traditional elements—here Conrad does not mention Henryson). In Part II Conrad treats the war plot, pointing out Sh's departures from Medieval and classical sources (e.g., in the single combat of Hector with Ajax) and his original use of those sources (e.g., Lydgate's account of the death of Troilus may have served as a model for the death of Hector, and Homer's account of Achilles' brutality to Hector's body gives Sh another precedent for the horrid scene). Conrad denies the influence of Caxton. He argues that Hector is Sh's ideal hero and hints that the Hector plot was intended to glorify Essex, who, like Hector, was foully killed. Equally unconvincing is the assertion that the play can be apportioned between 1594 and 1602; Conrad offers little evidence for these putative layers of composition. There are interesting comments on the characters of Achilles and Thersites and on the dramatic function of brief scenes in Act V. Conrad is not consistently reliable, but the best criticism in this essay justifies his opinion that Troi. is "ein wunderbares Werk."

1233. Conrad, H[ermann]. "[Zu Caesar III, 1, 105]," ShJ, XXXI (1895), 380-382.

There is no authority in Plutarch's three accounts of Caesar's death for Brutus' exclamation to his fellow conspirators: "let us bathe our hands in Caesar's blood / Up to the elbows and besmear our swords." Conrad suggests that it is Sh's modification of the ancient custom of drinking human blood (or eating human flesh) to ratify an oathtaking. The custom is described by Sallust, Pomponius Mela, Diodorus Siculus, Dio Cassius, and Plutarch ("Poplicola" and "Cicero"—the versions which Conrad thinks Sh adapted). The alternative which Conrad rejects seems to be a more plausible source: the custom of hunters' dipping their hands into the blood of the slain animal--Sh associates the conspirators with hunters several times in the play.

1234. Cook, Albert S. "The Character of Criseyde," PMLA, XXII (1907), 531-547.

In passing, pp. 539-540: Cressida's "shrewd maxims" in I ii "might have come straight from [Ovid's] Art of Love." Cook adds that Boccaccio's relationship with "Fiammetta" apparently established the tradition which dictated the character of Cressida as she appears in Sh.

1235. Cook, Albert S. "Marlowe, Faustus 13. 91-2," MLN, XXII (1907), 35-37.

Cook extends a discussion by Frederick Tupper (ibid., XXI [1906], 76-77) on Lucian and Marlowe's "Was this the face ..." to include Sh's reference in Troi. He ranges across a score of references in Greek and Latin literature to the thousand ships of the Greeks. The relation between the rape of Helen and the abduction of Hesione traces to Dares, as Cook shows. The art. appears in compressed paraphrase in NewShna, VI (1907), where it is ridiculed as pedantry by a somewhat petulant editor.

1236. Cook, Albert. "Shakespeare's Antony and Cleopatra, V,ii,338-341," Expl, VI (1947), item 9.

A brief note traces the lines "I am fire and air; my other elements / I give to baser life" (Antony V ii 292-293) to Aristotle; Cleopatra means that her soul will rise while her body sinks into the earth.

1237. "Coriolanus," TLS, July 27, 1922, pp. 481-482.

Though this leading art. descends without warning from interpretative criticism to quibbles over the punctuation of F_1, it nonetheless contains some most provocative observations on the play: (1) both Coriolanus and Aufidius are Homeric heroes--creatures of passion who but slenderly know themselves; (2) the failure of the play is that its hero is too human —we are annoyed by him as much as awed; (3) when Sh first read Plutarch for the play he thought of making an Iago out of Aufidius, but during the writing he neglected him for two and a half acts, and when he returned to the character he forgot his original purpose (because he was following North's prose so closely) and made him a warm and receptive host to the man in whose heart he had earlier wanted to steep his hands. By the time Sh reintroduced the original, crafty Aufidius,it was too late--the audience has a dual vision of the man,and ergo the great power of Othello's fall is lacking from Cor. About Aufidius it is difficult to agree--he is never completely generous of spirit, though of course he is no Iago.

1238. "The Coriolanus of Plutarch and Shakespeare," CornellR, IV (1876), 103-109.

"Evidently the play is the biography dramatized. The difference between the two is only that between historical narration and dramatic action," i.e., Sh compresses time and action while he invents dialogue. The author shows that Sh and Plutarch both confused Volumnia, Coriolanus' wife, with Veturia, his mother; he also shows that Sh misinterpreted North's sentence about Censorinus, making him an ancestor of Coriolanus when actually he lived two centuries later (see II iii 251-253). DLC

1239. Corson, H. Introduction to the Study of Shakespeare. Boston, 1889 (no complete pagination available—as abstracted in the New Variorum Antony).

Corson sees Antony as a perfect example of Hamlet's tragic figure flawed by a "vicious mole of nature." Cleopatra is attractive only sexually; her character is unattractive enough to assure that we remain undeceived about the morality of her relationship with Antony. Corson includes a quotation from De Quincey's study of the Roman political figures as Sh portrays them.

1240. Courtenay, T. P. Commentaries on the Historical Plays of Shakespeare. Ln, 1840 (no complete pagination available--as abstracted in the New Variorum Cor.).

Courtenay points out the debt Sh owes to Plutarch for Volumnia's influence over her son at the crucial moment and for the terrible price he pays for his compliance. Courtenay emphasizes the legendary characteristics of the story --neither Plutarch nor Livy was in a position to know accurately what had happened five hundred years B.C. Another account discussed briefly is that of Dionysius of Halicarnassus. He adds that other accounts, if there were such, doubtless perished in the sack of Rome.

1241. Craig, Hardin. "The Shackling of Accidents: A Study of Elizabethan Tragedy," PQ, XIX (1940), 1-19.

For Senecan Stoicism in Antony, see #1884.

1242. Craig, Hardin. "Shakespeare and the History Play," AMS, pp. 55-64.

For Titus as a rhetorical gateway to the early history plays, see #0997.

1243. Crawford, A. W. "A Note on Julius Caesar," MLN, XXXVII (1922), 164-167.

Crawford argues more effectively than Cobden-Sanderson (#1225) for the assignment of V iv 7-8 to Lucilius rather than to Brutus. Crawford brings Plutarch into the argument, but does not thereby obtain the support that he claims. It is not necessary that Lucilius "be" Brutus in these lines to show Sh consistently following Plutarch. What Plutarch says about Brutus' friends seeking to protect him by posing as their leader Sh may have dramatized in the later passage where Lucilius surrenders to Antony's soldiers claiming that he is Brutus.

1244. Crawford, Charles. "The Date and Authenticity of Titus Andronicus," ShJ, XXXVI (1900), 109-121.

Crawford denies that Peele, Greene, and/or Marlowe had a hand in Titus. He cites parallels of phrase between Titus and Peele's The Honour of the Garter (June, 1593) and concludes that Sh borrowed shamelessly from Peele. The logic of the paper is not consistent, and it is full of errors, typographical and grammatical, which cast doubt on Crawford's reliability. Most of the parallels are not compelling.

1245. Crundell, H. W. "Bacon and 'Troilus and Cressida'," NQ, CLXXXVI (1944), 226.

Crundell objects to two parallels cited by R. L. Eagle between Troi. and Bacon--neither proves Bacon's authorship of the play because both are classical concepts with broad Renaissance provenance: (1) "Amare et sapere vix deo conceditur," an aphorism from Publilius Syrus [cf. III ii 163-164]; (2) the confusion about Aristotle, young men, and moral philosophy. Eagle defends himself on (2) (ibid., 275-276) and Crundell shows (ibid., CLXXXVII [1944], 106-107) that Aristotle probably did mean "moral philosophy" in the first ch. of the Nicomachean Ethics. Crundell appears to have Eagle at a disadvantage.

1246. Cunningham, Dolora G. "The Characterization of Shakespeare's Cleopatra," SQ, VI (1955), 9-17.

The apparent change that takes place in Cleopatra's character toward the end of the play should be explained as a conversion from a life of sensuality to reverence for eternal values. In short, in this view Antony is Christianized Plutarch. But a more coherent reading might see Cleopatra as putting off the orient (hedonism) and putting on Rome (Stoicism) after her Roman (who, ironically, had not been Stoic enough) has been taken from her. Cf. Elizabeth Story Donno (SQ, VII [1956], 227-233), who attacks Dr. Cunningham's thesis sharply and effectively, but not from the vantage point of Stoicism.

1247. Curry, John T. "'Et Tu Brute!'," 10 NQ, V (1906), 125.

Curry believes that Sh borrowed Caesar's dying expression from Jonson's Every Man Out of His Humor (1599). Suetonius has him say καὶ σὺ τέκνον. Though Curry believes that it would be more natural for Caesar to speak Latin than Greek, the usual modern view is that Jonson's play postdates Caesar and that Jonson used as a joke the expression which Sh's small Latin had coined; Jonson knew his Suetonius and would regard Sh as a violator of received authority and ergo subject to ridicule.

1248. D., J. "Shakespeare's Mystical Plays--Julius Caesar," NIR, XII (1900), 372-377.

The author of this essay argues that "consciously or unconsciously," Sh conveyed in Caesar the traditional Christian interpretation of the man: he was born to prepare a temporal order which Christianity could inhabit. Like Christ he was to be martyred (cf. Antony's display of Caesar's mutilated body and garments), but like Christ he would live on in his achievements after his death because of the very violence of his enemies. D. implies that Sh shares Dante's view of the conspirators and he draws a parallel between the dream of Pilate's wife and the dream of Calphurnia. Sh makes Caesar an alter Christus by emphasizing his physical infirmity, thereby setting off his spiritual greatness. This interpretation will not bear scrutiny, though it is ingenious; more recent interpretations of Caesar in a Christian context have overlooked D's art. DLC

1249. D., L. "Antony and Cleopatra," NIR, XII (1900), 377-381.

A mystical interpretation of the play elicited by #1248. Antony is Adam, falling from greatness because of his commitment to an imperfect woman. Paradise Lost provides the author with his Christian parallels to Antony. D. does not consider that pagan Plutarch provided Sh with the theme of the fall of the tainted Antony. DLC

1250. Danby, John. "The Shakespearean Dialectic: An Aspect of 'Antony & Cleopatra'," Scrutiny, XVI (1949), 196-213. (Reprinted in Poets on Fortune's Hill [1952].)

The play is Antony's tragedy: he could not, like a colossus, for long bestride the space between Rome (the world) and Egypt (the flesh) without toppling. The play is "the deliberate construction of a world without a Cordelia, Shakespeare's symbol for a reality that transcends the political and the personal." Thus, stripped of redemption, Antony is "Shakespeare's study of Mars and Venus--the presiding deities of Baroque society." Sh's conception of Rome is exactly personified in Octavius, the uncomplicated, sober, resourceful, and triumphant soldier. This is an interesting conception of the tragedy, but Danby does not support it by any detailed analysis of (e.g.) Plutarch's attitude toward Octavius. See Knights (#1447), and also a letter from Wilson Knight (pages 323-327) claiming proprietorship of certain ideas in Danby's art.; Danby replies in the same issue.

1251. Davies, Thomas. "Julius Caesar"; "Antony and Cleopatra," Dramatic Miscellanies... (Ln, 2nd ed., 1785), II, 197-257, 334-371.

Davies cannot concur in Sh's (apparent) admiration for Brutus; he prefers Caesar, to whom he feels Sh has done scant justice. This commentary on Caesar repeatedly digresses into classical history and culture; a long excursus on Roman acting and actors and an awed enumeration of the luxuries of life in the dying republic have interest, but little relevance to Sh's play. Davies makes a comparison between the quarrel scene in Caesar and the quarrel between Agamemnon and Menelaus in Euripides' Iphigenia in Aulis. Davies also claims to be the first commentator to notice that Antony's funeral oration has almost no basis in Plutarch. If Davies wanders back from Sh into Roman history in his chs. on Caesar he wanders forward from Sh into Restoration and eighteenth-century stage history in his notes on Antony. There are perhaps fewer scholia of special interest on Antony than on most of the other plays in Davies' three vols. (see #1895, e.g.). There is an interesting digression on the character of the historical Fulvia and another on Cleopatra's talents. MnU

1252. Davis, E. "Troilus and Cressida," ESA, I (1958), 10-26.

A vigorous defense of the play which concentrates on language and on dramatic and thematic unity. To Davis the ordinariness of both Achilles' and Cressida's betrayals of others makes them satiric prototypes of masculinity and femininity. "Ulysses is a Polonius grown to Olympian stature," while Pandarus suggests in his epilogue that all men have something of the pander in them. Anachronistic references to Cressida as a "shopgirl" and to Troilus as a victim of "Weltschmerz" should be a caveat for the reader: Davis makes no attempt to place the play in its literary tradition and he does not explore the reasons why Sh should have elected the Trojan War as a vehicle for his satire on human nature and society.

1253. Dean, Leonard F. "Voice and Deed in Coriolanus," UKCR, XXI (1955), 177-184.

This interesting thematic analysis of Plutarch's "Coriolanus" and Sh's play shows that the former belongs to a group of lives in which Plutarch portrays extreme ethical positions, inadequate to the situations they are confronted with. Sh seizes this concept, making Coriolanus regard verbal arts (tact, deprecation, plea, persuasion) as hypocritical and evil contrasted with action (this dichotomy derives especially from the Comparison with Alcibiades). Then after the banishing scene the emphasis falls on solitude (the "lonely dragon") which Coriolanus mistakes for magnanimity. Here again Sh is appropriating a hint from Plutarch, who says that Plato spoke of arrogant, unyielding men as likely to live in solitude.

1254. Deighton, K. "Introduction," Timon of Athens (1905/1929), ArdenSh, pp. vii-xxxi.

Deighton anticipates a more recent critical consensus by assigning Sh the vast majority of Tim. and arguing that it is an unpolished draft possibly worsened in a few places by actors, but not supplemented in any major way by any of Sh's fellow dramatists. He mentions Painter, Plutarch, and Lucian as the major sources for the play and argues that Sh must have known Lucian (perhaps even in Greek) because there are verbal echoes of Misanthropos in Tim. (the passages are given in Greek--the evidence is not compelling). But Deighton iterates Boas' observation (in #0112) that Sh shows no real familiarity with the triumphs of Periclean Athens in this play.

1255. Deighton, K. "Introduction," Troilus and Cressida (1906/1932), ArdenSh, pp. vii-xxxii.

Deighton proposes as sources for Troi. Caxton, Lydgate, Chapman's Iliads, and, less certainly, Chaucer (he regards the love plot as most un-Chaucerian in tone). He is willing to accept the theory of revision in the play, but would not go so far as Fleay does. Hector's lines on "mad idolatry" are to be taken as the central thesis of the play: Sh's cynicism made an idolater of Troilus and Sh carried this cynicism over into the war plot, also, where men worship at the shrine of a woman not worth the having. An interesting comment calls attention to the similarity of expression among the Greek heroes, who are not individualized by their speech as Sh's characters normally are.

1256. Delius, N[icolaus]. "Shakespeare's Coriolanus in seinem Verhältniss zum Coriolanus des Plutarch," ShJ, XI (1876), 32-58. E-S HB

Delius can claim to be first to make a close comparison of the whole of Cor. with the whole of Plutarch's "Life of Coriolanus" to determine the extent of Sh's indebtedness for plot, characterization, and diction. He concludes that earlier critics have overestimated Sh's dependence on the source, although the section on language clearly shows Sh's fidelity to North's phrasing in many passages. Delius' thesis rests on Sh's manipulation of twelve main incidents in Plutarch (Sh fuses some and separates others in the interest of dramatic effectiveness) and on the approach to the protagonist (e.g., unlike Plutarch's Marcius, "altogether unfit for any man's conversation," Sh's hero is a warm friend to Menenius, Cominius, and Titus Lartius). This pioneer work has since been qualified by numerous commentators; for an excellent recent study, see #1390.

1257. Delius, Nicolaus. "Shakespeare's Julius Caesar und seine Quellen im Plutarch," ShJ, XVII (1882), 67-81. E-S

Delius provides a seriatim account of Caesar showing which incidents Sh invented and which he borrowed from Plutarch's "Antonius," "Brutus," and "Caesar." The emphasis falls almost entirely on events and encounters between characters rather than on philosophical issues or the personal characteristics of the principals in the action. This emphasis makes it appear that Sh deviates more from Plutarch's conception of the Caesar story than actually he does. Delius also magnifies Sh's originality by laying stress on incidents which Sh omitted, introduced, or rearranged instead of placing North's prose side by side with Sh's verse in the many places where Sh does follow his source closely. Delius explains that Sh wished to dramatize Caesar's death, not his life, and that therefore he drew only on the last fifth of the "Life of Caesar," but there is little other exploration of Sh's artistic or philosophical motives for departure from Plutarch.

1258. Delius, N[icolaus]. "Ueber Shakespeare's Timon of Athens," ShJ, II (1867), 335-361.

Delius here retracts an opinion he had formerly held that Tim. is a partial revision made late in his career of a play Sh had drafted in his earliest period. He holds in this art. that Sh made a partial revision of a play (now lost) by an unknown predecessor. Sh probably knew the accounts in Painter and Plutarch, but he doubtless relied almost exclusively on his source-play. The anonymous predecessor borrowed a good part of his plot from Lucian (scarcely accessible to Sh), but it seems doubtful whether he knew the academic Timon. The body of the art. is a seriatim analysis of Tim. with the object of segregating Sh's contribution to the play. Delius makes the interesting point that Tim. is most Shn when the protagonist is on stage. At ibid., III (1868), 175-204, Delius nominates George Wilkins as author of the original Tim. (as well as of the original Per.).

1259. De Selincourt, E. "Troilus and Cressida," Oxford Lectures on Poetry (OUP, 1934), pp. 78-105.

De Selincourt favors disintegrating Troi., but he does not make a special plea of the matter; he is particularly interested in the tone of the play as a product of Sh's vicarious experience with British political life and of his misinterpretations of the chivalry of Lydgate and Caxton. Cressida to De Selincourt is more guilty than to some of her critics, and Troilus is a tragic hero crushed as none of Sh's other heroes are. Yet the love plot is not the whole of the play; Cressida's infidelity is only an incident in the general corruption of Troy and Greece. The astute analysis of the war plot is more satisfying on the whole than the treatment of the love plot.

1260. Desmonde, William H. "The Ritual Origin of Shakespeare's 'Titus Andronicus'," IJP, XXXVI (1955), 61-65.

The author believes that three major episodes in Titus, the death of Titus' sons, the rape of Lavinia, and the cannibalistic banquet, derive mediately from Greek male and female puberty rites. The death of Titus' sons together with the horrid banquet and the butchery of Act V culminating in the death of Titus and the succession to power of his last living son is a reflection of the father-son conflict in the Greek mysteries typified by the legend of Pelops and Oinomaos and the other myths of the house of Tantalus. The rape of Lavinia is a descendant of a defloration ceremony typified in the myth of Persephone (the rape takes place by a pit--Hades carried Persephone beneath the ground). The probable immediate source for both episodes is Ovid's Meta. IV in which the two themes are united in the myth of Tereus, Philomela, and Procne.

1261. Deutschbein, Max. "Die Tragik in Shakespeares Julius Caesar," Anglia, LXII (1938), 306-320.

An interesting essay which sees Caesar as the gateway to the mature tragedies because of its emphasis on the paradoxical relationship between ideal "honor" and real "danger." These two terms (with "honesty") are central in the ironies of the play. The play is Brutus' tragedy because "es ist ganz klar, dass an Brutus sich die Auseinandersetzung von Schicksal und Charakter vollzieht." But in Caesar's murder also we see portrayed the constant threat to existence which marks the human condition. Deutschbein does not discuss warrants in Plutarch for Sh's theme except to quote a passage from the "Life of Caesar" which identifies Brutus' followers ("Bruti") with beasts; this may have offered Sh a hint for the "Et tu Brute" with its possible pun making Brutus beastly--the antithesis of honorable.

1262. Deutschberger, Paul. "Shakspere on Degree: A Study in Backgrounds," SAB, XVII (1942), 200-207.

A study of Ulysses' speech in Troi. (I iii) as a document of Medieval and Renaissance thought. Deutschberger goes no further toward the ultimate source in Platonic metaphysics than a passing reference to Boethius.

1263. Dibelius, Wilhelm. "Zur Stoffgeschichte des Titus Andronikus," ShJ, XLVIII (1912), 1-12. E-S

Sh's sources for Titus are not Roman but Byzantine: Sh combined details from the life of the Emperor Andronicus I (late twelfth century) with the legend of Thamar, the wild warrior queen of the Caucasian kingdom of Georgia (approximately contemporary with Andronicus), and the carnal concupiscence of her daughter, Rousoudan; both of the latter Sh combined in Tamora. There are sufficient echoes (e.g., the names "Bassianus," "Demetrius,"

"Chiron," "Aaron") to lend a certain plausibility to the argument that Sh borrowed from some Latin or Italian redaction of the Byzantine sources.

1264. [Dobree, Bonamy]. "Cleopatra and 'That Criticall Warr'," TLS, October 11, 1928, pp. 717-718. (Reprinted with minor alterations as Ch. IV of his Restoration Tragedy [1929].)

This leading art. compares Antony with Dryden's All For Love and Daniel's Cleopatra against the background of Plutarch as source and Aristotle as critical standard. Antony represents the romantic, or panoramic, form; All For Love the classical, unified, form; Cleopatra the Senecan, narrative, form. Sh does not come out best in this "criticall warr," but the essay contains several brilliant insights into Sh's conception of tragedy and his use of Plutarchian materials.

1265. Dorsch, T. S. "Introduction," Julius Caesar (1955/1958), ArdenSh, pp. vii-lxxiv.

An excellent introduction to the play, although in its extended character analyses it is perhaps unfair in denigrating Brutus, Casca, and Cassius while minimizing analogous faults in Caesar and Antony. Observations about the minor characters (especially Lucius, Portia, and Calphurnia) are very interesting. The commentary on Sh's manipulation of Plutarch is revealing; Dorsch suggests that Sh may have drawn on the "Caius Julius Caesar" in A Mirror for Magistrates as well. The discussions of the unity of the play and of the images which recur in it are both provocative criticism.

1266. Dowden, Edward. "The Roman Plays," Shakspere: A Critical Study of His Mind and Art (1875), 3rd ed. (N.Y., n.d. [1880?]), Ch. VI, pp. 245-299.

Dowden's Sh criticism is now sometimes labeled "personalist" and discarded, but this ch. contains intelligent analysis of Caesar, Antony, and Cor. with frequent reference to Plutarch. Dowden does not try to identify Sh with any single character or his experience with any set of circumstances in the action, but he does try to read Sh's politics through Cor. and his attitudes toward types of character through Caesar. Dowden is well informed--he knows for example that the speeches of Brutus and Antony have analogues in the Appian trans. of 1578. Perhaps Dowden's criticism has been largely assimilated by later writers, but its contribution should not go unrecognized.

1267. Draper, John W. "Cassius and Brutus," BHM, XIII (1943), 133-143.

Sh unified the respective characters of his two conspirators and contrasted them with each other by use of the classical humors. He altered Plutarch in details in order to emphasize the choleric temperament of Cassius and the sanguine humor of Brutus. An interesting and well-documented study, but there is more to Cassius than hot temper and more to Brutus than a positive cast of mind.

1268. Draper, John W. "The Psychology of Shakespeare's Timon," MLR, XXXV (1940), 521-525.

Sh made alterations in the classical tale to make it palatable to an Elizabethan audience. The chief of these is the domination of the hero by successive humors over which he has no control. He begins as sanguine, becomes choleric under severe misfortune, descends into melancholy when his choler has burned up bodily fluids, and then, verging on madness, he kills himself. All of this is orthodox Renaissance medical psychology and serves to excuse Timon for his extravagant behavior, especially his suicide. If Draper is correct in implying that Timon and Coriolanus (see #1270) are largely the sums of their respective humors, he may have an answer to the failure of audiences to respond to these two heroes: they may seem to audiences like automatons moved about by inexorable Necessity.

1269. Draper, J[ohn] W. "The Realism of Shakespeare's Roman Plays," SP, XXX (1933), 225-242. E-S SG

An analysis of Sh's three "Plutarch" plays shows that Caesar, the earliest, is by no means faithful to details of Roman life, while Antony successfully avoids anachronism. The difference can be accounted for by the growing influence of Jonson's accurate classicism. The anachronisms in Cor. are the result of Sh's ignorance of early Roman history. This is a thorough study with plausible conclusions.

1270. Draper, John W. "Shakespeare's Coriolanus: A Study in Renaissance Psychology," WVBPS, III (1939), 22-36.

"Greek simplicity of plot and character and style, and Greek restraint with Greek inevitability of outcome" are the striking features of Cor. Plutarch had suggested that Coriolanus was insolent, but Sh altered the source to dwell constantly on his pride. In Renaissance (ultimately Greek) psychology, pride leads to choler, to revenge, to shame and death. But Coriolanus is not alone in his choleric humor; the Plebeians, who in Plutarch's account had recently banished the Tarquins in anger at their pride, are also choleric as they show in Sh's action. Thus both leader and people totter on the "brink of ruin" because of a defect of humor. This inherent tendency to predictable behavior gives the play a pre-history like that of Oedipus: perhaps this is its most "Greek" feature.

1271. Draper, John W. "The Theme of 'Timon of Athens'," MLR, XXIX (1934), 20-31. E-S

Sh flies in the face of classical authority in the plot and characterization of Tim., but not through ignorance. He is consciously deploring usury, the vice of the play and the bane of Jacobean England. Thus, in a classical setting he writes "a sort of dramatic elegy on the ideals of chivalry that were succumbing in a capitalistic age." If accepted, this ingenious interpretation gives thematic unity to the play, supports the theory of sole Shn authorship, and suggests that Sh was not the blunderer with classical materials which he has often been thought to have been.

1272. Draper, R. P. "Timon of Athens," SQ, VIII (1957), 195-200.

A reading of the play as an unsatisfactory prologue to the last plays, with their theme of healing and regeneration. Timon behaves like an exile from the Saturnian Age who cannot accept "the fallen world in which he actually exists." This theme of the Golden World and the irony that "real" gold—the evil desideratum of almost everyone in the play--was discovered in the cruel Iron Age (according to Ovid), are the poles of an axis on which the play can be seen to turn. Thus the many references to the fecundity of the earth and Nature suggest the Golden World at the same time that they look back to Lear and ahead to the last plays. A very interesting interpretation of the play, which finds more unity in it than some others have found, but which candidly admits that the shift in emphasis late in the action from Timon to Alcibiades is an artistic blemish.

1273. Dreizen, Lester. Shakespeare: Mark Antony and Mass Persuasion, A Study of Attitudes and Their Transformation. Mesnil, 1953, 64 pp.

Not seen.

1274. Dryden, John. Prologue to Troilus and Cressida (1679), Munro, II, 251.

Here the ghost of Sh confesses that he "drain'd no Greek or Latin store."

1275. Dunkel, Wilbur D. "Shakespeare's Troilus," SQ, II (1951), 331-334.

Dunkel offers an interpretation of Troi. which is not so original as he assumes it to be: Troilus' conceptions of truth, honor, and value are all based empirically; but abstractions must be our guides, or at least Sh so hints by showing the unworthiness of the basis (Cressida) of Troilus' value system. Because the Greeks and Trojans are concerned about the relationship between the absolute and "the individual appraiser" the play is about "the various ways in which men think." The hypothesis may not be appealing, but Dunkel does show succinctly how uncomfortably Troilus finds himself an alter Menelaus when he sees Cressida/Helen give herself to Diomedes/Paris.

1276. Duthie, George Ian. "Imaginative Interpretation and Troilus and Cressida," Shakespeare, Hutchinson's University Library (Ln, 1951), pp. 89-114.

Duthie sides with those who find the Greeks and Trojans much alike in the disorderliness of their approach to war. Priam and Ulysses represent ordered sanity, but neither is capable of preventing the prideful, emotional men around him from doing their countries disservice. Troilus is irrational in his love, a parallel to the war plot. The most interesting point in this essay for the general reader is an ironic parallel between Hector and Achilles: the former plunges into his final battle because of misguided vows which he has made "to many Greeks"; the latter refrains from helping his allies because of a misguided vow he has sworn to the Trojans Polyxena and her mother.

1277. Dyboski, Roman. Rise and Fall in Shakespeare's Dramatic Art. Ln, 1923 (no complete pagination available—as abstracted in the New Variorum Cor.).

Dyboski believes that Sh's restricting emphasis on the isolation of the hero dries up the possibilities of variety in Cor., possibilities that Sh had realized in Caesar, which also dealt with republican Rome with its "simple" culture. Cor. is an ethical, not an aesthetic play. Dyboski, forgetting Temp., Cym., Per., and W.T., says that Cor. "terminates Shakespeare's poetic manhood."

1278. Eardley-Wilmot, H. "Coriolanus," TLS, October 13, 1950, p. 645.

The author would assign the three lines Menenius speaks in III i about gangrened feet to Sicinius because they do not suit Menenius' character. A. P. Rossiter ably defends the F_1 attribution of speeches (ibid., p. 661).

1279. Eckhardt, Eduard. "Zur Rolle des Thersites in Shakespeares Troilus and Cressida," ESn, LXIV (1929), 370-379.

Eckhardt observes that Thersites has no real function in the plot of Troi. and argues that his rôle is that of Sh's mouthpiece to denigrate Nestor, Ajax, Achilles, Patroclus, Diomedes, Menelaus, and Helen. As a witty coward Thersites is, therefore, a sort of vitriolic Falstaff. But Eckhardt also produces interesting parallels between Sh's Thersites and Heywood's (Iron Age I) which persuade him that Heywood's play may have inspired Sh's conception of Thersites. The depth of Sh's pessimism is indicated to Eckhardt by his willingness to let a foul-mouthed, repulsive character express his own view of the Trojan War.

1280. Eisenstein, Judith. "Thersites and the Abstraction," Westwind, I (Fall, 1957), [17]-[19]. GRS

Thersites, like Falstaff, Shylock, and Edmund, is a cynical questioner of accepted values. But unlike these men and unlike Ulysses (who also "comment[s] upon folly and confusion, and exercise[s] a 'corrective' function") Thersites' skepticism is motiveless. He does not stand to gain from denigrating the values of others. The essay does not discuss Thersites as a traditional character; indeed, it sees him as post-Copernican man. CLU

1281. Eitner, Karl. "Die Troilus-Fabel in ihrer literaturgeschichtlichen Entwickelung, und die Bedeutung des letzten Akts von Shakespeare's Troilus und Cressida im Verhältniss zum gesammten Stücke," ShJ, III (1868), 252-300. E-S

Eitner devotes two thirds of his art. to a detailed survey of the evolution of the legend. The emphasis here falls on the characters in the love plot: the growth of Troilus, e.g., is traced in antiquity from Homer and the pre-Homeric account of the death of Troilus through Sophocles, Virgil, Horace, Ausonius, Seneca, and a number of Alexandrian grammarians and rhetoricians to Dares and Dictys. Among Medieval authorities discussed are Benoît de Ste. Maure, Guido della Colonna, Lydgate, Boccaccio, Chaucer, Henderson's (sic) Testament of Cresseid, Jacques Milet's Istoire de la destruction de Troye la Grant, and Raoul Le Fevre (with Caxton's trans.). Sh used Chaucer, Lydgate, Caxton, and Chapman's Homer, but he added his own attitudes, sympathetic and elegiac (especially in the tragic fifth act), and antipathetic and satiric (in the bitter comedy of much in the first four acts). The assumption that a single tone must dominate a play has led critics to regard the fifth act as an intrusion, but the death of Hector and the disillusionment of Troilus elicit our sympathy and indicate that the world which Sh has been mocking through Thersites' railing now is about to come to an end.

1282. Eliot, T. S. "Vergil and the Christian World," SewR, LXI (1953), 1-14.

In passing (p. 5): Sh portrays all the Homeric heroes as "ruffian[s]" except Hector, whose lines in II ii beginning "If Helen then be wife to Sparta's king" indicate his human dignity.

1283. Ellehauge, Martin. "The Use of His Sources Made by Shakespeare in Julius Caesar and Antony and Cleopatra," ESn, LXV (1930), 197-210. E-S SG

A sketch of Sh's departures from Plutarch in action, characterization, and language. In almost every case the deviations were made in answer to the demands of dramatic form. Daniel's Cleopatra may have modified Sh's phrasing and ideas in Antony. Ellehauge appears to rely rather heavily on the impressionistic criticism of Georg Brandes, but on the whole his observations are valid, though not profound.

1284. Elliot, Robert C. "The Great Misanthropes: 2) Timon of Athens," The Power of Satire: Magic, Ritual, Art (PUP, 1960), pp. 141-167.

Elliott's satisfying interpretation of Tim. distinguishes Apemantus (a privileged Cynic railer like Thersites—discussed in the preceding section of this ch.) from Timon (after his misfortunes a satirist something like Marston and Hall), and both from Sh, who satirizes both (especially Timon) by pushing them into a flyting (IV iii 354-375) reminiscent of the contest in scurrility which amused Virgil, Horace, and Maecenas in the "Journey to Brundisium" (Satires I v 51-69). This is at least as plausible a view of the play and its hero as any that has been proposed in recent years.

1285. Ellis-Fermor, Una. "'Discord in the Spheres': The Universe of Troilus and Cressida," The Frontiers of Drama (Ln, 1945), pp. 56-76.

The theme of Troi. is disjunction, the absence from the universe of absolute value, and Sh reflects it in the juxtaposition of incompatibles: nobility and cowardice, faith and disillusionment, lethargy and violence, effeminacy and virility (this last in the verse as well as in the characters). Thus discord becomes an artistic principle in the play; Troi. is perhaps the only play ever written of which this is true. The thesis is argued with imagination and vigor, but the author's desire to move from the values of the play to Sh's opinions about the nature of value in the universe is not to be condoned, especially when she speaks of the form of Troi. as triumphing over the chaos of its concepts and then seeks to apply the principle of art as spiritual triumph to the plays which follow in the canon.

1286. Ellis-Fermor, Una. "The Shakespearian Transmutation," The Jacobean Drama: An Interpretation (1936), 4th ed. (Ln, 1958), pp. 247-271.

The essay considers inter alia Troi. and Tim. as studies in pessimism, Antony as a rebirth of optimism, and Cor. as a part of Sh's composite sketch of political man (as the state makes demands of him and as the state shapes him). But there is no attempt here to account for the tone of these plays in their sources. In passing Miss Ellis-Fermor suggests that Sh would have accepted Aristotle's division of virtues into the categories public and private, though he nowhere overtly makes such a division himself.

1287. Ellis-Fermor, Una. "Timon of Athens: An Unfinished Play," RES, XVIII (1942), 270-283.

This seriatim commentary on the structure, verse, and characterization concludes that the play was never finished, perhaps because Sh realized that in isolating Timon from his society he was imposing a dramatic difficulty on himself which he had surmounted in Ham. but which he knew could not be surmounted in Tim. An interesting suggestion, but not compelling, because Sh so obviously did surmount the same difficulty again in Cor.

1288. Elton, Oliver. "Shakespeare," The English Muse: A Sketch (Ln, 1933), Ch. IX, pp. 152-175.

There are remarks on Sh's classicism passim, but the most specific are the brief comments on the Roman plays, 160-161, 165-166. Caesar "is Shakespeare's most truly classic play"; Antony "is no romantic play . . . the world is neither well nor ill lost; it simply is lost"; in Cor. "the prose of North is well worthy of Shakespeare's respect for it."

1289. Elton, William. "Shakespeare's Portrait of Ajax in Troilus and Cressida," PMLA, LXIII (1948), 744-748.

An attempt to reinstate Fleay's defunct identification of Jonson with Ajax. Elton submits much evidence, external and internal, but none of it refutes Tatlock's arguments (#1718) for the historical basis of the tone of the play.

1290. Elton, William. "Two Shaksperian Parallels," SAB, XXII (1947), 115-116.

The second note finds an analogue to Menenius' fable in a Medieval French débat. The parallel is of interest, but Sh's source obviously was Plutarch.

1291. Emerson, Oliver F. "Antony and Cleopatra," PL, II (1890), 71-77, 125-129, 188-192.

Part I, on Sh's conception of the developing political situation in Rome during the sixteen years embraced by Caesar and Antony, concludes that as Antony's star sinks the star of empire rises and that Antony loses the empire when he loses mastery over himself (cf. #1516). Part II concentrates on situation and motive in Antony, suggesting that the political backdrop holds together two plots: the downfall of Antony through his sensuality, and the destruction of Egypt's queen "through the temptation she presents to another." Part III deals with the characters as moral agents: Sh's task was to keep the proper measure of audience sympathy with the protagonists at all times--not an easy task in a play in which patently immoral behavior everywhere predominates.

1292. Emerson, Oliver F. "Antony and Octavius: A Comparative Estimate," PL, II (1890), 516-523.

A well-balanced juxtaposition which is best summed up, perhaps, by two of its insights: (1) at Philippi, Antony praised his fallen enemy while Octavius "turned away ... with businesslike promptitude 'To part the glories of this happy day'"; (2) Antony's fault is that he is not "moderatissimus," as Cicero would have a Roman be.

1293. Empson, William. "Double Plots: Heroic and Pastoral in the Main Plot and Sub-Plot," Some Versions of Pastoral (Ln, 1950), pp. 25-86.

Part of this ch., pp. 34-42, is an analysis of the ironic relationship between the "heroic" main plot of Troi. and the "pastoral" subplot which becomes an acid commentary on it. Not only are Paris and Troilus, Helen and Cressida analogues, they are also the causes of the things they symbolize: e.g., Troilus symbolizes Troy and its status, but he is also the cause (in part) of its difficulties. This is a very interesting criticism of the play even if it sometimes considers too curiously. By Empson's standards Troi. may be regarded as a great play; he maintains that English drama died when the parallel subplot died.

1294. Empson, William. "Timon's Dog," Shakespeare Survey (Ln, n.d.), pp. 22-36. (This is not the periodical ShS.)

Empson interprets Tim. in the light of its canine imagery which, he feels, serves to characterize those who use it (i.e., Timon and Apemantus). The two chief connotations are flattery and cynicism. It is interesting that Empson does not mention the origins of Sh's imagery in Greek Cynicism; to Empson Diogenes the Cynic has no relevance to the play.

1295. Engel, Eduard. "Shakespeares Bibliothek," ShJ, XXXV (1899), 273-274.

Engel prints Sidney's account of Menenius' fable from the Apologie for Poesie and asserts that Sh used it in Cor. An alternative version from Camden's Remaines (1605) he considers an unlikely source. The apparent source of both Camden and Sidney, Plutarch's "Life of Coriolanus," is, it would seem, obviously Sh's source for the passage in I i.

1296. Enright, D. J. "Coriolanus: Tragedy or Debate?" EC, IV (1954), 1-19.

Because Coriolanus does not see into himself, the play must be regarded as a debate in which both sides are wrong and Rome, the tragic protagonist, suffers. Enright believes Plutarch's Coriolanus to be a simpler character even than the two-dimensional, "shadowy" figure Sh created. (On this point see Browning, #1188.) But Enright does not observe that if the hero is not introspective, Sh at least allows us to see in him a complexity that makes tragedy possible. Enright's view is too limited, though he makes an observant point when he calls Coriolanus the Shn hero most talked about by other characters.

1297. Etty, J. L. "Studies in Shakespeare's History: VI--Julius Caesar," MM, LXXXVII (1903), 350-360.

"Shakespeare's Caesar outrages both liberty and good taste, and is thus a most suitable victim for the daggers of the conspirators." Sh sided with the conspirators, but dwelt not so much on tyrannicide as on his "favourite subject," friendship (between Caesar and Antony, Caesar and Brutus, Brutus and Cassius, Brutus and Portia). This interpretation of the play may not bear scrutiny, but Etty makes a number of interesting points of which these three are typical: (1) Brutus "is the very type of the doctrinaire politician, and seems in his own person to stultify Plato's ideal of the philosopher-king." (2) Cassius hates Caesar because Caesarism deprives Cassius of the one thing he loves--practical politics. (3) Antony is a character more complex than anyone else in the play: Etty gives an excellent analysis of the man. Entirely an interesting study.

1298. Etty, J. L. "Studies in Shakespeare's History VII--Antony and Cleopatra," MM, LXXXIX (1904), 302-309.

Etty believes that Sh keeps the great political issues in the background; he himself pulls them to the fore, unearthing passages in Plutarch and Cicero which Sh did not use to show just what the tide of history was sweeping across and just what was at stake at Actium. The result is a paper on the whole convincing in its analysis of Antony, Cleopatra, and the action. Only on the structure of the play is the criticism badly deficient: Etty considers the multiplicity of scenes a liability when actually it suggests fragmentation of Antony's world, acceleration toward catastrophe, and especially the grandeur of the world Antony is losing.

1299. Evans, G. Blakemore. "Pandarus' House?: Troilus and Cressida, III.ii; IV.ii; IV.iv," MLN, LXII (1947), 33-35.

This note adduces internal evidence that Troilus and Cressida meet not at Pandarus' house, but at her (i.e., Calchas') house. The error in most modern eds. is traceable to Lewis Theobald, who may have been influenced by Chaucer, where the lovers do meet at Pandarus' home. A minor point, perhaps, but it is not without significance that Cressida gives herself to her lover on her own ground.

1300. Evans, G. Blakemore. "The Problem of Brutus: An Eighteenth-Century Solution," Baldwin Festschrift, pp. 229-236.

Evans prints his transcription of a manuscript draft of a letter (ca. 1712-19) signed by one T. Killigrew (not the theatrical producer), a letter which objects to Sh's portraits of both Brutus and Caesar. Killigrew suggests a number of revisions in Acts II and III, all calculated to make Caesar appear a greater offender against the commonweal and therefore to give Brutus greater justification for his tyrannicide. This letter was printed in Munro in 1932 and there attributed to T. Killigrew the Elder (1660-83?).

1301. Everett, William. "Six Cleopatras," AM, XCV (1905), 252-263.

A judicious criticism of plays by Sh, Fletcher, Corneille, Dryden, Alfieri, and Mme. de Girardin. Everett stresses the fidelity with which Sh follows Plutarch, yet he grants that Sh conveys the illusion of originality. The most provocative observation about Antony is that it contains no uninterrupted speech so long as twenty lines: Sh did not want declamatory rhetoric to obscure the characters whom he reveals through dialogue. Mme. de Girardin, Fletcher, and Dryden deserve praise for their "noble language" and "profound feeling," but for characterization Sh has no peer.

1302. Fansler, Harriott Ely. The Evolution of Technic in Elizabethan Tragedy. Chicago, 1914, 283 pp. SG

For Senecanism in Caesar, see #1919.

1303. Farnham, Willard. "The Beast Theme in Shakespeare's 'Timon'," CUPE, XIV (1943), 49-56. GRS

Farnham begins with the assertion that the concept of man as beast (or worse) in Tim. is Sh's contribution (a carry-over from Lear) despite the fact that the pre-Shn Timon story contains such elements. Later in the essay Farnham concedes Sh's possible indebtedness (ultimate) to legends about Diogenes the Cynic and Antisthenes the Cynic, and to Lucian's equation between Timon's flatterers and birds and beasts of prey.

1304. Farnham, Willard. Shakespeare's Tragic Frontier: The World of His Final Tragedies. California UP, 1950, 289 pp.

Farnham advances the thesis that Tim., Macb., Antony, and Cor. are a group of tragedies in which the heroes (and Cleopatra) are "deeply flawed," yet attractive with noble dignity. Farnham makes no special point of the fact that three of these plays deal with classical themes, nor does he observe that characters in Troi., R.III, R.II, and (crudely) Titus are also "deeply flawed." What Farnham sees as a philosophical development in Sh's art (he cites Chapman's ethical tragedies as a parallel) may only be a survival of the Machiavellian villain hero (Macbeth), of lust tragedy (cf. Gismond of Salerne and Antony), of the railing malcontent (cf. Jaques and Timon), and of Marlovian arrogance (cf. Tamburlaine and Coriolanus). But irrespective of the validity of the thesis Farnham's source studies for each of the plays are made with scrupulous care. He has thoroughly digested his predecessors and adds some new material: (1) Tim. contains a beast-in-man theme which is post-Plutarchian; Sh flouts tradition by eliciting sympathy for the hero; Apemantus is a variation on Diogenes the Cynic (dog). (2) In Macb. the Witches are not Norns or Parcae but probably fairies--descendants of nymphs or Erinyes who tempt men to evil, but do not force it on them. (3) Sh emphasizes the paradoxes of Cleopatra's character more than Plutarch does; he owes no apparent debt to the Countess of Pembroke's Antonius, but is definitely indebted to the Argument of Daniel's "Letter from Octavia to Marcus Antonius" (1599); Sh is not so obviously indebted to Daniel's Cleopatra, though Farnham would accept Daniel as source. (4) Plutarch's Coriolanus is the victim of a churlishness which a better education would have supplanted; Sh's Coriolanus is guilty of spiritual pride and its servant wrath--yet these evil qualities are also the source of his nobility. Farnham's is an important critical source study.

1305. Farquhar, Edward. "Shakespeare's Brutus," OC, XVIII (1904), 558-562.

An interpretation of Brutus' denial of knowledge of Portia's death (IV iii 181-192) as a sign of impending lunacy: "with all his grandeur of spirit Brutus is a fanatic; a man who follows his 'principle' without intelligence to match." Hardly a convincing explanation, either of the passage or of the play.

1306. Feldman, Harold. "Unconscious Envy in Brutus," AI, IX (1955), 307-335.

In a psychological study which until its last section is refreshingly pure of psychiatric jargon, Feldman examines Sh's departures from Plutarch in the motivation of Brutus' participation in the conspiracy. The hero is a self-lover so much that he does not recognize in himself the envy he feels toward Caesar. Feldman several times admits that his argument is perhaps not convincing, and the reader will agree, especially when he calls to the stand elements of Roman history which are external to the play and may well have been unknown to Sh.

1307. Felheim, Marvin. "The Problem of Time in Julius Caesar," HLQ, XIII (1950), 399-405.

A dogmatic, but unconvincing, exposition of the time scheme of Acts I and II. The crux is I iii, which Felheim believes to be the night of March 14, and which others have thought the night of February 15. The most reasonable explanation is one of which Felheim is unjustifiably contemptuous--see #1651.

1308. Feuillerat, Albert. "Titus Andronicus," The Composition of Shakespeare's Plays: Authorship, Chronology (Yale UP, 1953), pp. 142-184.

A minute examination of the Malmö Q of 1594 and of F_1 convinces Feuillerat that he can trace the evolution of the play: "It is an old play, written by author A ..., first touched up by author B to give it a Marlovian flavor [Aaron is an imitation of Barabas], and finally revised in an important way (as the mannerisms and images show) by Shakespeare." Feuillerat assumes that Sh had a distinctive, recognizable style in the early 'nineties, an assumption which appears unwarranted--Sh learned his craft by imitating closely classical and Renaissance models, and his early style is derivative. Feuillerat argues inter alia that one Shn characteristic is "compound words after the Greek and Latin manner" (e.g., "counsaile-keeping"); in another place Feuillerat reasons that "one author was familiar with classical history, the other ignorant of local color and speaking of Roman institutions in terms ["King" and "Queen" for "Emperor" and "Empress"] of the English court." A meticulous study, but it is founded on fallacious assumptions.

1309. Finsler, Georg. Homer in der Neuzeit von Dante bis Goethe: Italien, Frankreich, England, Deutschland. Leipzig, 1912, 530 pp.

Sh merits but one paragraph, in which Finsler discusses the "vielumstrittene Frage" of Sh's possible use of Chapman's Homer for Troi. Sh knew Caxton, but not Lydgate. Finsler regards as "wahrscheinlich" Small's suggestion (#1665) that details like the combat between Hector and Ajax come from Chapman, but he notes that Sh was not influenced by "die grossen homerischen Bilder" like the wrath of Achilles or the embassy. Finsler points out that Sh's response to the Homeric story was not sardonic in Ham. (Player's speech) and 2H.IV (Northumberland's analogy between himself and Priam). DLC

1310. Flatter, Richard. "Julius Caesar--ein Tyrann?" Triumph der Gnade: Shakespeare-Essays (Wien, 1956), pp. 129-133. GRS

Flatter argues that if Sh's Caesar is vain, superstitious, and vacillating, many great men have been also. This rationalization of Caesar's faults is followed by a more telling point: when Metellus Cimber pleads for his brother's return from banishment Caesar refuses to place personal influence above the state decree which banished Publius Cimber. Caesar, then, is not a tyrant, but a good sovereign: whether crowned or not, Caesar has the power of a king, and the requisite traits of character as well. Flatter does not discuss Plutarch's attitude.

1311. Fleay, F[rederick] G. "On the Authorship of Timon of Athens," NSST, I (1874), 130-194.

Fleay here first advances the theory that Sh wrote a skeletal version of Tim. which an unidentified hack writer completed. His attempt to dismember the play is largely intuitive (e.g., "ira furor brevis est" [I ii 28] is a hackneyed

Latin phrase "not at all in Shakspere's style," but not unlike the scraps of Latin in the non-Shn Titus, H.VI, and Shrew). Fleay says little about the sources. He reprints as "The Life of Tymon of Athens" those parts of the play which are Shn in his judgment (pp. 153-194).

1312. Foakes, R. A. "An Approach to Julius Caesar," SQ, V (1954), 259-270.

The leitmotiv of contrast between a man's public name and his private self, between the ideal principle and the real practice, suggests that Caesar should be interpreted not as a character study, but as the story of a rebellion—its inception, mission, and final defeat. This interpretation makes both Caesar and Brutus less important than some have thought them and Cassius both more important and less base. An interesting theory, which makes plot, not character, the focus of the play. Such an approach to the play is hardly consonant with Plutarch, who was intensely interested in character; Foakes does not explain Sh's putative rejection of Plutarch's emphasis.

1313. Foard, James T. "Shakespeare's Classical Plays," ManQ, XII (1893), 333-371.

With acerbity Foard attacks those who maintain that Sh disguised Englishmen as Romans and Greeks in Caesar, Antony, Tim., and Cor. His best (and most extended) criticism treats Caesar, finding a middle ground between those who think the play Brutus' tragedy and those who see it as a eulogy of Caesarism. He argues that the cast are much what the historical personages were; even when Plutarch gives only hints, Sh conveys the men we learn about in the letters of Brutus and Cicero, e.g. The comments on Antony are more brief and less satisfying, especially in the contrast between Juliet ("the heroine of the young and enthusiastic poet") and Cleopatra ("the idol of the middle-aged theatrical manager"). Antony is "the old, old tale. Hercules and Omphale, Venus and Mars, Dido and Aeneas, Solomon and the Queen of Sheba." Foard finds Tim. "a Titanic fragment, an unformed boulder of the Cyclopean Age," yet a more finished play than Cor. He denies Sh's indebtedness to the academic Timon, suggesting instead Painter and Lucian: "For so much as he was indebted to Lucian . . . the poet was also indebted to his little knowledge of Latin and less Greek." There is a brief contrast between Timon (who hates in the abstract) and Apemantus (who hates his concrete neighbors). The criticism of Cor. is an insensitive attack on the hero and a claim that Sh's sympathies lay with the commoners. Foard ends the essay with praise of Sh for breathing life into "what Time has left us of the ancient heroes."

1314. Foerster, Richard. Lucian in der Renaissance. Kiel, 1886, 25 pp.

Not seen. The monograph is presumed to consider the possible relationship between Misanthropos and Tim. NjP CtY NN ICarbS

1315. Ford, Daniel. "Shakespeare and Aristotle," Nation, XCVI (1913), 34. SG

Ford points out that the error Hector makes (Troi. II ii 165-167) in misquoting Aristotle's Nicomachean Ethics is traceable not to Bacon but to Erasmus' Colloquia (1526). In this discovery Ford was anticipated by twenty years (see #1542). Lily B. Campbell (#1197) appears to be aware neither of Ford nor of his predecessor, Neilson.

1316. Forster, E. M. "Julius Caesar" (1942), Two Cheers for Democracy (N.Y., 1951), pp. 154-158.

"Although it is not carefully constructed like a Greek play or a classical French play . . . [Caesar] does succeed in startling us and holding us . . . by three well-timed explosions": the assassination, Antony's oration, and the quarrel in Brutus' tent. Some of the characters are sympathetic (notably Brutus), but Sh did not care about character as much as we do; he altered Casca whenever it seemed convenient to do so and he made a radical change in Caesar after his death.

1317. Fowler, William W. "The Tragic Element in Shakespeare's 'Julius Caesar'," TRSL, XXX (1910), 31-58. (Reprinted in Roman Essays and Interpretations [1920].)

This refreshing essay is written from the perspective of an historian, who knows, for example, that Medieval education relied on Orosius for an account of the demise of Caesar; Sh's prejudices in favor of Caesar's greatness were doubtless mediately Orosian. Fowler makes other stimulating suggestions: Caesar's references to himself in the third person are probably due to Sh's recollection of this stylistic device in the Commentaries.

Fowler is not just a competent historian; he is also the possessor of an excellent critical sense. He follows Sh through his probable reading of North and he maintains that Sh would have regarded the life of Caesar as less promising dramatically than his death. When he found a more personal (and hence more appealing) Brutus immediately after the "Life of Caesar," he decided to combine the death of Caesar with the life of Brutus. The result is a hybrid tragedy, combining the old conception of the fall of a great man (Caesar) through the turning of Fortune's wheel with a new conception of the fall of a great man (Brutus) through his own well-intentioned mistake. It is this hybrid quality which limits the success of the play. It is not possible to agree completely that Plutarch's "Life of Caesar" portrays the man as only the sum of his titanic public achievements; episodes such as Caesar's adventure with the pirates, his remark to the boat captain at the mouth of the River Anius, his attitude toward the Rubicon, all are dramatically charged and reveal a human personality. But Fowler is basically right about the emphasis of the play and about Sh's reasons for the form it takes.

1318. Franke, Hans. "Vier Arten des heldischen Menschen: Zur Dramaturgie des Charakters," DD, I (1942), 107-110. GRS

Not seen. GRS lists this art. with other studies of the character of Coriolanus.

1319. Franz, W. "Klangwirkung und Wortstellung," ESn, LXX (1935), 129-131.

A comment on Sh's effective use of rhetoric, rhythm, repeated suggestion, and word placement in Antony's speech to the mob in Caesar III ii.

1320. Frenzel, Karl. "[On Antony and Cleopatra]," Berliner Dramaturgie, I (1871), 258 (as trans. and abstracted in the New Variorum Antony).

Frenzel's is surely among the most unqualified condemnations of Antony ever made. He regards the play as a total failure structurally because Sh does not focus on a few characters in his huge cast, because he does not contrast Antony and Octavius sharply, and because he never is able to make more of the epic theme of "political and social movement" than disjointed chronicle. Moreover, Frenzel does not like Cleopatra--he regards her as a "Fury" and a "fish-wife."

1321. Freytag, G. Technique of the Drama, trans. E. J. MacEwan, Chicago, 1895 (no complete pagination available--as abstracted in the New Variorum Caesar).

In a passage on Caesar Freytag emphasizes that the audience's loyalties are divided between Caesar and the conspirators. Caesar's greatness and the personal attractiveness of Brutus are incompatibles; yet "the characters are not entirely a mixture of incongruous elements."

1322. Fries, C[arl]. "Shakespeare und Buchanan," ShJ, XLVII (1911), 196.

Fries juxtaposes Antony's "The evil that men do lives after them; / The good is oft interred with their bones" with lines from Buchanan's Baptistes, Sophocles' Ajax, and a fragment of Stesichorus.

1323. Fries, Carl. "Zu Shakespeares 'Troilus and Cressida'," Archiv, CLXV (1934), 80-81.

In II i 18-20, where Thersites insults Ajax by saying that horses could learn an oration better than Ajax could memorize a prayer, Fries somewhat implausibly hears an echo of Achilles' talking horses, who expound the sic transit theme to him. But, says Fries, Sh did not know the Iliad, and his Thersites is entirely nonpolitical, whereas Homer's is a partisan; therefore the incidents of the Iliad must have been common knowledge in the sixteenth century. The "rugged Pyrrhus" passage in Ham. and the emphasis on mimicry in Ham. and Troi. show that the plays were written at about the same time. Not a very convincing thesis.

1324. Friesen, H. von. Shakspere-Studien. Wien, 1876 (no complete pagination available--as trans. and abstracted in the New Variorum Caesar).

Friesen follows a hint from Gervinus (#0264) in comparing Brutus with Hamlet--both are idealists but Brutus remains gentle in adversity while Hamlet becomes bitter and cruel. Sh is to be praised for his original additions to Plutarch in Caesar: Antony's rhetoric, Brutus' behavior after Caesar's death, his Forum speech, "the energy of his righteous indignation at the unworthy behaviour of Cassius."

1325. Frye, Roland. "Rhetoric and Poetry in Julius Caesar," QJS, XXXVII (1951), 41-48.

In an attempt to distinguish between the specific impact of rhetoric (oratory) and the generalized impact of poetry, Frye analyzes Marc Antony's funeral oration (which is both). Sh did not have more than Plutarch's hints about Caesar's mantle to develop, but "if Antony had had Shakespeare's [speech] ... it would have served him as well as his own."

1326. Fuller, Harold deW. "The Sources of Titus Andronicus," PMLA, XVI (1901), 1-65.

In a closely reasoned argument Fuller attempts to persuade that the sources of Titus were the same (lost) English sources which inspired the surviving German and Dutch plays on the same story. Fuller's examination of the documents is minute and his familiarity with a large corpus of previous opinion (especially Continental) lends weight to his findings. But even if he is right, he has not determined Sh's sources themselves. He makes an unwarranted rejection of the ballad on Titus without giving it adequate attention, and he never considers the possibility that Sh evolved the tone, if not the plot, from classical sources (Ovid, Seneca, Virgil). The art. remains, however, an important scholarly study.

1327. G., Mr. "On Shakespear by Mr. G.," Gentleman's Journal (1694), Munro Sup, No. 80, pp. 538-539.

A heated defense, in heroic couplets, of Sh against his critics. Sh "the nice Paths of Learning never knew," but nevertheless created an Antony and a Brutus greater than the historical originals. There is a vivid ten-line recapitulation of high points in the action of Caesar.

1328. Gallagher, Kate L. "A Plea for Cassius," Shna, VI (1889), 260-265.

An intelligent and moderate defense of Cassius which was doubtless more necessary in the 1880's than in the 1960's. The post-mortem tributes to him from Titinius and Brutus leave no doubt as to Sh's attitude. The author illustrates from the play Cassius' virtues as Plutarch describes them: greatness of spirit, hatred for tyranny, courage, patriotism, loyalty to his friends. On the whole a convincing interpretation, though it goes outside the play in introducing Caesar's unjust award of the Praetorship to Brutus although, as Caesar admitted, "Cassius has the stronger plea."

1329. Garnett, Richard. "[On Antony and Cleopatra]," English Literature (Ln, 1903) (no complete pagination available--as abstracted [from Vol. II] in the New Variorum Antony).

Garnett makes an interesting comparison between the ascendant Antony of Caesar and the declining Antony of Antony, and another between the sculptured characterization and set speeches of Caesar and the broad, masterful, almost casual sweep of Antony. He regards Cleopatra as the key to Antony and therefore to the play; she is various, as Enobarbus says, and the rôle demands a mature actress; it is surprising to hear Garnett say that Sh "follows Plutarch's delineation [of Cleopatra] closely."

1330. Gasquoine, T. "Shakspere's Timon: A Study of Character," The Christian Reformer (May, 1887), 296-307.

Gasquoine's thesis is that "Timon gives from love of giving, but it can scarcely be said from love of those on whom the gifts are lavished. He stands before us as the type of those ... cursed, with a defective amiability." Had Timon been more sensitive he would not have given indiscriminately to those who had no need, and he would at the same time have been capable of enduring ill fortune with equanimity. Tim. is, then, a tragedy of character, in which external action is less important than (and perhaps a function of) internal action. Gasquoine does not discuss Sh's sources for the character or the theme. MiU

1331. Gayley, Charles M. "Shakespeare and Hooker," Shakespeare and the Founders of Liberty in America (N.Y., 1917), Ch. VII, pp. 162-190.

This ch. is an exhaustive analysis of Ulysses' "degree" speech in the light of its probable sources. Gayley's main objective is to show that Hooker's reverence for natural law and the "degree" through which it operates is identical to Sh's respect for degree as a cohesive force in the natural order. (On this point T. W. Baldwin disagrees, #1141.) But Gayley is frank to admit that the core of the speech is in Odysseus' rebuke to Thersites in Iliad II (perhaps in Chapman). The probable sequence of Sh's agglomerations on the Homeric core is Chaucer's Troilus and Criseyde, Chaucer's Boethius (which is as close as Sh comes to drawing on the Platonic stream--Gayley doubts Sh's direct use of either Plato or Aristotle's Nicomachean Ethics), possibly Elyot, and Hooker (who transmitted to Sh some concepts in Boethius and Arnobius which are not in Chaucer). This is a persuasive argument, but one must note Baldwin's radical dissent (#1141) from Gayley's belief in Boethian (i.e., Platonic) influence. Gayley elaborates his major points in six appendices (pp. 234-259).

1332. Genouy, Hector. "Tradition romaine et

'Julius Caesar' de Shakespeare," RELV, XLVIII (1931), 201-216, 241-254. SG

A detailed seriatim analysis of the play in comparison with its sources in North's trans. The major departure from Plutarch is in the character of Caesar, whom Sh does not portray as deserving of his fate. Sh contracted a very large debt to North, but repaid it in part by making great poetry of North's prose. M. Genouy appears to be in better command of the play and of North than of the English Renaissance background. In his introduction, for example, he implies that almost no Englishmen could read the classics in the originals and that only a tiny fraction of Latin literature remained untranslated by 1600.

1333. Gérard, Albert. "Meaning and Structure in Troilus and Cressida," ES, XL (1959), 144-157.

Troilus is the character central to the structure of the play because he unites the two plots (it is interesting to note that he refers to both Cressida and Helen as pearls and dresses them both in mercantile imagery). Yet ironically the protagonist is full of inconsistencies (Gérard inclines toward Campbell's view of Troilus, #1199). Hector embodies the ethical principles which Sh expects us to value, yet he, too, is inconsistent. Gérard's analysis of the structure of each plot is worth following carefully—it appears to be a worthy antagonist to the view of Baldwin (#1140) that Sh organized the play around the Hector plot. As for tone, Gérard thinks the play a precursor of Beatness and Existentialism, though superior to both of them artistically.

1334. Gilbert, Allan H. "'A Thousand Ships'," MLN, LXVI (1951), 477-478.

The mediate source of Troi. II ii 81-82 is not only Lucian's Dialogues of the Dead, but also and especially Seneca's Trojan tragedies, where there are some six references to the thousand ships of the Greeks. The immediate source is, of course, Marlowe's three uses of the phrase.

1335. Giles, Henry. "[Cleopatra]"; "[Thersites]," Human Life in Shakespeare (Boston, 1868/1887), pp. 143, 197-199 (as abstracted in the New Variorum Antony, Troi.).

Giles's reaction to Cleopatra is an enthusiastic outburst of admiration. The paradoxes in her nature (vehemence and subtlety, ambition and sensuousness, e.g.) interest him, and he is fascinated by her ability "to combine politics with pleasure." On Thersites Giles is more restrained. The character is a cynical "impersonate ridicule on the Homeric heroes," but he does not represent only the modern world's rejection of the ancient, since he would rail at the modern world as well—if he were in it. His coarseness is comic, but we cannot laugh at him; Sh forces us to laugh with him.

1336. Gillet, Louis. "Shakespeare: viii Les tragédies romaines: 'Antoine et Cléopâtre'," RH, XXXIX, No. 4 (1930), 165-188, 313-329.

In this series of lectures the major emphasis falls on Antony, but there are critical discussions of Caesar and Cor. as well. If M. Gillet is not always convincing when he interprets, he is always interesting. Among his most gallant sorties is a defense of Sh against charges of anachronism in the Roman plays. Again, Antony revolutionized the attitude toward the amatory heroine; Cleopatra was the first "ripe" feminine lover since Virgil's Dido. "Coriolan demeure la satire immortelle de la démocratie." "Rien de plus faux que de comprendre Shakespeare à l'allemande, comme une sorte de génie barbare, le Luther de la poésie ... Shakespeare n'a rien tant aimé que l'Italie."

1337. Gilman, Albert. "Textual and Critical Problems in Shakespeare's Coriolanus," diss (Michigan, 1954), DA, XIV (1954), 673-674.

The chief textual problem is mislineation in F_1; Gilman's study leads him to believe that there is less mislineation in the play than has often been thought. Gilman studies the critical problems (the nature of the play and the interpretation of its protagonist), discussing the positions of successive critics, and outlining the contributions of twentieth-century methods.

1338. Glen, Enid. "A Note on 'Coriolanus'," NQ, CLXXIV (1938), 347.

A defense of the hero and his play by analogy with Oth., Tim., and Caesar. The tragedy is that of an idealist who ironically violates his own ideals. "The plan of 'Coriolanus' has the broad simplicity and grandeur which Shakespeare associates earlier, in 'Julius Caesar', with a Roman theme."

1339. Godwin, [William]. "Shakspeare Compared With Homer"; "Shakspeare and Chaucer Compared," Memorials of Shakspeare...

By Various Writers, collected by Nathan Drake (Ln, 1828), pp. 252-254, 261-267.

These two abstracts from the Life of Chaucer do not hesitate to give Troi. the palm over both the Iliad (which does not delineate character and is too soberly humorless) and Chaucer's Troilus, which "has the stately march of a Dutch burgomaster as he appears in a procession ..." (an odd figure for Chaucer, surely). Godwin makes the interesting observation that though Sh used Chapman's Homer, Lydgate, and Caxton, Chaucer must be regarded as the prime mover of Troi., because his poem was a national monument revered in Elizabethan England as the Iliad and the Aeneid were in ancient Greece and Rome. DFo MnU

1340. Goethe, Johann Wolfgang von. "Troilus and Cressida" (1824), Goethe's Literary Essays, ed. J. E. Spingarn (N.Y., 1921), p. 195.

A brief comment: Troi. is not a parody or travesty of the Iliad, but the product of an intellect of a different epoch. Homer is restrained and dignified; Sh is "romantic-dramatic," perhaps even prosaic under the influence of his Medieval sources.

1341. Golding, S. R. "'Timon of Athens'," NQ, CL (1926), 273-275.

A vigorous attack on the hypothesis that Sh performed a reviser's task on the work of Day and Middleton in Tim. Golding would assign Day's alleged part to Wilkins and deny Sh any part at all, since it is not conceivable that Sh as reviser would have left the play in such "execrable condition." H. Dugdale Sykes replies with verve in defense of Sh's hand as reviser (ibid., CLI [1926], 21-23); Golding responds (ibid., 167-170).

1342. Goldsmith, Robert Hillis. "Did Shakespeare Use the Old Timon Comedy?" SQ, IX (1958), 31-38.

The academic comedy, Timon, may have been a source not only for Sh's Tim., but also for Lear. Goldsmith prints a number of parallel passages, most of which are not striking. Though the old play contains much "pedantic buffoonery, ...the Greek quotations and rhetorical terms of Demeas the orator would not have troubled the former scholar from King Edward's School in Stratford."

1343. Goll, A. Criminal Types in Shakespeare, trans. C. Weekes, Ln, 1909 (no complete pagination available—as abstracted in the New Variorum Caesar).

Goll regards the last lines of Caesar as possibly ironic: Brutus was "a man" and no more, yet tried to make of himself "the judge and avenger of justice"—he paid with his life. Goll also speculates on what would have happened if Brutus had had the cunning of Cassius and Antony, or if he had won the civil war. History would have regarded him differently; but despite the possible irony of Antony's epitaph, Sh does leave us with Brutus' virtues remembered.

1344. Gomme, Andor. "Timon of Athens," EC, IX (1959), 107-125.

A frontal assault on the position assumed by Knight in The Wheel of Fire (#1444). Gomme is effective in his criticism of Knight's equation of Timon, Abraham, and Christ. But he is at his best building positions, not assailing them: e.g., he shows that Timon is as materialistic as his parasites because he can think in no terms but those of gold; again, Timon may have been practice for Coriolanus, who is Timon + Alcibiades. The view that Tim. was an abortive attempt to write a tragedy on a classical figure disenchanted with his culture seems more satisfying than Wilson Knight's "sentimentalized" approach.

1345. Granger, Frank. "Shakespeare and the Legend of Andronicus," TLS, April 2, 1920, p. 213.

Granger rebukes Elizabethan scholars for failing to note the probability that Titus drew on the Medieval Byzantine tradition and that Sh's classicism was sufficient to give him access to historians of the Eastern Empire. R. W. Bond makes a sternly critical reply April 16, 1920, p. 239, but as the controversy flows through subsequent issues, Bond at length admits (May 28, 1920, p. 335) that Granger could be right.

1346. Granville-Barker, Harley. "Antony and Cleopatra," Prefaces to Shakespeare: Second Series (Ln, 1930), pp. 111-233. E-S

Even more than usually, in this preface Granville-Barker writes from a seat in the theater. Perhaps the two most striking passages discuss the flowing action of the play on the Elizabethan stage and the qualities of Cleopatra which a boy actor could bring out best. There is even less of Plutarch in this essay than in the other two on Roman plays, but the analysis of Antony and of the minor characters is very good. Granville-Barker has much to say of the poetry and even something of the music and costuming for the play.

1347. Granville-Barker, Harley. Coriolanus: Prefaces to Shakespeare: Fifth Series. Ln, 1947, 195 pp.

As is his custom, Granville-Barker regards the play from the director's chair; he pays little attention to Sh's use of Plutarch or his reaction to Roman history. The primary emphasis falls on acute character studies and a very valuable seriatim analysis of the action; the book ends with a discussion of the spare, intense verse and some other technical details. The method of arrangement makes some repetition inevitable, but this remains as readable and intelligently moderate a piece of criticism as any on the play. Granville-Barker ranges himself between those who find Coriolanus a typical Shn tragic protagonist and those who think him a satirized portrait of what not to be in public life. He appears also to have found the proper balance between views that Cor. is a domestic tragedy and that it is a political problem-play. It is difficult to agree that Rome gradually becomes more important than Coriolanus, but otherwise Granville-Barker merits the reader's entire confidence.

1348. Granville-Barker, Harley. "From Henry V to Hamlet" (1925), PBA, XI (1924-25), 283-309. (Annual British Academy Shakespeare Lecture.)

Though he calls Caesar "the turning-point of Shakespeare's career," the point at which he subordinated rhetoric to his hero's interior conflict, Granville-Barker's remarks on Caesar and on Brutus in this famous address are brief. Brutus is not a successful tragic hero because he lacks emotional warmth and impulsiveness. Sh, "taking much of him ready made from Plutarch, never quite fathoms his stoicism."

1349. Granville-Barker, Harley. "Julius Caesar," Prefaces to Shakespeare: First Series (Ln, 1927), pp. 51-132. E-S

The play is Brutus' tragedy, but Sh did not really commit his attention to Brutus as he later was to commit it to Hamlet. As for Caesar, he is thin because he must be--too large a gap must not be left when the title figure leaves the stage. This does not mean that Sh depreciated him, however; indeed he may have hesitated to characterize him because he revered him. The studies of Cassius, Antony, Octavius, and even Casca and Calphurnia are equally good. Thinking of the play from a director's vantage point, Granville-Barker finds its structure excellent, especially under Elizabethan stage conditions. The discussion of construction is filled with perceptive observations such as that Antony is unleashed immediately after Caesar's death to engross the attention of the audience when a major focus of interest has departed. To make the explosion of Antony's soliloquy and oration more violent, Sh keeps him in the background during Acts I and II. This preface has all of the merits which have made its author's name a synonym for intelligent theater criticism. At the same time it suffers from an ill-considered attempt to read Sh's mind through the portal of his writing. This defect considered, the essay adds as much to the enjoyment and understanding of the play as anything ever written on it.

1350. Granville-Barker, Harley. "Verse and Speech in Coriolanus," RES, XXIII (1947), 1-15.

This essay, written just before Granville-Barker's death, is subsumed into #1347.

1351. Gray, Austin K. "Shakespeare and Titus Andronicus," SP, XXV (1928), 295-311.

Gray advances numerous arguments to prove that ca. 1593-94 Sh revised an old Senecan play belonging to the Pembroke Company and ended with Titus. The most important of the arguments are documentary (e.g. Henslowe's Diary) and comparative (Gray adduces a number of interesting parallels of situation, classical allusion, and phrasing between Titus and Venus and Lucr.). But Sh was not very interested in the task of revision; he did little to Act I, spent most of his energy on Act II (shifting the emphasis from Seneca to the more humane Virgil [Aeneid II] and Ovid [Meta.]), and then lost interest, allowing the old play to show through rather badly in the later acts. It is perhaps as easy to accept Price's theory of integrity (#1585) as this elaborate theory of revision--indeed, some of Gray's evidence would support Price's position.

1352. Gray, Henry David. "Antony's Amazing 'I Will To Egypt'," MP, XV (1917), 43-52.

Gray adduces reasons for believing that Sh intended the Soothsayer scene (Antony II iii), in which Antony decides to return to Egypt though he is not yet even married to Octavia, to appear at the end of Act II. This alteration in the F_1 text, Gray believes, would remove Antony's apparent duplicity. But, as Gray seems to admit, the alteration is fraught with as many difficulties as it removes; the text appears better left alone.

1353. Gray, Henry David. "The Authorship of 'Titus Andronicus'," FMV, pp. 114-126.

Gray argues that the main corpus of Titus is the work of Sh who was out-Kyding Kyd, and that Greene and possibly Peele revised the play, adding further scenes of horrid violence. Gray relies on the prosodic tests which were popular between Fleay and 1935 but are now generally discredited; his results are unconvincing, as Tucker Brooke points out with acerbity in a counterarticle in MLN, XXXIV (1919), 32-36. Brooke's harshness precipitates a flurry of correspondence ibid., pp. 244-247.

1354. Gray, Henry David. "Shakespeare's Share in Titus Andronicus," PQ, V (1926), 166-172.

Gray, who for ten years stood alone against other disintegrators in his belief that Sh wrote the original Titus to have it revised by Greene and Peele, here retracts his former position. He is persuaded by J. Q. Adams' Life (#0060) that Sh could have worked for the Pembroke Company and ergo could have made the revision of January 1593/1594. Gray still believes that other hands, Greene's and Peele's, are discernible in the play, and he still uses his verse tests (especially the percentages of feminine endings) to characterize respective contributors to the play.

1355. Gray, Henry David. "The Titus Andronicus Problem," SP, XVII (1920), 126-131.

Gray here repeats his argument published in the FMV (#1353): Sh wrote the play and it was then submitted to the revision of another hand (Greene's) or hands. The argument does not improve with age and repetition.

1356. Graydon, Joseph S. "Defense of Criseyde," PMLA, XLIV (1929), 141-177.

A brief note on the first page suggests that Sh's Cressida, unlike Chaucer's heroine, succumbs to Diomedes the first night she is in the Greek camp because Sh wished to preserve the Aristotelian hourglass; the action is to take place in "'a single revolution of the sun, or exceed it very slightly'."

1357. Greg, W. W. "Alteration in Act I of 'Titus Andronicus'," MLR, XLVIII (1953), 439-440.

Greg suggests that some minor changes in the punctuation of Q_1 (1594) of Titus I i would eliminate the ambiguity which makes Alarbus appear to be on stage and not on stage at the same time. The argument is persuasive, but Greg admits that it does not preclude the possibility that someone inserted the episode of the sacrifice of the silent Alarbus.

1358. Grierson, H. J. C. "The Drama: Comedy," Cross Currents in English Literature of the XVIIth Century, 2nd ed. (Ln, 1958), pp. 66-95.

The last six pages of the ch. deal with the Roman plays. With a hint of pejoration, Grierson says: "Shakespeare ... shows no clear interest in the political or moral principles which the story raises," and he contrasts Sh's interest in drama with Jonson's interest in ethics. The analysis of Brutus, and the more terse allusions to Cor. and Antony are intended as support for such statements as this: "And what to Shakespeare is the battle of Actium, the moral and political issues of which were to Virgil so tremendous? Merely an episode in the story of the loves of Antony and his Egyptian Queen, an episode in the rivalry between the great soldier and lover and the thin-blooded politician Octavius."

1359. Griffin, Nathaniel. "Un-Homeric Elements in the Medieval Story of Troy," JEGP, VII (1908), 32-52. E-S

As early as the first century, Dares and Dictys, the forgers who were thought more authoritative than Homer until the eighteenth century, reshaped the Troy story: (1) they injected realism—an attempt at probability; (2) they altered the emphasis—minor characters (like Troilus and Briseis in Dares) became major figures; (3) they wrote from bias—Homer had portrayed both sides objectively. These three alterations are characteristic features of both Chaucer's Troi. and Sh's. Dares and Dictys were apparently only the most prominent of a long tradition of anti-Homerici; Sh is in the tradition when he elevates Thersites from braggart to Chorus.

1360. Griffiths, G. S. "Antony and Cleopatra," Essays and Studies, XXXI (1945), 34-67.

Griffiths, who denies Bradley's interpretation of the action as Antony's tragedy, gives the protagonist's place to Cleopatra and suggests that Sh flew in the face of Plutarch's emphasis in order to make her the central character. The fallacy in this reading is that it demotes Antony to the rôle of reactor to stimuli and it takes no real account of themes and characters (especially in the "Roman" world) which Sh obviously considered important. Griffiths is sensitive, however, and if he is super-subtle or impressionistic at times, he does occasionally cast light in dark corners.

1361. Griffiths, L. M. "A Vindication of Titus Andronicus," Shna, I (1884), 201-204.

In his defense of the basic integrity of the play, Griffiths draws some interesting analogies between Titus and Coriolanus; between Marcus and Nestor, Antonio, and Prospero; and between Tamora and Cleopatra.

1362. Grosart, Alexander B. "Was Robert Greene Substantially the Author of Titus Andronicus?" ESn, XXII (1896), 389-436.

Grosart answers his question with an emphatic "Yes," alleging that Greene's Selimus and characteristic features of his tastes and style elsewhere are sufficiently close to Titus to prove that he wrote it; yet Grosart accepts the statement of Ravenscroft that Sh did have a hand in the play. Grosart's fallacy is that he does not dispose of the probability that a young dramatist would extensively imitate the style, tastes, plots, and diction of his betters while he was developing his Art and his reputation. Among the "proofs" are the large number of classical tags in Titus; Greene, who liked to label himself "Master of Arts in both Universities," was a classical-reference dropper. But so were Marlowe, Spenser, Jonson, Nashe, and indeed all Elizabethans. Sh is merely outdoing them in Titus in an effort to gain a foothold on the Ln stage.

1363. Guidi, Augusto. "'Creature' in Shakespeare," NQ, CXCVII (1952), 443-444.

Guidi believes that when Antony says of Lepidus (Caesar IV i 31) "It is a creature that I teach to fight" he means to characterize Lepidus as a domestic animal. Guidi does not observe that his contention is supported by Antony's other references to Lepidus as an ass and a horse.

1364. Gundolf, Friedrich. Caesar: Geschichte seines Ruhms. Berlin, 1924, 273 pp. E-S

See pp. 175-186. Sh "war kein Eigenbrödler und weicht nirgends von der geschichtlichen communis opinio seiner Zeit und gar seines Volks ab, die den Cäsar einhellig als grossen Helden und Herrscher anerkannte, einerlei ob sie politisch und sittlich seine Handlungen billigte." Gundolf gives little attention to the "thrasonical" strain which many recent critics have found in Caesar's speeches in the play. DLC

1365. Gundolf, Friedrich. "Cäsar und Brutus," EuropäischeR, IV (1928), 489-513. E-S

Gundolf sees Caesar as the first of Sh's spiritual tragedies, the conflict between the soul (Brutus) and the world (Caesar). "Die Stimmung des Brutus mehr als die Geschichte des Cäsar, der abendliche Schatten von Philippi mehr als der mittägliche Glanz von Rom sind der Ursprung dieser Tragödie." Gundolf maintains that the streets, Forum, Capitol, and battlefield of the play are less elements of Roman local color than places in which spiritual conflict can take place. There is a brief but interesting contrast between Plutarch's characterization of the two men and Sh's, and Gundolf also offers commentary on Cassius, Antony, and Octavius. MH

1366. Gundolf, Friedrich. "Shakespeares Antonius und Cleopatra: Festvortrag," ShJ, LXII (1926), 7-35. E-S

Like many who have interpreted Antony since, Gundolf sees the moral structure of the action as a set of polarities: the dionysiac "Lebenskraft," personified in Cleopatra, opposes the apollonian "Weisheit" or "Vernunft," personified in Octavius. That intellect should triumph over nature is inevitable in the scheme of things, but Sh reveres the loser as well as the victor. This interpretation grants more significance and more stature to Octavius than many recent critics would endorse; Gundolf, however, makes valuable comments on the structural rôle of minor characters like Lepidus, Pompey, Enobarbus, and Eros. There is little discussion of Plutarch here, and few detailed comments on individual scenes and passages.

1367. Gwynn, S. L. "A Theory of 'Troilus and Cressida'," [an address as reported in] Acad, XXXIX (1891), 374-375.

Gwynn observes that had Sh known Greek culture as he knew Latin he would never have written Troi., the most debased of his plays.

His Greeks are those of Juvenal, "imperfectly understood." Gwynn considers the camp scenes to be based on Homer. As irrelevancies to the love plot they were intruded in order to ridicule Chapman whom Sh hated for alienating his Dark Lady as Diomedes alienated Cressida. Gwynn's analysis suffers from his lack of careful attention to Sh's sources.

1368. Habart, Michel. "Clés pour Coriolan," Europe, No. 347 (1958), 103-113.

There are three keys to the meaning of Cor.: (1) it is not a tragedy, but a satire on its hero and his Patrician colleagues (Coriolanus is an anti-courtier: everything Castiglione would condemn); (2) the theme is the class struggle—Sh sides with the Plebeians; (3) Coriolanus is a puppet "teleguided" by the will of his psychic master—his mother. This essay is not to be recommended as a key to the meaning of Cor.—despite its title.

1369. Haines, Charles. Two Men With Four Faces. Milano, 1957, 87 pp. GRS

Not seen. The second man, apparently, is Sh's Brutus, discussed on pp. 55-85.

1370. Hales, John W. "'Caesar Doth Bear Me Hard'," Acad, XXIV (1883), 416.

Hales reiterates an earlier suggestion that the phrase "to bear [someone] hard" which occurs thrice in Caesar but nowhere else in Sh "is merely a rendering of the Latin aegre (or graviter) ferre." This suggestion is promptly assaulted by A. H. Bullen (ibid., p. 434). Hales and Bullen parry briefly in the early issues of 1884.

1371. Halio, Jay Leon. "Rhetorical Ambiguity as a Stylistic Device in Shakespeare's Problem Comedies," diss (Yale, 1956).*

It is presumed that Halio treats classical rhetoric in Troi.

1372. Hall, Vernon, Jr. "Julius Caesar: A Play Without Political Bias," SERD, pp. 106-124.

"His purpose being ethical, Plutarch was not interested in the struggle between Caesar and the Republicans from a political point of view. In this respect Shakespeare was his faithful disciple, and I believe that any attempt to read political attitudes, modern or Renaissance, into Julius Caesar falsifies the play." The leitmotiv of the play is virtus, which Plutarch admired in all the characters in the Caesar story. Sh and his audience shared this reverence for Roman grandeur. But Hall weakens the thesis by excusing all aberrations of the characters and especially by implying that Plutarch had no Hellenic bias and wrote (e.g.) his "Consolatory Letter on the Death of His Daughter" in conscious emulation of Cato's behavior when he had, of course, many a Greek philosopher on whom to model his attitude. Hall fails to consider also that to Plutarch, politics was the arena of the virtus of the classical world.

1373. Halliday, F. E. The Poetry of Shakespeare's Plays. Ln, 1954, 196 pp.

Halliday points out (pp. 130-131) the plethora of Latinate words in Troi.; he suggests that it is due to Sh's enthusiastic recognition of the possibilities of combining Latinisms with Anglo-Saxon diction, but that Sh quickly realized his excess (perhaps under the influence of the purge given Marston in Jonson's Poetaster) and in the later plays is more restrained. The implication that Sh "discovered" Latinity so late as Troi. is unwarranted. It is not difficult to find neologisms from Latin in Sh's earliest plays.

1374. Hanford, J[ames] H. "A Platonic Passage in Shakespeare's Troilus and Cressida," SP, XIII (1916), 100-109. E-S SG

Ulysses' "degree" speech (I iii 75-137) is traceable ultimately to Plato's Republic. So also is the incitement to war by Exeter and Canterbury in H.V I ii 178-213. Hanford leaves open the question of direct indebtedness, but is inclined to believe that Sh saw the Republic in a Latin, French, or Italian version before writing Troi.

1375. Harbage, Alfred. As They Liked It: An Essay on Shakespeare and Morality. N.Y., 1947, 238 pp.

Harbage makes the interesting suggestion (Ch. III, pp. 152-162) that the apparent moral inconsistency in the Greek and Roman plays (e.g., in Cor. the populace triumphs; in Caesar autocracy triumphs) results from Sh's large conception of ancient history: his classical plays "are not tragedies but segments of a larger tragedy—the fall of an ancient civilization." This book contains many stimulating remarks about the Greek and Roman plays, notably about Titus with its coincidental Senecanism.

1376. Harmatopegos. "'Troilus and Cressida': 'My Sacred Aunt'," NQ, CLV (1928), 134.

When Hector refers thus to Ajax' mother (IV v 134), he is thinking of Hesione, but though Telamon was married to Hesione, she was not Ajax' mother--Telamon was married three times. The vagueness of classical sources on the matter may excuse Sh from "indifference to classical orthodoxy."

1377. Harrier, Richard C. "Troilus Divided," SERD, pp. 142-156.

Troi. is a play in which the tension between honor and reason is thematic. Troilus, who rejects the premise that altered circumstances necessitate altered values, is contrasted with his polar opposite, Thersites, in whose opinion the values of chivalry are a cloak for bestiality. Both positions are extreme and between them stands the epic balance of Aeneas, the shadowy standard of measure, who, as founder of Troynovant, to the Elizabethans symbolized the best of the classical world. Troilus remains the tragic hero, however, and his flaw, passionate adherence to his values (Cressida, the honorableness of keeping Helen, his code of chivalry) in the face of reason, guarantees his destruction, but perhaps merits our tragic identification, much as Lear's unreasonableness does. The thesis is well argued, but there is much in the play which it does not embrace.

1378. Harrison, G. B. Shakespeare at Work, 1592-1603. Ln, 1933, 325 pp.

For Sh's sources for Caesar's character in Caesar, see #0794.

1379. Harrison, G. B. "Shakespeare's Topical Significances: II--The Earl of Essex," TLS, November 20, 1930, p. 974.

The last third of this lucid analysis of suspected Essex references in Sh's plays before 1600 explores the possibility that Achilles sulking in his tent in Troi. is a jibe at Essex sulking in his bed (1598) when the Privy Council had need of his services. Chapman's first installment of The Iliads appeared in 1598 and was dedicated to Essex, to whom Chapman ascribed "Achilleian virtues." Accordingly Harrison is prepared to infer that Troi. was performed for a private audience of Essex' enemies in 1598 or perhaps in 1600, when Essex was fomenting rebellion.

1380. Harrison, G. B. Shakespeare's Tragedies. Ln, 1951, 277 pp.

Harrison regards all six of the Greek and Roman plays as tragedies. His method is to give a running account of the action of each play, punctuated by comments on matters of topical interest or of dramatic importance. The essays are intended for the general reader; what Harrison says of sources is brief, but sometimes provocative (as in the suggestion that Titus owes something direct to Seneca's Thyestes as well as to Ovid). It is not easy to agree that Achilles is a portrait of Essex (though Harrison argues the point more persuasively than anyone else who has attempted it); nor does Harrison succeed altogether in convincing that Tim. is a Morality play (though his point--that Timon is a personification divorced from parents, children, wife, even mistress—is well taken). A fluent introduction to the tragedies.

1381. Hastings, William T. "The Hardboiled Shakespeare," SAB, XVII (1942), 114-125.

An effective defense (1) of Sh's authorship of Titus and (2) of the play itself, partaking as it does of the "sophisticated brutality" of Renaissance art. This brutality comes in part from the late Medieval world and in part from Apuleius, Petronius, Plautus, Terence, Ovid (and, he might have added, Seneca).

1382. Haug, Ralph A. "The Authorship of 'Timon of Athens'," SAB, XV (1940), 227-248. GRS

An able defense of the thesis proposed by Chambers (#0159) that Tim. is Sh's work left unfinished. Haug examines the various alternatives which have been proposed and rejects them chiefly because Tim. has, he maintains, a unity of tone which is Shn, a higher aesthetic value than the other unities which Sh neglected in the play. The protagonist, disillusioned by his discovery that he lives in a loveless universe, turns toward hatred. Everything in the play either precedes, supports, or follows from this turning point in the moral life of Timon. Haug does not discuss Sh's sources.

1383. Haynes, French. "Shakespeare and the Troy Story: History of the Troy Story from the Time of Homer to Shakespeare," HowardSHL, LXXX (1922), 67-131. HB SG

This extended study surveys the accretions to the legend from Dictys and Dares through Sh and Heywood and then gives a systematic allusion-list for Sh's references (outside of Troi.) to the events and persons of the tale. Then follows a survey of critical interpretation of Troi. and Haynes's own understanding of Sh's relationship to the legend. Haynes intelligently rejects poetomachia, ridicule of Chapman's Homer, and Shn melancholy as explanations of the tone of the play, suggesting the attempted fusion of classical, Medieval, and Renaissance versions as the cause of dislocations in the structure of the play and tradition as the cause of the crudities of tone. Haynes makes some dubious judgments (e.g., that the play was written as closet drama) but these are far outnumbered by thoughtful observations (e.g., Sh did not write a tragedy on Paris and Helen as he did on Antony and Cleopatra because tradition gave him a Trojan prince and a Greek queen whose carnality was unredeemed by intelligence or dignity). A plethora of errors in typography and other mechanics mars an essay which has the advantage of intelligent judgments and of its debts to Rollins, Tatlock, and many other students of the play.

1384. Haywood, Richard M. "Shakespeare and the Old Roman," CE, XVI (1954), 98-101, 151.

Haywood points out that Sh's Brutus is a specifically Roman hero, whereas Plutarch's is simply a virtuous man. Sh restores to the character the patriotism which Cicero and Livy had established for him but Plutarch, the Greek, had understandably omitted. Haywood does not insist that Sh read Livy or Cicero, being content to point out the disparity between Plutarch and Sh.

1385. Hazlitt, William. Characters of Shakespear's Plays (1817). Liber Amoris and Dramatic Criticisms, ed. Charles Morgan (Ln, 1947), pp. 159-426.

Hazlitt's impressionistic sketches are of great historical importance as the first effort to expand the technique of character analysis and appreciation founded by Morgann and Richardson (see supra, p. 7) to embrace the whole Sh canon. The personalism of Hazlitt's criticism is indicated by his depreciation of Caesar for lack of "interest and power" without thorough analysis and with no reference at all to Plutarch. Yet Hazlitt is modern in his suggestion that Tim. is a unified satire combining the spirit of Diogenes and the Stoics (Apemantus) with the furious imprecations of Juvenal (Timon). Hazlitt cannot resist reading the politics of the Romantic movement into Cor., but he does make some comparisons with North's Plutarch; he oddly considers Cressida and Pandarus real and interesting but Troilus a stick figure. His appreciation of Antony is warm. Of Errors, the only play other than the Greek and Roman plays about which Hazlitt makes "classical" remarks: "This comedy is taken very much from the Menaechmi [sic no ital.] of Plautus, and is not an improvement on it . . . [Errors] leads us not to feel much regret that Shakespeare was not what is called a classical scholar."

1386. Heine, Heinrich. "Shakespeare's Maidens and Women" ([1838?]), The Works of Heinrich Heine, trans. Charles Godfrey Leland (Ln, 1891-98), I, 249-441.

Heine begins his series of character sketches with the women from Sh's classical tragedies: Cressida, Cassandra, Helen, Virgilia, [Volumnia], Brutus' Portia, Cleopatra, and Lavinia. The brief essays are informal; Heine is as likely to discuss the reason why Faust, a German, chose a beauty millennia-old as to consider the supposed subject at hand. Yet his insights are sometimes penetrating: it is in Troi. that we should compare Sh with the Greeks because in Troi. Sh portrayed their story and heroes. Sh is less interested in form than in truth; with the Greek poets the emphasis is reversed. Heine's essays are pleasant reading in this fluent trans.

1387. Henderson, W. B. Drayton. "Shakespeare's Troilus and Cressida Yet Deeper In Its Tradition," PPV, pp. 127-156. E-S SG

Part I is Henderson's attempt to find unity in the play in the tension between individual values and social values. Part II traces elements in the play to Lydgate, whom he would add to Chapman's Homer, Caxton, and Chaucer as sources. Part III explains the character of Thersites (only hinted at by Chapman) and the large number of references to folly in the play as traceable to Erasmus' Encomium Moriae, the source of Sh's interest in the wise, critical fool. This effort to qualify the basic position of Tatlock (#1718, #1719) is not entirely successful, though Henderson argues with vigor.

1388. Herrington, Walter S. "A Plea for Coriolanus," 3 TRSC, XIV, No. 2 (1920), 97-104.

Herrington attempts to convince that Coriolanus is more sinned against than sinning. A good part of his argument is an analogy to conditions in Canada in the period following the First World War; the analogy obscures Elizabethan conventions and Sh's sources: though Herrington mentions Plutarch it is to dismiss his Coriolanus as only the germ of Sh's larger conception. The net effect of the art. is not to change radically the usual unsympathetic reaction to Coriolanus.

1389. Hertzberg, W. "Die Quellen der Troilus-Sage in ihrem Verhältniss zu Shakespeare's 'Troilus und Cressida'," ShJ, VI (1871), 169-225. E-S

Hertzberg offers extension and modification of Eitner's survey of classical accounts of Troilus (#1281); included is an excellent discussion of both Dictys Cretensis and Dares Phrygius. The survey of Medieval accretions which follows gives some attention even to minor works like The Gest Historiale of the Destruction of Troy (fourteenth century). Chaucer, however, dominates the discussion. Chaucer is the primary source of Sh's love plot; the close similarity of Caxton to Lydgate makes it uncertain whether Sh followed one or the other (or both) for his war plot. For details (e.g., the prominence of Ulysses, the stupidity of Ajax, Thersites as clown, the timing of Patroclus' death) which do not appear in these Medieval authorities, Hertzberg provides possible sources in such authors as Horace (Epistles), Ovid (Epistolae ex Ponto and especially Meta. XIII), Juvenal, Seneca, and "Pindarus Thebanus." He argues strongly against the theory that Sh parodies Homer in the play, and denies that Sh used Chapman's Iliads at all. Hertzberg's thesis on Sh's use of Homer requires modification (see, e.g., Presson, #1583), but otherwise this is an informative and interesting study.

1390. Heuer, Hermann. "From Plutarch to Shakespeare: A Study of Coriolanus," ShS, X (1957), 50-59.

Though he ends with the statement that the complexity and ambiguity of Sh's Coriolanus leave him "wrapped in a cloak of mystery defying rational analysis," Heuer has analyzed the "Volumnia scene" of Act V with critical judgment and sensitive perception to demonstrate the development of Sh's complex hero from the more simple character of Plutarch. To the latter, Coriolanus was a crude man lacking the virtues of political wisdom and self-discipline which Alcibiades had and which a Greek education could have imparted to him. Amyot injected into this simple portrait the polarities of "rigueur" and "raison" with all the associated antinomies of passion and logic. North's contribution to the scene was a reverent concern for "nature" which is associated in his trans. with decency and honor, and which leads to the possibility of "tragic greatness." "Coriolanus in Shakespeare's version is made to appear much more drastically as the 'foreign recreant', as the apostate and sinner against the laws of nature, than in North's prose version"; Sh opposes pride to pity, mercy to honor, in every case heightening and dramatizing the moral tenor of North's account. In this detailed study Heuer has made a valuable contribution to the understanding of Sh's creative process. Many have previously noted that Sh follows North at length in V iii; Heuer's critical microscope has first brought to view the minute differences between the play and the biography which reveal both the nature of tragedy and Sh's attitude toward it. This is constructive criticism.

1391. Heuer, Hermann. "Lebensgefühl und Wertwelt in Shakespeares Römerdramen," ZNU, XXXVII (1938), 65-90.

Heuer argues that the ethical structure of Sh's Roman tragedies is Germanic (i.e., Medieval) as much as classical. Many of the ethical standards (e.g., hospitality, attitude toward suicide, loyalty to one's leader, the ties of kinship) are un- (or perhaps sub-) rational and have analogues in feudal and chivalric values. Heuer offers one persuasive piece of evidence that Sh altered Plutarchian morality: Plutarch gives no model for the Enobarbus whom Sh makes a tragic case of treason and repentance. But in most other cases the Medieval ethical norms which Heuer introduces are exactly analogous to principles stated or implicit in Plutarch--it is very difficult to distinguish source from analogue here. The art. contains sections on character and fate, leadership and loyal obedience, "nobleness" as a heroic virtue, and the community as a political ideal. As always, Heuer is a stimulating critic, even if it is not possible to accept his hypothesis without reservation.

1392. Heuer, Hermann. "Shakespeare und Plutarch. Studien zu Wertwelt und Lebensgefühl im Coriolanus," Anglia, LXII (1938), 321-346. SG

An earlier and fuller version of the thesis of #1390, which can be regarded as an adequate condensation of this art.

1393. Heuer, Hermann. "Troilus und Cressida in neuerer Sicht," ShJ, LXXXIX (1953), 106-127.

Troi. "ist ein Stück, das zwar mit Ingrimm die Diskrepanz zwischen Ideal und Wirklichkeit aufreisst, aber in keinem Augenblick über die rechte Bestimmung der Werte im Zweifel lässt." Heuer discusses the treatment of both love and war in the play, focusing on the Medieval sources (more probably Lydgate than Caxton) and on Sh's allusions to the Trojan legend elsewhere in his works.

1394. Hibernicus. "The Wallet of Oblivion," *NQ*, CLXXIII (1937), 227.

Ulysses' disquisition to Achilles on worldly fame: "Time hath, my lord, a wallet at his back . . ." (*Troi.* III iii 145-146) is traceable to Aesop, not to Spenser. The concept of two bags, one in front and one behind, was popular in antiquity. Hibernicus cites variations on Aesop in Catullus, Persius, and Horace. Edward Bensly (ibid., 265) adds citations to Seneca, Plutarch, and Babrius; D. T. Starnes cites Erasmus and Withals' *Dictionarie* (ibid., CLXXVI [1939], 29-30).

1395. Hill, Archibald A. "Diomede: The Traditional Development of a Character," MichiganPLL, VIII (1932), 1-25.

Hill ends his study with Benoît de Ste. Maure, but he alludes to Sh's *Troi.* as the culmination of a Medieval tradition in the Homeric story which has since been obscured by the popularity of Virgil and Homer.

1396. Hill, N. W. "Shakespeare and Aristophanes," *Acad*, LXXII (1907), 76. SG

For Aristophanes in *Antony* IV xiv, see #1965.

1397. Hill, R. F. "The Composition of *Titus Andronicus*," *ShS*, X (1957), 60-70.

An inconclusive reopening of the question of authorship on the basis of parallels (this time with Sh's undisputed early work to see what in *Titus* is uncharacteristic of Sh). Hill relies chiefly on figures of classical rhetoric (asyndeton, epizeuxis, epanodos, etc.), and he finds *Titus* less sophisticated in its use of them than any other early Shn play. As he admits, however, explanations may lie in the nature of the theme and in the date of composition.

1398. Hodge, Harold. "Coriolanus," *Harper's*, CXVII (1908), 852-858.

It is impossible to determine Sh's political preferences because he portrays both good and evil in the Patricians as well as in the Plebeians. Coriolanus himself recalls the Achilles of Horace, "*inexorabilis, acer*," when he is abused by his countrymen. Neither the hero nor the people is in any way magnanimous, and "Coriolanus has not learned the meaning of *noblesse oblige*." Hodge writes with intelligence and fluency.

1399. Hodge, Harold. "Julius Caesar: Critical Comment," *Harper's*, CXII (1906), 362-368.

An indictment of Brutus: "We are forced to the conclusion that Marcus Brutus was a solemn humbug." Hodge bases this conclusion on an extended contrast with Cassius and an analysis of Brutus' behavior before and during the assassination. He is an "immaculate poser" who does not himself realize that he is posing as a virtuous man when in reality his carefully controlled conscience tells him that the right is whatever he wants to do. Among the more original suggestions: the story of the Gracchi would have been a better vehicle than *Caesar* for a portrayal of the inadequacy of idealism in politics, had Sh wanted to make such a portrayal—he did not: the theme of *Caesar* is Nemesis for a treacherous crime. Hodge's study of Brutus is less convincing than his essay on Coriolanus (#1398).

1400. Hodgson, Geraldine. "*Coriolanus* and Shakespeare's 'Tragic Course'," *CQR*, CXVII (1934), 292-303.

An effective rebuttal of Dover Wilson's contention that the "comparative emptiness" of *Cor.* indicates Sh's lack of concern for the play (*The Essential Shakespeare*). Miss Hodgson believes that Sh cared enough to add to Plutarch's plot and North's language the theme of *superbia*, insolence, or ὕβρις. Coriolanus' pride is perhaps borrowed from the Hellenism of the Italian Renaissance—it certainly does not come from Plutarch. Sh's hero has something in common with the defiant Sigismondo Malatesta; he reveals his *superbia* most plainly in his boast to Aufidius just before his death: "like an eagle in a dovecote, I / Flutter'd your Volscians in Corioles. / Alone I did it." The emphasis falls on "alone."

1401. Hodgson, Geraldine. "Enobarbus--the Enigma," *CQR*, CXXII (1936), 88-99.

An intelligent analysis of an "equivocal" character. Miss Hodgson thinks of Enobarbus as a Renaissance man—poet, soldier, cynic, friend, hedonist. "Sensuous, impulsive, he can sing Cleopatra's charms in immortal words; but he seems incapable of thinking out a sequence of inevitable consequences." The irony of his "place i' th' story" is that he earns it not for loyalty but for repented treason. He accuses Antony of having obeyed will and ignored reason, but dies brokenhearted after he is himself corrupted into obeying reason and ignoring will.

1402. Hoffmann, M. "Graceless Glosses on Shakespeare," RELV, XLVIII (1931), 260-262.

Three flippant comments on problems in Caesar. One treats the fact that Brutus has had no occasion to tell Portia of the conspiracy, yet she knows all by the time of the assassination; the second derogates Brutus with the other characters, all of whom are grey, not black or white; the third suggests that the pride of the conspirators after the murder may have been suggested by Grévin's Caesar, or more likely Muret's, which could have been the university play in which Polonius performed.

1403. Holland, Norman N. "The 'Cinna' and 'Cynicke' Episodes in Julius Caesar," SQ, XI (1960), 439-444.

Sh altered North considerably in Caesar in order to unify and concentrate the action; yet in two episodes, the death of Cinna and the intrusion of the Cynic on the quarrel scene, he included seeming irrelevancies from North. Holland indicates that Sh altered these passages, too, and tries to show that they have significance for the interpretation of the major action: Cinna's death is Caesar's in miniature; the Cynic's intrusion emphasizes the disparities between Cassius and Brutus which cause their downfall. So far Holland is convincing, but he vitiates his thesis by stretching it beyond probability: e.g., Cinna suggests the Good Thief to Caesar's Christ, and the Cynic forces open a closed door as Brutus' dagger forced its way into Caesar's mutilated body.

1404. Hollander, John. "Musica Mundana and Twelfth Night," Sound and Poetry, ed. Northrop Frye (Col UP, 1957), pp. 55-82.

For "classical" music in Caesar, see #0808.

1405. Honig, Edwin. "Sejanus and Coriolanus: A Study in Alienation," MLQ, XII (1951), 407-421.

An illuminating interpretation of both plays, especially of Sejanus. Coriolanus is alienated by a hatred for those he was destined to rule, and Sejanus is alienated by an ambition implemented neither by secular sanction nor by moral values. In both plays the people are, because of their selfishness, accessories to the evil in the protagonists; yet ironically they end by destroying the men who have isolated themselves. Jonson and Sh are linked also by a mutual tone of nostalgia for the Saturnian Age, overt in Sejanus, implicit in Cor. Perhaps the two playwrights also shared a common hatred of the Puritan demagogues who could sway a fickle English populace; this hatred of Puritanism is reflected in the mob scenes of these two Roman plays. The last point is less persuasive than almost all others in this stimulating essay.

1406. Honigmann, E. A. J. "Shakespeare's Plutarch," SQ, X (1959), 25-33.

An expansion of the thesis of Richard Büttner (#1195) that Sh borrowed material in Cor. from the Comparison of Coriolanus with Alcibiades. Honigmann points out some interesting echoes of thought and phrasing from the Comparison of Dion with Brutus (Caesar), "The Life of Pompey" (Caesar), the Comparison of Demetrius with Antonius (Antony), "Romulus" (Merch.), etc. The conclusion is that Sh read much more widely in Plutarch than his critics have. Some of the parallels cited are tenuous, but the general conclusion appears to be well founded; a more persuasive, and momentous, thesis than Büttner's.

1407. Hookham, G. "[On Coriolanus]," Will o' the Wisp (Oxford, 1922) (no exact pagination available—as abstracted in the New Variorum Cor.).

Hookham regards the play as "a monument of fallen greatness" (i.e., Sh in Cor. has fallen from the pinnacle of his achievement in, e.g., Ham. and Macb.). Coriolanus is a Pistol with courage, Volumnia is "repulsive," the language of the play exceeds the emotion, and, worst of all, in a "decadent mood" Sh "libels" the Roman crowd, which was really neither foolish nor cowardly. Hookham's contempt for Cor. tempts him to expel the play from the canon, but he does not yield to temptation because he can recognize Sh's hand in the play.

1408. Hooper, Henry. "'Cressida, Daughter to Calchas'," Shna, I (1884), 269-272.

An appreciation of the character which

amounts to a partial defense: e.g., Cressida's father, Calchas, a traitor, has set her a precedent which extenuates her treason to Troilus. Hooper is a personalist and does not discuss Cressida as a traditional character.

1409. Horn, F. "[On Coriolanus]," Shakespeare's Schauspiele erlaütert (Leipzig, 1826) (no exact pagination available--as trans. and abstracted in the New Variorum Cor.).

Though we may prefer others of Sh's plays, we must not ask of Sh in Cor. more than is just--he was working with intransigent material; everyone in the play is in the wrong, and as a result we are left with an unfulfilled longing to identify ourselves with some character. In the end Rome itself emerges as the focus of interest.

1410. Hoy, W. A. "Roman Life and Character ...in Shakespeare's Roman Plays," HLM, XVI (1882), 209-218.

Not seen.

1411. Hudson, H. N. Shakespeare: His Life, Art, and Characters. Boston, 1872 (no complete pagination available--as abstracted in the New Variorum Caesar, Cor., Antony).

Hudson regards Sh's Caesar as a "strange disguise" of the historical Caesar, for whom he cannot find sufficient praise—he concludes that Sh made his greatness "falsetto" to play up Brutus, an inferior man, and also to show Caesar as the perverse conspirators saw him. Hudson thinks Cor. the most perfectly constructed of the Roman plays—a worthy peer to the great tragedies. Antony he would have preferred to see tighter in structure.

1412. Hulme, Hilda M. "Three Notes on the Pronunciation and Meaning of Shakespeare's Text," Neoph, XLI (1957), 275-281.

The first note would emend F_1's "Ouerture" in Cor. I ix 46 to "ovator," which would be pronounced in the same way by Elizabethan actors. "Ovator," he who receives an ovation, is sixteenth-century Latin without classical authority. The argument is interesting, but not conclusive.

1413. Hulme, Hilda M. "Three Notes: Troilus and Cressida, V.vii.11; Midsummer Night's Dream, II.i.54; Measure for Measure, II.i.39," JEGP, LVII (1958), 721-725.

Note 1 (721-722) suggests that F_1 has the correct reading: "my double-henn'd sparrow" is Thersites' derisive name for Paris, whose two "hens" were Oenone and Helen.

1414. "Humanismus in Shakespeares Römerdramen," Germania, XVI, No. 6 (1938) (no pagination available). GRS

Not seen.

1415. Hunter, G. K. "Shakespeare's Hydra," NQ, CXCVIII (1953), 100-101.

Hunter asserts that the correct interpretation of Cor. III i hinges on our awareness that Sh knew the etymology of "hydra" (ὕδωρ) and thus used water as a political image in the scene. The "lesse Greeke" involved is not "an embarrassing amount of erudition."

1416. Hunter, Sir Mark. "Politics and Character in Shakespeare's 'Julius Caesar'," EDH, X (1931), 109-140.

This impressive approach to the play calls attention to the political atmosphere engendered by I i, where, significantly, Brutus is not even mentioned. There is no single hero: Sh is interested in a number of characters as they interplay in a political setting. But he also portrays them in their personal relationships where some of them are more attractive than their public behavior makes them seem. Hunter is at his best in character analysis, especially of Cassius and Antony, but there are many other merits: e.g., the discussion of Caesar as a history play in which the sweep of events is more important than the revelation of dominating personalities. A very satisfying address.

1417. Jenkin, Bernard. "Antony and Cleopatra: Some Suggestions on the Monument Scenes," RES, XXI (1945), 1-14.

The changes Sh made in Plutarch, especially in IV xv, were necessitated by the difficulty of producing on an Elizabethan stage the action as it appears in "The Life of Marcus Antonius."

1418. Jepsen, Laura. Ethical Aspects of Tragedy: A Comparison of Certain Tragedies by Aeschylus, Sophocles, Euripides, Seneca, and Shakespeare. Florida State UP, 1953, 130 pp.

Chs. V and VI, on Antony and Caesar respectively, compare the first with Euripides' Bacchae and the second with Seneca's Hercules

Oetaeus. In both Antony and the Bacchae there are ambiguities about moral worth. Cleopatra, who is like Dionysos, destroys Antony, who is like Pentheus, but the romantic irony is that the audience identifies with destroyer as much as with destroyed in each play. Sh's Brutus, like Seneca's Hercules, is a personification of the Stoic emphasis on will and intention rather than on the action which proceeds from will and intention. These two chs., like the three other major ones (#1976), are good criticism —they throw light on classical tragedy as much as on Sh.

1419. Jepsen, Laura. "A Footnote on 'Hands' in Shakespeare's Titus Andronicus," Writers and Their Critics: Studies in English and American Literature, FSUS, No. 19 (Florida State UP, 1955), pp. 7-10.

The play is unified by Sh's sixty references to hands, often in contexts of violence, mutilation, loss, bestiality, and then again in other contexts of competence and service. Perhaps Sh took the idea from Ovid's tale of Philomel where the skillful hands of the ravished girl tell a hideous story in the tapestry. But Sh greatly surpassed the horror of Ovid's version and in doing so delayed Lavinia's testimony and her vengeance; as a result tragic irony mounts toward the explosive catastrophe of Act V.

1420. Johnson, Samuel. Notes to Shakespeare Vol. III: Tragedies, ed. Arthur Sherbo, Augustan Reprint Society, Nos. 71, 72 (Los Angeles, 1958), 146 pp. (total).

The "Tragedies" annotated in these two numbers include Cor., Caesar, Antony, Tim., Titus, Troi. If the format of this series makes reading Johnson's notes difficult, one is rewarded by a completeness which Sir Walter Raleigh's samplings (#0351) cannot rival. Johnson is too often regarded today as a ponderous and opinionated historical curiosity; in fact he should be consulted for his insights on individual passages: e.g., he "illustrates" Antony III x 11 (Scarus' leprous curse on Cleopatra for fleeing from Actium) from Horace; and he makes an ingenious if not entirely correct guess at the source of the confusion in Brutus' sentiments on Cato and suicide (Caesar V i 97-112). Of equal interest are Johnson's brief general comments on the plays. He believes, e.g., that Sh drew on Caxton for Troi. but tempered Caxton with Chapman's Homer, a view now beginning to return to favor after many years of exile. Again, Johnson recognizes the stylistic austerity of Caesar, and, anticipating modern students of imagery, traces it to Sh's effort at "adherence to the real story, and to Roman manners."

1421. Jones, R. T. "Shakespeare's Julius Caesar," Theoria, XII (1959), 41-51.

Jones objects to the preference of "realist" critics for Cassius over Brutus, but as he seeks to restore Sh's intention in the play, he exhibits their chief fallacy: he discusses both Brutus and Cassius as if they were figures in a twentieth-century "political situation." It is certainly true that Cassius with his passionate yet calculating commitment is a type no modern revolution can live long without and that Brutus is a revolutionary likely to be a better leader than his predecessor ("had he been put on"), but to Sh the concept of revolution and revolutionaries was as alien as the Communists to whom Jones compares Cassius. It is perhaps significant that not a word is said of Plutarch in the essay.

1422. Jones, Robert E. "Brutus in Cicero and Shakespeare," CJ, XXXVIII (1943), 449-457.

Jones regrets that Sh did not "delve into the minutiae of Roman history" in quest of the true Brutus who is revealed better in Cicero's letters and in his Brutus than in Plutarch who is less interested in "sober history" than in "pointing a moral." If Sh had read the letters (especially the ones to Atticus) he would have found information about (1) Brutus' reputation, (2) "his previous relations with Caesar," (3) the causes Caesar gave Brutus for turning against him, (4) the influence on Brutus' republican sentiments of Cicero, Greek literature, and Portia, (5) Brutus' sullied financial dealings which could provide irony in the quarrel scene, (6) details absent from Plutarch about Brutus' obstinacy, idealism, impracticality, and his Attic oratory. An interesting study, but, as Jones admits, again and again Sh conveys the supposed real Brutus despite his ignorance of Cicero's Epistles.

1423. Jorgensen, Paul A. "Enobarbus' Broken Heart and The Estate of English Fugitives," PQ, XXX (1951), 387-392.

Sh deliberately departed from Plutarch and from his own practice when he protracted the scenes detailing Enobarbus' desertion, remorse, and death; he wished to suggest a topical analogue--the desertion to the Spaniards in the Low Countries of English officers so luridly and dramatically described by Lewkenor's Estate of English Fugitives. This piece of propaganda was immensely popular in the late 'nineties; Sh could expect his audience to make the analogy, Jorgensen thinks. But Antony was written ten years after the fact; how many theatergoers in the early 1960's would notice a parallel in an historical drama to the desertion to the Communist cause of American prisoners in Korea?

1424. Jorgensen, Paul A. "Shakespeare's Coriolanus: Elizabethan Soldier," PMLA, LXIV (1949), 221-235.

Jorgensen analyzes Coriolanus in the light of Elizabethan attitudes toward military men, and argues that the significant differences between Sh's version and Plutarch's can be traced to these attitudes. Jorgensen shows that the tragic flaw is not patrician pride but impulsiveness, which assures Coriolanus' failure both as general and as statesman. The interpretation seems plausible and it solves many of the critical problems in the play.

1425. Kannengiesser, Paul. "Eine Doppelredaktion in Shakespeares 'Julius Caesar'," ShJ, XLIV (1908), 51-64. E-S

Kannengiesser reasons that Sh's first version of Caesar IV iii made it plain that Brutus knew nothing of Portia's death before Messala informed him of it. His laconic response to the news was, however, found to be flat on stage: as Lessing once observed, "Alles Stoische ist untheatralisch." Accordingly Sh's second version showed Brutus revealing his grief after having kept his secret through the quarrel. The printer of F_1 set up both of the versions through inadvertance.

1426. Kaula, David C. "The Moral Vision of Shakespeare's Troilus and Cressida," diss (Indiana, 1956). DA, XVI (1956), 2150-51.

This diss argues that Troi. is a typical Shn play in its moral framework, the "post-medieval vision of the Augustinian earthly city." Troilus' love is self-seeking, and Cressida's behavior is a natural product of Trojan values in which Helen is "the paradigm of feminine excellence." The values of Stoicism, Cynicism, and Realpolitik are exemplified in Agamemnon and Nestor, Thersites, and Ulysses respectively. Kaula also discusses Sh's rejection of Chapman's "Achilleian virtues" of self-sufficiency, aloofness, reason, fortitude, self-control (i.e., his Stoicism); Sh indicates his rejection by making Chapman's Achilles into "a sadistic boor."

1427. Keightley, Thomas. "Transposition," 2 NQ, IX (1860), 358.

An exponent of phrasal metathesis as a means of restoring meter and meaning in corrupt passages, Keightley demonstrates the possibilities. Tampering with the word order in Troi. V ii 150-152 can excuse Sh from having written "Ariachne" for "Arachne." But the metathesis radically alters Sh's sense in a passage which renders meaning and meter as it stands.

1428. Keller, Wolfgang. "Der Schluss von Shakespeare's 'Troilus und Cressida'," ShJ, LVI (1920), 106-107.

Keller suggests that it was Henryson's Testament of Cresseid which induced Sh to depart from Chaucer's account of the death of Troilus at Achilles' hands. Henryson, whose sequel to Troilus and Criseyde was printed in eds. of Chaucer in Sh's time, casts doubt on Chaucer's accuracy as an historian of the Trojan War. Sh therefore followed Henryson in making Troilus survive the events of the play. The result, Keller believes, is a play without a definitive tragic ending.

1429. Keller, Wolfgang. "Shakespeares 'Troilus und Cressida'," ShJ, LXVI (1930), 182-207. E-S SG

Keller finds cynicism and grim satire in parts of Troi. and traces this tone to Sh's disillusionment over the Essex affair as well as to two of Sh's main sources: (1) Ovid's Heroides and Meta. (both of which view the Trojan War sardonically), (2) the post-Chaucerian tradition with its moralizing condemnation of Cressida. Keller doubts that Chapman's Iliads had anything to contribute; he reprints Troilus' complaint and Cressida's reply from The Paradise of Dainty Devices, calling them a neglected contribution to the Troy literature of the sixteenth century. A stimulating essay which provides, inter alia, insight into Sh's changing attitude toward the Troilus-Cressida story during his career, and into Ovid's presentation of the Homeric story.

1430. Keller, Wolfgang. "Zwei Bemerkungen zu 'Julius Caesar'," ShJ, XLV (1909), 219-228. SG

The first note suggests a possible influence of Caesar's Revenge on Sh's early conception of Brutus. Keller calls attention to Sh's emphasis on Brutus as a bastard son of Caesar (and therefore murderer of his father) in the early plays (2,3H.VI); Sh later obscured this bit of Plutarchian gossip completely in Caesar. Keller conjectures that Sh's interest in the Caesar story early in his career sprang from his having acted in Caesar's Revenge. The second note argues forcefully that Brutus is the hero of Caesar. Keller's main argument is that most of the action is based on Plutarch's "Life of Brutus," even when Sh could have used "Antonius" and "Caesar" just as well; it is apparent that it was Brutus the republican who dominated Sh's thinking as he wrote. Yet Sh retains the would-be monarch's name as title and moreover makes him nobler than Plutarch's Caesar; Keller hints that it was prudent of Sh to do so, living as he did in a monarchy. As for Antony, his "Life" is the dominant source for only one scene (IV i) and in that scene he is plainly evil: he certainly cannot be taken as the hero.

1431. Kellett, E. E. "Shakspere as a Borrower," Suggestions: Literary Essays (CUP, 1923), pp. 33-56.

The only "suggestions" about Sh's classical debts in this essay are (1) Cicero is unimportant to the conspirators before Caesar's death but important to Brutus and Cassius at the time of Antony's proscription. This is because Sh followed Plutarch's account of the purge closely in Act IV and forgot that he had assigned Cicero a minor rôle in the first three acts; (2) Macduff's "He has no children" (Macb. IV iii 216), taken to mean "Macbeth has no children for me to kill as vengeance," is a parallel to Medea's "Utinam esset illi frater ... " when she contemplates avenging on Jason the death of her brother (Seneca's Medea, 125).

1432. Kemp, Robert. "En Relisant 'Timon d'Athènes'," Le Temps, 4-5 avril, 1942, p. 3. GRS

Kemp finds Apemantus preferable to Timon, whose violent emotions far exceed the provocation—after all, ingratitude is an occurrence of little importance to a society which has witnessed the fall of Pericles, the Peloponnesian War, and repeated plagues. Kemp is amused by Sh's extravagant anachronisms in the play. On the other hand he finds the invective (some of it) impressive. He sees Plutarch's "Life of Antonius" as the primary source, though he mentions Lucian, Aesop, and Pliny (the latter two for animal allusions). He also favors disintegration though he refrains from designating Sh's collaborator or from specifying his contribution.

1433. Kendall, Paul M. "Inaction and Ambivalence in Troilus and Cressida," VirginiaES, pp. 131-145.

Kendall reads Troi. as if it were a nineteenth-century problem-play; not Sh's sources but Sh himself is responsible for the tone of the play. The peculiarities of that tone spring from the inconclusiveness of every action begun in the play and from the duality in all the major characters. Sh experimented again with duality in other plays but never again attempted suspended action, because his audience would not tolerate it. Kendall does not notice that suspended action, like suspended volition, is antidramatic and hardly a device to be praised in a competent dramatist; yet he says that "the chief problem" in Shn studies is solved—Troi. is a successful play.

1434. Kenny, Hamill. "Shakespeare's Cressida," Anglia, LXI (1937), 163-176.

A defense of the character, especially on moral grounds: Cressida committed no sin in Troy because she was handfasted to Troilus before she slept with him; in the Greek camp she resisted her carnal impulses, and if she appears to fall quickly that is because of the temporal necessity of the play. In short, there is little ground for the accusations of Ulysses or the revilings of Thersites (or, indeed, for the harsh slanders of modern critics). Kenny turns to the traditional basis of the legend for support, but he appears to overstate his exculpation.

1435. Kimbrough, Robert Alexander, III. "New Tricks and Old Decorum: Shakespeare's Troilus and Cressida in its Theatrical and Literary Setting," diss (Harvard, 1959).*

1436. King, A. H. "Notes on Coriolanus," ES, XIX (1937), 13-20.

The two most important notes appear to be (1) "Martius," as in North and F_1, not "Marcius," as in modern eds., is correct—the former spelling emphasizes the derivation from "Mars"; (2) in II i, where Menenius gives a character sketch of himself and then of the Tribunes, Sh is imitating Theophrastus' seventeenth-century imitators, possibly Jonson, but if Cor. is to be dated 1608 or later, the source could be any number of writings. At ibid., XX (1938), 18-25, King gives further notes of similar interest.

1437. Kirschbaum, Leo. "Shakespeare's Stage Blood and Its Critical Significance," PMLA, LXIV (1949), 517-529.

Modern directors make a serious error when they attempt to cleanse productions of Caesar and Cor. of the Grand Guignol effects which Sh intended for vivid portrayal on stage. By omitting the conspirators' ritual self-bedaubing with Caesar's blood the director glosses over Sh's implication that the assassination was an unworthy, inhumane slaughter. In Cor., the countless references to the protagonist as hacked and bleeding or covered with the blood of others are Sh's way of suggesting that he is a brutal man of blood, not a man of thought or sentiment. An interesting point, but not entirely convincing, especially when Kirschbaum injects "Christian brotherhood and mercy" as the antithesis of Coriolanus' "demented sensuality."

1438. Kirschbaum, Leo. "Shakspere's Cleopatra," SAB, XIX (1944), 161-171.

Sh is consistent throughout Antony in his portrayal of both lovers as "voluptuaries." Kirschbaum analyzes the sexual content of Acts IV and V and discusses the imagery of the play, citing and criticizing inter alia Schücking (#1639) and Stoll (#1706).

1439. Klein, David. "Has Cassius Been Misinterpreted?" SAB, XIV (1939), 27-36.

A vigorous defense of the character against his many detractors. In places Klein appears to consider too curiously, but he makes two good points: (1) his analysis of the quarrel scene convincingly shows that Cassius endures Brutus' insults when Brutus is at least as much in the wrong as he; (2) one piece of evidence for Cassius' malignancy can be dismissed: Antony's eulogy of Brutus Sh found in Plutarch and embodied faithfully at the end of the play after he had already made Cassius a sympathetic figure. Sh did not scruple over consistency in matters like this. Klein's apology will not revolutionize the interpretation of the play, but it may justifiably ameliorate the stigma which Cassius still bears in some critical quarters.

1440. Kleinstück, Johannes. "Ulysses' Speech on Degree as Related to the Play of Troilus and Cressida," Neoph, XLIII (1959), 58-63.

An ingenious argument that Ulysses is not Sh's spokesman, and that the hierarchical society which he postulates as "the good" in I iii is utopian since no man can discern the true worth of his neighbor (cf. the many false estimates of character in the play), and subordination is therefore guesswork. Ulysses "supports" Kleinstück's argument by completely disregarding his own advice; he inverts the normal subordination of Ajax to Achilles with the object of getting the latter to fight, a goal he prefers to "specialty of rule." He also falsely estimates Achilles as a man long on prowess and short on policy; Achilles avoids Hector and lets the Myrmidons do the killing for him. Some of the inconsistency which causes Kleinstück to pejorate Ulysses may be Sh's attempt to convey Homer's "wily" Odysseus, a somewhat devious manipulator of others.

1441. Knight, G. Wilson. "Brutus and Macbeth," The Wheel of Fire: Essays in Interpretation of Shakespeare's Sombre Tragedies (OUP, 1930), pp. 132-153. (Reprinted with some deletion and revision from CQR, CX [1930], 40-71. E-S)

Disregarding the relationship of Caesar to Plutarch and of Macb. to Holinshed, Knight finds some striking similarities between the two plays (the one time he mentions Plutarch it is to deny his relevance). Like Macbeth, Brutus suffers an internal "insurrection"; like him, he is an assassin; like him he loses his collaborator (Brutus loses both Cassius and Portia); like him he is visited by a ghost to torment his already disturbed conscience, etc. Knight has shown that the plays are similar in "rhythm" if not in ethical tone, but his dismissal of historical criticism leaves some interesting questions of indebtedness entirely unanswered.

1442. Knight, G. Wilson. The Imperial Theme: Further Interpretations of Shakespeare's Tragedies Including the Roman Plays. OUP, 1931, 367 pp.

A good part of this book is relevant to the Guide: there are two chs. on Caesar, the first delineating thematic patterns of language, the second opposing the themes of love and honor (Cassius and Brutus)—Knight prefers Cassius and Antony to Brutus and Caesar because the former are emotional while the latter are coldly rational. The ch. on Cor. argues that its theme is that of Antony, love and war as incompatibles (again in this ch. Knight uses imagery as a chief foundation of argument). Almost half the book is occupied by four essays on Antony, "probably the subtlest and greatest play in Shakespeare," with the possible exception of Temp. Here again Knight explores the images, the sounds, and the verbal paradoxes of the play to suggest methods by which Sh shows divinity emerging from sordidness. The difficulty with all of the essays in the vol. is that they treat Sh in a cultural vacuum: Sh's source in Plutarch is to Knight irrelevant; the classical biases and enthusiasms of the Elizabethan and Jacobean audiences are ignored and Sh's triumphs are never seen in the perspective of attempts by his dramatic contemporaries at similar subjects and themes. Yet, though Knight can be drastically wrong in his intuitions (e.g., at the "consummation" of Cor. "the whole is suddenly aglow with heating love"), his method does cast light on the plays; the analysis of the imagery of human trivia in Caesar, e.g., shows that this is not so lean and sparse a play as has sometimes been casually assumed.

1443. Knight, G. Wilson. "The Metaphysic of 'Troilus and Cressida'," DR, CLXXXV (1929), 228-242. E-S (Reprinted with some expansion in The Wheel of Fire [1930].)

Knight states his belief that in Troi. Sh explores the philosophical possibilities of the life of intuition (Troilus) and the life of reason (Ulysses and Hector). Each system of values has its limitations: Troilus shows that reason is the coward's excuse when Hector would abrogate honor and give over the war; yet Troilus' intuitive [perhaps "instinctive" is a better word] love demands infinite fulfillment and duration which are patently impossible in a finite world. Knight considers the play one of Sh's most successful efforts both in structure and in profundity of thought.

1444. Knight, G. Wilson. "The Pilgrimage of Hate: An Essay on Timon of Athens," The Wheel of Fire: Essays in Interpretation of Shakespeare's Sombre Tragedies (OUP, 1930), pp. 227-262.

This extraordinary critical essay, far from finding Tim. wanting, sees in it the most powerful of Sh's tragedies. The play begins with Sh's virtual announcement that he is writing a parable (I i 43-45), and from there Sh shows us Timon the great lover—not cold and saintly, but warm and personal in his philanthropy. When reversal comes, Timon moves from sublime love toward sublime hatred—from civilization down through various stages of being to chaos, which Sh symbolizes in the seas which wash over his grave. Modern critics seldom find Timon so attractive a character and seldom discover the coherent pattern in Tim. which Knight credits, in part, with its greatness.

1445. Knights, L. C. "Antony and Cleopatra and Coriolanus," Some Shakespearean Themes (Ln, 1959), Ch. VII, pp. 143-156. (Reprinted from SewR, LXI [1953], 43-55.)

"Shakespeare infused into the love story as he found it in Plutarch ... an immense energy, a sense of life so heightened that it can claim to represent an absolute value." The world of Cor. is "a familiar world; yet the evil at the heart of the state—though not, as in Macbeth, deliberately willed—is just as firmly stated. ... In cutting himself off from a responsive relationship to his society ... Coriolanus has diminished his own stature as a human being."

1446. Knights, L. C. "Beyond Politics: An Aspect of Shakespeare's Relation to Tradition," ShN, VI (1956), 14.

For Caesar and Cor. as political documents, see #1653.

1447. Knights, L. C. "On the Tragedy of Antony and Cleopatra," Scrutiny, XVI (1949), 318-323.

An attempt to sharpen the contrast which Danby makes (#1250) between what Antony's career might have been and what his love amounted to. Knights is convincing when he argues that Cleopatra's last scenes should not be interpreted as approval of her position in Antony's life but rather an evocation of "sympathy or even admiration for what, in [Sh's] final judgment, is discarded or condemned."

1448. Knights, L. C. "Shakespeare and Political Wisdom: A Note on the Personalism of Julius Caesar and Coriolanus," SewR, LXI (1953), 43-55.

Taken together, Caesar and Cor. teach two lessons about the relation between public and private life: (1) the human individual is worth more than the abstract political principle; (2) people as persons make politics, good or bad. Knights's hostility toward abstract dogmatism in modern political life is to be commended, but his enthusiasm has perhaps caused him to find more docere in the two plays than Sh's usual emphasis on delectare would warrant to be there.

1449. Knights, L. C. "Shakespeare: 'King Lear' and the Great Tragedies," The Age of Shakespeare, The Pelican Guide to English Literature, II (n.p.: Penguin Books, 1955), pp. 228-256. GRS

The thoughts on Antony and Cor. first appeared in SewR and Scrutiny (see #1445, #1447).

1450. Knights, L. C. "Shakespeare's Politics: With Some Reflections on the Nature of Tradition," PBA, XLIII (1957), 115-132. (Annual British Academy Shakespeare Lecture.)

In passing Knights quotes a passage from Chaucer's trans. of Boethius on love as the cohesive force in the body politic and calls it the best statement of the positive values of Sh's doctrine of degree. The body politic is discussed briefly as it appears in Caesar, Cor., and Troi.

1451. Knights, L. C. "The Theme of Appearance and Reality in Troilus and Cressida," Some Shakespearean Themes (Ln, 1959), Ch. IV, pp. 65-83.

Sh portrays in Ulysses' scheming man's public appearance and in Troilus' intuitive self-centeredness his private reality; but G. Wilson Knight is wrong to say that Sh prefers the second to the first. The Greeks must complement the Trojans—each is defective without the other. Sh manipulated the stock figures of the tale of Troy, ironically reversing some and leaving others as he found them in his sources, all with the object of playing Ulysses' world against Troilus'. In passing Knights suggests the pseudo-Platonic Alcibiades I as the (at least ultimate) source for III iii 95-111.

1452. Knights, L. C. "Troilus and Cressida," TLS, June 2, 1932, p. 408.

A suggestion, not accorded much favor now, that Troi. should be read (at least in part) as a Morality play in which Pandarus is a personification of his evil profession (a sort of comic Vice), Troilus is Constancy, and Cressida Infidelity. The theory can be applied more easily to Pandarus than to Cressida, and it hardly applies to the lyric outbursts of Troilus.

1453. Knights, L. C. "Troilus and Cressida Again," Scrutiny, XVIII (1951), 144-157.

Subsumed into the ch. on Troi. in Some Shakespearean Themes (#1451).

1454. Knoll, Robert E. "Drama of Fulfillment and Drama of Choice: A Note on Greek and Elizabethan Drama," WHR, XI (1957), 371-376. GRS

For Antony as a play "psychological" rather than Greek in spirit, see #1990.

1455. Knowland, A. S. "Troilus and Cressida," SQ, X (1959), 353-365.

Though Troi. is not a tract on Mutability or on Time or on Fate or on anything else (modern interpretations notwithstanding) all these "themes" are in the play, in which Sh seems to portray and sympathize with the human desire to erect something noble and enduring out of the chaos of actualities repeatedly frustrated by the gods. Knowland finds the Trojans much like the Greeks—the two camps are not symbols for opposed abstractions. Among the well-made points is Knowland's distinction between the bombast of Latinate diction (in the Prologue and in the speeches of Ulysses, Nestor, and Hector) and the triviality of colloquial speech (in the morning-after scene between the lovers, e.g.). An interesting study which wisely emphasizes the play as drama, not as statement, poetic or otherwise.

1456. Kreyssig, F. "[On Coriolanus]," Vorlesungen über Shakespeare [or possibly Shakespeare-Fragen, Leipzig, 1871—the New Variorum is not clear which work is abstracted]. (Berlin, 1874) (no exact pagination available—as trans. and abstracted in the New Variorum Cor.).

Kreyssig considers Cor. a triumph, but not justly to be ranked so high as Caesar. He admires the intellectual concepts in the play, its heightened language, and "the bold and the many-sided articulated characteristics." His defense of Sh against those who object to anachronism is stout, and he shows that the theme is a compelling one—the destruction of an aristocrat who fails to be truly aristocratic, i.e., to subordinate "personal ambition [to] patriotic interest." An interesting commentary.

1457. Latham, Grace. "On Volumnia," 1 NSST (1887-92), 69-90.

Miss Latham writes an appreciative essay; she prefers Volumnia to Virgilia, a preference which is seldom found now that society has rebelled against matriarchy. The chief fault in this extended eulogy is that it exceeds the play by discussing the possible relationships of Volumnia to her husband and to her son before the action. Yet, despite her enthusiasm, Miss Latham can find and admit faults in her heroine and she hints at the irony implicit in the reversal of rôles in IV i and IV ii where Volumnia becomes distraught and wrathful while (in IV i) her son assumes his mother's usual rôle of calm encourager and comforter.

1458. Law, R[obert] A. "The Roman Background of Titus Andronicus," SP, XL (1943), 145-153.

Law seeks to add the last six books of the Aeneid and Plutarch's "Life of Scipio Africanus" to Kittredge's list of sources (#0365). Law's evidence, especially for "Scipio," is interesting, but he shows no knowledge of H. deW. Fuller's research (#1326) into possible lost English sources for Sh's play. Law considers his thesis a weapon against disintegrators.

1459. Law, R[obert] A. "Some Books that Shakespeare Read," LCUT, I (1944), 14-18.

For Sh's use of North's Plutarch in Titus, see #0835.

1460. Law, R[obert] A. "The Text of 'Shakespeare's Plutarch'," HLQ, VI (1943), 197-203.

For a discussion of the ed. Sh probably used for the Roman plays, see #0836.

1461. Lawrence, William W. "The Love-Story in 'Troilus and Cressida'," ColSS, pp. 185-211. E-S

Lawrence sides with the historical critics, advancing the view that Sh had no freedom in the portrayal of Cressida; he could no more redeem her without incurring the ridicule of his audience than he could redeem Richard III. A large part of the essay is an elementary, but effective presentation of the conventions of courtly love in Boccaccio and Chaucer; Lawrence treats Henryson and the sixteenth century more briefly. The character of Pandarus (in Chaucer) is defended; the immutability of Troilus' lofty reputation is also noted. Though Lawrence gives no analysis of Sh's play, he calls the Greek plot the enveloping action to the main, or love plot. Some, but by no means all of this essay reappears in Shakespeare's Problem Comedies, #1462.

1462. Lawrence, W[illiam] W. "Troilus and Cressida," Shakespeare's Problem Comedies (N.Y., 1931), Ch. IV, pp. 122-173.

Though he insists early in the ch. that tradition as expounded by Tatlock and Rollins is not enough to account for the problems of the play, Lawrence spends a good portion of his space on Sh's conventional heritage in the legend; he does not add greatly to the work of his predecessors: what is based on the Iliad Sh may have taken from a lost play. When he does return to the interpretation of the play he makes a number of valid critical points, e.g., (1) Cressida and Achilles are mutual analogues as they selfishly betray trust to follow the bent of their passions; (2) the final seven scenes, though perhaps not by Sh, probably reflect his intention--if the play ends inconclusively, that was part of Sh's realistic conception of the Troy story: the guilty triumph, at least temporarily.

1463. Lawrence, William W. "Troilus, Cressida and Thersites," MLR, XXXVII (1942), 422-437.

Arguing for the influence on Sh of tradition and of the taste of the intended audience (perhaps a private one), Lawrence examines the three characters. Cressida is exactly what tradition made her--a faithless wanton--but she is sympathetically portrayed early in the play to give Troilus cause to love her. Troilus is more noble than he has sometimes been thought; if he desires his lover's body, this is no more than Romeo does. Thersites was expanded to appeal to an audience which liked coarse ribaldry cloaked as satire and especially to degrade the Greeks in conformity with British pro-Trojan prejudice (it is significant that Thersites does not flagellate the Trojans as he does the Greeks). Lawrence argues with poise, but it is difficult to see the Trojans as much more appealing than the Greeks.

1464. Leavis, F. R. "'Antony and Cleopatra' and 'All For Love': A Critical Exercise," Scrutiny, V (1936), 158-169.

A comparison of poetic merits to show Sh's superiority. Surprisingly, though the descriptions of Cleopatra in her barge are a major point of contrast, Leavis nowhere brings North's prose account into the discussion.

1465. Lee, Nathaniel. "Lucius Junius Brutus, Dedication" (1681), Munro, II, 264.

A brief reference to the difficulty Sh or any poet has in capturing and portraying "Greece or Old Rome." Sh's native wit enabled him to succeed with Brutus despite "a blockish Age."

1466. Lees, F. N. "Coriolanus, Aristotle, and Bacon," RES, n.s. I (1950), 114-125.

Lees attempts to show that Sh's conception of man as a social animal in Cor. is indebted to I.D.'s 1598 trans. of Aristotle's Politics and that Bacon possibly drew the concept from Cor. in his essay Of Friendship (1625). The similarities of thought are interesting, but Lees has hung a large case on a slender thread, especially in his verbal parallels.

1467. Legouis, Pierre. "Troïlus Devant le Mariage," LLM, XLII (1948), 1-13. GRS

Legouis considers the extramarital relationship of the lovers in Troi. in the light of their characters and of the tradition of courtly love. He rejects the thesis of Kenny (#1434) that a handfast marriage precedes the sexual consummation and he enumerates possible reasons why the lovers cannot marry (indeed do not consider doing so). In Legouis' interpretation Troilus is rather naïf, while Cressida is fully cognizant of the moral implication of her behavior. Pandarus is firmly characterized by his parody of the marriage service as the lovers are about to withdraw to bed. Legouis does not treat the connection, logical or analogical, of either of the lovers with the war plot.

1468. Lewis, Wyndham. "Thersites and Apemantus," The Lion and the Fox: The Rôle of the Hero in the Plays of Shakespeare (Ln, 1927), Part VII, pp. 229-262.

Lewis is concerned with the relationship between the heroic and the anti-heroic in Shn tragedy and history, and in this section he applies his criticism to the Greek and Roman plays with Troi. as a radial point. Thersites, Apemantus, and the Tribunes in Cor. all share the fox-like anti-heroism which Lewis believes Sh appreciated as much at least as he did the leonine heroism of Timon, Troilus, or Coriolanus. Lewis is more likely to cite Machiavelli, Cervantes, or Nietzsche than Plutarch, Lucian, or Homer, but his criticism does throw some light on these three "difficult" plays by reading them in the context of Renaissance (as opposed to Victorian) morality.

1469. Lindner, Albert. "Die dramatische Einheit im Julius Cäsar," ShJ, II (1867), 90-95. E-S

Lindner argues that the unity of Caesar stems from its theme: the rise of the monarchy, personified in the first three acts in an unattractive Caesar and in the last two acts in Caesar's inheritor, Octavius. After the assassination, Caesar's spirit becomes more than a principle, as it seeks a personal revenge on the conspirators. The structure of Caesar can therefore be contrasted with that of Sophocles' Ajax: in both plays the heroes die midway through the action, but in Caesar the hero assumes greatness after his death whereas in Ajax the hero becomes after death a mere object for men to fight over. Caesar has a unity which Ajax lacks. Lindner's account does not reckon with Antony, who plays so large a rôle in Acts III, IV, and V, but it merits praise as the earliest recognition of reversal of rôles as a structural principle in the play.

1470. Lloyd, Michael. "Cleopatra as Isis," ShS, XII (1959), 88-94.

Cleopatra, as a virtual personification of procreative power (the lover and the nurse), has the characteristics of Isis as they are described by Apuleius in The Golden Ass and by Plutarch in the Moralia. Isis was part Ceres and part Venus, as is Cleopatra; but Antony, whom Lloyd sees as a faithless lover, does not participate in the qualities of Osiris, the devoted lover, and his inconstancy accentuates the Isis-like majesty of Cleopatra. That Sh had access to Apuleius and to Holland's Moralia (1603) is unquestioned; it is debatable, however, whether the cult of Isis was familiar enough to the Elizabethans to be meaningful to an audience in the context of Antony. Perhaps Barroll (#1145) has a more probable thesis.

1471. Lloyd, Michael. "The Roman Tongue," SQ, X (1959), 461-468.

What the Roman characters in Antony say of Cleopatra characterizes them as hypocrites, for their behavior and their language are both distinctly inferior in moral tone to hers. It is ironic that the Romans speak of Cleopatra and of Egypt as lacking in moral fiber, while they themselves far outdo her (e.g., Octavius "sells" his sister; Roman statesmen carouse on Pompey's galley). Lloyd does not discuss the alleged anti-Roman bias of the play in the light of Plutarch's account.

1472. Lloyd, W[illiam] Watkiss. "Pyramid," 7 NQ, XI (1891), 283.

For Sh's possibly erroneous references to the pyramids in Antony, see #2008.

1473. Lloyd, W[illiam] Watkiss. "'Troilus and Cressida', II.ii.163," 7 NQ, II (1886), 304-305.

The passage on the young men to whom Aristotle would not teach moral philosophy is noteworthy for its accuracy. Sh even used the word "hear" (in the sense of "study" or "learn"), an accurate trans. of the Greek metaphor ἀκούω. Hector's reference may be an anachronism, but it suits its Shn context perfectly because both Troi. and the Nicomachean Ethics assert that passion defeats morality.

1474. Lord, Louis E. "Aristophanes' Influence on English Writers," Aristophanes: His Plays and His Influence, Our Debt, [No. 4] ([1925]/1963), pp. 155-173.

For mediate "Aristophanic" influence on Tim., see #0847.

1475. Lütgenau, F. "Troilus und Cressida," ESn, L (1916), 63-79. E-S

Lütgenau rejects the theory that Troi. is a record of Sh's personal disillusionment. He argues that the play is consistently and successfully a comedy until V v, and that the change in tone and action at that point is traceable to another hand in the play (probably Wilkins'), to be credited with the last six scenes and the epilogue. Lütgenau recognizes that his interpretation hinges on Troilus, but does not offer convincing evidence that Troilus is a comic character; and he certainly does not persuade that I iii is an irrelevant scene to be assigned to the collaborator.

1476. Lyman, Dean B. "Janus in Alexandria: A Discussion of 'Antony and Cleopatra'," SewR, XLVIII (1940), 86-104.

Lyman's intuitive criticism admittedly seeks to read greatness into the play. The result is an understanding of Antony as a Janus-figure with one face toward Rome and the other toward Egypt. There is nothing improbable or even original about this version, but Lyman gives the impression of distorting the play through oversimplification.

1477. MacCallum, M. W. Shakespeare's Roman Plays and Their Background. Ln, 1910, 656 pp. E-S HB SG

This is unquestionably the most painstaking and extensive study of Caesar, Antony, and Cor. in relation to their source in Plutarch that has yet appeared, and as such it has aged little in fifty years. MacCallum carries a very large burden of erudition with grace and uses it shrewdly in his observations on Sh's creative process and on his concepts of Rome, history, tragedy, character, and style in prose and poetry; these are observations which must still be considered today even if they are not universally accepted today. MacCallum's chief limitations are his undue reliance on the judgments of Coleridge, Gervinus, and Brandes; his omission of an index; and his reluctance to guide the reader's further study by means of bibliographical notes--but these limitations are amply balanced by the appendices, especially B which prints the Latin, Greek, French, Tudor, and Shn versions of Volumnia's dissuasion of her son from the sack of Rome, and C and D on Sh's debt to Appian in Caesar and Antony. In his critical interpretations of the plays MacCallum holds to a middle ground, and if he attains it (as especially on Caesar and Brutus) by contradicting himself, it is not the less a valid position, endorsed in the main by the more responsible of recent critics. Another asset is the brilliance of MacCallum's analyses of minor characters, especially in Caesar and Antony. This book repays careful study.

1478. Mackenzie, Agnes M. The Women in Shakespeare's Plays. Ln, 1924, 474 pp. E-S

This critical study treats the entire canon more or less chronologically, but though Miss Mackenzie conveys an occasional observation on Sh's classicism in other plays (e.g., Portia's classical allusions as she watches Bassanio choose are not inconsistent with Renaissance feminine gentility; Julia and her maid, Lucetta, in T.G.V. are descendants respectively of Psyche and of the competent servant of Roman comedy), the important relevant passages are the six on the Greek and Roman plays. Titus and Tim. she dismisses in haste because the women in them do not reward scrutiny, but the other four she treats in detail and she sees them as a group: Caesar and Cor. as studies of men (and women) in their relationship to the social order are a pair which open and close Sh's tragic period. Troi. and Antony are another pair in each of which a public figure is wrecked by an irresponsible, selfish, but fascinating woman. Miss Mackenzie surely writes from bias—her inability to find Cleopatra attractive is an indication—but she also has insights: Portia blames her sex for her faults; she attempts to emulate her husband's resolute Stoicism, but cannot, and kills herself to escape from her weakness. The analyses of Cressida/ Helen and Volumnia/Virgilia are also of special interest, though they inspire partial disagreement. Not the least of Miss Mackenzie's limitations is her hesitant, but real faith in Shn soul-sickness, but she has an amusing contempt for Victorian bardolatry and a vigorous, even racy style to commend her book.

1479. MacLure, Millar. "Shakespeare and the Lonely Dragon," UTQ, XXIV (1955), 109-120.

In three nonroyal political protagonists Sh exemplifies a truism of Plutarch's Lives and More's Utopia: a man must reconcile his private image of himself with his public duty— if he does not, he is dishonored. Achilles loses his honor because he conceives of the Trojan War as his private affair; Coriolanus loses honor and life because he cannot bear to let the public into his private glories (e.g., the wound-showing scene); Antony loses his honor and the verdict of history to Octavius at Actium because an affaire de coeur means too much to him. This art. does not attribute any significance to the fact that all three are classical heroes. Did Sh pursue the hint about a man's private and public character in Plutarch's introduction to the "Life of Alexander"?

1480. Macmillan, Michael. "Introduction," The Tragedy of Julius Caesar (1902/1934), ArdenSh, pp. ix-xciii.

Macmillan compares Caesar to Sophocles' Ajax (both plays reach a major focus of interest long before the end) and to the Iliad (an inexorable chain of cause and effect produces succeeding calamities in each story). Neither Brutus nor Caesar is to be regarded as the hero of the tragedy, because Sh keeps shifting the audience's sympathies as heroic characters succeed one another in the action. Yet Brutus is even more virtuous in Sh than the almost flawless Brutus of Plutarch while Caesar is less perfect in Sh than in Plutarch (though Plutarch does offer precedent for all of the Shn Caesar's limitations). The excellent character studies show one ironic similarity between Brutus and Caesar and discuss Sh's Plutarchian contrast between Brutus and Cassius, and between Brutus and Antony. Macmillan refers to the Ciceronian background of Antony's oration, though he doubts that Sh had read Cicero. He includes an admirable discussion of Sh's compression and idealization of Roman history in the play. The last thirty pp. of the introduction are extracts from North's three relevant Lives, carefully arranged to make a seriatim companion to the play.

1481. Maginn, William. "Timon of Athens," Shakespeare Papers (Ln, 1859), 187-231.

This illuminating essay begins with a caustic rejection of Richard Farmer's thesis that Sh was a contemptible ignoramus. Maginn's argument is not so much that Sh was knowledgeable as that Farmeresque pedantry would have ruined his art as it ruined Ben Jonson's. When he turns to Tim., Maginn analyzes the tone of Lucian's Misanthropos at length and argues that Sh did not borrow from him—Lucian is flippant and supercilious; Sh is somber and magniloquent. The outbursts of Timon come from Lear, Constance, and Margaret, not from Lucian. Maginn also discusses Molière's Alceste, who is more an Apemantus than a Timon. But the most rewarding part of the essay is Maginn's searching analysis of the character of Sh's Timon: he is a misanthrope from the beginning because he gives for his own pleasure, not for the delight of others, but his later misanthropy is sheer madness in the great imprecations of Act IV. Act V is a bit improbable because Sh tries to crowd in the bits of legend (e.g., the hanging-tree) which he found in his sources. A century has not lessened the value of this essay. MnU

1482. Main, William W. "The Dramatic Context of Shakespeare's Troilus and Cressida," diss (North Carolina, 1954).*

1483. Maizitis, Mara Ruta. "A Reading of Troilus and the Roman Plays," diss (Yale, 1960).*

1484. Markels, Julian. "The Public and Private Worlds of Shakespeare's Roman Plays," diss (Minnesota, 1957). DA, XVIII (1958), 221-222.

Markels sees the tension between individual aspirations and the demands of society as a major theme in the Roman plays (though he does not argue that it is a "classical" phenomenon). Antony successfully reconciles the two worlds in Antony (most critics disagree) while Julius Caesar and Brutus resort to self-deception in their efforts to make the reconciliation. Markels sees Coriolanus as Sh's evidence that a wholly public commitment "dehumanizes" a man. Many critics have argued that Coriolanus' commitment is not public enough.

1485. Marquand, N. J. "The Theme of Responsibility in Julius Caesar," Standpunte, IX, No. 4 (1955), 4-17.

A somewhat confusing essay which does not focus sharply on the theme of responsibility in the play. It is not clear, e.g., whether Marquand believes that Caesar's predisposition to tyranny is a violation of responsibility, or whether he would label "irresponsible" Antony's use of his own sincere emotions to inflame the Plebeians. He does point out that Brutus' perceptions, moral and intellectual, accord him a responsibility which he repeatedly fails through errors of judgment and through self-division. It is difficult to accept Marquand's portrait of a Brutus agonized by self-doubt and guilt. On the other hand the essay contains stimulating analysis: of the Cinna scene as a microcosm of what has gone before it; of the behavior of Antony immediately after the assassination; of Sh's systematic alterations in Plutarch's account of Caesar; and of the change in "the spirit of Caesar" after the assassination. MH

1486. Marsh, D. R. C. "The Conflict of Love and Responsibility in Antony and Cleopatra," Theoria, XV (1960), 1-27.

To Marsh the play presents neither the romantic view (the world well lost) nor the anti-romantic view (greatness vitiated by a strumpet); he finds its key in commitment—the man who is engagé, as both Antony and Cleopatra are at the end of their life together, has greatness in him that Caesar's expediency (and perhaps Enobarbus') never can approach. (It is possible that Marsh's interpretation is tinted by the fact that he wrote the essay while a prisoner during the South African racial disturbances.) One merit of the essay is that without florid enthusiasm it rejects the common notion that Cleopatra is simply an interesting harlot. But perhaps the chief merit is Marsh's alert and sensitive analysis of speeches, minor scenes, and characters which other critics ignore as though they were lagniappe of no importance; Marsh shows the contribution of even the smallest elements to the total impact of the play.

1487. Matthews, Brander. "The Plays from Plutarch," Shakspere as a Playwright (N.Y., 1913), pp. 254-275.

Writing with one eye on the theater, especially the actor in it, Matthews compares the three Roman plays more with each other than with Plutarch. He shows a marked preference for Caesar ("in 'Julius Caesar' we have world-politics, and in 'Coriolanus' only ward-politics"), and he prefers All for Love to Antony (at least in construction). Matthews sees the Roman plays as tragedies in the Bradleian sense, but presented in the chronicle manner of the history plays. He emphasizes though that Sh shows greater fidelity to Plutarch than he does to Holinshed. The ch. is uneven: Matthews' rejection of the view that Sh sympathized exclusively with aristocrats appears with his statement that Antony in Caesar is more dramatic than Antony in Antony because he has no interior conflict in the earlier play.

1488. Matthiessen, F. O. "North's Plutarch (1579)," Translation: An Elizabethan Art (HUP, 1931), Ch. III, pp. 54-102. E-S

Concerned primarily with "North's differences from his model" as an index of his artistic greatness, Matthiessen does not dwell at length on the uses to which Sh put the Lives. However in several places, notably in Section VI (pp. 95-98), he makes intelligent comments on Sh's direct use of North's idiom. Perhaps the chief merit of the essay is its juxtaposition of various versions: Plutarch, Amyot, North, Sh, Dryden, and Langhorne and Langhorne. One can see from one of these passages (Cleopatra at Cydnus—pp. 100-102—Langhorne and Langhorne, Dryden, and North) how much of Sh's response to Plutarch was a function of North's prose.

1489. Maurer, Wallace. "From Renaissance to Neo-Classic," NQ, CCIII (1958), 287.

The changes Dryden made in rewriting Ulysses' "degree" speech in Troi. emphasize Sh's "fresh[er] expanding infinitude."

1490. Maxwell, J. C. "Animal Imagery in 'Coriolanus'," MLR, XLII (1947), 417-421.

Cor. is unified by the ironic use of references to animals, often in contexts of preying and of mutual incompatibility. There is no sufficient basis for this language in Plutarch—Sh added it, thus manifesting his "cohesive imagination" though Maxwell does not speculate on what such imagery implies about Sh's attitude toward Plutarch's Coriolanus.

1491. M[axwell], J. C. "Introduction," The Life of Timon of Athens (1957), CSh, [XXIX], pp. ix-xlii.

Maxwell is inclined to favor the view that a Shn rough draft of Tim. is what survives in F_1. He follows Farnham's account of Sh's sources for the play (#1304), thinking it likely that Sh actually read Lucian, probably in trans. Maxwell doubts Sh's knowledge of Boiardo, but argues tentatively for his knowledge of the academic Timon; Plutarch also, of course, is in Maxwell's list of sources. The intelligent critical account of the play is an expansion of #1496.

1492. Maxwell, J. C. "Introduction," Titus Andronicus (1953/1961), ArdenSh, pp. xi-xlv.

Maxwell favors a date shortly before 1590 for Titus, is inclined to accept the chapbook on Titus as the major source (despite Sh's obvious effort to draw the audience's attention to Ovid), and recognizes Sh's controlling conception throughout the play (though he will admit that Peele could have had a hand in Act I). He argues against Dover Wilson's contention (#1784) that Sh was less than serious in writing this "Lamentable Romaine Tragedie" and points out that it shows dramatic promise "though it was not yet certain [when the play first appeared] whether he would steer clear of violent episodic melodrama on the one hand and exaggeratedly Ovidian narrative in dialogue on the other." An informed and conservative introduction.

1493. Maxwell, J. C. "'Julius Caesar' and Elyot's 'Governour'," NQ, CCI (1956), 147.

The source of Decius Brutus' characterization of Caesar as subject to flattery (II i 203-208) may be in part not Aesop, but Elyot, who juxtaposes, as Sh does, the flatterer with the lion-hunter who secretly lays a snare in the wood.

1494. Maxwell, J. C. "Shakespeare: The Middle Plays," The Age of Shakespeare, The Pelican Guide to English Literature, II (n.p.: Penguin Books, 1955), pp. 201-227. GRS

Maxwell remarks that Sh humanizes Caesar by beginning with Plutarch instead of with one or another of the doctrinaire pro- or anti-republican views which dominated the Renaissance controversy over Julius Caesar. Of Troi. he observes that the war plot is more consequential than the love plot, though Sh ironically fuses the two themes by relating love to war in the imagery. The imagery of food and of commerce also casts a pejorative light on love in the play. Maxwell objects to interpretations which make the Trojans representative of intuition and therefore of good; the Renaissance dichotomy between passion and reason is a better guide to the play. Despite their brevity the passages on Caesar and Troi. are valuable guides to the two plays.

1495. Maxwell, J. C. "Simple or Complex? Some Problems in the Interpretation of Shakespeare," DUJ, n.s. XV (1954), 112-115.

Near the end of this art. Maxwell challenges Dover Wilson's interpretation (#1782) of a passage in the quarrel scene of Caesar (ll. 69-75, on Cassius' financial resources). Wilson would have Brutus pure of heart and single-minded. Maxwell maintains that Sh made him illogical: he wants to share Cassius' extorted wealth, but is not himself willing to extort. Maxwell appears to have the better case.

1496. Maxwell, J. C. "'Timon of Athens'," Scrutiny, XV (1948), 195-208.

Maxwell conceives of the play as an unfinished tragedy of a man who violates Aristotle's μηδὲν ἄγαν by making the vice of prodigality out of the virtue of liberality and, when he perceives the world to be ungrateful, subsides into unwarranted and generalized misanthropy. The most brilliant hint in the essay is that Timon is guilty of hybris for appropriating to himself a divine prerogative: to give without receiving in return; it is typical of Timon that he thinks of the reciprocity of nature as "thievery" (IV iii 439-445).

1497. McDiarmid, Matthew P. "The Influence of Robert Garnier on Some Elizabethan Tragedies," EA, XI (1958), 289-302.

Section VI (p. 302) briefly suggests that MacCallum (#1477) may have been too positive about the influence of Garnier's Senecanism on the Roman plays. Sh's "power of transmitting the language of others into his own idiom" requires a cautious approach to source study.

1498. McElroy, J. G. R. "The Word 'Ceremony' in Shakspere," Shna, I (1884), 75-77.

A discussion of the meaning of Caesar I i 69-70 in the light of Sh's fusion of the Feast of Lupercalia, Caesar's triumph over Pompey, and Antony's attempt to crown Caesar, all of which are discrete events in Plutarch.

1499. McFarland, Thomas. "Antony and Octavius," YR, XLVIII (1958), 204-228.

An interpretative analysis of Antony which makes no reference to Sh's conception of Rome or to his use of Plutarch. But McFarland is percipient in his seriatim guide to the developing tone of the play; the balance of moral power shifts toward love (which gradually transcends lust) while the balance of material power is shifting toward the pragmatic world (which gradually reveals its pseudo-Machiavellian hollowness). The result is a noble magnificence in the immolation scenes of Acts IV and V. Among the interesting points is McFarland's remark on Aristotle and tragedy: "We may doubt whether the conception of catharsis ... is not too negative to account for the magnificence and intensity of the emotional process involved in Antony and Cleopatra. We may inspect our own emotions and conclude that the presence of joy, not the absence of pity and terror, describes our state at the end of the play."

1500. McGinn, Donald J. "Cleopatra's Immolation Scene," French Festschrift, pp. 57-80.

The apparent change in Cleopatra's character between Antony's death and her own is brought about by her love of Antony; but she cannot kill herself until she fully realizes that she is to be degraded in Caesar's triumph. Then "what her love for Antony is not strong enough to impel her to do her love for herself finally accomplishes." The seriatim analysis of the action, interior and exterior, from Antony's death to the closing tableau is imaginative, and in places convincing.

1501. McGuire, O. R. "Did Shakespeare Know His Julius Caesar?" TR, IX (1924), 277-280.

The answer is: "the poet had far greater knowledge of history than his critics." McGuire believes (as does Julia Wedgwood, #1757, whom he does not cite) that Caesar's enemies feared the cult of personality which had led centuries before to the ostracism of Aristides the Just from Athens. Sh shows that personality was the key to the future in Rome: (1) by playing down Caesar's greatness as a living man to emphasize the greatness of his personality ("Caesarism") after his death; (2) by ending the play not with the temporary triumph of the republicans, but with the restoration to power of lesser men than Caesar who would appropriate to themselves his name, his personality, and his greatness. An interesting comment.

1502. Megaw, Neill. "Shakespeare's Troilus and Cressida, I, iii, 354-356," Expl, XV (1957), item 52.

Megaw offers an interpretation of the tenuous syntax of these lines which makes them an expression of Nestor's grim concern lest Hector defeat the best the Greeks have to offer and thereby transmit the soul of Greek military prowess to the Trojans and guarantee defeat for the Greek expeditionary force.

1503. Megaw, Neill. "The Sneaking Fellow: 'Troilus and Cressida' I.ii.246-249," NQ, CCI (1956), 469-470.

An astute analysis of the subtle byplay between Cressida and Pandarus; Cressida pretends not to recognize Troilus (whom she already knows) so she can tease her uncle. There is some credibility in her pretense, as the warriors are wearing Medieval armor.

1504. Meinck, Carl "Shakespeares Römerdramen," Über das örtliche und zeitliche Kolorit in Shakespeares Römerdramen und Ben Jonsons "Catiline", SEP, XXXVIII (1910), pp. 3-56. E-S SG

A painstaking analysis of the three Plutarch plays in juxtaposition with their sources. The conclusion is that Sh drew heavily on those sources in his effort to establish local and temporal verisimilitude. The vast majority of his Roman and Egyptian allusions come from Plutarch, but not all of these from the four Lives he used for Antony, Caesar, and Cor.; Sh appears to have read widely in North. Sh also added bits of local color he acquired from Ovid, Pliny, and perhaps Renaissance dictionaries. Meinck's most interesting observation is that miscellaneous touches of local color are concentrated in the first act of each play (e.g., Cicero speaking Greek, eunuchs, the Nile, slaves, Lupercalia, cypress groves, centurions, tribunes, etc.); such illusion-building paraphernalia diminish once Sh has adequately set his stage in each play. Also interesting are Meinck's observations that: (1) Sh fails to describe Corioli and Antium because Plutarch fails to do so; (2) Sh seized on one or two central loci to characterize Rome (the Capitol--about which Sh, like his age, was in error--and the Tiber) and Egypt (the Nile). A valuable study. DFo

1505. Merchant, W. M. "Classical Costume in Shakespearian Productions," ShS, X (1957), 71-76.

Merchant indicates both at the beginning of this brief illustrated history of costuming the Roman plays and at the end that Sh had a reasonably clear idea of what a Roman would wear, even if his audience did not. The source of Elizabethan knowledge of such matters was the Italian archaeology of Mantegna and Vecellio.

1506. Merchant, W. M. "Timon and the Conceit of Art," SQ, VI (1955), 249-257.

The flyting between the Painter and the Poet in I i is of more importance to the meaning of Tim. than "commercial" interpretations of the play can allow. The debate reflects a contemporary effort to elevate painting to dignified status. It also states a theme, the relationship between appearance and reality, which is of great importance later in the play. Just as the Renaissance wondered whether to praise mimesis or whether to make "counterfeit" a pejorative term, so Timon moves from his early praise of art as imitation to a categorical condemnation of all appearance. Merchant attempts to tie this Platonic problem to strains of scriptural imagery in the play. The latter argument is less persuasive than the basic thesis about art and imitation.

1507. Messiaen, Pierre. "Qui Est le Héros de Jules César?" Culture, II (1939), 625-630. GRS

Not seen.

1508. Messiaen, Pierre. "Shakespeare et L'Histoire Romaine," Culture, II (1939), 351-357. GRS

Not seen.

1509. Meyer, George Wilbur. "Order out of Chaos in Shakespeare's Troilus and Cressida," TulSE, IV (1954), 45-56.

In an impressively coherent and forceful argument, Meyer advances the thesis that Troi. is unified: Sh wished to say "that war fought in an unworthy cause by opponents dedicated to false ideals of private honor results in folly, frustration, and disorder for both sides." The play is to be contrasted with H.V where wisdom, success, and ordered discipline are the hallmarks of a good cause. In Troi., Sh sees Helen as a strumpet and Cressida as her analogue. Troilus, like Menelaus, fights for a whore not worth the having. The sexual perversity of both Greeks and Trojans is a specific reflection of the general chaos of the senseless war. Even Ulysses, whose "degree" speech is good advice, neglects his own precepts when he further divides the Greek camp by fostering an Ajax clique. Meyer's interpretation makes sense out of most of the cruxes of the play, especially the inconclusive fifth act; altogether an intelligent piece of criticism.

1510. Meyerstein, E. H. W. "Was This the Face?" TLS, March 22, 1928, p. 221.

Marlowe's source for the "thousand ships" which were launched on behalf of Helen could well have been Lucian's Dialogues of the Dead, which appeared in sixteenth-century eds. with facing Latin. Sh's passage in Troi. (II ii 81-82) would thus have the same ultimate source. Cf. Gilbert (#1334), who notes that Seneca mentions the thousand ships several times.

1511. Meyn, Elisabeth. "Der Krieg bei Homer und Shakespeare," Die Frau, XXXVI (1929), 610-621.

Sh may have turned the heroism of the Iliad upside down in the shrill cursing of Thersites, but we should not forget that beneath Homer's surface portrayal of heroism lies an eloquent paean to peace which is not unlike Sh's apparent rejection of war in Troi. The bulk of the essay is an interesting analysis of the peace motif in the Iliad. MH

1512. Mills, L[aurens] J. "Cleopatra's Tragedy," SQ, XI (1960), 147-162.

In the course of interpreting Antony as the tragic and ironic position of Cleopatra, who learns selflessness when all is already lost and she therefore cannot grow in it, Mills suggests in passing, p. 158, that Cleopatra's "My resolution's plac'd, and I have nothing / Of woman in me . . . " (V ii 238-239) "reflects the contemporary popularity of Virgil's 'Varium et mutabile semper / Femina' (Aeneid, IV 569-570)."

1513. Modersohn, Anna B. "Cicero im englischen Geistesleben des 16. Jahrhunderts," Archiv, CXLIX (1925), 33-51, 219-245. E-S HB

See p. 228 for three Shn references to "Tully," two of them in 2H.VI and one in Titus. On p. 244, the author devotes a paragraph to Sh's portrait of Cicero in Caesar, essentially according to Plutarch, but stripped of political significance. Sh first exposed the duality of Cicero's nature: authoritative, wise, on the side of justice, but vain, timorous, and somewhat unpleasant.

1514. Moeller, Georg Hermann. Die Auffassung der Kleopatra in der Tragödienliteratur der romanischen und germanischen Nationen. Ulm, 1888, 94 pp. E-S

Moeller's book is an annotated catalogue of two score Cleopatra plays from 1540 to 1885. In a detailed plot summary, Antony is placed in close juxtaposition with the versions of Hans Sachs and Cinthio, Plutarch serving as a standard for all three. There are some interesting similarities between Sachs and Sh which tempt Moeller to consider a possible relationship between the two; he sees less similarity between Cinthio and Sh. Moeller contrasts Sh's Cleopatra ("ein begabtes, ehrgeiziges, bevorzugtes Weib") with the monsters or ethereal spirits some of his successors have left us. MnU

1515. Montgomerie, William. "English Seneca," LLT, XXXVI (1943), 25-28.

For Senecan elements in the ghost scene in Caesar, see #2028.

1516. Moore, Ella Adams. "Moral Proportion and Fatalism in 'Antony and Cleopatra'," PL, VII (1895), 613-619.

Antony is the titanic struggle of Antony's greatness against his "vicious mole of nature," his sensual passion. The struggle is the more momentous because the whole world is at stake. The conflict lasts until III ii, after which point Antony definitively ceases to struggle; thereafter he is the prey of "the outer things [which] will overwhelm him and carry him to destruction." An interesting reading.

1517. Moore, Ella Adams. "Moral Proportion and Fatalism in 'Coriolanus'," PL, VIII (1896), 86-90.

"In no drama is the inexorableness of the fatalism of passion more manifest than in this." "Shakespeare has made Coriolanus' death, not a sacrifice to his filial affection, but the legitimate outcome of his passion for revenge." Coriolanus, like Antony, gives in to his passion (at III iii 67) and from then on is a pawn of circumstances beyond himself. Despite Mrs. Moore's contention, the definition of catastrophe as an abdication of the moral struggle cannot be supported so easily for Cor. as for Antony, it would seem.

1518. Morgan, Appleton. "The 'Titus Andronicus': Was It Shakespeare's First Play? How Was It Mounted on the Elizabethan Stage? Did It Meet With Favor from Theatre-goers?" Shna, VI (1889), 20-39, 116-127, 157-179.

An intelligent and vigorous defense of Sh's sole and original authorship of the play. Morgan's judgment and critical acumen are discriminating and he is well informed about pre-Shn drama and its theater as well as about Sh's works. The most important relevant section is in the first of the three parts; Morgan discusses and lists many of the classical allusions in the play, calling them "juvenile signs" of "a school-boy's first tragedy." Somewhere Sh acquired knowledge of the two Byzantine emperors named "Andronicus" (twelfth and fourteenth centuries): the episode of Titus' shooting messages attached to arrows is based on the account of Nicetas in which Andronicus No. 1 is reported to have shot arrows with peace terms fastened to them into a city he was besieging; the clown with his pigeons reflects a story told of Andronicus No. 2 in which a peasant climbed the tower of Santa Sophia to catch pigeons and there discovered a codicil to the will of Athanasius the Patriarch laying Andronicus and the city under anathema for banishing him. It is noteworthy that neither Shn episode has a causal relationship to the plot. It appears to Morgan that Sh knew the two stories and inserted them somewhat arbitrarily into his play. If Sh's putative knowledge of Byzantine history is difficult to accept, the rest of Morgan's essay on the probable staging and reception of the play is illuminating as well as entertaining.

1519. Morris, B[rian] R. "Thomas Watson and 'Troilus and Cressida'," NQ, CCIII (1958), 198-199.

Morris cites Watson's free trans. of an Italian madrigal as evidence that others beside Sh could, in the 1590's, regard Troilus as the "centre of interest in the story." The allusion to "Troyilus ... dead for loue" "suggests that ... it was possible to interpret the story as a tragedy of love ... "

1520. Morris, Brian [R.] "The Tragic Structure of Troilus and Cressida," SQ, X (1959), 481-491.

Troi. is the tragedy of Troilus, who is the only character to develop as a result of his experiences, and who was associated by the

Elizabethans (including Sh in his other plays) with such tragic classical figures as Medea, Thisbe, Dido, and Leander. Cf. Martha H. Shackford (#1649), who prefers Ulysses as the central figure.

1521. Morsbach, Lorenz. Shakespeares Cäsarbild, SEP, LXXXVIII (1935), 32 pp. E-S SG

To Morsbach, Sh's Caesar shares the hero's rôle with Brutus, but Caesar is not the lesser of the two heroes. This is a seriatim summary and commentary on the parts of Caesar in which Caesar or his ghost appears or is alluded to. It is of interest that Morsbach's interpretation barely mentions Act IV, which therefore would become an intrusion in the main plot. Sh's Caesar is seen as fearless, warmhearted, strong-willed--in short a greater man than Plutarch made him. Morsbach's analysis takes account of speaker and context when doing so supports his thesis (e.g., in Casca's description of Caesar's refusal of the crown), but does not do so when doing so might weaken the argument (as in Antony's attacks on the conspirators in the funeral oration and in the prologue to battle, V i 39-44).

1522. Mott, Lewis F. "Note on a Passage in Julius Caesar," MLN, XII (1897), 160.

Mott believes that "honour" in Brutus' "set honour in one eye and death i' th' other / And I will look on both indifferently" (I ii 86) is a pun: "virtue" and "rank." Brutus thus means "I will take indifferently high position or death, for I love my personal integrity more than I fear death."

1523. Muir, Kenneth. "The Background of Coriolanus," SQ, X (1959), 137-145.

A discussion of what amounts to a brief Coriolanus allusion-list for the decade before Sh wrote the play. Muir is not so anxious to attribute indebtedness as to show that Sh "was ... writing within a literary tradition" in which the name of Coriolanus bore suggestions of disease in the commonwealth, the evils of banishment, the delights of fearless soldiering, etc. Sh's audience doubtless brought some of these associations with them to the theater.

1524. Muir, Kenneth. "Greene and 'Troilus and Cressida'," NQ, CC (1955), 141-142.

Following suggestions by C. H. Herford and R. K. Presson that Greene's Euphues His Censure to Philautus (1587) contributed details and atmosphere to Troi., Muir expands the list of possible debts Sh incurred. The most interesting of them is the language used by other characters in describing Helen and Cressida.

1525. Muir, Kenneth. "In Defense of the Tribunes," EC, IV (1954), 331-333.

Muir proposes that the Tribunes of Cor. are not so despicable as has generally been assumed; Sh was more impartial politically than his critics have been.

1526. Muir, Kenneth. "In Defence of Timon's Poet," EC, III (1953), 120-121.

In reply to those who call the Poet a complete hypocrite, Muir points out that early in the play he has composed "an allegory of Fortune" in which he perhaps candidly warns Timon that he will be deserted by fair-weather friends in foul weather. The Poet thus announces the theme of the play, though he himself joins the deserters later in the action.

1527. Muir, Kenneth. "Menenius' Fable," NQ, CXCVIII (1953), 240-242.

Muir adduces verbal evidence in tabular form to demonstrate multiplicity of sources for the famous fable of the Belly and the Body (Cor. I i 99-150). But there is little reason for searching far beyond North's Plutarch, which Sh follows very closely (as Muir himself admits).

1528. Muir, Kenneth. "Shakespeare and the Tragic Pattern," PBA, XLIV (1958), 145-162. (Annual British Academy Shakespeare Lecture.)

On Titus, Caesar, Antony, and Cor., see #2045.

1529. Muir, Kenneth. "Timon of Athens and the Cash-Nexus," MQM, I (1947), 57-76.

Not seen.

1530. Muir, Kenneth. "Troilus and Cressida," ShS, VIII (1955), 28-39.

This sturdy defense of the play is various in its approach. Muir discusses patterns of imagery, the characters, the relationship to Lucr., Sh's use of the traditional features of the legend, Sh's putative attitude toward the action, symbolic and allegorical attempts on the meaning of the play. At most points he is well informed of his precursors' opinions and moderately conservative in his own. An intelligent justification which convinces the reader that "the real problem about the play is the failure of most critics to appreciate it."

1531. Müller, A. Über die Quellen, aus denen Shakespeare den Timon von Athen entnommen hat. [n.p. available], 1873, [no pagination available].

Not seen. According to J. C. Maxwell (#1491) Müller was among the early advocates of the theory that Tim. is an unfinished play. Maxwell does not discuss Müller's view of the source problem.

1532. Muller, Herbert J. "Elizabethan Tragedy: 3. Shakespeare," The Spirit of Tragedy (N.Y., 1956), pp. 165-195. GRS

For Troi. as a reflection of Sh's personal tragic spirit, see #2047.

1533. Münch, W. "Aufidius," ShJ, XLII (1906), 127-147.

Münch finds in Aufidius a much more complex figure than the conventional villain whom critics have traditionally seen as the diametrical opposite of and foil to Coriolanus. This provocative essay examines Aufidius' motivation, discussing Sh's deviations from Plutarch's account. In the fierceness of their egotism at least the two national heroes are much alike; they should in some sense be regarded as counterparts.

1534. Munday, Mildred B. "Pejorative Patterns in Shakespeare's Troilus And Cressida," BR, V, No. 3 (1955), 39-49.

Dr. Munday believes that Sh uses the rhetoric of derogation (tapinosis, cacemphaton, meiosis, diasyrmus) to convey the disintegration of "a world where heroism is opportunism, character is reputation, and love is sensuality." The emphasis naturally falls on Thersites' use of these adoxiographic rhetorical formulae, but there are illustrations from the language of other characters as well. The focus only hovers on rhetoric, however; it touches also on imagery, characterization, and logic. It is not clear that the author has entirely established her thesis that pejorative language is "inevitable" for a play about social disintegration; Troilus speaks idealized poetry and so do Hector and Ulysses. It is not wise to ignore or discount these three.

1535. Munro, John. "Titus Andronicus," TLS, June 10, 1949, p. 385.

This art. discusses the famous Longleat drawing of Titus, Tamora, and Aaron. Munro believes it to be a composite drawing of Titus and Tamora as they appear in I i and Aaron as he appears in V i. That Alarbus does not appear in the I i part of the picture is to suggest that he never did appear in the play itself, being sacrificed off-stage. Mutius, an "extra" son of Titus, appears, like Alarbus, to be an addition to the dramatis personae provided by someone later than Sh. Munro's notes and opinions are interesting. J. Dover Wilson offers a vigorous rebuttal, ibid., June 24, 1949, p. 413. (See Wilson's previous art., #1785.) See also Munro's reply and the opinion of A. J. Perrett, ibid., July 1, 1949, p. 429. See also Greg's art. #1357.

1536. Murry, John Middleton. "Antony and Cleopatra," Shakespeare (Ln, 1936), Ch. XVII, pp. 352-379.

This startling reading of Antony centers on Sh's concept of royalty which is derived not from Plutarch, but from Sh's own ethic. Royalty is a product of loyalty: Antony convinces the audience that despite the harsh things the Romans say of him he is a loyal--and ergo royal--Titan, and for four acts his royal dignity lends greatness to its surroundings. Cleopatra, who has not been truly loyal until Antony's death, imbibes his spirit as it leaves his body and shows her royalty in her subsequent loyal death. The whole play is suffused by the tension between royalty and baseness. Murry makes some brilliant comments (e.g., on the analogy between IV ii 10-33 and V ii 317-330), but he also makes a repeated and jarring association of Antony with the Christ of the Last Supper and the Crucifixion.

1537. Murry, J[ohn] Middleton. "A Neglected Heroine of Shakespeare," Countries of the Mind: First Series (Ln, 1922), pp. 29-50. (Reprinted from LM, February, 1922; and later reprinted in Discoveries [1924].)

By reassigning some of the speeches in F_1 of Cor., Murry gives lines to Virgilia which are appropriate to her delicacy and loving nature. This is a sensitive character study, but it makes no reference to Sh's sources.

1538. [Murry, John Middleton]. "North's Plutarch," TLS, September 12, 1929, pp. 689-690. SG (Reprinted in Countries of the Mind: Second Series [1931].)

An extended critical comment on North's

merits and limitations as a stylist and on Sh's specific response to individual passages. There are a number of well-chosen quotations from North and Sh. The art. traces the "munificence of decoration" in Antony to Plutarch's "Life of Antony"--by far the richest in description of all the Lives.

1539. Musgrove, S. "Julius Caesar": A Public Lecture delivered for the Australian English Association, on August 19th, 1941. Sydney, 1941, 26 pp. GRS

Not seen. CtY.

1540. Nathan, Norman. "Caius Ligarius and 'Julius Caesar'," NQ, CCV (1960), 16-17.

Though Plutarch makes Ligarius prominent in the conspiracy, Sh gives him a minor rôle, and indeed does not include him in the assassination scene. In Sh's account, Ligarius is the only conspirator who has been unjustly treated by Caesar, and ergo the only man who has the motive of retributive justice. The fact that he does not participate in the murder by implication casts the other conspirators in an unfavorable light. The argument is not convincing.

1541. Nathan, Norman. "Flavius Teases His Audience," NQ, CXCIX (1954), 149-150.

When Flavius orders the artisans to go home in Caesar I i, Sh is teasing the groundlings in his audience, who ought to be at work; the Cobbler's justification of the holiday he has taken is the groundlings' vicarious reply. Sh has established a good-humored bond with his audience in this byplay, which is otherwise irrelevant to the action of Caesar.

1542. Neilson, Geo[rge]. "Bacon and Shakespeare's Mistake About Aristotle," Ath, No. 3403 (1893), 62.

Neilson shows that Erasmus' Colloquies is a probable source for the mutual error of Bacon and Sh about boys who were "unfit to hear moral philosophy." Neilson's discovery apparently has gone unnoticed, for both Ford (#1315) and Miss Campbell (#1197) fail to acknowledge it.

1543. Nel Mezzo. "'2 Henry IV.,' II.iv.21: Ulysses and Utis," 11 NQ, IV (1911), 83-84.

For a coincidence of epithets used by Sh's Thersites and Sophocles' Ajax, see #1060.

1544. Nelson, Lawrence Gerald. "Classical History in Shakespeare," diss (Virginia, 1943).*

1545. Newbolt, Henry. "Shakespeare's 'Antony and Cleopatra'," Studies Green and Gray (Ln, 1926), pp. 272-277.

Brief notes on the "greatness" of the protagonists especially with reference to the language they utter. The story Sh chose has "all the prestige of ancient Rome and of the gorgeous East."

1546. Nicholson, B[rinsley]. "'Troilus and Cressida'," 3 NQ, X (1866), 164-165.

An explanation of some ambiguous passages in the exchange of Cressida for Antenor (IV i; IV iv). Nicholson also discusses an image from surgery as applied to Cressida in I i.

1547. Nørgaard, Holger. "Shakespeare and Daniel's 'Letter from Octavia'," NQ, CC (1955), 56-57.

Sh borrowed from Daniel in Antony, I i, where Cleopatra teases Antony for his embarrassment at the prospect of receiving a message from Fulvia. North gives no basis for the passage. See Joan Rees (#1594) for an extension of the thesis, and see R. C. Bald (#1138), to whom Nørgaard refers.

1548. Norman, Arthur M. Z. "Daniel's The Tragedie of Cleopatra and Antony and Cleopatra," SQ, IX (1958), 11-18.

It was from Daniel's closet tragedy that Sh obtained (1) the daring double climax of Antony and (2) his conception of Cleopatra as high-minded (Plutarch had conceived her only as Antony's "evil genius"). Norman's argument rests on parallels, some verbal and some structural; Barroll (#1145) and others have shown that the tradition behind Sh's play is most complex—answers to the question of indebtedness must be tentative.

1549. Norman, Arthur M. Z. "Source Material in Antony and Cleopatra," NQ, CCI (1956), 59-61.

"Sundry observations" on Sh's manipulation of Plutarch; the most interesting are on Enobarbus and on Plutarch's conception of masculinity. On this latter point see Waith (#1749), whose thesis Norman seeks to modify.

1550. Nowottny, Winifred M. T. "Acts IV and

V of Timon of Athens," SQ, X (1959), 493-497.

Seizing Merchant's hints (#1506) about scriptural language in Tim., Mrs. Nowottny expands them into a defense of the unity of the play. She finds an ironic reversal of Christian sentiments in the language of Timon near the end of his life. The evidence is not compelling.

1551. Nowottny, Winifred M. T. "'Opinion' and 'Value' in Troilus and Cressida," EC, IV (1954), 282-296.

Mrs. Nowottny sees in Troi. Sh's dramatic consideration of the philosophical question: "What approach to life is valid in a world where hopes are not embodied?" He considers the Greeks' rage for order and their respect for the "general censure," but prefers the loyalty of Troilus to his values even when the event proves disappointing (i.e., Cressida's perfidy does not invalidate Troilus' love). Another polarity in the play is between creative imagination (the author tries to persuade that Troilus is a practicing poet) and social structure (the Greek camp as it ought to be). There are several interesting points here (e.g., Ulysses and Troilus take different views of the state of Chaos), but the play will not bear all the scrutiny Mrs. Nowottny gives it (e.g., Apollo may be god of poetry, but when Troilus invokes him it is because he is patron of Troy and lover of Daphne, not because he is a poet). For further strictures on the thesis of this art. see Frank Kermode (EC, V [1955], 181-187).

1552. Nyland, Waino S. "Pompey as the Mythical Lover of Cleopatra," MLN, LXIV (1949), 515-516.

Scholars have failed to note that Sh misread North in assigning Pompey the rôle of paramour to Cleopatra. Plutarch intended Pompey's son for the part, but it is probable that neither father nor son actually made love to her.

1553. Oliver, H. J. "Coriolanus as Tragic Hero," SQ, X (1959), 53-60.

Expounding the thesis "Shakespeare's Martius, like his Antony, is ... a far more admirable figure than Plutarch's," Oliver interprets Cor. as the tragedy of a man whose very goodness causes his fall. Oliver argues with conviction, but his conclusion is not likely to reverse the usual view of Cor. He makes the interesting comment that Sh read Plutarch's comparison of Coriolanus and Alcibiades, but, judging from Tim., reversed Plutarch's appraisal of the two men.

1554. Oliver, H. J. "Introduction," Timon of Athens (1959), ArdenSh, pp. xiii-lii.

The best bibliographical and aesthetic study, perhaps, yet made of the play. Oliver is persuasive in defending the thesis that Sh wrote Tim. unassisted but left it unfinished because his material was intractable to tragedy: his hero is less than perceptive and moreover withdraws into passivity midway in the action. Oliver also persuades that the play is better conceived and better executed (roughhewn though it remains) than almost any critics have been willing to grant; he will not go so far as Knight (#1444), but he shows plainly that the play is successfully constructed on contrapuntal principles: a single character is shown reacting to polarized stimuli and at the same time a group of characters are seen taking various reactions to a single stimulus. The commentary on sources is less commanding. Oliver lays heavy emphasis on Plutarch, minimizing the probable influence of Lucian (in French or Italian trans.), Painter, and the academic Timon. He even suggests that Sh, the author of the academic Timon, and Shadwell (who "improved" Sh's play) may all have separately drawn on some now-lost source. Oliver does not discuss Sh's response to Periclean Athens.

1555. Ornstein, Robert. "Seneca and the Political Drama of Julius Caesar," JEGP, LVII (1958), 51-56.

Though Sh could have synthesized his Brutus (not a convinced republican, but merely naïf politically) from widely scattered references in Plutarch's Lives, it is more likely that he conceived the man after reading De Beneficiis, where Seneca tersely portrays him as a man who fails in Stoicism because of bad political judgment. An interesting hypothesis, reinforced by the fact that Golding's trans. was available to Sh.

1556. Ornstein, Robert. "Troilus and Cressida," The Moral Vision of Jacobean Tragedy (Wisconsin UP, 1960), pp. 240-249.

Troi. is not so much a comical satire as an ironic examination of "the issues of tragedy ... a serious study of man's aspiration towards the ideal in love and war." But "chivalry is a luxury which only the winner can afford," even though there is a sad validity in Troilus' "romantic ideal that the only significant values are those intangibles which a man will not sell at the price of his own life." Helen is a commodity which neither side really wants but which both sides demand--a cloak "for the loathsome truth ... that men want to fight." Cressida, in ironic contrast, is a commodity easily bought and sold--evidence that Troilus' values cannot prevail over the realism of a Diomedes (or a Bolingbroke, or Octavius, or Hal). This is a fluent and perceptive essay.

1557. Oswald, Eugene. The Legend of Fair Helen as told by Homer, Goethe and Others. Ln, 1905, 211 pp.

Sh appears only twice, briefly. One reference (pp. 130-131) discusses Sh's tolerant attitude toward Helen's immoral behavior (in A.Y.L. and Troi.); the other (p. 50) suggests that Sh's portrayal of Cassandra raving had an influence on later interpretations of Cassandra. MnU

1558. Palmer, J. Foster. "On Certain Phases in the Evolution of Ethics from Homer to Christ, with Special Reference to the Reappearance of Some of Homer's Characters in the 'Troilus and Cressida' of Shakespeare," 2 TRSL, XV (1893), 48-83.

Palmer argues that in Troi. Sh criticizes the three cardinal virtues of Homeric ethics: ἀνδρεία, or valor (Achilles), μεγαλοπρέπεια, or magnificence (Agamemnon), and φρόνησις, or sagacity (Odysseus). The love plot is only a vehicle to carry Sh's criticism, in which Aristotelian ethics are a norm for measuring Homeric ethics. Sh is deliberately anachronistic, introducing Aristotle in Hector's speech (II ii 165-167) to call attention to the ethical norm. The implication of the play is that if Homeric virtues cannot be praised by Aristotelian standards, a Christian must surely condemn them. Palmer believes that Sh knew the 1598 ed. of Chapman's Iliads: Books III, IV, V, and VI (which Chapman did not translate in this first ed.) "are entirely passed over" in Troi., while Books I, II, VIII, XI, etc. are closely paralleled by events, characters, and phrasing in the play. A valuable interpretation of the ethics of Troi. Palmer's position on Sh's use of Chapman is abstracted in the New Variorum, pp. 421-422.

1559. Palmer, J. F[oster]. "Shakespeare and Cicero," 9 NQ, VI (1900), 316-317.

A vigorous reply to E. Yardley (ibid., 214) who had asserted that Sh did not know Homer through Chapman, but through Ovid's Meta. XIII.

1560. Palmer, John. "Caius Marcius Coriolanus," Political Characters of Shakespeare (Ln, 1945) pp. 250-310.

This essay could almost have been called "A Defense of the Roman People and Their Tribunes," so much it seeks to redress the bias which Palmer traces to Hazlitt's assumption that Sh showed his aristocratic sympathies by castigating the mob and their leaders. The argument is an effective one; it largely succeeds in drawing the reader toward Coleridge's view that Sh demonstrates magnificent impartiality in Cor., but Palmer finds little to praise in any aristocrat, including the hero. The seriatim analysis of the characters in action is almost as sensitive as in his study of Caesar (#1562). Palmer points out the significance of Sh's alteration in Plutarch's account of Coriolanus' abortive revenge: in Plutarch, Coriolanus wanted to destroy the people and their property; in Sh, he feels a general hatred that embraces the city itself. Perhaps the most challenging metaphor in the essay attempts to explain the cool reception the play often receives: "the English love pictures, but have no taste or discrimination in statues, and 'Coriolanus' has all the qualities of the finest statuary. It has the boldness and simplicity of a classic monument."

1561. Palmer, John. Comedy, The Art and Craft of Letters. N.Y., [1914], 64 pp.

For brief remarks on Troi. as a comedy, see #1063.

1562. Palmer, John. "Marcus Brutus," Political Characters of Shakespeare (Ln, 1945), pp. 1-64.

This extraordinary essay is one of the most percipient of all studies of Brutus; and, despite its title, it is much more: Palmer analyzes brilliantly all of the major figures of the action, and occasionally a minor one as well (Decius "is the junior minister or high official who seeks compensation for accepting the supremacy of an abler man by indulging a humorous perspicacity at his expense and airing an intimate acquaintance with his foibles"). Palmer avoids the heresy of worshiping the dramatis personae at the expense of the action by numerous comments on the structural effectiveness of individual scenes or speeches; and his briefly stated view of the whole action, that it is symphonic, Acts IV and V treating the themes of I and II in a minor key, is worth developing. Palmer still cannot avert the charge that he follows Bradley in his concern with private character; in the introduction, e.g., he implies that political subjects were forced on Sh by his audience and that, disliking them, he concentrated on the secret selves of his kings and statesmen. This ch. remains, however, a major contribution to Caesar criticism.

1563. Paolucci, Anne. "The Tragic Hero in Julius Caesar," SQ, XI (1960), 329-333.

Brutus, like Oedipus, gradually reveals himself to himself as the play progresses, and when he fully realizes that he has expropriated the prerogatives of the gods by executing justice on Caesar, he willingly pays the price. An interesting interpretation, but not entirely convincing, especially when the author uses it to justify the title of the play.

1564. Parrott, Thomas M[arc]. "Further Observations on Titus Andronicus," SQ, I (1950), 22-29.

A review of the controversy over the interpretation of the Longleat drawing of Titus. Parrott spells out the various views and lends his own support to Wilson (#1785). Appended are some strictures on Wilson's ed. of Titus with Wilson's rejoinders.

1565. Parrott, [Thomas Marc]. The Problem of Timon of Athens, Shakespeare Association Papers, No. 10 (OUP, 1923), 34 pp.

Parrott, like J. M. Robertson (#0493), believes that Chapman had a hand in Tim. As the former sees it, Sh began Tim. by writing the great monologues of the later acts thinking to create a part for Burbage to deliver as he had delivered Lear. But Plutarch did not provide Sh any plot but the climax and Sh found creating a prelude to Timon's abandonment and misanthropy difficult in the absence of a story to dramatize. Therefore he became interested in Macb. and never returned to Tim. which Chapman was assigned to pull together after 1616. Chapman bungled the difficult job and after someone else had tampered with the result, Tim. was left to Heminge and Condell. Like many disintegrationist arguments, this one is intuitive and quite unconvincing; Parrott does make two good points: (1) Sh may have been misled about the value of talents by Plutarch's "Life of Antony," where large sums in talents are mentioned several times; (2) Cor. and Tim. have in common the theme of a public who reject an obligation they have incurred to a prominent citizen. The essay contains some surprising lapses in spelling and diction.

1566. Parrott, T[homas] M[arc]. "Shakespeare's Revision of 'Titus Andronicus'," MLR, XIV (1919), 16-37.

On the basis of verbal, metrical, and thematic tests, Parrott parcels out the play more precisely than conservative critics today would consider wise. He discusses the classical allusions in the play passim; as one might expect, the best parts of the play are all assigned to Sh. Parrott gives no consideration to construction in the play.

1567. Parsons, Howard. "Shakespeare's 'Julius Caesar': Dramatis Personae," NQ, CXCIX (1954), 113.

The earliest authority for the dramatis personae of Caesar is Rowe, who supplied it. He erred in calling Flavius and Marullus "tribunes." They are Senators, as Sh shows by having them speak authoritatively to the Plebeians, as Patricians would.

1568. Paton, Allan Park. North's Plutarch: Notes as to a Copy of This Work in the Greenock Library, Supposed to Have Been Shakspere's. Greenock, 1871, 36 pp.

Paton argues, unconvincingly, that the copy of the 1612 North at issue belonged to Sh. It contains the initials "W.S." and some marginal symbols opposite passages which Sh used in his plays. Paton's thesis has been universally rejected in this century on the ground that Sh had written all of the Roman plays before 1612 and late in his career was pursuing other dramatic genres; ergo it is not probable that he would buy a new North when he already (presumably) owned a 1579, or 1595, or (less likely) 1603 ed. Paton does, however, provide interesting evidence for Sh's use of a marginal gloss in the "Life of Marcus Porcius Cato" for Titus Lartius' praise of Coriolanus (I iv 56-61). DFo

1569. Pearce, T. M. "Shakespeare's Antony and Cleopatra, V, ii, 243-359," Expl, XII (1953), item 17.

Though the name of Cleopatra's death-dealing "aspic" comes from North's Plutarch, the qualities of the snake itself are traceable to the basilisk of Pliny, which became confused with asps in the sixteenth century. This is the explanation of the sudden death of Iras, who collapses after gazing on her mistress after the latter has assumed the potency of the basilisk by her proximity to it. The argument is not convincing.

1570. Pearson, Norman Holmes. "Antony and Cleopatra," Shakespeare: Of an Age and for All Time, The Yale Shakespeare Festival Lectures (Shoe String Press, 1954), pp. 123-147.

Pearson suggests union as the leitmotiv of the play--union between Rome and Egypt, between Antony and Octavia, among the Triumvirs all are doomed to failure; it is the marriage of Cleopatra's return to Cydnus in Act V which is the true union in the play. Pearson briefly discusses Sh's Elizabethan predecessors in the legend, suggesting that they thought of Cleopatra as "a tanned Helen of the Nile."

1571. Peart, S. E. "The Comradeship of Antony and Cleopatra," PL, IV (1892), 217-221.

"Mad Antony," who is not really admirable, is partially redeemed by the affectionate companionship he shares with Cleopatra. "Surely there is a pathos in the history of those who are the greatest wrecks of all they leave behind them." If accepted, this reading makes sentimental melodrama out of what others regard as high tragedy.

1572. Penniman, Josiah H. "The Return from Parnassus and Troilus and Cressida," The War of the Theatres, PPPLA, IV, No. 3 (Boston and Halle, 1897), pp. 144-151.

Penniman wisely expresses doubt that Troi. should be read as a document in the War. He surveys a number of extravagant hypotheses and concludes that none of them can be substantiated. Elsewhere in this book he rejects efforts to identify Sh with Ovid or Virgil in The Poetaster. DFo TxHR

1573. Peterson, Henry. Caesar; A Dramatic Study in Five Acts. Philadelphia, 1879, 72 pp.

In the Preface to his play, Peterson states that Sh's "conception of [the historical] Caesar is essentially a mistaken one"; the conspirators were not lovers of liberty but lovers of the "right of the aristocracy to rule as it pleased." Sh's misconception was "undoubtedly drawn from Plutarch." DLC

1574. Pettet, E. C. "Coriolanus and the Midlands Insurrection of 1607," ShS, III (1950), 34-42.

Sh makes two important departures from Plutarch's account of the Plebeians' relations with the Roman aristocracy: (1) he strips away all grievances (such as usury) which the mob had against the Patricians except the shortage of corn, which he magnifies; (2) he makes the mob appear even less responsible in Cor. than Plutarch had made them. Pettet cautiously proposes that Sh's treatment had a basis in the revolt of the commoners of Northamptonshire and surrounding counties in the spring of 1607, a response to high prices and short supply of grain. Sh, who never trusted the lower classes en masse, was probably unsympathetic to the popular movement, and went out of his way to state his aristocratic leaning in Menenius' fable, among other places in the play. Pettet has an interesting theory, but it does not seem clearly proven. The thesis was partially anticipated by G. B. Harrison in "A Note on Coriolanus," AMS, p. 239, and to a considerable extent by Sidney Shanker in "Some Clues for Coriolanus," SAB, XXIV (1949), 209-213.

1575. Pettet, E. C. "The 'Dark' Comedies," Shakespeare and the Romance Tradition (Ln, 1949), Ch. VI, pp. 136-160.

A substantial portion (pp. 140-156) of this ch. is a study of the anti-romantic tenor of Troi., a tone which Pettet is prepared to trace to Sh's "disillusionment"; though he admits the influence of Henryson and other post-Chaucerians on Sh's portrait of Cressida, he does not consider the sixteenth-century tradition, and he juxtaposes Criseyde and Cressida almost as though there were no development of the character from Chaucer to Sh. Pettet also deals with Troilus and Pandarus, again comparing them with their Chaucerian counterparts, and he gives lesser attention to the war plot. Pettet is inclined to doubt that the Greeks and Trojans are an attack on Chapman's Homer. He proposes tentatively that the chivalrous warriors who appear as "'lustful brutes and stupid bullies'" may be Sh's response to those, like Spenser, who had a Cheevyesque fondness for "outmoded ideals of medieval chivalry."

1576. Pettet, E. C. "Timon of Athens: The Disruption of Feudal Morality," RES, XXIII (1947), 321-336.

Unaware that he has been anticipated, Pettet advances an interpretation very similar to that of John W. Draper (#1271), except that to Pettet the classical setting is "flimsy Athenian trappings" which can be "stripped" away, leaving "a straightforward tract for the times." This view is perhaps a bit extreme.

1577. Pettigrew, Helen P. "Troilus and Cressida: Shakespeare's Indictment of War," WVBPS, V (1947), 34-48.

"Mars, and not Venus, [is] the villain of the piece." Sh is condemning the war which warps Cressida's frail character, distorts Troilus, separates Achilles from Polyxena, rages around Paris and Helen. War and love are natural enemies; the former must violate the latter. Though war is her theme, Mrs. Pettigrew spends most of her space on love. She idealizes both Troilus and Cressida, excusing the latter for her behavior early in the play and suggesting Ulysses' contemptuous speech ("There's language in her eye ...," IV v 55-63) as the turning point after which she becomes base. This is not a convincing interpretation.

1578. Philips, Carl. Lokalfärbung in Shakespeare's Dramen. Köln, 1887 (no complete pagination available—as trans. and abstracted in the New Variorum Antony).

Philips is impressed by Sh's ability to evoke in Antony the luxury of Egyptian life through vivid references to climate, geography, flora, and especially fauna. The local color is as consistent as it is imaginative. Philips goes on to argue that this local color is intended by Sh to convey his supposed belief that races which become hedonistic under the influence of luxuriant natural surroundings are the prey of more rugged races. He forgets (1) that the climate of Italy and that of Egypt are both comfortable; (2) that in II vii Sh gives us a picture of la vie douce as it could be lived by Romans.

1579. Phillips, James E., Jr. The State in Shakespeare's Greek and Roman Plays, ColSECL, No. 149 (Col UP, 1940), 230 pp.

Phillips begins his study with a detailed examination of the state and law as they were conceived by Renaissance political theorists. He confines the historical study to the Tudor period, but occasionally shows the influence of Plato, Aristotle, Isocrates, and other classical authorities on the corpus of doctrine which Sh turned to dramatic use in Troi., Tim., and the Roman trilogy (Phillips does not consider Titus, a "Roman" play in which political mistakes made in Act I precipitate the avalanche of calamities which follows). After showing that analogy was a standard method of expounding political concepts (a method Sh uses in Ulysses' "degree" speech, Menenius' fable, and Canterbury's lecture on the ordered society in H.V), Phillips discusses the Renaissance attitude toward monarchy and then proceeds to the five plays which he regards as specifically, though not exclusively oriented toward politics. He reads Troi. as Oscar J. Campbell (#1199) does, as a satire on a society (the Greek camp) in which selfish passion is permitted to abrogate the "specialty of rule" and the ordered degree which together make fruitful action possible. More original is Phillips' interpretation of Tim. as a play in which the governors (the Athenian Senate) have allowed avarice (the classical vice of tyrants) to distract them from their obligation to the commonwealth. This reading of the play has the great merit of making sense of the shifting emphasis, first on Timon then on Alcibiades, toward the end of the play: Sh is showing that the one (a tragic figure) is so flawed by passion that he can only rant at the state which has betrayed him and its trust, while the other (a heroic figure) takes positive and effective action to purge that state of its vestiges of "pre-social" selfishness that the future may be purer. The difficulty with Phillips' reading of Tim. is the same for all his interpretations of the classical plays: as he admits, his view must inevitably come into conflict with any interpretation of the plays as tragedies in which individuals are the center of interest. In Cor., e.g., Phillips sees the moving force in the illegitimate desire of the Plebeians for a voice in the government, yet he ends by saying that the play is the tragedy of a Patrician who cannot subordinate himself to the common good. Again, in Caesar and Antony, taken together, Phillips sees a study of destiny selecting (after the death of Caesar) the man most fit to exercise the "specialty of rule"—even though this view does not fit with the minor rôle of Octavius, the sympathetic portraits of Brutus and of Antony (in Antony) or the centrality of Cleopatra. Yet Phillips' interpretations of the Greek and Roman plays have much to commend them—he is frank in his admission that politics is not the center of dramatic interest in any of the plays and he is obviously correct in his belief that Sh regarded Roman history as a storehouse of exempla to support orthodox theories of monarchy. This remains one of the most rewarding studies of the plays on classical themes as a group.

1580. Porter, Charlotte, and Helen A. Clarke. "Shakespeare's 'Antony and Cleopatra': A Study Program," PL, XX (1909), 315-320.

Like the other "programs" in this long series, this one is a succession of suggestions and leading questions calculated to prompt serious thought about the play; some of them throw light on Sh's understanding of the classical world: e.g., "Is the Antony of this play a direct development of the Antony of 'Julius Cesar' [sic]?"

1581. Potts, Abbie Findlay. "Cynthia's Revels, Poetaster, and Troilus and Cressida," SQ, V (1954), 297-302.

Following the suggestion of Oscar J. Campbell (#1199) that Jonsonian satire inspired the tone of Troi., Professor Potts aligns a large number of parallels, chiefly verbal, between Jonson's two plays and Troi. Some are close enough to attract interest, but some others are surely gratuitous. It does not appear that the author is justified in asserting that Sh's audience would have applied their recollection of Jonson as a catalyst to the comedy in Troi.

1582. Prenter, N. Hancock. "'Antony and Cleopatra,' II.ii.211-16.--" 9 NQ, IX (1902), 222-223.

Prenter wishes to explain the crux in the description of Cleopatra's barge by interpreting all the language as Elizabethan seamen's English. Two correspondents provide supplements, ibid., p. 342, but this is not a very rewarding approach to North's Plutarch.

1583. Presson, Robert K. Shakespeare's Troilus and Cressida & the Legends of Troy. Wisconsin UP, 1953, 165 pp.

This important study of Sh's probable sources begins with evidence that the Troy story was very popular in the 1590's and that Sh, wishing to capitalize on the popularity and at the same time wishing not to ape the chronicle plays based on Lydgate and Caxton, turned in 1601 or thereabouts to the recently published Iliads of Chapman. Sh did not, of course, abandon the Medieval sources altogether, even in the war plot, but Presson believes that the scholars who dismiss Sh's possible debt to Chapman have not read Chapman side by side with the Medieval versions. The first hundred pages of the book are a minute examination of key scenes and characters in the war plot in their relationship to Chapman, Heywood's Iron Age, Caxton, and, to a lesser extent, Lydgate. The cumulative evidence for Sh's use of Chapman is quite persuasive (Presson points to two or three details which recall Book XXII of the Iliad, which Chapman had not translated--he hesitantly suggests that Sh's "less Greek" might have been sufficient for Book XXII, but the more likely possibility is that the parallels are fortuitous). Perhaps the most interesting passage in this ch. is the study of Thersites as a lower-class expansion of hints in Homer; Thersites' association with his betters is a vivid instance of Ulysses' point about degree in the social order. Presson devotes much less space to the love plot, the structure of which he traces chiefly to Chaucer: the unpleasant Cressida Sh obtained ready-made from the post-Chaucerian tradition, while the theme (the destructive effect of passion) is the same for the love plot as for the main plot. Sh found this theme implicit in Chapman's Homer which is in effect a "humanist tract." This is a thorough and stimulating study.

1584. Presson, Robert K. "The Structural Use of a Traditional Theme in Troilus and Cressida," PQ, XXXI (1952), 180-188.

Presson is a conservative who believes that we must see Troi. in its historical context "out of which it may mean anything." That context, he feels, is the traditional Renaissance opposition of passion and reason. When passion triumphs as it does over Troilus, Achilles, and Priam's family, "disillusionment or deterioration" follows. Sh wished to make Troilus into passion's slave, so he chose to follow the traditional (un-Chaucerian) view of Cressida to emphasize the unworthiness of Troilus' passion. Presson believes that Sh knew Chapman's Homer "more than fairly well" and suggests that Sh's Achilles "as the exemplum of the proud emotional man" may have been derived from Chapman. An interesting approach.

1585. Price, Hereward T. "The Authorship of 'Titus Andronicus'," JEGP, XLII (1943), 55-81.

This brilliant defense of the integrity of the play is unquestionably the most convincing study of the subject. Price cleverly defeats the statisticians with their own methods, showing that metrically, verbally, and phrasally the play has more in common with Sh's other works than with Peele, Greene, and Marlowe, the favorite nominees of the disintegrators. But much more interesting and important are the other two arguments: (1) Titus contains more allusions to classical literature than either the other early plays or the other Roman plays; this is deliberate Shn artistry. Sh wished to establish a Roman setting and used the classics (notably those most easily accessible to him: Virgil, Ovid, Seneca) as texture; in the later Roman plays he found enough texture in Plutarch without going into classical literature. (2) The subtleties of construction and characterization mark the play as wholly Shn. Most significantly, Sh differentiates among his characters by a use of rhetoric indicative of his school training. The essay is filled with original insights: e.g., when Chiron says he read his Horace "in the grammar long ago" he characterizes himself as a dolt to whom poetry exists only in grammars; the passage certainly does not mean that Sh never read Horace outside of school. This art. is a major reference point in Titus criticism, in the disintegrationist controversy, and in the study of Sh's classicism.

1586. Price, Hereward T. "The Language of Titus Andronicus," PMA, XXI (1935), 501-507.

A part of the paper discusses Sh's use of Latinate diction--Price points to some free use of language and says, "Trained classical scholars do not make howlers like that." Price is particularly interested in the reference to the "palliament" as a white Roman robe in I i 182. Sh blended discrete references in Peele to the palliament and to the candidatus (the white-clad). "We see . . . with what consummate impudence he borrowed Roman-sounding words from his contemporaries in order to create a Roman atmosphere in his play."

1587. Proestler, Mary. "Caesar Did Never Wrong But With Just Cause," PQ, VII (1928), 91-92. HB SG

According to Cicero (De Officiis) and Suetonius (Lives of the Caesars), Caesar was fond of quoting a fragment from Euripides to the effect that if wrong is ever right it is wrong done to gain a throne. Sh may well have written the controversial line in the first place, and if he did Jonson blundered in ridiculing so apt a characterization of the historical Caesar.

1588. Pyle, Fitzroy. "Hostilius: 'Timon of Athens', III,ii.70," NQ, CXCVII (1952), 48-49.

Pyle argues that the name "Hostilius," applied by one "Stranger" to another, is a printer's misreading for "Lucilius" in a stage direction for the preceding line: "Exit Lucilius [for 'Exit Lucius']." Pyle reasons that the deletion of the proper name makes smooth verse out of rough, but it scarcely appears necessary to emend the F_1 text.

1589. Q., D. "Shakespeare's Little Latin," NQ, CXCIII (1948), 150.

For an "anti-Baconian" remark about classicism in Titus, see #0890.

1590. Rankin, H. F. "Cressida," [an address as reported in] Acad, XXXIX (1891), 375.

A vigorous condemnation of Sh's heroine who illustrates the truth of heredity by following in her father's traitorous footsteps. Mrs. Rankin gives no consideration to the long tradition of fickle Cressidas which produced Sh's perfidious heroine; this is not a very useful analysis.

1591. Ravenscroft, Edward. Titus Andronicus, or the Rape of Lavinia: To The Reader (1686), Munro, II, 319.

This brief passage casts doubt on Sh's authorship of Titus and is a very early document in the disintegrationist movement. The Rape of Lavinia is Titus "improved"; Ravenscroft finds the play he revised "the most incorrect and indigested piece in all [Sh's] Works."

1592. Rea, John D. "Julius Caesar II,i,10-34," MLN, XXXVII (1922), 374-376.

Rea points out that "adder" was a common trans. in the sixteenth century of the Latin "regulus" ("basilisk"). He suggests that Brutus' entire soliloquy turns on a Latin pun ("regulus" is also a diminutive of "rex"). Caesar is thus a "kinglet," a basilisk, a serpent who would be king (Sh later applies the same imagery to Claudius in Ham.). The Latin pun Sh may have obtained from a Latin Caesar play. Rea's is an ingenious suggestion, but if the Latin pun is there, it can hardly be expected to trigger our interpretation of the soliloquy; the audience, however educated and alert, could not be expected to retreat from "adder" to "basilisk" to "regulus" to "kinglet" all as a line is being delivered.

1593. Rees, Joan. "'Julius Caesar'—An Earlier Play, and an Interpretation," MLR, L (1955), 135-141.

The inconsistencies in the two problem characters of Sh's Caesar may be traceable to Kyd's Cornelia and its source, Garnier's Cornélie. In Kyd and Garnier, Caesar appears a cross between a Senecan tyrant and Plutarch's noble Roman; in Kyd, Brutus displays a tendency to wander away from concrete immediacy toward abstract principle. Mrs. Rees feels that she has interpreted the play; actually, she has discussed a possible source of confusion in it. Tracing one problem to its source in another does not necessarily solve either.

1594. Rees, Joan. "Shakespeare's Use of Daniel," MLR, LV (1960), 79-82.

Mrs. Rees makes two points: (1) Sh's debt to Daniel's Civil Wars is apparent not only in the history plays, but also in Caesar, where Brutus' soliloquy (II i 10-34) and Casca's portents (I iii) both contain elements found in the Civil Wars, but not in Plutarch. (2) Nørgaard (#1547) did not indicate the use which Sh made of Daniel's "Letter from Octavia" in Antony. It is the foundation of I i, which gives immediacy to the triangle and to the conflict between Antony's obligations and his preferences.

1595. "Remarks upon the Tragedy of Julius Caesar," BM, VIII (1767), 571-574.

The author sees many unclassical blemishes on the play (chiefly violations of the unities of time and action [i.e., tone]). Sh follows Plutarch slavishly, which is part of the cause for these blemishes (e.g., the Cinna episode is "trivial and ludicrous" and should have been omitted). Yet Sh is a better recorder of Roman character even than Tacitus and Livy. Cicero, Demosthenes, and Aeschines can "scarcely" equal the two funeral orations, and Brutus' repeated "If any, speak; for him have I offended" is unsurpassed as "an example of the Sublime cited by Longinus." The author also admires the quarrel scene, Brutus' soliloquy, and his apostrophe to conspiracy (II i 77-85). DLC

1596. Reyher, Paul. Essai sur les idées dans l'oeuvre de Shakespeare. BLM, I (Paris, 1947), 662 pp.

Some of the ideas which this book discusses have classical roots, but Reyher makes no special point of sources. The plays on classical themes are therefore the point of contact between the book and this Guide. Reyher shows that Titus owes something to Ovid and Seneca, but he is more interested in parallels between Tamora and Margaret, Titus and Richard II, Aaron and Marlowe's Barabas. In the section on Caesar, Reyher gives a comparison between Plutarch's accounts and Sh's play—especially interesting are the passage on Cinna and the character sketches of Caesar, Brutus, and Cassius. The criticism of Antony is very perceptive, especially on the differences between Plutarch's and Sh's accounts of Cleopatra's behavior after Actium, on the orgy in Pompey's galley, and on the differences in tone between Antony and Caesar. Reyher shows also that many concepts and phrases in Antony can be found in Sh's other plays. The political ideas in Cor., like those in Troi., Reyher believes to have a special topical significance in the relationships between Crown, Lords, and Commons on the Spanish question. He finds the Boethian distinctions between Fortune and Nature to be a key theme in Tim. This is an original, perceptive book.

1597. Ribner, Irving. "Political Issues in Julius Caesar," JEGP, LVI (1957), 10-22.

Caesar is a play with two heroes (Brutus, and to a lesser extent Caesar), and a villain (the mob). Caesar's flaw is his aspiration to kingship which, since he has no lineal claim to it, can only be tyranny. Brutus' flaw is that to do a public service he commits a private wrong—he kills his friend. Sh does not have any prejudice against republicanism; his lesson is that chaos results when a noble general aspires to the throne (as in the later Essex affair), and even greater chaos follows the use of evil means to bring about good political ends. Cf. Breyer's study (#1180) of Caesar as tyrant, of which Ribner shows no knowledge.

1598. Ribner, Irving. "Shakespeare and Peele: The Death of Cleopatra," NQ, CXCVII (1952), 244-246.

Cleopatra's application of the asp to her breast and the lovely lines she speaks are not in North or other classical sources. Ribner traces them to Peele's Edward I, but J. D. Reeves and especially Holger Nørgaard (ibid., pp. 441-443) show that this material was part of the Renaissance Cleopatra legend.

1599. Ribner, Irving. "The Tragedy of Coriolanus," ES, XXXIV (1953), 1-9.

Modern audiences and critics fail to appreciate Cor. because they no longer are awed by pride, the besetting sin of its hero. Sh shows us a basically good man "seduced" by pride and contriving a deadly cul de sac for himself. Cor. is less complex than Oth., e.g., because we do not see the hero being seduced, only the hideous results of the seduction; nor do we see him enlightened and repentant in Act V just before death. Cor. is thus a simple play thematically and structurally.

1600. Ribner, Irving. "The Tudor History Play: An Essay in Definition," PMLA, LXIX (1954), 591-609.

For Sh's plays on classical themes as history plays, see #1076.

1601. Richards, I. A. "Troilus and Cressida and Plato," Speculative Instruments (Ln, 1955), pp. 198-213. (Reprinted from HR, I [1948], 362-376.)

Richards finds numerous similarities between Sh's thought in Troi. and Plato's in the Republic. The relationship between "value" and stability in the state is apparent in both the play and the dialogue. Both Sh and Plato ask the difficult question, "What is aught but as 'tis valu'd?" and both deal with the envy of the gods. Richards also shows that Troi. is full of adumbrations of future events and he makes some interesting points about Ulysses, who is the secret service of the Greek army--he knows the truth about everyone. Richards never claims Sh's direct knowledge of Plato (he envisions a student reading Troi. as a follow-up to Homer and Plato); his prose is dense enough to make his meaning uncertain at times, but he appears to have established a definite parallel between the play and the dialogue.

1602. Richardson, William. "On the Dramatic Character of Timon of Athens," Essays on Shakespeare's Dramatic Characters of Richard the Third, King Lear, and Timon of Athens... (Ln, 1784), pp. 85-112.

Richardson does not refer to the origin of Sh's conception of Timon, contenting himself with an analysis of the motives behind the character's behavior. "He does some good, but it is to procure distinction; he solicits distinction, but it is by doing good." With this middle position Richardson sums up an essay which is among the pioneer character analyses in the eighteenth century. Richardson also admires the delineation of the flatterers and the frankness of Apemantus. His opinion of the play as a whole is considerably higher than that of most modern critics. MnU

1603. Richardson, William. "On the Faults of Shakespeare," Essays on Shakespeare's Dramatic Characters of Richard the Third, King Lear, and Timon of Athens... (Ln, 1784), pp. 113-146.

Sh's greatest fault is "want of taste" in violating the unity of tone characteristic of the ancients: the major examples are drawn from Cor.--Volumnia's reference to her son's enemies as "cats," Menenius' candor about his fondness for tippling hot wine, etc. Less important faults are the result of ignorance or carelessness: e.g., in Cor. Alexander the Great is represented as having already lived--a crass anachronism. MnU

1604. Ridley, M. R., ed. Antony and Cleopatra (1954/1956), ArdenSh.

The only major passage in the "Introduction" which appears neither in R. H. Case's original Arden (#1202), nor in Ridley's earlier study (#1605) is a discussion (pp. xlv-xlix) of Cleopatra's motives for suicide. Ridley believes that Cleopatra thinks impulsively of taking her life immediately after Antony's death but then hesitates as time passes and it occurs to her that Caesar might not display her. She arranges the scene with Seleucus to gain time and Caesar's confidence and when it is obvious that he regards her as a trophy she turns again to thoughts of Antony and dies royally.

1605. Ridley, M. R. Shakespeare's Plays: A Commentary. N.Y., 1938, 227 pp.

The passages on the Greek and Roman plays are not the most satisfying parts of a book of stimulating criticism: that Ridley should see in Brutus no more than a fool and in Troi. the personal expression of Sh's disillusionment with sex is indication enough of his blind spots. But he is equally capable of challenging insights: (1) Tamora has no subtlety, but she is credible, like Titus' grandson and the clown; (2) the division of interest among Caesar, Brutus, and Antony indicates that we should read Caesar as a transitional play (between chronicle and tragedy) and should object to the title figure's limitations as little as we do in John; (3) the debunking of the Greek and Trojan heroes in Troi. has precedent in Sh's portrait of Caesar; (4) in Antony Sh substitutes glorious poetry for the plot which Plutarch's account of Antony's vacillations denied him--his Octavius becomes another Aeneas, cold, unattractive, but personifying the destiny of Rome; (5) Coriolanus, who is magnificent in his single-mindedness, learns too late that yielding may be triumphant rather than degrading; (6) Timon's invective indicates his idealism--Thersites' indicates his complete cynicism. Outside of the plays on classical themes there is almost no commentary which embraces Sh's classicism.

1606. Rieschel, H. "Das Tragische Geschehen im Coriolanus," Junge Geisteswissenschaft. Arbeiten junger Göttinger Germanisten. Festgabe zur 200-Jahrfeier der Georgia Augusta (Göttingen: Turm Verlag, 1937), pp. 21-22. GRS

Not seen.

1607. Robertson, J. M. Did Shakespeare Write Titus Andronicus? A Study in Elizabethan Literature. Ln, 1905, 255 pp. SG (Republished under the title: An Introduction to the Study of the Shakespeare Canon [1924].)

See pp. 225-229: "The [classical] pedantries of Titus are as alien to the spirit and method of Shakespeare's real work as are its atrocities and moral stupidities." Peele is responsible for the passages in I i which are indebted to Euripides' Hecuba (136-138) and Sophocles' Ajax (379-381), because he was a Greek scholar and neither Attic tragedy was available to Sh in trans. Robertson is here as elsewhere a vehement controversialist, but this aspect of his attempt to purge the Sh canon is something less than convincing.

1608. Roeder, Ralph. "Timon of Athens," TAM, X (1926), 453-460.

Proposing that Tim. is "Shakespeare's farthest reach into the absolute," Roeder makes the acute observation that Timon's flaw is just that which Greece most abhorred, extremism: "the middle of humanity thou never knewest, but the extremity of both ends" (IV iii 300-301). Yet Roeder finds in Timon a sympathetic character--his is "a tragedy of loneliness."

1609. Röhrman, H. "Troilus and Cressida," Marlowe and Shakespeare: A Thematic Exposition of Some of Their Plays (Arnhem, 1952), pp. 60-87. GRS

Röhrman objects to any attempt to make Sh merely a participant in traditional attitudes toward the Troy story. Sh was himself responsible for the cynicism of the play because at bottom he was tormented by a consciousness of chaos. Troilus is an ideal hero and lover who is to be martyred not by death but by time, a far more cruel tragedy. The dissension among the Greeks is selfish and pragmatic, the dissension among the Trojans is selfless and principled--yet the Trojan disagreement is the more dangerous, because the Greeks at least agree on their war aims while the Trojans are not sure what value to place on what they are fighting for. There are interesting remarks on Cressida, Pandarus, and (especially) Diomedes. But Röhrman's contempt for historical criticism distorts his reading of Troi. and limits the value of this essay.

1610. Rohrmoser, Günter. "Antonius und Cleopatra," Shakespeare-Tage 1956 (Bochum), pp. 1-6. GRS

Not seen.

1611. Rolfe, W. J. "'Pompey's Statua' (Jul Caes. III, ii, 192)," Shna, I (1884), 175.

The reference may be to the actual statue, thought to be Pompey's, which was uncovered in 1553. Rolfe gives an account of the discovery and later history of the statue.

1612. Rolfe, W. J. "Shakespeare's 'Julius Caesar'," PL, V (1893), 169-176, 424-431; VI (1894), 7-13.

An interpretative essay which is full of thoughtful observations on the source, characters, and structure of the play. Typical are these major points: Ben Jonson doubtless had no hand in "correcting" Sh's play; otherwise North's two un-Roman blunders, "Calphurnia" and "Decius" (for "Decimus") Brutus, would not have been allowed to remain. Caesar, who has nothing to do and little to say before his death becomes important to the action after it. Brutus' tragedy is that he usurps the prerogatives of Providence by killing Caesar not for what he has been, nor for what he is, but for what he *might* be; the most telling irony in the play lies in Brutus' tacit condemnation of himself in V i 103-105, where he considers it "cowardly and vile, / For fear of what *might* fall, so to prevent / The time of life" (on this point Rolfe anticipates MacCallum [#1477, p. 246], who does not refer to him). In Caesar, Antony is "a profligate turned demagogue"; in Antony, "we find him a demagogue turned profligate again"--it is ironic that "he plays upon the Roman plebeians as upon a pipe . . . but he himself becomes a pipe on which the Egyptian Siren plays what tune she will." On the whole an illuminating commentary. The germ of this art. appeared in Shna, I (1884), 38-41.

1613. Rollins, Hyder E. "The Troilus-Cressida Story from Chaucer to Shakespeare," PMLA, XXXII (1917), 383-429. E-S SG

After a survey of fifteenth- and sixteenth-century sources so thorough that it amounts virtually to a Troilus-Cressida-Pandarus allusion-book, Rollins shows that, contrary to most critics' opinions, Sh treated Cressida mildly, without bitterness. The debased view of Cressida, traceable especially to Henryson and later ballad-mongers, was so widespread that it is surprising that Sh allowed her to make her final exit unmarred by leprosy. Rollins recognizes the great contribution of Tatlock to the interpretation of Troi. in the light of its sources, and he wisely rejects the war-of-the-theaters and satire-on-Chapman's-Homer interpretations of the play.

1614. Root, R. K. "Troilus and Criseyde," The Poetry of Chaucer, revised ed. (Boston, 1934/1957), Ch. VI, pp. 86-127.

A part of this interpretative ch. is a survey of the tale of Troy as part of the matter of Rome the Grand. Root carries the legend from the Ilias Latina of "Pindarus Thebanus" (first century) to Dryden. Sh is accorded only a paragraph, which labels his play "merely disgusting," Cressida "merely a confessed wanton," and Pandarus "merely repulsive." Some recent estimates are more generous to the play and its characters, and few would now agree that Troi. was written "in a spirit of bitter cynicism and blackest pessimism."

1615. Rosen, William. Shakespeare and the Craft of Tragedy. HUP, 1960, 231 pp.

Half of this book (pp. 104-207) is a study of the methods by which Sh influences audience opinion of his characters in Antony and Cor. (the first half of the book treats Lear and Macb.). In Antony Sh establishes a tension between Antony's radiant past and his shameful present by using a host of choric commentators (chiefly Romans) who frame his every move by predicting it and then reviewing it. This technique, in use until Act IV, assures that no one can miss Sh's point that a once great man is being destroyed by a wanton life with a royal whore (Cleopatra's past is uniformly described—even by herself—as a tissue of carnality, infidelity, and baseness). At the time of Antony's suicide, however, the choral expositors drop away and Antony is left to die remembering his past greatness; so, too, Cleopatra dies uncondemned, but also unredeemed--she is still the deceiver, still the temptress, still the actress. As a result of Sh's abandonment of the "chorus" halfway through the play, critics have been deluded into thinking that the play is ambiguous or that the characters (especially Cleopatra) undergo a regeneration. This is sound criticism of Antony; yet one feels that Rosen has minimized Cleopatra's achievement in Act V. She imbibes what vestiges of Stoicism remain in Antony at his death, and (ironically) becomes more Stoic than he as she dies in the high Roman fashion. Rosen applies essentially the same method to explain the pejorative view of Coriolanus which almost all critics take. He emphasizes that Coriolanus is contrasted with Menenius, commented upon by everyone in the play, and allowed himself to reveal his private virtues (excellent for war) which become public vices (disastrous in peacetime). Rosen shows that "opinion" is a key term in the play; that the citizens are a chorus supported by the Tribunes, Volumnia, Tullus Aufidius--indeed by everyone in the cast--all forming a composite picture of the hero which he himself reinforces by his every speech. The limitation of Rosen's approach both to Antony and to Cor. is that the "chorus" of each play is itself (unlike Greek Choruses) subject to criticism from the audience. We recognize that the Romans who condemn Antony are biased and that every character in Cor. is motivated by strong personal prejudices when he speaks of Caius Marcius. Nevertheless Rosen's two chs. are an illuminating criticism of the Roman plays, approaching them as they do from the point of view of an audience, not a reader.

1616. Rossiter, A. P. "'Troilus and Cressida'," TLS, May 8, 1948, p. 261.

Rossiter would rearrange the speeches at the close of II ii in order to make Hector's change of position on the morality of keeping Helen less sudden. "Hector is no weathercock --is indeed by no means deformed, defiled or degraded with all the other 'heroes of antiquity'." But Rossiter's readjustment implies a lacuna in the text; the passage is meaningful without any tampering.

1617. Rossiter, A. P. "Troilus and Cressida," ShN, V (1955), 3.

A report of a Summer Lecture (1954) at Stratford. Sh expected his private audience to remember Chaucer and Homer; the sordidness of Sh's reflection of these sources would suggest the decay of late Elizabethan England to them. Sh's central idea may be that "systems of thought do not apply to realistic behavior." In any case, Sh was depressed when he wrote Troi.

1618. Roussel, Louis. "Shakespeare's Greek," TLS, February 2, 1946, p. 55.

Roussel calls attention to the "analogy" between Aufidius' "the anvil of my sword" (Cor. IV v 115) and the phrase "λόγχης ἄκμονες" from Aeschylus' Persae 51. He is answered (ibid., p. 91) by Dosio Koffler, who points out three other verbal coincidences between Sh and Greek tragedy, but who accepts Sir Sidney Lee's contention that "The Greek language was unknown to [Sh]." Koffler (ibid., p. 115), Roderick Eagle (ibid., p. 127), John Berryman (ibid., p. 151), and A. De Quincey (ibid., p. 199) debate the meaning of Sh's phrase and the extent of his Greek until the editor ends the controversy with a call for facts, not opinions.

1619. Rücker, F. G. "The Spirit of Caesar," CR, CI (1912), 129-131.

A brief defense of Caesar's character as Sh portrays him: "the mightiness of Caesar is chiefly seen as reflected in the events which followed on his death. The Roman State was torn in two by the task of having to decide between Brutus's view and Antony's view of him whom all alike recognized as having been the foremost man in all the world."

1620. Rümelin, Gustav. "Zu den Dramen über Stoffe des classischen Alterthums," Shakespearestudien (1865), 2nd ed. (Stuttgart, 1874), pp. 133-156. E-S

The chief fault in the three Roman plays is that Sh's Romans are Englishmen in togas. Yet Sh does lend local color to the plays by vivid geographical and other physical allusions. Caesar is the most perfect of the three, although it contains many violations of historical truth; the most obvious is in the character of Caesar: "Hätte der Dichter auch nur ein Kapitel aus Cäsars Commentarien gekannt, er würde ihm nicht so plumpe, grosssprecherische Worte in den Mund gelegt haben." Cor. also violates history as it portrays an action too huge for the republic in which it supposedly takes place. Sh follows Plutarch in distorting the character of Antony and in tacitly ranking actions of great magnitude (e.g., Actium) with trivial affairs and relationships. Rümelin proposes that Sh wrote the Roman plays as moral exempla for Southampton. He places Titus among Sh's juvenilia and dismisses it. Despite the availability of Plutarch, Homer, and possibly Greek tragedy (all in trans.), Sh (like his contemporaries) never responded to Hellenic culture, as Tim. and Troi. show. The former is more like a children's fable than a tragedy. The latter is an enigma—the probability is that Sh wrote it for a private coterie of dilettantes, filling it with veiled personal satire which cannot be decoded now. Though Rümelin is reluctant to accept Sh's classicism on its own terms, his criticism is sometimes cogent--on the whole the essay has aged less than most nineteenth-century criticism of the Greek and Roman plays. DFo

1621. Ruppel, K. H. "Antonius und Cleopatra: Werkgestalt und Bühnenerscheinung," ShJ, XCIII (1957), 186-195. GRS

The first section (pp. 186-191) of this art. attributes the aura of magnificence in the play in part to the suggestions of divinity which attach to Cleopatra (who not only is costumed like Venus at Cydnus, but is actually an incarnation of Venus/Astarte), to Antony (who is identified with Hercules), and to Octavius (who soon after the play closes will become deified as Augustus--the principle of "Ordo" in the Roman state). The fusion of the gods of love and of death ("Eros Thanatos") underlines this apotheosis of the central characters, as does the almost godlike ease with which the action moves around the Mediterranean world. A most interesting view of the play. The balance of the art. is an account of three modern stage productions.

1622. Ryan, Pat M., Jr. "Appian's Civil Wars Yet Again As Source for Antony's Oration," QJS, XLIV (1958), 72-73.

Ryan makes the plausible conjecture that if Sh did model Antony's Forum speech on Appian's account he probably searched for clues outside the sections strictly relevant to the action of Caesar. Ryan points out a parallel between Antony's ironic "honorable men" and a similarly ironic "boni cives" in another oration delivered by Antony in Book V of Appian.

1623. Rymer, Thomas. "Reflections on the Julius Caesar," A Short View of Tragedy, [part of] Ch. VIII, in Critical Works of Thomas Rymer, ed. Curt A. Zimansky (Yale UP), 1956, pp. 164-170.

A scurrilous attack on Sh's Caesar, falling short only of the inappropriate vituperation of the essay on Oth. (#2087). Brutus and Cassius are clowns; the oratory is a stupid process of capping sentences; the search for a flint in Brutus' study (II i 1-9, 35-36) is ludicrous, etc. Among Sh critics it is difficult to find a man with worse taste than Rymer.

1624. S. "The Shakspearian Cowards: Thersites," Ath, No. 763 (1842), 526-528.

An interesting character sketch, specifying the chief difference between Homer's Thersites and Sh's: Homer's coward is like Parolles and Sir Andrew Aguecheek, quarrelsome and boastful of his prowess (if he is sure he will not have to prove his mettle); Sh's Thersites is publicly proud of his cowardice--he equates valiancy with idiocy and cowardice with intellect. S. cites a number of passages from Troi. which illustrate this significant difference. The two chief Homeric characteristics remain, however, "irreverence for authority and the volubility of a daring and bitter tongue." The intermediary between Homer and Sh was Chapman's trans. S. ends with a passage from Dryden's Troilus and Cressida in which Thersites speaks a gloriously Shn idiom.

1625. Sackton, Alexander H. "The Paradoxical Encomium in Elizabethan Drama," TSE, XXVIII (1949), 83-104.

For adoxiography in Tim., see #0908.

1626. Sandoe, James. "Troilus and Cressida," ShN, VIII (1958), 28.

This report of a lecture given at the Oregon Festival in 1958 interprets the play as love and honor both perverted. Sandoe makes a very strange defense of Cressida, who "becomes a wanton before our eyes because of desolation and vengefulness"; she did not want to leave Troy, and infidelity is her response to the Trojans' (especially Troilus') acquiescence in her departure.

1627. [Sargeaunt, George M.] "Troilus and Cressida," TLS, May 19, 1932, pp. 357-358. (Reprinted as Ch. XV of The Classical Spirit [1936].)

In this leading art., Sargeaunt is more interested in defending the character of Troilus and in touching the rhetorical magnificence of the poetry than in tracing Sh's manipulation of his sources, but he does make some very challenging passing remarks on analogies to the classics: (1) "No other writer except Sophocles has been so beset with the significance of Time in life, not . . . as a destroying or 'calumniating' power, but as a mysterious cooperator with the individual in bringing events to pass"; (2) Sargeaunt anticipates in part the approach of Oscar J. Campbell by calling Troi. a "Greek Satyric play . . . a half-serious, half mocking dramatization of a legendary subject which was thus divested of its heroic quality and presented in an atmosphere more closely corresponding to that of ordinary life."

1628. Sargent, Ralph M. "The Source of Titus Andronicus," SP, XLVI (1949), 167-183.

A thorough and critical examination of an eighteenth-century chapbook containing a prose version of the Titus story and a ballad apparently based on the prose version. Sargent considers that an ancestor of the prose tale could have been Sh's source and discusses at length Sh's putative additions to and deletions from this "source," all in the light of Sh's artistic process. Sh's most important addition was the language and the poetry, none of which is in either version, but Sh also changed the political import of the story to conform with his usual political ideas. Sargent appears to have a plausible case, but it can only be proved by the discovery of a copy of the tale which antedates ca. 1590.

1629. Sarrazin, G. "Shakespeare und Orlando Pescetti," ESn, XLVI (1913), 347-354. E-S SG

An implausible suggestion that Sh read or saw an English trans. (by Munday?) of Pescetti's tragedy Il Cesare (1594). There is no external evidence that the play was produced in Ln, but Sarrazin is tempted to identify it with one of the lost Caesar plays of the 'nineties. Parallels with Caesar are largely incidental and include the place and time of the conspirators' meeting, the decision to spare Antony, Portia's curiosity, and Caesar's decision to go to the Senate despite Calphurnia's dream.

1630. Schanzer, Ernest. "Antony and Cleopatra and the Countess of Pembroke's Antonius," NQ, CCI (1956), 152-154.

Schanzer adduces a number of parallels between the two plays to support Dover Wilson's contention (#1781) that Sh had read the trans. of Garnier's Marc Antoine. Most are not sufficiently close to justify the assurance of Schanzer's conclusion.

1631. Schanzer, Ernest. "'Antony and Cleopatra' and 'The Legend of Good Women'," NQ, CCV (1960), 335-336.

Sh refers three times in Antony to the fact that Cleopatra was the widow of her brother, Ptolemy. Schanzer skillfully untangles the confusions that have resulted from the fact that there were two brothers named Ptolemy, both of whom Cleopatra married and both of whom she survived. None of Sh's sources (Plutarch, Appian, the Cleopatra plays) could inform him about Cleopatra's marriages; Sh must have obtained his information from the opening lines of the story of Cleopatra in Chaucer's LGW. Chaucer's source in turn was doubtless Vincent de Beauvais, not Boccaccio as is often thought.

1632. Schanzer, Ernest. "A Neglected Source of Julius Caesar," NQ, CXCIX (1954), 196-197.

Though the anonymous Caesar's Revenge was not published until 1606, it probably dates from the 'nineties. Sh drew from his memory of it several elements in Caesar: the identification of Brutus' evil spirit with Caesar's ghost, the goddess Até (called "Discord" in the source), Antony's bombastic prophecy over Caesar's body, and "above all . . . the thrasonical traits in Caesar's character, the hubristic tragedy of his fall, and the revenge of his ghost on the field of Philippi." The Senecan elements in Caesar's Revenge (and therefore in Caesar) derive proximately from the French Senecans. This elevation of the importance of Caesar's Revenge as a source has met with reservations from J. C. Maxwell (#0030).

1633. Schanzer, Ernest. "A Plot-Chain in 'Antony and Cleopatra'," NQ, CXCIX (1954), 379-380.

"The habit of association, which exerted such a powerful influence on Shakespeare's method of composition, could extend beyond his choice of words to the very plotting of the play itself." A sequence of events (royal quarrel, peace-marriage, further breach, lament of the woman with divided loyalties) which Sh had used in John recurs in Antony (II ii, III iv). Consciously or not, he modified Plutarch so that the same events would occur in the same order.

1634. Schanzer, Ernest. "The Problem of Julius Caesar," SQ, VI (1955), 297-308.

Like T. J. Spencer (#1680), Schanzer believes that conflicting traditions in the 1590's fostered an ambivalence in the Elizabethan attitude toward Caesar. This ambivalence is notable also in Plutarch and Appian; and Sh, who had no thought of Caesar other than adulation in his earliest references to him (1,2,3H.VI), perhaps grew to some doubts after reading Plutarch and Appian. But an ambiguous Caesar in the play is not merely an accidental product of sources. Sh deliberately makes his Caesar the mysterious sum of men's conflicting opinions of him (Cassius', Casca's, Brutus', Artemidorus', Antony's) to capitalize on the ambivalence in his audience's attitude toward Caesar. The result is a play (like Meas.) in which an idealist (Brutus) chooses a course of action which we cannot approve, but which is hardly to be condemned outright. Caesar is by no means the "simple" play which high school teachers have assumed it to be. Schanzer's is a coherent and percipient analysis.

1635. Schanzer, Ernest. "Three Notes on 'Antony and Cleopatra'," NQ, CCV (1960), 20-22.

Note II discusses the origins of the names of some minor characters in Antony. Most can be found in North's Plutarch, but one is probably from Appian and another possibly from the Countess of Pembroke's Antonius.

1636. Schanzer, Ernest. "The Tragedy of Shakespeare's Brutus," ELH, XXII (1955), 1-15.

Caesar is Brutus' tragedy: the Aristotelian peripeteia of the play is that Brutus killed Caesar to protect the state he loved, but was afterwards unable to assure it the benefits he wished to bequeath it. This is not to make a doctrinaire republican of Brutus--he is not afraid of monarchy, but of what monarchy might do to his friend Caesar. The theme is not politics but the morality of Brutus' political decision. Sh has thus stripped Brutus of Plutarch's republican sentiments. There are numerous interesting observations on the sophistication of Brutus' speech to the people, on the imagery of hunting which dominates Act III and which Sh probably derived from a single hint in Plutarch, on the character of Caesar, which is neither tyrannical as in Lucan, nor saintly as in Orosius. An intelligent art.

1637. Schmidt, Wolfgang. "Die Wertlehre in Troilus und Cressida," NS, XLVII (1939), 181-188.

Schmidt sees Troi. as a crucial link between Caesar and Ham. In all three plays values are at issue and the relation between practical reality and absolute value is explored. Brutus and Hamlet, like Troilus and Hector, endorse absolute ideals which lead to disaster in their practical affairs. Yet, ironically, though Hector is an absolutist about chivalry and "fair play," he is a pragmatist in his desire to let Helen go; meanwhile, Troilus, who is an absolutist about Cressida and Helen, is a pragmatist on the field of battle (V iii 37-49). Moreover, Ulysses, who is a relativist in his disquisition on Time and reputation in III iii, is given Sh's own belief in absolute order to preach in I iii. Though values are constantly threatened by those who have none (Pandarus, Achilles, Thersites), Troi. is not a reflection of Shn disillusionment any more than Caesar and Ham. are.

1638. Schröder, Rudolf Alexander. "Troilus und Cressida: Eine Festrede," ShJ, XC (1954), 11-36. (Reprinted in Merkur, IX [1955] GRS.)

Schröder interprets the title as an ironic reflection of the two worlds in the play. Both the "Oberwelt" of Troilus and the "Unterwelt" of Cressida are darkened by shadows which are a result partly of sources, partly of early Jacobean malaise, and partly (perhaps) of Sh's personal Weltschmerz. Schröder gives more attention to the war plot and its place in the two worlds than to the lovers themselves. He does not assert that Sh read Homer in a Latin trans., but will not deny the possibility either (he does not discuss Chapman). Schröder's theory that Troi. is a Morality play has been advanced by others--Schröder adds the notion that James I was the intended recipient of the moral instruction.

1639. Schücking, L[evin] L. Character Problems in Shakespeare's Plays. Ln, 1922, [Caesar] pp. 40-52; [Antony] pp. 120-144. E-S SG

Sh's deviations from Plutarch in the character of Julius Caesar were in response partly to the dramatic conventions of the Elizabethan stage and partly to the necessity of making the colossus appear human. In the first three acts of Antony, Cleopatra is an erotic harlot, a much less attractive and less dignified woman than Plutarch's queen. Sh's departure from the source here was necessitated by Elizabethan morality which demanded that a woman convicted of adultery be lacking in other virtues as well. Yet, in Acts IV and V, Cleopatra behaves with dignity and dies well, as in Plutarch. The inconsistency in her character is to be explained as a reversal (cf. The Honest Whore or The Maid's Tragedy) induced by Antony's scathing condemnation of her (III xiii 105-122), and her later apparent wavering about suicide is Sh's attempt to be faithful to his source by having her die not on Antony's corpse, but later. Schücking's thesis on Cleopatra has been a center of controversy ever since it appeared; perhaps Schücking is right in saying that Cleopatra experiences regeneration but wrong in believing that Antony's tongue-lashing precipitates it. It is at the moment of her Roman's death that Cleopatra acquires the Roman virtues.

1640. Schwalb, Harry M. "Shakespeare's Antony and Cleopatra, I,ii,1-5," Expl, VIII (1950), item 53.

Schwalb highlights the unconscious irony of Alexas' predictions about Charmian's future husband. When we later realize that Charmian is a sacrificial bride of death, everything Alexas has said takes on mordant significance. Death and sex are closely identified all through the play.

1641. Schwamborn, Heinrich. "Brutus und Cassius, Einige Betrachtungen zu Julius Caesar," NS, I (1955), 24-32.

Sh "wusste . . . das alle politischen Institutionen und Zustände so gut und so schlecht sind wie die Menschen, die sie tragen." Therefore he concentrates on the men who make history, not so much on history itself. Caesar, Cassius, and Brutus are the three portraits from Sh's gallery of political types which Schwamborn comments on. His tendency is to avoid extreme positions: e.g., "Zwischen beiden Polen [i.e., Cassius' contemptuous denigration and Caesar's own lofty view of himself] . . . steht Cäsars wirkliche Grösse."

1642. Schwartz, Elias. "On the Quarrel Scene

in Julius Caesar," CE, XIX (1958), 168-170.

"Brutus never comes to know either himself or the scope of his betrayal," and the quarrel scene (IV iii) is proof. Brutus is thus a pathetic rather than a tragic figure. Schwartz does not discuss the extent to which this view of "great nobility and dullness of wit" can be justified from Plutarch.

1643. Scott, John A. "An Unnoticed Homeric Phrase in Shakespeare," CP, XXXIII (1938), 414. SG

Scott points out the striking similarity between Cor. IV vi 144-145 and Chapman's trans. of Iliad IV, 43. The lines deal with the paradox of unwilling willingness, and Chapman and Sh are very close in both thought and phrase. Scott does not note, however, that the volitional paradox is also cardinal in Greek tragedy (e.g., Aeschylus' Prometheus 671) and may have become a Renaissance commonplace.

1644. Seaton, Ethel. "Antony and Cleopatra and the Book of Revelation," RES, XXII (1946), 219-224.

An assertion that though Antony is Sh's most human play its language is given cosmic suggestions by echoes of the Apocalypse. Miss Seaton adduces a number of parallel passages, some of which are close and some of which are not. She estimates that "the facts and statements of Plutarch are the ground-bass of the theme; but the undertones of Revelation, like sunken bells under the tide, sound through the surge and swell of the poetry." Her estimate may be somewhat exaggerated, although Jack Lindsay in a letter to the editor (ibid., XXIII [1947], 66) points out that the Sibylline verses and the "millenary hopes" of the Near East were both associated in the time of Augustus with Cleopatra. He considers it "extraordinary" that Sh should have made a similar association "purely through intuitive insight."

1645. Sen, Sailendra Kumar. "What Happens in Coriolanus," SQ, IX (1958), 331-345.

An objection to the trend of recent criticism of Cor. which denies to Coriolanus any of that interior conflict which Sen regards as a criterion of Shn tragedy. Sen finds three points in the play where the hero undergoes an internal struggle and suggests that they are Sh's effort to impose his usual tragic conflict on Plutarch, an effort that is less than successful, since after each moment of conflict the hero "lapses" into resolution again. It is interesting to note (1) that in each case Volumnia precipitates the conflict: (a) when she proposes that he seek the Consulship, (b) when she urges him to dissemble to regain the public favor, (c) when she seeks to turn him back from his vengeful purpose; (2) that in none of the three cases does Plutarch so much as hint at the struggle with himself which Coriolanus undergoes in Sh. Sen's theory of intermittent conflict would explain first why we are both attracted and repelled by the play, and second why Bradley (#1175) can say that the hero suffers an internal civil war in Act V and Granville-Barker (#1347) can say that he is a surface character--and both of them seem to be correct. Sen is an astute critic.

1646. Sen Gupta, S. C. Shakespearian Comedy. OUP, 1950, 287 pp.

For comic elements in Troi., see #0915.

1647. Sewell, Arthur. Character and Society in Shakespeare. OUP, 1951, 149 pp.

An indictment of the critical methods of the psychologists, especially J. I. M. Stewart (e.g., #1701), which contains some brief but illuminating passages on Sh's plays on classical themes. Pp. 53-56 constitute a brief defense of Brutus as a man in a moral dilemma; pp. 122-133 emphasize that the moral posture of the later plays on classical themes is the measurement of man not sub specie aeternitatis, but sub specie temporis. The most provocative observations link the Roman plays to the Greek plays by thematic threads such as the abdication of duty (Coriolanus, Antony, Achilles) and the "general censure" of a man's conduct (Ulysses' admonition to Achilles, the Athenian view of Timon, Octavius' view of Antony and his lover). A stimulating section whose ramifications deserve further exploration.

1648. Sewell, Arthur. "Notes on the Integrity of Troilus and Cressida," RES, XIX (1943), 120-127.

The play is a "concoction" of three disparate elements: the romantic story of tradition, the philosophical exposition of moral positions (i.e., the debate material), and ribald cynicism. Sh, revising another's work, added the second and third elements to appeal to the sophisticates in his private audience. The argument is not persuasive; a good part of Sewell's hypothesis is, as he admits, "intuitive."

1649. Shackford, Martha H. "Dramatic Characterization of Ulysses: Troilus and Cressida," Shakespeare, Sophocles: Dramatic Themes and Modes (N.Y., 1960), pp. 84-96.

"Shakespeare's portrait of Ulysses ... is remarkable for its unconscious association with Greek tradition. Ulysses has that intellectual acuteness of mind, love of strategem, resourcefulness, strong will, interest in the genus homo, fondness for dramatic poses, and ironic humor which characterize Socrates. His more primitive traits, seen in Greek drama, have been transcended by his fitness to be a symbol of Renaissance humanism in his glowing eloquence, his concern for social and political philosophy, his belief that good government depends upon the alert minds and disciplined passions of both governors and governed. The most significant figure in Troilus and Cressida, Ulysses gives this problematical drama its chief excuse for being." The essay is a percipient analysis of four major scenes in each of which he plays a different rôle; Professor Shackford effectively demonstrates the "roundness" of his character.

1650. Shackford, Martha H. "Julius Caesar and Ovid," MLN, XLI (1926), 172-174. HB SG

Professor Shackford places Ovid's account of the stellification of Caesar and of the portents that preceded his death (Meta. XV) beside selected passages from Caesar. Most of Sh's references to the portents are obviously from North, but Sh apparently also recalled Ovid for four or five details not in Plutarch. Professor Shackford traces Caesar's speech about the northern star to this Ovidian stellification; she does not notice that her argument can be greatly reinforced by the fact that Sh had already discussed the stellification of Caesar's spirit in Bedford's invocation of the spirit of Henry V (1H.VI I i 52-56).

1651. "Shakespeare's Legerdemain With Time in 'Julius Caesar'," PL, XI (1899), 276-282.

Sh does not preserve unity of time in Caesar, which has a triple time scheme: (1) the historical time, ca. three years; (2) the acting time, ca. three hours; (3) the suggested time, ca. four days. Sh compresses Plutarch's historical time into his own briefer compass to gain intensity; he imposes the illusion of his time scheme by a system of references to hours, days, holidays, nights, etc.

1652. "Shakespeare's Plutarch," AMB, I (1882), 144-145.

A reprinting of a suggestion by Halliwell-Phillipps that Sh must have used an ed. earlier than 1603 for Cor. because the word "spite" in Coriolanus' explanation to Aufidius in IV v is omitted in the 1603 and 1612 eds. The evidence is impressive, but not quite so conclusive as Halliwell-Phillipps and the editor of the AMB assume.

1653. "Shakespeare's Roman Plays: & Other Subjects," ShN, V (1955), 41; VI (1956), 4, 14, 20.

This is "A report on the Seventh Shakespeare Conference ... held at the Shakespeare Institute, Stratford-upon-Avon September 4-9, 1955." Almost all of the papers summarized in ShN have since been published (see, e.g., #0654, #1680, #1553, #1390, #1750). The second installment contains a summary of J. M. Nosworthy's paper "Symbol and Character in 'Antony and Cleopatra'," the third gives an account of L. C. Knights's "Beyond Politics: An Aspect of Shakespeare's Relation to Tradition," and the fourth treats Nevill Coghill's "The Tragic Fact in the Roman Plays." Nosworthy argued that terrestrial imagery coupled with the imagery of fire suggests the theme of apotheosis (as in the Phoenix legend--Nosworthy related Antony to Phoenix) which, in the case of Antony, Sh added to Plutarch's account, expanding a reference to the Hercules/Omphale myth in the "Life of Marcus Antonius" to make a demigod of Antony. Knights proposed that Caesar and Cor. are documents of political morality which emphasize the necessity for personal, immediate action rather than abstract, mediate philosophizing. He traced Sh's interest in the ethics of politics and the personal element in civic life to his small-town background, and to the sixteenth-century homiletic tradition. Coghill advanced an interpretation of the Roman plays as "studies in [the] nobility" of adhering to one's principles and to oneself even at the cost of death. The usual conflict is between private and public values; Coghill traced the tone of the Roman tragedies ultimately to Medieval sources, especially Dante. The first two papers provoked considerable discussion which is also summarized.

1654. Shaw, [G.] Bernard. Three Plays for Puritans: The Devil's Disciple, Caesar and Cleopatra, and Captain Brassbound's Conversion. Ln, 1901, 314 pp.

The introductory essay (pp. v-xxxvii) is

the place in which Shaw makes his famous pronouncement that "it cost Shakespear no pang to write Caesar down for the merely technical purpose of writing Brutus up." He defends his own comic treatment of Cleopatra in love by attacking Sh's tragic treatment of the same theme; he insists that Antony is a failure because sexual love cannot be taken seriously. Shaw's effort to épater le bourgeois among critics is now taken no more seriously than Shaw takes love.

1655. Sherwood, John C. "Dryden and the Rules: The Preface to Troilus and Cressida," CL, II (1950), 73-83.

Sherwood shows that Dryden's impartiality in his judgments of Sh by classical standards is a product of the question he asks: can Sh be taken as a model by a dramatic poet? Sherwood also shows that most of the "classicism" which Dryden brings to bear on Sh is French. Yet Sh comes off well in Troi. on the very neoclassical standards by which the Restoration sometimes damned him. An interesting analysis.

1656. Shestov, Leo. "The Ethical Problem in 'Julius Caesar'," NA, I (1928), 348-356.

Shestov is to be numbered among those who think Sh wrote the plays in an effort to find relief from a spiritual agony that does not antedate the German Romantic Movement. Caesar was Sh's first experiment: an exploration of the pains and rewards of serving Morality wherever she may lead. Brutus is an alter Sh; Sh turned to Plutarch because his Platonic morality was momentarily satisfying (Shestov seems unaware of the Stoic element in Plutarch and Caesar). From this point the discussion is encumbered by such anachronisms as Kant, Fichte, Positivism, and Romantic republicanism.

1657. Showerman, Grant. Horace and His Influence, Our Debt, [No. 14] (Boston, 1922), 176 pp.

The great popularity of Horace in England is indicated by Sh's quotation in Titus IV ii 20-21 from the Odes. Even those with "small Latin" knew Horace (p. 123).

1658. Sidgwick, Henry. "Shakespeare's Methods, With Special Reference to Julius Caesar and Coriolanus," Miscellaneous Essays and Addresses (Ln, 1904), Ch. IV, pp. 91-119.

Sh "shows a reverent fidelity to the essential and vital facts of the history, though he allows himself some freedom in handling details"; Sh's purpose is to reproduce Plutarch on the stage as accurately as is consistent with dramatic form. Sh was, however, more faithful to Plutarch in characterization than in the concepts of Roman politics. MacCallum's analysis of Sh and Plutarch (#1477) convincingly attributes greater inventive license to Sh--at least in Cor.--than Sidgwick would agree to.

1659. Siegel, Paul N. "Foreshadowings of Cleopatra's Death," NQ, CCIII (1958), 386-387.

An interesting commentary on Sh's use of adumbration for ironic effect in Antony as he had used it before Juliet's death in Romeo. Siegel believes these foreshadowings concentrate the attention of the audience on Cleopatra's death at the expense of Antony's. The Elizabethans thought of her as they thought of Dido and Juliet--she was one of Love's martyrs. This interpretation is radically opposed to those of Barroll (#1145) and Rosen (#1615). Siegel appears to minimize the vast difference in moral nature between Juliet and Cleopatra.

1660. Simpson, Lucie. "Shakespeare's 'Cleopatra'," FR, CXXIX (1928), 332-342. E-S (Reprinted in The Secondary Heroes of Shakespeare and Other Essays [1951].)

Somewhat an enthusiast, the author sets out to interpret the play as Cleopatra's; Antony is only an appendage. Although Sh did not ennoble Cleopatra and portrays her more unfavorably even than Plutarch did, he is "condoning human frailty" in the play and concerns himself chiefly with his heroine. The political content of the play will not support so limited a reading.

1661. Simpson, Percy. "'Julius Caesar,' II.i. 204-5.--" 9 NQ, V (1900), 393.

Steevens' note on this passage traces to Claudian Sh's knowledge of the hunter's device of placing mirrors so as to confuse bears. Simpson cannot find the supposed allusion in Claudian; at ibid., VI (1900), 203 he partly settles the question by showing that Steevens might have confused Claudian with Pliny who is said to advise hunters carrying off a tigress' cubs to place mirrors so as to confound the mother with her own reflection. But once again he is unable to specify chapter and verse.

1662. Simpson, Percy. "Pluto in Shakespeare as God of Wealth," 9 NQ, IV (1899), 265.

The modern emendation "Plutus" for the F_1 "Pluto" in Caesar IV iii 102 and Troi. III iii 197 is unjustified. In Greek literature Pluto is said to hoard riches in Hades, while Renaissance literature is full of similar references to Pluto as wealthy. The most important source for Sh would doubtless be Marlowe's Hero and Leander, which speaks of "Dis, on heapes of gold fixing his looke." Subsequent correspondence (ibid., 402, 501; VI [1900], 17, 18) adds corroboration.

1663. Simpson, Percy. "The Theme of Revenge in Elizabethan Tragedy," PBA, XXI (1935), 101-136. (Annual British Academy Shakespeare Lecture.)

For Caesar and the revenge play, see #2111.

1664. Skottowe, A. Life of Shakespeare. Ln, 1824 (no complete pagination available--as abstracted in the New Variorum Antony).

Skottowe points out that Antony's mind remains clear enough to see his predicament despite the absolute enslavement of his body. The key passage is Antony's violent condemnation of Cleopatra (III xiii 105-122) followed by his tender forgiveness of her. Both his physical susceptibility and his intellectual awareness are well documented in history. Skottowe believes that Sh has not given his Cleopatra the talents and the "elegance" which Plutarch's Cleopatra has.

1665. Small, R. A. The Stage Quarrel Between Ben Jonson and the So-called Poetasters. Breslau, 1899, 204 pp. E-S

This book contains a discussion (pp. 154-169) of the sources of Sh's Troi. They are (1) Chaucer (with modification of Cressida to accord with Renaissance prejudice); (2) Caxton for a good many details (including the last seven scenes and the Prologue, which are not by Sh); (3) Chapman's Iliads for certain phrases and the character of Nestor, etc.; (4) Sh's own imagination for Ajax, who is a satirical caricature of Ben Jonson. As (2) and (4) show, Small is a special pleader, and his source study should be weighed against the findings of Tatlock (#1718), Presson (#1583), and other scholars.

1666. Smith, C. Alphonso. "The Dramatic Import of the Falling Sickness in Shakespeare's 'Julius Caesar'," PL, VI (1894), 469-470.

Smith points out that Plutarch affords no statement that Caesar had an epileptic fit when offered the crown; indeed the story appears nowhere in classical literature. Sh invented it (on the briefest of hints about Caesar's epilepsy in Plutarch) to suggest "that Caesar's fortune is waning, that the gods as well as men have conspired against him."

1667. Smith, Gordon Ross. "Authoritarian Patterns in Shakespeare's Coriolanus," L&P, IX (1959), 45-51.

Drawing his terminology, definitions, and clinical symptoms from Erich Fromm and T. W. Adorno, Smith finds that Menenius, Coriolanus, Virgilia (sic), and Volumnia are "authoritarians," i.e., people who would impose their wills on others without warrant in demonstrable superiority. This leads to a reading of Cor. as a political document in the restive years which preceded the Revolution. Plutarch provided Sh a story of a society without a middle class, and Sh capitalized on this social lacuna, writing an attack on the authoritarian aristocracy for the benefit of his largely bourgeois audience at the Globe. The Plebeians are criticized in this "realistic and grim satire" also, but not to the same extent as the villainous Coriolanus. Sh's demonstrated conservatism about the social order is sufficient ground for rejecting Smith's interpretation.

1668. Smith, Gordon Ross. "Brutus, Virtue, and Will," SQ, X (1959), 367-379.

An entirely unconvincing depreciation of the character. Smith magnifies trivial details in order to castigate Brutus, who emerges from this art. somewhere between a criminal and a Freudian case study. After citing fourteen cases of Brutus' overriding the advice of others, Smith goes on to twist the quarrel scene entirely in Cassius' favor, to make the scene with young Lucius in the tent a monstrous display of injustice on Brutus' part and to say of his famous reflection on Cato's suicide, "For lack of anything better, Brutus trots out his old trumpery again."

1669. Smith, J. E. "'Antony and Cleopatra,' II.ii.—" 7 NQ, X (1890), 402-403.

Smith suggests that the difficulties in Enobarbus' description of Cleopatra at Cydnus ("tended her i' th' eyes" and "made their bends adornings," both with reference to the Nereides, her gentlewomen) can be eliminated if the first expression is emended to "bended to the oars." The picture, for the last part of which Plutarch gives no authority, is then of some handmaidens tending the sails, some steering, and others rowing so gracefully that they adorn the ship as they bend to their work. A very long controversy follows: for opinions from Adolphus Trollope, R. M. Spence, W. W. Lloyd, Brinsley Nicholson, and several others, see ibid., p. 483; XI (1891), 82, 182, 362-364; XII (1891), 4, 62-63, 202-203, 261-263.

1670. Smith, Warren D. "The Duplicate Revelation of Portia's Death," SQ, IV (1953), 153-161.

Smith argues that both accounts of Portia's death in Caesar are canonical. In Plutarch's "Life of Brutus" a false report that Portia has died reaches Brutus just before the assassination of Caesar; this may have given Sh the idea of making Brutus privately doubt the report of Portia's death which he relays to Cassius at IV iii 144-157. The doubt would be underlined moments later (173-178) by the discrepancy between Brutus' and Messala's information about the proscription (in "Cicero," "Marcus Antonius," and "Brutus" respectively Plutarch gives the number killed as more than two hundred, three hundred, and two hundred). But Messala shatters Brutus' false hopes for Portia's safety (181-192), and Brutus' magnanimity appears the greater when he conceals his grief. Smith shows that Brutus protects others from knowledge of his private anxieties and griefs at numerous other points in the play and would interpret this behavior as evidence of Brutus' capacity for leadership. Smith's thesis is attacked by Brents Stirling (ibid., X [1959], 211-217).

1671. Snider, Denton J. "[On the Theme and Structure of Troilus and Cressida]," System of Shakespeare's Dramas (St. Louis, 1877), II, 197, 222 (as abstracted in the New Variorum Troi.).

The theme of Troi. is reflected in its structure--in each of the two plots disparate elements are brought together, but the union is only temporary as disparity again becomes dominant. The separated lovers are united, then re-separated; Achilles' detachment is overcome, but Troy remains standing; the Trojan council imposes community of purpose on the defenders, but no military success follows. The theme of unity versus discord is emphasized in the chaos of the last act in which discord triumphs and no conclusion is reached.

1672. Snider, D[enton] J. "The Tragedy of Julius Caesar," The Western, n.s. II (1876), 38-49, 77-87. (Reprinted from the Journal of Speculative Philosophy, VI, No. 1.)

Snider sees the play virtually as an allegory: Caesar ("World-Spirit" [i.e., the tide of history]) is unsuccessfully opposed by Cassius ("Politics" [i.e., the intellectual conviction that the state is the center of the universe]). Into this polarity intrudes Brutus ("Morality" [i.e., the will to do good without the intellectual equipment to know what the good is]). Though Caesar dies physically, the tide of history triumphs completely--the Roman world was ripe for a Caesar before Caesar crossed his Rubicon. Snider's depreciation of Brutus and elevation of Cassius anticipates some recent positions on the play, but few have gone so far as Snider in the direction of reading Caesar as an allegory in political ethics. DLC

1673. Soellner, Rolf [H.] "The Madness of Hercules and the Elizabethans," CL, X (1958), 309-324.

For Sh's use of conventions about Herculean insanity in Antony and possibly in Caesar, see #2120.

1674. Soellner, Rolf [H.] "The Troubled Fountain: Erasmus Formulates a Shakespearian Simile," JEGP, LV (1956), 70-74.

For the classical background of Troi. III iii 310-315, see #0928.

1675. Sommers, Alan. "'Wilderness of Tigers': Structure and Symbolism in Titus Andronicus," EC, X (1960), 275-289.

This effective defense of Titus interprets the play in Nietzschean terms as unified by the tension between Roman values and barbarian passions (cf. Antony). As Sh saw them, the Roman values are "justice, continence, and nobility" (I i 15), and the tragedy is that of Rome (the real protagonist), as her virtues are violated: the latter two in Lavinia and Bassianus by barbarians in the wood (Act II), and the former by Titus himself in Act I. It is the violation of justice which is the heart of the play, and the restoration of order in Act V is a matter of the restoration of justice.

1676. Soreson, C. "'Whom Everything Becomes'," The Silver Falcon (N.Y.: Hunter College, 1936), pp. 21-24. GRS

Not seen. GRS implies that this essay is a character study of Sh's Cleopatra.

1677. Spaeth, John W., Jr. "Caesar's Friends and Enemies Among the Poets," CJ, XXXII (1937), 541-556. GRS

Spaeth refers (p. 543) to the historical Caesar as a student of Euripides and Menander, who actually exclaimed "καὶ σὺ τέκνον" when Brutus stabbed him, "Shakespeare to the contrary notwithstanding." Spaeth characterizes the phrase as "Greek of the Attic tragedy."

1678. Spence, R. M. "'Troilus and Cressida,' III. iii. 223 5 [sic]," 8 NQ, VI (1894), 283.

Spence believes that an alteration in the punctuation of Calchas' plea to the Greek chieftains (III iii 3-5) can make better sense of the lines. He insists that Johnson's emendation of "love" to "Jove" is to be discarded, since Jove does not want Troy to fall, though fall it must. K. D. recommends (ibid., VIII [1895], 24) that "love" be emended to "lore" to make Calchas refer to his prophetic knowledge which warns him to abandon doomed Troy. Chaucer's Calchas is portrayed as a very learned man. Spence rejects D.'s suggestion (ibid., IX [1896], 423).

1679. Spencer, Benjamin T. "Antony and Cleopatra and the Paradoxical Metaphor," SQ, IX (1958), 373-378.

Antony is "the mirror held up to the disturbance of values when two large and incompatible cultures [Rome and Egypt] come into conflict." Sh sided with neither East nor West, but enjoyed reflecting the conflict in the paradoxes with which Antony is replete. Spencer adduces a large number of such paradoxes (especially of "synoeciosis, a yoking of seemingly incompatible terms"), but Sh is known as a master of irony of all kinds and one wonders whether an examination of Ham., e.g., might not produce as many paradoxical metaphors as Spencer finds in Antony, even though the former has no conflict of cultures (see #0424, pp. 135-136). Certainly, however, Spencer has shown that Sh added such expressions to Plutarch, e.g., in Enobarbus' description of Cleopatra in her barge.

1680. Spencer, T[erence]. "Shakespeare and the Elizabethan Romans," ShS, X (1957), 27-38.

"In spite of literary admiration for Cicero, the Romans in the imagination of the sixteenth century were Suetonian and Tacitan [i.e., imperial] rather than Plutarchian [i.e., republican]." Moreover their history was regarded as a succession of "garboyles," remote indeed from our notions of Roman grandeur. The kind of Rome depicted in Guevara's Dial of Princes is even more tumultuous than that in Titus, which "is a more typical Roman play, a more characteristic piece of Roman history, than the three great plays of Shakespeare which are generally grouped under that name." But Titus is not authentic of any one period; "it includes all the political institutions that Rome ever had. The author seems anxious, not to get it all right, but to get it all in." The three other Roman plays display a progressive independence from popular attitudes toward Rome, and a resulting verisimilitude which impressed the eighteenth century. Sh undertook a "serious" literary effort when he tackled the massive folio of North, and he deliberately moved tangentially to his time, which preferred Suetonius' gossip and the Moralia to the Parallel Lives. Spencer's is a very important study, full of original insights: e.g., (1) it took special courage for Sh to write on Coriolanus--he had no precedent as in Caesar and Antony; (2) it is a mistake to assume a unified opinion of Caesar in the sixteenth century--he was constantly being reappraised; (3) Sh's Caesar and Cor. have virtually alone formed the modern bias about the moral tone of ancient Rome. This essay, which includes a brilliant comparison between Sh and Jonson as "Roman" playwrights, is as original and as thoughtful as any that has appeared on the Roman plays; it makes an admirable complement in criticism to the historical scholarship provided by Barroll (#1144, #1145, #1148).

1681. Spencer, Terence. "Shakespeare Learns the Value of Money: The Dramatist at Work on Timon of Athens," ShS, VI (1953), 75-78.

To support his theory that Tim. represents, in part, a draft for the finished play that Sh never wrote, Spencer shows that in various places the text is inconsistent in its references to talents as units of money. This inconsistency Spencer believes to reflect uncertainty on Sh's part as to the value of a talent; during the course of composition he learned the large value of the classical talent and corrected his earlier errors in some places but not in others. Sh's knowledge of talents would be partly biblical and partly Plutarchian.

1682. Spencer, Theodore. "A Commentary on Shakespeare's 'Troilus and Cressida'," SEL(T), XVI (1936), 1-43.

An intelligent analysis of the play which takes account of conventional Renaissance attitudes toward the Trojan War but also recognizes that Sh's manipulation of those conventions is important as an indication of his craftsmanship. E.g., the Elizabethans thought of Thersites only as a railer, so Sh had to bring him on stage in that rôle if at all; but Sh saw that Thersites could be made a link between the war story and the love story (as he is not in Heywood's Iron Age, e.g.) and therefore introduced his contumelious comments into both plots. Spencer stresses the unity of the play, showing that the themes of love appear in the war plot while war dominates the love plot. He is also persuasive on the tone of the play, showing that seemingly irrelevant scenes (Pandarus with Paris and Helen in III i, e.g.) establish the color of the society in which the action takes place. The most interesting observation, perhaps, is that Greeks and Trojans are paralleled, but kept apart in separate scenes until the time comes for Cressida to join the Greeks, after which the enemy forces mingle in chaotic indiscriminacy as the action whirls toward catastrophe. This is one of the most original and thoughtful essays on the play; it merits reprinting in some more accessible place. MH

1683. Spencer, Theodore. "The Elizabethan Malcontent," AMS, pp. 523-535.

For the classical ranter in Tim. and Troi., see #2124.

1684. Spencer, Theodore. "The Isolation of the Shakespearean Hero," SewR, LII (1944), 313-331. GRS

Spencer discusses Timon, Antony (in Antony), and Coriolanus as isolated tragic heroes (pp. 327-330). Timon's alienation does not engage our emotions; Antony is isolated by Cleopatra from a public world the loss of which does not violate Antony's identity as a human being; Coriolanus, like Timon, fails to arouse our passions (though the political themes in the play may do so). Spencer does not discuss the fact that these three heroes are classical figures--he attributes the coldness of the plays to Sh's failure to dwell on "interior isolation" late in his career.

1685. Spiegelberg, Walter. "Shakespeares Cäsarbild," NM, X (1939), 177-189.

An emphatic rejection of the view that Sh wrote Caesar down. Spiegelberg defends the character against charges that he is superstitious and subject to flattery; less convincing are the comments on Caesar's infirmities and his thrasonical speeches. The best argument is briefly stated: Sh refers eight times before and after Caesar to the historical Julius as a great and admirable man; if we are to accept Sh's Caesar as "absichtlich verkleinert" we must posit also that Sh lowered his high opinion of the man in the late 'nineties and then later returned to that high opinion again. TxU

1686. Squire, John. Shakespeare as a Dramatist. Ln, 1935, 233 pp.

The most important ch. for Sh's classicism is IV, "Plot, Construction, Device," in which Squire discusses the Greek and Roman plays. He finds Troi. admirable except that Sh never decided on whom to concentrate (as he did in Antony, his other play about sensuality). Tim. has no action and partakes of "the crude psychology of the fabulists, Aesop among the bipeds." Caesar is "grossly misnamed" but it is unexcelled for the concentration and movement of its plot. Sh is largely to be excused from Titus (Squire has the pontifical tendency to excommunicate what he does not like). There are other scattered remarks of interest; perhaps the most stimulating is the observation that Sh used Holinshed, Plutarch, and the Italian novelists as the Attic tragedians used their inherited mythology--it is in the nature of drama to be derivative.

1687. Staedler, Erich. "Die klassischen Quellen der Antoniusrede in Shakespeares 'Julius Caesar'," NM, X (1939), 235-245. SG

A reprint of Antony's entire oration (except for the fourteen interruptions from the citizens) heavily annotated with parallels drawn from Suetonius, Dio Cassius, Plutarch, Cicero, and Appian; the notes introduce an occasional phrase also from Velleius, Tacitus, Florus, and Petronius. Some of the coincidental phrasing could be expected of any writer describing Antony's oration over Caesar's body, but some of the parallels are striking. Staedler quotes Appian, Dio, and even Plutarch in Greek and all the others in Latin; the anonymous Appian trans. is not mentioned. Staedler's conclusion suggests that a collaborator wrote Antony's speech, since "selbst die vorurteilsloseste Shakespeareforschung behauptet für ihren Helden nicht mehr als die Fähigkeit, klassische Texte in englischer Übersetzung verstanden zu haben." Staedler goes on to suggest that his evidence could be regarded as support for the theory of multiple authorship advanced by William Wells (#1759). The editor appends a note objecting to this obviously untenable hypothesis. TxU

1688. Stahl, E. L. "Shakespeares Römerdramen," Germania, XII, No. 9 (1937) (no pagination available). GRS

Not seen.

1689. Stamm, Rudolf. "Elizabethan Stage-Practice and the Transmutation of Source Material by the Dramatists," ShS, XII (1959), 64-70.

Stamm's interesting approach to Sh's use of his sources concentrates almost entirely on Plutarch and Antony. Taking particular note of the opening scenes, Stamm shows that the phrasing, the implied stage directions, and the rhetorical features of the speeches are all a result of Sh's effort to make drama out of Plutarch's opening description of Antony's voluptuous way of life. Stamm's observations on Sh's use of dramatic recapitulation and recollection of events which are narrated by Plutarch are especially telling, but the whole essay gives the unfortunate impression of having been telescoped by force from a larger whole.

1690. Stanford, W. Bedell. "Ulysses from Homer to Joyce," CAP, XLVI (1949), 31-33. (A summary of an address.)

Sh receives but one sentence: "Seneca dominated the French and English stage. But Shakespeare in his Troilus and Cressida, which appeared soon after Chapman's Seaven Bookes of the Iliades of Homere (1598), contains some striking developments of the Ulysses tradition, and seems to have been influenced by the Iliadic Odysseus." MnU

1691. Starnes, D[eWitt] T. "Shakespeare and Elyot's Governour," TSE, VII (1927), 112-132.

For the sources of concepts of order in Troi. and Cor., see #1088.

1692. Steadman, John M. "'Perseus upon Pegasus' and Ovid Moralized," RES, IX (1958), 407-410. GRS

For Pegasus and horsemanship in Troi., see #1090.

1693. [Steele, Richard]. The Tatler, No. 68 (September 15, 1709).

A brief passage in this number suggests that the power of the quarrel scene in Caesar stems from Brutus' restraint in not speaking immediately of his wife's death and, when he does tell Cassius of it, of suppressing his emotion.

1694. Stegmeyer, Franz. "Brutus oder: Das ethische Problem in Shakespeares Julius Cäsar," Europäische Profile: Essays (Wiesbaden, 1947), pp. 32-43. GRS

An adherent of the "Sturm und Drang" school of Shn criticism, Stegmeyer argues that a disillusioned Sh turned in 1601 (sic) to Plutarch in search of the idealism which Plutarch had imbibed from Plato. In Brutus he found a character whose morality was Duty and to whom Morality was everything. Plutarch himself could supernaturalize such ethical positions, but Sh (like Brutus, whom Stegmeyer sees as Sh's alter ego) could not. The foundation of Shn tragedy is the awareness Sh came to in writing Caesar: we may smile away a benevolent God, but we cannot do away with malevolence, the evil spirit which hovers over Brutus' later life. This is a reading difficult to accept in the light of Sh's earlier concern with Plutarch and the Caesar story. And it does not seem obvious that a spiritual crisis lies behind the composition of the play. DLC

1695. Stein, Arnold. "The Image of Antony: Lyric and Tragic Imagination," KR, XXI (1959), 586-606.

A commentary on the shifting images of Antony provided by Enobarbus, the other soldiers, Caesar, Cleopatra, and even Antony himself, all against the backdrop of Rome, which represents "fact." Antony's tragedy is that Rome will not "in Tiber melt"—the lyric imagination with which he would wish it away is incompetent to succeed in a world of fact. Yet tragedy does not invalidate lyricism. Stein appears to identify Antony's lyric imagination with Aristotelian magnificence, but he makes no reference to the classical ethics behind the play.

1696. Stein, Elizabeth. "Caxton's Recuyell and Shakespeare's Troilus," MLN, XLV (1930), 144-146. E-S

Professor Stein indicates several similarities between Caxton and Troi., especially in IV v. It was perhaps from Caxton, not from

Ovid that Sh derived the image of a ship as Perseus' horse in I iii 40-42.

1697. Stempel, Daniel. "The Transmigration of the Crocodile," SQ, VII (1956), 59-72.

Following the suggestion of Oscar J. Campbell (#1200), this art. interprets Antony as a "tragical satire" on both hero and heroine, both of whom are slaves of passion, a feminine vice. Like Phillips (#1579), Stempel sees Rome with all its virtues as a moral standard which Antony has subverted by his lust. Acts IV and V restore order in the state. Plutarch's depreciatory attitude toward Cleopatra would tend to support Stempel's argument, but he does not dwell on Sh's sources.

1698. Stemplinger, Eduard. Horaz im Urteil der Jahrhunderte, Erbe, Zweite Reihe, H. V (Leipzig, 1921), 212 pp.

For an echo of Horace's Odes in Antony, see #1092. DLC

1699. Sternfeld, Frederick W. "Troilus and Cressida: Music for the Play," EIE, 1952 (1954), 107-137.

Sternfeld discusses the ethical significance of music as Plato delineates it in the Republic, showing that Sh's practice indicates his belief in the Platonic theory. In Troi., Pandarus (a nobleman) sings erotic airs (considered effeminate compared with ballads and madrigals) even though in Sh's other plays a nobleman would leave singing in public to professionals. The effect is to underline the decay of the Trojan aristocracy. It is of interest that Sh refers less here to the other Platonic concept of music (cosmic music) because his interest lies more in the corrupt microcosm than in the harmonious macrocosm. Sternfeld supplies numerous details about Elizabethan music which make this an informative art.

1700. Stewart, J. I. M. "'Julius Caesar' and 'Macbeth': Two Notes on Shakespearean Technique," MLR, XL (1945), 166-173.

In the note on Caesar, Stewart points out that critics who think Sh's Caesar inferior to Plutarch's character because of his vainglorious boasting are forgetting the principle of "direct self-explanation," according to which a character conventionally types himself for the benefit of the audience. The play is an odd mixture of realism and convention.

1701. Stewart, J. I. M. "Professor Schücking's Fatal Cleopatra," Character and Motive in Shakespeare: Some Recent Appraisals Examined (Ln, 1949), pp. 59-78.

Schücking's view of Cleopatra as the product of Elizabethan conventions (#1639) comes under heavy fire in Stewart's attempt to read the character as psychologically believable. If she displays nobility in Act V, at least she isn't reading Plato on the immortality of the soul, and she does express herself in the same erotic and colloquial language she has used in earlier scenes. In short, she is consistent--no harlot in the early acts of the play and no saint at the close. For similar strictures on Schücking's approach to Caesar see part (pp. 46-55) of the preceding ch.: "Bottom's Dream." Perhaps the truth lies on neither side of this chasm--perhaps Schücking overstates Cleopatra's inconsistency and Stewart is wrong to ignore convention as the author of what inconsistency there is.

1702. Stirling, Brents. "'Or Else This Were A Savage Spectacle'," PMLA, LXVI (1951), 765-774.

Stirling interprets Caesar as the catastrophe of "the 'Elizabethan' Brutus who combined tragically wrong ends with high dignity of means." Brutus' failure is that he cannot dignify by sacrificial assassination the base motives of the butchers he conspires with. The play is unified by ceremonial rituals and by the ironic commentaries on them of Marc Antony and other characters. This ceremonialism is only hinted at in Plutarch; Sh makes it a central theme in the play. A lucid and perceptive analysis.

1703. Stirling, Brents. "The Plays," The Populace in Shakespeare (Col UP, 1949), pp. 19-63.

In the section on Caesar (pp. 25-35), Stirling suggests that many of the details of the mob scenes are "intuitive" (i.e., based on Sh's understanding of group psychology). Yet he is able to specify a source in the "Life of Brutus" for I i. He shows, moreover, that the pendulum-like emotions and loyalties of the mob in the Forum scene (for which Plutarch provides no basis) may not indicate Sh's antipopular prejudice (1) because it is dramatic to show the crowd manipulated (2) because Plutarch elsewhere gives indications of contempt for the fickle crowd. Stirling treats Cor. in much the same manner (pp. 35-45), and arrives at a similar conclusion: if Sh makes the Tribunes and the mob less competent politically than Plutarch does, it is because he wishes to create a force to balance against the inadequacies of Coriolanus. The conclusion is plausible: comparison between a source and a Shn play is not always a safe guide to Sh's political prejudices.

1704. Stockley, W. F. P. "A Study of 'Julius Caesar'," Mosher's, XXI (1902-3), 128-133, 199-203, 259-262, 325-330, 376-382; XXII (1903), 23-30, 84-98. (The periodical is retitled The Champlain Educator beginning with Vol. XXII.)

This essay, intended as a guide for teachers, begins with a justification of the title in the "external action" which is dominated by Caesar. But Caesar is a "Jove," cold, public, remote, while Brutus is a "Prometheus," human, capable of private emotion, tangible; therefore the interest of the play is personal, not political. In the section titled "Shakspere's Use of Plutarch in 'Julius Caesar'," Stockley depreciates North, maintaining that Sh supplied not only the poetry, but most of the characterization as well. Discussions of suicide and of the Epicureanism of Cassius and the Stoicism of Brutus follow; an elementary commentary on versification in the play completes the essay. DLC

1705. Stocks, John Leofric. Aristotelianism, Our Debt, [No. 20] ([1925]/1963), 165 pp.

In a note to pp. 100-101, Stocks quotes Hector's lines on "young men, whom Aristotle thought / Unfit to hear moral philosophy" (Troi. II ii 163-167) to illustrate Aristotle's belief that "intelligence, which is man's highest gift, is the last to achieve its perfection . . ."

1706. Stoll, Elmer Edgar. "Cleopatra," MLR, XXIII (1928), 145-163. E-S (Reprinted in Poets and Playwrights [1930].)

Here as clearly as Stoll expresses it in any other place is a critical manifesto: Sh puts plot above character as Aristotle would approve; he creates characters through speech and action but does not endow them with labyrinthine interior psychology; he is moral enough to approve or disapprove of his creatures' behavior but tolerant enough to elicit sympathy even for the depraved. As this applies to Cleopatra, Stoll argues that no Freudian or other psychological analysis is needed to explain the "change" in her character after the death of her lover. She has the right to change as any human does, but she does not show many new characteristics in Act V and she retains all the old ones. Stoll seems willing to wrestle with the play without Plutarch for an ally; yet his approach to Cleopatra is more convincing than Schücking's (#1639). See Murry, #1536, for a possible compromise between Schücking and Stoll.

1707. Storr, Ernest B. "Shakespeare's Brutus: A Character Study," LQHR, CLX (1935), 322-330.

Dante, who assigned Brutus to the lowest reaches of hell, was probably closer to the man's historical character than Sh, to whom Brutus was an idealist with a Stoic creed who became "the victim of his own magnanimity." Caesar gives structure to the play, but it is Brutus who is psychologically interesting. This view of the historical Brutus is not easy to reconcile with the accounts given by Plutarch and Cicero.

1708. Street, Ida M. "Coriolanus," NEYR, LI (1889), 266-274.

"In Coriolanus, Shakespeare seems to have turned his back upon his own time, and looking towards the ancient and guided only by his artistic instincts, to have written a pure tragedy, having a hero with classic singleness of character." But the author seems unable to settle the point, for she later qualifies: "He has not perfect classic singleness. His pride is not in opposition to an external fate, but in conflict with his own nobler nature." This indecision coupled with her failure to recognize Aufidius' servants as a low-comedy element (she believes Cor. to have a completely classical unity of tone), vitiates much of the author's criticism. But the essay is not without insights, the most illuminating of which is that before his banishment Coriolanus thinks of the citizens as an adjunct to Rome but after it he identifies them with the city.

1709. Stull, Joseph S. "Cleopatra's Magnanimity: the Dismissal of the Messenger," SQ, VII (1956), 73-78.

Cleopatra's treatment of the messenger in II v 102-106 is open to various interpretations. Stull thinks the commercial imagery of the lines refers to a casket of jewels which Antony has sent her to ease the news of his marriage; Cleopatra regards the "price" (i.e., his new wife) as too high, rejects the gift, and magnanimously gives it to its bearer. Thus her treatment of the messenger is not heartless and callous, but generous once she has vented her anger. When the messenger returns to describe Octavia (III iii) he again offers the casket of jewels which Cleopatra this time accepts, rewarding him with gold and an apology for her tantrum. An interesting speculation which Stull regards as a refutation of the view of Schücking (#1639) and others that Cleopatra is unregenerate in the early acts, only revealing magnanimity in Act V. But Stull's evidence is most slender.

1710. Swanston, Hamish F. G. "The Baroque Element in Troilus and Cressida," DUJ, n.s. XIX (1957), 14-23.

Swanston defines "the baroque" as a philosophical quest for unity (i.e., truth) in the disparities of life. The quest preoccupied poets from 1580 to 1650; Sh's Troi. is in the tradition. Swanston explores and lists the multitude of paradoxes which crowd the play and shows that a few are there only for the sake of the wit in them whereas most lead on to a concept more important than themselves. The whole course of the play is the falling from unity into disparity on the Trojan side and the apparent movement from disparity to unity in the Greek camp. It is therefore obvious that the Greeks will win; but they do not win at the death of Hector because disunity lurks beneath the harmony they think they have achieved when Achilles returns to battle. The love affair of Troilus and Cressida reflects and reinforces this baroque theme of dichotomy and harmony. An essay informed by insight, though, as Swanston admits, it leaves some mists undispersed.

1711. Swinburne, Algernon C. A Study of Shakespeare (1880). Ln, 5th printing, 1909, 309 pp.

Swinburne's violent prose and vague impressionism limit strictly the value of his criticism. The only relevant parts of this commentary on the canon are the passages on the classical plays: in Caesar personal relationships are subordinated to politics--in Cor. the reverse is true; the latter is a domestic tragedy. Pandarus and Thersites in Troi. are "Eternal Cesspools"--Sh wrote the play in the tub of Diogenes.

1712. Sykes, H. Dugdale. "The Problem of 'Timon of Athens'" (1921), Sidelights on Elizabethan Drama: A series of studies dealing with the authorship of Sixteenth and Seventeenth Century Plays (OUP, 1924), pp. 1-48. (Reprinted from NQ.)

Sykes adds his theory to the long list of attempts to dismember Tim. He maintains that Sh revised a clumsy play by Middleton and Day. The argument rests largely on intuition and assertion and is not persuasive. Sykes does not consider the problem of sources either for the "Shn" or for the "non-Shn" parts of the play. DFo

1713. Symons, Arthur. Studies in the Elizabethan Drama. N.Y., 1919, 261 pp. E-S

This collection of Symons' essays contains three of relevance to the Guide: "Antony and Cleopatra" (1889), "Titus Andronicus and the Tragedy of Blood" (1885), and "Troilus and Cressida" (1907--see #1714). To the modern reader all three may seem inconsequential; the essay on Antony has all the enthusiasm of the interpretations of Sh's characters in the Romantic period, the essay on Titus accepts Ravenscroft's dubious tradition and dismembers the play, and Manon Lescaut is the moral criterion against which Cleopatra and Cressida are tested; Symons reads Sh anachronistically.

1714. Symons, Arthur. "'Troilus and Cressida'," Harper's, CXV (1907), 659-664. (Reprinted in Studies in the Elizabethan Drama [1919].)

Symons accepts the theory of multiple authorship and is inclined to read Sh into his play, which he considers to be "an assaying of accepted values" about love and honor. "Thersites is the Falstaff of a world that tastes bitter"; Sh is merciless in his revelation of Helen's and Cressida's "shallow and troubled depths of woman"; Hector is the only truly noble character; Troilus' "I am giddy: expectation whirls me round" speech contains "perhaps the most sensitive lines in Shakespeare." The essay is stimulating in places, but it does not take a dispassionate view of the whole play. (See also #1713.)

1715. Tannenbaum, Samuel A. "Notes on 'Troilus and Cressida'," SAB, VII (1932), 72-81.

Of the thirty-eight notes, almost all suggest textual changes or interpret obscure passages. A sizable number discuss at least briefly Sh's attitude toward elements of the Troy story.

1716. Tassin, Algernon de V[ivier]. "Julius Caesar," ColSS, pp. 253-287. E-S

Tassin's detailed analysis of the action of Caesar and of the characters of Brutus and Cassius is based on a close comparison of Sh with Plutarch. From this comparison he concludes that Sh's mixed feelings about Brutus arise from the momentary lapse (in the Comparison of Dion with Brutus) from Plutarch's otherwise consistent adulation of the man. Tassin thinks that Sh also studied carefully Appian, Dio Cassius, Cicero, and other authorities on Caesar's death, a view not now generally accepted (except for Appian). The play is to be commended for its spareness in action, word, and speech—it is Sh's most carefully constructed play. Tassin's work is full of insights, but he has not considered his predecessors (he does not mention MacCallum) and he uses a modern trans. of Plutarch, which causes him to misinterpret Sh's portrayal of Brutus' attitude toward suicide.

1717. Tate, Nahum. Address to Edward Tayler prefixed to The Loyal General, A Tragedy (1680), Munro, II, 266-267.

Tate's lone voice testifies to Sh's learning as manifested especially in the Roman plays where "the Manners, the Circumstances, the Ceremonies, all are Roman." But he follows this daring rejection of the Restoration bias with the usual assertion that Sh was a student of Nature.

1718. Tatlock, J. S. P. "The Chief Problem in Shakespeare," SewR, XXIV (1916), 129-147. SG

The chief problem is the interpretation of Troi., which so many critics have regarded as a crux, the explanation of which would clarify Sh's middle (tragic) period. Alternative to the personal interpretations (pessimism, disillusionment, sorrow over Southampton's incarceration) which have been proposed is Tatlock's explanation: Troi. is an accurate reflection (1) of Sh's sources and (2) of the prejudices of his audience. The sources were chiefly Caxton, Chaucer, and perhaps a French trans. of the Iliad, but not Chapman. (Cf. #1719, the thesis of which is referred to here.) A coherent argument, expressed with wit.

1719. Tatlock. J. S. P. "The Siege of Troy in Elizabethan Literature, Especially in Shakespeare and Heywood," PMLA, XXX (1915), 673-770. E-S HB SG

Tatlock emphasizes the great popularity between 1598 and 1602 of the Troy legend and lists some twenty plays (lost and extant) current in the sixteenth and early seventeenth centuries. He discusses the sources, value, and authorship of the four major nondramatic Troy poems of the period and concludes that while some (especially Heywood's Troia Britanica, 1609) borrow directly from various classical authors, the spirit of all "is mediaeval or early modern, superficially chivalric ...not simple, dignified, unified." After brief consideration of minor plays there follows a learned discussion of Heywood's five "Ages" plays (Golden, Silver, Brazen, Iron I, and Iron II): dates and sources. This is an exhaustive study. Part IV (pp. 726-759) suggests that the striking similarities between Troi. and Heywood's Iron Age I (which he summarizes with Troi. in parallel columns) should be accounted for by a lost play as common ancestor. This hypothesis would also explain the clumsy and inconclusive fifth act of Troi. In the best scholarly fashion, Tatlock admits that his hypothesis is only that and presents the alternative view: Sh used Chaucer, Caxton, Heywood, and some trans. of the Iliad other than Chapman (he lists several possibilities). Part V is a thoughtful consideration of the critical problem of interpreting Troi. in the light of its sources. This art. is a work of thorough scholarship. Over two hundred footnotes testify to Tatlock's command of the Elizabethan documents and of his predecessors' opinions. Little has been done in the past fifty years to refute or supersede this learned work, though Ernest O. Schanzer argues (RES, XI [1960], 18-28 passim) that Heywood was indebted to Sh, and R. K. Presson (#1583, #1584) has argued effectively for Sh's knowledge of Chapman.

1720. Taylor, A. E. "Some Reflections on Shakspere's 'Julius Caesar'," MUM, IV (1905), 113-129.

Ostensibly a comparison between Caesar and Racine's Phèdre and Athalie, this interesting essay actually dwells chiefly on the affinity of Shn tragedy for Aeschylean (both placing emphasis on revelation of character through time, and both including tangential comic elements), and the parallel affinity of French tragedy for Sophoclean (both concerned with the tense revelation of a single aspect of character in a single situation, and excluding all that does not concentrate on that single situation). Taylor's conception of Attic tragedy is too categorical: Agamemnon is tense with unity of focus, and Sophocles never forgets the past which molds the present. But the art. makes some interesting points about Caesar and its relationship to Sh's other tragedies; the play is an abortive attempt to write a classically unified tragedy in which character does not develop. There are two "single-situations," Antony's oration and the quarrel scene, and accordingly the play is two, not one. Ignoring the first two acts, Taylor designates Antony the leading figure of Play No. 1; Brutus is the protagonist of Play No. 2. Sh never afterward attempted the Sophoclean mode, contenting himself with the portrayal of character in transition.

1721. Taylor, George C. "Shakespeare's Attitude Towards Love and Honor in Troilus and Cressida," PMLA, XLV (1930), 781-786.

Rejecting as unsatisfactory the doctrine of Lawrence (#1461), Tatlock (#1718), and Rollins (#1613) that the tone of the play is purely a product of tradition, Taylor expounds the thesis that Sh's plays all show the Hotspur/Falstaff polarity--a delicate balance between the idealization of love and honor and the castigation of both by realism. In Troi., Sh simply allowed the balance to become distorted, failing to temper the cynicism of Pandarus and Thersites with adequate idealism. An interesting approach and well argued, but the importance of tradition should not be underestimated.

1722. Ten Brink, B. Five Lectures on Shakespeare. N.Y., 1895 (no pagination available--as abstracted in the New Variorum Antony).

Ten Brink compares Cleopatra with Juliet and reluctantly admits that the former is enchanting. Cleopatra is Sh's feminine masterpiece, but at the same time she is an indication that his soul had suffered--he could not otherwise have created such a temptress.

1723. Thelemann, Anna. "Dictys als Mitquelle von Shakespeares Troilus," Archiv, CXXXIII (1915), 91-96. E-S SG

Because Sh's play preserves essentially the order of events of Dictys Cretensis' version of the tale of Troy, and because the play contains an element (Achilles' refusal to receive the Greek chieftains in his tent) found in no other source, the author would add Dictys to the list of accepted sources. Two Latin eds. (1552 and 1559) would have been available to Sh, and a French trans. by De la Lande (1556) is particularly close, she thinks, to some of Sh's phrasing. The case does not appear to be clearly established by the evidence.

1724. Thiselton, Alfred E. "'Troilus and Cressida,' I.i.31.--" 9 NQ, III (1899), 423.

Thiselton would restore the F_1 reading of the line to make Troilus accuse himself of treachery to Cressida; emendations and alterations of the punctuation have made him accuse himself of disloyalty to himself.

1725. Thomas, Mary Olive. "Plutarch in Antony and Cleopatra," diss (Duke, 1956).*

1726. Thomas, Mary Olive. "The Repetitions in Antony's Death Scene," SQ, IX (1958), 153-157.

In Antony IV xv, Cleopatra asks her maids twice for help in lifting Antony into the monument and Antony twice tells Cleopatra he is dying. In a complex argument Dr. Thomas considers alternative explanations of the evolution of the text using as a major criterion the fidelity with which various hypothetical versions of the scene conform with North's account of the action.

1727. Thompson, Dorothy B. "The Colossus at Rhodes," SQ, II (1951), 270.

A query as to Sh's source for the information he manifests in Caesar I ii 135-138, Troi. V v 9, and 1H.IV V i 121-124 about the appearance of the Colossus. "Classical authors and monuments do not indicate in any way" that the statue bestrode the harbor or held a torch. (The author might have added Antony V ii 82-83.) There has apparently been no answer to her question.

1728. Thompson, Karl F. "The Feast of Pride in 'Troilus and Cressida'," NQ, CCIII (1958), 193-194.

In the passage about "skittish Fortune's hall" in III iii, Thompson prefers the F_1 reading "pride is feasting" to the Q reading "pride is fasting." The latter refers only to Achilles' abstention from the banquet of war and its honors, but the former reading has more subtle suggestions. Despite Thompson's arguments "fasting" appears at least as good a reading in the light of the whole play.

1729. Thorndike, Ashley H. Tragedy, Types

of English Literature, ed. W. A. Neilson. Boston, 1908, 390 pp. E-S HB

For remarks on the Roman plays as tragedies, see #2145.

1730. Tillyard, E. M. W. "Troilus and Cressida," Shakespeare's Problem Plays (Toronto UP, 1949), pp. 36-93.

A thoughtful analysis of the play which considers the traditional background without neglecting interpretative criticism of the play as drama. Tillyard would emphasize the Medieval sources of the play as against Chapman and the other classicists; he points out that in Homer Sh was confronted with an approach to the legend so different from his own and his age's that he would have been bold to adopt it. Troilus and Ulysses are the pivots upon which the play turns (it is significant that together they witness Cressida's infidelity), but Sh refuses to sentimentalize either of them. There are many passing suggestions of considerable interest: e.g., Stephen Hawes's Pastime of Pleasure contains a brief recapitulation of the traditional aspects of the legend--especially of the rôle of Time, the destroyer; again, does the imagery of commerce in the play mean that Sh identifies the Greeks with the nouveau riche bourgeoisie and the Trojans with a nobler but dying feudal society? A satisfying essay which wisely rejects extreme positions.

1731. Tolman, Albert H. "The Fifth Act of 'Antony and Cleopatra'," Falstaff and Other Shakespearean Topics (N.Y., 1925), pp. 161-168. E-S

Perhaps the most original suggestion in this brief analysis of Cleopatra's behavior is that while loyal to Antony she cannot resist the urge to charm Dolabella, which she does to such effect that she completely ensnares him "in her strong toil of grace," obtaining from him the truth about Caesar's plans. Thus there is a special irony in Caesar's laudatio funebris.

1732. Tolman, Albert H. "Is Shakespeare Aristocratic?" PMLA, XXIX (1914), 277-298. (Reprinted in Falstaff and Other Shakespearean Topics [1925].) E-S

In an essay which answers the question two ways at once, Tolman includes Tim., Cor., Caesar, and Troi. as they reflect Sh's putative attitude toward the mass of men. Of Troi. he makes the surprising remark that "it seems to have been when the poet's mind was least wholesome that it was most aristocratic."

1733. Tolman, Albert H. "The Structure of Shakespeare's Tragedies With Special Reference to Coriolanus," MLN, XXXVII (1922), 449-458. (Reprinted in Falstaff and Other Shakespearean Topics [1925].) E-S

Stating that Sh's fidelity to Plutarch in Cor. has been overestimated, Tolman shows in some detail the changes Sh made, all of them calculated either to intensify the action or to delineate minor characters more fully. One or two he considers infelicitous--the distortion of the source to make the mob despicable accounts for the unpopularity of the play. Tolman's belief that in Cor. "there is no dead point" will not win agreement from those who think that Act IV limps toward Act V.

1734. Tolman, Albert H. "Studies in 'Julius Caesar'," Falstaff and Other Shakespearean Topics (N.Y., 1925), pp. 122-145. E-S

This is a group of ten notes on such questions as "The Relation of the Play to Its Source," the double revelation of Portia's death, and Brutus' soliloquy. None is extensive, but at least two contain interesting observations: (v) the episode of the intruding Cynic Poet and the attempt of Strato to secure service with Octavius are examples of Sh's "unwise acceptance of material found in the source"; (viii) the antecedents of Caesar's rodomontade need not be sought in classical or Renaissance literature--a precedent exists in the bombastic swagger of the Herod of the Mystery plays.

1735. Traversi, D[erek] A. "Coriolanus," Scrutiny, VI (1937), 43-58. (Reprinted in An Approach to Shakespeare [1956].)

An examination of the texture of the verse and prose in the play in pursuit of Sh's elusive attitude toward Rome, his hero, politics, etc. The results are not entirely satisfying, first because Traversi forgets that a play is heard, not read (he speaks of the end of a run-on line as a key position for a word) and secondly because he does not make any systematic examination of Sh's apparent approach to his source. Plutarch comes up once as background for the observation that the farcical treatment of the heroes of antiquity in earlier drama provided Sh a precedent for whatever satiric fun he pokes at his hero. Sh himself had travestied Homeric heroes in Troi. Traversi regards Cor. and Troi. as mutual analogues in language, tone, and theme (war and its heroes).

1736. Traversi, D[erek] A. "The Last Plays: (2) Antony and Cleopatra," An Approach to Shakespeare, revised ed. (Garden City, N.Y., 1956), pp. 235-261.

Through an expert examination of the imagery of Antony, Traversi accounts for the moral ambivalence of the action. The corruption--even rottenness--both of the protagonists and of Rome is made vivid in images of "dungy earth," "Nilus' slime," and "dotage." Yet we are at the same time to accept lust as love and mortal infirmity as transcendent "fire and air." The reconciliation of the paradox lies in Sh's repeated hints that out of slime, dung, and clay comes growth; the language of fertility animates the play, lending stature gradually to the protagonists and making plausible the apotheosis of Act V.

1737. Traversi, D[erek] A. "Love and War in Shakespeare's 'Troilus and Cressida'," Love and Violence, trans. from the French Amour et violence by George Lamb (N.Y., 1954), pp. 35-49. (Amour et violence is a number [by various authors] of Etudes carmélitaines [1946].)

A modified version of #1738.

1738. Traversi, D[erek] A. "'Troilus and Cressida'," Scrutiny, VII (1938), 301-319.

The verse of Troi., with its juxtaposition of hyper-Latinate and Anglo-Saxon diction, reflects the conflict between the "endless self-scrutiny" of the Greeks and the emphasis on will, nature, and desire in Troy. The imagery of food, digestion, and taste also reflects the theme of desire. Like Knight (#1443), to whom he admits indebtedness, Traversi places too much emphasis on the polarities in the play. It is significant, for example, that Achilles is as dominated by carnal desire as Troilus, while the Trojans analyze their motives in keeping Helen as the Greeks question their own behavior at the gates of Troy. Traversi qualifies his thesis, softening the distinction between Greeks and Trojans, in a revised version, #1737. This revised essay is reprinted with minor changes in An Approach to Shakespeare (1956).

1739. Trench, Richard Chenevix. "Plutarch's Parallel Lives," Plutarch: His Life, His Lives and His Morals--Four Lectures (Ln, 1873), pp. 29-72.

The passage (pp. 50-60) on Sh's use of North focuses on Caesar and Antony. Trench devotes more than two pages to a catalogue of incidents in Caesar which derive directly from Plutarch: "the whole play--and the same stands good of Coriolanus no less--is to be found in Plutarch." Yet Sh maintains his "royal pre-eminence" by elaborating hints in North's trans., e.g., Antony's theatrical display of Caesar's torn mantle. Sh had a greater problem in Antony: to dignify a Roman who had led a vile life. Sh solves it by leaving out Antony's early career, which was filled with wickedness, and by showing him under the influence of a "potent Eastern enchantress." Though idealized, Antony does recall the historical personage. Trench feels it necessary to defend Sh against possible charges of having plagiarized from North. DLC

1740. Trevelyan, R. C. "Thersites," LL, XI (1934), 202-210.

An amusing dialogue in Limbo between Cressida and Thersites (and others) which pokes good fun at modern decayed classicism. Trevelyan is a member of the archetypal school of interpreters and suggests that Thersites as a type existed in the experience of the human race before Homer uncovered a fraction of him and Sh a very great deal more.

1741. Tschischwitz, B. "Timon von Athen: Ein kritischer Versuch," ShJ, IV (1869), 160-197.

Tschischwitz disagrees with Delius (#1258) that Sh would have made a partial revision of another's work so late in his career. "Der Fall liegt ... durchaus nicht ausser dem Bereiche der Möglichkeit, dass ein anderer ungleich weniger Berufener sich mit seiner Arbeit könne befasst und sie so zugerichtet haben, wie sie uns leider überliefert worden." Tschischwitz analyzes selected passages and argues (especially on the basis of IV iii) that Sh fused the accounts in Lucian's Τίμων and Plutarch's "Life of Antonius," himself providing the somber tone. The Cynicism in Tim. probably derives from Lucian's βίων πρᾶσις. Sh could have found both of Lucian's works in French or Italian trans. Sh's fusion of sources would account for the duality in the character of Timon (Epicurean and misanthropist), and the other inconsistencies in Tim. could be explained as results of a clumsy cutting of the original play for production (perhaps after Sh's death).

1742. Uhler, John E. "Julius Caesar--a Morality of Respublica," MiamiSS, pp. 96-106.

Sh modified Plutarch's character portraits in order to present such a jaundiced view of the Roman republic as Appian gives. Thus Sh makes Brutus less perfect, Antony less immoral, Caesar less mighty. This leveling process calls attention to the State, the real hero, which Sh sees in a sixteenth-century context: the Respublica of the Tudor Morality play. The argument, especially in derogation of Brutus, is interesting, but despite the leveling of character, Uhler does not persuade that Caesar is an allegory.

1743. Ulrici, H. "Ist Troilus und Cressida Comedy oder Tragedy oder History?" ShJ, IX (1874), 26-40.

Ulrici answers his question with the first of the alternatives, arguing that Thersites, Ajax, and Pandarus establish the "parodisch-satirische Tendenz" of the play while the epilogue leaves the audience with a wry last impression.(See also Th. Bruns's commentary on Pandarus and his epilogue, ibid., XII [1877], 222-227.) Ulrici argues strongly for Sh's knowledge of Chapman's Homer and (perhaps) of a French trans. as well: (1) Thersites does not appear in the Medieval sources of the play, (2) the death of Patroclus is Achilles' motive for killing Hector in Homer and Sh, but not in the Medieval accounts, (3) in Dares and his Medieval imitators it is Troilus, not Hector (as in Homer and Sh) who falls at Achilles' hands as the story ends, (4) Sh's Ulysses as statesman appears to be modeled on the Homeric character. Ulrici insists that Sh is not parodying Homer, however; he suggests that Jonson's pedantry may have been the butt--this would account for the appearance of Aristotle in the Homeric age and for the "schulmeisterlich" tenor of Hector's speech about Aristotle.

1744. V., G. "Zu Antonius und Cleopatra," ShJ, XII (1877), 320-321.

Quoting Plutarch (in German trans.) as support, V. argues that the incident of Seleucus and the treasures (Antony V ii 138-175) has not been prearranged by Cleopatra. It impresses Caesar with her desire to live, but is nonetheless a spontaneous incident both in Plutarch and in Sh.

1745. Vatke, Theodor. "Shakespeare's Antonius und Kleopatra und Plutarch's Biographie des Antonius," ShJ, III (1868), 301-340. E-S

"Uns scheint die ganze in der Tragödie dargestellte Welt nur Folie zur Entwicklung des Liebesverhältnisses." The body of the art. is a detailed seriatim summary and analysis of Antony with frequent reference to Plutarch and occasional digressions on Sh's conception of history and character (the most interesting of these compares and contrasts Caesar the history play with Antony the personal tragedy). The seriatim treatment of the play has the advantage of giving due attention to numerous scenes and passages which are often neglected by criticism. Vatke insists on the tension between the heroic and the hedonistic in Antony; he argues that Sh's most radical departure from the historical facts in Plutarch comes in Act V where Sh's Cleopatra dies for love of Antony--Plutarch's Cleopatra dies because Fortune has deserted her. Many modern critics place morality and politics closer to the core of the play than Vatke places them.

1746. Viehoff, Heinrich. "Shakespeare's Coriolan," ShJ, IV (1869), 41-61.

This sensitive analysis begins with a rejection of the idea that Cor. is part of a Roman national tetralogy, corresponding with the history plays; Viehoff also rejects the theory that politics are the core of the play. He prefers to see Coriolanus (hero first, Patrician second, and Roman third) as the central concern of the action. Coriolanus is a hero of Achilles' type: his boldness, courage, anger, pride, and family loyalty all belong to the heroic age, but the Rome he lives in is anti-heroic. Viehoff offers excellent character sketches of Menenius, Aufidius (whose heroism reinforces Coriolanus' as Hector's parallels Achilles'), and Volumnia with her foil, Virgilia. The seriatim summary and analysis of the action in Aristotelian terms is equally rewarding as it shows Sh's artistry in first paralleling and later fusing two conflicts: Coriolanus' quarrel with the people and his relations with the Volscians. If Sh does not maintain unity of time and place he does have unity of character, the highest of the unities. Viehoff does not make Plutarch a major part of his discussion: had he done so he could have found evidence to support his reading of the play.

1747. Viehoff, Heinrich. "Shakespeare's Julius Cäsar," ShJ, V (1870), 6-36. E-S

Viehoff interprets Caesar much as he interprets Cor. (#1746): "Brutus' Charakter und sein in diesem Charakter wurzelndes verhängnissvolles Handeln und tragisches Geschick bilden den Angelpunkt des ganzen Dramas."

Sh is concerned here not with history or politics, but with psychology, which he found in Plutarch's account of a high-minded man who killed his friend and benefactor. But Plutarch's account was only a hint; the Brutus whom Viehoff eulogizes as "zugleich ein herrliches Mannes-Ideal und ein Musterbild edler Menschlichkeit, ein Gemüth voll selbstbewusster Kraft und zugleich voll Liebe," etc., is largely Sh's creation. Sh denigrates Caesar to emphasize Brutus' perfections, and uses Cassius and Antony as analogue and contrast, respectively, to focus interest on his protagonist. Viehoff provides a detailed seriatim analysis of the action with occasional reference to Aristotelian structural concepts. Caesar, he concludes, is magnificently unified by centrality of characterization, and portrays the paradoxical thesis about Brutus: "Seine Schuld ist zugleich seine Ehre."

1748. Voltaire, F. M. de. "[On Shakespeare's Julius Caesar]," Théâtre de Corneille (Paris, 1765), II, 262 (as trans. and abstracted in the New Variorum Caesar).

Voltaire's famous condemnation of the play as a "monstrous spectacle," "absurd," "barbarous," "bizarre," etc. This is the essay which excited the wrath of Mrs. Montagu (#0426) and many another of Johnson's contemporaries.

1749. Waith, E[ugene] M. "Manhood and Valor in Two Shakespearean Tragedies," ELH, XVII (1950), 262-273.

For classical attitudes toward masculinity in Cor. and Antony, see #2154.

1750. Waith, Eugene M. "The Metamorphosis of Violence in Titus Andronicus," ShS, X (1957), 39-49.

Waith explains the repellent combination of violent horror and florid rhetoric in Titus as Sh's deliberate attempt to dramatize the spirit of Ovid's Meta. as he understood it. Ovid portrays humans as transformed physically and psychically by unlimited passions induced by violent outrage. The rhetorical elaboration glosses the vivid narrative and description, putting a "psychic distance" between the reader and the pitiable and horrifying events Ovid describes. In Titus, however, the mutilated reality is presented to the view of the audience--rhetoric cannot establish the proper "psychic distance"; ergo the play fails. This is an ingenious explanation of the problem of the play. There are, however, many metamorphoses in Ovid and some characters and events in Titus which do not fit the pattern. Waith has selected from Ovid the metamorphoses of Niobe, Hecuba, and Philomela, Procne, and Tereus, probably because they are referred to in the play, but many of Ovid's other transformations (Baucis and Philemon, e.g.) have nothing to do with outrage or strong passions. Then, too, of the characters in Titus, only the hero, Tamora, and Lavinia fit Waith's scheme. Waith is surely illuminating the play by tracing it to Meta., but his interpretation does not account for as much of Ovid or of Titus as he assumes.

1751. [Walker, Alice]. "Introduction," Troilus and Cressida (1957), CSh, [XXV], pp. ix-xlvi.

Dr. Walker reads the play as a satire in which the Trojans "wear the motley with better grace but . . . are as much the victims of ruling passions as the Greeks." With the exception of Ulysses, Sh's "commentator," no one emerges unscathed (Dr. Walker does not note that Ulysses, like Hector, gives excellent advice and then takes himself an exactly opposed course of action). The lack of rational prudence among the Trojans may reflect Laocoon's criticism of his fellow citizens for accepting the wooden horse in Aeneid II. Sh's allusions to the Troy story in other plays show that he took the fall of the city seriously but regarded the lovers as comic material. This introduction contains a rewarding discussion of Sh's imagery in the play, a discussion which Dr. Walker regards as an argument against disintegration. In her consideration of sources she questions whether Sh used Homer and Chaucer; the major sources were clearly Caxton, Ovid (from whom Sh got his theme of Time as well as the beef-witted Ajax), and the Renaissance tradition (possibly including lost plays on the Trojan story). This is a valuable commentary, although it is not possible to agree with the editor that Troilus is entirely a ridiculous figure nor that Hector is the butt of satire; the play carries too large a burden of moral wisdom to be merely a scornful critique of a traditional legend.

1752. Walker, Roy. "Antony and Cleopatra," TLS, May 29, 1953, p. 349.

After discussing the problems of staging the dying Antony's elevation into Cleopatra's monument in IV xv, Walker points out that Plutarch's account has blinded critics to the dramatic effects Sh aimed at in the scene. He offers three alternatives: (1) the scene symbolizes Antony's apotheosis—he is raised up to Isis; (2) the scene symbolizes Antony's final enslavement by Cleopatra; (3) Sh deliberately left the scene ambiguous. Walker prefers (3).

1753. Wall, Annie Russell. "Is Shakespeare's Caesar Ignoble?" PL, IV (1892), 191-199.

This panegyric of the historical Caesar gives a biased account of the action and motivation of Sh's play in which Brutus is "a murderer and a traitor" while Caesar's greatness is deliberately clouded lest the audience refuse to tolerate his murderers on the stage. Not a very persuasive interpretation, especially when the author, like Dante, consigns Brutus' remains to deepest hell, where, to a greater extent than Cassius, he partakes of the vileness and the punishment of his confrere, Judas.

1754. Warner, Alan. "A Note on Antony and Cleopatra," English, XI (1957), 139-144.

Like Waith (#2154), whom he does not mention, Warner anticipates Barroll (#1145), who does not mention him, in interpreting Antony as a play about virility turned effeminate and *ergo* destroying itself. This theme of subjection of the male to the female (the personification of his own carnality) is exemplified in classical myth by the Hercules-Omphale legend. It is significant that Antony identifies himself with Hercules in both the play and its source.

1755. Way, Arthur S. "The Quarrel Scene in 'Julius Caesar'," LQR, CLI (1929), 50-58.

A reverent tribute to Brutus as the personification of Roman *virtus*. Sh avoided the realistic details of Plutarch in order to idealize his hero. The school of Way's criticism can best be indicated by a quotation: "As he faces Cassius in the tent, between him and those lowering eyes, that passion-writhen face, comes the vision of a darkened chamber far away, dim with a deadly mist of stifling fume, of a couch whereon a dear form lies stretched in awful stillness ..."

1756. Wecter, Dixon. "Shakespere's Purpose in Timon of Athens," PMLA, XLIII (1928), 701-721.

Wecter offers the suggestion that Timon, who resembles neither the Misanthrope of Lucian "whose delight is to jeer at humanity" nor the "silly voluptuary of the academic farce," is in reality a portrait of Essex, whom Sh wished to rehabilitate now that Elizabeth was dead. However, when similar efforts got other authors into difficulties, Sh suppressed the play and later a reviser hacked it to pieces for stage presentation to obscure the allegory. This extensively documented theory is now universally rejected—most of the evidence is unimpressive. Wecter believes that Sh did not know Lucian.

1757. Wedgwood, Julia. "Shakespere's 'Julius Caesar'," CR, LXIII (1893), 356-368.

From the time of the ostracism of Aristides the Just and the exile of the Tarquins until the advent of Christianity the classical world had a great distrust of personality in political life. The cult of personality as practiced by the admirers of Elizabeth was alien to the spirit of the ancient world. The remarkable achievement of Sh was to recapture that classical spirit in the attitude of Brutus and others toward Caesar's attempt to establish himself as a personality in Rome. This is the reason for Sh's portrayal of Caesar as thrasonical and idiosyncratic. An interesting approach to the problems of the play, but Miss Wedgwood gives no hint as to Sh's source of information about personality or its absence in classical politics.

1758. Weiss, John. "Troilus and Cressida (Ajax)," Wit Humor and Shakspeare: Twelve Essays (Boston, 1876), pp. 90-104.

In a lively, rambling characterization of the play, Weiss attempts to persuade that Sh parodies in the lovers the serious rape which caused the war and that Ajax is another Malvolio in his comic self-esteem. Weiss's facetious but charming depreciation of what is serious in the play almost convinces that "when the ugly thing stands thus stripped of its Homeric mantle, we hurry to demand that it shall be decently clothed in travesty." But the author's implausible theory of disintegration should put the reader on his guard against the enchantments of a witty style.

1759. Wells, William. The Authorship of Julius Caesar. Ln, 1923, 225 pp.

As extreme a case as one is likely to find of vivisection. Wells seriously believes that Caesar is "an old play by Marlowe (with the possible assistance of Peele), the present revision of which was commenced by Shakespeare and finished by Beaumont." The argument rests almost entirely on verbal parallels; Wells also makes something of his opinion that Caesar deviates from Plutarch more than Antony and Cor. do. The fallacy in both arguments is the assumption that literary figures can be counted upon to repeat closely what they have once succeeded at--to follow predictable patterns of language and source manipulation --and that playwrights do not consciously or unconsciously imitate one another. It is ironic that a play which is now regarded as one of Sh's most tightly knit dramatically should here be treated as the work of as many as four individualists. MnU

1760. Wendlandt, Wilhelm. "Shakepeare's [sic] Timon von Athen," ShJ, XXIII (1888), 107-192.

This detailed, somewhat verbose art. anticipates recent views (#1287, #1491, #1554) in arguing that Tim. as it appears in F_1 is Sh's unfinished work. Wendlandt rejects theories which would make Sh a collaborator, a reviser of another's work, or a victim of some hack's tampering. Two useful features are a full commentary on earlier scholarship and a painstaking seriatim discussion of the play. Wendlandt minimizes source study in favor of verse tests, bibliographical analysis, and thematic comparison with unquestionably canonical plays.

1761. Westbrook, Perry D. "Horace's Influence on Shakespeare's 'Antony and Cleopatra'," PMLA, LXII (1947), 392-398.

Sh's Cleopatra dies with a regal majesty absent from the account of Plutarch, but apparent in Horace's magnificent Ode ("Nunc est bibendum"). The conclusion is that the Cleopatra of the last two acts is based in part at least on Horace. Westbrook cites Baldwin (#0089) as evidence that Sh was capable of reading Horace in Latin.

1762. Westenholz, Friedrich von. Idee und Charaktere in Shakespeares Julius Cäsar. Stuttgart, 1897, 39 pp. E-S

Not seen. MiU NNU PU(F)

1763. Wetherell, J. "Shakespeare Reading," Ath, No. 1960 (1865), 692.

Wetherell suggests that in Caesar II i 28 (Brutus' soliloquy justifying the conspiracy) the word "sequel" makes a better reading in the light of Brutus' character than does "quarrel." This emendation does not appear necessary.

1764. Wherry, George. "Julius Caesar's Deafness," 10 NQ, XI (1909), 243.

Wherry guesses that Caesar may have had aural vertigo which his contemporaries confused with epilepsy. This might account also for the story of his deafness. B. Leake points out (ibid., 425) that no classical authority for Caesar's deafness exists; Sh invented the infirmity.

1765. Whitaker, Virgil K. "Julius Caesar and Tragedy of Moral Choice," Shakespeare's Use of Learning... [see #0635], Ch. X, pp. 224-250.

This detailed reading of the play finds in it Sh's first use of moral choice as a central pivot of drama. The tragedy is that of Brutus, who is a good man tempted by his pride to commit the sin of regicide. Sh deliberately altered details in Plutarch to make Caesar more noble and Brutus less so. The audience, trained in dialectic, would be expected to recognize the logical fallacies of Brutus' soliloquy and the logical merits of Antony's. About the soliloquies Whitaker is obviously correct, but in his exculpation of Caesar he is not entirely convincing: e.g., he compares Caesar's falling sickness to Roosevelt's paralysis and insists that both rulers gain in stature by surmounting physical defects; Whitaker has not considered that neither the Romans nor the Elizabethans were influenced by the Humanitarian movement. But this ch. is a valuable contribution to Caesar criticism.

1766. Whitaker, Virgil K. "Philosophy and Romance in Shakespeare's 'Problem' Comedies," Jones Festschrift, pp. 339-354.

Whitaker sees the "dark" comedies, especially Troi. and Meas., as extensions of Sh's tragic vision (the defeat of reason by passion). Sh tried to convey this tragic vision in plays based on romances, not appropriate to philosophical statement. Because he did not bother to alter his materials, he appears to be working toward mutually incompatible goals, but as Whitaker repeats in Shakespeare's Use of Learning (#1767), Troi. is nonetheless central in Sh's intellectual development.

1767. Whitaker, Virgil K. "Troilus and Cressida and Measure for Measure," Shakespeare's Use of Learning... [see #0635], Ch. IX, pp. 194-223.

The first part of this interesting ch. posits that "Troilus and Cressida is, in fact, the keystone in the arch of Shakespeare's intellectual development, however rough-hewn and misshapen it may be." It contains, as only partially assimilated statement, a large burden of wisdom about reason and passion and their relationship to order and chaos--a burden too heavy for the thin romance Sh chose to bear it. In the tragedies he was able to assimilate fully such moral concepts into the dramatic texture. Cf. Whitaker's earlier treatment of the same ideas, #1766.

1768. White, Richard G. "Glossaries and Lexicons," Studies in Shakespeare (Boston, 1886), pp. 280-363.

For Plato in Troi. and Caesar, see #1104.

1769. Whitney, Ernest. "Shakspere's Julius Caesar," NEYR, XLV (1886), 862-867.

Whitney believes there is evidence that Sh once intended Caesar as two plays (cf. 1,2 H.IV) and hastily welded the two together: it is noteworthy that fifteen characters drop out of the action with the death of Caesar while thirteen new ones are later introduced. Whitney also argues for major changes in the act-division of the first three acts, but his proposals would leave Act III devoid of a major turning point in the action.

1770. Wickert, Maria. "Antikes Gedankengut in Shakespeares Julius Cäsar," ShJ, LXXXII/LXXXIII (1948), 11-33.

Two excellent notes on the play. The first shows that Brutus' Forum speech is a masterful bit of oratory on the principles of Quintilian and Cicero; it relies heavily on tricolon which structures both the whole and the individual parts. Brutus is spoken of as a practiced orator by Antony (III ii 222-235) and Octavius (V i 28). It would be interesting to apply this analysis to Brutus' problematical soliloquy at II i 10-34. There are several thoughtful suggestions here: e.g., that the crowd's willingness to "let [Brutus] be Caesar" comes from a passage in the "Life of Caesar": "they that desired change ...wished Brutus onely their prince and governor above all other." It seems plain, however, that the conclusion that Brutus' oration puts Antony's in the shade is an overstatement. The second note treats "the spirit of Caesar," by which Sh meant what the Romans meant by genius and the Greeks by δαίμων. Sh fused his conception of Caesar's revenging spirit with Plutarch's statement that Caesar's "good fortune ...did continue afterwards in the revenge of his death ..." Sh, in making Caesar's revenge a personal triumph, follows in the tradition of Senecan revenges, avoiding the Renaissance Christian interpretation in which God punished the conspirators for murder. Sh unifies the play by investing Caesar's genius with a majesty unencumbered by the mythological apparatus which enlarges Henry in H.V II iv 99-101.

1771. Wilcox, John. "Love in Antony and Cleopatra," PMA, XXI (1935), 531-544.

An interesting interpretation of the alterations Sh made in Plutarch. The most important of them was the elimination of moral condemnation of hero and heroine. Antony is Everyman confronted with the impossible choice between a career (Adler) and love (Freud). No matter how he chooses he will later be dissatisfied. Cleopatra is never disloyal and only thwarts Antony to test his love. After she has definitively satisfied herself, at Actium, of his attachment to her, she becomes submissive and a generous, tender lover to him. But the irony for her is that the test has destroyed the man. Realizing this, she is patient with Antony even in his violent anger and gladly dies to join him. The emphasis which Wilcox places on the emotions of the characters minimizes the political import of the action; this may be unwise in the light of the political orientation of all Sh's other Greek and Roman plays.

1772. Wildenbruch, Ernst von. "Einleitende Worte zu einer Vorlesung von 'Antonius und Cleopatra'," ShJ, L (1914), 1-3. E-S

A vivid sketch of the historical events which lie behind Sh's play. There is no discussion of Sh's access to knowledge of these events, but Wildenbruch does recall a saying of Mommsen: "'Wenn Sie sich Persönlichkeit und Charakter des Antonius vorstellen wollen, so lesen Sie Shakespeares Antonius und Cleopatra'."

1773. Wiley, Edwin. "A Study of the Supernatural in Three Plays of Shakespeare (1) Julius Caesar," CUC, XV (1913), 490-501. SG

In writing Caesar, Sh came under the influence of Plutarch's supernaturalism, which is manifest throughout the play. In fact, Sh goes beyond Plutarch to make the spirit of Caesar greater than his body (which explains the references to his physical infirmities) and to emphasize its posthumous dominance over the events of Acts IV and V. The play is well titled, and only the distorted emphasis of "ambitious actors" has made the rôles of Brutus and Cassius seem the core of the play. The influence of Plutarch's supernaturalism continues through Ham. and Macb., though it is not borrowed directly in those plays. Wiley persuades that Caesar's spirit is the moving force in Acts IV and V, but it is difficult to agree with him that Brutus and Cassius are minor figures.

1774. Williams, Charles. "The Cycle of Shakespeare," The English Poetic Mind (OUP, 1932), pp. 29-109.

Williams examines most of the canon, treating it as a document stamped with "the growth of a poet's mind." The most important page of the document is Troi., in which Sh explores paradox as he had not done before, even in Ham. Troi. is a play in which discord and concord are one, yet disparate and opposed. Sh reflects the paradox in the language (Latinate and intellectual in passionate contexts), in inconclusive debates on philosophical issues, in vigorous action which leads to no goal, and especially in the agonized paradox uttered by Troilus, "This is, and is not, Cressid." Troilus' plunge into psychological chaos is an exemplification of the principles stated by Ulysses in Act I in the degree speech. Williams' criticism is challenging, if not always lucid.

1775. Williams, Talcott. "Shakespeare's Fidelity to History," PL, XIII (1901), 91-97.

The remarks on Sh's North are brief and general. Because North, like Plutarch, was an artist, Sh instinctively followed him more closely than need be, including characters who have little dramatic function simply because they appear in North.

1776. Wilson, Elkin. "Shakespeare's Enobarbus," AMS, pp. 391-408.

A sensitive analysis of the character. Wilson shows that Enobarbus is almost wholly Sh's creature, since Plutarch no more than mentions him in the "Life of Antony." His rôle is that of the Greek Chorus, speaking truth humanely.

1777. Wilson, F. P. "Shakespeare," Elizabethan and Jacobean (OUP, 1945), pp. 109-130.

The plays on classical themes are treated briefly passim in this allusive survey. Wilson makes two observations of special interest: (1) When he wrote the Roman plays Sh, for the first and almost the only time, used a great writer as source; yet Plutarch has no unity in his Lives--Sh's great contribution was organic form. (2) Troi. is not a satire, but "a tragedy of treachery and a tragedy of lechery." There is precedent for Sh's distortion of Homer in a 1599 pamphlet which accuses Homer "of making a dog of Agamemnon, a kitchen-fellow of Patroclus, a madman of Hector, and of Achilles a mere brothel humour ..."

1778. Wilson, H. Schütz. "Shakespeare's Two Characters of Antony and Cleopatra," The Theatre, n.s. IX (1887), 127-139.

This analysis of the characterization states that Sh is almost solely responsible for the protagonists: North's Plutarch provided only hints, though excellent ones. There are some interesting suggestions: Antony is a more various character than Cleopatra, whose duplicity, as a dominant trait, renders her less complex. Antony has the more imaginative nature--at least he speaks the more imaginative poetry. But Wilson is unable to see anything but evil in Cleopatra: he even maintains that she sent Mardian with the false report of her death knowing it would lead Antony to suicide; she hoped to please Caesar by procuring the death of her lover.

1779. Wilson, Harold S. On the Design of Shakespearian Tragedy, TST, V (Toronto UP, 1957), 256 pp.

Discarding the chronology of the canon as irrelevant, Wilson juxtaposes two main sets of tragedies, concluding that Antony and Lear are a synthesis of the two opposed sets. The first set is Christian in its values: Romeo and Ham. represent Providence bringing good out of evil; Oth. and Macb. represent Providence punishing evil. The second set is pre-Christian in its values: Caesar and Cor. show classical Nemesis pursuing and destroying men for hamartia; Tim. and Troi. show satirically, yet tragically, the pagan social order itself as corrupt and deserving of punishment. These pairs of theses and antitheses are resolved in Antony and Lear, which, while "classical" in their ethics, thematically announce the triumph of love, sexual and familial. The criticism of the individual plays is unusually provocative, readable, and well-informed. But it is surely cavalier to dismiss chronological development

—Sh did not waver among Hegelian theses, antitheses, and syntheses again and again over a fifteen-year period; artists do not work that way. Wilson also leaves out Titus and the tragic English history plays—they do not fit his matrix. But the book remains very valuable for its insights into Sh's classicism.

1780. Wilson, J. Dover. "Ben Jonson and Julius Caesar," ShS, II (1949), 36-43.

Jonson referred to Caesar four times, at least three times somewhat contemptuously; all four citations have to do with the classicism of Sh's play. But Wilson defends Sh's classicism in three of the four cases: i.e., (1) accurate Aristotelian psychology in "O judgment, thou art fled to brutish beasts," (III ii 110); (2) "orthodox Galenic physiology" in Antony's eulogy of dead Brutus (V v 73-75); (3) the famous "just cause" crux (III i 47). The passage Wilson does not defend is Caesar's dying Latin rather than Greek: "Et tu Brute" (III i 77) rather than "καὶ σὺ τέκνον." The general contention is that Jonson felt "rancor" because Sh had daringly surpassed him on his own classical ground by writing Caesar despite his "small Latine."

1781. W[ilson], J. D[over]. "Introduction," Antony and Cleopatra (1950), CSh, [XXXV], pp. vii-xxxvi.

Wilson discusses Sh's conception of Cleopatra the "gipsy," African rather than Greek; but he also shows that Sh transcended Plutarch's pejorative view, anticipating modern scholars to whom Cleopatra was a talented, intelligent, forceful, and charming woman beyond her considerable sexual magnetism. Sh seems to have known little more than Plutarch's account (perhaps Daniel's first version of Cleopatra and Leo Africanus' History of Africa, and very probably the Countess of Pembroke's Antonie): "The only deity he mentions is Isis, a name he finds in Plutarch, and it recurs so often that it is obvious he had no other to make play with." But the verisimilitude of the play is striking: "the universe in which Brutus and Cassius move is still post-medieval, while that of Antony and his mistress has become, with one exception, Roman; the exception being the ... contempt they both express for this 'little O, the earth,' and even that Shakespeare might have explained, had Jonson taxed him with it, as a kind of stoicism." Wilson argues that the Mediterranean world of the play is only a backdrop to the tragedy of the two lovers; at the same time he points out that Antony's soldiership is often underestimated by critics: Antony would doubtless be bearded like his ancestor, Hercules, and clothed in his lion's skin on Sh's stage. The character analyses and the discussion of Acts IV and V are particularly satisfying.

1782. W[ilson], J. D[over]. "Introduction," Julius Caesar (1949), CSh, [XXX], pp. vii-xxxiii.

Wilson argues that Suetonius and Lucan (both of whom he thinks Sh may have read) shaped the Renaissance approach to the assassination story, an approach which Sh takes when he denigrates Caesar. He denies that there was ambivalence in the connotations of Caesar's name in the Middle Ages and Renaissance (he regards Dante as "a Ghibelline and imperialist exception"). The story is not the tragedy of the conspirators but the tragedy of Roman republicanism which goes down to defeat at the hands of "Caesarism" (i.e., arrogant dictatorship) bringing a great era of commonwealth to an end. This political theme tightly unifies a play which at the same time is humanized by Sh's concern with the private lives of some of his cast. Wilson discusses Sh's manipulation of Plutarch to pejorate Caesar, and includes an illuminating interpretation of the quarrel scene and a defense of Brutus' soliloquy. There are several passing remarks on other Shn plays--one of special interest interprets Antony III xiii 111-115 as Sh's definition of Até, a principle which also operates in Caesar when Caesar struts before his fall. The equation which Wilson implies between Caesar and twentieth-century dictators has been much criticized; it is difficult to believe that Tudor Sh would have taken so dim a view of monarchy and empire as Wilson finds in Caesar.

1783. W[ilson], J. D[over]. "Introduction," The Tragedy of Coriolanus (1960), CSh, [XXVI], pp. ix-xl.

Wilson reasons that Sh used no other source for Cor. than Plutarch except in Menenius' fable, where traces of Livy (Holland's trans.) and Camden (Remaines) can be discerned. Sh did, however, take liberties with Plutarch, introducing the women and Aufidius early in the play, condensing and fusing incidents in the "Life," and blackening the character of the populace (not for political, but for dramatic reasons). Wilson argues further that criticism has been wrong to see Coriolanus as a proud man; he is choleric and too honest to conceal the contempt for the Plebeians which he shares with other Patricians. Wilson's view of the hero and of the dramatic structure in which he moves is not unlike that of S. K. Sen (#1645). A rewarding introduction to the play.

1784. W[ilson], J. D[over]. "Introduction: An Essay in Literary Detection," Titus Andronicus (1948), CSh, [XXVII], pp. vii-lxv.

Wilson dismisses the question of classical affinity by alluding briefly to Titus as a neo-Senecan "tragedy of blood" and by denying that Roman history lies at the foundation of the play. The bulk of the introduction is a complicated set of arguments intended to persuade that Sh and Peele were collaborators in a revision of an existing play in late 1593, Peele being largely responsible for Act I and Sh for the rest. Wilson relies heavily on stylistic judgments (which he admits are intuitive) and on verbal echoes. To protect Sh against possible charges of having given his approval as reviser to hyperbolic fustian, Wilson argues (1) that the revision was made in great haste, (2) that Sh wrote his parts of the play with tongue in cheek.

1785. Wilson, J. Dover. "'Titus Andronicus' on the Stage in 1595," ShS, I (1948), 17-22.

This is a preliminary attempt to account for the inconsistencies between the Longleat drawing of Titus and its text. Wilson admits that his conclusions are tentative and he welcomes controversy. He thinks the text may have been added after 1623 to a drawing made ca. 1595. The most important observation for this Guide is that the drawing gives strong evidence that Sh's Roman plays were staged with the aristocratic characters in classical costume and the lower classes dressed as Elizabethans.

1786. Wimsatt, W. K., Jr. "Poetry and Morals: A Relation Reargued," Thought, XXIII (1948), 281-299.

A part of this essay analyzes Antony to show that a work of art may be beautiful though its values are immoral. Sh might register surprise at Mr. Wimsatt's neo-Hegelian assumption that the play defends immoralism.

1787. Winchell, Walter B. "Shakspere's Two Delineations of Mark Antony," HLM, XV (1881), 205-209.

A rather sternly moralistic response to both Caesar and Antony. Antony would have been better off had Cassius and Brutus taken him at his word (Caesar III i 157-160); had they stabbed him then, he would not have been corrupted by Cleopatra. Antony is a "profligate" in Egypt, while he had been only a "'masker and reveller'" in republican Rome. The rôle of Antony in the two plays "tells us that there is a right that brings its sure reward: that there is a wrong that meets its just retribution." Winchell points out the ironic fact that Antony who is the conquerer in Caesar, becomes the conquered in Antony; he kills himself just as the conquered conspirators had done in the earlier play. DLC

1788. Winter, W. "[On Antony and Cleopatra]," Old Shrines and Ivy (N.Y., 1892) (no exact pagination available--as abstracted in the New Variorum Antony).

Winter's criticism is lyric, but he recognizes that Antony has moral overtones: though Antony and Cleopatra are magnificent in their utter commitment to love, the catastrophe is inevitable, and it is prefigured in their passion. Winter emphasizes the magniloquence of the play; he sees no reason to probe Sh's relationship to Plutarch, being content with Sh's fascinating language and the characters who speak it.

1789. Wölcken, F. "Shakespeares Julius Caesar und Marlowes Massacre at Paris," ShJ, LXIII (1927), 192-194.

Without discussing Sh's sources in Plutarch for Caesar's character, Wölcken suggests that "die Haltung des reineren Heros [Caesar] auf die Darstellung des minderen [Marlowe's Duke of Guise] abgefärbt hat." He compares speeches expressing contempt for death and places Sh's "Yet Caesar shall go forth" (II ii 28) beside the Guise's dying line, "Thus Caesar did go forth, and thus he died" (Scene xviii, l. 87 in H. S. Bennett's ed.).

1790. Wölffel, Heinrich. "Ueber Shakespeare's Coriolan," ALVN (1864), 1-54.

An eloquent defense of Coriolanus against charges that he is a selfish, proud, "junkerisch" contemner of the Roman people. Wölffel sees the hero as a great patriot who loves Rome far more than he loves himself and who is a needed surgeon to the city's diseases. The eulogy is overstated; it is surely a distortion to interpret Coriolanus' reaction to the appointment of five Tribunes (I i 219-225) as Wölffel does: "von Hohn und Dünkel ist an dieser Stelle wenigstens keine Spur in seinen Worten zu finden." The remarks on Sh's use of Plutarch are very brief. Wölffel begins with interesting observations about the numerous Coriolanus plays for which Sh's great tragedy provided a model—as yet unequaled. MH

1791. Wood, Frederick T. "Shakespeare and the Plebs," Essays and Studies, XVIII (1932), 53-73.

This defense of Sh against the frequent charge that he despised the lower classes identifies a number of honest, loyal, dignified commoners like Old Adam in A.Y.L. But the chief argument is that Sh liked the commoners as individuals but understood mob psychology enough to know that they are stupid and irresponsible in crowds. Cor. and Caesar are the two chief mob plays, and they show two stages of man's relation to the state: in Cor. the Plebeians have no real rights in the state—they are not Rome but its rats, and the Patricians abhor them; by the (historical) time of Caesar the mob has become the state, and Caesar, Brutus, Cassius, and Antony do not hesitate to cater to it. In both plays Sh draws the rôle of the Plebeians from Plutarch.

1792. Wright, Austin. "Antony and Cleopatra," Shakespeare: Lectures on Five Plays by Members of the Department of English, Carnegie Institute of Technology, CSE, No. 4 (1958), pp. 37-51.

Directed to undergraduates, this lecture is as much an appreciation as an analysis of the play. Wright does not mention Plutarch, though he does touch on the historical situation of Rome in the years after the death of Julius Caesar. The emphasis falls entirely on character at the expense of action; Wright speaks of the greatness of Antony which emerges only after his folly has reduced him to the point where he has nothing left to lose. Of Cleopatra he says less that contributes to an understanding of her character. There are remarks on Menas, Pompey, Ventidius, Enobarbus, and others.

1793. Wright, Ernest H. The Authorship of Timon of Athens. ColSE[CL?], 1910, 104 pp. E-S SG

Wright dissects Tim., excising ten scenes and passages which he considers inferior to Sh even at his worst. These he ascribes to an unnamed reviser of Sh's original, unfinished work. The reviser greatly misunderstood Sh's proposed plan which Wright attempts to reconstruct in a final ch. of speculation. The fallacy of Wright's hypothesis is common to most attempts at disintegration: the judgments as to what is characteristically Shn are of necessity subjective, even intuitive. But Wright's book has value because of his thorough and cautious development of the source problems in the play. He is inclined to reject Boiardo and his imitator del Carretto; if Sh read them he did not follow them when they deviated from Plutarch and Lucian (on this point cf. Bond, #1165). Sh definitely used both the "Life of Antonius" and the "Life of Alcibiades," and the evidence is strong that he knew the academic Timon (he includes the mock banquet and the loyal steward, both introduced by the author of the English play). Sh may also have read Lucian's dialogue, but it would not have been necessary if he knew the academic play. Lucian would be accessible in French and Italian. On the whole a persuasive argument about sources; not persuasive at all about dismemberment.

1794. Wyndham, George. "The Poems of Shakespeare," Essays in Romantic Literature, ed. Charles Whibley (Ln, 1919), pp. 237-388.

Section VIII (290-305) follows Small (#1665) in interpreting Troi. as a document in the "poetomachia": the Greeks are the neo-classicists (Chapman, Jonson = Ajax, and Marston = Thersites) while the decent Trojans are the romantic dramatists, who are "English" (and therefore Trojan). Wyndham's theory would account for the vigorous scurrility of the play and for its anti-Hellenic bias, but it must be remembered that both scurrility and bias were in the Medieval tradition out of which the play sprang.

1795. Yardley, E. "Shakespeare and Cicero," 9 NQ, VI (1900), 317-318.

Yardley points out two errors in Troi. but gives classical authority for one (Hesione as the mother of Ajax--IV v 132-135) and shows that Milton also made the other (a Greek refers to Boreas by his Latin name--IV v 9).

1796. Yates, Frances A. "Queen Elizabeth as Astraea," JWCI, X (1947), 27-82.

This enviably learned study treats the identification of Elizabeth with Astraea the just by her courtiers, poets, churchmen, and political propagandists. Miss Yates traces the political and religious connotations which accrued to the Greek myth from Ovid through the Italian Middle Ages to the English Renaissance, documenting her analysis at every point. Sh's two references to Astraea (1H.VI I vi 4; Titus IV iii 4) are discussed in two pages (70-72). The whole scene in which Titus shoots arrows at the constellations Miss Yates would interpret as a political and spiritual allegory: Lucius, who is namesake of the putative first Christian king of England, strikes Virgo with his arrow, and of course Virgo is Astraea's stellar name. The theme of the play is thus epitomized in the scene, for justice in the Empire is abrogated by Saturninus (Saturn's opposite) and restored at length by Lucius. The reference to Astraea in 1H.VI is an identification with Joan la Pucelle, and at this point Miss Yates dismisses it, but later points out that since Virgo was influential in the horoscope of France Sh's reference was appropriate.

1797. York, Ernest C. "Shakespeare and Nashe," NQ, CXCVIII (1953), 370-371.

The ghastly detail of having Lavinia raped across the butchered body of her husband is a close parallel to the rape of Heraclide in Nashe's Unfortunate Traveller. The detail does not appear in the Ovidian tale of Philomela, nor in other versions of Titus. In this discovery York was anticipated by John D. Ebbs (MLN, LXVI [1951], 480-481), who shows that the relationship has importance for dating Titus, regardless whether Sh or Nashe was the borrower.

1798. Zandvoort, R. W. "Brutus's Forum Speech in Julius Caesar," RES, XVI (1940), 62-66. (Reprinted in Collected Papers [1954].)

The examination of rhetorical features of the speech shows that it is rich in isocolon, parison, and paromoion, the three chief structural features of euphuism. Thus the contrast between Brutus' oration and Antony's is not the contrast between the Laconic and the Asiatic styles hinted at in Plutarch, but a more modern distinction between euphuism and the style of the Arcadia. Despite Zandvoort's evidence it is not obvious that Brutus' oration is euphuistic, and it is even less obvious that Antony's emotional rhetoric bears a resemblance to the stately prose of Sidney.

1799. Zielinski, Th. "Ovid und Shakespeare," Philologus, LXIV (1905), 17-20. SG

On pp. 17-18, Zielinski suggests that psychologically Cleopatra has something in common with the Dido of the Heroides. The parting scene (I iii) in Antony is modeled on Ovid, not on Virgil, but Sh mingles Cleopatra's childishness (from Ovid) with her crafty foxiness (from Plutarch).

THE TRAGEDIES

1800. Addington, M[arion] H. "Shakespeare and Cicero," NQ, CLXV (1933), 116-118. HB SG

This note compares Hamlet's "To be or not to be" soliloquy with John Dolman's 1561 trans. of Cicero's Tusculan Disputations and finds significant parallels. It is possible that Sh used Dolman, but, strangely, Q_1 is closer in language to Dolman than Q_2; the author does not explain this paradox. Sh apparently also knew Grimald's 1558 trans. of De Officiis. There is appended a useful list of supposed echoes of Cicero elsewhere in Sh.

1801. [Addison, Joseph]. The Spectator, No. 44 (April 20, 1711).

This critical objection to the stage business of contemporary and Elizabethan tragedy contains one of the first recorded comparisons of Ham. with the Orestes legend. Addison contrasts the versions of Sh and Sophocles, pointing out that Sophocles shrewdly has Orestes avenge his father on both Clytemnestra and Aegisthus off-stage, a more terrifying experience for the audience than the sight of Hamlet heaping the stage with "Carcasses" as he takes a similar revenge in Act V. Addison appeals to Horace (Ars Poetica) as a middle ground between Shn practice and the ridiculous extremes to which the French go to avoid showing death on-stage.

1802. Agate, James. "Iago's Ancestress," SatR, CXXXIV (1922), 583-584.

In a rev. of a production of Euripides' Medea, Agate takes occasion in passing to condemn the play by indicating that its dominant character is monstrous; Medea is like Iago, hopelessly insane, but Sh has put his maniac in a subordinate position, whereas Euripides allows his to rule the stage.

1803. Alexander, Peter. Hamlet, Father and Son, The Lord Northcliffe Lectures, University College, London, 1953 (OUP, 1955), 189 pp.

See especially Lectures II, III, and IV, the heart of the book which examines the nature of hamartia and catharsis with special reference to Ham. Alexander ranges widely, however, discussing A. C. Bradley, Greek tragedy, Freud, and the Romantic poets along the way. This is a well-written and provocative critical study.

1804. Allen, Don Cameron. "The Rehabilitation of Epicurus and His Theory of Pleasure in the Early Renaissance," SP, XLI (1944), 1-15. GRS

In passing: Sh's allusions to Epicureanism in Macb. (V iii 8) and Lear (I iv 265) show that he shared in the popular contemporary prejudice against Epicurus "as an advocate of gluttony and license." Allen does not mention Sh's allusions in Wives (II ii 300) and Antony (II i 24, II vii 58) which support his contention, or Cassius' reference (Caesar V i 76) which does not.

1805. Allen, Percy. "Drama Down the Ages," ShR, I (1928), 341-348, 438-444.

In passing: the "Elizabethan counterpart" of "nature tragedy," the seasonal ritual which pits Orestes (Winter) against Aegisthus (the Sun) and Clytemnestra (the Earth), is Ham., in which Hamlet is the equivalent of Orestes, Claudius of Aegisthus, Gertrude of Clytemnestra, Horatio of Pylades. The Greek ritual of

NOTE: Numbers preceded by # refer to entries in this Guide. Keys to abbreviations are found on pages xi-xvii and 381-387.

renewal following death is paralleled in Hamlet's voice for Fortinbras and Malcolm's plans for coronation (Macb. V viii 74-75). DFo

1806. Allinson, Francis G. "Lucian's Creditors and Debtors," Lucian: Satirist and Artist, Our Debt, [No. 8] (N.Y., 1927), Ch. VIII, pp. 121-187.

In this very broad survey of the Lucianic tradition in all of Western European literature, Sh finds only a brief paragraph which praises Fox on Ham. (#1926) and cites Parrott on Tim. (#1565). Allinson is apparently inclined to the view that Sh used John Rastell's English trans. of the Necromantia (i.e., Menippus).

1807. Anderson, F. M. B. "The Insanity of the Hero--an Intrinsic Detail of the Orestes Vendetta," TAPA, LVIII (1927), 43-62. HB

Mrs. Anderson begins where Gilbert Murray (#2049) ended; she finds the common Aryan link between Ham. and the Orestes vendetta in the heroes' psychoses, both of which take the form of cynanthropy. There is more anthropology and psychiatry here than literary scholarship, and though her pre-literary speculations are interesting, Mrs. Anderson has not established her point, especially when she suggests that Sh had some (unspecified) contact with the Orestes legend as he was revising the tale of Belleforest and the Ur-Hamlet.

1808. Apperson, G. L. "Some Shakespearean Names," GM, CCLXXXVII (1899), 278-283.

For the etymology and appropriateness of Ophelia's name, see #2182.

1809. Archer, William. "The Myths of Romeo and Juliet," NR, IV (1884), 441-450.

The stories of Romeo and Juliet, Hero and Leander, and Pyramus and Thisbe "are collateral outgrowths of some primitive legendary embodiment of the sweet vehemence of young desire," but "to credit Shakespeare with any knowledge of the mythic origin or relationships of his subject would be a graver anachronism than Hector's quotation from Aristotle." Sh believed the story to be "Veronese history," but recognized in it an elemental truth which makes his play great.

1810. Armstrong, W. A. "The Elizabethan Conception of the Tyrant," RES, XXII (1946), 161-181.

For Macbeth as a classical tyrant, see #0970.

1811. Armstrong, W. A. "The Influence of Seneca and Machiavelli on the Elizabethan Tyrant," RES, XXIV (1948), 19-35.

For further remarks on Macbeth as a classical tyrant, see #0971.

1812. Aronstein, Phil. "Die Hexen im englischen Renaissancedrama," GRM, IV (1912), 536-549, 582-597. E-S

Sh appears in Part I. Aronstein would regard the Hecate scenes in Macb. as spurious even though Sh alludes to the goddess in 1H.VI, Dream, Ham., and Lear, because Hecate is superfluous in Macb. and because the style is not Shn.

1813. Ashe, Geoffrey. "Hamlet and Pyrrhus," NQ, CXCII (1947), 214-215.

Ashe makes the ingenious suggestion that Sh included the Player's long speech on Pyrrhus (II ii) not only to satirize the Marlowe-Nashe Dido Queene of Carthage and to touch off the "rogue and peasant slave" soliloquy, but also to indicate to an alert audience that Hamlet is still thinking of revenge for a dead father, since Pyrrhus is seeking vengeance for his dead father, Achilles, whom Priam had "betrayed."

1814. Atherton, J. S. "Shakespeare's Latin, Two Notes," NQ, CXCVI (1951), 337.

The second of two notes finds an echo of Seneca's Phaedra (717-718) in Macb. II ii 60-61. The parallel is particularly compelling.

1815. Auden, W. H. "The Dyer's Hand," The Listener, LIII (1955), 1063-66. GRS

Auden distinguishes between poetry and history, at the same time drawing interesting contrasts between Macb. and Oedipus Tyrannus. In both plays prophecies come true, but the oracle states a fact while the Witches tell a lie which Macbeth's moral decisions turn into a truth. Sh's Oedipus would vow never to sleep with a woman or kill a man; temptation would then tease him to break his vow. Oedipus is only the sum of his actions in Sophocles' play; Macbeth is a real person, because we see him make (and agonize over) a succession of difficult choices. Oedipus does not change (though his status does); Macbeth degenerates gradually into a "guilt-crazed creature." To Auden, Sh's approach is more interesting and possibly more profound; Sophocles' approach produces the more perfect and beautiful work of art.

1816. Auerbach, Erich. "The Weary Prince," Mimesis: The Representation of Reality in Western Literature, trans. Willard R. Trask (PUP, 1953), Ch. XIII, pp. 312-333.

Though Sh, like the classical dramatists, conceived of tragic destiny as the prerogative of aristocrats, unlike the ancients he caused his noble protagonists to portray a range of reality much broader than the sublime: there is room in Sh's tragic art for the gross details of daily life, for pedestrian style, for buffoonery. "Thus Shakespeare's ethical and intellectual world is much more agitated, multilayered, and, apart from any specific dramatic action, in itself more dramatic than that of antiquity." In a sense Sh fulfilled the desideratum of the conclusion of the Symposium where Plato prophesied the fusion of comedy and tragedy. This is a provocative philosophical study.

1817. Awad, Louis. "Hamlet and Orestes," Studies in Literature (Cairo, 1954), pp. 77-110.

Not seen.

1818. Baker, J. E. "The Philosophy of Hamlet," PPV, pp. 455-470.

By way of refutation of the critics who would make Hamlet a Freudian case, an agnostic, or a materialist, Baker argues that Hamlet (though not perhaps Sh) espouses Platonic dualism in the Medieval Catholic realist tradition. He recognizes the validity of the material order but emphasizes the supremacy of the spiritual. This Platonism is melded in the character with a desire for the equanimity and fortitude of the Stoic, the qualities Hamlet admires in Horatio but cannot himself attain. Baker makes his points well.

1819. Bald, R. C. "'Thou, Nature, Art My Goddess': Edmund and Renaissance Free-Thought," AMS, pp. 337-349.

When Lear and the other "good" characters use the term "natural," they are referring to the ius naturale, founded on Christianized classical philosophy, which enabled man to assume a place in the cosmos between God and beast. When Edmund uses the term "natural" or "nature," he means physical nature, self-contained without reference to any higher order of being. Edmund's position can be traced to Lucretius and to Cicero (Pro Sestio), and would seem shockingly heretical to Sh's audience.

1820. Baldensperger, Fernand. "Was Othello an Ethiopian?" HSNPL, XX (1938), 3-14.

In arguing the affirmative, Baldensperger points out that in Aethiopica II Heliodorus alludes to Egyptian love charms; Othello's handkerchief is an amulet. A footnote observes that Cyprus was Venus' island--a fit home for Bianca (and, though Baldensperger does not say so, for adultery, real or suspected).

1821. Baldwin, T. W. Shakspere's Five-Act Structure: Shakspere's Early Plays on the Background of Renaissance Theories of Five-Act Structure from 1470. Illinois UP, 1947, 848 pp.

For the influence of Terence's dramatic structure on Romeo and also the influence of Ovid and neo-Senecanism on the play, see #0683.

1822. Banner, Friedrich. "Schicksal und menschliche Tragik (Betrachtungen zum Hamletproblem)," NZ, IV (1952), 365-369.

Not seen. This art. is presumed to consider the Greek concept of Fate.

1823. Barnet, Sylvan. "Some Limitations of a Christian Approach to Shakespeare," ELH, XXII (1955), 81-92.

Barnet would reject Christian interpretations, from the damnation of Othello to the regeneration of Lear. He draws an implicit analogy between Shn practice and Greek tragedy, where renewal is not to be anticipated at the close, despite the calm choric pronouncements of Sophocles and Euripides and the occasional "note of life" in Aeschylus. Barnet's evidence from the Greek tragedians is unacceptable: moral regeneration and subsequent happiness are obviously thematic in the Oresteia, the Iphigenia in Tauris, and the Alcestis, e.g.

1824. Barnett, George L. "'The Glass of Fashion and the Mould of Form'," NQ, CLXXXV (1943), 105.

This line (III i 161) in Ophelia's eulogy of Hamlet Barnett believes to be a conscious or unconscious borrowing from the first sentence of Plutarch's "Life of Paulus Aemilius" (North's trans., of course). The resemblance is very close, and there is no reason to doubt that Sh read far more widely in Plutarch than critics at one time thought.

1825. Battenhouse, Roy W. "The Ghost in Hamlet: A Catholic 'Linchpin'?" SP, XLVIII (1951), 161-192.

After giving seven reasons why the Ghost is inconsistent with Catholic teaching on purgatory, Battenhouse proposes that he is from a pagan "purgatory." Seneca, Virgil, Apuleius, Ovid, Cicero, and indirectly Plato's Phaedo and Republic (the myth of Er) contribute to the pagan basis of Sh's conception. Battenhouse is not so convincing here as in #1826. E.g., one of his arguments is that the Ghost is referred to as evil (i.e., "extravagant and erring"); in this context, however, "erring" obviously means "wandering" (from "errare"). See Hankins, (#0305) for a more convincing treatment of the pagan element in Sh's purgatory.

1826. Battenhouse, Roy W. "Hamlet's Apostrophe on Man: Clue to the Tragedy," PMLA, LXVI (1951), 1073-1113.

This brilliant study ranges far beyond the apostrophe to consider the intellectual history behind the philosophical concepts of the entire play. Beginning with a distinction between "two major and conflicting anthropologies, the Thomistic and the Neoplatonic," Battenhouse shows that Hamlet's thought early in the play is basically Platonic optimism: reason is godlike and beautiful; sensual experience is bestial and ugly--and man is rationis capax. But later the obverse of Hamlet's philosophical coin appears as he finds all men (and women) around him enslaved by passion and he assumes (especially in Act V) the posture of Stoic pessimism--reason cannot save him, but at least "the rest is silence." Mingled with these two basic philosophies of the play are such elements as the Calvinist sense of man's depravity and pre-Cartesian dualism of body and spirit. Battenhouse calls Hamlet's world "sub-Christian" and suggests that Sh implicitly criticizes its homocentricity. Perhaps Ham. is "the Tragedy of Unbaptized Man." The art. is documented with impressive erudition and contains some perceptive criticisms of its predecessors in interpretation.

1827. Bayliss, Wyke. "Shakespeare in Relation to His Contemporaries in the Fine Arts," Literature, V (1899), 387-389, 414-416.

These two essays discuss the paucity of works of talent in the visual arts in Sh's time contrasted with the plethora of great works in the time of Sophocles. The first essay places Hamlet against Orestes, Cordelia against Antigone, and Desdemona against Alcestis. Hamlet has no gods to solve his problems, Cordelia has no Chorus to encourage her, Desdemona has no Heracles to bring her back to life. And Sh had no Phidias to inspire him, but he did have Gothic architecture.

1828. Beckingham, C. F. "Seneca's Fatalism and Elizabethan Tragedy," MLR, XXXII (1937), 434-438.

Insisting that Seneca was uninterested in philosophical concepts unless they were an index to action, and that for him accordingly Fatalism was an incitement to take an ethical position, not "a philosophical theory of Possibility," Beckingham illustrates "ethical" Fatalism in several Elizabethan dramatists. Caesar, Ham., and Lear are the three Shn plays from which passages are briefly extracted.

1829. Bennett, Josephine Waters. "Characterization in Polonius' Advice to Laertes," SQ, IV (1953), 3-9.

The source of the maxims Polonius gives to his son is not Euphues, but Isocrates' Ad Demonicum, a standard schoolboy text. Thus the Elizabethan audience, familiar with the adages, would think of Polonius as a prattler of puerile cliché-wisdom rather than as a member of a passé generation. Mrs. Bennett does not consider that since Lyly also drew on Isocrates nothing was to prevent the audience from identifying Polonius as a euphuist, even if he does not speak the euphuistic style. For other strictures on Mrs. Bennett's thesis, and for her reply to them, see ibid., VI (1955), 362-364 and VII (1956), 275-276. Note that (as T. W. Baldwin [#0089, II, 604-606] points out) H. B. Lathrop (#0381) made the same point about Polonius in 1933.

1830. Berdan, J. M. "Shakespeare's Learning," Nation, XCII (1911), 241. SG

In a somewhat confused letter to the editor, Berdan first attacks the logic of Baconians and then uses the Hyrcanian tigers of Macb. III iv 101, 3H.VI I iv 155, and Ham. II ii 472 as evidence that Sh read the Aeneid (IV, 367), ridiculing all rival suggestions.

1831. Berry, E. G. "Hamlet and Suetonius," The Phoenix, II (1948), 73-81.

A close-packed juxtaposition of characteristics of the Emperor Claudius as Suetonius describes them with the behavior of Hamlet in Sh's play. The resemblances (some of them) are striking: both men are kept from power by murderous uncles; both are erratic in speech (from brilliant down to "wild and whirling"); both use insulting and obscene language at times, yet are sensitive, decent men; both court and win popular favor; both are philosophically inclined students; both lapse into inactivity when confronted by the avuncular obstacle. There are many other parallels of lesser significance. Berry believes that these parallels are closer than the ones Gollancz (#1935) cites between Ham. and Livy's account of Lucius Junius Brutus. His conjecture is that either Kyd or Sh read the "Life of Claudius" and incorporated striking features into his play; Sh had enough Latin to read Suetonius and he might have turned to him as the other great classical biographer after reading Plutarch. An interesting argument which has something in common with the theory of Montgomerie (#2031) that Sh based Ham. in part on the "Life of Nero."

1832. Bethell, S. L. "The Player's Speech and Hamlet as Dramatic Critic," Shakespeare and the Popular Dramatic Tradition (Ln, 1944), pp. 144-151.

The "rugged Pyrrhus" speech is a burlesque of "the ranting tragedy"; "Shakespeare ... has compressed into one brief speech the salient characteristics of the Senecan tragedy: rant, Latinity, the stock emotive word; classical reference; extended conceit; the classical simile." It is true that these Senecan elements are present, but as Bethell admits, the heroic verse is almost too good to be recognizable burlesque, as (e.g.) the Pyramus/Thisbe sketch is in Dream.

1833. Bickersteth, Geoffrey L. "The Golden World of 'King Lear'," PBA, XXXII (1946), 147-171. (Annual British Academy Shakespeare Lecture.)

This profound reading of the play begins with Sir Philip Sidney's distinction between the "brazen" world of nature and the "golden" world of poetry and proceeds to a consideration of both concepts in the play in the light of the three key words: "nature," "patience," and "love." The play is Stoic in that nature, the δαίμων in each Stoic, compels him to deal with others dispassionately in accordance with the truth (as Cordelia does with her father in I i, e.g.) and then to endure patiently the consequences. But when love is added to Stoicism we have Christianity, and this is the final impact of the play. Early in the play Cordelia is like Prometheus, a proto-Stoic, partly responsible for her own sufferings, but at the end her perfect love makes her more like Christ.

1834. Bloom, Allan D. "Cosmopolitan Man and the Political Community: An Interpretation of Othello," APSR, LIV (1960), 130-157.

In the course of an interpretation of Oth. as primarily a play of political philosophy, Bloom makes two appeals to the classics to justify his unorthodox position: (1) he places (pp. 143-144) Othello's love for Desdemona against the Platonic-Aristotelian conceptions of love as fulfillment of lack. Othello is unaware of his need, but feels it all the same; (2) he follows Shaftesbury (pp. 151-152) in deriving Desdemona's name from δεισιδαίμων ("superstitious") rather than from δυσδαίμων ("ill-starred") even though Cinthio obviously intended the latter meaning and Sh would have had to re-etymologize the word. Bloom's entire thesis elicits a caustic critique, "English Bards and APSR Reviewers," from Sigurd Burckhardt (ibid., 158-166) which in turn precipitates an elongated and somewhat heated controversy, only fragments of which are relevant to Sh and the classics.

1835. Blunden, Edmund. "The Madness of Lear," N&A, XLIII (1928), 458-459. SG

Subsumed into "Shakespeare's Significances" in The Mind's Eye (#1836).

1836. Blunden, Edmund. "Shakespeare's Significances" (1928), The Mind's Eye (Ln, 1934), pp. 195-215. E-S SG

This address on Lear attempts to illustrate "the richness, and intuitive complexity, and choral harmony" of the play. Blunden points out (pp. 201-203) that Lear is fond of recalling his classical education; he lapses into Latin, refers to Prometheus and other mythological figures, speaks of ancient philosophical problems ("nihil ex nihilo"; "what is the cause of thunder?"). But most interesting of all is Lear's interest in Horace's Odes and Epistles—Blunden indicates two cases in which Sh may have deepened the meaning of Lear's ravings by alluding to Horace. The parallels are quite close.

1837. Bodkin, Maud. "Archetypal Patterns in Tragic Poetry," Archetypal Patterns in Poetry: Psychological Studies of Imagination (OUP, 1934), Ch. I, pp. 1-25.

A good part of this first ch. is an attempt to apply to Ham. and Lear the theory of Jung on the Collective Unconscious, which "explains" their analogous relationship to the Orestes and Oedipus legends. Miss Bodkin draws on Murray (#2049) and on Jones (#1980), for both of whom she has praise with some reservations. As she admits, her hypothesis "cannot be investigated in accordance with a strict technique," and it therefore will be regarded with suspicion by those who distrust intuitive criticism.

1838. Borinski, Karl. "Regula poeseos," Die Antike in Poetik und Kunsttheorie I: Mittelalter, Renaissance, Barock, Erbe, IX (Leipzig, 1914), pp. 234-245. E-S

The last three sections of this ch. treat Sh's knowledge of and relation to Aristotle, especially in Ham. Borinski dismisses the notion of a Sh who kept his eyes turned away from the Medusa's head of classical literary theory. Though he was amused by the controversialists in Aristotelian theory (cf. Polonius' generic catalogue for the drama), Sh "die Schlagworte der gelehrten Dramaturgie vorführen will." Borinski suggests Sh's knowledge of Cicero, Donatus (on holding a mirror up to nature), and Plautus' Trinummus (as source for Polonius' opposition between "gravis" and "levis"), in addition to the Latin university drama of his time.

1839. Bowers, R. H. "Polonius: Another Postscript," SQ, IV (1953), 362-364.

Bowers does not dismiss Josephine Bennett's parallels between Isocrates and Polonius' advice (#1829), but he emphasizes their commonplace character by citing the advice of a fifteenth-century father to his son. Bowers also denies the hypothesis (originally proposed by Gollancz in 1916) that Sh knew Goslicius' De Optimo Senatore and borrowed for Ham. from it. According to Bowers, it contains chiefly generalized classical sentiments on statesmanship (Cicero, Plato, Aristotle, Seneca, etc.), not Renaissance immediacies. However, Sh may have given "Corambis" the Latin name "Polonius" as a nod toward Goslicius' reputation.

1840. Boyd, Catherine Bradshaw. "The Isolation of Antigone and Lady Macbeth," CJ, XLVII (1952), 174-177, 203.

An impressionistic comparison and contrast between Antigone, set apart by her sense of justice, and Lady Macbeth, set apart by her sense of guilt. The timidity of Ismene and the self-centeredness of the Chorus emphasize the moral solitude of Antigone; Lady Macbeth's willing abdication of her femininity makes her monstrous and underlines her separation from society.

1841. Bradbrook, M. C. "Lucrece and Othello," TLS, October 27, 1950, p. 677.

Sh apparently took Othello's comparison of Desdemona to chrysolite, whose purity supposedly made it indestructible, from Middleton's imitation of Lucr., The Ghost of Lucrece (1600). If so, the indication would be that Sh thought of Desdemona as an analogue to the Roman matron.

1842. Bradley, A. C. Shakespearean Tragedy: Lectures on Hamlet, Othello, King Lear, Macbeth. Ln, 1904, 498 pp. E-S SG

As Bradley says at the outset, he is not primarily interested in sources or in comparative criticism; yet in two important passages (pp. 389-390, 276-279) he studies respectively the Senecan contribution to Macb., and Shn fatalism (in Lear) contrasted with Aeschylean Fatalism. Moreover, in the introductory chs. on the substance and structure of Shn tragedy, there are numerous references to the plays on classical themes, though Bradley does not study Sh's use of Plutarch, e.g.

1843. Bradley, Henry. "'Cursed Hebenon' (or 'Hebona')," MLR, XV (1920), 85-87.

A survey of possible explanations of Sh's peculiar term for the poison that killed Hamlet's father. Bradley decides that henbane is meant, but that Sh assumed that Marlowe's "hebona" was a poetic synonym for the ignoble English word. "Another possibility is that hebenon is a pedantic attempt at correction, by some transcriber or proof-reader, who vaguely remembered the Greek ἔβενος and thought it was neuter."

1844. Brandl, Alois. "Zur Vorgeschichte der Weird Sisters im 'Macbeth'," Liebermann Festschrift, pp. 252-270. E-S

In passing Brandl notes Ovidian, Horatian, and Senecan references to "die Parzen" and to Hecate, though his major emphasis falls on Holinshed, Hector Boethius, and their antecedents.

1845. Brien, G. "The Oedipus in Exile of Sophocles Compared with King Lear," Prolusiones Literariae (Ln, 1841), pp. 19-30.

Not seen.

1846. Brock, F. H. Cecil. "Oedipus, Macbeth and the Christian Tradition," CR, CLXXVIII (1950), 176-181.

Oedipus is constrained by prophecies; Macbeth is tempted by them: the difference is Christianity, which intervened between the classical and modern worlds. Sh's world is modern, because there would have been no science, no Renaissance if Elizabethan Englishmen had believed as the Greek dramatists did that man's struggles do not alter, but only reveal, the web of Fate.

1847. Büchler, Hermann. Shakspeare's Dramen in ihrem Verhältnisse zur griechischen Tragödie. Nürnberg, 1856, 86 pp. HB

For "Hindeutungen" about the relationship of Ham. to Attic tragedy, see #1190. MnU

1848. Buchwald, O. "Medea und Othello," Propyläen, I, Nos. 40-43 (1869) (no pagination available).

Not seen.

1849. Buckley, W. E. "'Hamlet,' III.i.," 6 NQ, XII (1885), 423.

Buckley cites Aeschylus' reference to a "sea of troubles" (κακῶν θάλασσα) in the Septem contra Thebas and also a similar expression in Prometheus. "The idea may have suggested itself independently to many writers."

1850. Budd, F. E. "Shakespeare, Chaucer, and Harsnett," RES, XI (1935), 421-429.

In the first two parts of the art., Budd argues effectively that Edgar's reference to Nero as "an angler in the lake of darkness" (Lear III vi 8) is not a misreading of Rabelais as has been thought from the time of Upton (#0606), but, like all of Sh's four other references to Nero (1,3H.VI, Ham., John), is drawn from a passage of twelve lines on Nero in Chaucer's "Monk's Tale."

1851. Budd, Henry. "The Contrast of the Ancient and Modern Drama as Illustrated by Prometheus Vinctus and Macbeth," St. Mary's Hall Lectures and Other Papers (Philadelphia, 1898), pp. 114-137.

A detailed summary of the action of the two plays to show that each is representative of the tragic conception dominant in its time. Prometheus is free to defy Zeus in spirit, but must wait for Fate to take physical action for him: i.e., his tragedy is enforced passivity. Macbeth on the other hand himself sets in motion the train of cause and effect which destroys him: in Shn tragedy the protagonist initiates the tragic action though he has no control over its later course. Budd's is an oversimplified view of both plays--he does not emphasize Prometheus' initial act (stealing fire for man) which precipitated the ensuing calamities that we witness. Then, too, the atmosphere of Macb. is dominated by the equivocal prophecies of the Witches, even though Macbeth is tempted, not constrained to sin. Budd considers the plays in isolation, only comparing them in his conclusion. DLC

1852. Burr, Charles H., Jr. "'Hamlet' Once More," PL, III (1891), 615-626.

In passing: in deciding the question of the hero's madness, real or feigned, we should remember that Sh's audience knew the tale of "Hamblet" and his assumed madness just as a Greek audience knew the mythology which was dramatized for them.

1853. Bush, Douglas. "Hero and Leander and Romeo and Juliet," PQ, IX (1930), 396-399.

In refutation of the arguments of J. M. Robertson for Marlowe's authorship of Romeo, on which he supposedly based his Hero and Leander (Problems of the Shakespeare Sonnets [1926]; The Shakespeare Canon III [1925]), Bush points out the commonplace character of some conceits and other elements which the play and the poem have in common. Some are of classical origin, e.g., the Nurse (Marlowe borrowed his from the Heroides), the idea that a lover can breathe life into his beloved with a kiss (Romeo V i 8-9) from the Greek Anthology.

1854. Butler, James D. "Shakespeare and Plato," Shna, II (1885), 444-446.

In response to a query from F. J. Furnivall, Butler proposes that Sh obtained Iago's

Platonic conception of the ennobling power of love (Oth. II i 216-218) from the Symposium (a remark by Phaedrus), probably in a French or Latin version. As support he suggests that the Symposium may also have inspired "At lovers' perjuries, / They say Jove laughs" (Romeo II ii 92-93), but Sh's source for the latter is plainly Marlowe. Furnivall is not entirely satisfied by Butler's evidence.

1855. C., H. A. [Helen A. Clarke]. "Life and Letters," PL, XIV, No. 3 (1903), 7.

In a discussion of modern drama is a brief passage suggesting that the effect of Greek tragedy is "to relieve the victim of fate of any moral responsibility, and place the responsibility upon a state of things," whereas poetic justice is the moral criterion of Shn tragedy. On the face of it a greatly oversimplified view, especially of the Greek drama.

1856. C., T. C. "Hamlet, Three Notes," NQ, CLXXV (1938), 114. SG

Note (2) points to Cicero's De Oratore 101 as the ultimate source of the "mind's eye" of Ham. I i 112 and I ii 185. Sh doubtless acquired the expression orally from someone like Ben Jonson. Hibernicus (ibid., 158-159) proposes alternative loci in Cicero and Ovid, and P. L. Carver (ibid., 191 SG) suggests Cicero's Second Oration against Verres (V, 55, 144) as paraphrased in Acolastus, which in Palsgrave's 1540 ed. was a school text. Finally G. G. L. (ibid.) cites sixteenth-century English Bibles, Plato, and Aristophanes to establish the commonplace character of the expression. Cf. H. K. Baker (#0972), who attacks T. C. C. on the question of oral transmission.

1857. Cahill, Sister Mary Angeline, O. P. "Tragic Effect and Poetic Justice Theoretically and in King Lear," diss (Boston College, 1942).*

This diss is presumed to discuss Aristotle's Poetics in relation to Lear.

1858. Caine, T. H. Hall. Richard III and Macbeth: The Spirit of Romantic Play in Relationship to the Principles of Greek and of Gothic Art, and to the Picturesque Interpretations of Mr. Henry Irving: A Dramatic Study. Ln and Liverpool, 1877, 46 pp.

For Macb. as "Gothic" rather than classical in spirit, see #0985. DFo

1859. Cairncross, Andrew S. "The Tempest, III.i.15, and Romeo and Juliet, I.i.121-8," SQ, VII (1956), 448-450.

For a possible debt of Romeo to Cicero, see #2197.

1860. Caldiero, Frank M. "The Source of Hamlet's 'What a Piece of Work is a Man!'," NQ, CXCVI (1951), 421-424.

The proximate source is Pico della Mirandola's Heptaplus; perhaps indirectly Sh's passage derives from Photius' Life of Pythagoras. Plotinian Platonism exerted a greater influence (through the Italians) on English Renaissance literature than did neo-Aristotelianism. It is therefore not surprising, in Caldiero's judgment, that Sh should borrow a Pythagorean doctrine from an Italian.

1861. Camden, Carroll. "Memory, the Warder of the Brain," PQ, XVIII (1939), 52-72.

Camden documents the Renaissance interest in mnemonics, especially in artificial aids to the memory. The science is traceable to Simonides, who had a "local" (i.e., spatial) memory. The catalogue of ancient commentators includes Plato, Xenophon, Aristotle, Metrodorus of Scepsis, Cicero, the author of Ad Herennium, Seneca, and Quintilian. Hamlet's praise of Laertes, which would if itemized "dozy th' arithmetic of memory" (V ii 118-119), appears to allude to one of the Elizabethan mnemonic systems.

1862. Camden, Carroll. "Three Notes on Shakespeare," MLN, LXXII (1957), 251-253.

Note II suggests that Albany's proverb, "Filths savour but themselves" (Lear IV ii 39) is derived from Googe's trans. of Palingenius' Zodiacus Vitae.

1863. Campbell, Lewis. Tragic Drama in Aeschylus, Sophocles, and Shakespeare: An Essay. N.Y., 1904, 280 pp. HB

Expanding on the thesis that tragic themes, especially of familial life, recur in Greek and Shn tragedy because they are of the common stock of human concern, Campbell compares classical and Shn tragedy at many points: structure, action, diction, the conception of character, the rôle of Necessity, etc. The treatment is sometimes more general than might be desired, but Campbell frequently makes challenging comparisons: e.g., "the Wars of the Roses ...presented horrors comparable with 'the Tale of Thebes or Pelops' line', while the Roman background of European civilization had its counterpart in the epic tale of Troy." The essay ranges beyond Sh to consider in passing his contemporaries and the tragedians of France, Spain, and Germany. But Campbell never strays far from Sh; in Part II, after chs. on Aeschylus and Sophocles, he concludes with six chs. on Sh's tragic art, measuring it against the critical dicta of the first hundred pages. The major emphasis falls on Ham., Macb., Oth., and Lear.

1864. Campbell, Lily B. "Polonius: The Tyrant's Ears," AMS, pp. 295-313.

Claudius, as an immoral usurper, fits the pattern of classical tyrants; like a tyrant he surrounds himself with a coterie of informers. Polonius is Claudius' chief spy, a busybody modeled on the type in Plutarch's "De Curiositate" from the Moralia. Sh could have seen Holland's trans., written before 1600, though not published until 1603; he also borrowed Claudius' "consolation" to Hamlet in I ii from the Moralia. Plutarch's description of the overly curious is a sketch of Polonius: he is so busy looking for the hidden that he misses the overt; he has too much confidence in his wisdom, but can't apply it; he must bleat out what he knows; and his espionage leads him into trouble eventually. The argument is for a consistent Plutarchian Polonius, whose advice to Laertes is of no avail to himself. It is noteworthy that "he is accepted by the king as his ears but never as his brain. The king listens to his reports but never acts on his decisions." An interesting interpretation.

1865. Campbell, Lily B. Shakespeare's Tragic Heroes: Slaves of Passion. CUP, 1930, 248 pp. E-S

This pioneer work on Elizabethan psychology documents thoroughly the commonplaces of sixteenth-century thought on reason and passion as they were related to the Christianized classical tradition. The classical authorities most often cited are Aristotle and Plutarch, but the Stoics and the Peripatetics are referred to as well. Professor Campbell then analyzes the four great tragedies, Ham., Oth., Lear, Macb., each as a study of the evil effects of a passion (grief, jealousy, wrath, fear, respectively). That she is correct in placing Shn tragedy within its own psychological framework there can be no doubt, but the reader feels that there is more to Hamlet than his grief or to Othello than his mad jealousy; and certainly there is more to the two plays than the passions of their heroes. See Waldock on Sophocles (#2155) for a more unfavorable judgment which may not entirely be deserved, and see also the entry (#0148) on Professor Campbell's ch. on Renaissance conceptions of drama.

1866. Campbell, Lily B. "Theories of Revenge in Renaissance England," MP, XXVIII (1931), 281-296.

For classical attitudes toward revenge in Ham., see #0988.

1867. Campbell, Oscar J. "The Salvation of Lear," ELH, XV (1948), 93-109.

Campbell sees Lear as a Medieval "morality play upon which has been grafted a view of the unwise man of stoic morality." He finds in the play parallels to the Stoic pronouncements of Cicero's De Officiis I and II, of Epictetus, and of Plutarch. The parallels are interesting, but the Stoicism of Pauline moral theology is often indistinguishable from pagan Stoicism. Who is to say which Sh is thinking of at any given point in the play? For the view that Sh's apparent Stoicism in Lear is actually the Christian patience of the Renaissance homiletic tradition, see John F. Danby, "'King Lear' and Christian Patience," CamJ, I (1948), 305-320.

1868. Campbell, [Thomas]. Life of Mrs. Siddons. Ln, 1834, 2 vols. (as abstracted in the New Variorum Macb.).

At II, 6 Campbell compares Macb. to Aeschylus in the beauty and "fault of excess" of its metaphor. Like Aeschylus' tragedies, Macb. is almost too sublime to present on stage. But since it has been proved that Sh did not study Greek drama, one must attribute the similarities to "consanguinity of nature."

1869. Cardwill, Mary E. "Hecate in 'Macbeth'," PL, X (1898), 532-543.

This vigorous defense of Shn authorship of the Hecate passages concludes that so far from being an interpolation, "if not the keystone of the play [Hecate] is at least the summing up of its evil." The author makes an interesting case of it based on the classical concept of "triple Hecate," together with Medieval popular superstitions about her. Sh brilliantly combined both elements in the play. Among the salient points: (1) her speech, crude and blunt, is that way by Sh's intention: Macbeth is to be led to destruction not by ethereal shadows, but by real substance; (2) Macbeth does not revere the supernatural powers who have prophecies to offer him--the Nemesis of this hybris is that he achieves only seeming success: Hecate was traditionally accorded a special authority to deal with men according to the degree of their reverence for her; (3) the cauldrons are quite possibly the debased popular form of the classical propitiatory hecatombs offered to Hecate at wayside altars in Greece. An interesting and informed criticism of the play. (See objections to it by W. J. Rolfe, PL, XI [1899], 602-605.)

1870. Chapman, Raymond. "Hamlet and Fortune," TLS, October 25, 1947, p. 549.

Chapman would emend "slings" to "stings" in association with the arrows of "outrageous Fortune" and he insists on the initial capital to emphasize that Fortune is a goddess. He also cites a passage from Dekker (1623) where Fortune is the authoress of "a sea of troubles." The proposal to emend is unconvincing.

1871. Charlton, H. B. "Romeo and Juliet as an Experimental Tragedy," PBA, XXV (1939), 143-185. (Annual British Academy Shakespeare Lecture.)

Measured against the Aristotelian doctrine of "probability or necessity" as understood by the sixteenth century, the sonnet-prologue to Romeo takes on special importance. In it, Sh emphasizes the feud and Fate as necessary agents in the destruction of his protagonists and his protagonists as necessary agents in the resolution of the feud; Sh thereby aimed to assure τὸ φιλάνθρωπον in his audience and achieve the tragic effect. But the difficulties in the story were insurmountable: (1) to make probable a bloody feud in a sophisticated city-state was not so easy as in (e.g.) the barbarian Scots border culture; (2) the Christian Renaissance could accept classical Fate only as a literary convention. The play is saved, partly, by its poetry and characterization, but Sh recognized its inadequacies and turned away from Aristotle to comedy and history. This is a learned and, in part, convincing approach to the play, but two reservations can be made: (1) the Elizabethans had heard rumors of men like Sigismondo Malatesta and could surely accept the Italian as at once cultured and bloody; (2) the general acceptance of astrology in the Renaissance argues against the inability of Sh's audience to accept Fate as real in the play.

1872. [Charlton, H. B.] "The Senecan Tradition in England," [part of the Introduction to] The Poetical Works of Sir William Alexander Earl of Stirling, ed. L. E. Kastner and H. B. Charlton, PUM, No. X (Manchester UP, 1921), pp. cxxxviii-cc. (Reprinted as Charlton's in The Senecan Tradition in Renaissance Tragedy, PUM, No. XXIV [1946].) E-S HB

For Senecan Fatalism in Romeo, see #1209.

1873. Charosky, Graciela Susana. "Macbeth: Classical and Medieval Drama," LV, III (1959), 21-28.

This rather disjointed commentary on the play indicates "classical" elements: violent action off-stage (for the most part), Greek tragic dignity in the inexorable movement of the action, a Senecan Chorus (the Sergeant, Ross, and Angus as commentators), pervasive irony (as in Sophocles), and Greek and Roman names and allusions. The classical elements are seen to dominate the play, though Medieval concepts are important also in the action. This is not an entirely satisfactory study of the classical background of Macb. FCU

1874. Chesterman, Frances. "Romeo in Humoral View," SatR, CXV (1913), 12-13.

Reading the play as a lesson in Senecan temperance, Miss Chesterman finds in Romeo, especially, "a studied example of Sanguine Humour in pathological degeneration," which produces "a rush to headlong ruin." This view, while it contains a kernel of truth, is untenable as an exclusive guide to the tragedy because it ignores altogether the inexorable Necessity on which Sh lays so much stress throughout the play.

1875. Childs, Ralph de S. "Influence of the Court Tragedy on the Play Scene in Hamlet," JEGP, XXXII (1933), 44-50.

Childs believes that the entire play scene is a miniature court tragedy, inserted as masques were inserted in later plays to suggest the flavor of entertainment at court. Sh prefixed the dumb show to the playlet as an imitation of the dumb shows which in Gorboduc and Tancred and Gismund are vestiges of the Senecan Chorus, prefacing the events of each act. This is as reasonable an argument as any on this thorny question.

1876. Coad, O. S. "Shakespeare and Aeschylus," JEGP, XX (1921), 556-557. HB

Coad points to two coincidental parallels between Sh and the Choephori: (1) Antony's dramatic use of Caesar's robe (Caesar III ii) is like Orestes' use of his father's; (2) the ghost scene of Macb. (III iv) recalls Orestes' vision of the Furies.

1877. Conley, C. H. "An Instance of the Fifteen Signs of Judgment in Shakespeare," MLN, XXX (1915), 41-44. SG

Conley indicates that Sh's portents (Caesar II ii 17-24; Ham. I i 113-120) can be found in Holinshed as well as in Lucan. He suggests a third source: the Doomsday literature of the Middle English period which survived to Sh's time. He quotes extensively from an Anglo-Norman poem, but his suggestion is not so plausible as the alternatives.

1878. Cook, Albert S. "Notes on Shakespeare," MLN, XXI (1906), 147-149.

The second note points out a parallel between Romeo II iii 3-4 ("And flecked darkness like a drunkard reels / From forth day's path and Titan's fiery wheels") and a passage in Nonnus' Dionysiaca.

1879. Cook, Albert S. "Shakespeare, Haml. 3.4.56," MLN, XX (1905), 216-217.

"Hyperion's curls; the front of Jove himself" is probably an echo of Kyd's Soliman and Perseda rather than a debt to Meta. III.

1880. Coulter, C. C. "The Plautine Tradition in Shakespeare," JEGP, XIX (1920), 66-83. E-S HB SG

For the influence of Latin comedy on Romeo, see #0728.

1881. Cox, Ernest H. "Shakespeare and Some Conventions of Old Age," SP, XXXIX (1942), 36-46.

Cox believes that Sh's view of death, old age, and the transitoriness of life was entirely conventional, with roots in the Middle Ages. Hamlet's speech to Polonius (II ii 198-203) is not from Juvenal's tenth Satire, but from "the native traditions of describing age." Most authorities believe Sh knew Juvenal; Cox does not appear to have established his point.

1882. Craig, Hardin. "The Ethics of King Lear," PQ, IV (1925), 97-109.

The ethical system which Sh and his age recognized as the foundation of the moral order is traceable to Socrates and Aristotle, though Aquinas defended it in theological terms as well. The four primary virtues according to this Platonic-Aristotelian canon are wisdom, justice, temperance, and fortitude; in Lear, all four are standards against which the failures of characters are to be measured. Lear's first mistake is a violation of wisdom, which is followed by offenses against temperance and (especially) against justice by other characters; fortitude is a goal for both Lear and Gloucester. Sh need not have read the Greeks--the philosophy was available everywhere in Elizabethan times --but he followed Greek ethics at every moral crux in the play.

1883. Craig, Hardin. "Hamlet's Book," HLB, VI (1934), 17-37. SG

The book which Hamlet is said to be reading in Q_1 just before the "To be or not to be" soliloquy is (as Francis Douce suggested) Girolamo Cardano's De Consolatione. The whole play is permeated by the pessimism and quasi-Christianized Stoicism of the consolation writers, and most of the passages which source-seekers have traced to Montaigne, Cicero, Seneca, and Plutarch were gathered and assimilated in Cardano, who would have been available in English trans. Some of the parallels cited are significant, but perhaps Craig has gone beyond his evidence, especially in the light of the plethora and popularity of consolation books in the sixteenth century.

1884. Craig, Hardin. "The Shackling of Accidents: A Study of Elizabethan Tragedy," PQ, XIX (1940), 1-19.

Critics who have read Shn (and other Elizabethan) tragedy with Aristotle's Poetics in one hand have failed to see that the primary impulse of Renaissance drama is Senecan (pessimistic) rather than Aeschylean (optimistic). Seneca's Stoicism portrays defeat as inevitable; it is the posture of the defeated that "shackles the accidents." This is the key to Lear, Ham., and Antony, in all of which a protagonist learns that "ripeness is all." Craig also discusses most effectively the influence of Senecan rhetoric, plot, and characterization on Sh, but his major contribution appears to be the segregation and definition of a Renaissance "tragedy of titanism" in which a protagonist (like Prometheus or Hercules) can find no relief: "the terms of his contract call for suffering." Cf. H. W. Wells (#2162) for an analogous reappraisal of Seneca's influence.

1885. Crane, William Ward. "The Allegory in 'Hamlet'," PL, III (1891), 565-569.

Crane believes that the play can be read as a triangle of (1) Hamlet, the fore-thinker who thinks too much (Prometheus), (2) Laertes, the after-thinker who thinks too late (Epimetheus), and (3) Fortinbras, the strong-in-arm who does not think but preserves (Atlas). In addition to this unusual analogy with the classical Titans, Crane makes some comparisons between Hamlet and Orestes, but his conclusions are vitiated by his belief that Gertrude was an accomplice in the murder of Hamlet's father.

1886. Crundell, H. W. "The Rugged Pyrrhus and Hamlet," TLS, November 23, 1935, p. 770.

Crundell emphasizes the analogy between Pyrrhus' situation and Hamlet's, and suggests that the speech is not an interpolation--Sh deliberately inserted it to give Hamlet further cause for self-torment when he considers that Pyrrhus hesitated and then acted, while he, Hamlet, has only (so far) hesitated. C. R. N. Routh, unaware that he has been anticipated, makes a virtually identical suggestion (ibid., August 5, 1944, p. 379).

1887. Cumberland, Richard. "[Macbeth and Richard III]," The Observer, II (1808), Nos. 69-72, pp. 117-144. (The essay may antedate 1808; it is reprinted in part by Nathan Drake in Memorials of Shakspeare [1828].)

Cumberland compares Macbeth with Claudian's Rufinus and Lady Macbeth with Clytemnestra, and he finds occasion to illustrate R.III and Macb. from Horace, Diphilus, Philonides, Claudian, and Aeschylus. In a digression Cumberland finds Aeschylus and Sh each the father (if not the inventor) of his national drama. If Aeschylus is less varied in character portrayal, it is because he was confined by the Chorus and "the simplicity of the Greek fable." Sh lacked the corpus of mythology which Aeschylus shared with his audience and his achievement must therefore be more highly praised. Cumberland forgets that Sh and his audience had community of thought about the Wars of the Roses just as Aeschylus and the Athenians did about the Trojan War. DFo

1888. Cuningham, Henry. "Introduction," Macbeth (1912), ArdenSh (Ln, 4th ed., 1928), pp. vii-l.

The Editor rejects (inter alia) the Hecate scenes as uncanonical, but he does not discuss Hecate as a classical goddess. He iterates Malone's two notes on Sh's use of Plutarch in the play; passages in "Marcus Antonius" for the "insane root" of I iii 84 and for "under him / My Genius is rebuk'd . . ." (III i 55-57).

1889. Cunningham, James V. "Tragedy in Shakespeare," ELH, XVII (1950), 36-46.

In the course of his argument that to Sh and his contemporaries the term "tragedy" meant violent death producing fear and woe in the audience, Cunningham points out that Polonius in Ham. II ii 415-421 shows Sh's knowledge of classical critical theory on dramatic form, though Cunningham's analysis of Sh's twenty-four uses of the term "tragedy" would indicate that Sh ignored that classical critical theory at will.

1890. Cunningham, James V. Woe or Wonder: The Emotional Effect of Shakespearean Tragedy. Denver UP, 1951, 136 pp.

Cunningham shows that Sh's conception of the impact of tragedy on its audience is derived from tradition. In Chs. III and IV he gives a survey of critical doctrine on the tragic emotions from Aristotle through Donatus and Diomedes Grammaticus to the Medieval and Renaissance rhetoricians. Sh's relatively simple view was that tragedy is death and that the tragic emotions of fear, pity, and wonder are responses to death as it is portrayed on the stage. Cunningham brings the tradition to bear especially on the last scene of Ham.; this is good criticism informed by scholarship.

1891. D., C. "An Essay upon Shakespear's Learning," BM, II (1761), 404-405.

A letter which argues, as John Hales is said to have argued, that if Sh was not familiar with the classics, his works nevertheless can rival or surpass the ancients at every point. Virgil's lines on Caesar's death in the Georgics can "not be thought superior" to Horatio's lines on the portents in "the most high and palmy state of Rome" (Ham. I i 113-120). Terence on the subject of dying at the moment of supreme happiness in love lest grief follow is less strong and "pathetic" than Othello expressing the same thought (II i 191-195). Ham. "is allowed even by the professed admirers of the Classics, to be superior to the Electra of Sophocles." Sh's difficulties in plot construction which have earned him the label of ignorance do not exist in Wives, the only Shn play which is (like Jonson's comedies) purely comic. DLC

1892. Dannenfeldt, Karl H. "Egypt and Egyptian Antiquities in the Renaissance," SR, VI (1959), 7-27.

For Shn Egyptology in Oth., see #0735.

1893. Davidson, Sarah Anne. "King Lear, Scapegoat," VJ, V (1931), 117-136.

A disciple of Gilbert Murray and Janet Spens, Miss Davidson traces the Lear story beyond Holinshed and Geoffrey into Celtic mythology in which Llyr, the god of the sea, is connected with annual vegetation-fertilization rites: the cult of the year daemon. From this point, she draws a number of interesting (but not compelling) analogies with the myth of Cecrops and his daughters, but wisely declines "to put Cordelia up on the West Pediment of the Acropolis." Sh obviously was unaware of the scapegoat pre-history of his protagonist, but some instinct made him strip away the veneer of Christianity which had concealed it in his sources. An attractive thesis presented with responsible documentation.

1894. Davies, Thomas. "Hamlet," Dramatic Miscellanies... (Ln, 2nd ed., 1785), III, 1-159.

This commentary contains fewer references to classical culture than several of the shorter essays (see #1004, e.g.). Of special interest are two parallels to Lucian (neither in the grave scene), a digression on the ghost of Darius in the Persae, an analogy between Hamlet's eulogy of Horatio and Orestes' praise of Pylades as "unfever'd" in Euripides' Electra, and a similarity between Socrates' eagerness for death (Apology 32) and "To be or not to be." MnU

1895. Davies, Thomas. "Macbeth"; "King Lear," Dramatic Miscellanies... (Ln, 2nd ed., 1785), II, 112-196, 258-333.

These two commentaries draw on Aeschylus, Sophocles, and Euripides more than on any other sources for illustrations and comparisons. Lady Macbeth is like Clytemnestra in character, if not in situation; Cordelia has filial piety rivaled only by that of Antigone in Oedipus Coloneus; the blinding of Gloucester has precedent in the fates of Oedipus and Polymnestor, but Sophocles and Euripides had the good sense to perform the act off-stage, though both allowed their victims to lament on-stage after the fact. Lines on sleep and night in Macb. remind Davies of the "Hymns of Orpheus"; the hawk and the "mousing owl" recall Atossa's vision of the hawk and the eagle in the Persae. Like Davies' other scholia (see #0738, #1004, #1894) these have fluency and charm. MnU

1896. Detter, Ferd. "Die Hamletsage," ZDA, XXVI (1892), 1-25.

At the beginning of this learned study, Detter discusses the parallels between the L. J. Brutus and Hamlet stories and casts doubt on a putative Indo-European source for both tales, as neither contains that element of mythology which one would expect from prehistoric legend: "wir haben es hier lediglich mit einem novellenstoff [sic, l.c.] zu tun." Detter concentrates on the development of the legend after it migrated to Scandinavia and offers very little comment on Sh's place in the tradition. MdBJ

1897. Domincovich, H. A. "Macbeth, V,ii,3-5," MLN, XXIX (1914), 94-95.

A proposal that in "their dear causes / Would to the bleeding and the grim alarm / Excite the mortified man," the term "excite" has its Latin sense "excito," "to call up from the dead," as in Cicero's In Catilinam II. The lines mean that Macbeth's enemies have such cause to fight as would raise even the dead to participate.

1898. Donoghue, Denis. "Shakespeare's Rhetoric," Studies, XLVII (1958), 431-440.

A discussion of the rhetorical nature and impact of Ham. and Oth. in the imaginative form of two post-mortem addresses: "Hamlet to the Mob" and "Desdemona to Emilia." Hamlet stresses and exemplifies Aristotelian Logos, Pathos, and Ethos in "his" play; Desdemona emphasizes that her function in Oth. derives from the third "office" of a Ciceronian orator, permovere as opposed to docere or delectare.

1899. Doran, Madeleine. "That Undiscovered Country: A Problem concerning the Use of the Supernatural in Hamlet and Macbeth," PQ, XX (1941), 413-427. (Also in Craig Festschrift, pp. 221-235.)

Miss Doran contends that a believable supernatural is coupled with "the problem of the suffering and aspiring heart ..." in Shn tragedy, as in Aeschylus. She illustrates the simplicity of tragic suffering briefly from Euripides' Alcestis 911: ὦ σχῆμα δόμων, πῶς εἰσέλθω, which is implicitly compared to Lear's "You must bear with me. ...I am old and foolish."

1900. Dowden, Edward. "Introduction," The Tragedy of Romeo and Juliet (1900/1935), ArdenSh, pp. ix-xxxix.

Dowden mentions Xenophon of Ephesus as the ultimate source of "the escape from enforced marriage by the use of a sleeping potion," but indicates the indirectness of the connection between Sh and the Greek romance by pointing out that Anthia and Habrocomes was first printed in 1726.

1901. Dowlin, Cornell M. "Two Shakspere Parallels in Studley's Translation of Seneca's Agamemnon," SAB, XIV (1939), 256. SG

One is proverbial (A.Y.L. and W. R.'s prefatory verses) and therefore not significant; the other is a close verbal and situational parallel (Macb. and the Chorus of Agamemnon I) and suggests the possibility "that Shakspere was indebted to the Tenne Tragedies of 1581 rather than to the Latin ..." See also ibid., XV (1940), 128 for a correction.

1902. [Drake, J.] The Antient and Modern Stages survey'd... (1699), [a refutation of Jeremy Collier], Munro, II, 424-428.

An amusing defense of Ophelia, who like maids since the time of Sophocles "longed to know, what was what, before [she] died." Ham. as a whole surpasses everything in "Antiquity ...for the admirable distribution of Poetick Justice."

1903. Draper, John W. "The Old Age of King Lear," JEGP, XXXIX (1940), 527-540.

In Lear, Sh, "like a Greek dramatist, condense[s] the normal evolution of years into a brief time." Lear, who is over eighty, opens the action in choler which in the Galenic system of medicine is appropriate to the middle-aged man, not to the dotard. Thus Lear is younger than his years; yet the choler exhausts his vital powers and he falls precipitously into melancholy (appropriate to the very old) and thence into madness. Draper's interest in Galenic medicine (this paper was read before the American Association of the History of Medicine) perhaps blinds him here as it does elsewhere to larger values and themes in the plays he writes on. His reading makes the play almost trivial.

1904. Draper, John W. "Patterns of Style in Romeo and Juliet," StN, XXI (1949), 195-210.

An analysis of eight major scenes in Romeo to show that Sh used the "colors of rhetoric" to characterize his speakers and set the tone of the action. Draper follows Baldwin (#0089) and Sister Miriam Joseph (#0424) in asserting a classical basis for the rhetoric, but he does not elaborate the point.

1905. Draper, John W. "Shakespeare's 'Star-Crossed Lovers'," RES, XV (1939), 16-34.

In Romeo, Sh utilized the pseudo-science of astrology and the doctrine of the humors, traceable to Greek medicine, "to give the plot of his drama something of the inevitable sequence of Hellenic tragedy." Draper analyzes the humors of the dramatis personae and then traces the plot step by step with close reference to the time scheme to show that events take place at inauspicious times: e.g., Romeo is banished and Juliet pushed into marriage with Paris on Tuesday, Mars's unpropitious day. "Thus the theme of the play is not the evils of civil faction, as in Paynter, or the wickedness of 'stolne contracts', as in Brooke, but rather, as in Greek tragedy, the hopelessness of defying the heavens' will." Draper's argument is uneven, on some points persuasive, on others decidedly not.

1906. Dryden, John. "Dedication," The Satires of Decimus Junius Juvenalis (1693), Munro, II, 179-180.

Though Virgil and Homer have not been equaled since their time, Sh surpasses the ancients in tragedy.

1907. Dugit, E. "Oreste et Hamlet," AESG, I (1889), 143-186.

A detailed comparison of the Choephori, Sophocles' Electra, and Euripides' Electra serves as a prologue to a consideration of modern interpretations of the theme. Ham., written in ignorance of the Greek plays and their spirit, is chief of these. Dugit makes some odd assumptions (e.g., Gertrude was Claudius' accomplice in the murder of King Hamlet) and he labors under the venerable French bias that makes Sh a barbarian genius writing to please a crowd who demanded violence above all. In Dugit's judgment, if Sh is more violent than the Greeks, he is also more reflective (in this sense more like Sophocles than like Aeschylus or Euripides), but Hamlet's meditations are often irrelevant to the task before him, producing a play profound but diffuse. Dugit also believes that Sh is a fatalist (Hamlet passively allows Fate to take its course) while the Greeks defined Fate as an inexorable law of cause and effect which leaves room for human freedom--indeed demands that man's will be its agent. In his remarks on suspense (a major element in Sh which the Greeks deliberately eliminated) and on religion (the English drama, unlike the Greek, did not have a religious basis), Dugit shows that he understands Greek culture better than Elizabethan. DLC

1908. Dunn, E. Catherine. "The Storm in King Lear," SQ, III (1952), 329-333.

Professor Dunn sees in the play an example of Empedoclean dualism: Love and Hatred (Ingratitude) war for control of the universe. In the storm scenes both microcosm and macrocosm are distorted by the battle. Professor Dunn makes much of the classical interest in the morality of gratitude, cf. her dissertation cited in the notes to this art. On the war of the elements in Lear, cf. also George W. Williams (#2167).

1909. D[uthie], G[eorge] I[an]. "Introduction," Romeo & Juliet (1955), CSh, [XXVIII], pp. xi-xxxvii.

Duthie points briefly to Xenophon of Ephesus as the ultimate source of "the heroine's use of a potion to escape an enforced marriage." He makes much of the rôle of Fate or Fortune's wheel in the play, comparing Chaucer's Troilus and Criseyde, where not character but Fortune precipitates calamity.

1910. Eagle, R[oderick] L. "Sun Moving Round the Earth," NQ, CLXXXIX (1945), 43. GRS

In response to a query, Eagle points out that the context of Hamlet's "Doubt that the sun doth move" (II ii 117) is evidence of Sh's belief in Ptolemaic astronomy.

1911. Easy, Benj. "Hamlet," 3 NQ, VIII (1865), 126.

Sh is thinking of the derivation of "disaster" in Ham. I i 118; the phrase "disasters in the sun" means "dis-stars in the sun" or sunspots. Sh, like his age, enjoyed hyper-subtle etymologizing in Latin and Greek.

1912. Eidson, John O. "A Senecan Parallel in 'Hamlet'," SAB, X (1935), 105. SG

Eidson finds parallels in Seneca to Hamlet's "there is nothing either good or bad but thinking makes it so." But he does not note that the superiority of mind to Fortune was a Stoic commonplace, and that Sh could have found the idea and phrasing in a number of contemporary writers.

1913. Ellison, Paul. "Reason to the Dane," BUSE, I (1955), 20-37.

An analysis of the dialectic (most often Aristotelian syllogisms) of Ham. shows that in the protagonist as the action proceeds a tension develops between Stoicism, the ethical system he professes in Act I, and Christianity, toward which he is moving later in the play. In the scene of carnage in Act V he reveals that both sets of values are mingled in him, but that Christianity is dominant. The argument is not persuasive, especially about V ii.

1914. Elton, Oliver. "Hamlet the Elizabethan: A Popular Lecture," A Sheaf of Papers (Liverpool UP, 1923), pp. 17-35.

This portrait of Hamlet as an Elizabethan courtier is concerned with philosophy (he is no Stoic as Brutus was--at least not in respect to suicide), letters (Hamlet's classical allusions are hackneyed, especially when he is emotionally stirred, and he likes outdated heroic tragedy on classical themes) and, among many other things, humanism (the "What a piece of work" speech is Greek in its affirmation of human worth, but Sh may well have obtained the ideas indirectly, through Montaigne's Essais). Elton's is an interesting approach to the character.

1915. Erskine, John. "'Romeo and Juliet'," ColSS, pp. 213-234. E-S

In passing Erskine compares the love of Romeo and Juliet with those of three other pairs of famous lovers, Hero and Leander, Tristan and Iseult, Pyramus and Thisbe. But, more interesting, he adds Paris and Helen, who are destroyed not by Menelaus, but by "the rising tide of Greek destiny" as Romeo and Juliet are destroyed by enmity between their houses, not by individual malice.

1916. Fairchild, A[rthur] H. R. "'Mummy' in Shakespeare," PQ, I (1922), 143-146.

Fairchild attempts to establish that "mummy" meant to the Elizabethans the dead embalmed body itself, not any gum which might ooze from it, as other commentators have thought. Sh refers to mummy in Oth. III iv 74-75, Macb. IV i 23, and Wives III v 19. The reference in Oth. makes it clear that Sh associated the term with ancient Egypt.

1917. Fairchild, A[rthur] H. R. "A Note on Macbeth," PQ, IV (1925), 348-350.

The expression "[Let] The eye wink at the hand" (I iv 52) does not mean "Let me appear not to see what I do" but rather "Let me refuse to see what I do." The passage can be illustrated from one of Alciatus' Emblems (XVI), a drawing of a hand with an open eye in its palm. The accompanying verses (Greek and Latin) contain at one point the phrase "Ecce oculate manus credens id quod videt," which may have been in Sh's mind as he was writing this aside of Macbeth's. Fairchild's hypothesis is surely not necessary to explain Sh's use of the phrase, but Sh did know the emblem literature.

1918. Fairchild, Arthur H. R. Shakespeare and the Tragic Theme, MUS, XIX, No. 2 [incorrectly numbered XXIX, No. 2] (1944), 145 pp.

The tragic theme in Sh is the conflict between "sentimentalism" (i.e., self-centered emotionalism) and "will" (i.e., intellectual awareness and directed energy). The tragic heroes (Fairchild concentrates on Ham., Oth., Lear, and Macb.) all are "sentimental" while their antagonists succeed temporarily because in them the intellect is dominant. Insofar as the tragic theme is ethical, the virtues at stake are Greek: wisdom, fortitude, temperance, and justice. All of these are intellectual virtues, yet Sh always reserves a place for the emotional virtues (e.g., conscience, love, humility), which are Christian, rather than classical. Therefore Fairchild's thesis contains a central paradox which he does not fully explain: Sh's heroes fail because of passion (i.e., neglect of reason), yet the "rational" characters are the evil ones in each tragedy. In Ch. II Fairchild places Sh's "subjectivism" (the homocentricity of his philosophy) in a tradition which goes back as far as the Odyssey. Though many of the observations here are significant (especially on Platonic and Neoplatonic attitudes toward love and the ideal), it is not apparent that this discussion of Sh's classical heritage supports the main thesis of the book.

1919. Fansler, Harriott Ely. The Evolution of Technic in Elizabethan Tragedy. Chicago, 1914, 283 pp. SG

Though the book deals with technique in many Elizabethan dramatists, it gives more attention passim to Sh than to anyone else, ending the account with his retirement. The most significant point about Sh and classical form is that Sh (with Marlowe) revolted against Senecanism in the 'nineties, "sought other themes and a freer technic, yet gradually, nevertheless, conformed somewhat to the best conventions of Seneca and partly remade them. This fact is especially manifest in 'Romeo and Juliet', in the Senecan elements of 'Hamlet' and in the structure of 'Othello'." There are references as well to the Senecanism of Caesar and R.III. This is a plausible thesis.

1920. Farnham, Willard. Shakespeare's Tragic Frontier: The World of His Final Tragedies. California UP, 1950, 289 pp.

For the classical antecedents of the Witches in Macb., see #1304.

1921. Fergusson, Francis. "Hamlet: The Analogy of Action," HR, II (1949), 165-210.

This somewhat repetitive essay (which later appeared as a ch. in The Idea of a Theater) divides roughly into two theses: (1) Ham. is constructed on the principle of analogy which Aristotle describes in the Poetics when he takes up the structure of the Odyssey; i.e., each subplot or character is related to the central theme not causally or logically but by analogy (Laertes' troubles are a parallel to Hamlet's). (2) The ritual aspect of the play (reception, ceremony, procession, funeral, etc.) gives it a solemnity worthy of Greek tragedy (with which Fergusson compares it). The theme is that of Oedipus: the state must be purged by a man who suffers for the truth, and the man himself must uncover the disease in that state. This ritual approach is provocative, especially in the emphasis it gives to "The Mousetrap," but it takes no account whatever of the materials of plot, theme, and character which came ready-made in Sh's sources. For some strictures on Aristotle as a key to Ham., see Hardin Craig's "The Shackling of Accidents" (#1884).

1922. Fergusson, Francis. "Macbeth as the Imitation of an Action," EIE, 1951 (Col UP, 1952), pp. 31-43.

Fergusson defines "πρᾶξις" as "purpose," "aim," or "motive" and suggests that the unifying motive in Macb. is the extra- or suprarational elements in the plot, not just the Witches, but also the faith of Macduff and Malcolm, the "unsexing" of Lady Macbeth, and especially the effort of Macbeth to outstrip everything and everyone, reflected in the metaphor "The expedition of my violent love / Outrun the pauser, reason." An interesting approach to the Poetics, but it is not obvious that Aristotle would applaud Fergusson's definition of his term.

1923. Fischer, Rudolf. Zur Kunstentwicklung der englischen Tragödie von ihren ersten Anfängen bis zu Shakespeare. Strassburg, 1893, 192 pp. E-S

Fischer traces the evolution of English dramatic structure and technique under Senecan influence through Marlowe. In brief but illuminating comparisons with Marlowe near the end of the book (see analytical "Inhalts-Übersicht"), Sh is portrayed as a "feinfühlig Meister" whose maturity enabled him to manipulate the devices of Senecanism to better structural effect than Marlowe could. The emphasis falls on such matters as ratio of men to women in the cast, number of actual speakers on the stage at any given time, length and number of scenes, balance between monologue and dialogue. A satisfying approach to Seneca and his English inheritors.

1924. Flanagan, Sarah Patricia. "A Reinterpretation of King Lear," diss (Brown, 1957). DA, XVIII (1958), 581.

The abstract alludes to discernible parallels between Lear and Greek tragedy, especially the Oedipus cycle.

1925. Flatter, Richard. "Who Wrote the Hecate-Scene?" ShJ, XCIII (1957), 196-210. GRS

Flatter defends the integrity of Macb., rejecting the theory of Middleton's collaboration, and arguing that Sh not only wrote III v, but made the scene central to the spiritual crisis in the play. He argues that Sh's conception of Hecate as the queen of witches comes from Spenser's Daphnaida (Stanza 3), where Hecate appears accompanied by three witches. At ibid., XCIV (1958), 200-202, John Cutts argues for Middleton's hand in Macb., and Flatter replies, ibid., XCV (1959), 225-237, pointing out further possible sources in Meta. VII and XIV and in FQ for Sh's Hecate and for the number three which is so much associated with her and her Witches in Macb. Flatter is inclined to doubt Sh's classical obligations: Sh "did not identify his Witches with the Fates of Greek mythology; he did not regard them as the 'Parcae', as Boece calls them, nor as the 'goddesses of destinie', as they are described by Holinshed." The controversy continues through ibid., XCVI (1960), 173-176, 192-193. Flatter appears to have the better case on the authorship question.

1926. Fox, W. S. "Lucian in the Grave-Scene of Hamlet," PQ, II (1923), 132-141. HB SG

Fox cites ten elements or references in the grave scene which recall Lucian (chiefly the Dialogues of the Dead), and asserts that Sh knew Lucian in an English, Latin, or French trans. Perhaps Fox gives undue weight to his evidence, for many of the references were Elizabethan commonplaces (e.g., "ubi sunt," death as a leveler of persons, mutability). The analogy between Alexander the Great in Lucian and in Ham. is interesting, though not compelling.

1927. Fox, W. S. "Sources of the Grave-Scene in Hamlet," 3 TRSC, XVII (1923), Section 2, pp. 71-80. SG

Though grave scenes are common in the Senecan tragedies of the Elizabethan and Jacobean periods and though there probably was one in the Ur-Hamlet, Lucian is nonetheless a major source of inspiration for Ham. V i. Most of this art. is a survey of Lucian allusions and eds. in the sixteenth century calculated to demonstrate the accessibility to Sh of a Latin, English, or French version of the Dialogues of the Dead. See Fox's analysis of the grave scene itself (#1926).

1928. French, J. Milton. "Othello Among the Anthropophagi," PMLA, XLIX (1934), 807-809. E-S SG

French attempts to establish that Othello's description (I iii) of his romantic adventures was based on maps in Ptolemy's Geography rather than on the verbal pictures in Pliny. T. W. Baldwin (#0084) a year later firmly established that Sh did read Pliny. French's theory is interesting (as is the map he reproduces as evidence), but his fanciful speculation on the meaning of the word "antres" does not command belief.

1929. Furnivall, F. J. "The End of Hamlet's 'Sea of Troubles'," Acad, XXXV (1889), 360. SG

Furnivall wishes to reinterpret Ham. III i 59-60 as a reference to the ancient custom of the Celts of demonstrating their courage by opposing the incoming tide with drawn swords, even though they be drowned by it. He cites references to the custom in Aristotle, Nicolaus of Damascus, Strabo, and Aelian. Sh's most likely access to the information would be Abraham Fleming's 1576 English version of Aelian. Inviting as Furnivall's explanation may be in the context of the soliloquy, it is difficult to agree when he says "some of Sh's audience at the Globe would have understood his 'by opposing, end them,' better than some of his successors have done." This bit of Celtic lore is too recondite to be common knowledge then, or now.

1930. Gaither, Mary Elizabeth. "Ancient and Modern Concepts of the Tragic Hero," diss (Indiana, 1953). DA, XIII (1953), 547.

This diss considers inter alia the chief difference between Shn and Greek tragedy: Greek tragic heroes are scapegoats who fall through ignorance or blindness; Shn tragic heroes are themselves fully responsible for what befalls them.

1931. Geoffroy, [Julien Louis]. "Ducis: Hamlet" (1809), Cours de littérature dramatique ..., 2nd ed. (Paris, 1825), IV, 1-8.

As prologue to a review of Ducis' production, Geoffroy advances the opinion (pp. 1-4) that Sh was, by contrast with Sophocles, a complete barbarian, even though Hamlet has "plus d'humanité et de naturel que le Grec Oreste." Geoffroy finds it revolting that Hamlet should hold a double standard vis à vis his mother and uncle when both are equally guilty of his father's murder (Gertrude may, indeed, be more guilty than Claudius). Sh did not know Sophocles, or any other classics but North's Plutarch, and therefore could not profit from the single-minded remorselessness of Sophocles' hero. Geoffroy is disturbed that French dramatists should imitate Sh rather than Sophocles. DFo

1932. Gilkes, A. H. School Lectures on the Electra of Sophocles and Macbeth. Ln, 1880, 148 pp.

Gilkes treats each play in isolation; there are no comparisons between them. But at one point (p. 137), he makes the passing observation that in Macb. V iii 61-62, the uneasy Doctor is reminiscent of the Watchman of Antigone who reluctantly brings to Creon the news of Polynices' burial. However, the Doctor's part should be played seriously; if the Watchman has a tinge of the comic in him, the Doctor does not.

1933. Glasson, T. Francis. "Did Shakespeare Read Aeschylus?" LQHR, CLXXIII (1948), 57-66.

Glasson resurrects the hypothesis of Churton Collins (#0173) that Sh knew the Greek tragedians. He cites fourteen parallels to Choephori in Sh (eight of them in Macb., the others in Ham. and Romeo), but he is convinced that Sh did not get at Aeschylus through Sanravius' Latin trans. and is forced to leave his own question unanswered. Glasson is familiar with Murray (#2049), Farmer (#0238), Root (#0497), and Dover Wilson (#2173, #2174), but surprisingly makes no mention at all of Baldwin's Small Latine (#0089), which appeared four years earlier than this art., and he sees little to object to in Farmer. He does not notice that some of his fourteen passages were transmitted through Seneca (e.g., the "multitudinous seas incarnadine"). But he refrains from making extravagant claims for Sh's learning.

1934. Goldsmith, Robert Hillis. "Did Shakespeare Use the Old Timon Comedy?" SQ, IX (1958), 31-38.

For possible influence on Lear, see #1342.

1935. Gollancz, Israel. The Sources of Hamlet. OUP, 1926, 321 pp. E-S

In pp. 27-33 of his introductory essay on the legend, Gollancz points out the similarity between the Hamlet story and the legend of Lucius Junius Brutus, who feigned imbecility to protect himself from the Tarquins. Saxo Grammaticus introduced the Roman material, possibly from Livy, but more likely from his own contemporary Zonaras, who recapitulated earlier versions. Gollancz does not discuss Sh's play, but since the Roman elements were already in Saxo, the classical connection with Sh is mediate.

1936. Grace, William J. "The Cosmic Sense in Shakesperean Tragedy," SewR, L (1942), 433-445.

Grace attempts to show that Sh's tragic vision is at least partly Platonic: Good is a norm which permeates the universe through transcendent correspondences; Evil breaks these correspondences, isolating the sinner (villain) from the rest of the harmonious cosmos. The view appears in Castiglione's Courtier. An allusive and speculative art. rather than a thorough analysis of the question.

1937. Gray, Henry D[avid]. "Did Shakespeare Write a Tragedy of Dido?" MLR, XV (1920), 217-222.

Gray discusses the "interesting possibility" that the "rugged Pyrrhus" speech in Ham. represents a survival of his own putative tragedy on Aeneas and Dido, written perhaps in the 1580's in imitation of Marlowe (and surpassing him). If this is the case, the speech would be drawn from a scene which contained Aeneas' long epic narrative of the sack of Troy.

1938. "A Greek Hamlet," FM, n.s. XXII (1880), 511-527.

An imaginative and vivid retelling of Herodotus' story of the tyrant Periander and his vengeful son Lycophron. The author does not suggest any indebtedness, but stresses the striking similarities: the passivity of the avenger coupled with an inexorable rigidity of will, the effect on the mind of the culprit (Claudius/Periander), the implications for succession to the throne, the rôle of friends and family of the avenger, the trip to a foreign island (Corcyra/England), the almost gratuitous death of the hero at the moment of triumph. But he is frank in pointing out some differences: the Greek hero has neither humor nor madness, neither "brutality of fact" nor doubt of his victim's guilt, and where Hamlet succeeds in his vengeance Lycophron is "the only victim of his own tragedy."

1939. Hadas, Moses. "Clytemnestra in Elizabethan Dress," CW, XXXII (1939), 255-256.

Hadas traces Lady Macbeth back to Aeschylus' Clytemnestra by way of Hector Boece's Historia Scotorum and Livy's bloodthirsty Tullia. An interesting succession but not a compelling argument.

1940. Hadzsits, George D. Lucretius and His Influence, Our Debt, [No. 12] (N.Y., 1935), 372 pp.

In a footnote (p. 277) to his ch. on Lucretian influence on the Renaissance, Hadzsits speaks of the many parallels between Sh and Lucretius perhaps traceable to Sh's reading in Montaigne, who was directly indebted. He cites (p. 106) only Lear's speech about the baby crying as it first enters "this great stage of fools" (IV vi 180-187).

1941. Halliday, William Reginald. "The Classical and the Medieval Traditions," Greek and Roman Folklore, Our Debt, [No. 44] (N.Y., 1927), pp. 115-144.

The ch. contains two allusions to Sh: (1) the Witch's "I'll do, I'll do, and I'll do" (Macb. I iii 10) is comparable to the traditional superstition of repeating a form of the verb "τελῶ" ("to do"). This repetition was regarded as magical in ancient times and is the etymological source of the word "talisman." (2) Jaques's metaphor "the world's a stage" has a "literary ancestry ... which can be traced in the diatribes or popular sermons of the Cynics," and his division of life into seven ages is perhaps ultimately traceable to the folklore of the lunar month; Halliday mentions Solon and Hippocrates as ancient authorities on the number seven.

1942. Hamilton, Marie P. "A Latin and English Passage on Dreams," SP, XXXIII (1936), 1-9. SG

Sh, like Chaucer, Shelley, Swift, and Fitzgerald, makes use of the classical concept that dreams are a nocturnal reiteration of a man's waking concerns. The concept goes back as far, perhaps, as Epicurus, but Sh's debt is to Claudian (Panegyric on Honorius) when he has Mercutio discuss the question (Romeo I iv 53-94); it is noteworthy that Sh Anglicizes, introducing Queen Mab, and adopting a lighthearted tone. An interesting art.

1943. Hamilton, Richard Winter. "On the Tragic Genius of Shakspeare," Nugae Literariae: Prose and Verse (Ln, 1841), pp. 185-235.

In language which he admits may be "too elated" Hamilton glorifies Sh at the expense of the Greek dramatists. He "was by no means learned" (Hamilton has praise for Farmer); yet he surpasses the Greek tragedians in his scope and in his creation of individuals. The essay lingers over Macb. and Ham. and touches many other plays lightly. Brief comparisons between Shn and Greek tragedy are numerous (e.g., the tomb scene in Romeo and the dénouement of Antigone). DFo

1944. Hankins, John E. "The Character of Hamlet," The Character of Hamlet and Other Essays (North Carolina UP, 1941), pp. 1-92.

In the course of a detailed argument to prove that Hamlet delays until he is sure of the justice of what he has been told to do, Hankins observes: "It is no accident that Shakespeare has made Hamlet a student of philosophy," and passim he shows Hamlet's reflections on problems posed by Seneca, Aristotle (Nicomachean Ethics), Lucretius, and Plato (the Gorgias). The two most interesting passages are (1) the thorough analysis of "To be or not to be ..." as a philosophical problem ("aut esse aut non esse") seen in Stoic and Epicurean terms; and (2) the conclusion, which juxtaposes the problems of justice in Ham. with Socrates' observations to Polus and Callicles on Archelaus of Macedonia, who killed his brother and went unpunished. Sh could have found the Gorgias in any of three Latin versions, including Ficino's.

1945. Hankins, John E. "Hamlet's 'God Kissing Carrion': A Theory of the Generation of Life," PMLA, LXIV (1949), 507-516.

A thorough examination of Hamlet's mystifying remarks to Polonius about carrion, the sun, and pregnancy (II ii 181-187). Hankins explores the classical antecedents of belief in spontaneous generation by sunlight in dead matter and in a woman's womb. Both beliefs had Aristotelian authority and were widespread in late classical and Medieval "scientific" writings.

1946. Hankins, John E. "On Ghosts," The Character of Hamlet and Other Essays (North Carolina UP, 1941), pp. 131-171.

In section 4, Hankins lists among five approaches to the Ghost in Ham. the view that he is "the actual soul of the elder Hamlet." There are illustrative or supporting citations from such classical authorities on pneumatology as Lucian (on Diogenes and Heracles in the Dialogues of the Dead), Macrobius (Commentarii in Somnium Scipionis), Porphyry, Iamblichus, Apuleius (De Deo Socratis), and (in the Renaissance) Ficino, who Christianized the Neoplatonic concepts.

1947. [Hanmer, Thomas?]. Some Remarks on the Tragedy of Hamlet... (1736). (Reprinted by The Augustan Reprint Society. Series Three: Essays on the Stage, ed. Clarence D. Thorpe, 1947.)

This anonymous essay, traditionally attributed to Hanmer, is distinguished for its disregard of the unities of time, place, and action in favor of unity of "design" (centrality of purpose). In this rejection of Restoration canons of Shn criticism Some Remarks... anticipates Johnson's "Preface" (#0351). The author refers twice to classical parallels to the play: (1) Horatio, like Achates in the Aeneid, is a friend who never is required to prove his loyalty by sacrifice, but in the last scene Sh hints that much will be demanded of Horatio in after time; (2) Sh shows a restraint absent from the Oresteia--Hamlet is not required by the story to perform the shocking act of matricide.

1948. Harrison, Frederic. "Greek and Elizabethan Tragedy," De Senectute: More Last Words (Ln, 1923), pp. 79-102. HB

What made Attic tragedy piteous (and pity is what makes tragedy) was its concentration on the action, its concern with the catastrophe, its restraint from excess (of visual horror, multiple deaths, and lyric outbursts in dialogue). Romantic tragedy (Sh is almost the only dramatist mentioned) may be greater as poetry, but can never rival Attic drama for piteousness because it lacks centrality. Only Macb. of all Sh's plays is an approximation of the Greek spirit--or would be if one eliminated the Porter and the Witches.

1949. Harrison, Jane Ellen. Mythology, Our Debt, [No. 26] ([1924]/1963), 155 pp.

Miss Harrison quotes twice from Sh in passing: (1) Ham. III iv 58-59 to indicate Sh's conventional conception of Hermes as a messenger; (2) W.T. IV iv 116-118 to indicate that Sh, like Milton and other modern poets, "sees deeper" into the Ceres/Persephone myth than

Homer, who portrays Persephone only as Queen of the Underworld.

1950. Harrison, Thomas P., Jr. "The Folger Secret of Secrets, 1572," AMS, pp. 601-620.

For possible influence on Lear, see #1021.

1951. Harrison, Thomas P., Jr. "'Hang Up Philosophy'," SAB, XXII (1947), 203-209.

The principles of moderation and of man's potentiality for good or evil, two major themes in Romeo, are underscored by Friar Laurence in II iii, when he indulges in his meditation on botany, poisons, and human nature. Mandrake (the sleeping potion) and aconite (the deadly poison) are the potent liquors the Friar refers to, and his observations about their capacities are drawn from the natural histories of Pliny and Bartholomaeus. Like the liquors, Romeo has latent potentiality within him; thus, though Fate is a factor in the tragedy, Romeo is responsible for his destiny. A valuable exegesis of the passage.

1952. Harrison, Thomas P., Jr. "Shakespeare's 'Hebenon' Again," MLR, XL (1945), 310-311.

Harrison quotes Pliny both in the original and in Holland's trans. as evidence that Sh was thinking of the drastic effects of hemlock in the Ghost's description of his death (Ham. I v 59-73). One of these effects, the "vile and loathsome crust," Sh may have expanded from the word "maculae" in Pliny which Holland renders "certain spots or specks." It is significant that Pliny also discusses henbane; there is no reason why Sh could not have "reinforced" this passage from his knowledge of "other dangerous plants," but Harrison appears correct in his belief that Pliny's hemlock is the primary poison here.

1953. Harrison, W. A. "Hamlet's Juice of Cursed Hebona," NSST, [IX] (1880-85), 295-321.

With an impressive display of medical, literary, linguistic, and botanical erudition, Harrison lends support to the contention of Nicholson (#2055) that Sh meant "hebon," "yew," by the "hebona" which killed Hamlet's father. Harrison, like Nicholson, marshals the ancients in his behalf, but Thomas P. Harrison, Jr., may have a better argument for hemlock (#1952) than W. A. Harrison does for yew.

1954. Hart, H. C. "Introduction," The Tragedy of Othello (1903/1934), ArdenSh, pp. ix-xliv.

Suggesting a date in or around 1602, Hart calls attention to several passages in Oth. which seem to be indebted to Holland's Pliny (1602). Among them are the "chrysolite" of V ii 145, the "Anthropophagi" of I iii 144, the "Pontic Sea" reference (III iii 453-456), and the "med'cinable gum" of "Arabian trees" (V ii 350-351). "Indeed, outside Plutarch's (North's edition) Lives, it would be difficult to produce an author so definitely honoured by Shakespeare's recognition as Philemon Holland [is] in this play." Hart also calls attention to the Greek root of Desdemona's name (p. xxxi).

1955. Heilman, Robert B. "The Lear World," EIE, 1948 (Col UP, 1949), pp. 29-57.

A view of Shn tragedy as the tension between those who accept myth defined broadly (e.g., Desdemona, Lear, Cordelia) and those who hyperrationally ignore or reject it (e.g., Iago, Edmund, Goneril). Heilman makes a number of interesting remarks about classical myth: e.g., (1) Goneril, Regan, and the other purveyors of evil in Lear do not mention the gods at all; they are outside the world of justice and love which Sh conveys in the pagan gods. (2) Gloucester is a reincarnation of Tiresias--only when blind does he see. (3) Oedipus and Macbeth both hear prophecies and both Sophocles and Sh "proclaim certain limits to the efficacy of a rational management of life" but "whereas the Greek emphasis is upon what man cannot escape, the Elizabethan emphasis is upon what he cannot capture." A thoughtful piece of criticism.

1956. Heilman, Robert B. Shakespearian Tragedy and the Drama of Disaster. British Columbia UP, 1960, 27 pp.

Heilman distinguishes between true tragedy, produced by a flawed protagonist who acts upon others, and "disaster," in which pathetic characters are acted upon. He marshals Sh and the Attic tragedians on the first side and Ibsen, Synge, O'Neill, and numerous others on the second. The comparisons between Greek and Shn characters are mainly brief allusions (e.g., Cordelia is in Antigone's position, faced with a choice between hybris and humiliation).

1957. Heilman, Robert B. "The Sight Pattern in Oedipus Rex," This Great Stage: Image and Structure in King Lear (LSU Press, 1948), pp. 20-24. (Part of Ch. I.)

A brief but illuminating analysis of Oedipus Tyrannus, which like Lear has as one leitmotiv the paradox that the blind perceive better than those who have eyes. Heilman points to two or three similarities of phrasing, which are "something more than an accident ... a certain complex of raw materials may always, as it were, exact from the artist a certain kind of aesthetic strategy."

1958. Henderson, W. A. "Shakspeare and Sophocles," 8 NQ, IV (1893), 345. HB

Henderson asserts that Sh wrote Ham. as an exercise in filial piety after his father's death just as Sophocles (so legend says) wrote Oedipus Coloneus as a protest against his ungrateful son. He points to similarities of theme between Ham. and Electra, but defers to Collins' (at that time projected) essays (#0173, #0174) on the question of direct indebtedness.

1959. Heninger, S. K., Jr. "Shakespeare's King Lear, III,ii,1-9," Expl, XV (1956), item 1.

In this speech ("Blow winds ... "), Lear conveys universality by including each of the four elements. The phrase "thought-executing" (line 4) refers to the capacity of lightning to destroy contents without damaging containers, a capacity described by Seneca and Pliny: Lear wants the thought of his ungrateful children to be struck by lightning.

1960. Hense, Carl Conrad. "Shakespeare und die Philosophie (Pythagoras)," Shakespeare: Untersuchungen und Studien (Halle, 1884), pp. 619-641.

For Brabantio, Romeo, and Hamlet as critics of classical philosophy, see #0800. DFo

1961. Herpich, Cha[rle]s. A. "'Bellona's Bridegroom,' 'Macbeth,' I.ii.54," 10 NQ, III (1905), 426.

Herpich attributes Sh's error in mating Mars with Bellona to a similar error in Chapman's Homer, Book V. But the expression in Macb. refers not to Mars, but to Macbeth; Herpich's explanation is unnecessary.

1962. Herpich, Cha[rle]s. A. "The Source of the 'Seven Ages'," 9 NQ, IX (1902), 46-47.

For a possible relation between Holland's Pliny and the wailing child on "this great stage of fools" in Lear, see #0802.

1963. Herzberg, Max J. "Sources and Stage History of Romeo and Juliet," A-VG, XXI (December, 1954), 21-27.

At the beginning of this commentary for college students on the film version of the play, Herzberg remarks that the story originates in Ephesus in Asia Minor, "has roots in Ovid's Pyramus and Thisbe," and finds an analogue in the Anthia and Habrocomes of Xenophon of Ephesus. There is no elaboration.

1964. Hewitt, Douglas. "The Very Pompes of the Divell--Popular and Folk Elements in Elizabethan and Jacobean Drama," RES, XXV (1949), 10-23.

"Just as Greek tragedy, which originated in the worship of Dionysos, derived part of its force from its religious associations, so Elizabethan drama, when performed to an audience responsive to the folk ceremonies from which the plays partly sprang, may have had certain appeals which are now lost." The discussion centers on Lear, in which the protagonist is: (1) the fool as king driven out to usher in a fertile new spring; (2) the scapegoat suffering (as every tragic protagonist suffers) Christlike for all mankind. There is an analogy between the British deposed-lunatic-king folk theme and similar themes in primitive Greek and Roman religion which Hewitt does not point out. Cf. #2029, #2049, #2126, and #1893. The connection with the classics probably lies in Indo-European pre-history which has left no documents to substantiate the hypothesis.

1965. Hill, N. W. "Shakespeare and Aristophanes," Acad, LXXII (1907), 76. SG

Hill sees a direct debt to Aristophanes' Clouds (345-348) in Hamlet's comic remarks to Polonius (III ii 393-399) on the shapes of clouds and in Antony's serious comparison between his shifting fortunes and shifting clouds (Antony IV xiv 2-11). Sh presumably found a Latin trans. Arthur Chapman observes in a sarcastic reply (ibid., 123) that Sh needed no prodding to recognize that clouds often look now like one animal and again like another.

1966. H[olland], N[orman] N. "Macbeth as Hibernal Giant," L&P, X (1960), 37-38.

The episode where Birnam Wood approaches Dunsinane and the large number of references to planting, growth, seeds, fruit, and decay (e.g., "the yellow leaf") suggest to Holland that Macb. should be interpreted as a ritual in which winter (Macbeth) gives place at last to spring (Malcolm). Holland stresses Germanic folklore, but mentions also the relevance of Frazer's Golden Bough which traces the rituals of the sacrificial king in primitive Mediterranean religion.

1967. Horton-Smith, Lionel. Ars Tragica Sophoclea cum Shaksperiana Comparata: An Essay on the Tragic Art of Sophocles and Shakspere... Cambridge, 1896, 146 pp. (The Latin Prize Essay at Cambridge, 1894.)

This is a scholarly essay which profits from earlier criticism of both dramatists. Horton-Smith considers various aspects of "tragic art" from the use of pun to metrics to catharsis (though oddly he does not discuss hamartia), and he extends the scope of the essay to include the social and physical settings in which the "tragic art" of both dramatists was conceived. A number of allusions to other Greek and Roman classics are introduced incidentally to illustrate various points. A useful essay which sees as many points of difference as of similarity and which refrains from patronizing either dramatist. DFo

1968. Howell, W. B. L. "Ajax and Hamlet," CM, VI (1896), 205-211.

The chief connection between Sophocles' play and Sh's is the madness of their heroes. But insanity takes one form in Ajax, who is violent and active, and another in Hamlet, who is voluble but passive. Both men treat beloved women cruelly, but Ajax' indifference to Tecmessa is less reprehensible than Hamlet's abuse of Ophelia. Ajax is a primitive man led astray by Intellect (Athena deceives him into attacking the sheep); Hamlet is a sensitive man in whom "resolution / Is sicklied o'er with the pale cast of thought." Howell makes some interesting observations, especially about Ajax, but he is not justified in calling Ham. "roughhewn"; nor are the two plays as comparable as he assumes.

1969. Hunter, G. K. "Isocrates' Precepts and Polonius' Character," SQ, VIII (1957), 501-506.

Josephine Bennett (#1829) is in error when she assumes that Sh expected his audience to be contemptuous of Polonius' advice as wisdom from a schoolboy's collection of sententiae. The ultimate source is Isocrates, but the same precepts were very common in serious contexts at the time Sh was writing; indeed he seriously repeats several of them in All's W. The delayed impact of the speech is not its folly, but its tragic inadequacy to cope with the massive evil of the play. An interesting argument.

1970. Hunter, Grace. "Notes on Othello's 'Base Indian'," SAB, XIX (1944), 26-28.

This note suggests two possible explanations of Othello's phrase at V ii 347: (1) Ammianus Marcellinus' history of Rome recounts the story of an ignorant near-eastern (Indian?) soldier who threw away the pearls in a captured satchel, keeping only the less valuable leather. (2) Herod was "base" of birth in the eyes of the Romans and intensely jealous of his wife, Mariamne, who died because of his suspicion of Sohemus, who like Cassio was innocent, but thought to be guilty. Herod was half Jewish, an Idumean--"Idumean" may be the word Sh wrote.

1971. Hyde, Isabel. "A Note on 'King Lear' and 'Timon of Athens'," NQ, CCV (1960), 19-20.

The reference in Lear to "tell[ing] tales" (II iv 230-231) to Zeus of one's enemies that he may punish them is, according to this note, a direct echo of Lucian's Misanthropos, which Sh used as a source for Tim. It is possible, accordingly, that Tim. antedates Lear, if one can accept the author's contention about Sh and Lucian. But note that as early as Titus Sh had suppliants shoot arrows at the gods to call their attention to injustices which needed righting.

1972. James, M. R. "Understood Relations," NQ, CLXV (1933), 380.

This phrase (Macb. III iv 124) means "overheard conversations." Part of the evidence James offers is the classical legends of Bessus and Ibycus, as related by Lewis Theobald.

1973. Jameson, [Anna]. Characteristics of Women, Moral, Political, Historical (1832), 2nd ed., 1833, II, 88-114. (As abstracted in the New Variorum Lear.)

A warm appreciation of Cordelia, contrasted in places with Antigone. "To Antigone our admiration [for what she does], to Cordelia our tears [for what is done to what she is]."

1974. Jeffreys, M. D. W. "The Weird Sisters in Macbeth," ESA, I (1958), 43-54.

Not seen. According to the SQ bibliography--#0042--(1959, for 1958), Jeffreys traces the Witches to Hecate and the Erinyes; though later scenes are more "mundane," the classical background "'strikes the grand note in the opening scene, elemental forces and a man at the crossways'."

1975. Jenkins, Raymond. "The Tragic Hero of Aristotle and Shakespeare," ShN, IX (1959), 30.

This report of a paper read at the Southeastern Renaissance Conference (1959) indicates Jenkins' belief that Sh's tragic heroes, frank, aspiring, truthful, and honorable, are more like the ideal man of Aristotle's Ethics than like the tragic protagonist of the Poetics. The very virtues of Sh's heroes are the seed of their flaws; it is not the case with the hamartia of Aristotle's hero. A difference between Aristotle's ethical man and Sh's is that the former has temperance, the latter has not; but a greater similarity overshadows the differences: both are magnanimous.

1976. Jepsen, Laura. Ethical Aspects of Tragedy: A Comparison of Certain Tragedies by Aeschylus, Sophocles, Euripides, Seneca and Shakespeare. Florida UP, 1953, 130 pp.

Beginning with a consideration of ethos, which she defines as the moral implication of tragic action viewed emotionally by the audience, Professor Jepsen divides her subject into five parts, the first three of which are relevant to Sh's tragedies. (For the last two, see #1418.) First is poetic justice, exemplified in Aeschylus' Oresteia and Macb.; second is poetic (tragic) irony, exemplified in Oedipus Tyrannus and Oth., Oedipus Coloneus and Lear, and Antigone and Ham.; third is pathos, exemplified in Hippolytus and Romeo. The comparative judgments are made with Aristotle as a standard. Typical are these two points: (1) the "ethical" situation of Hamlet vis à vis Claudius, his uncle, unaided by Ophelia or Horatio despite their good will is strikingly similar to the "ethical" situation of Antigone vis à vis Creon, her uncle, unaided by Haemon and Ismene despite their good will. (2) "Like Euripides' Hippolytus, the tragedy of Romeo and Juliet represents the pathos of youth with unswerving devotion to an ideal, perishing through no fault of its own. The death of the young lovers brings about a reconciliation of members of the warring houses. The sins of the fathers are forgiven, as Hippolytus forgave his erring father. And as Artemis promised perpetual homage to Hippolytus after his untimely destruction, so old Montague and old Capulet will erect statues symbolic of the pathos of unmerited death." If the treatment of Greek and Shn tragedy seems sketchy in important respects, the author has aimed only at comparing "ethical" postures of drama to throw light on the tragic experience and on the ethos of Sh and the Greeks. This much she has accomplished admirably.

1977. Jiriczek, Otto L. "Hamlet in Iran," ZVV, X (1900), 353-364. E-S

Jiriczek shows that in some particulars an Iranian folk tale is closer to Saxo's version of the Hamlet story than is the story of L. J. Brutus (see #1935). While Jiriczek does not consider it impossible that the Persian tale should have migrated northwestward, the fact that ancient Celtic analogues also exist suggests to him that a common Indo-European ancestor should be postulated and that the question of indebtedness must be left unanswered. MnU

1978. Johnson, Francis R. "Shakespearian Imagery and Senecan Imitation," AMS, pp. 33-53.

A prolegomenon to a full study of Sh's creative imagination, based on the assumption that Sh was capable of reading Seneca's tragedies in Latin. Johnson's method is to cite Elizabethan imitations of Seneca and compare Sh's transmutation of the same material. The examples here are mainly from Macb. A rewarding approach to Sh's language, as much as to his poetic and dramatic sense.

1979. Jones, Ernest. "Hamlet's Place in Mythology," Hamlet and Oedipus (N.Y., 1949), Ch. VII, pp. 127-151.

This ch. is an attempt to relate Hamlet to the archetypal myth of the oedipal child who hates the father and desires the mother. Orestes, Oedipus, and Lucius Junius Brutus are the chief classical prototypes. Jones arrays the authorities, psychoanalytic, anthropological, and literary on his side, but the ch. is as unsatisfactory as the whole book. The three chief fallacies of the psychoanalytic approach are everywhere in evidence: (1) by equivocation Jones explains any deviation from predetermined behavior as disguise, repression, sublimation, so that he is automatically right no matter how Hamlet behaves; (2) amidst his array of documentable fact he often blandly slips in a "fact" which has not the slightest objective support: e.g., Sh never forgave his wife for conceiving premaritally and thus precipitating his "o'er hasty marriage" to her; (3) most annoying of all is the tacit assumption that the psychoanalytic approach is omni-sufficient--Jones is like a physicist who thinks he has disposed of a rose garden because he can recite the physical and chemical properties of the petals. The entire book contains comparisons with classical material passim, though most of them are in this ch.

1980. Jones, Ernest. "The Oedipus-complex as an Explanation of Hamlet's Mystery: A Study in Motive," AJPsy, XXI (1910), 72-113. E-S

Subsumed into #1979.

1981. Jones, William M. "Shakespeare's Source for the Name 'Laertes'," ShN, X (1960), 9.

Jones points out that the name "Laertes" appears neither in extant sixteenth-century lists of personal names nor, apparently, in Renaissance literature. Sh could have borrowed it from Ovid (Meta. XIII or Heroides I), but in neither place is Laertes more than mentioned. Jones argues that Sh, concerned with father-son relationships in Ham., thought of the Laertes/Odysseus/Telemachus relationship in the Odyssey and chose "Laertes" rather than "Telemachus" for Polonius' son because he did not wish to make too obvious an analogy for the audience. Sh could have read the Odyssey in Latin. Jones points to some interesting analogies between the two works, not the least of which is that in Book I of the Odyssey the Orestes story is told; Jones may have hit upon the link between the Greek myth and Ham., though his suggestion would require further study before it could be accepted as probable. Cf. #2132.

1982. Justesen, P. T. "Telemach und Hamlet," WBFA, VI (1931), 75-76.

Not seen. Justesen apparently believes that the Scandinavian originals of Sh's story were founded on the legend of Telemachus, brought north from Byzantium by itinerant merchants ca. 1000 A.D. [Information from Raven, #0038.]

1983. Kalepky, Theodor. "'Die Freude am Tragischen'--Shakespeare--Aristoteles," GRM, XVI (1928), 168-171.

Kalepky argues that Max J. Wolff was wrong to deprecate tragedy (by contrast with the lyric mode) as an artistic representation of reality (see GRM, XIV [1926], 390-397). Aristotle in the Poetics and Sh in Ham. (III ii 1-50, especially 23-28) consider the creative process in drama, both dealing with the question of the artist's (or, in Ham., the actor's) fidelity to nature. It is plain from Theseus' lines in Dream (V i 12-17) that, like Aristotle, Sh advocated a reflection of nature which leaves room for the poet's creative imagination.

1984. Keil, Harry. "Scabies and the Queen Mab Passage in Romeo and Juliet," JHI, XVIII (1957), 394-410.

A learned study which seeks to document the hypothesis that Mercutio's "round little worm / Prick'd from the lazy finger of a maid" is the acarus scabiei which Keil traces back into classical literature (especially scientific literature). But he points out that Sh's sources are not literary; if anything Queen Mab herself is Teutonic and it is in folklore that the connections lie.

1985. Kellett, E. E. "Shakspere as a Borrower," Suggestions: Literary Essays (CUP, 1923), pp. 33-56.

For an echo of Seneca's Medea in Macb., see #1431.

1986. Kemble, J[ohn] P[hilip]. Macbeth and King Richard the Third: An Essay in answer to Remarks on some of the Characters of Shakespeare [by Thomas (erroneously given as "William") Whateley]. Ln, 1817, 171 pp.

This book is a reply not only to Whateley, but also to Steevens, Whateley's ally in the effort to prove Macbeth a coward ("In Richard [III] it [courage] is intrepidity, and in Macbeth no more than resolution . . ."). Two very long footnotes on classical allusions in Macb. support Kemble's counter-argument; (1) the reference in I ii to "Bellona's bridegroom" is not to Mars, as Steevens appears to think, but to Macbeth, who is worthy to be mate to the war goddess; (2) the reference to Banquo's spirit, capable of "rebuking" Macbeth's as Octavius' did Antony's (III i 55-57) is drawn from Plutarch's "Life of Marcus Antonius" (in the North trans., Kemble recognizes). Kemble also cites references from Suetonius to emphasize the analogy of Antony to Macbeth and Octavius to Banquo. MnU

1987. Kitto, H. D. F. "A Classical Scholar Looks at Shakespeare," More Talking of Shakespeare, ed. John Garrett (N.Y., 1959), pp. 33-54.

A stimulating piece of criticism calculated to show that modern analyses of Greek (and Shn) tragedy err in placing too much emphasis on character at the expense of theme, which in Sh as in the Attic dramatists is "nothing less than the terms on which the gods will let us live." Beginning with a convincing interpretation of Antigone as a play with a theological (universal) theme, Kitto shows that Ham. should be read in the same way, and then proceeds to discuss Sh's history plays as illustrative of the Aeschylean theme that "blood spilt on the ground ... invokes fresh blood." Kitto places much emphasis on tragic irony in man's relation to the gods, and makes many thoughtful suggestions: e.g., III iii 73-98 is the ironic turning point in Ham., because Hamlet appropriates to himself the prerogative of Heaven when he seeks the damnation as well as the death of the king. Cf. #1988, where Kitto makes many of the same points.

1988. Kitto, H. D. F. "Hamlet," Form and Meaning in Drama: A Study of Six Greek Plays and of Hamlet (Ln, 1956), pp. 246-337.

This brilliant essay is the climax to a series of chs. depicting Greek tragedy as "religious drama," i.e., drama in which the universe is more important than the characters who are its antagonists. Ham. is not a play about a melancholy Dane, but the story of the catastrophic and total fall of two houses, Polonius' and Hamlet's, through the pervasive infiltration of evil as manifested in Gertrude's lust, Claudius' foul ambition, and Polonius' treachery and lewd-mindedness. Three decent people, Ophelia, Hamlet, and Laertes, are suborned or otherwise sucked into the vortex of evil and others, Rosencrantz and Guildenstern, even Osric, are tainted by the "complexive" movement of rottenness through the state of Denmark. Ham. is, therefore, a Greek tragedy, though Kitto emphasizes the linear progression of evil in Greek drama by contrast with the concentric progression in Ham. The most fruitful comparisons are to "the two Greek revenge plays," Electra and Choephori, to Oedipus, Antigone, Agamemnon, and (surprisingly) Ajax. This is one of the most rewarding correctives to the traditional concentration on the title figure at the expense of the play. See also #1987.

1989. Knight, G. Wilson. "The Poet and Immortality," ShR, I (1928), 407-415.

In passing: implicit in Macb. and Lear is the mystery in the final Chorus of Alcestis --what men seek they do not find; they find what they do not seek. Shn, like Greek tragedy reveals "the deepest significance of life" in its plots. DFo

1990. Knoll, Robert E. "Drama of Fulfillment and Drama of Choice: A Note on Greek and Elizabethan Drama," WHR, XI (1957), 371-376. GRS

Knoll makes a clear and valid distinction between Attic tragedy which reveals the inexorable results of decisions taken before the action begins and Elizabethan tragedy which portrays man at the moment of choice itself. Because events and character are predetermined, the interest of Greek tragedy is in large, moral questions and in metaphysics; by contrast the Renaissance drama poses questions of psychology (motivation, will). Sh's psychological bent is represented by Ham. and Oth. (with a glance at Antony). But in Lear Knoll observes a classical structure as Lear makes his decision in I i and endures the consequences thereafter. It is interesting to note that Lear is also Sh's most cosmological play. Knoll's distinction between moral and psychological questions may be a bit forced, since to the Elizabethans choice is a moral as well as a psychological matter.

1991. Koeppel, E. "Shakespeares Juliet Capulet und Chaucers Troylus," ShJ, XXXVIII (1902), 238-239.

As Juliet laments (III ii 114-124) the banishment of Romeo, she exclaims that she would prefer the death of her parents to the banishment of her lover. Troilus, also lamenting a banished lover, expresses virtually the same thought: "Why ne haddestow my fader, kyng of Troye / Byraft the lif, or don my bretheren dye?" (Troilus and Criseyde IV 276-277). Sh seems to have had the Trojan legend on his mind as he worked on Romeo. Koeppel also prints the passage from Il Filostrato which served Chaucer as source.

1992. Korner, Sinclair. "'Hamlet' as a Solar Myth," PL, III (1891), 214-216.

Korner points out that Hamlet refers repeatedly to the sun, especially to sun myths like that of Hyperion. Korner then suggests that the play can be read as a dramatization of the Aryan solar myth: Hamlet the King (the sun) is killed by Claudius (winter) who carries off Gertrude (Flora, the sun's bride). As in his art. on Dream (#0824), Korner offers little documentary evidence and gives no explanation for the appearance of Aryan materials of which "it is altogether absurd to suppose that Shakespeare had grasped the principles."

1993. Krappe, Alexander H. "Shakespeare Notes," Anglia, LII (1928), 174-182. SG

Notes 2 and 3 respectively trace the sleepwalking scene in Macb. to Lucretius and Macb. V v 24-26 ("Life's but a walking shadow . . .") to Lucian's Menippus. Neither suggestion is convincing. Cf. #0306, Chs. IV, VII. Note 4 finds the source of part of Polonius' advice to Laertes (Ham. I iii 58-69) in Hesiod's Works and Days, and suggests that "the direct channels of [Sh's] own learning" may have been less clogged than we sometimes think. But though Polonius may seem to paraphrase Hesiod, Krappe has forgotten the huge corpus of sententiae which occupy the millennia between them--a corpus which Sh possibly is satirizing here, though Krappe apparently does not think so.

1994. Kröger, Ernst. "Tabellarische Quellen-Übersicht," Die Sage von Macbeth bis zu Shakspere, Palaestra, XXXIX (1904), pp. 226-229. E-S SG

Kröger's list gives Plutarch as source for Macbeth's contempt for suicide, for the moving stones of III iv 123, and for Antony's genius "rebuked" by Caesar (III i 55-57). He detects the influence of Medea, both Seneca's and Ovid's (Meta. VII) in several places in the play (especially IV i). And he suggests Sententiae Pueriles as source for "sleep, death's counterfeit" (II iii 81).

1995. Kuhl, E. P. "Hercules in Spenser and Shakespeare," TLS, December 31, 1954, p. 860.

For the topical significance of a reference to Hercules in Ham., see #0827.

1996. Latham, R. G. "On the Double Personality of the Hamlet of Saxo Grammaticus --The Hamlet of Shakespear--Its Relation to the German Hamlet," 2 TRSL, X (1874), 214-317.

Near the end of this involved study of the Hamlet legend, Latham submits two pieces of evidence that Sh did not write the Ur-Hamlet (a point which needed demonstration in 1874 more, perhaps, than it does today). Both of them are "classical": (1) Der bestrafte Brudermord refers to the Roman actor Roscius as "Marus Russig," which Latham interprets as a corruption of the "Sextus Roscius Amerinus" of Cicero's oration. This Roscius was not an actor and has been confused by the author of the Ur-Hamlet with the Roman actor--Sh's play makes no error in this matter. (2) The passage in which Hamlet gets Osric to contradict himself about the weather is much more emphatic in Der bestrafte Brudermord; in Latham's opinion it recalls Juvenal's third Satire, whereas Sh's passage did not strike even Samuel Johnson as Juvenalian, and Johnson himself made a verse paraphrase of the third Satire. Latham's whole essay is not so coherent logically as it might be; his conclusion is the right one, but his evidence leaves something to be desired.

1997. Latham, R. G. "On the Pyrrhus and Hecuba in 'Hamlet'," Ath, No. 2296 (1871), 561.

The detail in Marlowe's Dido in which Hecuba attempts to claw out Pyrrhus' eyes is based on the passage in Euripides' Hecuba in which the same queen blinds Polymnestor. Thus there is evidence that Euripides was "known to the players of Shakespear's time." Latham goes so far as to propose that the Ghost in Ham. was suggested by the ghost of Polydorus, who opens the Hecuba.

1998. Lathrop, H[enry] B. "Shakespeare's Anthropophagi," Nation, C (1915), 76-77. SG

Lathrop claims positively to have discovered the source of Othello's "travel's history" in I. A.'s 1566 trans. of Pierre de Changy's French summary of Pliny. The elements are there, but so are they elsewhere. Cf. #2136, #1928, #0084.

1999. Law, Robert A. "Tripartite Gaul in the Story of King Leir," TSE, IV (1924), 39-48.

Caesar's famous division of Gaul was transmitted to Geoffrey of Monmouth, who refers to it in the Leir story and in turn passed it on to Spenser and to the author of King Leir. It is quite possibly responsible for the contrast between Burgundy and France (who apparently rule separate countries) in Sh's Lear (I i). An interesting and well-documented study.

2000. Leighton, William, Jr. "Shakespeare's and Greek Tragedy," Shna, I (1884), 241-244, 306-309; II (1885), 69-75.

In the first two of these three essays of impressionistic appreciation, Leighton draws numerous analogies between the Greek tragedies on the Orestes story and Shn tragedy, especially Ham. and Macb.; in the third he concentrates on the Oedipus cycle. Some of the analogues are so remote as to border on the fantastic, and none of them warrants Leighton's implication that Sh may have learned from the Greeks.

2001. L[eo], F. A. "'As stars with trains of fire'," ShJ, XV (1880), 433-437.

Leo suggests that a line has dropped out of the text of Ham. I i between 116 and 117. Using Plutarch's "Life of Caesar" as a guide, he proposes the insertion either of "Ev'n in the element above were signs" or of "Ev'n in the element were dreadful signs." There is nothing implausible in this suggestion, but the text renders adequate sense without it.

2002. Levin, Harry. "The Antic Disposition," ShJ, XCIV (1958), 175-190.

Here are several references to the classics in Ham., notably: (1) Hamlet's assumed madness has a precedent in Plautus' Menaechmi, which Sh had used twice before; (2) Hamlet's book is more likely to be Erasmus' Praise of Folly than the tenth Satire of Juvenal. About (1) Levin makes no claims as he indicates the vast popularity of madness, real or feigned, on the pre-Shn stage.

2003. Levin, Harry. "An Explication of the Player's Speech: (Hamlet, II, ii, 472-541)," KR, XII (1950), 273-296. (Reprinted in The Question of Hamlet [1959].)

A lucid and percipient piece of criticism which seeks to establish the functional significance of the "rugged Pyrrhus" passage in Ham. by consideration of its sources, internal logic, and verse. For Hecuba, Sh is more indebted to Ovid's Heroides and Seneca's Troades (and perhaps to Meta. XIII) than to either Virgil or Dido Queene of Carthage. Perhaps one difficulty the modern reader encounters in this passage is the result of his failure to respond as Sh's audience would to "the mobled queen," who was the archetype of suffering.

2004. Levin, Harry. "The Heights and the Depths: A Scene from 'King Lear'," More Talking of Shakespeare, ed. John Garrett (N.Y., 1959), pp. 87-103.

At several points in this provocative address Levin compares Lear with the classical world, especially with Sophocles: e.g., Sh flagrantly defies classical decorum in blinding Gloucester "coram populo"; Sophocles had blinded Oedipus back-stage. Edgar is compassionate to Gloucester as Antigone is to Oedipus at Colonus; Edgar's "The worst is not" is Sh's "variation on the tragic theme of Sophocles, 'Call no man happy until he is dead' . . ." Finally, Sh rejects in Lear the Stoic approval of suicide which he treats sympathetically in Caesar and Antony.

2005. Lewis, C. S. "Hamlet, the Prince or the Poem," PBA, XXVIII (1942), 139-154. (Annual British Academy Shakespeare Lecture.)

On p. 149 Lewis explains Hamlet's "since no man knows aught of what he leaves . . ." (V ii 234-235) "by the assumption that Shakespeare had come across Seneca's Nihil perdis ex tuo tempore, nam quod relinquis alienum est (Epist lxix)."

2006. Lewis, C. S. "Othello," TLS, June 19, 1948, p. 345.

The puzzling phrase "her motion / Blush'd at herself" (Oth. I iii 95-96) may echo Meta. X, where Ovid describes Pygmalion's statue; similar concepts appear in Shirach and Dante.

2007. Lloyd, W[illiam] Watkiss. "[Notes on Hamlet]," 7 NQ, IX (1890), 503.

Lloyd finds in Ham. echoes of Aeschines, Longinus, and Homer, and suggests that unless the occurrences are coincidental, Sh obtained his material from the University Wits. The parallels are not striking; the former possibility would seem the more plausible of the two.

2008. Lloyd, W[illiam] Watkiss. "Pyramid," 7 NQ, XI (1891), 283.

Lloyd argues that by "pyramid" Sh understood the obelisks for which Egypt is noted.

References are to Macb. and Antony. Lloyd points out this same confusion in Doctor Faustus, but Marlowe's reference is more clearly to an obelisk than the Shn ones are. Further suggestions ibid., 373, 498.

2009. Lodge, Oliver W. F. "Dido, Queen of Carthage," TLS, September 4, 1930, p. 700.

Sh had no desire to burlesque Marlowe's Dido in the "rugged Pyrrhus" speech (Ham. II ii 474-541). The turgid style is to be accounted for by Sh's desire to make the lines seem poetry when the rest of the play (to which the passage is to be contrasted) is already verse. It is noteworthy that Hamlet's surrounding commentary on the passage is in prose to heighten the contrast. Hamlet speaks without irony (454-471) when he praises the play. An interesting point of view which now has many adherents.

2010. Lord, George de F. "The Odyssey and the Western World," SewR, LXII (1954), 406-427.

In passing: Nausicaa's farewell speech to Odysseus contains hints of her love and desire for him which are "Desdemona-like."

2011. Lowell, James Russell. "Shakespeare Once More," Among My Books (Boston, 1898), pp. 151-227. (First published in 1870, the essay has been reprinted in various places.)

Beginning at p. 177 of this widely ranging essay, Lowell draws parallels and contrasts passim between Sh and the Greek tragedians. He suggests at p. 190 that some of the similarities and even identities of phrase may be a result of Sh's having "contrived to worry some considerable meaning out of [the Attic tragedies]" with the help of a Greek-Latin ed. Collins (#0173) thinks that Sh read the Greeks in Latin, and Sandys (#0512) refers to Lowell's suggestion, but it has been largely ignored in this century.

2012. "[Macbeth and the Oresteia]," Monthly Review [?] LXXXI [?] (1789) [?], 119-120 [?] (As quoted in Drake, #0210, II, 473-474. Drake's bibliographical information is inaccurate--the art. does not appear loc. cit. and a search has not turned it up.)

The author regards Macb. as having, like the Oresteia, a tripartite action: the murder of Duncan, the murder of Banquo, and the death of the hero are separate actions, "the first serving to shew how [Macbeth] attained his elevation, the second how he abused it, and the third how he lost it." The Witches correspond to the Furies, hovering "over the fate of the hero." To Sh must go the palm for plot interest and characterization (although Clytemnestra is Lady Macbeth's equal); to Aeschylus the palm for dignity of style, though Sh is more rich and versatile in diction.

2013. [MacKenzie, Henry]. "[On Hamlet]," The Mirror, No. XCIX (April 18, 1780), 393-396; No. C (April 22, 1780), 397-400.

In passing MacKenzie contrasts Hamlet, the center of interest in Sh's play, with Orestes, who is only a cipher to Sophocles. The audience is identified with the vengeance to be executed on Clytemnestra and Aegisthus, not with the agent of that vengeance; but when Hamlet is dead we think of him, not of the death of Claudius. MacKenzie also speaks of Sh's "ignorance of those critical rules which might have restrained him . . . " but points out that confining Sh to Aristotle would be like applying "the minute labours of the roller and the pruning-knife, to the noble irregularity of trackless mountains and impenetrable forests." DFo

2014. Major, John M. "Desdemona and Dido," SQ, X (1959), 123-125.

Desdemona and Dido have in common that (1) they fell in love while their respective men were recounting perilous adventures; (2) they fell in love with foreigners; (3) neither understood that her man put duty above his feelings (i.e., each is in an ironic position); (4) each is initially reluctant to yield to love. Since Dido was one of Sh's favorite classical heroines (she is referred to in six plays), it is not fallacious to draw the analogy, an analogy which lends added stature to Desdemona, making her more "worldly" and "majestic." The point appears well taken.

2015. Mangold, W. "Zu Hamlet, II, 2, 321," ShJ, XLIV (1908), 146-147. SG

The sarcasm of Hamlet's remark to Rosencrantz is heightened if we recognize the echo of Horace's Odes IV i 29.

2016. Marindin, G. E. "Shakespeare and Plutarch," Ath, No. 3572 (1896), 487-488.

Marindin cites a parallel between a passage on the tyrant Alexander of Pherae in Plutarch's "Life of Pelopidas" and the play scene in Ham. and also Hamlet's "What's Hecuba to him, or he to Hecuba, / That he should weep for her?" Marindin gives the Plutarch in Greek; North's English runs, "And an other time being in a Theater, where the tragedy of Troades of Euripides was played, [Alexander] went out of the theater ... saying, that he came not away for any misliking he had ... of the play, but bicause he was ashamed his people shoulde see him weepe, to see the miseries of Hecuba and Andromacha, and that they never saw him pity the death of any one man, of so many of his citizens as he had caused to be slaine. The guilty conscience therefore of this cruell and heathen tyran, did make him tremble at the only name and reputacion of Epaminondas ..." Although it is possible that Sh read the "Life of Pelopidas" and though there are other similarities between Alexander and Claudius, Marindin has not established beyond question that Plutarch "must have furnished Shakespeare with the idea."

2017. Marsh, John F. "A Few Notes on 'Hamlet'," 5 NQ, IX (1878), 203-204.

The third note points to the similarity between Hamlet's identification of death with sleep (III i 64-68) and a remark by Socrates (Apology 32). But the metaphor was a Renaissance commonplace.

2018. Marshall, Ed. "'The Undiscovered Country from Whose Bourn' etc.," 6 NQ, I (1880), 53.

Marshall calls attention to a passage in Euripides' Hippolytus "closely parallel" to Hamlet's fears of the undiscovered country of death. He also prints a Euripidean fragment which contains similar thoughts, but neither passage is strikingly close to Sh's thought and phrasing.

2019. Martin, L. C. "Shakespeare, Lucretius and the Commonplaces," RES, XXI (1945), 174-182.

For possible Lucretian influence on passages in Lear and Ham., see #0851.

2020. Maury, Lucien. "Hamlet, Héros Méditerranéen," RB, LXII (1924), 134-136.

Following the research of Emile Henriot, Maury observes that Saxo Grammaticus passed down legends which were not Danish, but "Mediterranean." Among them is the story of Lucius Junius Brutus, whose name (like Hamlet's) means "feeble-witted." Parallels between the Brutus and Hamlet stories "ne peuvent être l'effet du hasard." Other influences on the Hamlet story are a Byzantine poem and a lost Greek romance which survives in a Medieval French redaction. It may even be that oriental legend is discernible in the tale. Maury argues that Scandinavian traders brought these stories back from the shores of the Mediterranean.

2021. Maxwell, J. C. "Chaucer in the Queen Mab Speech," NQ, CCV (1960), 16.

Despite Nevill Coghill's contention (#0993), Chaucer's Parlement of Foules is a more probable source for the dreamers in Mercutio's famous speech (Romeo I iv 53-94) than is Claudian, on whom Chaucer drew.

2022. Maxwell, J. C. "The Technique of Invocation in 'King Lear'," MLR, XLV (1950), 142-147.

Sh does not oppose Christianity to paganism in Lear as Aeschylus opposes Prometheus to Zeus, but Christianity nonetheless is implicit as the moral basis of regeneration in the play. The gradual movement from paganism toward a Christian ethic can be seen in the invocations (not merely prayers, but curses, interjections, etc.) spoken by various characters at various times.

2023. McCollom, William G. "The Downfall of the Tragic Hero," CE, XIX (1957), 51-56.

In this attempt to isolate the cause of tragic catastrophe, McCollom points out that Hamlet, like Antigone, is destroyed by external circumstances. Yet, though neither could really be called guilty, each aids Fate in the precipitation of his own destruction.

2024. McEachran, F. "The Roots of Tragedy," The Bookman, LXXI (1930), 129-137.

Beginning with the distinctions Babbitt makes in Rousseau and Romanticism among the religious life, the human life, and the naturalistic life, this short philosophical essay strives to define tragedy as an expression of an attitude toward the dignity of man. Sh, like Racine, though to a lesser extent, understood and conveyed the humanist's sense of human dignity--this makes him "Greek." Hamlet may not be "moral," but he is ethically aware "and he leaves us, like Oedipus and Phèdre, with no sense of depression or of the lowliness of men."

2025. McKenzie, James. "A Shakespearean Interpretation," NQ, CXCVII (1952), 160.

McKenzie makes the assumption that because in his first soliloquy Hamlet mentions his uncle and Hercules in the same breath, he must be referring to Claudius when he mentions Hercules in the quarrel with Laertes at Ophelia's grave almost four acts later.

2026. Melchinger, Siegfried. "Antigone und Hamlet bleiben: Der Formzerfall im modernen Drama," WW, XI (1956), 210-220.

As a standard by which to measure the decadence of the modern stage, Melchinger proposes Antigone and Ham., both of which appeal to man's awareness of the opposition between heaven and hell. "Die griechische Tragödie und Shakespeare haben kein anderes Programm gehabt." Melchinger does not define the shared ground of Sh and the Greeks in specific detail.

2027. Meyerstein, E. H. W. "Othello and C. Furius Cresinus," TLS, February 7, 1942, p. 72.

Meyerstein traces Othello's defense in the trial scene (I iii) to an obscure passage in Holland's Pliny. The parallels are not so close as to necessitate agreement that Holland is the source. The irony in Othello's defense is a rhetorical trick which a shrewd man need not learn from a locus classicus, although Baldwin (#0089, II, 198-200) makes a case for Quintilian's influence on the rhetoric of the passage.

2028. Montgomerie, William. "English Seneca," LLT, XXXVI (1943), 25-28.

Montgomerie traces a detailed connection between "The Mousetrap" in Ham. and Senecan tragedy, especially Octavia, which lent Sh the name "Claudius," and Oedipus. The Lucianus who plays Hamlet in "The Mousetrap" is named for Seneca (a contraction of "Lucius Annaeus"). Though this theory presupposes an unusually alert Elizabethan audience, it is the more attractive when Montgomerie points out that the Ghost scene in Caesar (based on Seneca) introduces the two servants Lucius and Claudius. Montgomerie attaches much importance to the mirror motif in Ham., and traces it also to Seneca, with connotations of necromancy. Cf. Montgomerie's 1960 art., #2031, which makes an entirely different interpretation of "The Mousetrap."

2029. Montgomerie, William. "Folk Play and Ritual in Hamlet," FL, LXVII (1956), 214-227.

The art. is really sixteen brief notes on folklore elements in Ham., the second of which, "Hamlet and Ritual," suggests rather vaguely that Hamlet's problem of choosing between healing and revenge is a reflection of the Jupiter-Saturn polarity in classical mythology. The tenth note, "The Regifugium," connects Claudius' horrified flight from "The Mousetrap" with the ancient custom among the Romans of annually forcing the king to flee for his life. These anthropological connections are somewhat tenuous.

2030. Montgomerie, William. "Lucianus, Nephew to the King (Hamlet, III.ii.238)," NQ, CCI (1956), 149-151.

A somewhat disjointed discussion of Sh's possible indebtedness to Lucian and/or Apuleius in "The Mousetrap." It is puzzling that Montgomerie should, within the space of eighteen years, trace the same passage in Ham. to four discrete classical sources (cf. #2028, #2029, #2031). In neither this present essay nor in his more recent one does he make reference to his previously stated opinions. This interpretation is not the most satisfying of the four.

2031. Montgomerie, William. "More an Antique Roman Than a Dane," HJ, LIX (1960), 67-77.

Ham. III ii 410-417, where Hamlet compares his situation vis à vis Gertrude to Nero's vis à vis Agrippina suggests to Montgomerie that the whole play should be seen as an intentional analogue of the Nero story as told by Suetonius, Tacitus, and the author (Seneca?) of the Apocolocyntosis Divi Claudii. King Claudius is the Emperor Claudius, who "committed incest with Agrippina, married her and adopted her son Nero." The two Claudiuses have several traits in common (drunkenness, violent temper, love of gambling, e.g.). Ernest Jones (#1979) and Gilbert Murray (#2049) were both partly right in seeing connections between Hamlet and Oedipus and Orestes respectively. But both failed to recognize the missing link, Nero, who was conscious of his relation to both Greek myths. In two appendices, Montgomerie defends Q_2 against F_1 in the stage directions for "The Mousetrap," insisting that two separate poisonings are portrayed: the first of King Hamlet, the second of Claudius by Lucianus-Hamlet-Nero. The whole art. is an original and provocative approach to the play, but it is difficult to agree that Sh's audience would have recognized the many parallels with the Nero story. Cf. Montgomerie's 1943 art. (#2028), which takes a different approach to "The Mousetrap."

2032. Montgomery, Marshall. "'Cursed Hebenon' (or 'Hebona')," MLR, XV (1920), 304-306.

A criticism of Henry Bradley (#1843). Sh meant ebony, which he identified with the lignum vitae (lignum sanctum). He thought the juice capable of causing leprosy (a traditional view) and perhaps wrote "cursed" as "a daring reversal of the ordinary 'blessed'" (i.e., "sanctum"). See #1952 for a more plausible hypothesis.

2033. Montgomery, Marshall. "The Text of Hamlet," TLS, November 29, 1928, p. 938.

Montgomery examines Cooper's Thesaurus to show that the word "solid" ("this too too solid flesh") had a wide range of meaning in the sixteenth century, at least in the Latin form "solidus." "Hamlet deplored his corpus solidum, the too robust casket that enclosed his mens insolida."

2034. Moore, Gilbert Stuart. "The Theme of Family Disaster in the Tragedies of Euripides and Shakespeare," diss (Southern California, 1959). DA, XX (1960), 3731.

Like Euripides, Sh was obsessed with genealogy, and his great tragic theme is the obliteration of a family line (Ham., Macb., e.g.). Sh, then, is more like the Greeks (Aristotle praised Euripides for his concentration on this most tragic theme) than like the Medieval tragedians, who focus on the fall of a man, not of a house. Sh may well have known of Euripides, who is highly praised by Plutarch in the "Life of Pelopidas"; an episode in that Life "may have been a source of Hamlet's mousetrap" (cf. #2016).

2035. Morgan, Roberta. "Some Stoic Lines in Hamlet and the Problem of Interpretation," PQ, XX (1941), 549-558.

This defense of the F_1 reading of Ham. V ii 230-235 against the often-accepted Q_2 reading hinges on the Stoic (not necessarily Senecan) doctrine that man's life and the good things in it are merely a loan from Fortune which must be repaid by death. The author also analyzes the internal logic of the lines ("If it be now, 'tis not to come . . .") in Stoic terms. This is an interesting and convincing essay.

2036. Moss, Leonard Jerome. "The Dialectic of Tragedy: Heroic Integrity in Shakespeare, Sophocles, and Corneille," diss (Indiana, 1959). DA, XX (1959), 1353-54.

Moss tests Hegel's thesis on the distinction between Greek and "modern" tragedy by placing Sophocles (Ajax, Antigone, Oedipus Tyrannus, Philoctetes, Oedipus Coloneus) in juxtaposition with Sh (Ham., Oth., Macb., Lear) and with Corneille (Le Cid, Horace, Cinna, Polyeucte). He finds it somewhat an oversimplification, but is willing to credit this Hegelian proposition: Sophocles and Sh both measure the integrity of the tragic hero by challenging it gravely; the Greek challenges are "institutional" (social, religious), while the Shn challenges are "psychological" (reason, passion, will).

2037. Muir, Kenneth. "A Borrowing From Seneca," NQ, CXCIV (1949), 214-216.

Muir points out a number of verbal echoes in Macb. of the Chorus at the end of Act I of Seneca's Agamemnon in the Studley trans. Only "one hurly burly done, another doth begin" ("When the hurlyburly's done," Macb. I i 3) is compelling, but Muir reinforced his argument by further and more convincing parallels in 1956 (#2044).

2038. Muir, Kenneth. "Buchanan, Leslie and 'Macbeth'," NQ, CC (1955), 511-512.

In the course of criticizing Henry N. Paul's evidence that Sh had read Buchanan and Leslie on Scottish history, Muir suggests that Seneca's verses: "Qui sceptra saevus duro imperio regit / Timet timentes, metus in auctorem redit" may have inspired Sh's conception of Macbeth's tyranny. Sh might have found them in Sidney's Apologie.

2039. Muir, Kenneth. "Holland's Pliny and 'Othello'," NQ, CXCVIII (1953), 513-514.

Muir accepts the contention of Meyerstein (#2027) that Oth. I iii owes much to Holland's trans., and then goes on to draw some very tenuous parallels between Holland and the rest of the play. Muir is more certain than his evidence warrants that Holland provided Sh with phrasing, and he ignores Baldwin's pronouncements on Pliny and Sh (#0084, #2321).

2040. Muir, Kenneth. "Introduction," King Lear (1952/1959), ArdenSh, pp. xv-lxiv.

Muir comments briefly: (1) on the opening scene of Seneca's Phoenissae as an analogue to Gloucester's wish to plunge to death from a cliff (p. xlii); (2) on the presence of "Horatian allusions and ... Latin puns" in III vi (p. xlviii)--see notes on the scene; (3) on Philemon Holland's comments on the shallow philosophy of Nature in Pliny's Naturalis Historia as a possible source for the doctrines of Nature in Lear (p. lxii).

2041. Muir, Kenneth. "Introduction," Macbeth (1951/1957), ArdenSh, pp. xiii-lxxiv.

Muir notes briefly (pp. lxi-lxiii) the Senecan theme of tyranny in Macb. and suggests that Sh's contemporaries, more aware of Seneca than of Aristotle, would think the overthrow of an evil man tragic material; yet Sh was not restricted in form or content by Senecan antecedents to Macb. Muir also prints a passage on guilt and conscience from the Moralia and implies that Plutarch is a precedent, if not a source, for Macbeth's spiritual torments.

2042. Muir, Kenneth. "Latin Derivatives in English Verse," TLS, March 13, 1943, p. 127. GRS

This letter points out that the word "acerbe" (i.e., "acerb") appears in Q_1 of Oth. where F_1 has "bitter" (I iii 355). Muir considers Sh the coiner of this Latinate neologism.

2043. Muir, Kenneth. "Portents in 'Hamlet'," NQ, CXCIII (1948), 54-55.

Muir suggests a number of loci which in various combinations could have produced Horatio's grim description (I i 113-120). Included are Ovid (Meta. XV), Lucan (Pharsalia), Virgil (Georgics I), and Plutarch ("Life of Caesar"). An interesting application of Muir's theory of "polygenesis" (see Introduction, supra, p. 13).

2044. Muir, Kenneth. "Seneca and Shakespeare," NQ, CCI (1956), 243-244.

Here Muir points out verbal similarities between Cassandra's prophetic speech in Act V of Studley's trans. of Seneca's Agamemnon and two of Macbeth's speeches (his aside on murder I iii 139-142; his dagger soliloquy II i 36-45). The contexts are similar enough to give credibility to the inference that Sh remembered Studley.

2045. Muir, Kenneth. "Shakespeare and the Tragic Pattern," PBA, XLIV (1958), 145-162. (Annual British Academy Shakespeare Lecture.)

Muir's address is designed to extend "Shakespearean tragedy" to include two histories (R.II, R.III), the four Roman plays, and, though he barely mentions it, Tim. All these he would add to Bradley's core of Lear, Macb., Ham., and Oth.; with Romeo, one counts twelve in all. The references passim to the Senecan and Plutarchian background are brief but challenging. Typical is the plausible suggestion that Macb. is Sh's most unified play and at the same time a tragedy full of echoes of Seneca, both of these because it was intended for a royal command performance and Sh repolished his Seneca to please King James. There are perceptive brief passages on the "Pyrrhus" speech in Ham., on rhetoric as a barrier between audience and horror in Titus, and especially on Sidney's version of classical tragic theory as a basis for the criticism and perhaps the disease imagery of Ham.

2046. Muir, Kenneth. "Shakespeare's Use of Pliny Reconsidered," MLR, LIV (1959), 224-225.

The note brings forward verbal parallels between Othello's "Pontic Sea" simile (III iii 453-460) and three widely separated passages in Holland's Pliny. This is another instance of Muir's theory of coalescence (see #2043 and supra, p. 13).

2047. Muller, Herbert J. "Elizabethan Tragedy: 3. Shakespeare," The Spirit of Tragedy (N.Y., 1956), pp. 165-195. GRS

Muller takes Ham., Troi., and Lear as representative of Shn tragedy, which he sees as pessimistic in spirit. The remarks about classical analogues or contrasts are scattered: Lear's madness is "much more varied, subtle, and profound" than Ajax' in Sophocles' play. Sh cared more for character qua character than the Greeks did. The section on Troi. sees the play as most unattractive in tone, but more a reflection of Sh's state of mind than a satire; Helen and Cressida are "glorified slut[s]," a reflection of Sh's sexual nausea. Muller makes only brief allusions to the traditional background of the play, preferring to see Sh's personal emotions in it. He has kind words for (and some strictures on) Fergusson's thesis on Ham., Aristotle, and ritual (#1921).

2048. Murray, Gilbert. "Greek and English Tragedy: A Contrast," English Literature and the Classics, ed. G. S. Gordon (OUP, 1912), pp. 7-24.

Ancient tragedy is religion; modern tragedy is entertainment. Yet Sophocles may remind us a bit of Sh, for he "cautiously and delicately" moved away from the rigid formalities of Greek vegetation religion toward flexibility, psychological realism, and variety.

2049. Murray, Gilbert. "Hamlet and Orestes: A Study in Traditional Types," PBA, VI (1914), 389-412. (Annual British Academy Shakespeare Lecture; reprinted with some revision in The Classical Tradition in Poetry [1927].) E-S

Murray indicates many remarkable similarities of character and situation between Sh's Ham. and the seven Greek tragedies in which Orestes appears. He then traces the figures of Hamlet and Orestes to prehistoric myth, identifying both heroes with the ritual slayer in the cult of the year daemon. The hypothesis that striking parallels between Sh's play and the Greek tragedies stem from a common body of Indo-European myth is not capable of documentation; a preliterate culture leaves few documents to posterity. But Murray argues effectively by analogy.

2050. Murry, John Middleton. "The Blunt Monster," Shakespeare (Ln, 1936), Ch. V, pp. 118-140.

In passing: for the "rugged Pyrrhus" speech in Ham. Sh used lines from one of his own since-vanished failures of ten years before. "Perhaps we have in them a glimpse of the youthful classical tragedy he wanted to (and did) write; while Titus Andronicus is the classical tragedy he had to write ..." This is not a convincing hypothesis.

2051. Murry, J[ohn] Middleton. "A Shakespeare Problem," TLS, July 12, 1928, p. 520.

Murry points out the similarity between part of the "rugged Pyrrhus" speech in Ham. and Marlowe's Dido. Murry asks whether there is a classical basis for Priam's falling before the wind created by the brandished sword of Pyrrhus; the detail is common to Sh and Marlowe. Subsequent correspondence indicates (1) Sh's debt to Marlowe in Macb. (G. Wilson Knight, ibid., p. 568); (2) the parallel between what Pyrrhus does and what Hamlet wishes to do (William Poel, ibid., p. 581); and (3) some parallels between Dido and Dream (see #0764).

2052. N., B. "Scraps: Union sb. pearl. Hamlet V.ii.283.," NSST, [VIII] (1880), 56.

Sh's use of the term "union" for "pearl" has authority in Pliny, who explains that a pearl having matchless qualities was so called by the Romans to emphasize its uniqueness.

2053. N., N. "[Coincidence of Shakespear, with Seneca, and Lucretius]," Monthly Magazine, VIII (1799), 790.

N. indicates the exactness with which Macbeth's "Will all great Neptune's ocean wash this hand" coincides with the "Quis Tanais, aut quis Nilus" passage from Hercules Furens. He regards a parallel between Lucretius and a passage from Lear's ravings in the storm as only accidental. MnU

2054. Neilson, Geo[rge]. "'Macbeth,' I. iii. 32, I. v. 7, III. i. 2: 'Weird Sisters'," 7 NQ, X (1890), 403.

Neilson cites evidence from Barbour's Trojan War that "weird" implies that the sisters are goddesses of destiny, not mere witches. E. Yardley argues that they are witches ibid., XI (1891), 25, and the controversy continues ibid., 283-284, XII (1891), 3-4.

2055. Nicholson, Brinsley. "Hamlet's Cursed Hebenon," NSST, [VIII] (1880-82), 21-31.

An attempt to identify the poison that killed King Hamlet with the juice of the yew, which was sometimes called "ebenus." Nicholson turns to some classical authorities, including Dioscorides Pedanius, Pliny, and Suetonius, for evidence. For support for this view see W. A. Harrison (#1953).

2056. Nørgaard, Holger. "The Bleeding Captain Scene in Macbeth and Daniel's Cleopatra," RES, n.s. VI (1955), 395-396.

The bleeding Sergeant is indebted for his heroic speech not only to the First Player in Ham., but to Daniel's Cleopatra (for the image of two swimmers who choke each other's art). The hypothesis is that Sh was reading for Antony as he wrote Macb. A plausible argument.

2057. Nosworthy, J. M. "The Bleeding Captain Scene in Macbeth," RES, XXII (1946), 126-130.

There is no need to suspect the hand of a collaborator in the "heroic verse" of I ii, since Sh had already written such verse in Ham. (II ii 474-541: the "rugged Pyrrhus" speech). Sh learned the technique from Virgil's description of the fall of Troy and from Senecan tragedies [English? Latin?].

2058. Nosworthy, J. M. "The Hecate Scenes in Macbeth: Macbeth III.v; IV.i," RES, XXIV (1948), 138-139.

Regarding the character of Hecate as intrusive, Nosworthy nevertheless denies that she bears any relationship to Middleton's crude "brusque" Hecate; Sh's goddess delivers "polished speeches of distinctly Senecan flavor." Sh is ultimately responsible for the intrusion, for he refers to "pale Hecate" in Macbeth's soliloquy in II i. Indeed, it is possible that Sh himself wrote her part as a means of blending into the play the two songs (in which she is mentioned) which his company borrowed from Middleton for performance.

2059. Oeftering, Michael. "Heliodor auf der Bühne: c) England," Heliodor und seine Bedeutung für die Litteratur, LHF, H. XVIII (1901), pp. 149-155.

For an analogue in Heliodorus to Ham. I ii 141-142, see #0870. DLC

2060. O'Hora, Edward. "Klytemnestra and Lady Macbeth," HCP, XVII (1904), 24-29.

More a contrast than a comparison. Lady Macbeth is, in part, redeemed by her filial piety ("Had he not resembled / My father as he slept, I had done't"), by her loyalty to Macbeth, by the selflessness of her ambition, by her femininity, and by the fact that she is "broken" by her crime. Clytemnestra, however, is loveless (she loves neither Aegisthus nor Iphigenia), and also acts viciously out of a base and vengeful motive; worst of all she revels in her crime as Lady Macbeth does not. DLC

2061. Olive, W. J. "Sejanus and Hamlet," Taylor Festschrift, pp. 178-184.

A suggestion that Ham. is indebted to Sh's stint as actor in Jonson's Roman play. Among the interesting points: both plays repeatedly utilize the imagery of cosmetics; Sh exactly reflects Jonson's (classical) attitudes toward decorum and imitation in Hamlet's advice to the players; perhaps Hamlet refers to Sejanus, which failed on the stage, when he speaks of the play which was "caviary to the general." An additional possibility which Olive does not discuss is that Sejanus could have been the catalyst for the large number of "Roman" allusions and concepts in Ham. (e.g., "more an antique Roman than a Dane," "the most high and palmy state of Rome," Nero, etc.). On the other hand, Sh had, himself, recently written a Roman play when he sat down to Ham.; and moreover, the problem of the respective dates of Sejanus and Ham. must weaken Olive's argument.

2062. Paris, Jean. Hamlet: Ou les personnages du fils. Paris, 1953, 188 pp.

This interpretation of Ham. is a symbolic one: Fortinbras, Hamlet, and Laertes each represents an aspect of the filial state and (pp. 55-56) also a stage of the process of creation as the Greeks conceived it. Hamlet (chaos, Uranus) is supplanted by Laertes (time, Kronos) who in turn yields to Fortinbras (manifestation, Zeus). The small rôle assigned to Fortinbras in Sh's play and the fact that the three young men succeed their fathers, not one another, militate against the plausibility of this interpretation.

2063. Parr, Johnstone. "The 'Late Eclipses' in King Lear"; "Edmund's Birth Under Ursa Major," Tamburlaine's Malady and Other Essays on Astrology in Elizabethan Drama (Alabama UP, 1953), pp. 70-79, 80-84.

In both of these essays Parr invokes Claudius Ptolemy as the authority behind the Renaissance assumptions Sh reflects. He cites the Quadripartitum on the effects of eclipses on various kinds of people and he shows that though Edmund may scoff, he reveals his accurate knowledge of Ptolemy when he jeers that his birth under Ursa Major makes him "rough and lecherous"; men so born were liable to villainy and adultery under the respective influences of Mars and Venus.

2064. Parrott, T[homas] M[arc]. "'God's' or 'gods'' in King Lear, V. iii. 17," SQ, IV (1953), 427-432.

The F_1 reading "Gods" should be emended to "gods'," not to "God's"; Sh's pagan polytheism is self-consistent in this play. For rebuttal, see Alwin Thaler, in RenP (1955), 32-39.

2065. Parrott, Thomas M[arc]. "Hamlet's Sea-Voyage--Bandits or Pirates?: A Reply to Professor Lawrence," SAB, XIX (1944), 51-59.

A defense of Plutarch's "Life of Caesar" (2., the account of Caesar's adventure with the pirates) as source for Hamlet's encounter with pirates at sea; W. W. Lawrence had rejected Plutarch as a source (PMLA, LIX [1944], 54). Parrott's argument is convincing; this episode from the "Life of Caesar" appears to be one more in a long list of "Roman" elements in Ham.

2066. Parsons, A. E. "The Trojan Legend in England: Some Instances of Its Application to the Politics of the Times," MLR, XXIV (1929), 253-264, 394-408.

This learned survey of the Trojan legend, especially since Geoffrey of Monmouth, discusses its importance as propaganda. The legend was repeatedly invoked in Western Europe to "prove" a common ethnic origin of peoples, justifying political unification (e.g., of English and Normans, Scots and English). Sh uses the legend in Macb. IV i (see pp. 406-407 especially), where Macbeth sees the prophetic pageant. James I as a babe holds his genealogical tree tracing his ancestry to Troy and ergo justifying the union of England and Scotland as the land of Brut under one monarch.

2067. Pattee, Fred Lewis. "Fear in Macbeth," PL, X (1898), 92-95.

Macbeth is "the type of a pure and noble man driven by circumstances to crime and living the rest of his life in fear of the consequences. ...It is Aeschylus over again; it is the old Greek idea of Fate. When once the fatal step has been taken, the Eumenides are on the trail."

2068. Peebles, Rose Jeffries. "A Note on Hamlet," MLN, XXXI (1916), 117-120.

At ibid., 1-3, J. Q. Adams had suggested that when Hamlet speaks of the sun breeding maggots in a dead dog (II ii 181-187) he is cautioning Polonius that Claudius may attempt to seduce Ophelia. The author reinforces this suggestion by reviewing variations on the Danae myth current in Sh's time. The traditional identification of the sun and kings would hammer home the concept of Claudius as seducer when Hamlet speaks of the sun as an impregnator. An interesting observation; however it might not be as clear in the theater as in the study that Claudius is referred to here.

2069. Perrett, Wilfrid. The Story of King Lear from Geoffrey of Monmouth to Shakespeare, Palaestra, XXXV (1904), 308 pp.

Perrett suggests (pp. 250-251) that "Gods spies" (Lear V iii 17) means "gods' spies" "with gods' a subjective genitive." This interpretation preserves the pagan coloring of the play and the F_1 reading finds precedent in the Elizabethan trans. of Seneca's tragedies and in earlier Tudor drama. Cf. Thomas M. Parrott and Alwin Thaler, #2064.

2070. Platt, Isaac Hull. "[Polonius and Corambis]," NewShna, III (1904), 83-84.

Platt makes the fanciful suggestion that "Corambis" means (from Latin "coram" and "bis") "Mr. Seeing Double," a play on "Cecil," Lord Burghley's family name, which in Latin means "dim-sighted." At the same time he would derive "Polonius" from "πολέω" ("to busy oneself"), or from "πωλέω" ("to sell," as in "fishmonger," the fish deriving from Burghley's insistence that Englishmen eat fish to bolster the sagging British fisheries industry). The editor objects, as well he might.

2071. Porter, Charlotte, and Helen A. Clarke. "Fatherhood in Literature: The Oedipus Story in the Greek Drama; Shakespeare's 'Lear', Ibsen's 'Borkman'," PL, XI (1899), 102-116.

Intended as a skein of hints to provoke study of the theme, the outline contains fewer statements of fact or opinion than leading questions. Some of these questions are quite elementary, but others demand more than superficial thought: e.g., "How far do Shakespeare and Euripides lay themselves open to the charge that they make goodness passive?"

2072. Pott, C. M. "Parmenides Quoted by Hamlet," Shna, IV (1887), 510-512.

Pott believes that "To be or not to be" echoes the concern of Parmenides with the problem and nature of being. Why Pott should fasten on the Parmenidean fragments is a puzzle, since all metaphysicians are concerned with ontology: "aut esse aut non esse."

2073. Prema, B. S. "Lady Macbeth and Clytemnestra," The Literary Criterion, I (1952) (no pagination available).

Not seen. TU

2074. P[rescot], K[enrick]. Shakespear. n.p., 1774, 16 pp.

Prescot sets out to prove "the learning of Shakespear, from his leading us through the Lyceum and porch at Athens, where none but best scholars could appear or be esteemed." Sh's affinity for the Lyceum is in Hamlet's "To be or not to be," which translates exactly Socrates' thoughts on dreamless death in the Apology: "εἰ οὖν τοιοῦτον ὁ θάνατός ἐστι, κέρδος ἔγωγε λέγω"--"'Tis a consummation / Devoutly to be wish'd." Catullus also has lines on this subject, and "Tully, in the latter part of his treatise on old age, transfers much of the foregoing apology of Plato," but he leaves out Socrates' observations on dreams after death. Prescot also quotes Prospero's "cloud-capp'd towers" lines in Temp. IV i, which Sh "copies" from an eschatological passage in Seneca. This essay, which also contains astronomical speculations, was described by Halliwell-Phillipps as "the rarest of all ... modern Shaksperiana." DFo

2075. Prior, Moody E. "The Elizabethan Tradition," The Language of Tragedy (Col UP, 1947), Ch. II, pp. 16-153.

Prior is concerned with verse as a vehicle of tragedy and he relates the Elizabethan success with verse to rhetoric (when it is integrated into the dramatic structure) and moral didacticism (to which the loftiness of verse is appropriate). Sh is represented by Romeo and Lear (see pp. 59-93). Romeo is less sententious than the early history plays because it is not political: political issues evoked the solemn sentences which abound in Seneca. In Lear the integration of language, theme, and character is excellent, as Caroline Spurgeon's studies of Sh's imagery show. Prior makes occasional remarks of great interest: e.g., Benvolio's account to the Duke of the deaths of Mercutio and Tybalt has the stiffness of a Nuntius' speech.

2076. Prior, Moody E. "The Thought of Hamlet and the Modern Temper," ELH, XV (1948), 261-285.

See especially Section 3 (276-280) for the assertion that "Hamlet's thinking carries him beyond the essentially rationalistic order of the stoic metaphysics. His final position has quite as much in common with the 'ataraxia', the freedom from the perturbations of the mind and passions, which was the goal of ancient and later pyrrhonists." Sh's debt to none of them (including Montaigne) can be established, but the thought is basically skeptical in a non-pejorative sense of that term. The tranquility of the Stoic and the "ataraxia" of the pyrrhonist have more in common than Prior will admit. Prior is adding another ethical posture to the already snarled relationships in Ham. among Pauline ethics, New Testament trust in Providence, and Senecan Stoicism. The additional complication is welcome, but it is perhaps more wisely regarded as a philosophical analogue than as a source.

2077. Putney, Rufus. "What 'Praise to Give?' Jonson vs. Stoll," PQ, XXIII (1944), 307-319.

Putney argues that Stoll and the other "conventional" critics wrongly deny a basis in reality for the characters and plots of Sh's tragedies; Ben Jonson showed in his F_1 eulogy of Sh that he regarded the plays as grounded in Nature as well as contrived by Art. "His praise--magnificent and sincere, for flattery did not require him to rank Shakespeare with the Greeks and Romans--implies moral and spiritual qualities which modern criticism depreciates." The illustration and defense of the thesis are drawn from the four great tragedies, especially Oth. In them, Sh is "the peer of Sophocles."

2078. Rea, John D. "Notes on Shakespeare," MLN, XXXV (1920), 377-378.

The first note defends the F_1 reading "Cyme" for the purgative referred to at Macb. V iii 55. Holland's Pliny uses this term for tendrils of the colewort, a purgative plant.

2079. Reed, Robert R., Jr. "The Fatal Elizabethan Sisters in 'Macbeth'," NQ, CC (1955), 425-427.

Though the "broth-boiling scene" is probably traceable to Seneca's Medea, the hags are Elizabethan as much as classical. Sh wishes to associate them with the Roman Parcae to give them stature, but he also wishes us to think of them as witches, minions of the Devil, who tempt Macbeth into evil. Both views of the fatal sisters are valid. Reed's middle position on the genealogy of the Witches seems attractive in view of the fact that Macb., like Ham.

and Lear, is a tragedy in which Sh deliberately establishes a tension between pagan/classical and Christian/"modern" approaches to life.

2080. Ribner, Irving. "Then I Denie You Starres: A Reading of Romeo and Juliet," SERD, pp. 269-286.

Ribner proposes that Romeo is a milestone because it is Sh's first successful attempt to transmute source material. Brooke's Romeus and Juliet emphasized just punishment for sin; the Senecan dramatic tradition emphasized Fate and Fortune as manipulators of men's lives. Sh took the Senecan and Christian versions of love tragedy and transcended both by showing Romeo's growth from a belief in fickle Fortune to the Christian Stoicism of his belief in Divine Providence in Act V. Romeo does not "defy" the stars, he "denies" them: i.e., he refuses to be subject to Fate or Fortune but accepts Providence as the guide of men's affairs. "Like the tragedies of Aeschylus, Romeo and Juliet proclaims also that man learns through suffering, but even more strongly than in Greek tragedy, there is affirmation in Shakespeare that the ultimate plan of the universe is good, for out of the suffering of individuals the social order is cleansed of evil." This is a challenging reading of Romeo; it is reinforced by those interpretations of Ham. which emphasize that by Act V Hamlet is ready to "defy augury" and speak of Providence, but it neglects Juliet, minimizes the importance of the Prologue, and meets an awkward obstacle in the unchristian suicide with which Romeo follows his putative rejection of classical ethics.

2081. Ridley, M. R. "Introduction," Othello (1958), ArdenSh, pp. xv-lxx.

In having a "theatrically effective plot," Oth. is unique among Sh's tragedies and in a class with Oedipus Tyrannus (p. xlvi). In discussing the "simple and straightforward" Othello, Ridley compares him to Homer's Ajax, quoting Iliad XVII 645-647 to illustrate Othello's desire for certitude (p. lv). The play has unity of time, place, and action if we regard Act I as a prologue. Ridley's discussion of the unities is particularly interesting (p. xlvii).

2082. Rinehart, Keith. "The Moral Background of King Lear," UKCR, XX (1954), 223-228.

"Cordelia, Kent, and Edgar and Edmund, Goneril, and Regan are all 'flat' characters whose primary purpose it is to establish the moral background upon which the tragedies of Lear and Gloucester are played--a stoic background." Dying as they do of an excess of feeling, the latter two remain ignorant of the Stoic truth that reason must master passion--the first three know this truth--the second three openly flout it. Nature as goddess is another key to the Stoicism of the play, because to the Roman Stoics the physical world was divine. An interesting interpretation of the play, though it unquestionably diminishes the stature of Lear and Gloucester.

2083. Robertson, J[ohn] M. "A Marlowe Mystification," TLS, December 11, 1924, p. 850. SG

An error in Douce (#0207) on Romeo II ii 92-93 has passed unnoticed through eight editors. Douce called Marlowe the translator of the Ars Amatoria when he actually translated the Amores. Arthur M. Clark (ibid., July 16, 1925, p. 480 SG) assigns to Thomas Heywood the trans. of the Ars Amatoria from which Sh got these lines about Jove laughing at lovers' perjuries.

2084. Ross, Lawrence J. "The Meaning of Strawberries in Shakespeare," SR, VII (1960), 225-240.

For classical symbolism in the strawberries on Desdemona's handkerchief, see #1077.

2085. Rudé, Jack L. "Poetic Justice: A Study of the Problem of Human Conduct in Tragedy from Aeschylus to Shakespeare," diss (Harvard, 1934).*

2086. Rule, Fredk. "Imperious," 4 NQ, X (1872), 292.

Rule wonders whether Sh meant Hamlet to say, "Imperious Caesar, dead and turn'd to clay" or "Imperial Caesar ..." (Ham. V i 236); the quartos and folios disagree. Rule attempts to answer his own question (ibid., XI [1873], 72) in part by suggesting that the two terms meant much the same thing in the sixteenth century. For this view there is some support from Brinsley Nicholson, who points out (ibid., 166) that "imperious," like "curious," retained its Latinate suggestions in Sh. It did not become an epithet of personality until later. Meanwhile another correspondent (p. 106) complains against Rule's tampering with what he regards as a textus receptus.

2087. Rymer, Thomas. "Othello," A Short View of Tragedy, Ch. VII. In Critical Works of Thomas Rymer, ed. Curt A. Zimansky (Yale UP, 1956), pp. 131-164.

Rymer's outrageous condemnation of Oth. as lacking in every dramatic excellence is a classic of misguided Sh criticism. The ludicrousness of his vitriolic judgments appears plainly on every page. Rymer's relevance here is a result of his fondness for justifying his excoriation of Oth. from classical authority. His quotations from the classics range from Aristophanes to Horace, but, as Zimansky points out in his notes, they are by no means all relevant to Sh's play.

2088. S. "Greek and English Tragedy: Oedipus, —King Lear," The Reflector, II (1811), 127-139.

This critical essay treats both Oedipus Tyrannus and Oedipus Coloneus as (like Lear) manifestations of great genius. But S. observes that Sh did not borrow from Sophocles and that the point is not important (pace Malone and Steevens) once we submit to the grandeur of Sh's conception and poetry. Sh probably "knew and disdained" the unities, but then Sophocles, too, may have merely followed his materials, not "any predilection for doctrines so horrible, and errors so disgusting" as those which Aristotle forced on later generations. The criticism of all three plays is sound: S. rejects Tate's Lear as an abomination and sagely observes that the conclusion of Oedipus Coloneus is more clumsily contrived than Sophocles' usual skill would lead us to expect; by contrast Lear with Cordelia in his arms is sublime. S. also makes interesting observations on Sophocles' failure to show Oedipus insane and on the parallels between Lear's curses and Oedipus'. Altogether a rewarding essay. DFo

2089. Sargeaunt, G[eorge] M. "The Substance of Greek Tragedy," QR, CCLI (1928), 242-255.

In passing: Sh, unlike the Attic dramatists, portrays the facts of life without regarding the "spiritual and religious consciousness" which "can interpret the sorrows of existence." It is difficult to agree that Sh's plays are spiritually impoverished.

2090. Schacht, Theodor. Über die Tragödie Antigone nebst einem vergleichenden Blick auf Sofokles und Shakspeare. Darmstadt, 1842, 126 pp.

The juxtaposition of the two dramatists (pp. 85-114) is primarily a contrast, which dwells on the emotional effects produced by their respective techniques (e.g., Chorus, narrated action, brief time span in Sophocles; portrayed action, fully developed character, shifting locale in Sh). Sh fares well in the comparisons, but Schacht hesitates to deprecate Sophocles; he points out, e.g., that the presence of the Ghost in Ham. is deeply moving, yet observes that some scenes in Sh might better have been narrated than portrayed. There is an extended comparison between Antigone and Othello as characters who carry the seeds of their catastrophes within them, but the essay is, on the whole, stated in general terms without discussion of dramatic themes or analysis of passages. DFo

2091. Schadewaldt, Wolfgang. "Shakespeare und die griechische Tragödie: Sophokles' Elektra und Hamlet," ShJ, XCVI (1960), 7-34. (The essay appears with slightly different title in the author's collected writings, Hellas und Hesperien [1960].)

The first section, "Das Problem," contains several significant parallels between the two plays and mentions Murray's thesis (#2049). But the body of the essay treats each play largely in isolation, and the conclusion explains the presence of the same themes in both plays in quasi-mystical terms: Sh's genius, akin to the Greek genius, reconstructed Greek concepts from the kernels which Senecan and neo-Senecan drama offered him. Though Schadewaldt mentions Stoll's essay (#2132) in his notes he does not take cognizance of Stoll's theory that the Orestes legend came down to Sh in some specific form through Kyd's Ur-Hamlet. There are interesting observations, however, on grief in Ham. and on Fate as an aspect of character in Greek tragedy.

2092. Schadewaldt, Wolfgang. "Shakespeares 'König Lear' und Sophokles' 'König Ödipus'," Hellas und Hesperien, Gesammelte Schriften zur Antike und zur neueren Literatur (Zurich, 1960), pp. 570-578.

The link between plays which at first seem unlike is that in both man is confronted by ineffable evil and is stripped of the superficialities of life, falling back on more important realities which lie within the self. Similar awareness comes to sufferers in the two plays: "'Reif sein ist alles'," "'Rein sein ist alles'." Other similarities are the darkened backdrops against which the dramas are played, the theme of moral blindness and the anger which accompanies it, the paradoxes of reason in madness and freedom in constraint. Schadewaldt attributes the similarities to the fact "dass es ein festes Grundwesen des Tragischen gibt, das sich auch ohne unmittelbare Berührungen über die Zeit hinweg--Shakespeare hat Sophokles kaum gekannt--in ähnlichen geschichtlichen Lagen im Genie gleichsam von selbst wiedererzeugt."

2093. Schanzer, Ernest. "Four Notes on 'Macbeth'," MLR, LII (1957), 223-227.

The fourth note points out an ambiguity in Hecate's lines about the "vap'rous drop profound" that hangs "Upon the corner of the moon" (III v 23-29). She means either that she can use the drop to call up evil spirits, or that she can use it to create artificial ones, as Apollo and Juno do in Iliad V and Aeneid X. Schanzer prefers the first explanation.

2094. Schaubert, E[lse] v. "Die Stelle vom 'Rauhen Pyrrhus' (Hamlet II, 2, 460-551) in ihrem Verhältnis zu Marlowe-Nashes 'Dido,' zu Seneca und dem 'Urhamlet' und damit ihrer Bedeutung für Datierungsfragen, Quartoproblem und Nashes Angriff auf Thomas Kyd," Anglia, LIII (1929), 374-439. E-S SG

This elaborately reasoned art. begins with a meticulous examination of classical (Seneca, Ovid, Virgil, Dares, Dictys), Medieval, and Renaissance accounts of the death of Priam in search of a source for elements which the Player's speech has in common with Marlowe's Dido. These are chiefly Pyrrhus' hesitation in a statuesque posture, the wind of Pyrrhus' sword which blows Priam down, the mincing of Priam's limbs, and the nature of Hecuba's grief. No single account has all of them; Marlowe seems to have gathered them from several sources, some of them possibly from the bloody murder of Oronte and his young sons in Cinthio's Orbecche. The argument goes that Aeneas' tale to Dido in Marlowe's play provided Kyd with materials for his version of the death of Priam in the Ur-Hamlet; Sh then took over Kyd's passage virtually intact when he rewrote the Ur-Hamlet. But Kyd's main inspiration was Seneca--not passages on Priam, but scattered devices, especially in the Phaedra. Therefore the passage in Ham. not only echoes Marlowe but also the Tenne Tragedies (Kyd used the trans. of Seneca). An interesting hypothesis, but Sh could surely himself have fused his recollection of the Tenne Tragedies with Marlowe's lurid details; as the author admits, "Es ist anzunehmen, dass Shakespeare Seneca--zum mindesten in der englischen Übersetzung--gelesen hatte."

2095. Schöll, Adolf. "Shakespeare und Sophokles," ShJ, I (1865), 127-137. E-S HB

A somewhat romantic comparison of the two dramatists which restricts its observations to general statements; only Ham. and Macb. are mentioned and neither is analyzed. Poetry is a function of the culture against which it is written, though a classic transcends its cultural circumscriptions; yet, partaking to some extent of the ephemeral culture, classics fall into neglect when culture changes and are revived to be dissected by scholars and misunderstood by critics. This common fate Sophocles and Sh have shared.

2096. Schulze, Karl Paul. "Die Entwickelung der Sage von Romeo und Julia," ShJ, XI (1876), 140-225.

In passing (pp. 153-156), Schulze recounts Xenophon's tale of Anthia and Habrocomes which Douce (#0207) recognized as the ultimate source of the sleeping-potion-and-living-burial device in Romeo. Schulze emphasizes, however, that the device is the only similarity between the two stories and points out that it also appears in Chariton's Chaereas and Callirhoe, where the heroine, mistaken for dead, is entombed alive.

2097. Seeley, John Robert. "A Parallel between Shakespeare's Tragedy of King Lear and The Oedipus in Colono of Sophocles; Stating the General Design of Each Play, and Contrasting the Characters Introduced, in their Points of Similarity and Dissimilarity," Three Essays on Shakespeare's Tragedy of King Lear by Pupils of the City of London School (Ln, 1851), Essay I, pp. 1-51.

Seeley begins with the assertion that the death of Oedipus is a result of divine retribution while the deaths of Lear and Cordelia are gratuitous; ergo Lear is entertainment whereas Oedipus Coloneus is tragedy in the strict (i.e., religious) sense. Chs. II and III summarize the actions and cultural backgrounds of the two plays. Toward the end of Ch. IV Seeley compares Oedipus, who has borne his guilt like Promethean chains long before the play opens, with Lear, who discovers the meaning of guilt and love on-stage, and with Gloucester, who bears his suffering (like Oedipus) "erect and unshaken," though he does not have Oedipus' "unresisting dignity." Cordelia, whose filial loyalty reminds us of Antigone's, is more feminine and timid in her heroism. Creon and Edmund are both cast in the antagonist's rôle, but the "anomalous" character of Creon is very different from the purposeful, intellectualized evil of Edmund. Edgar and Theseus both are "protectors of wandering misery," but Theseus is a mere personification of Athens while Edgar is "real," though he embodies the virtues of Medieval chivalry. Seeley generalizes that "Sophocles is the poet of religion and human nature united; Shakespeare, of human nature alone." MB

2098. Semper, I. J. "The Ghost in Hamlet: Pagan or Christian?" The Month, n.s. IX (1953), 222-234.

A vigorous rebuttal of Battenhouse (#1825), who found classical elements in King Hamlet's Ghost. "The theory that the Ghost rises from a mythological Tartarus does scant justice to Shakespeare's artistic achievement, inasmuch as it brackets his noble creation with the Senecan spectres of his predecessors." This argument by association is not persuasive. It is noteworthy that Semper does not fully account for the Ghost's admonition to commit sin; nor does he attack Battenhouse where he is truly vulnerable—on the meaning of "extravagant and erring."

2099. Sensabaugh, G. F. "John Ford and Elizabethan Tragedy," PQ, XX (1941), 442-453. (Also in Craig Festschrift, pp. 250-261.)

Sensabaugh contrasts Ford's tragedy (physical forces in conflict with the laws of society) with Shn tragedy which participates in both the Greek and Medieval traditions--the tragedy of "man's free will in a world of human values"; Ford's characters are sick men and women who purge no pity or fear in us. Sh's heroes are fully responsible for their destinies and elicit our sympathy and awe as they fall. Sensabaugh illustrates briefly from Macb.

2100. Seronsy, Cecil C. "Shakespeare's King Lear, I, i, 159-163," Expl, XVII (1958), item 21.

The correct interpretation of these lines depends on the double meaning of the word "sight" in line 159 and on Apollo's dual function as patron of archery and "as god of light and wisdom." This is a valid contribution to the understanding of the rôle of the pagan gods in Lear.

2101. Shackford, Martha H. "Discovery, Recognition, Reversal: King Oedipus and Othello," Shakespeare, Sophocles: Dramatic Themes and Modes (N.Y., 1960), pp. 45-59.

Despite critics' traditional identification of the two terms, "discovery" reveals the unknown whereas "recognition" is "a becoming aware of something hitherto known." Each has a distinctive impact in tragedy. Analysis of Oedipus Tyrannus and Oth. shows that Sophocles and Sh utilize both discovery and recognition; there is, of course, no question of indebtedness. Professor Shackford's distinction is an important one; an interesting essay.

2102. Shackford, Martha H. "Foreshadowing and Suspense: Agamemnon and King Lear," Shakespeare, Sophocles: Dramatic Themes and Modes (N.Y., 1960), pp. 71-83.

Another of Professor Shackford's enlightening comparisons between Sh and the classics. Though Aeschylus' Agamemnon and Lear have much in common, one important difference is that the former engrosses by recapitulation of past horror with vague foreshadowing of more in the future, whereas the latter plunges into an action (I i) and then manipulates our suspense about the effects of this cause.

2103. Shackford, Martha H. "Sources of Irony in Hamlet," Shakespeare, Sophocles: Dramatic Themes and Modes (N.Y., 1960), pp. 9-24. ("This essay was first published in The Sewanee Review.")

Sh's innate sense of the ironic was implemented by the lessons he learned from Lyly, whose "irony of dissimulation" is traceable through Renaissance Italy and Spain back to Plautus and Terence and finally to Aristophanes and Lucian. This thoughtful piece of Ham. criticism attempts no direct connection with Greek drama; the definitions are crisp and the expression lucid.

2104. Shelley, P[ercy] B. Defence of Poetry (1821) (as abstracted in the New Variorum Lear).

In passing: Lear is a greater play than Oedipus Tyrannus and Agamemnon because in it Sh has incorporated comedy which is "universal, ideal, sublime."

2105. S[heppard], J[ohn] T. "Agamemnon and Macbeth," PRI, XXXV (1954), 560-569.

Sheppard begins with a three-page assertion that Sh knew more Latin and Greek (and liked them better) than some critics have believed. Sh's Greek would include bits of the Gospels, Theocritus, Hesiod, Homer, Lucian, and Isocrates. The critical study of the two plays is brilliant. The opening lines of Agamemnon, with their call for respite, prefigure the theme of the trilogy just as the "Prelude" of Macb., with its juxtaposition of foul and fair and its emphasis on dishonest, deceptive Fortune (I ii 14-15), outlines the horrid events to follow. Both plays make much of sleep and the loss of sleep. The threats which the Furies offer to Orestes in the Eumenides describe accurately what happens to Macbeth (he ends by believing that life is meaningless). An unusually rewarding essay which deserves wider circulation than it has had.

2106. Siegel, P[aul] N. "Adversity and the Miracle of Love in King Lear," SQ, VI (1955), 325-336.

Siegel interprets the play in Christian terms, hinting that Boethius' fusion of Stoic and Christian philosophies lies behind Sh's conception. Siegel does not examine this aspect of the question at any length, however, and his major argument is for the specifically Christian coloring of the play. There is a corpus of classicism in Lear which Siegel's critical approach cannot account for.

2107. Sigismund, R[einhold]. "Ueber die Bedeutung des Mandrake bei Shakespeare, sowie über die historische Entwickelung dieses Begriffes," ShJ, XX (1885), 310-319.

For the classical provenance of the shrieking mandrake alluded to in Romeo IV iii, see #1083.

2108. Sigismund, R[einhold]. "Ueber die Wirkung des Hebenon im Hamlet und eine damit verglichene Stelle bei Plutarch," ShJ, XX (1885), 320-324.

Sigismund argues that yew sap was the poison which produced horrid effects on King Hamlet while he slept in his garden. In Quaestiones Convivales (III i) Plutarch maintains that sleeping under a yew tree is fatal; Sigismund believes that Sh adapted the Plutarchian passage. He rejects Pliny as source despite the fact that Pliny speaks of henbane (hyoscyamus) poured into the human ear as an enemy to the reason.

2109. Sigismund, Reinhold. "Ursprung der Stelle: 'Was ist ihm Hekuba?'" ShJ, XVII (1882), 288-290.

Sigismund is apparently first among those who have noted the parallels between the Hamlet story and the account of Alexander of Pherae in Plutarch's "Life of Pelopidas" (see #2016, #2137). A fratricidal usurper who leaves a theater because of its dangerous emotional impact on him appears in each story. Alexander saw the miseries of Hecuba portrayed in Euripides' Troades; Hamlet hears the miseries of Hecuba recounted in the Player's description of the fall of Troy. Sigismund feels sure that Sh drew on Plutarch's account for Ham.

2110. Silberschlag, Karl. "Shakespeare's Hamlet, seine Quellen und politischen Beziehungen," ShJ, XII (1877), 261-289. E-S

In passing, Silberschlag calls attention to the difference in character between Sh's Hamlet and Saxo's by contrasting "no more like my father / Than I to Hercules" (I ii 152-153) with Saxo's summary of Amlethus' character: "Had his fortune equalled his gifts he would have attained the brilliance of the gods and surpassed the deeds of Hercules." Sh's lines are "offenbar im Hinblick auf diese Worte des Saxo." In a later passage, Silberschlag also compares Hamlet with Orestes. The situation is the same in Ham. as in the Oresteia, but Christian concepts forbid that Hamlet should take vengeance on his mother, so Sh and Aeschylus handle the conflict of loyalties differently.

2111. Simpson, Percy. "The Theme of Revenge in Elizabethan Tragedy," PBA, XXI (1935), 101-136. (Annual British Academy Shakespeare Lecture.) E-S

After a discussion of the Elizabethan understanding (and misunderstanding) of the Greek concepts of Até and Nemesis, Simpson goes on to an engrossing analysis of the major revenge tragedies from Kyd to Tourneur. Ham. is the only great play in the tradition. Unlike R.III, Ham. is not indebted to Seneca. Simpson also briefly discusses the other history plays and Caesar. The address is filled with astute criticism and informative suggestions: e.g., Spenser is the source of Sh's conception of Até; the great difficulty in constructing the revenge play was what to do with the Aristotelian "middle"--the beginning was a crime and the end its avenging--Ham. was the only play to fulfill all three parts of the Aristotelian requirement adequately. A very interesting critical essay, though it neglects the Roman (Senecan?) element in Ham. and ignores the probability that Sh learned of Até from Appian.

2112. Sitwell, Edith. "'Nero is an Angler'," TLS, February 2, 1946, p. 55.

Edgar's babbling in Lear III vi about Nero angling in the lake of darkness seems to Dame Edith to be drawn from a passage in Pausanius II xxxvii describing the Alcyonian Lake which Nero was said to have attempted in vain to plumb. But John Berryman (ibid., 151) quite correctly cites Budd's evidence (#1850) that Sh learned about Nero from Chaucer.

2113. Sledd, James. "A Note on the Use of Renaissance Dictionaries," MP, XLIX (1951), 10-15.

For a statement by Juliet's Nurse of a classical "fact" from a Renaissance dictionary, see #0923.

2114. Smith, Gerald. "A Note on the Death of Lear," MLN, LXX (1955), 403-404.

That both Lear and Gloucester should die of a combination of grief and joy has some precedent in the pseudo-classical Problems of Aristotle (1597) where the question is raised why men die of grief or of joy but not of anger.

2115. Smith, Grover. "The Tennis-Ball of Fortune," NQ, CXC (1946), 202-203. GRS

For Gloucester and the spirit of Euripidean tragedy, see #2290.

2116. Smith, Philip A. "Othello's Diction," SQ, IX (1958), 428-430.

Sh deliberately makes Othello speak an Ausländer's English to emphasize his lack of familiarity with Venetian ways and to give credibility to his inability to deal with Iago. The two chief characteristics of his speech are (1) a sentence structure out of Lily's Grammar and (2) a trick of combining native and Latinate words in hybrid compounds. Smith's point is interesting, but Othello says little that is any more "foreign" than the "multitudinous seas incarnadine" of Macbeth, e.g.

2117. Smith, Robert Metcalf. "Three Interpretations of Romeo and Juliet," SAB, XXIII (1948), 60-77.

In passing Smith points out the Boethian basis of Sh's conception of Fortune in Romeo: Providence ultimately controls men and it also controls the Fortune which proximately controls them. Thus Sh utilizes a Christianized classical Fatalism.

2118. Smyth, Albert H. Shakespeare's Pericles and Apollonius of Tyre: A Study in Comparative Literature. Philadelphia, 1898, 112 pp.

For Greek romance conventions as the mediate source of Romeo, see #2294. DFo

2119. Snuggs, Henry L. Shakespeare and Five Acts: Studies in a Dramatic Convention. N.Y., 1960, 144 pp.

For Snuggs's rebuttal of Baldwin's arguments (#0683) for the Terentian structure of Romeo, see #0926.

2120. Soellner, Rolf [H.] "The Madness of Hercules and the Elizabethans," CL, X (1958), 309-324.

Soellner traces the legends of Hercules through antiquity, emphasizing the portrayal by Seneca of his madness in the Hercules Furens and by Seneca and Ovid of his death agonies on Mount Oeta in the Hercules Oetaeus and Meta. IX. The Elizabethans extracted from these three sources and from classical medical treatises: (1) the notion that Hercules was a passionate raver (actually the Stoics revered him for his self-control); (2) the belief that his madness was induced by physiological, not supernatural causes, i.e., by melancholia. To these concepts some added (3) a Platonic identification of frenzy with creative inspiration and the gift of prophecy. The resulting complex was greatly different from the Hercules of any one of the classical authorities it was based on. Sh refers to Hercules' madness in the funeral of Ophelia and in Antony IV xii where Antony, who is Hercules' descendant, uses "Herculean" language when he raves that Cleopatra has betrayed him. The epileptic seizures of Caesar and Othello may also be modeled on the frenzied seizures of Hercules in antiquity. Soellner believes that Sh submerges this convention of Herculean madness in his characters as he submerges every convention he appropriates; for contrast he offers four other Elizabethan plays. This is a valuable study.

2121. Soellner, Rolf [H.]. "Shakespeare and the 'Consolatio'," NQ, CXCIX (1954), 108-109.

A reasoned and credible examination of the sources of Romeo III iii 54-56. The source of this consolatio is not Brooke or Lyly's Euphues, but Erasmus' De Conscribendis Epistolis (traceable in turn to Boethius).

2122. Spearing, Evelyn M. "The Elizabethan 'Tenne Tragedies of Seneca'," MLR, IV (1909), 437-461. (Reprinted in extended form as a pamphlet [CUP, 1912].) E-S HB SG

Though she suggests that the merit of this trans. is not in itself but in its influence, the author's remarks on that influence are most brief. Sh (Ham., Romeo) is accorded passing mention (pp. 459, 460, 461).

2123. Spencer, Terence. "Three Shakespearian Notes," MLR, XLIX (1954), 46-51.

Note III, "Like to the Pontic Sea," argues that Sh need not have acquired Othello's knowledge of the current in the Hellespont from Pliny, either in the original or in Holland's trans. This bit of lore was as often related by Renaissance geographers as it had been by their classical forebears.

2124. Spencer, Theodore. "The Elizabethan Malcontent," AMS, pp. 523-535.

Though the Elizabethan interest in the five types of melancholics (of which the malcontent makes one) has a foundation in the uncertain social conditions of the time, the view that man is better off not born is as old as Cicero, Seneca, Plutarch, and Boethius. Spencer does not elaborate their views. Sh portrays the malcontent (a man displaced from society) in Iago, and the satirical ranter (derived from the malcontent) in Apemantus, Timon, and Thersites.

2125. Spencer, Theodore. "Hamlet and the Nature of Reality," ELH, V (1938), 253-277.

The key to the thought and tone of Ham. is the Renaissance tension between Ptolemy and Copernicus, Cicero and Machiavelli, [presumably] Aristotle and Montaigne. These three pairs reflect the three orders of being: cosmos, state, and man; of each pair, the Elizabethans feared that the latter would prove to be a reality making mere appearance of the former. Spencer does not mention Platonic dualism and its contribution to the appearance/reality problem in the Renaissance, but this is a very stimulating art.

2126. Spens, Janet. An Essay on Shakespeare's Relation to Tradition. Oxford, 1916, 102 pp.

Part II (55-102) interprets Sophoclean tragedy as a dramatization of the quasi-religious rite of the scapegoat for the city and then suggests that some of the features of Attic revenge tragedy (e.g., the old avenger succeeded by a younger) were transmitted to Kyd and Sh (Ham., Macb., Lear) and Marston through the medium of Seneca, who exaggerated these ritual aspects (scapegoat, revenge code) which he took from Sophocles. A plausible argument lucidly expressed.

2127. Stampfer, J. "The Catharsis of King Lear," ShS, XIII (1960), 1-10.

The catharsis in the play springs from the fact that despite his purgation (Lear is a penitent, not hybristic), the hero must die and thereby experience the ultimate violation of Justice. But if this quasi-Christian interpretation is accepted, would not Lear's death represent the mercy of Providence, not its injustice? (see Kent's lines on Lear's death: "Vex not his ghost. O, let him pass! ...").

2128. Stapfer, Paul. Shakespeare et l'antiquité: Deuxième partie, Shakespeare et les tragiques grecs. Paris, 1880, 320 pp. (New ed., 1888.) The central thesis is summarized in PL, VI (1894), 187-196.

A detailed and critical study in comparative literature which concludes that Sh has more in common with Euripides than Euripides has in common with Aeschylus and Sophocles. "Euripide a consommé la plus grande revolution qui se soit jamais faite dans l'art dramatique, lorsque, au lieu du conflit extérieur des dieux, où résidait avant lui l'essence du drame, il transporta le théâtre de la lutte tragique dans l'âme des personnages." Apollo and the Furies are the real actors in the Oresteia; Antigone's gods from Hades are in conflict with Creon's patron Zeus in the Antigone; but in Euripides as in Sh, the struggle is interior. Like Sh, Euripides had in him more humanism than piety. By contrast the protagonists of Aeschylus' and Sophocles' Orestes tragedies are monolithic; undivided in mind they take their vengeance as an act of religious ceremony, unlike Hamlet, who is paralyzed by the division within him and only takes his revenge at the moment of death, thus stripping that revenge of solemnity and making it a personal, not a divine retribution. There are a large number of other comparisons and contrasts between Greek and Shn characters (including some from Homer: Penelope and Imogen, Eumaeus and Kent). Macb. receives the most extensive treatment, three chs. Stapfer also introduces the French tragic dramatists and Goethe. This remains a landmark of comparative criticism, though Kitto (#1988) and other recent commentators have modified its extreme emphasis on the affinity between Shn and Euripidean tragedy.

2129. Starnes, D[eWitt] T. "Actaeon's Dogs," Names, III (1955), 19-25.

For a possible reference to the Actaeon myth in Macb., see #0931.

2130. Steadman, John M. "The 'Faeries' Midwife': 'Romeo and Juliet', I,iv," NQ, CCI (1956), 424.

There is an analogue to Mercutio's metaphor about Queen Mab in Plato's Theaetetus, where Socrates speaks of himself as a midwife to men's thoughts; Queen Mab, of course, delivers dreams.

2131. Stoll, E[lmer] E[dgar]. "The Characterization," Shakespeare Studies: Historical and Comparative in Method (N.Y., 1927), pp. 90-146.

See Section 2 (93-96) for a discussion of the characterization of Othello, and of the Attic tragic protagonist. Stoll briefly points to similarities and differences.

2132. Stoll, Elmer E[dgar]. Hamlet: An Historical and Comparative Study, RPUM, VIII (Minnesota UP, 1919), 76 pp. E-S SG

To defend his interpretation of Hamlet as a "conventional" hero without German or Coleridgean psychological problems, Stoll advances a great number of parallels from classical revenge stories (and from their English and Continental descendants). The Odyssey; the Orestes plays of Aeschylus, Sophocles, and Euripides; the tragedies of Seneca; and part of the Oedipus cycle are among the analogues. But far the most important suggestion is that made in an appendix: Ham. and the Orestes stories have themes and incidents in common which are not in Belleforest because Kyd, who was educated at Merchant Taylors', read Euripides in Greek (or in a Latin trans.), and Sh simply borrowed the details from Kyd's Ur-Hamlet. If Stoll is correct there is no need for the anthropological hypothesis of Murray (#2049). Stoll specifies four elements in Ham. which Kyd could have found in Euripides but not in his "other" sources: (1) the character of Horatio (Pylades); (2) the hero's fear of not being honorably buried when dead; (3) the hero's father's death without due religious rites; (4) the Ghost's admonition to the hero not to taint his mind or harm his mother; this appears to refer to the Orestes story generally. This is an important book. The suggestion about Kyd has not received adequate scholarly attention, it would seem. For Homer as a possible link between Orestes and Ham., see #1981.

2133. Stoll, E[lmer] E[dgar]. "Oedipus and Othello: Corneille, Rymer, and Voltaire," RAA, XII (1935), 385-400. (Revised as Ch. VI in Shakespeare and Other Masters [1940].)

A defense of Oedipus and Othello from the critics who have thought them too stupid to penetrate the realities in the circumstances they are in. Stoll draws illuminating comparisons between the two and emphasizes the impact on the audience of Fate in each play. No indebtedness is implied.

2134. Stoll, E[lmer] E[dgar]. "'Reconciliation' in Tragedy: Shakespeare and Sophocles," UTQ, IV (1934), 11-33. (Revised as Ch. II of Shakespeare and Other Masters [1940].)

"Aeschylus ... is religious, and provides a solution, justifying the ways of God to men. Sophocles is religious, without attempting to do that. Shakespeare, as dramatist, keeping more in the background, is reverent but reticent and hardly religious at all." The reconciliation in Shn tragedy comes through the dignity with which the protagonists meet destiny and through the calm, implicit sense that "order, something solid, is behind or above."

2135. Stoll, E[lmer] E[dgar]. "Source and Motive in Macbeth and Othello," RES, XIX (1943), 25-32.

It is precisely because Sh deviates from his sources in stripping Iago of any adequate motive and in giving Macbeth no cause for crime in Duncan's behavior--because of this that the two plays succeed in emulating the Greek spirit, for Hellenic tragedy is the consequences of a horrid deed committed by a basically good man. In the case of Macbeth it is a horrid deed premeditated (as is Clytemnestra's); in the case of Othello it is simply hamartia (like Oedipus') --as a result Othello retains our sympathy throughout whereas only the great poetry of Macb. sustains our identification with the protagonist. A very interesting essay.

2136. Stroup, T. B. "Shakespeare's Use of a Travel-Book Commonplace," PQ, XVII (1938), 351-358. SG

With impressive erudition, Stroup cites analogues in a wide range of classical, Medieval, and Renaissance literature to Othello's romantic tale of his adventures. Indeed, the cannibals and headless men were so much a donné of travel-literature by 1598 that Bishop Hall ridiculed them in one of his satires. Sh could have obtained the material easily in any one of a dozen places.

2137. Stull, Joseph S. "Shakespeare and Plutarch's 'Life of Pelopidas'," NQ, CXCVIII (1953), 512-513.

Stull finds parallels to the "Life of Pelopidas" in Lady Macbeth's encouragement of her faltering husband, Mistress Page's readiness to hallow the cudgel that had beaten Falstaff, and Hamlet's rebuke to Gertrude for her relationship with Claudius. None of this evidence for Sh's knowledge of this one of Plutarch's Lives is so convincing as that offered by Marindin (#2016), of whom Stull appears not to be aware, though he discusses some of his predecessors.

2138. Symonds, John A. "The Rise of Tragedy," Shakspere's Predecessors in the English Drama (Ln, 1884), Ch. VI, pp. 211-245. E-S HB

In his survey of the "followers of Seneca" between Gorboduc (1561) and The Misfortunes of Arthur (1587), Symonds glances ahead momentarily at Sh, "who omitted nothing in the tragic apparatus of his predecessors, but with inbreathed sense and swift imagination woke those dead things [e.g., the ghost] to organic life." Symonds alludes briefly to a Senecan line transmuted in Macb. It is significant that in a preceding ch. Symonds minimizes the influence of Roman comedy on Sh and his predecessors. Modern scholarship would not be able to accept this lack of emphasis; at the same time, many modern scholars depreciate the Senecan influence which is the focus of Symond's interest.

2139. T., D. C. "'Lear,' IV.vi.278," 6 NQ, VI (1882), 262.

The phrase "indistinguish'd space of woman's will" can be "illustrated" from Aeschylus' Agamemnon, 485.

2140. Taylor, E. M. M. "Lear's Philosopher," SQ, VI (1955), 364-365.

Taylor explains that in III iv Lear is thinking of the Cynics when he refers to Edgar as a philosopher. The Cynics "were a byword for frugality and contempt for creature comforts"; interpreted in this way, the hitherto obscure babble about philosophy becomes an integral part of the scene, and a key to Lear's transformation. This is a point well made.

2141. Taylor, William Edwards. "The Villainess in Elizabethan Drama," diss (Vanderbilt, 1957). DA, XVII (1957), 1756-57.

Three traditions of feminine villainy influenced the Elizabethan drama: the native, theological anti-feminism, the Italian portrayal of lust in novelle, and the four Senecan types (revenger, agent of Fate, devil woman, and victim of guilty passion). Lady Macbeth, though in a native tradition, is "enrich[ed]" in her evil by Senecan associations.

2142. Tesch, Albert. "Das Nachleben der Antike in Shakespeares Dramen," WBFA, VII (1930), 38. E-S

Not seen. According to R[ichard] N[ewald], writing in #0053 (I, 241, item 998), Tesch believes that the Greek root of Desdemona's name is evidence of an ancient provenance for the plot of Oth. The facts that Pyramus/Thisbe parallels Romeo and that the Orestes story parallels Ham. are, he believes, reinforcing.

2143. Tesch, Albert. "Zum Namen Desdemona," GRM, XVII (1929), 387-388. E-S

Desdemona is the only character in Cinthio's version of the Othello story who has a name. In Greek, it means, of course, "the unfortunate one." Tesch postulates that Cinthio found the story in a Greek source in which the girl was continually referred to as unfortunate (δυσδαίμων). Cinthio mistook the epithet for her proper name. An amusing irony results from the fact that in 1609 "a stage-loving parent" named his daughter for Sh's Desdemona, obviously unaware of the Greek root-meaning. See commentary by Max J. Wolff and Alexander Krappe, ibid., XVIII (1930), 231-232.

2144. Thaler, Alwin. "'In my Mind's Eye, Horatio'," SQ, VII (1956), 351-354.

A brief, but interesting enumeration of references to the imagination as an interior eye in classical, biblical, Medieval, Renaissance, and modern literatures. Thaler does not mention Cicero, though he deals with Plato; he shows no knowledge of the controversy over Sh's putative source for the phrase and concept which took place in NQ in 1938 (see #1856), though he says "no adequate account has hitherto been taken of the provenience and influence" of the phrase.

2145. Thorndike, Ashley H. Tragedy, Types of English Literature, ed. W. A. Neilson. Boston, 1908, 390 pp. E-S HB

The first of the two chs. on Sh (pp. 136-195) is allusive rather than analytical; but when Thorndike notes a classical theme or antecedent in Sh, the remark is ordinarily pointed: Hamlet is a Senecan hero, "a strong man brought to face the enmity of chance ... who finds himself afflicted with a temperamental weakness that makes failure possible or indeed inevitable"; Macb. "coincides with the Senecan plan of a crime committed and then revenged through the accompaniment of supernatural agencies" --it combines "the destiny tragedy of the Greeks and the villain tragedy of the Elizabethans." Thorndike sees the Roman plays as constructed on essentially the same plan as the other tragedies except that Plutarch's art circumscribed Sh somewhat. The second ch. attempts an overview in which Thorndike brings classical drama to bear more broadly on his judgments of Sh: Antony is the most Medieval of the tragedies, Macb. the most classical; what Fate was to the Greeks, "incompatibility of temperament with conditions of life" was to Sh. Thorndike's respect for Fleay makes his judgment suspect, but he is not an insensitive critic.

2146. Trienens, Roger J. "The Symbolic Cloud in Hamlet," SQ, V (1954), 211-213.

An attractive suggestion that the protean cloud in Ham. III ii which is first like a camel, then a weasel, and finally a whale is symbolic of lust, which is uppermost in Hamlet's mind as he considers the pending meeting with his incestuous mother. Trienens cites numerous Medieval and Renaissance authorities to show that all three animals were regarded as voracious in their carnal appetites. The whale especially, as devourer of virgins in classical mythology, would be an emblem of lechery. An alternative but less attractive suggestion is made by David R. Cheney, ibid., X (1959), 446-447.

2147. Turner, Leslie Morton. Du Conflit tragique chez les grecs et dans Shakespeare. Paris, 1913, 268 pp. Thèse (Université de Paris, 1913).

This study, as Turner admits, is more a philosophical and psychological treatise than a work of literary criticism. The thesis is that Aristotle's definition of tragic conflict is inadequate; it is static, denying the dynamic process of becoming which Turner would call tragic drama. Sophocles and Euripides in Ch. II and Sh in Ch. V are merely evidence to support Turner's definitions; but Turner does argue that Sh shares with the Greeks a sense of tragic "devenir" which pits volition against Necessity (everything which opposes will) in a dynamic conflict. Macb., Oth., and Ham. are the Shn tragedies analyzed. It is perhaps noteworthy that Turner's diagrams of the "conflit-devenir" in all three of Sh's plays closely resemble the pattern of rising/falling action which classical and post-classical commentators have associated with Aristotle's Poetics; indeed, Sh's plays as Turner diagrams them fit Aristotle better than Sophocles' and Euripides' do. MH

2148. Turner, Paul. "True Madness (A Note on 'Hamlet', II.ii.92-95)," NQ, CCII (1957), 194-196.

Turner points to a number of interesting parallels between Ham. and Horace's Satires II iii on the theme that all the world is mad. If Polonius is referring to Horace in these lines on Hamlet's madness, a meaningless passage can be seen to make sense; Turner is of the opinion that Sh got his knowledge of the Satires from Drant's 1566 trans., but he "might have struggled through [the Latin] at Stratford Grammar School."

2149. Tyler, Thomas. "Hamlet and Plato's Republic," Acad, LIII (1898), 693-694.

Tyler explains Ophelia's description of

Hamlet's disarray (II i 78-84) as a reflection of Plato's parable of the cave (Republic VII). Tyler suggests that if Sh read Le Roy's French version of the Republic (1600), a number of cruxes in the play could be explained, including the problem of Hamlet's age. The parallels are distant at best; the conclusion does not command belief.

2150. Uhr, Leonard. "Hamlet's 'Coold Mother'," NQ, CCIII (1958), 189-190.

Uhr argues for the Q_2 epithet "coold" in Hamlet's first use of the word "mother" in I ii; F_1 gives "good." If Q_2 is preferred, the suggestion is given early to the audience that this play concerns the alternations of heat and cold in passion and underlines the sexual themes of Orestes, Hecuba, Oedipus, Nero, and Osiris hinted at elsewhere in the play. It seems that Uhr is considering too curiously.

2151. Vaganay, Hugues. "Quatre noms propres dans la littérature: Délie, Philothée, Ophélie, Pasithée," RLC, XV (1935), 279-288.

In contrast to those who have maintained that Sh derived Ophelia's name from its Greek root, Vaganay suggests an Italian original, Le Nuove Fiamme of Lodovico Paterno, who rhymes the name with "Delia."

2152. Vining, Edward P. "Shakespeare's Latin Derivatives," Shna, VIII (1891), 104-107.

An enumeration and explication of more than a score of words in Ham., each used in such a way as to indicate Sh's knowledge of its meaning in Latin. The most original paragraph is the first, in which Vining attempts to derive "Hamlet" from "ambulare," "to proceed at a slow pace." This suggestion has not won concurrence, but the rest of the etymologies are sound as is the conclusion: Sh "must have had a thorough acquaintance" with Latin; "even the apparent mistakes are of a nature which it would require quite as much scholarship to commit as to avoid."

2153. Vollhardt, W. "Italienische Parallelen zu Shakespeares 'Hamlet'," ShJ, LXII (1926), 132-157. SG

The art. begins with a denial of Senecan influence on the Ghost in Ham.; Vollhardt suggests Italian alternatives (though he admits a possible connection between Seneca's letters and other passages in Ham.--e.g., "To be, or not to be"). The English Senecans are, of course, a third possible source. Any denial of classical influence on Ham. must be made in the face of a very large number of references to ancient Rome in the play.

2154. Waith, E[ugene] M. "Manhood and Valor in Two Shakespearean Tragedies," ELH, XVII (1950), 262-273.

In the opening passage of his "Life of Coriolanus," Plutarch says that the Romans equated manliness with valor. Sh draws on the concept repeatedly in the tragedies: Hamlet is a man who makes this false equation; Coriolanus makes it, as does Macbeth (though Macduff is aware of the manliness of rationality and sensibility as well as of valor); Octavius, who makes the false equation, is contrasted with Antony who learns during the play to expand his definition of virility. An interesting discussion; was Sh reading the "Life of Coriolanus" earlier than critics have always assumed?

2155. Waldock, A. J. A. Sophocles the Dramatist. CUP, 1951, 228 pp.

Ch. I, "The Historical Method and Its Limitations" (1-10), is in part a very acid criticism of the "excesses" to which Professor Lily Campbell (#1865) goes in attributing elements in Shn tragedy to the influence of Seneca and Plutarch.

2156. Waldron, John. "'Machine': Hamlet, II. ii.124," NQ, CXCIX (1954), 515-516.

The word is usually glossed "bodily frame" without reference to its etymology. In Plautus and Cicero "machina" has the figurative sense: "device," "trick," "contrivance." It is therefore likely that Sh intended both meanings: Ophelia is to understand the second (i.e., the device of Hamlet's insanity) and should the letter be intercepted, Hamlet's enemies are to understand the first. This is perhaps a bit subtle, but it is an interesting possibility.

2157. Wales, Julia G. "Horatio's Commentary: A Study in the Warp and Woof of Hamlet," SAB, XVII (1942), 40-56.

Horatio's enumeration of the portents which anticipated the death of Caesar (Ham. I i 113-120) may have been indebted to Marlowe's trans. of Lucan's Pharsalia as well as to Plutarch, though the matter cannot be resolved with certainty. The belief that Sh drew on more than one source for this passage and for the portents in Caesar is now generally regarded with favor.

2158. Wallace, Charles William. "A New Play by Ben Jonson Quoted in 'Hamlet'," ESn, XLIII (1911), 378-379.

Wallace believes that "Aeneas' tale to Dido" in Ham. II ii is a quotation from the lost Dido and Aeneas which he is at pains to attribute to Ben Jonson. But in the absence of a text such conjectures are hardly fruitful.

2159. Warton, Joseph. "King Lear," The Adventurer, No. 113, No. 116, No. 122, December 4, 15, 1753; January 5, 1754. (Reprinted with some deletion in Shakespeare Criticism: A Selection, ed. D. Nichol Smith [OUP, 1916], pp. 68-79.)

The remarks on Euripides and Sophocles are very brief--perhaps the most important of them praises both Sh and Sophocles for permitting their characters to say little when stunned by disaster: Jocasta discovering the truth is like Lear discovering Kent in the stocks (i.e., realizing that both his daughters are villainous).

2160. W[arton], T[homas]. "Shakespear Vindicated from the Imputation of wanting Art," BM, VIII (1767), 57-59.

A demonstration that the Ghost scenes in Ham. are arranged climactically, the most terrifying being in Gertrude's closet. "Neither Sophocles, Aeschylus, or Euripides, whose well-conducted plots are the chief beauties of their works ... can produce any thing superior ..." Sh introduces the Ghost at moments of tension: e.g., following the description of the portents of Caesar's death ("which for exquisite poetry is greatly superior to the admired one in Virgil's Georgics"). Sh, then, is as capable of "art and contrivance" as any of the ancients, despite the ill-considered pronouncements of several generations of critics. The argument is briefly reinforced by remarks on climactic structure in Oth. DLC

2161. Wedgwood, Julia. "Aeschylus and Shakespeare: The Eumenides and Hamlet," Shna, III (1886), 65-74. (Reprinted from CR, January, 1886.)

An interesting contrast between two portrayals of essentially the same theme. The great difference lies in scope: Sh portrays "the heart of man"; Aeschylus portrays "the mind of God." To Sh the state is an aggregate of individuals; the Greeks "conceived the individual as a fragment of the state." The groping for universality in the Oresteia makes its pre-history more important to us than the pre-history of Ham. Yet Orestes is wooden and lacking in individuality compared to Hamlet.

2162. Wells, Henry W. "Senecan Influence on Elizabethan Tragedy: A Re-Estimation," SAB, XIX (1944), 71-84.

This lucid and reasoned essay attempts to moderate the extreme views of English Senecanism taken by Eliot, Mendell, and Cunliffe who stress it on the one hand and Farnham and Baker who deny it on the other. Actually, Wells shows, neither camp is right, for both misunderstand Seneca's appeal to the English Renaissance: (1) the "Senecan" elements of English drama (bombast, ghosts, violence, gore) are indigenous to the Morality and Mystery plays. The appeal of Seneca was in (2) his satirical pessimism--he saw the spiritual shallowness of his age as Sh did of his or T. S. Eliot of his --and in (3) his emphasis on the solitary individual--Seneca's heroes are lonely giants. The most "Senecan" period of English drama is 1599 (Caesar) to 1611 (Catiline), and the great central play is Ham.--a satiric, pessimistic, Stoic, rhetorical tragedy about a solitary protagonist. This corrective to biased criticism has not received the attention it deserves.

2163. Welsford, Enid. "The Court-Fool in Elizabethan Drama," The Fool: His Social and Literary History (Ln, 1935), Ch. XI, pp. 243-270.

For Erasmus and the Fool in Lear, see #0955.

2164. West, Robert H. "King Hamlet's Ambiguous Ghost," PMLA, LXX (1955), 1107-17.

West believes that it is impossible to determine whether the Ghost is pagan or Christian and that Sh did not wish us to know. Sh deliberately left the Ghost a puzzle to Hamlet and to the audience to make it suggest the controversies over pneumatology which were in fashion and especially to convey the terror which the unlabeled always inspires. Thus Sh obtains more dramatic force from his Ghost than any of his dramatic contemporaries or predecessors do from theirs. By contrast with the stagy Senecan ghosts who cry "vindicta" in a prologue and then take no part in the action, Sh's Ghost is a vital part of the action and of the mystery in the play.

2165. White, Beatrice. "Claudius and Fortune," Anglia, LXXVII (1959), 204-207.

When Claudius speaks of his having "one Auspicious and one Dropping eye" in his first appearance on stage (Ham. I ii 11: the F_1 reading), he immediately characterizes himself as a treacherous hypocrite, because the audience would think immediately of the goddess Fortuna, who in late classical and Medieval literature was portrayed as having one laughing and one weeping eye. A very interesting point.

2166. Williams, Edwin Everitt. Tragedy of Destiny: Oedipus Tyrannus, Macbeth, Athalie. Editions XVII Siècle: Cambridge, 1940, 35 pp.

Not seen. A substantial quotation in the rev. (CW, XXXV [1941], 9-10) by G. M. Harper, Jr., indicates that Williams regards the three plays as very much alike, not only because destiny is crucial in each but also because (1) tragic irony proceeds from the protagonists' vain efforts to elude destiny--efforts which only aggravate their positions; (2) the catastrophe of each play is precipitated by revelation of identity; (3) each play has political or religious overtones which reach down through time to the dramatist's own age; (4) the protagonists are paradoxical: noble criminals; (5) an evil councilor is a foil to the protagonist in each play. Harper regards the thesis as to some extent an oversimplification.

2167. Williams, George W. "The Poetry of the Storm in King Lear," SQ, II (1951), 57-71.

An analysis of III ii 1-9 ("Blow winds ...") to show that a sense of universality is achieved by (1) combining Teutonic monosyllables with polysyllabic loanwords ("cataracts"--Greek; "germens," "rotundity," "ingrateful," "sulphurous"--Latin, e.g.); (2) allusion to the story of Deucalion-Noah (which, of course, portrays punishment for ingratitude); and (3) Neoplatonic cosmology ("nature's moulds"). An interesting exegesis.

2168. Williams, Philip, Jr. "'Romeo and Juliet': Littera Canina," NQ, CXCV (1950), 181-182.

Williams points out that the letter "R" has been called the "littera canina" or "dog's letter" ever since it was so referred to by Persius in the first Satire. The nickname comes from the growling sound one makes in naming it. The Nurse in Romeo II iv 223 stops short of naming a part of the body which begins with the sound of the name of the littera canina.

2169. Williams, W. H. "Shakespeare, 'King Lear,' IV,vi,70-72," MLR, VI (1911), 88.

Williams illustrates Sh's use of "wealked" ("twisted") from Golding's Meta.; at ibid., 209-210, W. W. Skeat points out that he has anticipated Williams in his Etymological Dictionary. Skeat is able to supply two further instances of Golding's use of "welk." No suggestion is made by either correspondent that Sh borrowed the term from Golding's Ovid.

2170. Williamson, George. "Senecan Style in the Seventeenth Century," PQ, XV (1936), 321-351. GRS

In passing: "Polonius was a Senecan in theory when he observed that 'brevity is the soul of wit,' and in practice when he recognized Hamlet's 'points' by remarking, 'How pregnant sometimes his replies are'." Williamson observes, however, that this interpretation is "more than [Sh] intended."

2171. Wilson, H. Schütz. "Parallel Passages," Ath, No. 2527 (1876), 474.

The first of two notes points to the parallel between Mercutio's dissertation on Queen Mab and dreams and a forty-line passage from the fourth book of De Rerum Natura of Lucretius, whom Sh did not know, "it may with certainty be contended."

2172. Wilson, Harold S. On the Design of Shakespearian Tragedy, TST, V (Toronto UP, 1957), 256 pp.

For Lear as a "classical" play on love, and for a contrast between the Christian ethics of the tragedies and the pagan ethics of the Roman plays, see #1779.

2173. W[ilson], J. D[over]. "Hamlet: Introduction," Hamlet (1934), CSh, [XXXII], pp. vii-lxvii.

Wilson points briefly (p. xiii) to "striking points of similarity" between the feigned madness of Hamlet and the feigned idiocy of Lucius Junius Brutus; he suggests that Saxo Grammaticus colored an existing Hamlet tale with "embellishments" from Livy's account of L. J. Brutus.

2174. W[ilson], J. D[over]. "Introduction," Macbeth (1947), CSh, [XXXI], pp. vii-lxviii.

In passing (pp. xlii-xliii) Wilson calls attention to the Senecan flavor of Macb.: it deals with a tyrant, it probes the inner man, and it shows Nemesis pursuing the criminal. Sh may have derived this Senecanism from Sidney's Apologie which quotes the lines from Seneca's Oedipus which fit Macb. so exactly: "Qui sceptra saevus duro imperio regit / Timet timentes, metus in auctorem redit." But Wilson also notes that Sh knew the Hercules Furens (at least) in the original.

2175. W[ilson], J. D[over]. "Introduction," Othello (1957), CSh, [XXXIV], pp. ix-lvi.

In passing (p. li), Wilson suggests that Eliot is correct in seeing Senecan influence on Othello's last speech (#0228, p. 111), but wrong to conclude that Othello is "cheering himself up." Wilson believes there is Senecanism elsewhere in the scene as well, though he does not specify it.

2176. Wright, Louis B. "Handbook Learning of the Renaissance Middle Class," SP, XXVIII (1931), 58-86.

In passing: "Polonius should not be blamed too harshly for his proverbs. He doubtless had been trained in a typical grammar school" where he would be required to keep a commonplace book of "sentences culled from the classics for use in future orations or learned epistles."

2177. Yardley, E. "'Hamlet', I.i.117,118," 9 NQ, VIII (1901), 480.

Yardley quotes Iliad XVI, where Homer describes falling drops of blood as a portent of disaster; the parallel is to the "dews of blood" which presaged Caesar's death. Yardley also remembers that Virgil refers to blood flowing from wells before the assassination. See Yardley's further remarks ibid., IX (1902), 343, and those of J. E. Smith, loc. cit., who would like to read "asters" for "as, stars," suggesting that Sh uses the Greek word ἀστήρ to refer to portentous astronomical appearances. Yardley reacts unfavorably to Smith's suggestion ibid., X (1902), 224-225.

2178. Yardley, E. "'Romeo and Juliet', II.ii.," 9 NQ, IV (1899), 221-222.

The famous quip, "At lovers' perjuries, / They say Jove laughs," goes back much further than Ovid. Apollodorus quotes Hesiod, who says that Zeus lied to Hera about having seduced Io and as a result is never angry when lovers swear falsely. Apollodorus is quoting from one of Hesiod's lost works.

2179. Yates, Frances A. "Shakespeare and the Platonic Tradition," UEJ, XII (1942), 2-12.

An elaboration of points more briefly stated by Wilson (#0655). Miss Yates focuses on Sh's adherence to the Platonic conception of the composition of the firmament (expressed in Hamlet's letter to Ophelia). She demonstrates clearly that, contrary to common belief, Platonism was never completely displaced by Aristotelianism in the Middle Ages. Sh's Platonism is, like that of pseudo-Dionysius, anti-intellectual (see L.L.L., with its criticism of intellectual pretensions, and the skepticism of Hamlet's negative proposals in the letter to Ophelia). Another Shn inheritance, however, is from Renaissance Neoplatonism, the tradition (truncated by the Reformation) which began with Ficino and Pico and came to England in the early sixteenth century. Bruno, whose influence on L.L.L. and Ham. "has long been justifiably suspected," is "the last link in the chain by which the Platonic tradition can be traced up to, and including, the age of Shakespeare." There is one very odd suggestion here: that Jonson may have meant that Sh's Latin was "small" because it was barbarous (i.e., Medieval, rather than classical). MdBJ MH

2180. "'Young Abram Cupid'," PM, IV (1873), 482-489.

This comment rejects the frequent emendation of the peculiar name which Mercutio gives to Eros in the early Quartos and Folios of Romeo (II i 13). The suggestion is that in the sixteenth century "abram" meant "auburn"; the expression means "the auburn-haired beggar, Cupid." A very similar suggestion is made by an anonymous writer in CathW, XVII (1873), 234-241. Gerard E. Jensen (MLN, XXX [1915], 62) believes the word means "naked" as in "abram beggar."

THE LAST PLAYS

2181. A., J. "[Shakespear and Lucian]," Monthly Magazine, I (1796), 91.

A., a correspondent, points out the coincidence between a passage from Lucian's Tragodopodagra and Prospero's orders to Ariel about how to torment the conspirators. It is only an accidental similarity, he believes. MnU

2182. Apperson, G. L. "Some Shakespearean Names," GM, CCLXXXVII (1899), 278-283.

Among the names with classical connections are Greek "Ophelia" ("utility" or "profit," "words which certainly have no suggestiveness as regards Ophelia's character"); Latin or Italian "Miranda" ("wonderful," "an appropriate name for the daughter of Prospero"); Greek "Autolycus" (unmistakably a "descendant" of Ulysses' grandfather in the Odyssey).

2183. Arnold, Paul. "Esoterisme du Conte D'Hiver," MdeF, CCCXVIII (1953), 494-512.

This brilliant and daring interpretation suggests that Sh's two major departures from Greene (the pastoral festival and the revival of Hermione) are the key to the meaning of W.T., which is an imaginative recreation of the Dis-Proserpina myth: Perdita/Proserpina; Hermione/Ceres; Autolycus/Pluto. Thus the emphasis on chastity throughout the play, on winter, on flowers, fertility, resurrection. Sh derived his spiritualized allegorization of the myth from Heywood's Silver Age (1610), which echoes the Eleusinian concept that Proserpina is the soul cyclically alternating between an earthly vesture (hell) and celestial perfection (earth). This mythological reading explains a number of difficult passages in the play. Arnold is certainly less convincing when he tries to add the Psyche legend to the sources and when he explains Hermione's resurrection scene as reflecting the occult creation rituals of the Rosicrucians.

2184. Arthos, John. "Pericles, Prince of Tyre: A Study in the Dramatic Use of Romantic Narrative," SQ, IV (1953), 257-270.

This intelligent defense of the construction of the play points out that the cities of the ancient world and the conventions of the Greek romances (e.g., innocence in a brothel) are only a complementary framework for the real concern—the spiritual progress of Pericles. While the plot is developing the hero's mental state is developing also, and when Marina and her mother are "reborn" in Act V, Pericles' spirit is reborn too.

2185. Ashton, J. W. "The Fall of Icarus," PQ, XX (1941), 345-351. (Also in Craig Festschrift, pp. 153-159.) GRS

Faustus, Friar Bacon, and Prospero are the three characters in Renaissance drama who convey the tragic possibilities of the quest for knowledge and for the power it brings. The Renaissance identified these possibilities with the fate of Icarus, deriving the concept from the Ovide moralisé. Of the three only Faustus is directly linked to Icarus, perhaps because Friar Bacon and Prospero both virtuously abandon the quest before their plays are over.

2186. Baum, Bernard. "Tempest and Hairy Ape: The Literary Incarnation of Mythos," MLQ, XIV (1953), 258-273. GRS

Baum demonstrates (pp. 258-265) that

NOTE: Numbers preceded by # refer to entries in this Guide. Keys to abbreviations are found on pages xi-xvii and 381-387.

Temp. is permeated by the opposition between good and evil implicit in Renaissance cosmology, but he alludes only briefly to the Neoplatonic foundation of this polarity. He makes the point that Juno and Ceres preside over the union of Ferdinand and Miranda; Venus, "Mars's hot minion," is omitted, as more appropriate to Caliban's attempted rape than to Ferdinand's intended marriage.

2187. Bennett, Josephine Waters. "Britain Among the Fortunate Isles," SP, LIII (1956), 114-140. GRS

For Sh's reflection in Cym. of an ancient commonplace about Britain, see #0974.

2188. Bethell, S. L. The Winter's Tale: A Study. Ln, n.d., 128 pp.

To support his contention that Sh wrote for an audience which had "multi-consciousness" (a delight in ambiguity and levels of meaning), Bethell analyzes W.T. "not as a mixture but a compound" of Hellenistic erotic romance and chivalric romance, of Hellenic oracles and Christian supernaturalism, of Gothic horrors and Jacobean manners. Bethell sees more Christianity and less pseudo-classicism in the play than some critics do; the book is written with charm, vigor, and insight.

2189. Bond, R. Warwick. "The Puzzle of 'Cymbeline'," Studia Otiosa (Ln, 1938), pp. 69-74.

Bond offers the extraordinary argument that Cym. is a "keystone," holding together the British-English plays (Macb., Lear, and the histories) and the Greek-Roman plays (Errors, Dream, Troi., Per., Tim., Caesar, Antony, Cor.). Sh deliberately mingled Roman and British, ancient and modern to emphasize the unity of his own works and the ancient heritage of modern Britain. The eclecticism of Cym. is not usually regarded so highly.

2190. Bonjour, Adrien. "The Final Scene of The Winter's Tale," ES, XXXIII (1952), 193-208.

Bonjour is dubious of the validity of mystical interpretations (like Knight's, #2242) of the statue scene. Bonjour doubts the presence of Christian immortality themes; he does not dwell on the Persephone legend. The statue motif itself he would interpret as an artful fusion of the Pygmalion story and the sleeping beauty fairy tale. A reasonable essay full of perceptive criticism.

2191. Bowling, Lawrence E. "The Theme of Natural Order in 'The Tempest'," CE, XII (1951), 203-209.

Bowling makes the interesting suggestion that Temp. is a dramatization of the abrogation of "specialty of rule" which Ulysses expounds in Troi. The disruptions in the lives of the characters in Temp. originate with Prospero's abdication, a violation of the obligation of a ruler to rule. Bowling calls Ulysses' concept of degree "Aristotelian"; most critics think first of Plato as Ulysses' ultimate source. Bowling does not mention Merton (#2261), who finds a different kind of relationship between Prospero and Ulysses.

2192. Brockbank, J. P. "History and Histrionics in Cymbeline," ShS, XI (1958), 42-49.

This is an ingenious explanation of Sh's use of diverse elements in Cym.: the hints for all of them were patent in the "Brutan material" in Holinshed. E.g., the fusion of British with Italian legends was suggested by a passage which speaks of the Britons as ingenuous (Posthumus) and desirous of educating their sons at the Imperial Court (Italian journey). Sh remembered that the Roman Brutus whose ancestry was mysterious had to flee to Britain because he had killed his royal father in a hunting accident. "And Cymbeline touches, in a different order and to changed effect the motifs of mysterious descent, hunting, murder (a boy killing a prince), banishment, and chance (or providential) encounter with offspring of the same lineage." The argument is reinforced by the derivation from the Chronicle of names of characters in the nonhistorical plots: Cloten, Imogen, Posthumus. On the whole a convincing presentation of the case.

2193. Brower, R[euben] A. The Fields of Light: An Experiment in Critical Reading. OUP, 1951, 218 pp.

Ch. VI (pp. 95-122) in part interprets Temp. as a philosophical approach to the concept of metamorphosis (the "sea change"). Sh based his transformations in Temp. on Ovid, but he transcended Meta. by implying philosophy where Ovid was content with narrative and rhetorical decoration. Some other critics have detected philosophical values beneath Ovid's rhetorical irony (see, e.g., #1750, #2355).

2194. Brower, Reuben A. "The Heresy of Plot," EIE, 1951 (Col UP, 1952), pp. 44-69.

To Brower the heresy is separating "plot" from the characters whose actions make it, and both from the words in which they are revealed. Aristotle appears to fall into this heresy in the Poetics when he analyzes drama into its elements, but the neo-Aristotelian can avoid the heresy by noticing the integration of all the elements of a play in metaphorical language. Brower illustrates from Temp., where the theme is metamorphosis and where the metaphor which holds character, action, language, and theme together is the concept of dissolving. Brower borrows here from his essay on Temp. in The Fields of Light (#2193).

2195. Buchin, Erna. "Sidney's Arcadia als Quelle für 'Cymbeline'," Archiv, CXLIII (1922), 250-252. SG

As an alternative to The Golden Ass, proposed by Reich (#2281) as a source for the wicked-queen motif in Cym., this art. suggests the Arcadia Books II and III. It would appear that Reich has the better case, though there is no reason why Sh could not have read both sources and combined them in his recollection.

2196. C., P. A. "A Study of Shakespeare's 'Winter's Tale': Considered in Connection with Greene's 'Pandosto' and the 'Alkestis' of Euripides," PL, IV (1892), 516-521. (Reproduced almost exactly as by Charlotte Porter and Helen A. Clarke in PL, XIV [1903], 132-137.)

A series of eleven notes and hints for possible arts. on W.T. Nos. II and IV deal with Sh's use of the Alcestis theme of the loyal wife who "dies" because of her husband and is resurrected when he proves worthy of her; V suggests the antiquity and provenience of the outcast child myth; VI hints at the relationship between Autolycus and Hermes and/or Sisyphus.

2197. Cairncross, Andrew S. "The Tempest, III.i.15, and Romeo and Juliet, I.i.121-8," SQ, VII (1956), 448-450.

Cairncross turns to Cicero's De Officiis for support for an emendation in Temp. and an insertion in Romeo. In each case the alteration would provide a Ciceronian paradox, indeed a virtual trans. of the passage in De Officiis.

2198. Camden, Carroll. "A Note on Pericles," MLN, XLVIII (1933), 110-111.

An analogue to Antiochus' astrological reference to his daughter (I i 10-11) is in Lyly's The Woman in the Moone where Pandora is also endowed by a conclave of planetary influences.

2199. Chislett, William, Jr. "On Shakespeare's 'Julius Caesar'," FMV, pp. 76-78.

For anti-Roman sentiments in Cym. as a key to the interpretation of the character of Caesar in Caesar, see #1219.

2200. Conway, R. S. "The Classical Elements in Shakespeare's Tempest" (1917), New Studies of a Great Inheritance: Being Lectures on the Modern Worth of Some Ancient Writers (Ln, 1921), Ch. VIII, pp. 165-189. HB SG

Conway supplies a large list of supposed echoes of the classics in Temp. The materials range from the unities advocated by the Poetics to the tempest in Book I of the Aeneid. Ovid, Greek mythology, and classical onomastics are among the contributors to the play, but the real affinity is between Sh and Virgil: both believed in the ties that bind men together, in the mystery of things, in the power of hope, in the value of civilization. Conway recognizes the importance of Virgil's Georgics for a proper understanding of Temp., an importance which has gone largely unnoticed in much criticism of the play. Among the liabilities of the essay is Conway's fanciful speculation about Sh's preference for the classical gods in certain plays (chiefly later); he is apparently unaware that after 1606 it was illegal to name the Christian deity on the English stage. MnU

2201. Corin, Fernand. "A Note on the Dirge in Cymbeline," ES, XL (1959), 173-179.

The dirge for Cloten and the supposedly dead Fidele in IV ii has been thought by most to be Christian and therefore to be one of a long list of anachronisms in the play. Corin attempts to show that the scene can be read as entirely pre-Christian. Such details as burial with the head to the East and covering the grave with flowers are Celtic and Graeco-Roman respectively; in each case they are details exactly opposed to Christian practice. An interesting point, but Corin does not entirely succeed in stripping the scene of Christian suggestions.

2202. Craig, Hardin. "Pericles Prince of Tyre," Hunt Festschrift, pp. 1-14. GRS

Craig makes brief remarks (pp. 3-4) about the relationship of Apollonius of Tyre to other Greek and Latin romances. Per. is in the tradition: it "secures its credibility from the tacit popular belief that, in old times and faraway lands, life may be at once gentle and adventurous, fortunate and calamitous, disordered and beautiful." The play violates the unities, as Dryden saw, but Sh did remake the rambling legend "into a single action."

2203. Crundell, H. W. "Shakespeare, Lyly and 'Aesop'," NQ, CLXVIII (1935), 312. SG

For Aesop in Cym. III iii, see #0999.

2204. Curry, Walter Clyde. "Sacerdotal Science in Shakespeare's 'The Tempest'," Archiv, CLXVIII (1935), 25-36, 185-196.

Reprinted with minor changes as Ch. VI of Shakespeare's Philosophical Patterns (1937/1959). See #2205.

2205. Curry, W[alter] C[lyde]. Shakespeare's Philosophical Patterns. Louisiana State UP, 1937/1959, 261 pp.

Ch. V is an admirably erudite commentary on the nature and origins of Neoplatonism in the Renaissance. In Ch. VI Curry expounds the thesis that Temp. reveals Sh's assimilated knowledge of Plotinian and Iamblichan Platonism. Prospero is a theurgist, Sycorax a practitioner of goetical art, Ariel a rational δαίμων, the elves and fairies (as in Golding) lower δαίμονες. Neoplatonic cosmology permeates the whole even though Sh "is always primarily the creative artist and not the philosopher." Curry has surveyed an impressive range of scholarship, and his convictions must carry weight, though for some reservations, see J. C. R[ansom], KR, I (1939), 75-80.

2206. Cutts, John P. "Music and the Supernatural in 'The Tempest': A Study in Interpretation," M&L, XXXIX (1958), 347-358.

Cutts, who believes that the symbolic function of music in Temp. has been underestimated, suggests that Sh uses it in Act I and indeed throughout the play to evoke an ironic comparison of Prospero's Island with Circe's. Ariel functions as the Sirens do—to lure men where he will; but the purposes of Prospero are benevolent and the love he fosters between Ferdinand and Miranda is chaste, not wanton as Circe's was. The banquet scene, drawn from Aeneid II, adds another classical island association. Cutts might have reinforced his "Circean" argument by pointing to the irony that Prospero tries to make men of beasts like Trinculo, Stephano, and especially Caliban, whereas Circe made beasts of men.

2207. Cutts, John P. "Pericles' 'Most Heavenly Musicke'," NQ, CCV (1960), 172-174.

Pericles alone hears the music of the spheres in the presence of Marina (V i 225-236) because the microcosm of his soul has been restored to harmony with the universal macrocosm. This interpretation makes of Diana's subsequent theophany more than a dea ex machina; because he is in harmony with the macrocosm, she appears. An interesting argument.

2208. Danby, John. "Sidney and the Late-Shakespearian Romance," Poets on Fortune's Hill: Studies in Sidney, Shakespeare, Beaumont & Fletcher (Ln, 1952), pp. 74-107.

Danby's major point (and a striking one) is that the last plays, especially Per., are deeply indebted for theme and characterization to Sidney's Arcadia. But he traces one major theme, patience in the gusts of Fortune, back beyond Sidney to the Christianized Stoicism of Boethius. Danby also shows that Diana is the presiding deity of the last plays, but that sacred virginity (Marina, Miranda, Perdita) is only a subordinate theme, as are the Golden Bough fertility themes and the Christian resurrections.

2209. Dowden, Edward. "Introduction," Cymbeline (1903/1930), ArdenSh, pp. vii-xliii.

Dowden provides a useful summary of the account of Cunobelinus in Holinshed and of Boswell-Stone's comments on this account; special emphasis falls on the relations between Britons and Romans in the post-Julian period. Dowden discusses Sh's deviations from accepted "history" in Cym. In a later passage (p. xxxix) appears the hesitant conjecture that someone in Sh's company expanded V iv, inserting the "doggerel" (ll. 30-92) to prolong the spectacular dumb show and theophany of Jupiter which Sh had originally written.

2210. Eagle, R[oderick] L. "The Oracle in 'The Winter's Tale'," NQ, CLXXX (1941), 135.

Eagle points out that Cleomenes and Dion are sworn as to the authenticity of the statement they bring from the Oracle of "Delphos" in the same words used in Sh's time in a common oath-taking ceremony in the House of Lords. An interesting anachronism to add to the list in W.T.

2211. Fay, Edwin W. "Further Notes on the Mostellaria of Plautus," AJP, XXIV (1903), 245-277. HB

For a parallel between Temp. and the Mostellaria, see #0757.

2212. Finney, Gretchen L. "Ecstasy and Music in Seventeenth-Century England," JHI, VIII (1947), 153-186.

For the ecstatic power of music in Cym., see #0760.

2213. Flint, M. K., and E. J. Dobson. "Weak Masters," RES, n.s. X (1959), 58-60.

Prospero's reference to his elves as "Weak masters" (Temp. V i 41) needs no emendation. The words "master" and "mister" (from Latin ministerium) had become confused in the sixteenth century with the result that "master" came to mean "instrument."

2214. Genouy, Hector. L'Élément pastoral dans la poésie narrative et le drame en Angleterre, de 1579 à 1640. Paris, 1928. E-S HB

For Theocritean realism in the pastoral act of W.T., see #0775. MnU

2215. Gesner, Carol. "The Tempest as Pastoral Romance," SQ, X (1959), 531-539.

"The conventional romance of the situation and the elements of magic in Prospero's characterization" have concealed from critics that the play is actually a pastoral, springing (perhaps even directly) from Longus' Daphnis and Chloe, which would have been accessible to Sh in Amyot's French or in Angel Day's English. Some significant elements are common to Sh and Longus: e.g., attempted rape, attempted kidnaping, a tempest (supernaturally induced) followed by ethereal music, a wedding masque with nymphs and reapers. Dr. Gesner does not insist that Temp. is direct imitation, but cites Wolff (#2316) as authority for Sh's use of Longus in W.T., which immediately preceded Temp.

2216. Goddard, Henry P. "The Lesson of 'Cymbeline'," PL, III (1891), 572-577.

In passing: like Euripides' Alcestis, Sh's Imogen in later years would have difficulty subduing the contempt she could not help feeling for Posthumus, who, like Admetus, doubted her. This observation, like the question of Lady Macbeth's children, has no apparent relevance within the dramatic limits of the play on which it is based.

2217. Goolden, P. "Antiochus's Riddle in Gower and Shakespeare," RES, n.s. VI (1955), 245-251.

The confusion in the riddle in Per. I i can be traced to Gower's trans. of a corrupt Latin text (based on the lost Greek original). Whether Wilkins or Sh wrote the passage is immaterial; whoever did tried to make sense of Gower by altering the wording and writing from the point of view of the daughter rather than of the father.

2218. Greenlaw, Edwin. "Shakespeare's Pastorals," SP, XIII (1916), 122-154. E-S

This argument (against Greg and others) for the influence of pastoral conventions in A.Y.L., Cym., and W.T. emphasizes Sh's debt to Spenser (FQ VI) and Sidney (Arcadia). Sidney derived his pastoral elements ultimately from Longus' romance Daphnis and Chloe, while Spenser learned from Sidney. Of the seven building blocks in Longus, Sidney borrows all (e.g., foundling, attack by wild beasts, captivity, boorish rival in love, etc.) and Sh appropriates some, even when they do not appear in his romance sources, Lodge and Greene. An argument worthy of consideration (cf. Gesner, #2215, and Wolff, #2316).

2219. Griffin, William J. "Names in 'The Winter's Tale'," TLS, June 6, 1936, p. 480.

Although the classical association of Sicily with the pastoral life would suggest that it should be the locale for the pastoral scenes of Act IV, Sh deliberately reversed the Sicilia and Bohemia of Greene's romance. Griffin maintains that the motive was to enforce an identification of England with Sicily and Leontes (British Lion?) with James, who was notoriously jealous of his wife's chastity. Griffin notes that Leontes' is the only name in the play found neither in Plutarch nor in the source. Surely such an insult to his sovereign on Sh's part would be audacious beyond belief.

2220. Grimm, Herman. "[On the Sources of The Tempest]," Fünfzehn Essays (1875), pp. ca. 206- ca. 221 (no exact pagination available—as trans. in the New Variorum Temp.).

Grimm notes that Calderón, Corneille, Sh (in both Temp. and Cym.), Dryden, and Davenant all draw on the same basic myth of innocence in the wilderness which can perhaps be traced all the way to the Hindu legend of Samata. The most distinguished Greek exemplar is Adonis, but Longus' "Daphne" (sic for "Daphnis") and Narcissus and Hermaphroditus (the last two of whom Grimm does not cite) are other Greek echoes of the same basic folk motif.

2221. Grismer, Raymond L., and Elizabeth Atkins. The Book of Apollonius Translated into English Verse. Minnesota UP, 1936, xx + 113 pp. GRS

The introduction to this trans. of the Medieval Spanish version of the Apollonius story contains a section on "The Legend in English Literature." It mentions Sh's use in Per. of Gower (whose account is summarized in Macaulay's précis) and of "prose versions of the legend current in and before his time." There is no implication that Sh knew El Libro de Apolonio.

2222. Haight, Elizabeth Hazelton. "Apollonius of Tyre and Shakespeare's Pericles, Prince of Tyre," More Essays on Greek Romances (N.Y., 1945), pp. 142-189.

Professor Haight makes a detailed and sensitive analysis of the Latin romance, commenting on its themes, structure, characterization, and style, and its intimate relationship to Xenophon's Anthia and Habrocomes, with which it shares an extraordinary number of elements. Sh's Per. is seen as a classical play in its use of the Chorus, its flexible yet faithful treatment of a traditional story, and its dignified lower-class characters (cf. Euripides). The treatment of Sh's additions to his sources is perceptive, and Professor Haight makes some excellent points about Sh's use of antithesis in the manner of the Second Sophistic as a structural device (e.g., chastity in a brothel is opposed to incest in a palace; the riddle at the beginning of the play is ironically echoed in Pericles' exclamation at the end that Marina has begotten her begetter). The essay also calls attention to Sh's interest in Greek romance materials in other plays and finds occasion to define "small" and "less" in Jonson's aphorism as most recent commentators do: granting Sh some Greek and as much Latin as a grammar school pupil would know after studying Lily's Grammar, Mantuan, Ovid, Virgil, Plautus, Terence, Caesar, Sallust, Horace, and Seneca. It is not possible to agree that Sh knew the Greek tragedies in Latin trans. or that Sh became acquainted with Euripides through Gascoigne's Jocasta in 1566, when he was two years old, but this is in almost every other way a reliable and stimulating guide to the Apollonius story and to Sh's use of it.

2223. Hankins, John E. "Caliban the Bestial Man," PMLA, LXII (1947), 793-801.

Hankins shows that if Caliban's "appearance and environment are suggested by writers on distant lands" and "his parentage is taken from contemporary demonology," "his character results from Aristotle's conception of the bestial man" probably by way of St. Thomas' Commentarium in De Anima Aristotelis. An interesting demonstration.

2224. Harrison, Jane Ellen. Mythology, Our Debt, [No. 26] ([1924]/1963), 155 pp.

For the Persephone myth in W.T., see #1949.

2225. Henneberger, Olive Pauline. Proximate Sources for the Italianate Elements in Shakespeare. Urbana, Illinois, 1937, 14 pp. SG (An abstract of a University of Illinois diss.)

For Temp. as a product of the classics rather than of Italian comedy, see #0799. DLC

2226. Hense, C[arl] C[onrad]. "Das Antike in Shakespeare's Drama: Der Sturm," ShJ, XV (1880), 129-155. E-S (Reprinted in Shakespeare: Untersuchungen und Studien [1884] HB.)

A stimulating commentary on a large number of classical analogues to elements in Temp. In some cases (the theophany, the storm followed by recovery of lost men) it is probable that Sh drew directly on the classics (Ovid, Virgil, respectively). But in other cases the commentary is not source study but illuminating comparative criticism: e.g., the insular unity of Temp. is like that of Philoctetes; Prospero's island exile, Miranda's naïveté in love, Ariel's music, and the anagnorises of the play all are reminiscent of episodes in the Odyssey; the madness suddenly imposed by Ariel on Alonso,

Antonio, and Sebastian is like madness in Greek tragedy (Sophocles' *Ajax*, Euripides' *Hercules Furens*), originating in divine will. Hense is conservative: e.g., he suspects, but does not assert Sh's knowledge of Plautus' *Rudens*. He anticipates the commonly held modern view that *Temp.* is an eclectic play with strong affinity for classical themes and conventions.

2227. Herrick, Marvin T. *Tragicomedy: Its Origin and Development in Italy, France, and England*, ISLL, No. 39 (1955), 331 pp.

Herrick begins with a fifteen-page ch. on the classical origins of tragicomedy in (1) Plautus' facetious reference to his *Amphitruo* as a "*tragicocomoedia*"; (2) Euripides' tragedies which end happily; (3) the Greek satyr plays and Horace's remarks about them; (4) Aristotle's reference to "double issue" tragedy, in which the good are rewarded and the evil punished; (5) Donatus' commentary on Terence. Herrick then traces developments through Cornelius Schonaeus' *Christian Terence*, Cinthio and his Italian successors, and the French tradition to the Elizabethans, Jacobeans, and onward to Davenant. Sh's participation in the conventions is discussed in *All's W.*, *Meas.*, *Per.*, *Cym.*, and *W.T.*, with passing allusions to *Much*, *T.G.V.*, *A.Y.L.*, and *Merch*. This is an erudite study of a classical tradition, but the passages on Sh are as much plot summary as logical analysis.

2228. Hirschberg, Julius. "The Valley (The Winter's Tale, 2, 3, 100)," *ShJ*, LVI (1920), 107.

Hirschberg anticipates Tannenbaum's interpretation of this word (#2300). He quotes a sixteenth-century medical dictionary: "'φίλτρον dicitur a nonnullis eo nomine cavitas quae superiori labro inest, valleculae similis . . .'"; he points out that Englishmen, "wegen ihrer meist kurzen Nasen," would be particularly conscious of this facial depression.

2229. Hodgen, Margaret T. "Montaigne and Shakespeare Again," *HLQ*, XVI (1952), 23-42.

A re-examination of Montaigne's "Of the Caniballes" and Gonzalo's description of his proposed utopia (*Temp.* II i 147-168) in the context of other descriptions of primitive peoples. The ultimate source of the chief convention (i.e., a catalogue of elements of civilized society and a denial that the barbarians possess them) is Hesiod's description of the earliest men on earth. Plato (*Protagoras*), Philo Judaeus (describing Essenes), Agatharchides (describing Ethiopians), Homer and Strabo (both describing Scythians), and the *Roman d'Alexandre* (fourth century A.D., describing Brahmans of India) all are in a tradition which produced numerous Renaissance treatises besides Montaigne's. The thesis here is that Sh drew on more than Montaigne in this passage: Gonzalo's description contains some elements which are lacking in Montaigne but are prominent in other (earlier) treatises.

2230. Hoeniger, F. David. "The Meaning of *The Winter's Tale*," *UTQ*, XX (1950), 11-26.

Interpreting the play as an allegory of creation, destruction, and recreation, Hoeniger shows that the myth of Proserpine and Ceres is one aspect of the analogy. Others are the antithesis between true creative art and false art, and the cycle of innocence, evil, and redemption with its parallel cycle of life, death, and resurrection (the Eleusinian interpretation of the Proserpine legend). A very interesting approach to the play; but Hoeniger is wrong to assume that only he and Wilson Knight take *W.T.* seriously--cf. Helen A. Clarke (#2196), Charlotte Porter (#2275), Paul Siegel (#2288), and Samuel Wolff (#2316), e.g., among his predecessors and contemporaries.

2231. Honigmann, E. A. J. "Secondary Sources of *The Winter's Tale*," *PQ*, XXXIV (1955), 27-38.

The relevant part of this art. is the third (33-38), in which Honigmann refurbishes the argument of Wigston (#2312) for the central symbolic function of the Persephone-Ceres myth in *W.T*. Among the more interesting points: (1) Sh reread his Golding before writing *W.T.*, as verbal echoes show; perhaps Ovid suggested the Proserpina theme to him. (2) Digges's version of Claudian's *De Raptu Proserpinae*, though not published until 1617, may have been in progress much earlier, and Digges and Sh were well known to each other; Digges allegorizes the legend in his preface. (3) It is noteworthy that almost all versions of the legend localize it in Sicily: Sh deliberately reversed the countries of Greene's tale to emphasize the Sicilian locale of the story; this accounts for the "seacoast of Bohemia," which was the coast of Sicily in Greene (about this point Honigmann is in error--see IV, 236, Grosart's ed. of Greene).

2232. Hughes, Merritt Y. "A Classical vs. a Social Approach to Shakspere's Autolycus," SAB, XV (1940), 219-226.

Hughes suggests that in creating the character of Autolycus for W.T., Sh was less interested in portraying an English social type than in reflecting the Autolycus of Greek mythology (grandfather of Odysseus) who was transmuted into a cunning rogue by Plautus and Martial. Natalis Comes' Mythologiae is the likely source of Sh's information. Cf. William T. Hastings, "The Ancestry of Autolycus," ibid., 253, who finds prototypes for Autolycus in "the stock characters of earlier [English] drama."

2233. James, D. G. "The Failure of the Ballad Makers," Scepticism and Poetry: An Essay on the Poetic Imagination (N.Y., 1937), pp. 205-241. GRS

James believes that Sh's attempt to formulate a human mythology in the last plays is less than successful. The symbols (quest, resurrection, recovery of what was lost, etc.) may appear trivial unless supernaturalized. Yet when Sh supernaturalizes them (e.g., in Jupiter's theophany in Cym.), the effect is wooden. James minimizes the rôle of classical mythology in W.T. and Temp., a position difficult to justify (especially for W.T. where Apollo's oracle, symbolizing truth and clear sight, is an ethical yardstick for the entire action of the play).

2234. Johnson, Skuli. "The Poetry of Ovid," MAR, IV (1945), 12-23.

For Fasti and W.T. IV iv, see #2353. MnU

2235. Johnson, W. Stacy. "Folklore Elements in 'The Tempest'," MF, I (1951), 223-228.

That Sh knew Ficino's Neoplatonism "is both doubted and doubtful"; Curry (#2205) is premature to express confidence that Temp. is a reflection of theurgy. It is more probable that Prospero is drawn from the native superstitions about witches and magicians: Sh makes him acceptable by removing him from civilization, by cleansing his motives, and by sending him home less powerful in Act V. This is not a convincing argument: Temp. is steeped in the world of Theocritus, Virgil, Ovid, the Odyssey, and Plautus (see #2244); it is more reasonable to assume that Sh reflects classical philosophy than to introduce the native superstitions.

2236. Johnson, W. Stacy. "The Genesis of Ariel," SQ, II (1951), 205-210.

Ariel is "the superb combination of a philosopher's attractive formulation [i.e., a Neoplatonic spirit] with a folk tale's palpable humanity ... " Among the antecedents which may have coalesced in Sh's mind are devil lore, occult magic, the Bible (Isaiah xxix), and cabalism. Here Johnson appears willing to admit the influence of Neoplatonism; he denies it in #2235, published in the same year.

2237. Johnston, Mary. "Cymbeline III, v, 70-74," TLS, January 22, 1938, p. 60.

The author supports a proposed emendation of the lines (Cloten's "I love and hate her ...") by asserting that altered they would echo two epigrams of Catullus. The assertion appears gratuitous.

2238. Jorgensen, Paul A. "Alien Military Doctrine in Renaissance England," MLQ, XVII (1956), 43-49.

H.V, with its "happy few" prevailing without strategy over multitudes of enemies, represents the sentimental, foolhardy prejudice of the Elizabethans against military tactics; indeed Fluellen's pedantry in the play is a parody of writers on strategy who attempted to jolt the English out of their complacent confidence that God's might will fight for the virtuous and the ingenuous. By the time of Cym., however, Sh appears to value a disciplined cadre of troops trained in military skills and capable of fighting with intelligence (II iv 20-26). The change was doubtless brought about through the influence of books on the art of war, some of them classics translated into English (e.g., Caesar's Commentaries, Sextus Julius Frontinus' Strategemata, and Aelianus' Tactica).

2239. Kemp, Robert. "En Relisant 'Cymbeline'," Le Temps, 28-29 mars, 1942, p. 3. GRS

Kemp is amused by the absurdities of the play, especially the anachronisms which casually leap over fourteen hundred years. But he finds verisimilitude in the Roman part of the play: "Les courtes scenes qui se passent à Rome [II v ?, III vii ?] semblent tombées de Coriolan ou de Jules César."

2240. Kermode, Frank. "Introduction," The Tempest (1954/1958), ArdenSh, pp. xi-xciii.

Kermode asserts the formative influence of contemporary voyage literature on Temp., but he anticipates Marx (#2255) in seeing a connection between Renaissance geographical literature about the New World and the works of the ancient geographers. The play for all its topicality is rooted in the ancient world. Most of the comments on things classical in the play have been made also by others (e.g., Neoplatonism in Prospero; Aristotle's bestial man in Caliban; the first six books of the Aeneid in the whole play—from Tunis to Naples by way of a purgatorial experience). But some are striking and original: e.g., Caliban's name recalls "the Chalybeates, savage cannibals of the ancient world, whom Virgil mentions twice, and whom Pliny situates near the Coraxi." To Kermode the central theme of the play is the ancient quarrel between Nature and Art; Caliban is the central figure because his uncivilized Nature points by contrast to the Art of others. Sh conveys this theme in a structure specifically Terentian, preserving the unities and adhering rigidly to the sequence of protasis, epitasis, and catastrophe. An excellent introduction to the play, filled with good criticism as well as facts. See also Appendices B (for Ariel's relationship to Mercury) and D (for evidence that Ovid's Latin was Sh's primary source for the "elves of hills" speech).

2241. Klebs, E. Die Erzählung von Apollonius aus Tyrus. Berlin, 1899, 532 pp.

Not seen. Discussed briefly by J. C. Maxwell in his introduction to the CSh Per. and by F. D. Hoeniger in the Arden Per. Maxwell notes the exhaustiveness of the study and at the same time the failure of Klebs to persuade later scholars that the story does not go back to a lost Greek romance. Hoeniger speaks of Klebs's as the best account of the history of the legend.

2242. Knight, G. Wilson. The Crown of Life: Essays in Interpretation of Shakespeare's Final Plays. Ln, 1948, 336 pp. (First published by OUP in 1947.)

Knight regards the last plays, including H.VIII, as Sh's recapitulation of his earlier work. Having portrayed death as a triumphant experience in Antony, he could not return to the gloom of Lear, Ham., and the other somber plays; therefore he blended themes and incidents from various parts of the earlier canon so as to form a different kind of drama. Many of the themes and other echoes Knight so interestingly discusses are classical: e.g., pastoralism; the use of pagan theophanies in stilted verse (Hecate and Hymen set a precedent for Jupiter, Diana, and Apollo); classical mythology with symbolic significance (the Proserpine legend). But Knight makes no special point of Sh's classicism in the last plays; indeed, of Perdita's famous speech he says, "Dis may be classical, but his 'wagon' is as real as a wagon in Hardy." All of the essays in this vol. are filled with insights, but the ch. on Per. deserves special praise—Knight gives intelligent attention to a play which has been much neglected by other critics.

2243. Knight, G. Wilson. "The Vision of Jupiter in 'Cymbeline'," TLS, November 21, 1936, p. 958.

A unifying principle in Sh's last plays is the concept of the pagan gods as personally involved in the affairs of men; the theophany of each play is a central core. In Cym. Sh regarded the vision scene as essential; it is certainly not the work of any collaborator. A convincing critical treatment. The same thesis elaborated somewhat is to be found embedded in Ch. IV, Part ii of The Crown of Life (#2242).

2244. Knox, Bernard. "'The Tempest' and the Ancient Comic Tradition," VQR, XXXI (1955), 73-89. (Reprinted from EIE, 1954.)

In this brilliant and lucid essay, Knox shows the debt of Temp. to the Plautine and Greek comic traditions. Concentrating on the theme of slavery which dominates the play, his analysis shows clearly the debt to Roman comedy; Prospero is the master while Ariel and Caliban represent two kinds of Roman slaves and Stephano a third (the custodian of the wine cellar who drinks his master's store). Knox does not consider the question of Sh's access to Plautus, but the indebtedness seems apparent.

2245. Lambin, G. "L'île de Prospero ou les Faux Prodiges," LLM, LII (1958), 245-252.

Lambin argues, unconvincingly, that Prospero's island is one of the islets in the Lipari Archipelago off the coast of Sicily, near a direct line from Naples to Tunis. In ancient times they were referred to as Aeolus' domain.

Homer depicts them as stormy in the Odyssey (Lambin points out that Scylla and Charybdis are nearby and can account for the barking noises in Temp.); Diodorus Siculus describes the communal life of their Greek inhabitants (providing a source for Gonzalo's utopia); the pseudo-Aristotelian Book of Marvels records that strange music of tambourines and cymbals is to be heard near a tomb on one of the Aeolian isles. Without suggesting a source for Sh's putative knowledge of the Liparis, Lambin maintains that Sh adapted the prodigious feats of Prospero and Ariel from these classical legends and from natural phenomena of the region which Lambin describes from the accounts of eighteenth- and nineteenth-century visitors.

2246. Lancaster, H. Carrington. "Hermione's Statue," SP, XXIX (1932), 233-238.

Sh's source for the woman-posing-as-a-statue motif in W.T. is not Ovid's Pygmalion story, much less Euripides' Alcestis: in the latter there is no statue and in the former the woman is not alive before the statue enters the story; in neither is a love triangle any part of the plot. Lancaster points out a number of instances, especially French, of the use of the statue motif in the first four decades of the seventeenth century and proposes a lost story of the Empress of Rome type as common source for W.T. and the other statue plays. Lancaster's thesis leaves something to be desired; when we already know that Sh must have known the Pygmalion story, it seems unnecessary to conjecture a "lost story" into existence.

2247. Langenfelt, Gösta. "'The Noble Savage' until Shakespeare," ES, XXXVI (1955), 222-227.

For satire on Golden Age idealism in Temp., see #1038.

2248. Lascelles, Mary. "Shakespeare's Pastoral Comedy," More Talking of Shakespeare, ed. John Garrett (N.Y., 1959), pp. 70-86.

For eclectic pastoralism in the last plays, see #0834.

2249. Lawrence, W. J. "The Vision in 'Cymbeline'," TLS, August 24, 1933, p. 561.

The vision of Jupiter on his eagle in V iv was an interpolation made by someone other than Sh at a time after the middle of 1611. This interpolation was doubtless homage to the popularity of similar theophanies especially in Heywood's Silver Age (which Sh's company helped to produce). The deus ex machina was a response to the Jacobean craving for sensational theatrical effects. See Wilson Knight's arguments (#2242, #2243) for the integrity and importance of this theophany and of the others in the last plays.

2250. Lord, John Bigelow. "Certain Dramatic Devices Studied in the Comedies of Shakespeare and in Some of the Works of His Contemporaries and Predecessors," diss (Illinois, 1951). DA, XII (1952), 66-67.

For ultimately Greek and Roman dramatic devices in Temp. and W.T., see #0846.

2251. Lovejoy, Arthur O., and George Boas. Primitivism and Related Ideas in Antiquity [A Documentary History of Primitivism and Related Ideas, Vol. I], Johns Hopkins UP, 1935, 482 pp.

In two passing references (pp. 166, 207), the authors suggest that Plato and Democritus anticipated Polixenes' discussion in W.T. IV iv of the priority of nature to art. There is no discussion of Sh's access to this classical commonplace.

2252. Luce, Morton. "Introduction," The Tempest (1902/1926), ArdenSh, pp. ix-lxx.

Relevant notes are brief: Sh is portrayed as somewhere between amusement and defiance in his obvious adherence to the unities; Ariel's ancestry includes "the classic faun, satyr, and divinity"; Caliban's "deformity is, in part, a Platonic convention"; seventeen lines from Golding's Ovid are quoted as source for the "elves of hills" speech.

2253. Lynn, W. T. "Cunobelinus or Cymbeline," 8 NQ, X (1896), 474.

Cymbeline's challenge to Caius Lucius (III i 70-77) in which he points out that in his youth at Rome he was knighted by Augustus, is a "monkish fable" traceable to Geoffrey of Monmouth; Sh's immediate source is Holinshed. Cunobelinus was never at Rome, though his son Caractacus was.

2254. Mackail, J. W. "Mother and Son in 'Cymbeline'," Homage, pp. 193-196. E-S

An interesting analysis of the scene with the Roman ambassador, for which Cloten has been "primed" with a set speech by his mother. When he forgets his part and in characteristically brutal fashion makes a fool of himself over

Julius Caesar, his mother cuts in and delivers the speech herself. She is a ministering protectress, attempting to cover her son's blunders. She dies because of her one virtue: love for unworthy Cloten.

2255. Marx, Leo. "Shakespeare's American Fable," MR, II (1960), 40-71.

Advancing the thesis that Temp. is a preview of the American literary theme of spiritual restoration in the wilderness, Marx shows that the play bears a close relationship to the reports of voyagers which in turn were greatly influenced by the pastoral tradition of Golden Age idealism. Thus there is a link between Theocritus and Virgil, Arcadia, Elysium, Atlantis, and the garden of the Hesperides on the one hand and the concept of America as a pristine garden of fertile beauty on the other. Temp. stands somewhere between the two. Marx calls the entire play "pastoral" without distinguishing georgic elements (like the "foison" of Ceres which is attainable because it is striven for with the virtues of Virgil's farmer, while the "foison" of Gonzalo is not, since it is awaited, like manna). Marx's is, nevertheless, a stimulating and original interpretation of the play.

2256. Matthews, C. M. "The True Cymbeline," HT, VII (1957), 755-759.

"Shakespeare did less than justice to the greatest king of ancient Britain," whose forty-year reign contemporaneous with Christ is sketched here. "Ancient Rome was exciting to Shakespeare and he clearly enjoyed throwing a few tribunes, senators and classical allusions into his mixture, and even a vision of Jupiter, but he made no concessions to Ancient Britain," not reflecting its culture at all. Critics seldom distinguish between Sh's portrayal of the ancient Britons in the play and his portrayal of the ancient Romans; Matthews has made a contribution of some significance.

2257. M[axwell], J. C. "Introduction," Cymbeline (1960), CSh, [XXXVI], pp. xi-xlii.

In passing: the historical element in Cym. "is least satisfactory when it brings us into contact with the realities of the Roman empire." The audience expects ancient Rome to be something other than romantic, yet Sh handles his historical materials in a "cavalier ... fashion" as he does the pastoral element and, indeed, all the ingredients of the play.

2258. M[axwell], J. C. "Introduction," Pericles Prince of Tyre (1956), CSh, [XXXVII], pp. ix-xxix.

Maxwell mentions briefly that the remotest sources lie in Greek and Latin romances (p. x), and he takes note of the thesis of Simpson (#0543) that Sh may have drawn on Plautus' Rudens.

2259. Megaw, Robert N. E. "Shakespeare's Last Plays: An Inquiry Into the Artistic Form of Pericles, Cymbeline, The Winter's Tale, and The Tempest," diss (Chicago, 1950).*

It is assumed that five-act structure is discussed in this diss.

2260. Meier, Konrad. "Über Shakespeares Sturm," NS, XVI (1907), 193-210, 271-279, 321-336. E-S

In passing (p. 328), Meier derives Caliban's name from τὸ κᾶλον (firewood) and ὁ βαῦνος (oven). The name, then, suggests Caliban's duty to Prospero. Meier supports his argument by noting (as others have noted) that Caliban's mother also has a Greek name: σῦς + κόραξ or swine-raven. Sh's "less Greek" would perhaps be sufficient to coin the name as Meier suggests he did, but the thesis does not appear clearly proven; βαῦνος is not a common Greek term.

2261. Merton, Stephen. "'The Tempest' and 'Troilus and Cressida'," CE, VII (1945), 143-150.

Merton, who accepts the view of Campbell (#1199) that Troi. is a "comicall satyre," believes that Sh evolved Temp. from his experience with "commentators" in Troi. Prospero is modeled on Ulysses, who in turn is Aristotle's virtuous, reasonable man. Both Prospero and Ulysses philosophize on mutability, both stand au dessus de la melée, both are manipulators of others, both are known for wisdom, and especially both speak Sh's thoughts. When Sh appropriated Ulysses, he naturally inherited his opposite, Thersites, the Carlo Buffone of Troi. But Sh made some changes in him because Temp. is not a satire; Caliban is a curser, a railer, foulmouthed, but he also speaks poetry, feels no envy, and is capable of bright dreams. Thus one may account for Caliban's lack of self-consistency. An interesting theory, which can be further supported by the recognition that the pairing of characters in Temp. which Merton comments on has precedent in the pairing of characters in Troi. (Hector/Ulysses, Pandarus/Thersites, Helen/Cressida, etc.). Merton might also have explored thematic reasons why the Troy story should have seemed to Sh an obverse to Temp. (e.g., love and strife; the "golden" age vs. the "iron" age).

2262. "Miscellany: From the Norfolk Herald," PF, n.s. II (1806), 248-249.

Not being aware of Golding's trans. of the Meta., the unknown author of this short note confidently assumes that Temp. V i 33-50, the famous "elves of hills ..." passage, is a very literal trans. of Medea's invocation (Meta. VII). Curiously, by modern attitudes toward Sh's creativity, he calls it "direct plagiarism" and speaks of Sh as having "fled to antiquity for aid" when he had "exhausted his own prodigious powers." This short note is in effect all that A. V. R. Westfall (#0055) can adduce as evidence of Shn source study (classical) in America before 1865. MnU

2263. Moorman, F. W. "Introduction," The Winter's Tale (1912/1933), ArdenSh, pp. ix-xxxiii.

Moorman devotes considerable attention to the Greek romance materials which filtered into W.T. through Greene's Pandosto. He regards the oracle as central to the play and points out that oracles appear in Parthenius' ἐρωτικὰ παθήματα, Photius' abstract of Antonius Diogenes' τὰ ὑπὲρ θούλην ἄπιστα, Xenophon's Anthia and Habrocomes, Heliodorus' Aethiopica, and Achilles Tatius' Leucippe and Clitophon. Another romance element is pastoralism which Greene may have acquired from Longus' Daphnis and Chloe; a third is sensational adventures which may stem from Achilles Tatius and Heliodorus. The Greek heritage survives especially in the religious atmosphere of Sh's play, which is pervasive and consistent, and through proper names, some of them from Sidney's Arcadia, and one ("Autolycus") from the Odyssey by way of Ovid's Meta. Moorman also notes that Per. and T.N.K. both are set on Greek soil and are both indirectly traceable to the Greek romances (T.N.K. by way of Chaucer and Boccaccio). Among the possible sources for Act V, Moorman mentions Ovid's Pygmalion story and Euripides' Alcestis story (which Sh could have known from versions in LGW and Pettie's Petite Palace of Pleasure).

2264. Muir, Kenneth. "Pericles II.v," NQ, CXCIII (1948), 362.

Muir calls attention to the large number of references to Diana in Per. and suggests that the events of the action are precipitated by her wrath either (1) at Simonides for lying to the Knights in II v about Thaisa's vow of celibacy (if it is a lie), or (2) at Thaisa for making such a vow and then breaking it with Pericles. Muir suggests that some lines directing the audience's attention to Nemesis may have dropped out of the text. If accepted, Muir's view of the play would harmonize it more nearly with W.T. and Cym., in each of which temporary calamity is precipitated by human sin.

2265. Nearing, Homer, Jr. "The Legend of Julius Caesar's British Conquest," PMLA, LXIV (1949), 889-929. GRS

For allusions to Caesar's British adventures in Cym., see #1058.

2266. Newell, W. W. "Sources of Shakespeare's Tempest," JAF, XVI (1903), 234-257. E-S

The outline of Temp. stems mediately from the same pre-historic folk myth which produced the legend of the Argonauts and the Cupid-Psyche tale. Basic elements are magic (Cupid, Medea, Prospero), labors to prove worth (Psyche's punitive tasks, Jason's slaying of the dragon-soldiers, Ferdinand's woodpile), and exile with a return and happy ending. Newell cites analogues as far apart as India and New England, but does not specify the immediate source of Sh's plot.

2267. Nosworthy, J. M. "The Integrity of Shakespeare: Illustrated From Cymbeline," ShS, VIII (1955), 52-56.

Nosworthy makes three observations on Sh's classics: (1) Underdowne's trans. of the Aethiopica of Heliodorus must be regarded as a source of Cym. (2) The diction of the Chorus in H.V III shows that it was based on the same passage in North's Plutarch out of which Sh fashioned Enobarbus' description of Cleopatra at Cydnus and Iachimo's description (II iv) of the arras in Imogen's bedchamber. (3) In the romances, Sh returned to the poetic diction of the 1590's; when he did, he also returned to the classical materials he was interested in in the 'nineties: both Philomela (Titus) and Tarquin (Lucr.) are mentioned in Iachimo's monologue in the bedchamber. An interesting art.

2268. Nosworthy, J. M. "Introduction," Cymbeline (1955), ArdenSh, pp. xi-lxxxiv.

Nosworthy provides an illuminating account of the Elizabethan confusion about Cymbeline's reign; he points out that Sh made no effort to reconcile the inconsistencies in various accounts of the British relationships with the Romans, as he followed Holinshed for the most part. In a later passage (pp. xxxiii-xxxvii) Nosworthy ably defends the authenticity of the theophany of Jupiter in V iv, pointing out that the verse is rhymed fourteeners, setting the god's speech off from that of mortals. Similar fourteeners appear in a theophany of Jupiter in The Rare Triumphs of Love and Fortune (1582), a play which, it seems probable on other grounds, Sh exhumed to draw on for Cym. Nosworthy observes that a deus ex machina is necessary in so immensely involved a dénouement, and is, moreover, appropriate in a play which abounds with classical allusions. The prevalence of these classical references is noted at several points: see, e.g., the excellent discussions of echoes from the world of Venus in Cym. and of the rôle of the phoenix myth in the play. Altogether an intelligent introduction.

2269. Nosworthy, J. M. "The Narrative Sources of The Tempest," RES, XXIV (1948), 281-294.

Nosworthy presents (pp. 287-294) a better argument for the influence of the Aeneid on Temp. than that offered by Conway (#2200). Nosworthy believes that Sh used the early books of the Aeneid to launch his plot. Ferdinand, like Aeneas, is isolated from his companions by a supernaturally induced storm; his meeting with Miranda is based on Aeneas' meeting with Venus (Ferdinand even translates Aeneas' exclamation, "o dea certe"). Since Ferdinand is not to abandon Miranda, Sh carefully made sure that the audience would not connect her with Dido; this he did by adopting a lighthearted tone in the "Widow Dido" passage (which is based on the Aeneid, not on Marlowe's Dido). Once Sh had launched his plot, other narrative sources came into the spotlight, but such reminiscences of the Aeneid as the Harpy (III iii) and the speech of Ceres to Iris (IV i) are later echoes of the earlier material. Nosworthy argues effectively that Sh read the Latin. An excellent piece of scholarly criticism.

2270. "Notes and News," PL, III (1891), 224-225.

This brief discussion of earlier opinions on Sh's classical source for Autolycus, the master thief of W.T., concludes: "To discuss the probable originality with Shakespeare of a conception which is one of the universal inheritances of the Aryan race is futile; the type existed, and Shakespeare's part was to make an individual of the type." The author shows the similarity between Autolycus and the Hermes of the Homeric Hymn.

2271. Osborn, E. B. Our Debt to Greece and Rome. Ln, 1924, 192 pp. (Not the same as the series, Our Debt.)

Despite its title, the book is not a study of western indebtedness so much as a brief introduction to some of the achievements of classical culture; yet though the comments on Sh are very brief, one at least is provocative: Plautus' Rudens "recalls both 'the Tempest' and 'The Winter's Tale' of our arch-dramatist, who derived so much, directly and indirectly, from the Plautine comedy." MnU

2272. Parrott, Thomas Marc. "Pericles: The Play and the Novel," SAB, XXIII (1948), 105-113.

This is a clear and moderate brief statement of the complicated problems of Per.: its inception, ancestry, and peculiar publication history. Parrott discusses briefly the lost Greek romance and the Latin adaptations from it which form the mediate source of the play. Whoever wrote the play must have been a classical scholar, for he changed the names of characters in consistency with Greek and Latin onomastic practice. Perhaps the changes can be attributed to Heywood, if Per. is a revision of a Heywood play.

2273. Perry, Henry Ten Eyck. Masters of Dramatic Comedy and Their Social Themes. HUP, 1939, 428 pp. GRS

For a comparison between Temp. and Aristophanes' Birds, see #0880.

2274. Pettet, E. C. "The 'Romances'," Shakespeare and the Romance Tradition (Ln, 1949), pp. 161-199.

To Pettet, the last plays (including T.N.K.) are deeply indebted to the same Medieval materials that produced the comedies. He barely alludes to the classical themes and settings of these plays. The most interesting relevant observation is that the last plays are Sh's closest approximation to Aristotle's category of episodic drama "'in which the episodes or acts succeed one another without probable or necessary sequence'."

2275. Porter, Charlotte. "Old and New Ideals of Womanhood: The Iphigenia and Alkestis Stories," PL, III (1891), 269-280.

This interesting comparative study treats the theme of woman sacrificed by man for what he thinks is the public good. The exemplars are Aeschylus' Agamemnon (sacrifice of Iphigenia), Sophocles' Electra (the same), Euripides' Iphigenia at Aulis and in Tauris and Alcestis, Chaucer's Legend of Hypermnestra, Sh's W.T., and Goethe's Iphigenia in Tauris. Euripides' Alcestis and Sh's Hermione are very close in spirit, and Paulina, like Heracles, is the wonder-worker who tests the worthiness of him for whom she works wonders. Leontes and Admetus both assume that their welfare is the commonweal and ergo make selfish misjudgments; both are tempted to remarry by considerations of state, but each is loyal because he has learned wisdom "by the smart thereof." An illuminating study.

2276. P[rescot], K[enrick]. Shakespear. N.p., 1774, 16 pp.

For Prospero and Senecan eschatology, see #2074. DFo

2277. Q[uiller-Couch, Sir Arthur]. "The Tempest: Introduction," The Tempest (1921), CSh, [I], pp. xlv-lv.

In passing: the unity of time which characterizes Temp. is Sh's successful effort at "taking up the glove thrown down by Sir Philip Sidney" in the Apologie for Poesie.

2278. Q[uiller-Couch, Sir Arthur]. "The Winter's Tale: Introduction," The Winter's Tale (1931), CSh, [XIV], pp. vii-xxvi.

This introduction contains several observations on classical background: the editor points out that Sh found the shrine of Apollo located at "Delphos" (i.e., a fusion of "Delphi" and "Delos") in Greene's Pandosto; Sh has been much ridiculed for this blunder, but Greene, after all, was a Cambridge M.A. The ultimate sources of the themes in W.T. are the Greek romances, and Sh maintains the spirit of the ancient world despite his anachronisms. Christianity is not permitted to intrude. Autolycus' name comes from the Odyssey by way, perhaps, of Lucian's De Astrologia and Meta. XI. But Quiller-Couch finds "no warrant for tracing Hermione's restoration back to the Alcestis." The mutual anagnorisis of Leontes and Perdita in the fifth act violates Aristotelian canons because (1) it takes place off-stage and (2) it is "rescue and recognition by the aid of tokens."

2279. Rea, J[ohn] D. "A Note on The Tempest," MLN, XXXV (1920), 313-315.

Sh's island was suggested to him by Florio's trans. of Montaigne "Of the Canniballes," where Montaigne gives a description of a supposed Carthaginian island outside the Straits of Gibraltar and names Aristotle as his source. Rea's evidence is interesting, but it should be observed that classical literature is full of islands, and Temp. (it is coming to be recognized) is full of reminiscences of classical literature.

2280. Rea, John D. "A Source for the Storm in The Tempest," MP, XVII (1919), 279-286. E-S

According to Rea, the source of the storm is "Naufragium," one of the Colloquia of Erasmus, translated into English by William Burton in 1606. The parallels are quite close: St. Elmo's fire, an account given in a monologue punctuated by interruptions from the listener, names of some characters, etc. Rea shows that Erasmus could have provided Sh some details; it seems probable, however, that the primary source is Aeneid I.

2281. Reich, Hermann. "Zur Quelle des 'Cymbelin'," ShJ, XLI (1905), 177-181. E-S SG

Cymbeline's wicked queen, the step-relationship, the attempted poisoning, and the doctor's frustration of the attempt all were drawn from Apuleius' Golden Ass (X), which Sh knew from his use of the book in Dream. Reich makes out a convincing case which is not seriously damaged by the objections and alternatives proposed by Erna Buchin (#2195) and Friedrich Brie (ibid., XLIV [1908], 167-170).

2282. Rolfe, John C. "Sicca Mors, Juvenal x, 113," TAPA, XL (1909), lxxvi-lxxviii [of the Proceedings].

The phrase, which in Juvenal means "a bloodless (i.e., natural) death," comes to mind at Temp. I i 70, where Gonzalo "would fain die a dry death"; the meanings are different, but both passages have grim humor about them, especially when it is remembered that in English superstition the man marked by destiny for hanging could not drown.

2283. Rose, Brian W. "The Tempest: A Reconsideration of Its Meaning," ESA, I (1958), 205-216.

Rose argues that Prospero is not Sh, but a magician brought on stage to entertain James, who disapproved of demonology, but was interested in it. He argues in passing that James would recognize the "elves of hills" speech as a redaction of Medea's incantation in Meta. VII, and therefore would connect Prospero with his famous classical predecessor in witchcraft.

2284. Ruegg, August. "Caliban und Miranda," ShJ, LXXXIX (1953), 128-131.

Ruegg argues persuasively that the contrast between barbarous, monstrous Caliban and ethereal, gracious Miranda reflects the comic contrast between the repulsive Cyclops sick with love and beautiful Galatea in Ovid's Meta. XIII (764-870). Especially interesting is the apparent echo of Cyclops' catalogue of dainties offered to Galatea in Caliban's catalogue of dainties offered to Stephano (II ii 164-176). Ruegg also calls attention to thematic parallels between A.Y.L. and Temp.

2285. Rushton, W[illiam] L[owes]. "'Gods Have Taken Shapes of Beasts'," 4 NQ, IX (1872), 197.

Rushton considers Florizel's observation in W.T. IV iv 25-35 a direct recollection of Lyly's Gallathea (I i). The phrasing is close, but this truism about pagan deities is illustrated repeatedly in the Meta. Sh could surely have formulated it himself after reading Ovid.

2286. Schlauch, Margaret. "Roman 'Controversiae' and the Court Scene in Shakespeare's 'Merchant of Venice'," KN, VII (1960), 45-56.

For Per. as a descendant of the Controversiae of Seneca the Elder, see #0912. DLC

2287. Shackford, Martha H. "Nature and the Supernatural: Iphigeneia in Tauris and The Tempest," Shakespeare, Sophocles: Dramatic Themes and Modes (N.Y., 1960), pp. 97-112.

The essay points to some similarities and differences between Euripides' play and Sh's, and then, through an analysis of each play, attempts to establish each as a prototype of its religious culture. Prospero in Temp. symbolizes the Renaissance belief in man's potency to control his environment (nature), whereas Iphigenia and Orestes, each under the orders and power of a god, typify the Greek emphasis on the influence of the gods in the affairs of men. Professor Shackford perhaps recognizes that this thesis is an oversimplification for she ends by qualifying: "but when the necessity arose Iphigeneia showed herself superior to the emergency, and the gods approved her."

2288. Siegel, Paul N. "Leontes a Jealous Tyrant," RES, n.s. I (1950), 302-307.

Siegel applies the thesis of Armstrong (#0970, #0971) to W.T., in which Leontes' behavior exactly follows the traditional pattern of the tyrant including the (attempted) murder of a child (cf. Macb. and R.III) and the Senecan debate between the tyrant and an epitome of virtue and reason (Camillo in I ii 212-350). The chief difference is that in W.T. Sh sees evil as inherently and mysteriously pregnant with good. An illuminating commentary on the character.

2289. Singer, S[amuel]. "Shakespeare's drama und Wilkins' novelle [sic l.c.]," Apollonius von Tyrus: Untersuchungen über das Fortleben des antiken Romans in späteren Zeiten (Halle, 1895), pp. 33-67. HB

Singer makes a detailed comparative study of Per. with numerous versions of the romance including, inter alia, Gower, Twine, Wilkins, some Medieval Greek redactions, three Latin accounts, and Robert Copland's account (1510). His conclusion is that Sh used Gower and some version (perhaps now lost) other than Twine. Singer's research is meticulous—altogether he discusses nearly fifty accounts of Apollonius in this book—and if he appears to assume that Sh could not stir without a source, even for trivial and commonplace details, his parallel passage method does produce convincing conclusions in some cases. MH

2290. Smith, Grover. "The Tennis-Ball of Fortune," NQ, CXC (1946), 202-203. GRS

The Renaissance concept of man as a tennis ball batted about by Fortune may have originated in a misinterpretation of a passage in Plautus' Captivi. Pericles describes himself (II i 63-65) as a man made the tennis ball of the waves and wind. In passing Smith also observes that Gloucester's "They kill us for their sport" (Lear IV i 36-37) is reminiscent of the "fickle and relentless Destiny" of Euripidean tragedy.

2291. Smith, Homer. "Pastoral Influence in the English Drama," PMLA, XII (1897), 355-460. E-S

For a denial of pastoral influence on W.T., see #0924.

2292. Smith, Irwin. "Ariel as Ceres," SQ, IX (1958), 430-432.

There is no special significance to Sh's having Ariel "present" Ceres in the Masque (Temp. IV i) aside from the fact that the company was doubtless short of boys who could play women's parts, so Ariel had to "double," even though this necessitated two rapid costume changes. Sh did not have any classical symbolism in mind when he identified the two characters.

2293. Smith, Warren D. "Cloten with Caius Lucius," SP, XLIX (1952), 185-194.

To interpret Cloten's refusal to pay tribute to Caius Lucius in Cym. III i as the behavior of a prudent councilor is to miss the significance of Sh's source material, which portrays British-Augustan relations as almost cordial. Smith also discusses James I's diplomatic policy as a guide to the interpretation of the scene.

2294. Smyth, Albert H. Shakespeare's Pericles and Apollonius of Tyre: A Study in Comparative Literature. Philadelphia, 1898, 112 pp.

An erudite survey of the many versions of the Apollonius story which, Smyth shows, maintained the integrity of the original Greek and Latin romance as it migrated throughout Europe during the Middle Ages and the Renaissance. Smyth devotes rather less attention to Per. than might be expected; and little of that attention is focused on Sh's use of the conventions of the Greek romance that Smyth sketches elsewhere in the book. One passage of special interest (pp. 11-13) enumerates the elements common to the Apollonius story and to Xenophon's story of Anthia and Habrocomes (the mediate source of Romeo); "A correspondence so exact and even verbal is only explicable upon the theory that one of the narrators was the imitator of the other." DFo

2295. Spencer, Terence. "Shakespeare's Isle of Delphos," MLR, XLVII (1952), 199-202.

Spencer shows that Sh's reference to "Delphos" as an island (W.T. III i 1-3) is not a mark of his illiteracy, since the common Renaissance English name for Delos (island birthplace of Apollo, site of one of his oracles --cf. Aeneid III, 73-101) was "Delphos." This is the name Greene uses in Pandosto. Thus Sh was not referring erroneously to the oracle of Delphi (on the mainland), but correctly to the oracle on the island of Delos.

2296. Spencer, Theodore. "Appearance and Reality in Shakespeare's Last Plays," MP, XXXIX (1942), 265-274.

The hierarchy of being which Spencer traces to Aristotle, placed man between angels and beasts, capable of ascending or descending at will. In the early seventeenth century, many people looked down and, like Iago, saw primarily the beast in man. This vision was sufficiently shocking to demand balm; four balms were offered in Jacobean times: (1) Baconian scientism, which simply ignored the ethical-metaphysical problem; (2) Stoicism (especially in Chapman), which adopted the Platonic belief in godlike right reason; (3) the frivolity of Beaumont and Fletcher; (4) the poetic idealism of Sh's last four plays. In Shn tragedy, reality is always worse than appearance; in the last plays, appearance is always worse than reality. The discussion centers on Temp., in which Caliban's unredeemable bestiality is contrasted with Prospero's right reason. But it is noteworthy that in Act V Prospero abandons his angelic status and returns to the Aristotelian middle position occupied by man.

2297. Stapfer, Paul. Shakespeare et l'antiquité: Deuxième partie, Shakespeare et les tragiques grecs. Paris, 1880, 320 pp. (New ed., 1888.)

Contains a comparison of Imogen with Homer's Penelope (see #2128).

2298. Still, Colin. Shakespeare's Mystery Play: A Study of "The Tempest". Ln, 1921, 248 pp.

This is a first draft of the argument which Still advances in #2299. Large parts of this book are incorporated without change into The Timeless Theme, but the later book is given a broader scope by the inclusion of the "formulation" of Still's hypothesis about the spiritual significance of imaginative literature.

2299. Still, Colin. The Timeless Theme: A Critical Theory Formulated and Applied. Ln, 1936, 244 pp.

Advancing the proposition that all great art deals with the theme of man's spiritual pilgrimage upward from sin and error toward beauty and wisdom, Still devotes the second half of the book to an interpretation of Temp. as an allegory of this spiritual quest. He draws on Aeneid VI, on the Eleusinian mysteries, on Greek mythology generally, on the Old and New Testaments, on Dante, and on Milton, to say nothing of the many occult writers of the Near East who have treated the theme of initiation which Still finds in Temp. The hypothesis does not depend on Sh's having known the materials which are brought to bear on Temp., because Still believes "that the essence of individual genius lies in its affinity with the universal spirit which is collective genius and in its clear and direct apprehension of the eternal things with which the imagination of mankind has always been concerned." The Court Party are initiated into the Lesser Mysteries (the realm of Air—Ariel), while Ferdinand is privileged to move higher into the Greater Mysteries (the realm of Aether—Prospero's cell), and Trinculo and Stephano (like Adam and Eve) undergo the fall from the realm of air into the world of the senses. The fallacies in this vigorously advanced argument are numerous; perhaps chief among them is the quantitative approach to documentation: Still believes that weak pieces of evidence reinforce one another as they accumulate, an attitude toward proof which responsible scholars are not likely to endorse. Again, Still recognizes the Virgilian impress on the play, but he intrudes Book VI of the Aeneid which actually is far less in evidence than Books I-IV, which he hardly mentions. He begins his attack on orthodox critics by rejecting their proposed sources for Temp., as if identifying sources correctly were important to his argument, but then proceeds to ignore source study in favor of analogical criticism. This is not an acceptable thesis: it is obvious that Temp. deals in general with the theme of regeneration through penitence; it is very much less obvious that Greek rites or Christian ceremonies are implied in the moral context of the play.

2300. Tannenbaum, Samuel A. "The 'Valley' in 'The Winter's Tale'," SAB, VII (1932), 192-193.

Tannenbaum explains the word (II iii 100) as deriving from Latin vallecula, which refers to the indentation in the upper lip. On a beautiful woman's face, this groove was regarded as so charming that it was sometimes also called the philtrum or φίλτρον.

2301. Tew, Edmund. "[Shakspeare and Lucretius]," 4 NQ, XI (1873), 234.

Tew compares Prospero's "cloud-capp'd towers" speech (Temp. IV i) with a passage from De Rerum Natura I i and adds some lines of similar import from Lucan's Pharsalia. However, "it is hardly to be supposed that Shakspeare ever read Lucretius in the original."

2302. Thorndike, Ashley H. "Influence of the Court-Masques on the Drama, 1608-15," PMLA, XV (1900), 114-120.

Pointing out that anti-masques performed at court by professional players were sometimes introduced afterwards into public plays, Thorndike suggests (1) that the intrusive dance of twelve Satyrs in W.T. IV iv was borrowed from Jonson's Oberon produced at court January 1, 1611. If so, the date of W.T. is established as somewhere between January and May, 1611. (2) Temp. is indebted to the masques: Prospero, Ariel, the dance of goddesses, and the elaborate stage machinery all are masque elements which Sh wove into a romantic plot. Thorndike does not emphasize the pseudo-classical aura of these intrusive masques, but it is obviously an indirect link between Sh and classicism.

2303. Thorndike, A[shley] H. "The Pastoral Element in the English Drama before 1605," MLN, XIV (1899), 228-246. E-S

In his attempt to show the vitality of a native pastoral tradition independent of Italian models, Thorndike suggests in passing that Ariel is very similar to the unlustful satyrs of Fletcher. This places Ariel in the Elizabethan tradition of wild sylvan dwellers who were originally classical fauns, not satyrs; "the Elizabethans appear to have confused the two."

2304. Tillyard, E. M. W. Shakespeare's Last Plays. Ln, 1938/1951, 85 pp.

In expounding his thesis that Sh's last plays are a fulfillment of the great tragedies,

Tillyard draws an analogy to Greek tragedy in which the third play of the trilogy constitutes a reconciliation of the conflicts and pains of the preceding two plays (e.g., Eumenides, Aeschylus' lost play on Prometheus' reconciliation to Zeus). But the analogy is not entirely valid, as Tillyard has forgotten that the Greeks completed their cycles with satyr plays, as uninhibited and lewd as Sh's romances are delicate, if we are to judge by Euripides' Cyclops. Tillyard also makes incidental observations on Sh's indirect debt to Greek romance, on the importance of the Pantheon in the last plays, etc.

2305. Tinkler, F. C. "'The Winter's Tale'," Scrutiny, V (1937), 344-364.

This interpretative essay emphasizes the thematic complexity of W.T., its "air of sober restraint," and its richness of association with the primitive life. Tinkler speaks of rebirth, maturation, fertility, and other vegetation themes, but does not emphasize a connection with classical religion, nor (refreshingly) with occult pseudo-religions. Yet this essay is ordinarily cited as important by later critics who do postulate such connections.

2306. Tompkins, J. M. S. "Why Pericles?" RES, n.s. III (1952), 315-324.

Pericles' name and his virtue of patience are both to be found in Plutarch's "Life," which precedes "Coriolanus" and "Alcibiades," who as examples of impatience are implicitly contrasted with Fabius Maximus and Pericles. Sh probably read "Fabius" and "Pericles" while working on Cor. and Tim. Plutarch's Pericles is, of course, more complex than Sh's, but the two have much in common. This thesis provides at least as good an explanation of the name and the character as that which traces Sh's hero to the Pyrocles of Sidney's Arcadia or to the Pyrochles of FQ II.

2307. Vollhardt, W. "Zur Quellenkunde von Shakespeares 'Sturm'," AngliaM, XXXVII (1926), 337-342. E-S

To suggest the debt of Temp. to Italian pastoral drama and comedy, Vollhardt cites numerous Italian analogues, some of which have classical sources. Of some interest are his citations to Pliny and Pomponius Mela on the subject of half-human monsters like Caliban.

2308. Waith, Eugene M. "Pericles and Seneca the Elder," JEGP, L (1951), 180-182.

In modification of an argument by William Elton (ibid., XLVIII [1949], 138-139) that Lazarus Pyott's The Orator may have been the source of the brothel scenes in Per., Waith points out that Pyott's mediate source, one of Seneca's declamations, was itself doubtless based on the same Greek declamations which scholars believe exerted a great influence on the Greek romances. The Greek romances in turn are the sources of the Apollonius tradition on which Sh drew for Per. So it is impossible to demonstrate any direct connection between Sh and Seneca the Elder, though Per. and Seneca's declamations may well have a common ancestor.

2309. Warton, Joseph. "The Tempest," The Adventurer, No. 93, No. 97, September 25, October 9, 1753. (Reprinted with some deletion in Shakespeare Criticism: A Selection, ed. D. Nichol Smith [OUP, 1916], pp. 60-67.)

Sh has insight into human nature such as only Homer can rival; unlike Virgil and Horace he mingles blemishes with his excellences, making criticism rewarding. Though Sh attains consistency of character, realism in portrayal of emotions, and creative imagination, he violates the unities of time and place; but where in Temp. he achieves his normal virtues and adds the unities to them, he is so much the grander. This analysis of the characters and action is astute, but does not try to trace them to classical antecedents; at one point Warton speaks of Prospero's "We are such stuff . . ." as Euripidean in its sententiousness.

2310. White, Roderick. "Autolycus and Odysseus," TLS, November 22, 1957, p. 705. GRS

White corrects a TLS reviewer (ibid., p. 656), who identified Autolycus as the father of Odysseus. He was Odysseus' maternal grandfather. The reviewer expressed the opinion that Sh "knew a great deal of classical mythology" and that Autolycus in W.T. is named for Odysseus' forebear.

2311. Wigston, W. F. C. "The Winter's Tale," Bacon, Shakespeare and the Rosicrucians (Ln, 1888), pp. 139-155.

A restatement and acknowledgement of his earlier, anonymous thesis (#2312) on the significance of the Persephone myth in W.T. MnU

2312. [Wigston, W. F. C.] "The Winter's Tale," A New Study of Shakespeare: An Inquiry into the Connection of the Plays and Poems, with the Origins of the Classical Drama, and with the Platonic Philosophy through the Mysteries (Ln, 1884), Ch. I, pp. 1-39.

Wigston's first statement of his theory that the myth of Persephone and Ceres holds the key to W.T. (and to the other last plays as well). He restates the same basic thesis in briefer compass in his later work (#2311). Though Wigston has chs. on Sonn., Phoenix, Romeo, Dream, Temp., Cym., L.L.L., etc., as a Baconian he lies outside the scope of this Guide and is included only because of the references to him in Honigmann (#2231). MnU

2313. Wilson, Harold S. "'Nature and Art' in Winter's Tale IV, iv, 86-103," SAB, XVIII (1943), 114-120.

Following the lead of Lovejoy and Boas (#2251), Wilson cites Democritus, Plato, Aristotle, Cicero, and Pindar to demonstrate "that the idea of 'art' as a part of cosmic nature or as made by nature was a commonplace in antiquity." He then cites numerous Renaissance precursors of Polixenes' thought in W.T. IV iv 89-97; it is impossible to attribute indebtedness among so many potential creditors.

2314. Wilson, Harold S. "Some Meanings of 'Nature' in Renaissance Literary Theory," JHI, II (1941), 430-448. GRS

Of the thirty-five distinguishable meanings of the term "Nature" in the Renaissance, Sh intends the ninth in W.T. IV iv where Polixenes and Perdita discuss Art and Nature: "That which appoints and controls the 'laws' of literary art (as of all else) according to its own purpose, process, or form." Plato's Laws 890D is "a possibly relevant background" for this concept.

2315. Wincor, Richard. "Shakespeare's Festival Plays," SQ, I (1950), 219-240.

This confident anthropological approach to the last plays reads them as rediscoveries by Sh of the death-and-resurrection themes of ancient fertility plays including such classical ritual as the marriage of Diana at Nemi (cf. Frazer's Golden Bough) and the revival of Proserpine. But Wincor suggests no direct connection with classical religion; the common source is the heritage of the race.

2316. Wolff, Samuel L. The Greek Romances in Elizabethan Prose Fiction, ColSCL (Col UP, 1912), 529 pp. E-S

Wolff indicates passim Sh's indirect debt to themes and plots of the Greek romances in Lear, A.Y.L., and Romeo. On pp. 448-458 he makes a detailed comparison of three versions of Longus' Daphnis and Chloe, Greene's Pandosto, and W.T.; the conclusion is that though Sh's major debt is to Greene, he may well also have consulted Angel Day's English trans. of Longus' tale.

2317. Wright, W. Aldis. "Shakspeare: 'Cymbeline,' V.v.447,448," 7 NQ, II (1886), 85.

Wright points out that Sh's derivation of mulier from mollis aer has a precedent in A World of Wonders... (1607). Earlier Lactantius had identified mollis and mulier and attributed the identification to Varro, but Wright does not know who first added aer. F. C. B. Terry indicates (ibid., IV [1887], 105) that Caxton in Game and Playe of the Chesse (1474) gives the same etymology as Sh.

THE POEMS AND SONNETS

2318. Allen, Don Cameron. "On Venus and Adonis," Wilson Festschrift, pp. 100-111.

With exhaustive documentation in classical and Medieval sources, Allen sets out to explain Sh's deviations from Ovid in Venus. His most interesting suggestions concern Adonis (whose chastity and love of the hunt are traceable to Hippolytus, not to Hermaphroditus), the horses (who are Plato's passionate steeds running away with man's chariot), and Wat the hare (who is a classical fertility symbol). The irony of Venus as huntress (in the soft hunt of love) hunting the hunter (who prefers the hard hunt of death) is the axis of the poem. Allen's is one of the more satisfying of recent interpretations.

2319. Alvarez, A. "William Shakespeare: The Phoenix and the Turtle," Interpretations: Essays on Twelve English Poems, ed. John Wain (Ln, 1955), pp. 1-16. GRS (Apparently first published in Mandrake, II [1955-56], 395-408.)

The explication makes only the briefest reference to the classics. "Property" (line 37) may be "taken to be one of the five Predicables of Aristotelian logic"; the poem is too weighty to celebrate "merely the usual courtly Platonic passion."

2320. Baldwin, T. W. On the Literary Genetics of Shakspere's Poems and Sonnets. Illinois UP, 1950, 399 pp.

This book is an extension of Baldwin's William Shakspere's Small Latine & Lesse Greeke (#0089), intended to analyze in detail Sh's debt to Ovid in the nondramatic verse. Chs. I-III, on Venus, show Ovidian influence and propose the thesis that the poem turns on the hinge of Venus' sermon on the carpe diem theme with Platonic (ultimately Hesiodic) overtones: chaos + beauty/love = order. Ch. IV is an attack on Ewig's evidence (#2338) that Sh used Livy direct in Lucr. Ch. V partly reverses IV as Baldwin gives his own evidence for Sh's direct use of Livy, though he emphasizes the magnitude of Sh's debt to the Fasti. The rhetorical embellishments of the poem (e.g., Tarquin's doubts, Lucrece's lamentations) are standard school exercises. Chs. VI-XV, on Sonn., are less satisfying. Baldwin wanders progressively further from consideration of Ovidian influence into exegetical paraphrase and involved arguments about sequentiality and relationship to certain early plays in the canon. This section relies rather too heavily on verbal echoes and makes the fallacious assumption that the more complex thought is always the later one. Some of the speculations (e.g., the identity of the Dark Lady) are unconvincing. Baldwin does, however, show the debt to Ovid, Horace, and (mediately) Plotinus. The most interesting observation on Sonn. is that Sh's four-part structure accurately reflects the Renaissance oration as based on Cicero and Quintilian. Ch. XVI traces the sources of Phoenix. The summary maintains that the poems exemplify "the fundamentals of composition as they were taught in [Sh's] day," that is, analysis and genesis through "imitative variation." Though this book is uneven, it is an important contribution to understanding the means by which Sh put his cultural heritage to artistic use.

2321. Baldwin, T. W. "Phoenixities," TLS, June 14, 1941, p. 287.

There is no evidence that Sh drew on

NOTE: Numbers preceded by # refer to entries in this Guide. Keys to abbreviations are found on pages xi-xvii and 381-387.

Holland's Pliny in Phoenix or elsewhere. The "ultimate and probably proximate chief source" is the "Incerti Auctori Phoenix" usually printed by Sh's contemporaries with Lactantius' works. Cf. On the Literary Genetics... (#2320) Ch. XVI. See also (#2323, #2371, #2374, #2392) for other points of view expressed in TLS that year.

2322. Bartlett, Phyllis. "Ovid's Banquet of Sense?" NQ, CXCVII (1952), 46-47.

Unable to find in any of Ovid's works a passage which could have elicited Chapman's poem, Professor Bartlett suggests that Chapman was criticizing Venus 427-450 for its pseudo-Ovidian sensuality. If so, we have an early instance of criticism (implicit, at least) of Sh's classicism.

2323. Benham, Gurney. "The Phoenix and the Turtle," TLS, July 19, 1941, p. 352; July 26, p. 364.

A critical exegesis of the poem with special emphasis on possible topical references. There are remarks on precedents in Lucretius, Pliny, and Hesiod for individual passages in the poem.

2324. Bensly, Edward. "'The Phoenix and the Turtle'," NQ, CL (1926), 412.

In response to a query from George MacNaughton (ibid., 330), Bensly points out that "sable gender" refers to the belief that crows "generated their young by means of their beaks." The reference is to Aristotle's De Generatione Animalium, where the belief is called ludicrous and to Pliny's Naturalis Historia. Sh need not have consulted these loci: the belief was common knowledge in his time.

2325. Borinski, Ludwig. "The Origin of the Euphuistic Novel and Its Significance for Shakespeare," Baldwin Festschrift, pp. 38-52.

"Apart from the Latin classics we may distinguish four literary traditions which became important in Shakespeare's development: Senecan tragedy, the tradition of the Fall of Princes, the euphuistic novel, and the Arcadian novel with its background of Greek romance. Clearly the euphuistic novel is the most important of all four." The source of euphuism is not Lyly, but Pettie, who derived it partly from Aeneas Sylvius, partly from the débat tradition of Medieval literature, and partly from the rhetoric of Seneca. (Borinski does not discuss Isocrates' possible influence.) The significance for Sh is apparent especially in Venus and Lucr., the two most euphuistic of his works.

2326. Brown, Carleton. "Shakespeare and the Horse," 3 Library, III (1912), 152-180. E-S

Tracing descriptions of the good points of horses as far back as Xenophon, Brown cites nearly a dozen such catalogues in classical times and a great many more in the Middle Ages and sixteenth century. The probability appears to be that for Venus 271-300 Sh drew on Blundeville's "Arte of Ryding," which is in this long tradition, and that he supplemented it from Virgil's Georgics, perhaps in Googe's trans. Brown is aware of the alternative hypothesis that Sh picked up his information in the Stratford market place, but feels confident that there is a literary basis for the description. A learned and convincing study.

2327. Bush, Douglas. "Shakespeare: Venus and Adonis and The Rape of Lucrece," Mythology and the Renaissance Tradition in English Poetry (Minnesota UP, 1932; reprinted by Pantheon, 1957; revised ed., 1964), Ch. VII, pp. 139-155. E-S SG

Reading both Venus and Lucr. as conventional "literary exercises," Bush emphasizes that in both passion is defeated by rhetoric, which "is like that of Senecan declamation, like an explosion in a vacuum." There are some Ovidian elements (e.g., balance and paradoxical antithesis) in both poems, but on the whole they are less classical than Medieval and Elizabethan. Bush's footnotes constitute an informed survey and appraisal of opinion on Sh's sources for the epyllia; his own opinion is that both poems are tissues of commonplaces: Sh's "way was to accept the current fashion and excel in it." The critical consensus of the past twenty-five years accords the poems a higher place than Bush will grant them.

2328. Cantelupe, Eugene Benjamin. "Representations of Venus in Italian Renaissance Painting and English Renaissance Poetry," diss (Washington [St. Louis], 1959). DA, XX (1960), 3724-25.

Drawing on the iconographic tradition in representing classical mythology, Cantelupe interprets Venus as "an original Ovidian tragicomedy," Sh's departure from the usual portrayal of the myth of Venus and Adonis in the sixteenth century.

2329. Clark, Donald L. "Ancient Rhetoric and English Renaissance Literature," SQ, II (1951), 195-204.

A general, but informative address. Sh is represented by Lucr., Venus, Sonn., and Merch., all of which are briefly related to the rhetorical tradition.

2330. Colvin, Sidney. "The Sack of Troy in Shakespeare's 'Lucrece' and in some Fifteenth-Century Drawings and Tapestries," Homage, pp. 88-99. E-S SG

Sh's vivid picture of the fall of Troy in the tapestry which Lucrece gazes on (Lucr., 1366-1456) is not Homeric, but an accurate reflection of fifteenth-century tapestries which were based on Dares and Dictys. Sh probably is remembering such an arras in this passage. Colvin provides three excellent plates to illustrate his point.

2331. Cummings, Laurence A. "The Purpose and Style of The Rape of Lucrese [sic]," ShN, III (1953), 37.

A précis of a paper read at the Rocky Mountain MLA meeting (1953). Cummings discussed Sh's use of rhetoric, particularly the oration, and his identification of Lucrece with Troy and Tarquin with the Greeks, specifically Sinon.

2332. Cunningham, J[ames] V. "'Essence' and the Phoenix and Turtle," ELH, XIX (1952), 265-276.

According to Cunningham's belief, the source of the mystery in the poem is not Neoplatonic but Scholastic--the doctrine of the Trinity. Cf. T. W. Baldwin, #2320, Ch. XVI.

2333. D., A. "Shakespeare's Sonnets," NQ, CXCVI (1951), 5-6.

The second of two notes adds Sonn. 104 to T. W. Baldwin's list (#0089) of Shn echoes of a sundial passage in Lily's Grammar.

2334. Davenport, A. "Weever, Ovid and Shakespeare," NQ, CXCIV (1949), 524-525.

Davenport finds significant previously unnoticed parallels between Ovid's Meta. XIV and both Venus and Dream. His evidence that Sh used the original as well as Golding is convincing.

2335. Davidson, Thomas. "Aeschylus and Shakespeare," Shna, V (1888), 356-357.

The last two lines of Sonn. 87 Davidson regards as a borrowing from Aeschylus' Agamemnon. He also cites an analogue from the Iliad, but deceptive dreams and morning disillusionment are surely common to all men.

2336. Dunn, Esther C. "Poetry in the Nineties: 1. Narrative Poetry: Marlowe, Daniel and Shakespeare, with Special Attention to Shakespeare," The Literature of Shakespeare's England (N.Y., 1936), pp. 36-64.

Among the most interesting suggestions: (1) Venus is post-Ovidian in that it shows indebtedness to "the insipid prettiness of Sicilian shepherdesses on the flowery hillsides of late Greek pastoral; the rhetorical trifles of the Greek Anthology; the oratory of Seneca's plays" among other things. (2) "It is useful to think of [Lucr.] as a narrative poem, very closely approaching the form of the dramatic poems which Seneca, nearly sixteen centuries earlier, had the temerity to call plays, when they were declaimed for his master, Nero."

2337. Elmen, Paul. "Shakespeare's Gentle Hours," SQ, IV (1953), 301-309.

The "howers" of line 1 of Sonn. 5 are both units of passing time and the Horae of classical mythology. Seen with this double meaning, the poem takes on a special richness. Elmen discusses the Horae and their history and function at some length, pointing out that the NED is incorrect in assigning first reference to them to Milton. He gives references in Golding's Ovid, Spenser's Epithalamium and FQ among the more accessible sources. Elmen digresses to speculate whether Sh attended a stage in the Queen's progress at Elvetham in 1591, where he might have seen the Horae represented. But his reading of Sonn. 5 is plausible and attractive.

2338. Ewig, Wilhelm. "Shakespeare's 'Lucrece': Eine litterarhistorische Untersuchung," Anglia, XXII (1899), 1-32, 343-363, 393-455. E-S

In Part I Ewig offers evidence for Sh's use of Livy's account of the rape and suicide of Lucrece either in the original or in Painter's virtual trans. He then shows that Sh also knew the story in Ovid's Fasti and in Chaucer's LGW. All other versions (of which he discusses several) Ewig regards as doubtful sources at best. Ewig's thesis basically is sound; it has, however, been modified by Baldwin (#2320, Ch.

IV), who shows that Sh probably derived some of the Livian material from Marsus' annotated ed. of Ovid's Fasti, a standard text in Sh's day. Sh could also have picked up hints from Dionysius of Halicarnassus in Marsus' notes. Parts II and III of Ewig's art. show how Sh built on the Livian and Ovidian foundation by inventing details to lend verisimilitude and by elaborating the plot and characterization rhetorically. The rhetoric in the poem is (some of it) classical. A valuable art.

2339. Fairchild, Arthur H. R. "The Phoenix and Turtle: A Critical and Historical Interpretation," ESn, XXXIII (1904), 337-384.

Fairchild argues for Medieval and Renaissance sources for Phoenix (The Parlement of Foules and Latin emblem literature), but he also makes several references to classical bird lore as a part of the tradition behind the poem. Lucretius on the long life of crows, Ovid on owls (Sh seems to have drawn on Ovid directly), and Plato, Aristotle, Euripides, Cicero, and Ovid on swans are among the authorities. Fairchild argues convincingly that the poem is conventional, and should not be racked for topical allusions.

2340. Furness, Horace H. "The Meaning of 'Talents' in 'A Lover's Complaint'," PL, III (1891), 196-201.

After a survey of proposed interpretations, Furness settles on the Latin root and reads line 204 as "And, lo, behold these weights (of money; ergo "wealths") of their hair."

2341. Galinsky, Hans. Der Lucretia-Stoff in der Weltliteratur, SKGV, III (1932), 235 pp. E-S

In his discussion of Lucr. (pp. 91-101), Galinsky states that Sh certainly used Livy and very probably used Ovid's Fasti. But Sh's poem is colored also by Medieval chivalric ethics and by the Renaissance glorification of the beautiful, chaste woman. Platonic concepts of the relation between love and the soul also inform the poem. Galinsky sees unmerited sorrow and mutability as Sh's two dominant motifs. Though Sh keeps a delicate balance between tragedy and comedy, his basic intent is serious: "Nie wieder wird der Lucretia-Stoff Gefäss für tiefere menschliche Erlebnisse."

2342. Gundolf, Friedrich. "[Sh's Venus and Lucr.]," Shakespeare: Sein Wesen und Werk (Berlin, 1928), I, pp. 175-180. (As trans. and abstracted in the New Variorum Poems.)

Gundolf offers the interesting hypothesis that Venus and Lucr. are a transition between the earliest Sonn. and Romeo, between lyric and drama. What is stated emotion in Sonn. is personified emotion in Venus, Lucrece, Tarquin, and Adonis, and finally becomes "finished human beings" in Romeo, Meas., and Macb. (all of which echo themes, characters, and emotions from the two epyllia). An unusual approach to Sh's artistic development; Gundolf does not relate the two poems to the classical mythology and legend on which they are based --he might have reinforced his argument about characterization in Venus and Lucr. by referring to techniques of characterization in Ovid and Livy.

2343. Harrison, John S. Platonism in English Poetry of the Sixteenth and Seventeenth Centuries. Col UP, 1903, 235 pp. E-S

Sh's only appearance here is in brief illustrations from Sonn. (pp. 128-129, 134-135) of the use of the concept of Ideal Beauty. Harrison ignores whatever Platonic basis Sh may have had for the tension between love and friendship in Sonn.

2344. Hatto, A. T. "'Venus and Adonis'--and the Boar," MLR, XLI (1946), 353-361.

"Despite the classical theme of Venus and Adonis and its elusive Italian inspiration I discern it through a faint lingering mist of medieval courtliness," an aspect of which is the symbol of the noble boar supreme in his sexual prowess. Hatto cites Gottfried von Strassbourg, Boccaccio, and Chaucer to show that the boar was traditionally a symbol for a triumphant rival in love, who made the frustrated suitor jealous. Sh uses the symbol in this sense when Posthumus calls Iachimo "a full-acorn'd boar" in Cym. Thus, Venus is jealous of the boar's ability to attract Adonis. The fact that a similar sexual suggestion inheres in the pseudo-Theocritean Idyl on Adonis and the boar would suggest the probability of polygenesis (see "Introduction," supra, p. 13). This is a rewarding essay.

2345. Hegedüs, Stephen v. "Die griechische Quelle zu Shakespeares zwei letzten Sonetten," UngR, II (1913), 586-596. SG

Hegedüs proposes a number of paths by which the conceit in Marianus' epigram (Palatine Anthology IX 637) could have reached Sh. One suggestion is that Sh drew on Ovid's earlier tale of Arethusa and Alpheus (Meta. V) in which love and a spring are also identified. Another is that Sh saw some graphic representation of Marianus' demi-myth. A third is that he found access to a Latin version (on this point see #2350). But the difficulty with these alternatives is that Sh's two Sonn. are closer to the Greek version than to the putative intermediaries. Hegedüs is not convincing when he asserts that Sh's creative talent somehow reached back to Marianus' conceit through hints in the intermediaries. DLC

2346. Hertzberg, W. "Eine griechische Quelle zu Shakespeare's Sonetten," ShJ, XIII (1878), 158-162. E-S HB

In searching for a classical source for a passage in Herder about sleeping Cupid, Hertzberg discovered in the Palatine Anthology (IX, 637) an epideictic poem by Marianus (5th century A.D.) of which Sonn. 153 and 154 are a very close rendering. Sh obviously did not know the Greek original (cf. Ne Quid Nimis, #2370), but could have had easy access to Latin extracts (e.g., Selecta Epigrammata, Basel, 1529) of which eight Continental eds. were issued before the end of the sixteenth century. "Eine und die andre derselben wird schon den Weg nach England gefunden haben."

2347. Hubler, Edward. The Sense of Shakespeare's Sonnets, PSE, No. 33 (PUP, 1952), 169 pp. GRS

Like Diotima in the Symposium, Sh believed that love reveres not only beauty, but creativity, because creativity makes immortality possible. The concept appears in Sh's Sonn. urging the young man to marry, but Sh need not have read the Neoplatonists: "he could have picked up his ideas on propagation anywhere." Hubler is not primarily concerned with classical analogues to Sonn., but he makes several similar observations in passing: e.g., like Socrates in the Lysis, Sh had a passion for friendship; those anti-Stratfordians who argue that Sh could not have known what his works imply might remember that Terence was absolved by many in Sh's own age of having written the comedies--and on exactly the same ground; Sonn. 9 echoes the Narcissus myth.

2348. Hubler, Edward. "Three Shakespearean Myths: Mutability, Plenitude, and Reputation," EIE, 1948 (Col UP, 1949), 95-119.

The philosophical basis of Sh's first seventeen Sonn., with their emphasis on procreation as an obligation, can be found in Plato's Timaeus. From the Symposium (mediately) comes Sh's related attitude toward reputation. Hubler is among the few scholars who have recognized the classical precedents for themes in Sh's Sonn.

2349. Hunter, G. K. "A Source for Shakespeare's 'Lucrece'?" NQ, CXCVII (1952), 46.

Everything scholars say Sh got from Livy in Lucr. he could as well have found in Barnaby Googe's The Prouerbes of the noble and woorthy souldier Sir John Lopez de Mendoza... which recounts the Lucrece story with the detail of transporting Lucrece's body to Rome for public display after her death, a detail which appears in none of Sh's putative sources (though LGW 1866-67 does speak of a public display of her body). Hunter recognizes the possibility that Sh needed no source at all for such a dramatically effective detail as the solemn procession from Collatium to Rome; he has certainly not disposed of the probability that Sh drew on Livy and Chaucer.

2350. Hutton, James. "Analogues of Shakespeare's Sonnets 153-54: Contributions to the History of a Theme," MP, XXXVIII (1941), 385-403.

With enviable erudition and his characteristic thoroughness, Hutton examines the fourteen analogues he has discovered of Sh's two versions of an epigram by Marianus in the Greek Anthology. He shows that Hertzberg (#2346) was entirely wrong about the accessibility to Sh of this epigram in a Latin trans., and then proceeds to an exhaustive comparative study in the Renaissance treatment of the theme (French, Italian, German, neo-Latin, English). He points to two interlocking traditions and shows that Sh's immediate source has not been found, but holds out definite hope that it can be. Not the least important contribution here is the light Hutton throws on Sh's creative process: he makes a minute comparison of the two Sonn. with each other and with their possible sources. This art. is everything good scholarship should be.

2351. Hynes, Sam. "The Rape of Tarquin," SQ, X (1959), 451-453.

Sh's metaphorical identification of the sack of Troy with Lucrece's violation by Tarquin is reversed in the poem when the siege imagery is applied to Tarquin's soul after the lustful act, though his citadel is destroyed from within, not from without as Lucrece's was. Yet Sh speaks of Tarquin's shameful burden as Lucrece speaks of hers. The spiritual conflict in Lucr. suggests that Sh was foreshadowing the moral concerns of the great tragedies. Hynes was anticipated by the very similar thought of Christopher Devlin in The Month (n.s. IV [1950], 169-180). In an art. on "Robert Southwell and Contemporary Poets--I," Devlin speaks of Tarquin as raping his own soul and suggests "that Shakespeare, piqued by Southwell's example [in St. Peter's Complaint], had tried his hand at tapping a loftier [than Venus] and more metaphysical vein" which led him on to the spiritual conflicts in the great tragedies.

2352. Jackson, Robert Sumner. "Narrative and Imagery in Shakespeare's Venus and Adonis," PMA, XLIII (1958), 315-320.

An attempt to extend the conclusions of H. T. Price (#2376) by taking into consideration the characters of the central action. The polarity of the images in the poem reflects not only "nature with herself at strife" but also the conflict between nature and supernature--between man and god. The theme is not a simple one, however, for Venus has human passions while Adonis is godlike; thus the conflict takes place within the characters as well as between them. Jackson does not discuss the ancient basis of his interpretation, except to trace "Adonis" to Hebrew, where it means "the Lord."

2353. Johnson, Skuli. "The Poetry of Ovid," MAR, IV (1945), 12-23.

"His share in the shaping of the mind and art of Milton and of Shakespeare should in itself secure for Ovid permanence of fame." The formative influence of the Meta. is not discussed; Johnson makes two comments on the Fasti: (1) Sh used it directly in Lucr.; (2) its tale of the rape of Proserpine bears close comparison with W.T. IV iv. MnU

2354. Kuhl, E. P. "Shakespeare's 'Rape of Lucrece'," PQ, XX (1941), 352-360. (Also in Craig Festschrift, pp. 160-168.)

Kuhl shows that the political implications of the legend were considered important in the Renaissance; they were drawn from Ovid, Livy, and Cicero. Sh follows tradition by emphasizing the public consequences of Tarquin's crime. This is a worthy piece of historical criticism.

2355. Lee, Sidney. "Ovid and Shakespeare's Sonnets," QR, CCX (1909), 455-476. (Reprinted in Elizabethan and Other Essays [1929]. E-S HB SG)

The essentially pagan cosmic concern of many of Sh's Sonn. is traceable to Book XV of the Meta., where Ovid expresses the Neopythagorean doctrines (especially the concept of time as a cyclic process) which are the basis of Sh's thought. Sh also learned from Ovid's fifteenth book the conceit of immortality through verse and a vivid conception of the maturation process in man. All of these concepts were to be found in FQ and the sonneteers, but Lee shows that Ovid is at least a major source by indicating some striking parallels of phrase between Sonn. and Golding's trans. of Book XV. This is one of the most important studies of the sources of Sh's Sonn.; it has not been given sufficient attention by recent scholarship.

2356. Lee, Sidney. "Shakespeare and the Italian Renaissance" (1915), PBA, [VII] (1915-1916), 121-143 (Annual British Academy Shakespeare Lecture).

Lee, who emphasizes the Greek roots of Italian Renaissance literature, regards Italian culture as one route by which Sh acquired his classicism. Lee's most important example is the Platonism of Sonn. The references to his friend's beauty as a "shadow" show that Sh knew the Platonic belief that the phenomenal world is only a reflection of ideal reality; Bruno uses the word "umbra" for the same concept. Sonn. also contain the Platonic equation of Truth and Beauty. Again, in Merch. V i, "the mythological reminiscences, the praise of music, the neo-Platonic and pseudo-scientific theory of the spheres, are all Italian or Greco-Italian echoes." This is an interesting essay.

2357. Leishman, J. B. "Variations on a Theme in Shakespeare's Sonnets," Wilson Festschrift, pp. 112-149.

"Shakespeare's sonnets ... are filled with a sadness ... resembling that which breathes from so much of the great poetry of the ancient world: an almost overwhelming sadness at the fact of human transience." But like the ancient poets, Pindar, Ovid, and Horace, Sh dwelt on the "topic of poetry as the Defier of Time," and with Horace, he is the greatest who ever did so. There are differences: e.g., Horace's poetry is "outward," celebrating public greatness; Sh's is "inward," expressing private feelings. But the "great triad" (vii, viii, ix) of odes in Book IV is brother to the two pairs of Sonn., 64-65, 73-74. Leishman's thematic analysis continues with a treatment of Petrarch, Tasso, and Ronsard, ending with a brief commentary on the lesser capabilities of Elizabethan poets, at all points drawing analogies to Sh. This essay is as valuable for its sensitive criticism as for its extensive information.

2358. Lever, J. W. "Chapman and Shakespeare," NQ, CCIII (1958), 99-100.

The prefatory verses to Chapman's Homer very closely resemble Sonn. 55 ("Not Marble nor the Gilded Monuments"). The ultimate source of both poems is Horace Odes III xxx and/or Ovid Meta. XV. The probability is that Chapman drew on Sh.

2359. Lever, J. W. "Shakespeare," The Elizabethan Love Sonnet (Ln, 1956), pp. 162-272.

Lever's analysis of the Shn sequence wisely avoids speculation on the identities of the characters or the realities of the passions and concentrates fruitfully on the cultural background of the poems. Typical is the tracing of the emphasis on fertility in copulation to Erasmus' praise of natural sexual relations at the price of virginity in De Conscribendis Epistolis, which Sh may have found in Wilson's Arte of Rhetorique. Again, though Sh had said in L.L.L. that he preferred Ovid (i.e. romance) to sonnets, after writing Venus and Lucr. he returned to the sonnet form, ironically enough drawing on another aspect of Ovid, the Neopythagorean philosophy of time. (On this point Lever does not acknowledge the scholarship of Lee, #2355.) When Sh came to borrow the Ovidian/Horatian boast that poetry confers immortality, he altered it: Sh maintains that his verse confers immortality on the theme, not on the poet. Lever finds the Platonic influence superficial. Such concepts as identity, idealism, friendship as opposed to heterosexuality, etc., are a mere gloss on a surface substantially Ovidian. The findings of L. J. Mills (#0423) should modify Lever's stand on Platonism, but Lever's is nonetheless a rewarding study.

2360. Lewis, C. S. English Literature in the Sixteenth Century Excluding Drama. OUP, 1954, 696 pp.

The passage on Sh's poems and Sonn. (498-509) is not primarily concerned with their genetics or their affinity for classical culture. But Lewis points to the differences between Sh's Venus and the Aphrodite of Greece and to the fact that Lucr. is twelve times as long as the passage in the Fasti on which it is based. There are also some brief remarks on rhetoric as a structural device in Sonn.

2361. Loane, G. G. "Notes on Shakespeare's Poems: New Variorum Edition," NQ, CLXXVIII (1940), 188-189.

One of the notes asks whether Lucr. line 1612, "Begins the sad dirge of her certain ending," may not echo the "certa mori" with which Virgil characterizes Dido.

2362. Marschall, Wilhelm. "Das 'Argument' zu Shakespeares 'Lucrece'," Anglia, LIII (1929), 102-122. E-S SG

The "Argument" condenses the prolix Bandello and the already terse Livy into a straitened prose which Marschall regards as a significant passage in which to study Sh's art. He makes a phrase-by-phrase comparison between the "Argument" and these putative sources; he finds that Ovid's Fasti had little to contribute to the "Argument," though it provided the germs for Tarquin's lustful thoughts and for his praise of Collatine (106-112) in the poem itself. Marschall also searches for traces of the vocabulary of the "Argument" in the poem. He would entertain the possibility that inconsistency in naming characters (Lucrece, Lucretia; Collatine, Collatinus) indicates interpolation in the poem.

2363. Marschall, Wilhelm. "Das Troja-Gemälde in Shakespeares 'Lucrece'," Anglia, LIV (1930), 83-96. E-S

Marschall argues that the mural of Troy which Lucrece gazes at is an idealized picture, showing (despite the detail with which it is described) that Sh had only an amateur's knowledge of painting. The digression Marschall believes is modeled on Virgil's account of sorrowing Aeneas who gazes at the Trojan story on the wall of the temple in Carthage (Book I) and later tells Dido of the fall of Troy (Book II). Sh need not have read Virgil as he worked on Lucr.: Titus V iii 80-87 shows that Sh remembered Book II of the Aeneid from his schooldays.

2364. Mauntz, Alfred von. "Leuchtfeuer oder Irrlichter? Der Phönix und Turteltaube,"

Heraldik in Diensten der Shakespeare-Forschung (Berlin, 1903), pp. 163-311.

Mauntz is primarily concerned with heraldry as a clue to possible topicalities in Phoenix, but he briefly discusses the phoenix legend as it appears in Hesiod, Plutarch, Herodotus, and Philostratus (pp. 184-185). Sh's response is, he believes, to the Hebrew-Christian tradition in which the phoenix is an emblem for immortality and enduring truth. DFo

2365. Miller, Paul W. "The Elizabethan Minor Epic," SP, LV (1958), 31-38. GRS

Miller argues persuasively that Elizabethan "Ovidian" narratives were not just reflections of Roman poetry in general, but intentional imitations of the erotic epyllion which originated with Theocritus, Callimachus, Moschus, and the Alexandrians. Ovid represents the high water mark of the form in antiquity; its Elizabethan revival had a brief floruit (the conventions rose to popularity in 1589 and fell into decadence by 1602). Chief features of the classical genre are digression (often the digression is more significant than the main narrative), erotic love, rhetorical set speeches (the Elizabethans made much of this feature), and brevity (Elizabethan fondness for elaboration makes the average Renaissance epyllion far longer than its Alexandrian counterpart). Venus stands with Hero and Leander as the greatest English achievement in the form; Lucr. is an adaptation, combining the epyllion with the complaint. Miller's analysis focuses on Hero and Leander; Sh's poems are referred to only briefly.

2366. Miller, Robert P. "The Double Hunt of Love: A Study of Shakespeare's Venus and Adonis as a Christian Mythological Narrative," diss (Princeton, 1954). DA, XIV (1954), 2338.

Miller reads the poem as an allegory in which Christian positions on the relationship of flesh to spirit are conveyed under the "emblem" of Ovid's tale in Meta. X. Sh is orthodox (by Renaissance standards) in moralizing Ovid, and in expressing "ironic amusement at human aberration."

2367. Miller, Robert P. "The Myth of Mars's Hot Minion in Venus and Adonis," ELH, XXVI (1959), 470-481.

Miller maintains that readers who think of Venus as a tale without moral basis miss its delightful irony. In lines 97-114, where Venus speaks of Mars's submission to her wiles, the irony depends on our recognition of the moralized mythology in the Renaissance tradition. Mars (Virtus, manliness, rationality) is enslaved (in Vulcan's net, which Venus characteristically neglects to mention) by Venus (voluptas, effeminacy, sensuality). Venus' code of values makes this moral slavery a desideratum: therein lies the paradoxical wit of Sh. Miller exhaustively documents the allegorical interpretation of the myth in late classical, Medieval, and Renaissance sources. This is an enlightening essay.

2368. Miller, Robert P. "Venus, Adonis, and the Horses," ELH, XIX (1952), 249-264.

The digression on the courser and the jennet, Sh's only extended interpolation in Ovid's story, is a "conditional parallel" to the main action and contains the key to Sh's meaning in the poem as a whole. The horses, who are traditional symbols of lust, court in the romantic tradition, but Sh's imagery ironically portrays this tradition as a thin veil cast over lechery. The courser is Plato's horse deprived of reins and rider (reason) and ergo the follower of his passions. An effective coherent argument, which makes Sh an exponent of orthodox Renaissance morality.

2369. Muir, Kenneth. "Shakespeare and Erasmus," NQ, CCI (1956), 424-425.

Muir extends slightly a suggestion made by T. W. Baldwin (#2320, pp. 134-136) that Erasmus is the connecting link between passages on avarice in Horace and St. Luke which are combined in Lucr., 855-861.

2370. Ne Quid Nimis. "[Shakespeare and Cicero]," 9 NQ, VI (1900), 317.

This note suggests that since Sonn. 154 is a version of a poem in the Greek Anthology, Sh could read Greek fluently. Some modern critics (e.g., T. W. Baldwin, #2320) dispose of the problem by ostracizing 153 and 154 from the Sh canon, while others (e.g., Hutton, #2350) have shown that Sh had other means of access to the material in the two Sonn.

2371. Newdigate, B. H. "'The Phoenix and the Turtle'," NQ, CLXXIX (1940), 459.

In response to a query from W. P. D. about Sh's access to Pliny's Naturalis Historia and his use of the work in Phoenix, Newdigate supplies a brief discussion of Philemon Holland's 1601 trans. and of a Pliny passage on ravens which Sh may have used. His discussion is supplemented by G. Catalani (ibid., 459-460) and W. Jaggard (460). R. L. Eagle maintains (ibid., CLXXX [1941], 51) that Sh used the original: he hears an echo of Pliny's Latin in R.II.

2372. Oppel, Horst. "Das Bild des Brennenden Troja in Shakespeares 'Rape of Lucrece'," ShJ, LXXXVII/LXXXVIII (1951/1952), 69-86.

The bulk of the essay concerns Sh's understanding of and attitude toward painting in his description of Lucrece's mural. But Oppel observes that the passage appears based on Virgil, whose description of Troy in ruins became popular in England after the publication of Surrey's Aeneid. Oppel also comments on the Ovidian background of the poem as a whole, on the Trojan digression as a quiet space before the catastrophe, and on Sh's departure from Renaissance conventions in making the conflict between characters a central feature of the poem.

2373. Peterson, Douglas L. "A Probable Source for Shakespeare's Sonnet cxxix," SQ, V (1954), 381-384.

Peterson suggests that because the theme of "enslavement of reason and will by lust" has been a commonplace since St. Augustine, it is impossible to trace the ideas in the poem to any single source; but conceived as a literary exercise in which Sh sought "to adapt a theme to a given rhetorical scheme," the Sonn. can be shown to exemplify the rhetorical principles discussed by Wilson in Book III of his Arte of Rhetorique. The relationship is not so patent as to be unmistakable, but the argument is reinforced when Peterson shows that an epigram of Petronius on carnal pleasure may have reached Sh through Wilson.

2374. "Phoenixities," TLS, April 26, 1941, p. 203.

This is the editor's reaction to an art. by Osbert Sitwell, ibid., suggesting Marco Polo as the source of "the sole Arabian tree" of Phoenix. The editor believes that Pliny is a more probable source of this reference to the phoenix and of the one in Temp. T. W. Baldwin (#2321) attacks the editor's position. The editor takes up the cudgels again July 19, p. 347, and Sitwell re-enters the controversy July 26, p. 359. See also Margaret Cooper, May 24, 1941, p. 251.

2375. Pooler, C[harles] Knox. "Introduction," Shakespeare's Poems (1911/1927), ArdenSh, pp. vii-xciii.

"Classical literature ... seems to have affected Shakespeare much as it affected Keats, not as it affected, for example, Ben Jonson. It was an influence on the subject rather than on the style and treatment." Sh's plot for Venus is Ovidian (probably from Golding's trans. of the stories of Venus and Adonis and Salmacis and Hermaphroditus), but his setting is English. Pooler denies that Italianate classicism, "allegorical and fantastic," exerted an influence on the poem; he does provide a list of Latin, Italian, French, Spanish, and English predecessors of Venus. Pooler makes an acute distinction among the tones and emphases of the Lucrece stories in Ovid's Fasti, Chaucer's LGW, and Sh's poem: Ovid is far more political than either Chaucer or Sh. Sh almost certainly used Livy in addition to Ovid; he probably did not know Dio Cassius, Dionysius of Halicarnassus, Valerius Maximus, Zonaras, or Diodorus Siculus. He may, however, have known Chaucer and/or Gower, as well as Painter. Virgil may have provided the inspiration for the tapestry of Troy. Sh "probably had more than enough" Latin to read Livy and the Fasti, neither trans. in his time (unless one considers Painter Livy's translator). Of the poems with classical antecedents in Pass. Pil., all are either uncanonical or of doubtful authorship; the discussions are informed. Pooler mentions Pliny and Lactantius, ancient authorities on the phoenix bird, as background to Sh's Phoenix.

2376. Price, Hereward T. "Function of Imagery in Venus and Adonis," PMA, XXXI (1945), 275-297.

Venus, like its contemporaries, 2,3H.VI, Romeo, and Lucr., treats of "something exquisite destroyed by what is vile." The imagery, of nature at strife with itself, is consistent throughout the poem. "Whether by accident or design, Venus and Adonis resembles no poem so closely as it does the [Adonis] elegy of Bion." (On this point cf. Jiriczek, #2444.) Like Bion's, Sh's poem is not about Venus and her lover, but about "a process of nature." Sh also took many details from Ovid, but added much of his own. The result is the most pagan of Sh's works. This paper is characteristic of Price's criticism; it combines excellent critical judgment with thorough exploration of the background of the problem.

2377. Prince, F. T. "Introduction," The Poems (1960), ArdenSh, pp. xi-xlvi.

Prince relegates the sources and Sh's response to them to footnotes; he defers to Bullough (#2414) for Venus and Lucr. and mentions Baldwin's argument (#2320) that Ovid's Amores was the source of Phoenix mainly to question its validity. The criticism is not as illuminating in this ed. as in most of the other recent Arden vols. Prince sees Venus as a slightly blemished success and Lucr. as a failure relieved by a few good touches.

2378. Putney, Rufus. "Venus Agonistes," ColoradoSLL, No. 4 (1953), pp. 52-66.

An argument that Venus is Sh's first comic character, made laughable, but not unlovable, by the extremes of her unsuccessful attempt to seduce a mere mortal. Adonis, too, is comic with his protestations of youth and his sullen recalcitrance. Putney's reasoning is acceptable until we encounter Adonis' sermon on lust and love which one surely cannot discount as burlesque of pulpit mannerisms; Putney does not escape this one snare. Otherwise his argument has the attraction of making merits of the "defects" which many critics have exposed in the poem.

2379. Putney, Rufus. "Venus and Adonis: Amour with Humor," PQ, XX (1941), 533-548.

To substantiate his argument that Sh intended as comedy the rhetorical exaggerations which have irritated the critics of Venus, Putney examines numerous similar Ovidian narrative poems of the period. "[Sh] changed Ovid's legend, and his alterations are essentially comic." Putney's interpretation makes the poem inconsequential, "but it is far better to possess a flawless trifle than a superannuated failure." See the reservation made about Putney's similar argument in #2378.

2380. Reardon, James P. "Shakespeare's 'Venus and Adonis,' and Lodge's 'Scilla's Metamorphosis'," SSP, III [XXXVI of the continuous series] (1847), 143-146.

Reardon points to the similarities between the two epyllia: i.e., the stanzaic form, the subject of attempted seduction and metamorphosis, and the references to dying Adonis and Venus' grief in Lodge's poem. He assumes that Venus antedates 1589 and that it influenced Lodge when he saw it in manuscript. It is now generally agreed that the influence worked the other way, Sh being Lodge's debtor (for the formal elements of the poem if not for the story of Adonis).

2381. Remarks on the Sonnets of Shakespeare, with the Sonnets, showing that they belong to the Hermetic Class of writings and explaining their general meaning and purpose. By the author of "Remark's on Alchemy". N.Y., 1865, 286 pp.

Not seen.

2382. Rollins, Hyder. "[On the Sources of Sonnets 153 and 154]," New Variorum Sonn. I, pp. 392-394.

Rollins here summarizes the involved and often erroneous statements of a long succession of scholars about the possible relationships between these two Sonn. and the Greek and Latin Anthologies. A useful survey, sound in its criticism of the authorities.

2383. Rollins, Hyder. "The Sources [of Venus and Lucr.]," New Variorum Poems, pp. 390-405; 416-439.

Like Rollins' précis of opinion on the antecedents of Sonn. (#2382), these two summaries are excellent. It is noteworthy that Rollins relies heavily on eds. (especially of Venus); the paucity of books and arts. in the field is obvious. Rollins' critical observations are especially worth reading. Appended to the surveys of scholarship are excerpts from Golding's Meta., FQ III, Livy, Ovid's Fasti, LGW, and The Palace of Pleasure.

2384. Sachs, [no Christian name given]. "Shakespeare's Gedichte," ShJ, XXV (1890), 132-184.

A most informative guide, summarizing both known facts and received opinion (and sometimes rejected opinion) on matters of interpretation, sources, aesthetic criticism, etc. Sections on Venus, Lucr., Sonn., Lov. Com., Pass. Pil., Phoenix, apocryphal poems. Typical are the useful list of classical authorities on the phoenix and Sachs's transmission of a suggestion that Lov. Com. is reminiscent of the Heroides—leaving aside Ovid's epistolary form.

2385. Sidgwick, Arthur H. The Influence of Greek Philosophy on English Poetry: The Chancellor's Essay, 1906. Oxford: Blackwell, 1906, 30 pp.

Ch. III treats the period 1500-1660. Sidgwick labels allusions to classical philosophy in such Renaissance plays as Faustus and Merch. (Portia's Stoic mercy speech and the music of the spheres) "dead shoots grafted on to a living stem." What is truly Greek about the Elizabethan drama is its unconsciousness of any distinction between reality and the ideal. But in Sonn. Sh is a formal Platonist of the Italian school which elevated Eros into the binding force in the universe; indeed, "the most successful answer to the vexed question of their [Sonn.'s] order is that which exhibits them as a systematic exposition of Platonism —the six ascending stages of ideal love, and the six descending stages of vulgar love." A general, but provocative essay. MH

2386. Siegel, Paul N. "The Petrarchan Sonneteers and Neo-Platonic Love," SP, XLII (1945), 164-182. GRS

In a terminal footnote, Siegel remarks that Sonn. are neither in the courtly tradition of pleasurable lust nor in the Neoplatonic tradition of spiritual love which anticipates marriage. In the later Sonn. Sh expresses a "feeling of disillusionment with Platonic ideals" as he conveys "a tragic awareness of the power of lust."

2387. Spencer, Hazelton. "Shakespeare's Use of Golding in Venus and Adonis," MLN, XLIV (1929), 435-437. E-S HB SG

Spencer criticizes Max Dürnhöfer (Shakespeares "Venus and Adonis" im Verhältnis zu Ovids Metamorphosen und Constables Schäfergesang. Halle, 1890—not seen) for two unscholarly blunders in transcription which, together with some weak verbal parallels, persuaded him that Sh used only the Latin Meta. in writing Venus. Spencer demonstrates the probability that Sh used the Golding trans., but he suggests that Sh's imagery is his own contribution to the poem. See also #2334.

2388. Starnes, D[eWitt] T. "Shakespeare's Sonnet 60: Analogues," NQ, CXCIV (1949), 454.

It has not been noticed that Buchanan's Jephthes (a Latin playlet: ca. 1554) imitates Meta. XV in Scene ii. Perhaps Sh derived the conception of Sonn. 60 from Jephthes, not directly from Ovid.

2389. Staton, Walter F., Jr. "The Influence of Thomas Watson on Elizabethan Ovidian Poetry," SR, VI (1959), 243-250.

Watson's Amyntas (1585), either in its original Latin or in Abraham Fraunce's verbose trans., is the ancestor of the combination of pastoral, eroticism, mythological ornament, and metamorphosis which characterizes the epyllia of the 1590's; Marlowe added rhetoric to Watson's ingredients. Venus is thus an imitation of Marlowe and Watson (Watson especially in the complaint and metamorphosis of ll. 835-1194) more than of Ovid. Staton is quite correct in emphasizing the Elizabethan contribution to the tone of the erotic epyllion, but it can clearly be shown (see #2387, e.g.) that Sh was thinking of Ovid in Venus.

2390. Steadman, John M. "'Like Two Spirits': Shakespeare and Ficino," SQ, X (1959), 244-246.

Sh's comparison of his two loves to good and bad spirits (Sonn. 144) is traceable to Plato's Symposium perhaps through the Commentary of Ficino, who speaks of "duo amores": a "calodaemon" and a "cacodaemon." The references to angels in this Sonn. suggest that Sh was fusing Neoplatonism with "the medieval conception of good and evil spirits contending for man's soul." Steadman does not note that Sh's antinomy could also be Manichaean; it does not seem certain that Sh is indebted to Plato here.

2391. Straumann, Heinrich. Phönix und Taube: zur Interpretation von Shakespeares Gedankenwelt. Zurich, 1953, 63 pp.

Straumann argues for the principle of Mehrdeutigkeit (or multiple meaning) in Phoenix. The poem is a personal allegory, a symbol of ideal spiritual union, and a synthesis of literary traditions (of which court Platonism with its emphasis on the relation between beauty and truth is one) all at once. This argument is persuasive, but when Straumann goes on to suggest that after Phoenix Sh portrayed women as incapable of the Platonic union of beauty and truth he is not convincing; he appears embarrassed by the last plays (he considers their heroines miraculous exceptions to the rule) and he does not account for Desdemona, Cordelia, and other fair-but-true heroines.

2392. Thompson, D'Arcy W. "The Phoenix and the Turtle," TLS, August 16, 1941, p. 397.

In response to a comment by Osbert Sitwell (#2374), Thompson discusses the crow whom Sh addresses, "[thou] that thy sable gender makest / With the breath thou givest and takest." The reference is to the superstition that the crow procreates by exchanging breath with his mate. Thompson's authorities are Pliny, Aristotle, and Martial.

2393. Tolbert, J[ames] M. "The Argument of Shakespeare's Lucrece: Its Sources and Authorship," TSE, XXIX (1950), 77-90.

The Latinized prose in the Argument indicates that it is a trans. made from some Latin text. The discrepancies between the Argument and both the poem and its sources in Livy, Painter, and Bandello indicate (1) that Sh did not write it; (2) that it was based on the same Latin epitome of Livy which Thomas Lanquet used in his account of Lucrece in Cooper's Chronicle (1549). The hypothesis appears demonstrable only with the discovery of Lanquet's source.

2394. Tolbert, James M. "Shakespeare's Lucrece: Its Antecedents, Sources, and Composition," diss (Texas, 1950).*

2395. Tolbert, J[ames] M. "A Source of Shakespeare's 'Lucrece'," NQ, CXCVIII (1953), 14-15.

Tolbert traces Lucr. 1478-84 to the Illustrium Poetarum Flores, a sixteenth-century thesaurus of quotations from the ancient poets, but wisely does not claim too much for his evidence. The ultimate source is presumed to be passages in Seneca's Phaedra and Thyestes.

2396. Truitt, Warren. "Who Wrote 'Venus and Adonis'?" PL, VII (1895), 28-31.

An enthusiastic defense of Sh against the disintegrators. Part of the argument rests on the classical content of the poem in relation to the doctrine of untutored genius.

2397. Tyler, Thomas. "The Date of Shakespeare's Fifty-Fifth Sonnet," Ath, No. 2759 (1880), 337-338.

Tyler believes that the conceits in Sonn. 55 which trace ultimately to Ovid (Meta. XV) and Horace (Odes, "Ad Musam Melpomenen") have a proximate source in Meres's Palladis Tamia (1598) in which the relevant lines are quoted together with Meres's own Latin sentiments on the immortality of verse. Tyler does not explain why Sh could understand the Latin verses in Meres but could (or would) not read Horace and Ovid in the originals. The verbal parallels between Meres's Latin and Sh's English are not compelling, and the resulting argument for a date after 1598 for this Sonn. is weak. The art. is trans. into German in ShJ, XVI (1881), 411-412.

2398. Walley, Harold R. "The Rape of Lucrece and Shakespearean Tregedy [sic]," ShN, IX, X (1959/1960), 3.

A report of a paper read before the MLA meeting, 1959. Walley emphasized the three-part structure of Lucr.: the rape, the psychological effects on Lucrece and Tarquin, and the catastrophe. The long central section is the tragedy--the poem gives us an insight into Sh's early view of tragic conflict. R. H. Goldsmith added a comment on Lucrece's tragic flaw, overconcern with her reputation.

2399. Werner, Bruno E. "Venus und Adonis: Beitrag zur stilgeschichtlichen Betrachtung Shakespeares," Das Inselschiff, VI (1925), 99-114.

Werner sees the poem as a reflex of themes which the Renaissance inherited from the classics; the central one is the destructive and disruptive power of Time which Sh obtained from Ovid's Meta., the source of the poem. Sh shows a classically tranquil setting at the beginning of the poem and emphasizes the passing of time (the sun in his course through the sky) as disorder grows toward the horrifying chaos of Adonis' death and Venus' curse and flight. The Adonis tradition lent itself readily to Sh's ironic purposes as Adonis was a vegetation and fertility figure in the ancient legend which Ovid adopted. The theme of the poem, then, is the theme of Sh's earliest Sonn.: the war between Time and Order. Werner emphasizes metaphors of harmony (music) and dissonance as they delineate the tension within the poem. "Der Dualismus, der dem klassischen Ideal von der Einheit von Körper und Geist so sehr widerspricht, wird wie ein Schlüssel für die ganze Dichtung." DLC

2400. Wilkinson, L. P. "Shakespeare and Horace," TLS, May 6, 1955, p. 237.

Wilkinson points to a close verbal echo of Horace Epodes XI in Sonn. 104 as supplement to Percy Simpson's essay on "Shakespeare's Use of Latin Authors" (#0543).

2401. Wolff, Max J. "[On Venus and Lucr.]," Shakespeare der Dichter und sein Werk, 2 vols. (Munich, 1907, 1908) I, 270-273, 276-278 (as trans. and abstracted in the New Variorum Poems).

Wolff regards Venus as inferior to Ovid's account of the story because Sh emphasizes the reversal of sexual rôles while "Ovid's facile style glides easily over this obstacle." Sh's Venus is "only a woman babbling of love." Yet the rhetoric of the poem is sufficiently sophisticated to indicate that Sh did not write it before leaving Stratford. Wolff compares Lucr. with Venus, but he does not discuss the classical materials in the later poem.

2402. Wolff, M[ax] J. "Zu den Sonetten," ShJ, XLVII (1911), 191-192. E-S SG

Wolff indicates an Italian path to the Palatine Anthology which could have served Sh as well as the Latin one suggested by Hertzberg (#2346). Claudio Tolomei, Versi et Regole della Nuova Poesia Toscana (1539), translates the verses about Cupid's firebrand which are the source of Sonn. 153 and 154.

2403. Wolff, Max J. "Zu Shakespeares Sonetten," ESn, LXVI (1932), 468-469.

Wolff believes that Sh's leitmotiv of love for a beautiful young man is indirectly traceable to Tibullus, whose elegies in the Delia are a locus classicus. Propertius and Domitius Marsus are perhaps also ultimately responsible for the Dark Lady. But Wolff emphasizes that Sh's direct obligation is not to the Roman poets, but to their Italian imitators.

2404. Wyndham, George. "The Poems of Shakespeare," Essays in Romantic Literature, ed. Charles Whibley (Ln, 1919), pp. 237-388.

Section xii (315-330) interprets Venus as a "Renaissance" poem: i.e., a harmonious fusion of classic myth, Medieval "liquidity of diction" and contemporary realism in the depiction of physical nature. Section xvi (355-373) maintains that though Sh employs the language and some of the concepts of Spenser and of Hoby's Castiglione, "his Sonnets are no more a treatise of philosophy than they are a treatise of law" and it is unwise to interpret them as a document of Platonism.

2405. Yardley, E. "'The Rape of Lucrece'," 9 NQ, XII (1903), 323-324.

Yardley objects to the efforts of commentators to label Sh a scholar because they find parallels to his thought or phrasing in the ancients. He observes that there is no classical lore in Lucr. aside from the legend itself and references to Tereus and Philomel, Tantalus, and "a few of the best-known characters of the Trojan war." Yardley regards his argument as a weapon against Baconians.

2406. Young, G. M. "Master Holofernes," TLS, July 3, 1937, p. 496.

Young prints some lines in the punning, alliterative, logic-chopping manner of Holofernes--he discovered them on a portrait painted in 1575. In the same place he found a Latin sentence of which "the silver moon doth her eclipse endure" is so close a rendering that Young facetiously suggests that Sh "stole" from the unknown painter when he wrote (Sonn. 107) "The mortal moon hath her eclipse endured."

2407. Zocca, Louis R. Elizabethan Narrative Poetry. Rutgers UP, 1950, 306 pp.

Discussion of Lucr. centers in Ch. V, pp. 47-57, and of Venus in Ch. XX, pp. 248-261. In general, Zocca adheres to the theory of coalescence of sources, though he does not concern himself primarily with Sh's source material. In discussing both of Sh's "classical" poems, he emphasizes their participation in sixteenth-century conventions such as Italianate diction and euphuism in Venus and the Mirror and the Complaint in Lucr. Zocca makes an intelligent critical appraisal of each poem.

SHAKESPEARE'S CLASSICS

2408. Alden, Raymond M. A Shakespeare Handbook, revised ed. by Oscar J. Campbell (N.Y., 1932), 302 pp.

In the section headed "Source Material" there are modernized passages from North's trans. of the lives of Antony, Brutus, Caesar, and Coriolanus to illustrate the Roman plays. Alden himself comments that he has only excerpted; while this section is certainly not worthless, others have provided a more adequate means of comparing Sh with Plutarch.

2409. Blach, S. "Shakespeares Lateingrammatik: Lily's Grammatica Latina nach der ältesten bekannten Ausgabe von 1527 und der für Shakespeare in Betracht kommenden Ausgabe von 1566 (London, R. Wolfius)," ShJ, XLIV (1908), 65-117; XLV (1909), 51-100. E-S

Following brief citations of loci for Sh's eight quotations from Lily, Blach prints the two texts in juxtaposition, with some supplement from a 1572 ed. Then he appends an eight-page list of allusions to the Grammar, some as recent as the nineteenth century. Until 1945 (see #2433), Blach's arts. were the only easily accessible reprint of Lily; this work appears to have been carefully, if unpretentiously, done.

2410. Boas, Frederick [S.], ed. The Heroycall Epistles of the Learned Poet Publius Ovidius Naso. Translated Into English Verse by George Turberville [1567] Ln, 1928, xxiv + 349 pp. E-S SG

This is a beautiful (but, unfortunately, strictly limited) ed. of Turberville's vigorous trans. of the Heroides. Boas places Sh with Marlowe and Drayton as probable inheritors of Turberville's Ovid. The Shn passage in question is part of the "duet ... in the garden at Belmont" (Merch. V i 9-14). MnU

2411. Boas, Frederick [S.], ed. The Tragedie of Caesar and Pompey or Caesars Reuenge (1607), MSR, [XXVII] (1911), xiii pp. + [no pagination]. E-S

Boas' introduction suggests that the play is based on Appian and that it possibly antedates the turn of the century. If it dates from the 1590's there is a possibility that Sh could have drawn on it for Caesar, though Boas does not say so.

2412. Bond, R. W[arwick], ed. The Birth of Hercules [post-1597?], MSR, [XXIII] (1911), xi + 91 pp. E-S

The play is a close rendition of Plautus' Amphitruo; though the evidence seems clear that it postdates Errors, it is included here because of the very close parallels between the two plays. Its author (in Bond's judgment) perhaps borrowed some of his Plautus from Sh.

2413. Brooke, C. F. Tucker, ed. Shakespeare's Plutarch. 2 vols., N.Y., 1909. E-S SG

Vol. I: text of North's "Caesar" and "Brutus"; Vol. II: "Antony" and "Coriolanus." Caesar is indebted to North for subject and characterization, but not for language. In Antony and Cor., on the other hand, Sh borrows whole passages from North's racy, vigorous prose because he is too interested in grandeur of conception to bother formulating his own phrases. The grandeur of conception and the sense of destiny in Antony and Cor. he also learned from

NOTE: Numbers preceded by # refer to entries in this Guide. Keys to abbreviations are found on pages xi-xvii and 381-387.

Plutarch. North probably provided the first hint for Tim. as well. (See Skeat, #2471.)

2414. Bullough, Geoffrey, ed. Narrative and Dramatic Sources of Shakespeare: Vol. I, Early Comedies, Poems, Romeo and Juliet. Col UP, 1957 [Vol. I of proposed VII], 532 pp.

This first vol. of an important series contains sources and analogues of Errors, Shrew, Venus, Lucr., T.G.V., Romeo, Dream, L.L.L., and Merch. Obviously, Errors, the poems, and Dream call for more "classical" materials than the other plays, but included in the brilliant commentary on some of the other plays is occasional reference to a connection with ancient culture (e.g., Romeo and Xenophon of Ephesus; Sh's alteration of locale in Shrew from Athens to Padua, perhaps because he was working on Dream, an "Athenian" play, at the same time). The brief introductions to the reprinted texts are conservative and exceptionally well informed, but at the same time imaginative. The first three vols. of Bullough's set (see also #2415, #2416) promise that the finished work will be one of the most useful contributions to Shn scholarship to appear in recent years.

2415. Bullough, Geoffrey, ed. Narrative and Dramatic Sources of Shakespeare: Vol. II, The Comedies 1597-1603. Col UP, 1958 [Vol. II of proposed VII], 543 pp.

Though there are occasional comments passim on the classical foundation of the Renaissance themes in the comedies, only for Wives does Bullough give any connected treatment of classical sources. He prints the Actaeon story from Meta. III (Golding's trans.), labels it "probable source" and shows that the hunter hunted theme and the play on the horned man are related to the joke on Falstaff in Act V. He also discusses briefly, p. 9, the relation of Plautus' Casina to Wives, outlining and modifying the thesis of Forsythe (#0763). Bullough is sufficiently dubious as not to print any of Plautus' play.

2416. Bullough, Geoffrey, ed. Narrative and Dramatic Sources of Shakespeare: Vol. III, Earlier English History Plays: Henry VI, Richard III, Richard II. Col UP, 1960 [Vol. III of proposed VII], 512 pp.

This vol., like its two predecessors, is an immensely valuable compilation of sources (probable, possible, and definite) and analogues. Because it deals only with history plays its dependence on the classics is small, but Bullough prints some of the wooing dialogue (with English trans.) from Legge's Richardus Tertius which he labels an analogue. This is followed by Jasper Heywood's metrical version of Lycus' attempted seduction of Megara from Hercules Furens, labeled "possible source" (both selections pp. 306-317). In the introduction to R.III (pp. 221-248; see esp. 233-237) Bullough discusses the relationship between the wooing scenes in Legge, the one in Seneca, and the two in Sh. His belief is that Sh may have followed Legge in giving special prominence to women and to wooing in R.III, but that Legge is not otherwise a major influence on the play.

2417. Bush, Douglas, ed. The Eclogues of Mantuan Translated by George Turberville (1567), SFR, [I] (1937), vii + [190] pp.

Bush barely mentions Sh's "half affectionate, half satirical" allusion to Mantuanus in L.L.L., and he makes no suggestion that Sh used Turberville's Mantuan as a pony in Stratford School. The facsimile is clearly reproduced.

2418. Carr, R. H., ed. Plutarch's Lives of Coriolanus, Caesar, Brutus, and Antonius in North's Translation. Oxford: Clarendon, 1906, xxxv + 280 pp.

The sections in the introduction on Sh's use of North are IV-VII (pp. xv-xxxii). Carr feels it necessary to spend space on the date of Caesar, but his criticism of this play is sound, as it is of Antony and Cor. He points to Plutarch's ambivalent attitude toward Caesar as the source of moral ambiguity in Sh's play, and he shows briefly the process by which Sh evolved minor characters (Enobarbus, Menenius) from bare hints in Plutarch. His soundest observation is that Sh followed North more closely in Antony and Cor. than in Caesar, where he was working with three Lives. Carr reprints the 1595 text, "because it is a priori more likely to have been accessible" to Sh. DFo

2419. Case, R. H., ed. The Tragedy of Antony and Cleopatra (1906/1930), ArdenSh.

The prefatory material concludes with thirty-four pages of "Extracts from North's 'Plutarch' (1579)." See also #1202.

2420. Clements, [Arthur Frederick]. Tudor

Translations: An Anthology. Oxford: Blackwell, 1940, xv + 215 pp. GRS

This book is a sampler, providing a few pages each from B.R.'s Herodotus, Hobbes's Thucydides, Underdowne's Heliodorus, Newton's Cicero (De Senectute), Harington's Cicero (De Amicitia), Heywood's Sallust, Holland's Suetonius, Livy, and Pliny, Savile's Tacitus, Grenewey's Tacitus, and Adlington's Apuleius. North's Plutarch is represented by about seventy-five pages. The balance of the book consists of trans. from such "modern" classics as Rabelais, Cervantes, and Commines. The introduction barely mentions Sh's use of North and Florio's Montaigne. Several of the trans. here were, of course, made too late for Sh to have known them.

2421. Collier, J. P. Shakespeare's Library: A Collection of the Romances, Novels, Poems, and Histories, used by Shakespeare as the Foundation of his Dramas. 2 vols., Ln, 1843, 1850. E-S (The pagination in the 1843 printing is garbled.)

Though in the preface he disavows any intention of dealing either with classical or with English historical sources, in printing Twine's version of Apollonius of Tyre (for Per.) Collier includes a tale classical in origin. In the introduction to the tale he notes that Belleforest, who translated it, traced it to a Greek source: Collier recommends Douce (#0207) on this subject. MnU

2422. Collier, J. P., and W. C. Hazlitt. Shakespeare's Library: A Collection of the Plays, Romances, Novels, Poems and Histories Employed by Shakespeare in the Composition of his Works. 6 vols., 2nd ed., Ln, 1875. E-S

When Hazlitt speaks of this revised ed. of Collier's original work (#2421) as "greatly enlarged," he understates. Hazlitt adds immense quantities of material to Collier's skeletal two vols. Plutarch and Holinshed are instated and large numbers of analogues have been admitted; there are even ballads, etc., based on Sh. The result is that material (such as the old academic comedy of Timon from Dyce's manuscript) not readily attainable elsewhere is made available. Hazlitt's exclusion of 1H.VI and Titus is doubtless in accord with disintegrationist influence, but the omission of R.II is more mysterious, and T.N.K. is included. Hazlitt makes some patent errors (about the sources of Troi., e.g.) which have since been discredited, but he also has excellent insights: e.g., he includes Plutarch's "Life of Pericles" from which some now think Sh drew the virtue of patience and the name of his hero in Per. MnU

2423. [Craig, W. J., ed.] "The Life of Caius Martius Coriolanus (Extracted from North's Plutarch, ed. I, 1579)," The Tragedy of Coriolanus (1922), ArdenSh, pp. xxvii-lxiii.

Plutarch's "Coriolanus" is given complete, including North's marginalia, but without other annotations. Appended is a brief excerpt from Camden's Remaines, which many believe influenced Sh's wording of Menenius' fable.

2424. Cuningham, Henry, ed. The Comedy of Errors (1907/1933), ArdenSh.

As Appendix II, pp. 131-177, Cuningham reprints W.W.'s trans. of the Menaechmi without annotations. See #0731 for Cuningham's comments on the relationship of Errors to this trans.

2425. Cuningham, Henry, ed. A Midsummer-Night's Dream (1905/1930), ArdenSh.

As Appendix IV, pp. 167-175, Cuningham reprints (a) Golding's trans. of the story of Pyramus and Thisbe from Meta. IV and (b) "A New Sonet [sic; i.e., ballad] of Pyramus and Thisbe" by I. Thomson. See #0732 for Cuningham's view of the source question.

2426. Darton, F. J. Harvey, ed. The Golden Ass of Lucius Apuleius in the Translation by William Adlington. Ln, 1924, 359 pp. (privately printed for the Navarre Society).

Darton takes considerable liberties with the text, modernizing and bowdlerizing. The sixteen-page introduction does not mention Sh.

2428. Dorsch, T. S., ed. Julius Caesar (1955/1958), ArdenSh.

Appendix A, pp. 131-166, consists of extracts from Skeat's modernized reprint (#2471), arranged so as to call attention to Sh's sources for characterization and incident in Caesar. See #1265 for Dorsch's comments on Sh's manipulation of the source.

2429. Duckett, Eleanor S. Catullus in English Poetry, Smith College Classical Studies, VI (1925), 199 pp.

This anthology of passages from Catullus with facing English verse which translates or imitates them contains some dozen brief passages from Sh. There is no critical or analytical commentary, but the reader is provided the materials with which to judge Professor Duckett's implication of indebtedness.

2430. Dyce, Alexander, ed. Timon, A Play. Now First Printed. Ln: Shakespeare Society, 1842, vii + 95 pp.

Dyce prints from manuscript the "academic Timon," and he cites in a brief preface the opinion of Steevens that "the piece itself (though it appears to be the work of an academick) is a wretched one" and that of Malone, that the play provided Sh "the faithful steward, the banquet-scene, and the story of Timon's being possessed of great sums of gold which he had dug up in the woods"; the latter story is in Lucian's dialogue, but no trans. was available to Sh, in Malone's opinion. Dyce is content to leave the debate on indebtedness to others, but he has "considerable doubts" that Sh ever had access to the play. MnU

2431. Eliot, T. S., ed. Seneca His Tenne Tragedies Translated Into English Edited by Thomas Newton Anno 1581, The Tudor Translations, 2nd ser., ed. Charles Whibley, XI (Ln, 1927), liv + 231 pp.

The introduction is Eliot's famous essay usually titled "Seneca in Elizabethan Translation" (#0227).

2432. Fest, Otto. Über Surrey's Virgilübersetzung, nebst Neuausgabe des vierten Buches. . . , Palaestra, XXXIV (1903), 128 pp. GRS

The text itself occupies pp. 98-128. The introductory material does not discuss Surrey's possible influence on Sh or other later writers.

2433. Flynn, Vincent J., ed. A Shorte Introduction of Grammar by William Lily, SFR, [XXI] (1945), xii pp. + [no pagination].

Flynn makes only a very brief allusion to Sh's knowledge of and use of the Grammar, but his informed introduction clearly indicates the importance Lily's textbook had for three centuries in introducing Englishmen to Roman culture. An excellent photographic facsimile of the text.

2434. Forrest, H. T. S. The Original Venus and Adonis. Ln, 1930, 132 pp. E-S SG

At the end of an argument calculated to disintegrate the poem into Sh's original work and some seventy-two "interpolated" stanzas, Forrest reprints in appendix the relevant passages from Golding's Meta. The same materials are available in the New Variorum Poems (#2383), and of course in #2468 and its 1961 facsimile.

2435. Gaselee, S., ed. and reviser. Apuleius: The Golden Ass Being the Metamorphoses of Lucius Apuleius with an English Translation by W. Adlington (1566) (The Loeb Classical Library). Ln and N.Y., 1915, xxiv + 608 pp.

The trans. has been much altered to make it conform to the facing Latin. Gaselee makes no reference to Sh's possible debt to Adlington, or to Apuleius.

2436. Gordon, R. K., ed. and trans. The Story of Troilus as told by Benoit de Sainte-Maure Giovanni Boccaccio (translated into English Prose) Geoffrey Chaucer and Robert Henryson. Ln, 1934, xviii + 383 pp. E-S

The Henryson and Chaucer are in a form similar to the one in which Sh might have seen them, but both Boccaccio and Benoît are in modern English. In his introduction Gordon traces the story from Dares and Dictys through Henryson, ending with a brief remark which implies that Sh's debased Cressida is chiefly the descendant of what the ballad-makers made of Henryson.

2437. Greg, W. W., ed. Alexander and Campaspe By John Lyly (1584), MSR, [LXXVI] (1933), xii pp. + [no pagination]. E-S

The prefatory material contains no commentary on the influence of the play on contemporary views of Alexander and Diogenes, but Sh is thought by some to have been influenced by Lyly's play.

2438. Haines, C. R. The Carmina of Quintus Horatius Flaccus (Together with Satire I, 1x) Rendered into English Rhyming Verse and Accompanied by the Latin Text with "a full list of Shakespeare's allusions to . . . Horace". Ln, 1933, xxx + 211 pp. SG

Not seen. According to SG the introduction contains five pp. on Sh's debt to Horace, which, though less than Collins (#0173) would have it, is still visible in some half of the plays.

2439. Hammond, Eleanor Prescott. "A Pyramus-and-Thisbe Play of Shakespeare's Time," The Drama, V (1915), 288-300.

The author prints from the British Museum manuscript a transcript of the Tragoedia Misserima which Arthur Acheson thought to be by Matthew Roydon, early enough to be the model for Sh's parody in Dream. But, as the author indicates, the evidence points to a seventeenth-century date. In any case this English playlet makes an interesting analogue to the clumsiness and bombast of the Mechanicals' interlude.

2440. Harrison, G. B., ed. Julius Caesar in Shakespeare, Shaw, and the Ancients, Harbrace Sourcebooks (N.Y., 1960), 215 pp.

Intended for undergraduate students as a collection of source materials for the writing of term papers, this book contains the passages from North's trans. of the lives of Caesar, Brutus, and Antonius which Sh used for Caesar. In addition, there are relevant passages from Suetonius, Appian, Cicero (Letters and Philippics II), and the pseudo-Caesarian account of Caesar in Egypt. The brief introduction discusses the character of Caesar and the difference between history as narrative account and history as dramatic portrayal. Harrison states that Sh relied "almost wholly" on North; "he could (but probably did not) have had access to the other classical sources."

2441. [Hillebrand, H. N.] "Sources: III--Caxton and Lydgate," New Variorum Troi., pp. 424-447.

A generous selection from Caxton's Recuyell with much slighter relevant passages from Lydgate's Troy Book is a welcome means of studying Sh's possible use of either or both. Prefixed to the texts is a two-page discussion of the putative contributions of Caxton and Lydgate to Troi.

2442. Hooper, Richard, ed. The Iliads of Homer, Prince of Poets,...Truly Translated...by George Chapman (1863?), Library of Old Authors, 2 vols., 2nd ed., Ln, 1865, xcv + 268, 302 pp.

The complete Iliads. The detailed and extensive discussion of the trans. and its reputation does not include comment on Sh's possible use of Chapman in Troi.

2443. The Iliads of Homer Prince of Poets... by George Chapman, 2 vols. Oxford: Blackwell, 1930, 262, 289 pp.

A handsome reprint of the 1616 Folio with some emendation. No prefatory material.

2444. Jiriczek, O[tto] L. "Die erste englische Theocritübersetzung," ShJ, LV (1919), 30-34. E-S

Jiriczek reprints the thirty-first Idyl ("On the Death of Adonis") from the Sixe Idillia of 1588 with its "Argument" and facing Greek. Nevertheless, following Anders (#0073), Jiriczek emphasizes Sh's debt to Ovid, not to pseudo-Theocritus.

2445. Jiriczek, Otto L. Specimens of Tudor Translations From the Classics With a Glossary. Heidelberg, 1923, 200 pp. E-S

Intended more for comparative philological study than for literary evaluation, these "specimens" are nonetheless valuable partly because of the rarity of many of them and partly because different versions of the same classical passage appear together. Thus the opening 172 lines from Aeneid IV appear in the trans. of Douglas, St. Gelais, Surrey, Piccolomini, Phaer, and Stanyhurst. Jiriczek is not concerned with the imaginative use to which such trans. were put by Sh and his contemporaries, but both the Narcissus story and Medea's herb-gathering are given in Golding's verse, and some other less obvious Shn sources are included. MnU

2446. Johnson, Francis R., ed. The Foundacion of Rhetorike by Richard Rainolde, SFR, [XXV] (1945), xxiv + [124] pp.

Johnson's introduction makes only the briefest reference to Sh, but it constitutes as intelligent and clear an introduction to Renaissance rhetorical principles as can be found anywhere. As Johnson points out, Rainolde's book is an adaptation of Aphthonius' Progymnasmata; Sh is now generally thought to have been familiar with Aphthonian formulas. Johnson's introduction was printed as an art.: HLQ, VI (1943), 427-444.

2447. Kish, George, ed. The Excellent and Pleasant Worke "Collectanea Rerum Memorabilium" of Caius Julius Solinus; Translated from the Latin (1587) by Arthur Golding. SFR, 1955, [no pagination]. GRS

A facsimile. The three-page introduction points out that Solinus Polyhistor's book is ninety per cent a redaction of Pliny's Naturalis Historia. It was a sixteenth-century grammar text. Sh is not mentioned in the introduction.

2448. A lamentable Tragedie, mixed full of plesant mirth, containing the life of Cambises king of Percia... [by Thomas Preston] [ca. 1560], OEP, [XII] [n.d.], [no pagination]. E-S

The source, of course, of "King Cambyses' vein." No prefatory material.

2449. Lederer, M., ed. Daniel's The Tragedie of Cleopatra: nach dem Drucke von 1611, Bang's Materialien, XXXI (1911), xvi + 99 pp. E-S

The introduction to Daniel's Pembrokist tragedy does not discuss the possible mutual influences of Cleopatra and Antony, but the text is well printed.

2450. [Lennox, Charlotte]. Shakespear Illustrated: Or the Novels and Histories On which the Plays of Shakespear Are Founded Collected and Translated from the Original Authors with Critical Remarks in Two Volumes. By the Author of the Female Quixote. Ln, 1753, 292, 274 pp. E-S [A third vol. appeared in 1754 (not seen); it is said to contain Chaucer's Troilus as source for Sh's Troi., but no other "classical" materials.]

Shakespear Illustrated is the first attempt to compile Sh's sources. In this first ed. the only play with a classical source is Errors, for which Mrs. Lennox prints a trans. of a French version of the Menaechmi. She considers Sh's plot less probable, more arbitrarily complex than its source, and therefore less artistic. She is aware of W.W.'s trans., but assigns it to 1593 and assumes that Sh used it. In another passage Mrs. Lennox recognizes Plautus as the source of the confusion between Sebastian and Viola in Twel., but takes the occasion to retail the legend of Sh's ignorance of Latin and Greek. MnU

2451. Leo, F. A., ed. Four Chapters of North's Plutarch Containing the Lives of Caius Marcius Coriolanus, Julius Caesar, Marcus Antonius and Marcus Brutus as Sources to Shakespeare's Tragedies Coriolanus, Julius Caesar, Antony and Cleopatra and Partly to Hamlet and Timon of Athens. Ln and Strassburg, 1878, [iv] pp. + discontinuous pagination.

This folio-size photographic facsimile from the 1595 North was, unfortunately, published in an ed. of fifty copies. In his preface Leo praises Skeat (#2471) but observes the necessity for a facsimile, into which typographical errors cannot intrude. Endnotes provide collation of 1579 with 1595 and 1603 issues and in parallel columns Sh's use of North's wording in the five plays (in Ham. see I i 113-120). DFo

2452. MacCallum, M. W. Shakespeare's Roman Plays and Their Background. Ln, 1910, 656 pp. E-S HB SG

For Sh's sources for the dissuasion scene in Cor., see #1477.

2453. Macmillan, Michael. "Introduction," The Tragedy of Julius Caesar (1902/1934), ArdenSh, pp. ix-xciii.

For Macmillan's extracts from North's Plutarch, see #1480.

2454. MacNeice, Louis, ed. The Golden Ass of Apuleius: Translated Out of Latin by William Adlington in the Year 1566, Chiltern Library, No. 1. Ln, 1946, xi + 239 pp. GRS

Not seen.

2455. Matthiessen, F. O. "North's Plutarch (1579)," Translation: An Elizabethan Art (HUP, 1931), Ch. III, pp. 54-102. E-S

For a reprinting of a number of versions of passages from Plutarch, see #1488.

2456. McKerrow, Ronald B., ed. The Virtuous Octavia (1598) by Samuel Brandon, MSR, [XV] (1909), ix pp. + [no pagination]. E-S

McKerrow does not mention Sh, but he does observe the closeness with which Brandon follows Daniel's Cleopatra, which is usually thought to bear a relationship to Antony. Some have argued for Sh's knowledge of Brandon's play.

2457. Morley, Henry, ed. Homer's Iliad Translated by George Chapman, Morley's Universal Library, [No. 17], 4th ed. Ln, 1890, 320 pp.

The complete Iliads. Morley makes no comment on Sh's use of Chapman, but he does observe that "the generation that produced a Shakespeare best knew how to translate Homer."

2458. Mühlfeld, Wilhelm, ed. "The Tragedie of Caesar and Pompey or Caesars Reuenge [1607], Ein Drama aus Shakespeares Zeit zum ersten Male neugedruckt," ShJ, XLVII (1911), 132-155; XLVIII (1912), 37-80.

The comparisons with Caesar are incidental, and Mühlfeld does not discuss the possible influence of this play on Sh, though he does indicate the probability that it was written in the early 1590's. He also notes that he was impelled to reprint the play by Wolfgang Keller's "Bemerkung" (#1430) which does propose that Sh's conception of the Caesar story was shaped by this play.

2459. Nadeau, Raymond E. "The Progymnasmata of Aphthonius in Translation," SM, XIX (1952), 264-285. GRS

Nadeau translates from the Greek, not from the Latin version which Sh doubtless studied at Stratford. This trans. is included here (though modern) because it is the only one available (Richard Rainolde's Foundacion of Rhetorike [1563] is "a very free adaptation of the 'Latin Aphthonius' of Lorich[ius] ..."). Donald L. Clark's essay, "The Rise and Fall of Progymnasmata in Sixteenth and Seventeenth Century Grammar Schools" (ibid., pp. 259-263) does not mention Sh.

2460. Newbolt, Henry. "The Poet and His Raw Material: Prose," The Tide of Time in English Poetry (Ln, 1925), pp. 18-32.

In these pages Newbolt prints the scenes portraying the last moments of Antony and of Cleopatra in the poetry of Sh and in the English prose of North and the Greek prose of Plutarch. A brief introduction discusses individual phrases as they were developed by North out of hints in the original. Newbolt gives Amyot no consideration at all.

2461. Nicoll, Allardyce, ed. Chapman's Homer: The Iliad, The Odyssey and The Lesser Homerica, 2 vols., Bollingen Series XLI. N.Y., 1956, Vol. I, Homer's Iliads, xxii + 741 pp. GRS

A scholarly ed. "with Introductions, Textual Notes, Commentaries, and Glossaries." The introduction does not discuss Sh's possible use of the trans.

2462. Oliver, H. J., ed. Timon of Athens (1959), ArdenSh.

Appendices A, B, and C (pp. 141-151) are reprints respectively of relevant passages from North's trans. of the "Life of Marcus Antonius," from his "Life of Alcibiades," and from Lucian's Timon the Misanthrope (in a modern trans.). For Oliver's view of the source question see #1554.

2463. Osborn, E. B., ed. The Golden Asse of Lucius Apuleius Translated Out of Latin by William Adlington. Ln, 1923, 282 pp. E-S

Sh is not mentioned in the thirteen-page introduction to this limited ed.

2464. Pooler, C[harles] Knox, ed. Shakespeare's Poems (1911/1927), ArdenSh.

As part of his introduction, Pooler reprints Constable's "Shepherd's Song of Venus and Adonis" and excerpts from FQ III and Golding's Ovid--possible sources for Venus; the account of Lucrece in Painter's Palace of Pleasure, Chaucer's story of Lucrece from LGW, and the relevant excerpt from the Fasti (in Latin)--certain or possible sources for Lucr. See also #2375.

2465. Prince, F. T., ed. The Poems (1960), ArdenSh.

The appendices consist of (1) Golding's rendition of Ovid's stories of Venus and Adonis and Salmacis and Hermaphroditus, (2) Chaucer's account of Lucrece in LGW, (3) Painter's trans. of Livy's version of the Tarquin story, (4) the relevant passage from Fasti II in Latin and in a modern trans. See also #2377.

2466. [Rollins, Hyder]. "The Sources [of Venus and Lucr.]," New Variorum Poems, pp. 390-405, 416-439.

For reprints of Sh's supposed sources, see #2383.

2467. Rouse, W. H. D., ed. The Menaechmi: The Original of Shakespeare's "Comedy of Errors": The Latin Text Together With the Elizabethan Translation, The Shakespeare Library, ed. I. Gollancz. Ln, 1912, xiv + 122 pp.

The two texts are printed on facing pages. In the introduction, Rouse asserts that William Warner was "W.W.," but leaves unsettled the question whether this trans. preceded Errors. He notes only one verbal parallel (reference to a wife as a "stale"). A brief survey of the actions of Errors and the Menaechmi shows clearly that it is the addition of the second Dromio which makes Sh's play nearly three times as complex as Plautus' (in Sh's play characters encounter "strangers" fifty times; in Plautus', seventeen). Rouse defends Sh's introduction of the second set of twins: if one can accept Plautus' highly improbable plot, why not a yet more improbable one? TxU

2468. Rouse, W. H. D., ed. Shakespeare's Ovid Being Arthur Golding's Translation of the Metamorphoses. Ln, 1904 (Limited Edition), 321 pp. E-S SG

In the six-page introduction, Rouse briefly asserts Sh's use of both the Latin Meta. and Golding, and credits Sh with knowledge of the Fasti, the Heroides, and the Amores (presumably all in Latin). He also accepts as genuine the Shn ownership of the Bodleian Meta. and gives a useful list of sixteenth-century trans. of Ovid's works. Yet Rouse does not believe Sh's debt to Ovid to be so extensive as scholars normally do. See Ath, No. 4019 (1904), 617-618 SG for reservations. Rouse's important reprint was long a collector's item; in 1961 it was reissued in a welcome facsimile by Southern Illinois UP.

2469. Schanzer, Ernest. Shakespeare's Appian: A Selection from the Tudor Translation of Appian's Civil Wars (Liverpool UP, 1956), 101 pp.

On pp. xix-xxviii Schanzer constructs an argument for Sh's use of Appian in Caesar and Antony. From Appian Sh got his ambivalent attitude toward the conspiracy on Caesar's life, the duplicity and boldness of Antony in Caesar, the histrionics of Antony's funeral oration, some details about Pompey's character and relative power in Antony, the wars which Antony's wife, Fulvia, and his brother, Lucius, made on Octavius, and some less significant details. Sh may have first been led to Appian by a gloss in North which mentions him or perhaps by Caesar's Revenge, which shows indebtedness to Appian. Schanzer also makes one less plausible comment on a possible echo of Appian in Macb. Schanzer's extracts from the anonymous Tudor trans. are the best means available of judging Sh's possible debt.

2470. Sidgwick, Frank. The Sources and Analogues of "A Midsummer-Night's Dream", The Shakespeare Library, ed. Sir I. Gollancz (N.Y., 1908), 196 pp. E-S SG

Sidgwick's major emphasis falls on Chaucer, the tale of Robin Goodfellow, and Reginald Scot's Discovery of Witchcraft (as source for the ass's head), but he does print the Pyramus-Thisbe story in Golding's version from Meta. IV, and he refers to Plutarch's "Life of Theseus" and to Apuleius and Lucian, though he prints none of these.

2471. Skeat, W. W. Shakespeare's Plutarch: Being a Selection from the Lives in North's Plutarch which Illustrate Shakespeare's Plays. Ln, 1875, 332 pp. E-S

Complete: "Coriolanus," "Julius Caesar," "Marcus Brutus," "Marcus Antonius," "Octavius Caesar Augustus." Extracts: "Theseus," "Alcibiades." The preface (vii-xxi) discusses North and his source, describes the various eds. of North, gives a list of names in Sh's plays possibly drawn from Plutarch, and indicates a number of passages in the plays which may show indebtedness. Skeat accepts (xii-xiii) Allan Park Paton's contention (#1568) that Sh's autograph and jottings appear in a copy of the 1612 (4th) ed.; he should certainly have known that all three Roman plays long antedate 1612. Tucker Brooke (#2413) contemptuously dismisses Paton's argument, but refers erroneously to the ed. in question as the 3rd (1603).

2472. Smith, G. C. Moore, ed. Pedantius: A Latin Comedy Formerly Acted in Trinity College Cambridge, Bang's Materialien, VIII (1905), 1 + 164 pp. E-S

Some, notably Churchill and Keller (#0719), have thought Holofernes to be modeled on Pedantius and Nathaniel on Dromodotus. Smith's introduction doubts any connection between L.L.L. and Pedantius, but leaves the question open.

2473. Sonnenschein, E. A., ed. T. Macci Plavti Mostellaria: With Notes Critical and Exegetical and an Introduction. CUP, 1884, xxxv + 163 pp. SG

Brief comments propose that Sh borrowed the names "Grumio" and "Tranio" from the Mostellaria because they are not in A Shrew; that Sh borrowed the passage (I i 160-163) in which Lucentio repeats the name of Tranio with a hint of threat in his voice from lines near the opening of the Mostellaria; that Sh either saw Plautus' play produced or read Berardo's Italian trans. (1530). It is odd that Sh can be given credit for Italian which was not taught in grammar school, but not for Latin which was.

2474. Spearing, E[velyn] M., ed. Studley's Translations of Seneca's Agamemnon and Medea, Bang's Materialien, XXXVIII (1913), xxiii + 252 pp. E-S SG

In the introduction is a striking argument for the influence of Studley's Agamemnon on Ham. by way of the Ur-Hamlet. The editor introduces six structural parallels between Ham. and the Agamemnon and five verbal parallels. The cumulative effect is impressive, though of course "the character of Hamlet owes nothing to any predecessor ..." and the structural elements appear also in Belleforest. The editor thinks it probable that Kyd first was attracted to the theme of the Ur-Hamlet by the resemblance it bore to themes treated by his mentor, Seneca. This is a valuable ed. of "English Seneca."

2475. "The Speeches of Brutus on Caesar and of Antony over Caesar's Dead Body, from the Englisht Appian's Chronicle of 1578," NSST, Part II (1875-76), Appendix IV, pp. 425-439.

The relevant parts of the trans. are reprinted without critical commentary. The publication of more extensive extracts in Schanzer's Shakespeare's Appian (#2469) supersedes this appendix.

2476. Starnes, DeWitt T., ed. Proverbs or Adages by Desiderius Erasmus Gathered out of the Chiliades and Englished (1569) by Richard Taverner. SFR, [XXXIII] (1956), xvi + [142] pp.

Starnes's introduction to this valuable reproduction points to three probable echoes of Taverner in Sh: (1) Lucrece on Opportunity; (2) the Epilogue to A.Y.L.; (3) "the wallet of oblivion" from Troi. Taverner would appear to be one of Sh's indirect routes to the classics.

2477. Taylor, W. Cooke, ed. The Iliads of Homer, Prince of Poets... Translated...by George Chapman, 2 vols. Ln, 1843, 265, 243 pp.

The complete Iliads with Chapman's commentaries, and the Flaxman illustrations. The introduction does not discuss Chapman's possible influence on Sh.

2478. The Tragedie of Caesar and Pompey or Caesars Reuenge. Privately acted by the Studentes of Trinity Colledge in Oxford (1607), OEP, [XI] [n.d.], [no pagination]. E-S

This quarto is perhaps too late for Caesar (see Boas, #2411, for the opinion that the play dates from the 1590's). But it is not too late for Antony. As usual in this series the collotype reproduction is clear. No prefatory material.

2479. The Tragedie of Dido Queene of Carthage Played by the Children of her Maiesties Chappell. Written by Christopher Marlowe, and Thomas Nash. Gent. (1594), OEP, [XXVII] [n.d.], [no pagination]. E-S

No prefatory material.

2480. The Tragicomoedi of the vertuous Octavia Done by Samvel Brandon (1598), OEP, [CLXII] [n.d.], [no pagination]. E-S

No prefatory material.

2481. Vocht, Henry de, ed. The Earliest English Translations of Erasmus' Colloquia 1536-1566, HL, II (Louvain, 1928), 319 pp.

A scholarly ed. Sh is not mentioned as an inheritor of the Colloquia.

2481a. Vocht, H[enry] de, ed. Jasper Heywood and His Translations of Seneca's Troas, Thyestes and Hercules Furens. Bang's Materialien, XLI (1913), lvi + 355 pp. E-S.

A good scholarly ed. De Vocht speaks of Heywood's possible influence on Marston, Gorboduc, and The Misfortunes of Arthur, but he ignores the possibility that the alliterative rant of Bottom's "Ercles' vein" is a travesty of Heywood.

2482. Vollmer, Adolf. "Shakespeare und Plutarch," Archiv, LXXVII (1887), 353-403; LXXVIII (1887), 75-114, 215-270. E-S

Vollmer's extensive reprint contains the relevant passages from North's Plutarch with facing Greek under act-scene references which account for virtually all of the action in the Roman plays (first installment Cor., second Caesar, third Antony). Much of the prefatory material has been assimilated into later scholarship: e.g., Vollmer feels it necessary to show that Sh did not use Livy, Dionysius of Halicarnassus, or Zonaras for Cor. But these discussions are informed and conservative.

2483. Wallace, Malcolm W. The Birthe of Hercules: With An Introduction on the Influence of Plautus on the Dramatic Literature of England in the Sixteenth Century, Chicago, 1903, 183 pp. [of which 96 are introduction]. HB

Errors is accorded only three and one half pages, of which almost two are plot summaries. Wallace doubts that Sh read the Menaechmi in Latin (because he did not have enough Latin to do so), denies that Sh shows much indebtedness to Plautus outside Errors, and believes that he probably also knew the scene in the Amphitruo in which Mercury locks Amphitryon out of his own house. The value of this widely ranging introduction is in chance remarks on less commonly discussed matters such as the fact that Whetstone's Promos and Cassandra contains a Plautine courtesan and her circle; probably the low-life characters in Meas. can be traced indirectly to Plautus. There is also an extended passage on Lyly's debt to Plautus, interesting in the light of Sh's debt to Lyly. The text of The Birthe of Hercules is well printed and sufficiently annotated. MnU

2484. Whibley, Charles, ed. An AEthiopian History Written in Greek by Heliodorus Englished by Thomas Underdowne Anno 1587, The Tudor Translations, ed. W. E. Henley, V. Ln, 1895, xxix + 290 pp.

Whibley's colorful critique of Heliodorus and Underdowne observes in passing that Sh knew the Tudor trans. "you may be certain." His evidence is Twel. V i 120-122. The text reprinted here is the quarto "newly corrected and augmented." Whibley speculates that Q_1 may have appeared as early as 1577.

2485. Whibley, Charles, ed. The Golden Ass of Apuleius Translated Out of Latin by William Adlington Anno 1566, The Tudor Translations, ed. W. E. Henley, IV. Ln, 1893, xxx + 249 pp.

The introduction to this diplomatic reprint of the 1566 ed. is an intelligent appraisal of Apuleius and of Adlington, but it makes no mention of Sh.

2486. Whibley, Leonard, ed. The Famous Hystory of Herodotus Translated Into English by B.R. Anno 1584, The Tudor Translations, 2nd ser., ed. Charles Whibley, VI. Ln, 1924, xxxiii + 242 pp.

A reprint of B.R.'s trans. of Herodotus, Books I and II. Sh is not mentioned in the introduction, though Spenser and Ascham are. A passage in Book II has sometimes been thought to be the source of Orsino's lines in Twel. V i about the Egyptian thief who must kill the one he loves.

2487. Wyndham, George, ed. Plutarch's Lives of the Noble Grecians and Romans Englished by Sir Thomas North Anno 1579, The Tudor Translations, ed. W. E. Henley, VII-XII. Ln, 1895.

The "Introduction," a sensitive, one-hundred-page study of Plutarch and his translators, discusses "North's debtor-in-chief" in the last fourteen: "Shakespeare has taken over North's vocabulary, and that is much; but it is more that behind that vocabulary he should have found such an intensity of passion as would fill the sails of the highest drama." Among the more unusual suggestions is the remark that Sh may well have chosen his three Roman plays out of Plutarch because they deal with woman in her relationships to men--Calphurnia and Portia as wives, Volumnia as mother, Cleopatra as mistress. The emphasis falls on Cor. and Antony.

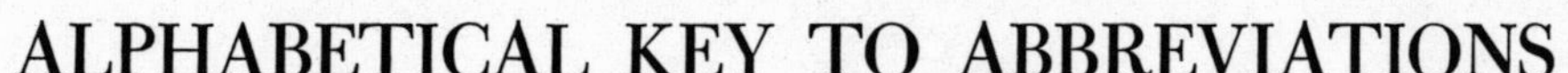

ALPHABETICAL KEY TO ABBREVIATIONS

ALPHABETICAL KEY TO ABBREVIATIONS

AA--Anglistische Arbeiten hrsg. L. L. Schücking
Acad--The Academy (Ln)
Acad (N.Y.)--The Academy (N.Y.)
Accent
The Adventurer
AESG--Annales de l'enseignement supérieur de Grenoble
AFLA--Annales de la faculté de lettres d'Aix
AI--American Imago
AJP--American Journal of Philology
AJPsy--American Journal of Psychology
All's W.--All's Well That Ends Well
ALVN--Album des literarischen Vereins in Nürnberg
AM--The Atlantic Monthly
AMB--Antiquarian Magazine and Bibliographer (Ln)
AMS--Joseph Quincy Adams Memorial Studies, ed. James G. McManaway, Giles E. Dawson, and Edwin E. Willoughby. Washington: The Folger Shakespeare Library, 1948.
Anglia
AngliaM--Beiblatt zur Anglia: Mitteilungen über englische Sprache und Literatur und über englischen Unterricht
Anglo-Americana--Anglo-Americana: Festschrift zum 70. Geburtstag von Professor Dr. Leo Hibler-Lebmannsport, hrsg. Karl Brunner. WBEP, LXII [1955?].
Die Antike--Die Antike: Zeitschrift für Kunst und Kultur des klassischen Altertums
Antike und Abendland
Antony--The Tragedy of Antony and Cleopatra
APSR--American Political Science Review
Archiv--Archiv für das Studium der neueren Sprachen und Literaturen
ArdenSh--The Arden Edition of the Works of William Shakespeare (both the original Arden Edition and the so-called "New Arden")
art(s).--article(s)
AshSS--Ashland Studies in Shakespeare
Ath--The Athenaeum (Ln)
A-VG--Audio-Visual Guide
A.Y.L.--As You Like It
AYR--All the Year Round
Baldwin Festschrift--Studies in Honor of T. W. Baldwin, ed. Don Cameron Allen. Illinois UP, 1958.
Bang's Materialien--Materialien zur Kunde des älteren englischen Dramas, hrsg. W. Bang. 44 vols., Louvain, 1902-13.
Bd.--Band
The Bee--The Bee, or Literary Intelligencer
BEM--Blackwood's Edinburgh Magazine
BFLS--Bulletin de la faculté des lettres de Strasbourg
BHM--Bulletin of the History of Medicine
BJRL--Bulletin of the John Rylands Library
BLM--Bibliothèque des langues modernes
BM--British Magazine
BNYPL--Bulletin of the New York Public Library
The Bookman
Boswell's Malone--William Shakespeare, Poems and Plays...with the corrections and illustrations of various commentators ...ed. after Mr. Malone's death by James Boswell the Younger. 21 vols., Ln, 1821.
BPLB--Boston Public Library Bulletin
BR--Bucknell Review
BRLC--Bibliothèque de la revue de littérature comparée
BUS--Bucknell University Studies
BUSE--Boston University Studies in English
Caesar--The Tragedy of Julius Caesar
Cahiers du sud

CalcuttaR—Calcutta Review
CamJ--The Cambridge Journal
CAP--Classical Association Proceedings
CarrollQ--Carroll Quarterly
CathW--Catholic World
CBEL--Cambridge Bibliography of English Literature
CE--College English
The Censor
ch(s).--chapter(s)
CH--Church History
The Christian Reformer (Ln)
CJ--Classical Journal
CL--Comparative Literature
CLU--University of California at Los Angeles Library
CM--The Canadian Magazine
Col UP—Columbia University Press
ColoradoSLL—Colorado University Studies: Series in Language and Literature
ColSCL—Columbia University Studies in Comparative Literature
ColSECL--Columbia University Studies in English and Comparative Literature
ColSS--Shaksperian Studies by Members of the Department of English and Comparative Literature in Columbia University, ed. Brander Matthews and Ashley H. Thorndike. Col UP, 1916.
Cor.—The Tragedy of Coriolanus
CornellR--The Cornell Review
CP--Classical Philology
CQR—Church Quarterly Review
CR--Contemporary Review
Craig Festschrift—Renaissance Studies in Honor of Hardin Craig, ed. Baldwin Maxwell, et al. Stanford UP, 1941. A reprinting of part of PQ, XX (1941).
CRAS--The Centennial Review of Arts and Science
The Criterion
CSE—Carnegie Series in English
CSh—The Cambridge Shakespeare, ed. Sir Arthur Quiller-Couch and J. Dover Wilson. CUP, 1921- (in progress).
CSt--Stanford University Library
CT--Canterbury Tales
CtY--Yale University Library
CU--University of California (Berkeley) Library
CUC--California University Chronicle
CUCE--Columbia University Contributions to Education: Teachers College Series
Culture (Paris)
CUP—Cambridge University Press
CUPCP--California University Publications in Classical Philology
CUPE--California University Publications in English
CU Riv—University of California (Riverside) Library
Curry Festschrift--Essays in Honor of Walter Clyde Curry, Vanderbilt Studies in the Humanities, No. 2 (Vanderbilt UP, 1954).
CW--Classical Weekly
Cym.--Cymbeline
DA--Dissertation Abstracts
Darmstädter Tageblatt
DD--Deutsche Dramaturgie: Zeitschrift für die Probleme der darstellenden Künste
DDAAU--Doctoral Dissertations Accepted by American Universities
DFo—The Folger Shakespeare Library
Discussion (South Africa)
diss—dissertation
DLC—The Library of Congress
DR--Dublin Review
The Drama
Dream—A Midsummer Night's Dream
DUJ—Durham University Journal
DVLG--Deutsche Vierteljahrsschrift für Literaturwissenschaft und Geistesgeschichte
EA--Etudes anglaises
EC--Essays in Criticism
ed(s).—edition(s), edited by, editor(s)
Edda—Edda: Nordisk Tidsskrift for Litteraturforskning
EDH--Essays by Divers Hands: Being the Transactions of the Royal Society of Literature
EH--Ewiger Humanismus: Schriften der österreichischen Gesellschaft in Innsbruck
EIE--English Institute Essays
ELH--ELH: A Journal of English Literary History
EM--English Miscellany (Rome)
Encounter
English
ER--Essex Review
Erbe--Das Erbe der Alten
Errors—The Comedy of Errors
E-S—Walther Ebisch and Levin L. Schücking. A Shakespeare Bibliography. OUP, 1931. With Supplement, 1937. See #0014.
ES--English Studies (Amsterdam)
ESA—English Studies in Africa (Johannesburg)
ESn—Englische Studien
Essays and Studies—Essays and Studies by Members of the English Association
Euphorion
EuropäischeR--Europäische Revue
Europe
Expl—Explicator
F_1—The First Folio, 1623

FCU--University of Miami (Coral Gables) Library
FL--Folk-Lore
FM--Fraser's Magazine
FMV--The Flügel Memorial Volume, Stanford University Publications: University Series [XXI], Stanford UP, 1916.
FQ--The Faerie Queene
FR--Fortnightly Review
Die Frau--Die Frau: Monatsschrift für das gesamte Frauenleben unserer Zeit (Berlin)
French Festschrift--Essays in Literary History, Presented to J. Milton French, ed. Rudolf Kirk and C. F. Main. Rutgers UP, 1960.
FSUS--Florida State University Studies
GBE--Giessener Beiträge zur Erforschung der Sprache und Kultur Englands und Nordamerikas
Germania (Berlin)
GM--The Gentleman's Magazine
GR--Greece and Rome
GRM--Germanisch-Romanische Monatsschrift
GRS--Gordon Ross Smith. A Classified Shakespeare Bibliography, 1936-1958. Pennsylvania State UP, 1963. See #0047.
H.--Heft
1H.IV--The First Part of King Henry the Fourth
2H.IV--The Second Part of King Henry the Fourth
H.V--The Life of King Henry the Fifth
1H.VI--The First Part of King Henry the Sixth
2H.VI--The Second Part of King Henry the Sixth
3H.VI--The Third Part of King Henry the Sixth
H.VIII--The Famous History of the Life of King Henry the Eighth
Ham.--The Tragedy of Hamlet, Prince of Denmark
HarLB--Harvard Library Bulletin
Harper's
HB--Huntington Brown. "The Classical Tradition in English Literature: A Bibliography," HSNPL, XVIII (1935), 7-46. See #0011.
HCP--Holy Cross Purple
Hermathena--Hermathena: A Series of Papers on Literature, Science, and Philosophy by Members of Trinity College Dublin
HJ--Hibbert Journal
HL--Humanistica Lovaniensia
HLB--The Huntington Library Bulletin
HLM--The Hamilton Literary Monthly
HLQ--The Huntington Library Quarterly
Homage--A Book of Homage to Shakespeare: To Commemorate the Three Hundredth Anniversary of Shakespeare's Death MCMXVI, ed. Israel Gollancz. OUP, 1916.
Home University (Ln)
HowardSHL--Howard College Bulletin: Studies in History and Literature
HR--Hudson Review
hrsg.--herausgegeben von
HSCL--Harvard Studies in Comparative Literature
HSCP--Harvard Studies in Classical Philology
HSE--Harvard Studies in English
HSNPL--Harvard Studies and Notes in Philology and Literature
HT--History Today
Hunt Festschrift--If By Your Art: Testament to Percival Hunt. Pittsburgh UP, 1948.
HUP--Harvard University Press
HWL--The History of the Works of the Learned
IADD--Index to American Doctoral Dissertations
IaU--University of Iowa Library
IBK--Innsbrucker Beiträge zur Kultur-wissenschaft
ICarbS--Southern Illinois University Library
IJP--International Journal of Psycho-Analysis
Das Inselschiff--Das Inselschiff: Zeitschrift für die Freunde des Insel-Verlags (Leipzig)
IowaHS--University of Iowa Humanistic Studies
Isis
ISLL--Illinois Studies in Language and Literature
Italica
IU--University of Illinois Library
IUS--Indiana University Studies: Contributions to Knowledge Made by Instructors and Advanced Students of the University
JAAK--Jahrbuch für Ästhetik und allgemeine Kunstwissenschaft
JAF--Journal of American Folklore
JEGP--Journal of English and Germanic Philology
JFKA--Jahresbericht über die Fortschritte der klassischen Altertumswissenschaft
JHI--Journal of the History of Ideas
JHUC--Johns Hopkins University Circulars
Jimbungaku--Jimbungaku: Studies in Humanities (Doshisha University, Kyoto)
John--The Life and Death of King John
Jones Festschrift--The Seventeenth Century: Studies in the History of English Thought and Literature from Bacon to Pope, by Richard Foster Jones and Others Writing in his Honor. Stanford UP, 1951.

JP--Journal of Philology
JWCI--Journal of the Warburg and Courtauld Institutes
Klaeber Festschrift--Studies in English Philology: A Miscellany in Honor of Frederick Klaeber, ed. Kemp Malone and Martin B. Ruud. Minnesota UP, 1929.
KN--Kwartalnik Neofilologiczny
KR--Kenyon Review
KSA--Die klassischen Schriftsteller des Altertums in ihrem Einflusse auf die späteren Literaturen
LCUT--Library Chronicle of the University of Texas
Lear--The Tragedy of King Lear
LGW--Chaucer's The Legend of Good Women
LHF--Litterarhistorische Forschungen hrsg. Josef Schick und Frh. v. Waldberg
LHM--American Society Legion of Honor Magazine
Library--The Library: A Bibliographical Quarterly
Liebermann Festschrift--Texte und Forschungen zur Kulturgeschichte: Festgabe für Felix Liebermann. Halle, 1921.
The Listener
The Literary Criterion (Mysore)
Die Literatur--Die Literatur: Monatsschrift für Literaturfreunde
Literature
LL--Life and Letters
L.L.L.--Love's Labour's Lost
LLM--Les Langues modernes
LLT--Life and Letters Today
LM--London Mercury
Ln--London
Lov. Com.--A Lover's Complaint
L&P--Literature and Psychology
LQHR--London Quarterly and Holborn Review
LQR--London Quarterly Review
LSU--Louisiana State University
Lucr.--The Rape of Lucrece
LV--Lenguas Vivas (Buenos Aires)
MA--Converse Memorial Library, Amherst College
Macb.--The Tragedy of Macbeth
MAH--Mélanges d'archéologie et d'histoire
ManQ--Manchester Quarterly
MAR--Manitoba Arts Review
MAS--The Manly Anniversary Studies in Language and Literature. Chicago UP, 1923.
MB--Boston Public Library
MCMP--The University of Michigan Contributions in Modern Philology
MdBJ--Johns Hopkins University Library
MdeF--Mercure de France
Meas.--Measure for Measure
Mélanges--Mélanges de linguistique et de philologie, Fernand Mossé in memoriam. Paris, 1959.
Merch.--The Merchant of Venice
Merkur (Stuttgart)
Meta.--Ovid's Metamorphoses
MF--Midwest Folklore
MH--Harvard University Libraries
MHRA--The Modern Humanities Research Association
MiamiSS--Studies in Shakespeare, University of Miami Publications in English and American Literature. Miami UP, 1953.
MichiganPLL--University of Michigan Publications: Language and Literature
MicroA--Microfilm Abstracts
The Mirror
MiU--University of Michigan Library
M&L--Music and Letters
MLA--Modern Language Association
MLN--Modern Language Notes
MLQ--Modern Language Quarterly
MLR--Modern Language Review
MM--Macmillan's Magazine
MnU--Walter Library, University of Minnesota
The Month
Monthly Magazine
The Monthly Mirror
Monthly Review
Mosher's--Mosher's Magazine
MP--Modern Philology
MQM--Modern Quarterly Miscellany
MR--Massachusetts Review
MSR--Malone Society Reprints
Much--Much Ado About Nothing
MUM--McGill University Magazine
Munro--see #0044
Munro Sup--John Munro. "More Shakspere Allusions," MP, XIII (1916), 497-544. See #0031.
MUS--University of Missouri Studies: A Quarterly of Research
Museum (Leyden)
Mutschmann Festschrift--Shakespeare-Studien: Festschrift für Heinrich Mutschmann, hrsg. Walther Fischer und Karl Wentersdorf. Marburg, 1951.
mythol.--mythological person(s), place(s), etc.
NA--New Adelphi
N&A--Nation and Athenaeum
Names
Nation
NBR--North British Review
NC--The Nineteenth Century
NcD--Duke University Library

n.d.—no date given
NED--The New English Dictionary
Neoph--Neophilologus
NER--New English Review
NewShna--New Shakespeareana
New Variorum—A New Variorum Edition of Shakespeare, ed. Horace H. Furness, his son, and MLA. 27 vols. Philadelphia, 1871- (in progress)
NEYR--New Englander and Yale Review
n.F--neue Folge
NIR—New Ireland Review
NJKA--Neue Jahrbücher für das klassische Altertum, Geschichte, und deutsche Literatur, und für Pädagogik
NjP—Princeton University Library
NM--Neuphilologische Monatsschrift
NN--New York Public Library
NNC--Columbia University Library
NNU--New York University Library (Washington Square)
n.p.—no place of publication given
NQ—Notes and Queries
NR--National Review
n.s.—new series
NS--Die neueren Sprachen
NSST--New Shakspere Society Transactions
NZ--Neuphilologische Zeitschrift
The Observer
OC--The Open Court
Occult Observer
OEP--Old English Plays: Students' Facsimile Edition...under the General Editorship of John S. Farmer. 184 vols. n.p., 1907-14.
Oth.—The Tragedy of Othello, the Moor of Venice
OU--Ohio State University Library
OUP--Oxford University Press
Our Debt—Our Debt to Greece and Rome
Palaestra—Palaestra: Untersuchungen und Texte aus der deutschen und englischen Philologie
PartR--Partisan Review
Pass. Pil.—The Passionate Pilgrim
PBA--Proceedings of the British Academy
PC--Publishers' Circular
Per.—Pericles, Prince of Tyre
PF--Port Folio
Philologica--Philologica: The Malone Anniversary Studies, ed. Thomas A. Kirby and Henry B. Woolf, Johns Hopkins UP, 1949.
Philologus
Phoenix--The Phoenix and Turtle
The Phoenix--The Phoenix: The Journal of the Classical Association of Canada
PJ--Preussische Jahrbücher
PL--Poet Lore
PM--Penn Monthly
PMA--Papers of the Michigan Academy of Science Arts and Letters
PMLA--Publications of the Modern Language Association of America
pp.--pages
PPPLA--Publications of the University of Pennsylvania: Series in Philology, Literature, and Archaeology
PPV--Essays in Dramatic Literature: The Parrott Presentation Volume By Pupils of Professor Thomas Marc Parrott of Princeton University, Published in his Honor, ed. Hardin Craig. PUP, 1935.
PQ--Philological Quarterly
PR--Poetry Review
PRI--Proceedings of the Royal Institution of Great Britain
Propyläen
PS--Philippine Studies: A Quarterly
PSE—Princeton Studies in English
PTPN--Poznanskie Towarzystwo Przyjaciol Nauk: Wydzial Filologiczno-Filozoficzny Prace Komisji Filologicznej
PUB--Princeton University Bulletin
PU(F)--University of Pennsylvania Library (Furness Memorial Library)
PUM--Publications of the University of Manchester, English Series
PUP--Princeton University Press
Q_1, Q_2, etc.—First Quarto, Second Quarto, etc.
QJS--Quarterly Journal of Speech
QR--The Quarterly Review
R.II—The Tragedy of King Richard the Second
R.III--The Tragedy of King Richard the Third
RAA--Revue anglo-américaine
RB--Revue bleue
RCC--Revue des cours et conférences
The Reflector--The Reflector: A Quarterly Magazine, on Subjects of Philosophy, Politics, and the Liberal Arts
RELV--Revue de l'enseignement des langues vivantes
RenP--Renaissance Papers
RES--Review of English Studies
rev.—review
RG--Revue germanique
RGF--Revue germanique et française
RH--Revue hebdomadaire
RIP--Rice Institute Pamphlet
RLC--Revue de littérature comparée
Romeo—The Tragedy of Romeo and Juliet
RPUM--Research Publications of the University of Minnesota

RSH--Revue des sciences humaines
SAB--Shakspere Association Bulletin
SAQ--South Atlantic Quarterly
SatR--The Saturday Review
SBAW--Sitzungsberichte der bayerischen Akademie der Wissenschaften: Philosophisch-historische Klasse
Scrutiny
SEL(T)--Studies in English Literature (Tokyo)
SEP--Studien zur englischen Philologie hrsg. Lorenz Morsbach
SERD--Studies in the English Renaissance Drama, ed. Josephine W. Bennett, Oscar Cargill, and Vernon Hall, Jr., "In memory of Karl Julius Holzknecht." New York UP, 1959.
SewR--The Sewanee Review
SFR--Scholars' Facsimiles and Reprints
SG--Selma Guttman. The Foreign Sources of Shakespeare's Works: An Annotated Bibliography of the Commentary Written on this Subject Between 1904 and 1940... Col UP: King's Crown, 1947. See #0019.
Sh, Shn, Sh's--Shakespeare, Shakespearean, Shakespeare's
ShJ--Jahrbuch der deutschen Shakespeare-Gesellschaft
ShN--The Shakespeare Newsletter
Shna--Shakespeariana
ShR--The Shakespeare Review
Shrew--The Taming of the Shrew
ShS--Shakespeare Survey
SKGV--Sprache und Kultur der germanisch-romanischen Völker, germanistische Reihe
SM--Speech Monographs
Sonn.--Shakespeare's Sonnet(s)
SouthernR--Southern Review
SP--Studies in Philology
The Spectator
SQ--Shakespeare Quarterly
SR--Studies in the Renaissance
SSP--Shakespeare Society Publications
Standpunte (Kaapstad)
StN--Studia Neophilologica
Studies--Studies: An Irish Quarterly Review of Letters Philosophy and Science
TAM--Theatre Arts Monthly
TAPA--Transactions of the American Philological Association
The Tatler
Taylor Festschrift--A Tribute to George Coffin Taylor: Studies and Essays Chiefly Elizabethan, by His Students and Friends, ed. Arnold Williams. North Carolina UP, 1952.
TBS--Transactions of the Bibliographical Society
T-D--More Seventeenth Century Allusions to Shakespeare and his Works [collected by George Thorn-Drury]. Ln, 1924. See #0051.
Temp.--The Tempest
Le Temps (Paris)
TennSL--Tennessee Studies in Literature
T.G.V.--The Two Gentlemen of Verona
The Theatre
Theoria--Theoria: A Journal of Studies in the Arts, Humanities and Social Sciences (University of Natal)
Thought
Tim.--The Life of Timon of Athens
Titus--The Tragedy of Titus Andronicus
TLS--The [London] Times Literary Supplement
T.N.K.--The Two Noble Kinsmen
TR--The Texas Review
Traditio--Traditio: Studies in Ancient and Medieval History, Thought and Religion
trans.--translation(s), translated
Troi.--The Tragedy of Troilus and Cressida
TRSC--Transactions of the Royal Society of Canada
TRSL--Transactions of the Royal Society of Literature of the United Kingdom
TSE--University of Texas Studies in English
TST--University of Toronto Department of English: Studies and Texts
TT--Time and Tide
TU--University of Tennessee Library
The Tudor Translations
TulSE--Tulane Studies in English
Twel.--Twelfth Night; or, What You Will
TxHR--Fondren Library, Rice University
TxU--Mirabeau B. Lamar Library, University of Texas
UEJ--University of Edinburgh Journal
UKCR--University of Kansas City Review
UMFR--The University Magazine and Free Review (Ln)
UngR--Ungarische Rundschau für historische und soziale Wissenschaften
The Universal Magazine
UP--University Press
UR--The University Review
UTQ--The University of Toronto Quarterly
Venus--Venus and Adonis
VirginiaES--English Studies in Honor of James Southall Wilson, [ed. Fredson Bowers], University of Virginia Studies, V [incorrectly numbered IV], 1951.
VJ--Vassar Journal of Undergraduate Studies
VM--Vassar Miscellany
vol(s).--volume(s)
VQR--Virginia Quarterly Review

WBEP--Wiener Beiträge zur englischen Philologie

WBFA--Wiener Blätter für die Freunde der Antike

The Western

Westwind (UCLA)

WHR--Western Humanities Review

Wilson Festschrift—Elizabethan and Jacobean Studies Presented to Frank Percy Wilson ..., ed. Herbert Davis and Helen Gardner. OUP, 1959.

Wives--The Merry Wives of Windsor

WSLL--University of Wisconsin Studies in Language and Literature

W.T.--The Winter's Tale

WU--University of Wisconsin Library

WUS--Washington University Studies: Humanistic Series

WVBPS--West Virginia Bulletin of Philological Studies

WW—Wort und Wahrheit

YR--Yale Review

YSE—Yale Studies in English

YWES--The Year's Work in English Studies

ZDA--Zeitschrift für deutsches Alterthum und deutsche Literatur

ZNU--Zeitschrift für neusprachlichen Unterricht

ZVLG--Zeitschrift für vergleichende Literaturgeschichte

ZVV--Zeitschrift des Vereins für Volkskunde

*—(following a diss entry): the compiler has not seen an abstract of the work; he cannot assure the reader of access to this unpublished material. The entries normally come from DDAAU or IADD.

INDEX

INDEX

In this Index, as elsewhere in the book, four-digit Arabic numbers are entry numbers of the Guide. Underscored four-digit Arabic numbers are dates. Capital Roman numerals refer to acts of plays or other major parts of works. Small Roman and one- and two-digit Arabic numbers refer to the Preface and Introduction, respectively. Acts, scenes, and lines from Shakespeare's plays appear thus: IV iii 181-193. The abbreviation mythol. designates persons, places, etc., as they appear in mythology (as opposed to literature). Greek-language main entries appear at the end of the Index.

Greek-Language Entries